The **Rough Guide** to

Slovenia

written and researched by

Norm Longley

NEW YORK • LONDON • DELHI

www.roughguides.com

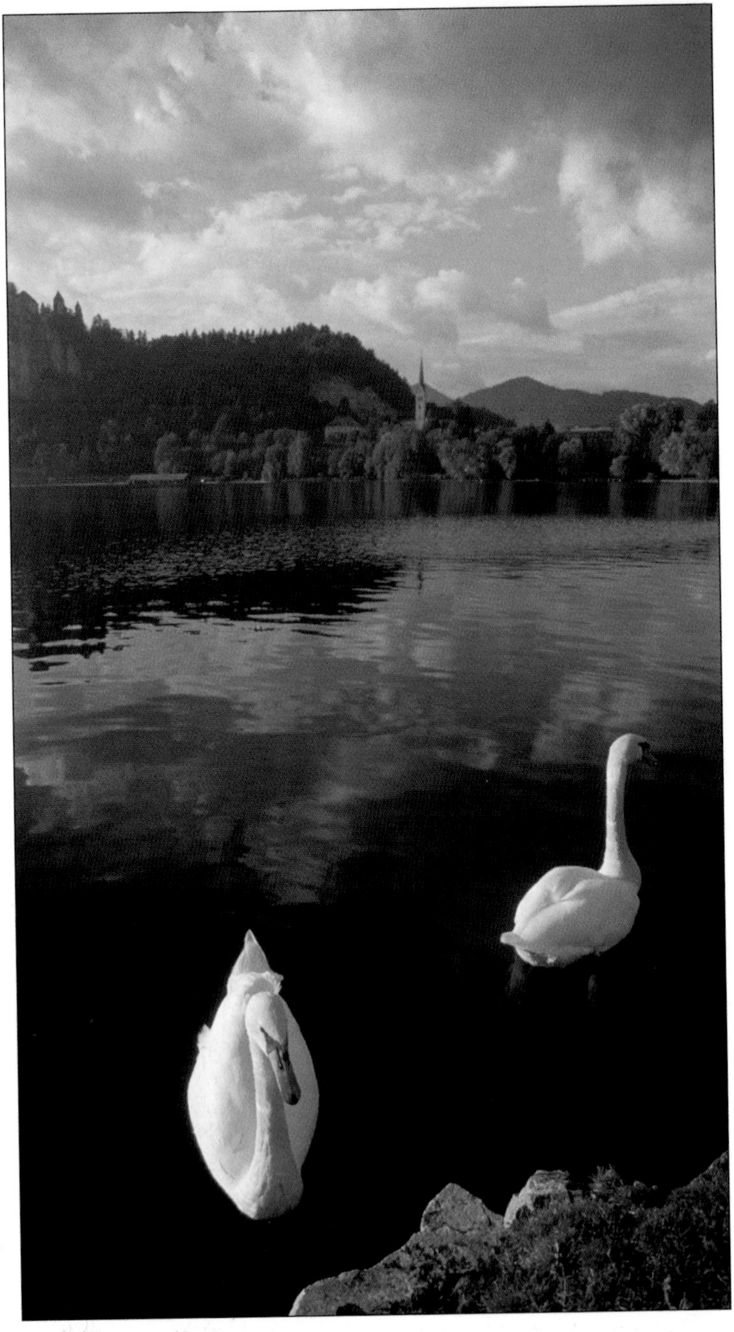

△ Swans on Lake Bled

Introduction to Slovenia

Roughly the size of Wales and with a population of less than two million, Slovenia sports a geographical diversity unmatched in many countries twice its size – imperious white limestone mountains, spectacular underground curiosities, sweeping vineyards, and a craggy coastline punctuated by historic coastal resorts are just some of the attractions packed cheek-by-jowl into this tiny country.

With distances so small, in a single day you could be hiking in the Alps in the morning, downing a few glasses of wine in a local cellar over lunch, and relaxing by the beach at the end of the day. Moreover, as one of Europe's greenest nations – over half the country is forested – there are limitless opportunities for outdoor pursuits, everything from skiing, climbing and hiking in the Alps, to white-water rafting, kayaking and canyoning on the country's many rivers, or cross-country cycling through rolling hills and forests.

Dominated by Germanic, and to a lesser extent, Hungarian and Italian influences from the Middle Ages until the end of World War I, the country spent the best part of the next seventy years locked into a less than harmonious Yugoslav federation. When the federation began to fracture in the late 1980s, Slovenia was the first to cede, and, save for the so-called Ten-Day War of independence in the summer of 1991, the country emerged more or less unscathed from the bloodbath that tragically engulfed Croatia and Bosnia. Slovenia was by far and away the most liberal and progressive of Yugoslavia's erstwhile republics, which partly accounted for its relatively painless transition from one-party rule to multiparty democracy, and from

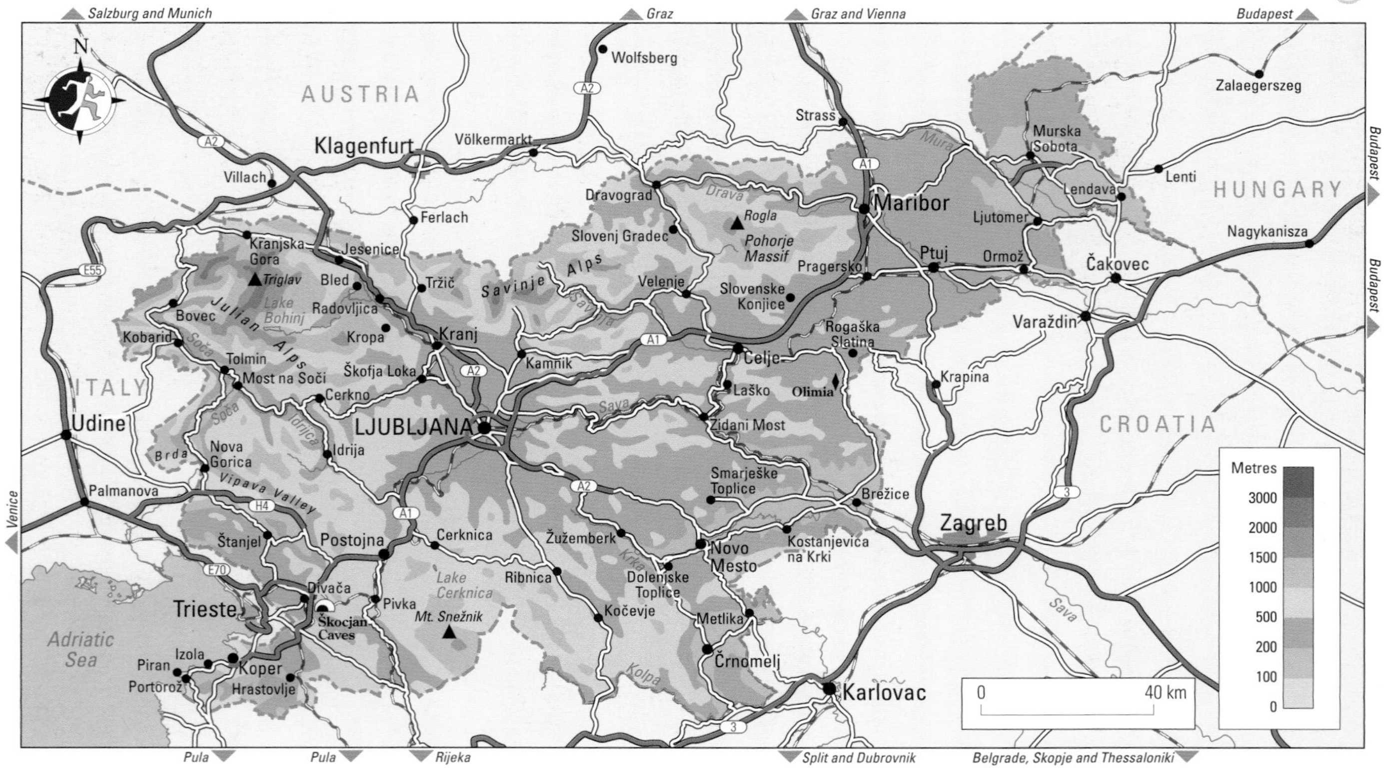

Salzburg and Munich
Graz
Graz and Vienna
Budapest
Budapest
Budapest
AUSTRIA
HUNGARY
ITALY
CROATIA
Wolfsberg
Zalaegerszeg
A2
Strass
Murska Sobota
Klagenfurt
Völkermarkt
Mura
A1
Lenti
Villach
Lendava
Dravograd
Drava
Maribor
Ferlach
Rogla
Ljutomer
Nagykanisza
Kranjska Gora
Slovenj Gradec
Pohorje Massif
Jesenice
E55
Savinje Alps
Pragersko
Ptuj
Ormož
Čakovec
Triglav
Bled
Tržič
Velenje
Slovenske Konjice
Lake Bohinj
Radovljica
Savinja
Bovec
Julian Alps
Varaždin
Kropa
Kranj
Rogaška Slatina
Kobarid
Soča
Celje
Tolmin
Škofja Loka
Kamnik
A2
Krapina
Most na Soči
Olimia
Cerkno
Laško
Sava
Udine
Soča
Idrijca
LJUBLJANA
Zidani Most
Nova Gorica
Idrija
Brda
Smarješke Toplice
Metres
3000
2000
1500
1000
500
200
100
0
Vipava Valley
Palmanova
A2
Brežice
3
H4
A1
Zagreb
Venice
Štanjel
Postojna
Cerknica
Žužemberk
Kostanjevica na Krki
Novo Mesto
E70
Krka
Lake Cerknica
Ribnica
Dolenjske Toplice
Divača
Trieste
Pivka
Kočevje
Sava
Škocjan Caves
Mt. Snežnik
Metlika
Adriatic Sea
Izola
Koper
Črnomelj
Piran
Kolpa
Portorož
Hrastovlje
Karlovac
0
40 km
3
Pula
Pula
Rijeka
Split and Dubrovnik
Belgrade, Skopje and Thessaloniki

communist to market economy, following independence. Having finally achieved its long-desired goals of NATO and European Union membership in 2004, Slovenia's place within the wider international community is assured, though what benefits this will bring to ordinary Slovenes – most of whom are broadly in favour of greater integration – remains to be seen.

△ Ljubljanica riverside, Ljubljana

Where to go

Most visitors to Slovenia begin with a trip to the country's sophisticated capital, **Ljubljana**, whose engaging blend of Baroque and Habsburg architecture, and river cafés and restaurants, could quite happily detain you for a few days. From here most visitors make a beeline for the stunning alpine lakes and mountains northwest of the capital, namely **Lake Bled**, with its fairytale island church and cliff-top castle, and the even more beautiful **Lake Bohinj**, less than 40km to the west. Both lakes lie on the fringe of the **Julian Alps**, whose magisterial peaks are as popular with climbers and hikers in the summer as they are with skiers in the winter. Most of the Alps are contained within **Triglav National Park**, which extends south to the imperious **Soča Valley**, whose river, the Soča, draws adventure sports enthusiasts to its foaming waters each summer.

South of the Soča Valley, beyond the enchanting **Goriška Brda** and **Vipava Valley** wine-growing regions, you're in the **Karst**. This rugged limestone plateau is scattered with ancient stone villages, but famed above all for its dramatic underground rivers, streams and depressions, manifested most spectacularly in the **Škocjan Caves**. The Karst is also home to the world-famous **Lipica stud farm**. Although just 47km long, the Slovenian **coast** packs in a multiplicity of little resorts, the

▽ Lipica stud farm

Fact file

• With an **area** of less than 21,000 square kilometres (roughly the size of Wales), and a **population** of just two million, Slovenia is one of Europe's smallest nations. Forty percent of the country is **mountainous**, around a quarter of which is alpine, with three major mountain groups: the Julian Alps, the Kamniške-Savinja Alps and the Karavanke mountains. The highest peak is Triglav (2864m) in the Julian Alps. The remainder of the country is comprised of subalpine hills, karst plateaus, forests and flat plains, whilst the coastline, facing the Adriatic, is just 47km long.

• The country is divided into eight geographical **regions** – Bela Krajina, Dolenjska, Gorenjska, Koroška, Notranjska, Prekmurje, Primorska and Štajerska – the boundaries of which are very fluid.

• On June 25 1991, Slovenia became an **independent republic** for the very first time. The 1991 constitution set in place a **parliamentary system of government**, elected every four years, with the prime minister at its head. The head of state, the president, is elected every five years. Slovenia became a full member of the EU in May, 2004.

• **Tourism** is one of the fastest growing sectors of the Slovenian economy, with alpine, coastal and health spa resorts absorbing the bulk of the country's tourist traffic. Slovenia's most important **exports** are vehicles, electrical appliances and pharmaceutical goods, and its main trading partners are Germany and Italy.

most enjoyable being **Piran**, a town brimming with Venetian architecture, and **Portorož**, the country's major beach resort. A short way north of these is the workaday port town of **Koper**, which conceals an appealing medieval centre.

Returning inland, there are more subterranean wonders to explore, few of which, anywhere in the world, can hold a candle to the breathtaking **Postojna Caves**, which lie within striking distance of another of Slovenia's remarkable natural phenomena, the "disappearing" **Lake Cerknica**. South of here, the dark forests and deep river valleys ranged along the Croatian border offer further possibilities for outdoor pursuits, whilst those seeking cultural diversions can take their pick from a rich tapestry of historical sites – churches, castles and ancient monasteries.

By comparison, the eastern part of the country is much less visited, and though it might not possess the clear-cut attractions of other regions, there are some rewarding places to visit. Chief amongst these

▽ Haymaking, Stara Fužina

△ Trenta Valley in the Julian Alps

is the country's most historic town, **Ptuj**, which is just a short ride away from Slovenia's second city, **Maribor**, and the **Pohorje Massif**, a major resort. Eastern Slovenia abounds in **spas**, the most popular of which are

Slovenian wine

Slovenian wine (*vino*) is little known beyond its own borders, yet its vineyards cover roughly the same area as the Bordeaux region in France and produce about half the quantity of wine of that region, much of which is of extremely high quality. Slovenia has three distinct wine-producing regions, each of which is subdivided into separate districts (there are fourteen in total): the largest of these regions is **Podravje** in the northeast, where white wines, such as Laški Rizling, Sauvignon and Šipon predominate; whereas the **Posavje** region in the southeastern corner of the country is known for its reds, in particular the rich and velvety Metliška črnina from Bela Krajina, and the blended, juice-like **Cvicek** from Dolenjska. The Primorje, or coastal, region yields a prolific number of both red and white wines, foremost of which are the excellent Merlot, the straw-yellow Zlata ("Golden") Rebula, and the dry Tokaj, all of which emanate from the gorgeous Goriška Brda hills bordering Italy. Meanwhile, no visit to the Karst region is complete without a drop of the full-blooded, ruby-red **Teran** wine.

By far the most enjoyable place to sample wine is in one of the many **wine cellars** (vinska klet) that abound along the country's twenty or so **wine roads** (vinske ceste). Alternatively, most towns and cities have a vinoteka (wine shop), where you may also be offered tasting, while most decent restaurants will have a healthy complement of Slovenian wines.

Rogaška Slatina and **Čatež**, two of the largest in the country. Moving further east, across the Mura River and towards the Hungarian border, the undulating hills of the **Podravje** wine-growing districts give way to the flat plains of **Prekmurje**, a lovely, rural region of smooth fields interspersed with pretty villages distinguished by Hungarian-style farmhouses and little white churches.

▽ Rafting on the Soča

When to go

Most visitors come to Slovenia in **summer**, when the weather is at its most reliable, the full range of sights are open, and the country's numerous festivals are in full swing. However, many of Slovenia's attractions, including the capital, Ljubljana, are just as enjoyable outside the peak summer months, and in particular during **spring** and **autumn**, when the countryside colours are at their most resplendent, hotel prices (at least in the resort areas) are slightly lower and the crowds are a little thinner.

▽ Lake Cerknica

Subterranean Slovenia

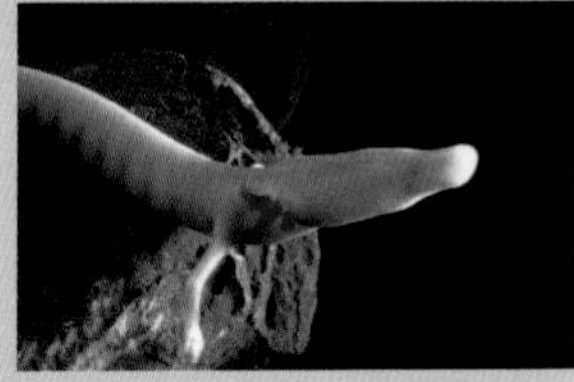

From the magnificent show caves at **Postojna** and **Škocjan**, to the **Ravenska** aragonite and **Križna water caves**, Slovenia boasts some of the finest underground systems in the world. To date, more than seven and a half thousand caves have been catalogued, the majority of which are located in the **Karst region** in southwest Slovenia. Although caves have been visited since the Middle Ages, it wasn't until the seventeenth century that systematic exploration and documentation of Slovenia's caves began. Foremost amongst the scholars of that time was the celebrated Slovene polymath Janez Vajkard Valvasor, who explored and wrote extensively on the mysterious subterranean phenomena, though it wasn't until a visit to Postojna by Emperor Franz Ferdinand in 1819 that caves as a mass tourist destination came into fashion. Today there are around two dozen caves open to the general public, some of which rank amongst Slovenia's most popular tourist attractions.

Slovenia's **climate** follows three distinctive patterns: in the northwest, an **Alpine** climate predominates, characterized by very cold winters, often with heavy rainfall and snow, and moderately warm summers, occasionally interspersed with short, violent storms. However, with the wide range of pursuits on offer here – skiing between December and March, and climbing, hiking and adventure sports between April and September – a visit to the mountain regions can be enjoyed at pretty much any time of the year. Aside from Kranjska Gora in the winter, and Lake Bled and Lake Bohinj in the height of summer, few resorts get so full that finding accommodation becomes a problem.

The Primorska region (from the Soča Valley down to the coast) has a typically **Mediterranean** climate – very warm summers with consistent sunshine, and pleasantly cool winters, though this is the one part of the country that can feel a little pressured by crowds, particularly in August when hordes of vacationing Italians arrive from just across the border. Booking accommodation around this time is therefore recommended. Whatever the season, there's a good chance you'll

▽ Predjama castle

▽ Piran harbour

experience the infamous *burja*, a vicious wind that whips down through the Karst on its way to the Bay of Trieste.

The remainder of the country subscribes to a **continental** climate of hot, dry summers – particularly in the south and east of the country – and bitterly cold winters.

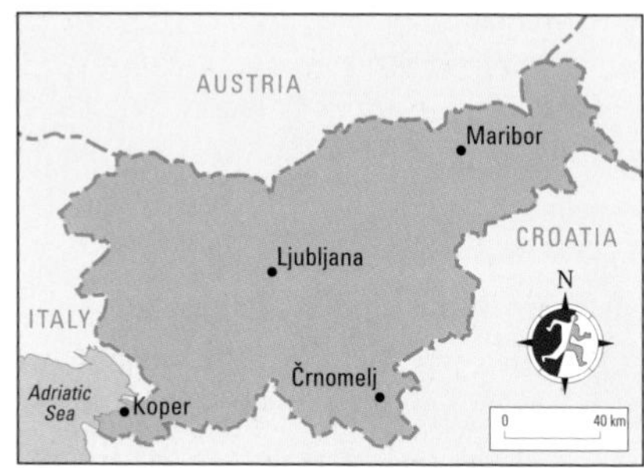

Average temperatures

	Jan	Feb	Mar	Apr	May	Jun	Jul	Aug	Sep	Oct	Nov	Dec
Črnomelj												
Temp. °C	1	4	7	11	16	19	21	20	16	11	6	2
Temp. °F	34	40	46	52	61	66	70	68	61	52	43	36
Koper												
Temp. °C	5	6	9	12	17	20	23	23	20	16	10	7
Temp. °F	41	43	48	54	62	68	74	74	68	61	50	46
Ljubljana												
Temp. °C	-1	0	5	9	14	17	19	19	15	10	4	0
Temp. °F	30	33	41	48	57	62	66	66	60	50	40	33
Maribor												
Temp. °C	-3	-1	4	9	14	17	19	18	14	9	3	-1
Temp. °F	26	30	40	48	57	62	66	64	57	48	37	30

things not to miss

It's not possible to see everything that Slovenia has to offer in one trip – and we don't suggest you try. What follows is a selective taste of the country's highlights: outstanding architecture, natural wonders, historic sites and great food. They're arranged in five colour-coded categories, which you can browse through to find the very best things to see and experience. All highlights have a page reference to take you straight into the guide, where you can find out more.

01 The Karst Page **183** • Explore dry-stone villages and a mysterious subterranean world of rivers, streams and caverns.

02 Logar Valley Page **276** • Impossibly picturesque glacial valley, carpeted with meadows and forests and hemmed in by the raw peaks of the Kamniške-Savinja Alps.

03 Gibanica Page **305** • Stuffed with cottage cheese, poppy seeds, walnut and apple, this irresistible sweet pie from Prekmurje is the definitive Slovene dessert.

04 Wine Page **vii** • From the sunny Goriška Brda hills in the west to the beautiful Ljutomer–Ormož vineyards in the east, Slovenia possesses some terrific wine-growing regions.

05 Ljubljana's Old Town Page **64** • Enjoy fabulous Baroque and Habsburg architecture, a hilltop castle and leafy riverside cafés in the enchanting Slovene capital.

06 Franja Partisan Hospital Page **181** • Once a clandestine World War II hospital, this is now a fine memorial museum.

07 Pršut Page **183** • The delicious dry-cured ham from the Karst goes down a treat with a drop of the local Teran wine.

08 Soča Valley Page **153** • Snow-dusted peaks, a magical river and a raft of historical sites combine to make this a truly memorable place.

09 Lake Bohinj Page **127** • Encircled by majestic mountains, Bohinj is the pearl of the Alpine lakes, less visited and more serene than Lake Bled.

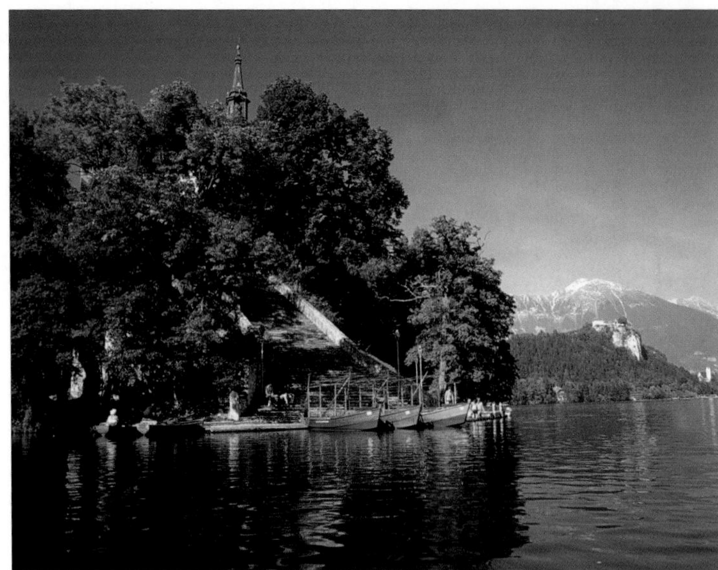

10 **Lake Bled** Page **118** • Fairytale lake complete with island church and atmospheric castle – take a dip, a stroll or just kick back on a gondola.

11 **Škocjan Caves** Page **186** • Carved out by the thrashing Reka River, the world's largest underground canyon is Slovenia's most amazing natural wonder.

12 **Ptuj Kurent** Page **300** • Slovenia's most vibrant and entertaining winter spectacle, featuring spooky masked figures dressed in chunky costumes parading through town.

13 Hiking in the Julian Alps Page **133** • One of Europe's most stunning and least spoilt mountain ranges, these mountain wilds are Slovenia's prime hiking region, with trails to suit walkers of all abilities.

14 Skiing Page **38** • Take your pick from over twenty ski resorts, with slopes and facilities to suit all abilities.

15 Lent Festival in Maribor Page **293** • Two vibrant weeks of music, theatre and art around the squares, streets and waterfront district of Slovenia's second city.

16 Piran Page **199** • An atmospheric coastal resort strewn with gorgeous Gothic–Venetian architecture, pretty little churches and quaint squares.

17 Cycling Page **24** • From the tough-going mountain climbs of the Julian Alps and Koroška, to the less demanding trails in Dolenjska and Prekmurje, Slovenia's countryside presents endless cycling possibilities.

18 Ptuj Page **294** • Slovenia's oldest and most appealing town is run through with over two thousand years of history.

19 Predjama Castle Page **218** • Dramatically sited castle with a labyrinth of rooms, secret passages and underground caves.

20 Planica ski-jumping Page **142** • Enjoy daring feats, beer and music at one of the world's great ski-jumping venues.

21 Adventure sports on the Soča Page **155** • This fabulous, foaming river is a first-rate venue for any number of adventure sports, from white-water rafting, kayaking and canoeing to hydrospeeding.

Contents

Using this Rough Guide

We've tried to make this Rough Guide a good read and easy to use. The book is divided into six main sections, and you should be able to find whatever you want in one of them.

Colour section

The front colour section offers a quick tour of Slovenia. The **introduction** aims to give you a feel for the place, with suggestions on where to go. We also tell you what the weather is like and include a basic country fact file. Next, our author rounds up his favourite aspects of Slovenia in the **things not to miss** section – whether it's great scenery, amazing architecture or a special museum. Right after this comes a full **contents** list.

Basics

The Basics section covers all the **pre-departure** nitty-gritty to help you plan your trip. This is where to find out which airlines fly to your destination, what paperwork you'll need, what to do about money and insurance, about Internet access, food, security, public transport, car rental – in fact just about every piece of **general practical information** you might need.

Guide

This is the heart of the Rough Guide, divided into user-friendly chapters, each of which covers a specific region. Every chapter starts with a list of **highlights** and an **introduction** that helps you to decide where to go, depending on your time and budget. Likewise, introductions to the various towns and smaller regions within each chapter should help you plan your itinerary. We start most town accounts with information on arrival and accommodation, followed by a tour of the sights, and finally reviews of places to eat and drink, and details of nightlife. Longer accounts also have a directory of practical listings. Each chapter concludes with **public transport** details for that region.

Contexts

Read Contexts to get a deeper understanding of what makes Slovenia tick. We include a brief history, introductions to **music** and **film**, and a further reading section that reviews **books** relating to the country.

Language

The **Language** section gives useful guidance for speaking Slovenian and pulls together all the vocabulary you might need on your trip, including a comprehensive menu reader. Here you'll also find a glossary of words and terms peculiar to the country.

Index + small print

Apart from a **full index**, which includes maps as well as places, this section covers publishing information, credits and acknowledgements, and also has our contact details in case you want to send in updates and corrections to the book – or suggestions as to how we might improve it.

Chapter list and map

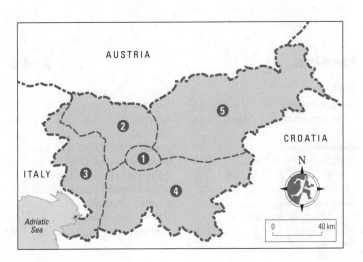

Contents

Colour section i–xvi

Basics 7–46

Guide 47–312

Contexts 313–335

Language 337–346

small print and Index 359–368

Basics

Basics

Getting there

Flying is by far the easiest way to reach Slovenia, though not many airlines fly direct to Ljubljana; possibilities do exist, though, with one no-frills airline flying direct, and a couple of others who fly to neighbouring countries, from where it's a short hop across the border. Flying from North America, Australia or New Zealand will entail one or more changes. Travelling overland from Britain is a rather long, though not unattractive haul, and you'll save little, if anything, by taking the train; however, with a rail pass you can take in Slovenia as part of a wider European trip. Bus trips offer another reasonably cheap alternative, but can be hard-going. The other option is driving, a journey of some 1500km from Britain, a trip best covered slowly over a couple of days.

Air fares always depend on the **season**, with the highest being around June to August; fares drop during the "shoulder" seasons – March to May & Sept–Oct – and you'll get the best prices during the low season, November to February (excluding Christmas and New Year when prices are hiked up and seats are at a premium). Note also that flying at weekends ordinarily adds to the round-trip fare; price ranges quoted on p.10 and p.14 assume midweek travel.

You can often cut costs by going through a **specialist flight agent** – either a consolidator, who buys up blocks of tickets from the airlines and sells them at a discount, or a **discount agent**, who in addition to dealing with discounted flights may also offer special student and youth fares and a range of other travel-related services such as travel insurance, rail passes, car rentals, tours and the like. Some agents specialize in **charter flights**, which may be cheaper than scheduled flights, but often have fixed departure dates and high cancellation penalties. For Ljubljana, you may even find it cheaper to pick up a bargain **package deal** from one of the tour operators listed on p.11 and p.14 and then find your own accommodation when you get there. A further possibility is to see if you can arrange a **courier flight**: in return for shepherding a parcel through customs, you can expect to get a deeply discounted ticket, although you'll need a flexible schedule and preferably be travelling alone with hand-baggage only. You'll probably also be restricted in the duration of your stay.

Online booking

Many discount travel websites offer you the opportunity to book flight tickets and holiday packages online, cutting out the costs of agents and middlemen; these are worth going for, as long as you don't mind the inflexibility of non-refundable, non-changeable deals. There are some bargains to be had on auction sites too, if you're prepared to bid keenly. Almost all airlines have their own websites, offering flight tickets that can sometimes be just as cheap, and are often more flexible. For specialist agents please see the relevant sections in this chapter.

Online booking agents and general travel sites

ⓦ **www.cheapflights.co.uk** (in UK & Ireland), ⓦ **www.cheapflights.com** (in US), ⓦ **www.cheapflights.ca** (in Canada), ⓦ **www.cheapflights.com.au** (in Australia). Flight deals, travel agents, plus links to other travel sites.

ⓦ **www.cheaptickets.com** Discount flight specialists (US only). Also at ⓣ 1-888/922-8849.

ⓦ **www.ebookers.com** Efficient, easy-to-use flight finder, with competitive fares.

ⓦ **www.etn.nl/discount.htm** A hub of consolidator and discount agent links, maintained by the non-profit European Travel Network.

ⓦ **www.expedia.co.uk** (in UK), ⓦ **www.expedia.com** (in US), ⓦ **www.expedia.ca** (in Canada). Discount air fares, all-airline search engine and daily deals.

ⓦ **www.flyaow.com** "Airlines of the Web" – online air travel info and reservations.

Ⓦ **www.geocities.com/thavery2000** An extensive list of airline websites and US toll-free numbers.
Ⓦ **www.kelkoo.co.uk** Useful UK-only price-comparison site, checking several sources of low-cost flights (and other goods & services) according to specific criteria.
Ⓦ **www.lastminute.com** (in UK),
Ⓦ **www.lastminute.com.au** (in Australia),
Ⓦ **www.lastminute.co.nz** (in New Zealand). Good last-minute holiday package and flight-only deals.
Ⓦ **www.opodo.co.uk** Popular and reliable source of low UK air fares. Owned by, and run in conjunction with, nine major European airlines.
Ⓦ **www.priceline.co.uk** (in UK),
Ⓦ **www.priceline.com** (in US). Name-your-own-price website that has deals at around forty percent off standard fares.
Ⓦ **www.skyauction.com** Bookings from the US only. Auctions tickets and travel packages to destinations worldwide.
Ⓦ **www.travelocity.co.uk** (in UK),
Ⓦ **www.travelocity.com** (in US),
Ⓦ **www.travelocity.ca** (in Canada),
Ⓦ **www.zuji.com.au** (in Australia). Destination guides, hot fares and great deals for car rental, accommodation and lodging.
Ⓦ **www.travelshop.com.au** Australian site offering discounted flights, packages, insurance, and online bookings. Also on ⓣ1800/108 108.
Ⓦ **travel.yahoo.com** Incorporates some Rough Guides material in its coverage of destination countries and cities across the world, with information about places to eat and sleep.

From the UK and Ireland

The quickest and simplest way of getting to Slovenia from the UK or Ireland is to **fly**, and whilst travelling **overland** – be it by bus, train or car – is perfectly feasible, it's not necessarily cheaper.

Flights

Flying to Ljubljana from the UK takes approximately two hours. There are currently two airlines flying from the UK to Slovenia: the Slovenian national carrier Adria Airways, with one **direct scheduled flight from London Gatwick to Ljubljana** each day (and vice versa); **fares** vary widely depending on time of year and length of stay; economy-class return fares start from around £120 in low season and £240 in high season; and the no-frills airline, easyJet, who also have one scheduled flight each day from **Stansted to Ljubljana** – return fares start from around £40.

Indirect flights with other airlines (including Air France, Austrian Airlines and Lufthansa – the last of these usually has the cheapest flights) are worth looking into – they do take longer and connection times are often very tight, but they can be fairly competitive in price, with tickets from around £240.

Another alternative, so long as you don't mind a little extra travelling, is to fly with a **no-frills** airline into one of the neighbouring countries. Ryanair currently fly from London Stansted to Trieste, in Italy, and Graz and Klagenfurt, in Austria, all three of which are within easy reach of Slovenia, and its capital, Ljubljana. Both Ryanair and easyJet also fly to Venice, from where it's a slightly longer journey into Slovenia, via Trieste. Onward connections to Slovenia are simple enough: flying into Trieste you can catch a train direct to Ljubljana or take one of the regular buses to the coast (Koper). In eastern Austria there are trains and buses to Maribor, from where you can catch an onward train or bus to numerous destinations within the country; whilst, from Klagenfurt you'll have to take a train into Slovenia. These flights do fill up quickly, however, and you should think about booking a couple of months ahead for the summer; moreover, the earlier you book, the cheaper the flight is likely to be. **Tickets** for all three destinations can be obtained for as little as £40, including tax. Another no-frills airline, Sky Europe, flies direct from London to Budapest, with return fares from as little as £60; from Budapest there are direct trains to Ljubljana (see p.15).

There are no direct scheduled flights from either Dublin or Belfast to Slovenia, so you'll have to take a flight to London and an onward flight from there.

Airlines

Adria Airways UK ⓣ020/7734 4630 or 7437 0143, Ⓦwww.adria.si.
Air France UK ⓣ0845/359 1000, Republic of Ireland ⓣ01/605 0383, Ⓦwww.airfrance.com.
Austrian Airlines UK ⓣ0845/601 0948, Republic of Ireland ⓣ1800/509 142, Ⓦwww.aua.com.
easyJet ⓣ0870/600 0000, Ⓦwww.easyjet.com. Low-cost flights London Stansted to Venice.

Lufthansa UK ⓣ0845/773 7747, Republic of Ireland ⓣ01/844 5544, ⓦwww.lufthansa.com.
Ryanair UK ⓣ0871/246 0000, Republic of Ireland ⓣ0818/30 30 30, ⓦwww.ryanair.com. Low-cost flights London Stansted to Graz, Klagenfurt, Trieste and Venice.
SkyEurope UK ⓣ020/7365 0365, ⓦwww.skyeurope.com. Low-cost flights London to Budapest.

Travel agents

Flightcentre UK ⓣ0870/890 8099, ⓦwww.flightcentre.co.uk. Rock-bottom fares worldwide.
Flights4Less UK ⓣ0871/222 3423, ⓦwww.flights4less.co.uk. Good discount air fares. Part of ⓦwww.lastminute.com.
Holidays4Less UK ⓣ0871/222 3423, ⓦwww.holidays4less.co.uk. Discounted package deals worldwide. Part of ⓦwww.lastminute.com.
North South Travel UK ⓣ01245/608 291, ⓦwww.northsouthtravel.co.uk. Friendly, competitive travel agency, offering discounted fares worldwide. Profits are used to support projects in the developing world, especially the promotion of sustainable tourism.
Premier Travel UK ⓣ028/7126 3333, ⓦwww.premiertravel.uk.com. Discount flight specialists.
STA Travel UK ⓣ0870/160 0599, ⓦwww.statravel.co.uk. Worldwide specialists in low-cost flights, overlands and holiday deals. Good discounts for students and under-26s.
Top Deck UK ⓣ020/7244 8000, ⓦwww.topdecktravel.co.uk. Long-established agent dealing in discount flights and tours.
Trailfinders UK ⓣ020/7938 3939, ⓦwww.trailfinders.com, Republic of Ireland ⓣ01/677 7888, ⓦwww.trailfinders.ie. One of the best-informed and most efficient agents for independent travellers.
Travel Bag UK ⓣ0870/890 1456, ⓦwww.travelbag.co.uk. Discount deals worldwide.
Travel Care UK ⓣ0870/112 0085, ⓦwww.travelcare.co.uk. Flights, holiday deals and city breaks around the world.
USIT Northern Ireland ⓣ028/9032 7111, ⓦwww.usitnow.com, Republic of Ireland ⓣ0818/200 020, ⓦwww.usit.ie. Specialists in student, youth and independent travel – flights, trains, study tours, TEFL, visas and more.
World Travel Centre Republic of Ireland ⓣ01/416 7007, ⓦwww.worldtravel.ie. Excellent fares to Europe.

Tour operators

Balkan Holidays ⓣ0845/130 1114, ⓦwww.balkan-holidays.co.uk. Southeastern Europe specialists, offering weekly package trips to Bled, Bohinj, Kranjska Gora and Portorož, from around £340. Ski package also available. Flight-only deals too.
Crystal Holidays ⓣ0870/166 4951, ⓦwww.crystalholidays.co.uk. Ski holidays in Bled, Bohinj, Kranjska Gora, and packages to the Adriatic Coast. Flight-only deals too.
Exodus ⓣ020/8675 5550, ⓦwww.exodus.co.uk. Eight-day trekking/climbing tour – including an ascent of Mount Triglav – and white-water adventure sports week on the Soča River. In Republic of Ireland, contact Worldwide Adventures ⓣ01/679 5700.
Explore Worldwide ⓣ01252/760 000, ⓦwww.explore.co.uk. Eight-day tour taking in Ljubljana, the Julian Alps, Škocjan Caves and the Adriatic coast (£500).
Inghams ⓣ020/8780 4400, ⓦwww.inghams.co.uk. Seven- to fourteen-day lakes and mountains package tours from around £340.
Mercian Travel ⓣ01562/883795 ⓦwww.merciantravel.co.uk. Bridge holidays for senior travellers in Bled and Portorož each September.
Peakland Walking Holidays ⓣ01298/872801, ⓦwww.walkingholidays.org.uk. Week-long walking tours in the Julian Alps (£899), running concurrently with a Natural and Local History week (£850); they also organize a couple of long weekends each year (£399).
Ramblers Holidays ⓣ01707/331133, ⓦwww.ramblersholidays.co.uk. Fifteen-day hikes in the Alps (moderate/difficult), based in two centres, Bohinj and Jezersko (£630).
Slovenija Pursuits ⓣ0870/2200 201, ⓦwww.slovenijapursuits.com. UK's premier Slovenia specialist, offering tailor-made holidays, including fights, accommodation (including tourist farms), sports and activities/recreational pursuits, and car hire.
Thermalia Travel ⓣ020/7586 7725, ⓦwww.thermalia.co.uk. Spa holiday specialists offering seven-day treatment programmes at the Rogaška Slatina spa in eastern Slovenia; prices from £540.

By rail

Travelling **by train**, the shortest journey from London to Ljubljana takes about eighteen hours, but it is likely to be even more expensive than flying. However, stopovers on the way are possible, and prices are more attractive if you're a student, under 26 or over 60. If you have an InterRail train pass, you can take in Slovenia as part of a wider trip around Europe (see the "Getting around" section on p.22 for details of rail passes).

A standard second-class **return ticket**, incorporating Eurostar, will cost around £260. Arriving in Paris, you take a train to Venice and change there for the final leg to Ljubljana. Tickets are usually valid for two to three months and allow for unlimited stopovers (as long as you stick to the prescribed route), unless that is, you travel the London–Paris part by Eurostar, in which case you'll have to commit yourself to reservations on specific services on this leg to qualify for the cheapest tickets.

Rail agents

Eurostar UK ⓣ0870/160 6600, ⓦwww.eurostar.com. Trains depart more or less hourly (roughly 6am–7.30pm) from London Waterloo through the Channel Tunnel to Paris Gare du Nord (2hr 40min) or Brussels-Midi/Zuid (2hr 20min). Up to 24 trains a day to Paris; up to 10 a day to Brussels. The cheapest return ticket to Paris or Brussels is currently £59 (Lille £55), though restrictions apply. You can take a bike – if it folds, it can go in the carriage with you; if not, you should register it as "Registered Baggage" a day in advance (£20 per cycle per journey). You can get through-ticketing from stations around Britain – including the tube journey across London to Waterloo – from Eurostar, many travel agents and mainline stations. InterRail, Eurail, Britrail and Eurodomino passes give discounts on Eurostar trains.
International Rail UK ⓣ0870/751 5000, ⓦwww.international-rail.com. Offers a wide variety of rail options, including Eurostar, all European passes and tickets, Motorail, international sleepers, ferry crossings and more.
Rail Europe UK ⓣ0870/584 8848, ⓦwww.raileurope.co.uk.

By bus

Although **buses** can be an economical alternative to taking the train, journeys this length can be incredibly arduous. Eurolines do not operate buses to Ljubljana but there is a service from London to Maribor in eastern Slovenia (from where there are fast bus and train connections to Ljubljana). The journey time is a stamina-sapping thirty hours, with one change in Frankfurt; a standard return fare will cost around £140, though look out for promotional fares which can bring the cost down considerably.

Bus companies

Eurolines UK ⓣ0870/514 3219, ⓦwww.eurolines.co.uk, Republic of Ireland ⓣ01/836 6111, ⓦwww.eurolines.ie. Eurolines isn't a company – it's a brand name under which thirty-plus companies operate international buses all around Europe; National Express is the UK operator, Bus Éireann is the Republic of Ireland operator. In the UK, tickets can also be purchased on the Eurolines number & website, from National Express (ⓣ0870/580 8080, ⓦwww.nationalexpress.com) and from Eurolines agents nationwide.

By car

If you have the time and inclination, **driving to Slovenia**, a distance of 1500km from London, can be a pleasant proposition. However, it's really only worth considering if you are planning to travel around Slovenia extensively – another very attractive proposition in itself – or want to take advantage of various stopovers en route.

Once across the channel, the most direct **route** to Ljubljana (around 30 hours at a leisurely pace with plenty of stops) is via Brussels, Stuttgart, Munich and Salzburg before crossing into Slovenia at the Karavanke Tunnel border. Detailed printouts of the route can be obtained from the websites of the AA (ⓦwww.theaa.com), or RAC (ⓦwww.rac.co.uk). See p.24 for details of driving within Slovenia.

There are numerous **ferry services** between Britain and Ireland, and between the British Isles and the European mainland. Which service you use will depend on where exactly you are coming from and which part of Europe you are aiming for. Ferries from the southeast of Ireland and the south coast of England connect with northern France and Spain; those from Kent in the southeast of England reach northern France and Belgium; those from the east coast and northeast of England cross the North Sea to the Netherlands, Germany and Scandinavia.

Ferry prices vary dramatically according to the time of year, time of day, length of stay and, for motorists, the size of your car. Whilst Hoverspeed is more expensive, the journey time is half that of the ferry. Look out for frequent special offers on both Hoverspeed and ferries.

Via the Channel Tunnel

Eurotunnel UK ⓣ0870/535 3535, ⓦwww.eurotunnel.com. Operates drive-on drive-off shuttle trains through the Channel Tunnel for vehicles and their passengers only. Trains run continuously between Folkestone and Coquelles, near Calais. There are up to four departures per hour (one per hour midnight–6am). Journey time is 35min (45min for some night departure times). It is possible to turn up and buy your ticket at the toll booths (exit the M20 at junction 11a), though at busy times booking is advisable; if you've booked, you must arrive at least 30min before your scheduled departure. Fares depend on the time of year, time of day and length of stay; it's cheaper to travel between 10pm and 6am, while the highest fares apply at weekends and in July and August. Bikes are carried on a specially adapted carriage that makes the crossing twice a day – see website for details.

Ferry companies in the UK and Ireland

Hoverspeed UK ⓣ0870/240 8070, ⓦwww.hoverspeed.co.uk. Dover to Calais.
P&O Ferries UK ⓣ0870/520 2020, ⓦwww.poferries.com. Dover to Calais.
SeaFrance UK ⓣ0870/571 1711, ⓦwww.seafrance.com. Dover to Calais.
Stena Line Britain ⓣ0870/570 70 70, Northern Ireland ⓣ028/9074 7747, ⓦwww.stenaline.co.uk, Republic of Ireland ⓣ01/204 7777, ⓦwww.stenaline.ie. Harwich to Hook of Holland.

From the USA and Canada

There are no direct flights from either Canada or the USA to Slovenia, so you'll have to rely on using one of the bigger European airlines (Lufthansa, Air France) to fly you into their home hub, from where you can continue the journey. Another alternative is to fly into the capital city of one of the neighbouring countries, such as Budapest in Hungary, or Vienna in Austria, from where there are onward train connections into Slovenia. Malev, the Hungarian carrier, fly direct from New York's JFK to Budapest, with fares from around $550 low season and $700 high season, whilst they also schedule direct flights from Toronto, with fares from around Can$900 low season and Can$1300 high season.

Airlines

Air Canada ⓣ1-888/247-2262, ⓦwww.aircanada.com.
Air France US ⓣ1-800/237-2747, Canada ⓣ1-800/667-2747, ⓦwww.airfrance.com.
American Airlines ⓣ1-800/624-6262, ⓦwww.aa.com.
Austrian Airlines ⓣ1-800/843-0002, ⓦwww.aua.com.
British Airways ⓣ1-800/AIRWAYS, ⓦwww.ba.com.
Lufthansa US ⓣ1-800/645-3880, Canada ⓣ1-800/563-5954, ⓦwww.lufthansa.com.
Malev Hungarian Airlines ⓣ1-800/223-6884 or 212/566-9944, ⓦwww.malev.hu.
United Airlines ⓣ1-800/538-2929, ⓦwww.united.com.

Travel agents

AESU Travel ⓣ1-800/695-AESU or 410/366-5494, ⓦwww.aesu.com. Discount air fares and student/low-budget travel.
Airtech ⓣ212/219-7000, ⓦwww.airtech.com. Standby seat broker; also deals in consolidator fares.
Educational Travel Center ⓣ1-800/747-5551 or 608/256-5551, ⓦwww.edtrav.com. Low-cost fares worldwide, student/youth discount offers, and Eurail passes, car rental and tours.
Flightcentre US ⓣ1-866/WORLD-51, ⓦwww.flightcentre.us, Canada ⓣ1-888/WORLD-55, ⓦwww.flightcentre.ca. Rock-bottom fares worldwide.
New Frontiers US ⓣ1-800/677-0720, ⓦwww.newfrontiers.com. Discount firm, specializing in travel from the US to Europe.
STA Travel US ⓣ1-800/329-9537, Canada ⓣ1-888/427-5639, ⓦwww.statravel.com. Worldwide specialists in independent travel; also student IDs, travel insurance, car rental, rail passes, and more.
Student Flights ⓣ1-800/255-8000 or 480/951-1177, ⓦwww.isecard.com/studentflights. Student/youth fares, plus student IDs and European rail and bus passes.
TFI Tours ⓣ1-800/745-8000 or 212/736-1140, ⓦwww.lowestairprice.com. Consolidator with global fares.
Travel Avenue ⓣ1-800/333-3335, ⓦwww.travelavenue.com. Full-service travel agent that offers discounts in the form of rebates.

Travel Cuts US ⓣ1-800/592-CUTS, Canada ⓣ1-888/246-9762, ⓦwww.travelcuts.com. Popular, long-established student-travel organization, with worldwide offers.
Travelers Advantage ⓣ1-877/259-2691, ⓦwww.travelersadvantage.com. Discount travel club, with cashback deals and discounted car rental. Membership required ($1 for 3 months' trial).
Travelosophy US ⓣ1-800/332-2687, ⓦwww.itravelosophy.com. Good range of discounted and student fares worldwide.

Tour operators

Adventure Center ⓣ1-800/228-8747 or 510/654-1879, ⓦwww.adventurecenter.com. Hiking and "soft adventure" specialists worldwide. Nine-day tours of the mountains and lakes, and a sixteen-day tour combined with a cruise along the Croatian Dalmatian coast.
Cross-Culture ⓣ1-800/491-1148 or 413/256-6303, ⓦwww.crossculturalinc.com. Small-group cultural tours of the country.
Geographic Expeditions ⓣ1-800/777-8183 or 415/922-0448, ⓦwww.geoex.com. Thirteen-day multi-country walking tours, Ptuj, the Lakes and Alps, and Piran on the Slovene leg.
Insight International Tours ⓣ1-800/582-8380, ⓦwww.inusa.insightvacations.com. Ljubljana as part of a multi-country tour (Austria, Italy and Croatia).
Rail Europe ⓣ1-877/EUROVAC, ⓦwww.raileurope.com. Rail passes and advice, plus good air fares, bookings for hotels and rental cars, and flexible, multi-centre vacation packages.
Wilderness Travel ⓣ1-800/368-2794, ⓦwww.wildernesstravel.com. Hiking in the Slovenian Alps included as part of a multi-country trip (with Austria and Italy).

From Australia and New Zealand

There are **no direct flights** to Slovenia from Australia or New Zealand so you'll have to change airlines, either in Asia or Europe, although the best option is to fly to a Western European gateway and get a connecting flight from there. A standard return fare from eastern **Australia** to Ljubljana, via London, with Quantas, is around Aus$ 2200 low season and Aus$ 2700 high season. Most flights typically require a stop in London, Paris or Frankfurt, continuing onwards from there. The same routeings apply for flights from **New Zealand**, with a standard return fare from around NZ$ 3300.

Airlines

Aeroflot Australia ⓣ02/9262 2233, ⓦwww.aeroflot.com.au.
Air France Australia ⓣ1300/361 400, New Zealand ⓣ09/308 3352, ⓦwww.airfrance.com.
Air New Zealand Australia ⓣ13 24 76, ⓦwww.airnz.com.au, New Zealand ⓣ0800/737 000, ⓦwww.airnz.co.nz.
Austrian Airlines Australia ⓣ1800/642 438 or 02/9251 6155, New Zealand ⓣ09/522 5948, ⓦwww.aua.com.
British Airways Australia ⓣ1300/767 177, New Zealand ⓣ0800/274 847, ⓦwww.ba.com.
Lufthansa Australia ⓣ1300/655 727, New Zealand ⓣ0800/945 220, ⓦwww.lufthansa.com.
Qantas Australia ⓣ13 13 13, New Zealand ⓣ0800/808 767 or 09/357 8900, ⓦwww.qantas.com.

Travel agents

Flight Centre Australia ⓣ13 31 33, ⓦwww.flightcentre.com.au, New Zealand ⓣ0800 243 544, ⓦwww.flightcentre.co.nz. Rock-bottom fares worldwide.
Holiday Shoppe New Zealand ⓣ0800/808 480, ⓦwww.holidayshoppe.co.nz. Great deals on flights, hotels and holidays.
OTC Australia ⓣ1300/855 118, ⓦwww.otctravel.com.au. Deals on flights, hotels and holidays.
STA Travel Australia ⓣ1300/733 035, New Zealand ⓣ0508/782 872, ⓦwww.statravel.com. Worldwide specialists in low-cost flights, overlands and holiday deals. Good discounts for students and under-26s.
Student Uni Travel Australia ⓣ02/9232 8444, ⓦwww.sut.com.au, New Zealand ⓣ09/379 4224, ⓦwww.sut.co.nz. Great deals for students.
Trailfinders Australia ⓣ02/9247 7666, ⓦwww.trailfinders.com.au. One of the best-informed and most efficient agents for independent travellers.
travel.com.au and **travel.co.nz** Australia ⓣ1300/130 482 or 02/9249 5444, ⓦwww.travel.com.au, New Zealand ⓣ0800/468 332, ⓦwww.travel.co.nz. Comprehensive online travel company, with discounted fares.

Tour operators

Eastern Eurotours Australia ⓣ1800/242 353 or 07/5526 2855, ⓦwww.easterneurotours.com.au.

Several excellent week-long escorted tours throughout the country, including the Alps and Slovenian Castles.

Russian Gateway Tours Australia ⓣ02/9745 3333, ⓦwww.russian-gateway.com.au. Russian specialists who also organize seven-day summer and winter trips to Slovenia; can also help arrange any aspect of your trip to Slovenia.

Overland from neighbouring countries

Slovenia is conveniently placed for easy access from a number of neighbouring countries. Travellers from the UK (or Ireland) on a no-frills flight (to Budapest, Trieste, Graz or Klagenfurt) will be required to continue the onward journey by train. Travellers from North America or Australia/New Zealand are likely to fly into one of the European gateway cities (for example Paris or Frankfurt), also necessitating an onward journey to Slovenia by train or bus.

Five trains a day make the short one-hour journey from **Graz** to **Maribor**, from where there are high-speed connections to Ljubljana. From **Trieste** there are two daily trains (originating in Venice) to Ljubljana, with two more from the border town, Villa Opicina (three to five hours). Alternatively take one of the regular buses from Trieste to Koper, which is well connected to the capital by bus and train. From **Budapest** (Keleti and Deli stations) there are half a dozen trains a day to Ljubljana, with a journey time of around nine hours. If you're looking to head south from Slovenia into Croatia or Serbia, there are currently five trains a day from Ljubljana to **Zagreb** (two hours thirty minutes), continuing on to **Belgrade** (nine hours).

Red tape and visas

Citizens of most European countries, as well as citizens of Australia, Canada, New Zealand and the USA, do not require visas for stays of up to ninety days, whilst citizens of some neighbouring countries, such as Italy and Austria, require only an identity card. However, visa requirements do change, and it is always advisable to check the situation before leaving home; all the latest information can be obtained from the Slovene Foreign Ministry website at ⓦwww.gov.si/mzz.

Assuming that you do require a visa, applications can be made to any Slovenian consulate abroad in person, or by post. Ninety-day stay **tourist visas**, with the option of single, double or multiple entry, currently cost £21/€30; **transit visas**, valid for five days, cost £7/€10. Should you wish to stay longer than ninety days, then leave the country at the nearest exit and re-enter.

Slovenian embassies and consulates abroad

Australia Embassy: Level 6, Advance Bank Centre, 60 Marcus Clark Street, Canberra ACT 2601 ⓣ02/6243 4830; Consulate: 86 Parramatta Road, Camperdawn NSW 2050, Sydney ⓣ02/9517 1591.

Britain 10 Little College Street, London, SW1P 3SH ⓣ020/7222 5400.

Canada Embassy: 150 Metcalfe Street, Suite 2101, Ottawa, Ontario K2P 121 ⓣ613/565-5781; Consulates: 4300 Village Center Courts, Main Floor, Toronto, Ontario L4Z 1S2 ⓣ905/804-9310.

Ireland Embassy: Morrison Chambers, 2nd Floor, 32 Nassau Street, Dublin 2 ⓣ01/670 5240.

New Zealand Consulate: PO Box 30247, Eastern Hutt Road, Pomare, Lower Hutt, Wellington ⓣ04/567 0027.

USA Embassy 1525 New Hampshire Avenue N.W. Washington DC 20036 ⓣ202/667-5363; Consulates: 600 Third Avenue, 21st Floor, New York, NY 10016 ⓣ212/370-3006.

Customs

Customs inspections, be they at Brnik airport or at one of the land border crossings, are minimal if not nonexistent most of the time. There is no **import duty** on items intended for personal use such as bicycles, cameras and video cameras. Up to 500,000SIT may be brought into, or exported from, the country.

Travellers are entitled to **VAT refunds** (known as DDV in Slovenia) on goods (but not alcohol or tobacco products) that exceed 15,000SIT, but make sure that you obtain a DDV form or document from the retailer following your purchase; both this and your receipt must be handed over to customs officials when making a claim – this can be done at Brnik airport as well as many border crossings.

Information, maps and websites

A large number of free brochures and special-interest pamphlets are produced by the Slovenian Tourist Board, and distributed by their offices abroad as well as their excellent, and extensive, network of local authority-run tourist offices within Slovenia. As well as providing local information and maps, many offices – which you'll find in pretty much every town, city and tourist site – supply information on other parts of the country. Almost without exception the staff, most of whom speak excellent English, are extremely knowledgeable and unfailingly helpful.

The tourist board's main publication is the superb *Next Exit* booklet, which plots six different routes throughout the country, each of which lists tourist offices, places to eat and sleep, and key sites of natural and cultural interest. The booklet also contains a range of discount coupons for use in hotels, restaurants and museums. Although there are exceptions, and these are listed throughout the guide, tourist offices do not deal in private accommodation (see p.28); for this you're best off heading to local tourist agencies, which can be found in most towns and cities. They, too, can sometimes be a good source of information.

Information offices abroad

Britain Slovenian Tourist Office New Barn Farm, Tadlow, Royston, Hertfordshire, SG8 0EP ⓣ0870 2255 305, ⓦwww.slovenia-tourism.si.
USA Slovenian Tourist Office 345 East 12th Street, New York NY 10003 ⓣ212/358 9689, ⓔslotouristboard@sloveniatravel.com.

Useful websites

The following sites have English language versions unless otherwise stated.

ⓦ**www.amzs.si** Site of the Automobile Association of Slovenia, including up-to-the-minute updates on local traffic conditions. Definitely worth consulting if you are planning driving in Slovenia.

ⓦ**www.bled.si** Comprehensive site of Slovenia's most popular tourist destination.

ⓦ**www.burger.si** Virtual reality site, with shiny pictures of landscapes, sites of natural and cultural interest, as well as interactive maps.

ⓦ**www.ljubljana.si** Key things to see and do in the capital.

ⓦ**www.ljubljanalife.com** Reasonably informative website of the capital's quarterly English-language magazine, with useful nightlife section, as well as weekly news bulletins and features.

ⓦ**www.matkurja.com/slo** Slovenian directory of websites.

ⓦ**www.slonews.sta.si** Website of *Slovenia News*, the country's best English-language news magazine, with domestic politics, cultural news and general interest articles. Updated weekly.

ⓦ **www.sloveniatimes.com** Another news magazine, though less regular and not as good as *Slovenia News*.
ⓦ **www.slovenia-tourism.si** Excellent, official site of the Slovenian Tourist Board, with information on all aspects of travel within the country, and good links to accommodation (hotels, tourist farms and campsites), museums, activities, events and so on.
ⓦ **www.uvi.si** Government public relations and media website, but not as dull as it sounds.

Maps

The best country **maps** of Slovenia are the 1:300,000 maps by Freytag & Berndt, and the GeoCenter Euro Map of the Dalmatian Coast and Croatia (but which also covers Slovenia); the latter is particularly useful if you're thinking of combining the two countries. **Town and city maps**, as well as a few regional ones (all around 1250–1500SIT) can usually be obtained from tourist offices and bookshops.

The Alpine Association of Slovenia (Planinska zveza Slovenije; PZS – see p.38) publishes a wide range of 1:50,000 **hiking maps**, such as Triglav National Park, the Julian Alps, and the Karavanke mountains; you can order these directly from PZS, or obtain them from tourist offices and bookshops. If you're driving, the best **road map** currently available is the 1:270,000 Tourist Road Map (*turistična avtokarta*), published by the national motoring organization AMZS.

If possible, and if you haven't got them in advance of your trip, you're best off trying to obtain any maps you need in the bookshops in Ljubljana (see p.85) as bookshops in the rest of Slovenia tend not to be particularly well stocked. If you do want to buy Slovenian maps in advance, try one of the specialist map suppliers listed below.

Map outlets

In the UK and Ireland

Stanfords 12–14 Long Acre, London WC2 ⓣ020/7836 1321, ⓦwww.stanfords.co.uk. Also at 39 Spring Gardens, Manchester ⓣ0161/831 0250, and 29 Corn St, Bristol ⓣ0117/929 9966.
Blackwell's Map Centre 50 Broad St, Oxford ⓣ01865/793 550, ⓦmaps.blackwell.co.uk. Branches in Bristol, Cambridge, Cardiff, Leeds, Liverpool, Newcastle, Reading & Sheffield.
The Map Shop 30a Belvoir St, Leicester ⓣ0116/247 1400, ⓦwww.mapshopleicester.co.uk.
National Map Centre 22–24 Caxton St, London SW1 ⓣ020/7222 2466, ⓦwww.mapsnmc.co.uk.
National Map Centre Ireland 34 Aungier St, Dublin ⓣ01/476 0471, ⓦwww.mapcentre.ie.
The Travel Bookshop 13–15 Blenheim Crescent, London W11 ⓣ020/7229 5260, ⓦwww.thetravelbookshop.co.uk.
Traveller 55 Grey St, Newcastle-upon-Tyne ⓣ0191/261 5622, ⓦwww.newtraveller.com.

In the US and Canada

110 North Latitude US ⓣ336/369-4171, ⓦwww.110nlatitude.com.
Book Passage 51 Tamal Vista Blvd, Corte Madera, CA 94925 ⓣ1-800/999-7909, ⓦwww.bookpassage.com.
Distant Lands 56 S Raymond Ave, Pasadena, CA 91105 ⓣ1-800/310-3220, ⓦwww.distantlands.com.
Globe Corner Bookstore 28 Church St, Cambridge, MA 02138 ⓣ1-800/358-6013, ⓦwww.globecorner.com.
Longitude Books 115 W 30th St #1206, New York, NY 10001 ⓣ1-800/342-2164, ⓦwww.longitudebooks.com.
Map Town 400 5 Ave SW #100, Calgary, AB, T2P 0L6 ⓣ1-877/921-6277, ⓦwww.maptown.com.
Travel Bug Bookstore 3065 W Broadway, Vancouver, BC, V6K 2G9 ⓣ604/737-1122, ⓦwww.travelbugbooks.ca.
World of Maps 1235 Wellington St, Ottawa, ON, K1Y 3A3 ⓣ1-800/214-8524, ⓦwww.worldofmaps.com.

In Australia and New Zealand

Map Centre ⓦwww.mapcentre.co.nz.
Mapland 372 Little Bourke St, Melbourne ⓣ03/9670 4383, ⓦwww.mapland.com.au.
Map Shop 6–10 Peel St, Adelaide ⓣ08/8231 2033, ⓦwww.mapshop.net.au.
Map World 371 Pitt St, Sydney ⓣ02/9261 3601, ⓦwww.mapworld.net.au. Also at 900 Hay St, Perth ⓣ08/9322 5733.
Map World 173 Gloucester St, Christchurch ⓣ0800/627 967, ⓦwww.mapworld.co.nz.

Health

Travelling in Slovenia should present few problems: the country has high standards of hygiene and health care, inoculations are not necessary, and tapwater is safe everywhere.

Most problems tend to be weather-related; summers can be blisteringly hot, particularly in central, southern and eastern regions, so a high-factor sun cream is a useful aid. Conversely, inclement weather in the mountainous regions, particularly at higher altitudes, can present potentially serious dangers – hence the usual provisos apply, namely, suitable clothing, sufficient provisions and equipment, and a watchful eye on the forecast. If you're planning to spend time in the mountains or forested areas, you may wish to consider being inoculated against tick-borne encephalitis.

All towns and most villages have a **pharmacy** (*lekarna*), with highly trained staff, most of whom invariably speak a good standard of English. Opening hours are normally from 7am to 7 or 8pm; signs in the window give the location or telephone number of the nearest all-night pharmacy (*dežurna lekarna*). In **emergencies** dial ⓣ112 for the ambulance service, who will whisk you off to the **hospital** (*bolnica*) where you should be attended to fairly rapidly.

Insurance

As an EU country Slovenia has free reciprocal health arrangements with other member states on production of your passport. However, you'd do well to take out an insurance policy before travelling to cover against theft, loss, and illness or injury. Before paying for a new policy, though, it's worth checking whether you are already covered: some all-risks home insurance policies may cover your possessions when overseas, and many private medical schemes include cover when abroad. In Canada, provincial health plans usually provide partial cover for medical mishaps overseas, while holders of official student/teacher/youth cards in Canada and the US are entitled to meagre accident coverage and hospital inpatient benefits. Students will often find that their student health coverage extends during the vacations and for one term beyond the date of last enrolment.

After exhausting the possibilities above, you might want to contact a specialist travel insurance company, or consider the travel insurance deal we offer (see box, opposite). A typical travel insurance policy usually provides cover for the loss of baggage, tickets and – up to a certain limit – cash or cheques, as well as cancellation or curtailment of your journey. Most of them exclude so-called dangerous sports unless an extra premium is paid: in Slovenia this could mean, for example, skiing, scuba diving,

Rough Guides travel insurance

Rough Guides Ltd offers a low-cost travel insurance policy, especially customized for our statistically low-risk readers by a leading British broker, provided by the American International Group (AIG) and registered with the British regulatory body, GISC (the General Insurance Standards Council). There are five main Rough Guides insurance plans: No Frills for the bare minimum for secure travel; Essential, which provides decent all-round cover; Premier for comprehensive cover with a wide range of benefits; Extended Stay for cover lasting four months to a year; and Annual multi-trip, a cost-effective way of getting Premier cover if you travel more than once a year. Premier, Annual Multi-Trip and Extended Stay policies can be supplemented by a "Hazardous Pursuits Extension" if you plan to indulge in sports considered dangerous, such as scuba-diving or trekking. For a policy quote, call the Rough Guides Insurance Line: toll-free in the UK ⓣ0800/015 09 06 or ⓣ44 1392 314 665 from elsewhere. Alternatively, get an online quote at www.roughguides.com/insurance.

white-water rafting, and trekking, though probably not activities such as canoeing or kayaking. Many policies can be chopped and changed to exclude coverage you don't need – for example, sickness and accident benefits can often be excluded or included at will. If you do take medical coverage, ascertain whether benefits will be paid as treatment proceeds or only after return home, and whether there is a 24-hour medical emergency number. When securing baggage cover, make sure that the per-article limit (typically under £500) will cover your most valuable possession. If you need to make a claim, you should keep receipts for medicines and medical treatment, and in the event you have anything stolen, you must obtain an official statement from the police.

Costs, money and banks

Of the ex-Yugoslav republics, Slovenia was always quite comfortably the most well-off. In the intervening years since independence, and as Slovenia has moved closer to full membership of the European Union, this gap has widened, although many Slovenes complain about the ever-increasing costs of living, especially in the capital, where rents are sky-high and house prices unaffordable for the majority. It is anticipated that Slovenia will convert to the euro in 2007; for the time being, and although prices for accommodation and tours are sometimes given in euros (payment is actually made in tolars), euros are usually only accepted in the casinos near Italy.

Some basic costs

Although Slovenia can by no means be classified as a bargain destination, it's still very good value on the whole, though prices in the capital, as well as in some of the more popular destinations such as Bled and Bohinj and the coastal resorts, are invariably higher than the rest of the country.

As with most destinations, your biggest expenditure will be on **accommodation**; outside Ljubljana and the coast, the average three-star hotel (in high season) comes in at around the 14,000SIT mark (see below for current exchange rate) for a double, whilst for a private room, or a night on a tourist farm, expect to part with around 3000SIT per person. Eating out in a decent **restaurant** will set you back 2500–3000SIT, including drinks, whilst you can get a more basic, but no less substantial meal for around 1500SIT in most places. You'll find foodstuffs in supermarkets and convenience stores on a par with western European prices.

Transport is inexpensive; as a rule buses are cheaper than trains, but, given the country's size, you'll not be travelling long distances. Fuel is currently amongst the cheapest in Europe (see p.25). **Museum** admission charges vary between 400SIT and 600SIT. Of course, by being a little more frugal in certain departments, you can cut costs considerably.

Youth and student discounts

Once obtained, various official and quasi-official **youth/student ID cards** soon pay for themselves in savings. Full-time students are eligible for the International Student ID Card (ISIC, ⓦwww.isiccard.com), which entitles the bearer to special air, rail and bus fares and discounts at museums, theatres and other attractions. For Americans there's also a health benefit, providing up to $3000 in emergency medical coverage and $100 a day for 60 days in the hospital, plus a 24-hour hotline to call in the event of a medical, legal or financial emergency. The card costs $22 in the USA; Can$16 in Canada; Aus$16.50 in Australia; NZ$21 in New Zealand; £6 in the UK; and €12.70 in the Republic of Ireland.

You only have to be 26 or younger to qualify for the **International Youth Travel Card**, which costs US$22/£7 and carries the same benefits. Teachers qualify for the **International Teacher Card**, offering similar discounts and costing US$22, Can$16, Aus$16.50 and NZ$21. All these cards are available in the US from Council Travel, STA, Travel Cuts and, in Canada, Hostelling International (see pp.13–14, 29 for addresses); in Australia and New Zealand from STA or Campus Travel; and in the UK from STA.

Several other travel organizations and accommodation groups also sell their own cards, good for various discounts. A university photo ID might open some doors, but is not as easily recognizable as the ISIC cards. However, the latter are often not accepted as valid proof of age, for example in bars or liquor stores.

Currency and exchange rate

Slovenia's unit of **currency** is the **tolar** (SIT), divided into 100 stotini. Coins come in denominations of 1, 2, 5 and 10 tolars; and there are notes of 10, 20, 50, 100, 200, 500, 1000, 5000 and 10,000 tolars. These large and colourful notes depict eminent Slovenes such as poet France Prešeren, architect Jože Plečnik, artist Rihard Jakopič and writer Ivan Cankar. (Prices are usually followed by the initials SIT.) The exchange rate is currently around 340SIT to £1, 230SIT to €1, and 200SIT to $1.

Banks and changing money

As a rule you're best off changing money in **banks** (*banka*), which you can find in all but the smallest towns, and which are generally open 8.30am–12.30pm and 2–5pm weekdays, and 8.30–11am or noon on Saturdays. Otherwise, you can change money at numerous small exchange offices (*menjalnice*), tourist offices, tourist agencies, post offices and hotels, though you may end up paying considerably more in commission. Changing **travellers' cheques** is a relatively painless process, although some banks do insist on seeing your issuing receipt in order for the transaction to go ahead. Make sure that you get rid of any unwanted tolars before you leave the country, as it's unlikely you'll be able to change them once outside.

Cash and travellers' cheques

If taking **cash**, a modest amount of low denomination euros is advisable. If carrying **travellers' cheques**, then by far the most recognized are American Express, either sterling or dollars. The usual fee for travellers' cheque sales is one or two percent, though this fee may be waived if you buy the cheques through a bank where you have an account. It pays to get a selection of denominations. Make sure to keep the purchase agreement and a record of cheque serial numbers safe and separate from the cheques themselves. In the event of lost or stolen cheques, report the loss forthwith to the American Express office in Ljubljana, which is opposite the train station at Kolodvorska 16 (Mon–Fri 8am–5pm; ⓣ01/430-7720); lost or stolen cheques can usually be replaced within 24 hours.

Credit and debit cards

Credit cards are a very handy backup source of funds, and can be used either in ATMs or over the counter. Mastercard, Visa and American Express are accepted just about everywhere, but other cards may not be recognized in Slovenia. You'll have little trouble finding ATMs (*bančni avtomat*), even in the smallest towns, whilst most hotels, restaurants and shops now accept plastic. Remember that all cash advances are treated as loans, with interest accruing daily from the date of withdrawal; there may be a transaction fee on top of this. However, you may be able to make withdrawals from ATMs in Slovenia using your **debit card**, which is not liable to interest payments, and the flat transaction fee is usually quite small – your bank will be able to advise on this. Make sure you have a personal identification number (PIN) that's designed to work overseas.

A compromise between travellers' cheques and plastic is Visa TravelMoney, a disposable prepaid debit card with a PIN which works in all ATMs that take Visa cards. You load up your account with funds before leaving home, and when they run out, you simply throw the card away. You can buy up to nine cards to access the same funds – useful for couples or families travelling together – and it's a good idea to buy at least one extra as a backup in case of loss or theft. There is also a 24-hour toll-free customer assistance number: there's a list online at ⓦusa.visa.com/personal/secure_with_visa/lost_your_card.html#numbs. The card is available in most countries from branches of Thomas Cook and Citicorp. For more information, check the Visa TravelMoney website at ⓦusa.visa.com/personal/cards/visa_travel_money.html.

Wiring money

Having money wired from home using one of the companies listed below is never convenient or cheap, and should be considered a last resort. It's also possible to have money wired directly from a bank in your home country to a bank in Slovenia, although this is somewhat less reliable because it involves two separate institutions. If you go this route, your home bank will need the address of the branch bank where you want to pick up the money and the address and telex number of the Ljubljana head office, which will act as the clearing house; money wired this way normally takes two working days to arrive, and costs around £25/$40 per transaction.

Getting around

Travelling around Slovenia by any mode of transport is wonderful, and whether you travel by train, bus or car, any journey you undertake will rarely be anything other than extremely scenic; moreover, the country's tiny scale means that you'll never have to travel long distances. On the whole, both trains and buses are clean, reliable and inexpensive, and although trains are cheaper, buses do cover a far greater number of destinations. Driving brings the obvious advantages of allowing you to visit pretty much anywhere you please, and in your own good time. Approximate times and frequencies are given in the "Travel Details" section at the end of each chapter.

Trains

Slovene railways (*Slovenske železnice*) run a smooth, efficient and inexpensive service covering a modest 1200 kilometres, almost half of which is electrified. All the key lines, as well as international trains, run through Ljubljana, but even if you're not intending to travel to the capital, you'll often save yourself a lot of hassle by heading to Ljubljana first and changing there, instead of messing about changing at a host of small regional stops.

Trains (*vlaki*) are divided into **slow trains** (*potniški*), which stop at every halt, **Intercity trains** ("IC") which are faster, more comfortable, and stop at fewer stations, and the relatively new, and very fast, **Inter City Slovenia** ("ICS"), three-carriage tilting trains which run between Maribor and Ljubljana, stopping at Pragersko, Celje and Zidani Most, covering the journey in just one hour forty-five minutes; air-conditioned, these trains also have catering and are wheelchair accessible. Given the short distances covered, there are no domestic overnight trains in operation. There are good rail links with neighbouring countries, with regular trains passing through Ljubljana to/from Belgrade, Budapest, Munich, Venice, Vienna and Zagreb; some of these trains – InterCity ("IC"), EuroCity ("EC") and EuroNight ("EN") – may require a supplement.

Although there are no special carriages for them, **bicycles** (*kolo*) can be carried on all trains (except the ICS), for which you have to pay an extra 550SIT. You can also check train information on the **website** Ⓦwww.slo-zeleznice.si. Most **timetables** (*vozni red*) have explanations in English, and timetable leaflets, which only indicate routes that trains from that station take, are sometimes available from counters. The yellow boards with *Odhodi* are departures, the white boards with *Prihodi* arrivals. If you're planning to travel extensively on the railways you might want to invest in a timetable (*Vozni Red Slovenske Železniške*; 1250SIT), available from most stations.

Tickets

Tickets for domestic train services can be bought at the station (*železniška postaja*) on the day of departure and up to two months in advance. If you enter a train without a ticket (for a good reason) you will have to pay a supplement of around 400SIT on top of the ticket price. Otherwise, fare dodging (not advised) could cost you anything up to 10,000SIT. Some stations now accept payment by credit card (currently Visa only) for both domestic and international tickets.

Fares are calculated by distance travelled, with a return ticket (*povratna vozovnica*) exactly double that of a single (*enosmerna vozovnica*). To give you some idea, a journey of 50km costs around 800SIT (1200SIT first class), a journey of 100km, 1130SIT (1700SIT first class), and a journey of 200km, 1880SIT (2820SIT first class). ICS trains, however, are more expensive; the second class fare for the journey between Ljubljana and Maribor (156km) currently costs around 2600SIT. **Concessionary**

fares on domestic services are available for children under the age of 6 (free), and for children aged between 6 and 12 (fifty percent discount).

Seat reservations (*rezervacije*) are obligatory for services marked on a timetable with a boxed R (in effect all ICS trains and some international services), and optional for those designated by an R. It's best to buy **international tickets** a day or so in advance. Aside from the train station, **tickets** for international services can also be purchased at certain agencies. Slovenian railways do not issue any passes for travel within the country.

Rail passes

There's a huge array of European rail passes available, covering regions as well as individual countries. Some have to be bought before leaving home while some can only be bought in the country itself. The national rail companies of many European countries also offer their own passes, most of which can be bought in advance through Rail Europe or direct from the national rail company or tourist office. Rail Europe is the umbrella company for all national and international rail purchases, and its comprehensive website (Ⓦwww.raileurope.com) is the most useful source of information on which rail passes are available; it also gives all current prices.

Inter-Rail pass

These passes are only available to European residents, and you will be asked to provide proof of residency before being allowed to purchase one. They come in over-26 and (cheaper) under-26 versions, and cover 28 European countries (including Turkey and Morocco) grouped together in zones:

A Republic of Ireland/Britain
B Norway, Sweden, Finland
C Germany, Austria, Switzerland, Denmark
D Czech & Slovak Republics, Poland, Hungary, Croatia
E France, Belgium, Netherlands, Luxembourg
F Spain, Portugal, Morocco
G Italy, Greece, Turkey, Slovenia plus some ferry services between Italy and Greece
H Bulgaria, Romania, Yugoslavia, Macedonia

The passes are available for 22 days (one zone only), or 1 month and you can purchase up to 3 zones or a global pass covering all zones. You can save £5 by booking via the InterRail website (Ⓦwww.inter-rail.co.uk). InterRail passes do not include travel between Britain and the continent, although InterRail Pass holders are eligible for discounts on rail travel in Britain and Northern Ireland and cross-Channel ferries, free travel on the Brindisi–Patras ferry between Italy and Greece, plus discounts on other shipping services around the Mediterranean, Scandinavia and the Balearics. The InterRail Pass also gives a discount on the London–Paris Eurostar service.

Euro Domino pass

Only available to European residents. Individual country passes provide unlimited travel in 28 European and North African countries. The passes are available for between 3 and 8 days' travel within a one-month period; prices vary depending on the country, but include most high-speed train supplements. You can buy as many separate country passes as you want. There is a discounted youth price for those under 26, and a half-price child (age 4–11) fare.

Rail contacts

In the UK and Ireland

Rail Europe (SNCF French Railways) UK Ⓣ0870/5848 848, Ⓦwww.raileurope.co.uk. Discounted rail fares for under-26s on a variety of European routes; also agents for Inter-Rail, Eurostar and Eurodomino.

In North America

CIT Rail US Ⓣ1-800/CIT-RAIL or 212/730-2400, Canada Ⓣ1-800/361-7799, Ⓦwww.cit-rail.com. Eurail and Europass passes.
DER Travel US Ⓣ1-888/337-7350, Ⓦwww.dertravel.com/rail. Eurail and Europass passes.
Europrail International Canada Ⓣ1-888/667-9734, Ⓦwww.europrail.net. Eurail and Europass passes.
Rail Europe US Ⓣ1-877/257-2887, Canada Ⓣ1-800/361-RAIL, Ⓦwww.raileurope.com/us. Official North American Eurail Pass agent; also

Useful timetable publications

The red-covered *Thomas Cook European Timetables* details schedules of over 50,000 trains in Europe, as well as timings of over 200 ferry routes and rail-connecting bus services. It's updated and issued every month; main changes are in the June edition (published end of May), which has details of the summer European schedules, and the October one, (published end of Sept), which includes winter schedules; some have advance summer/winter timings also. The book can be purchased online (which gets you a ten percent discount) at ⓦwww.thomascookpublishing.com or from branches of Thomas Cook (see ⓦwww.thomascook.co.uk for your nearest branch), and costs £9.50. Their useful Rail Map of Europe can also be purchased online for £6.95.

sells Europass, multinational passes and most single-country passes.

ScanTours US ⓣ1-800/223-7226 or 310/636-4656, ⓦwww.scantours.com. Eurail and European country passes.

In Australia and New Zealand

CIT World Travel Australia ⓣ02/9267 1255 or 03/9650 5510, ⓦwww.cittravel.com.au. Eurail and Europass passes.

Rail Plus Australia ⓣ1300/555 003 or 03/9642 8644, ⓦwww.railplus.com.au. Sells Eurail and Europass passes.

Trailfinders Australia ⓣ02/9247 7666, ⓦwww.trailfinder.com.au. All Europe passes.

Buses

Slovenia's **bus** network consists of a slightly confusing, but generally well-coordinated, array of small local companies. On the whole, buses are clean, reasonably comfortable, and, except for some departing on a Friday evening, rarely crowded. Whilst not as comfortable or relaxing as travelling by train, they do have the advantage of being able to reach significantly more destinations than trains; moreover, services tend to be more frequent. That said, services, particularly those on rural routes, are dramatically reduced (or even nonexistent) at weekends, and especially on Sundays.

Towns such as Ljubljana, Maribor and Koper have large bus stations (*avtobusna postaja*) with computerized booking facilities where you can buy your tickets hours (if not days) in advance – recommended if you're travelling between Ljubljana and the coast in high season. Otherwise, simply pile onto the bus and pay the driver or conductor. If you need to store items of baggage in the hold you'll be charged a little extra. Like trains, **fares** are calculated according to distance travelled; typical fares are around 1300SIT for 50km and 2500SIT for 100km.

By bicycle

Slovenia's wonderfully varied topography presents endless opportunities for cyclists. From the tough mountain climbs in Triglav National Park to the iron-flat landscapes of Prekmurje, there are a number of well-organized recreational routes and trails all over the country – see p.39 for more on cycling in the countryside. Otherwise, cycling is permitted on all roads except motorways. Most urban centres have, to a greater or lesser degree, well-integrated cycle lanes or paths, though the traffic in most towns and cities is rarely threatening. On a practical note, bikes can be taken onto trains, except ICS, for a small fee, whilst some buses might allow you to store your bike in the luggage compartment.

By car

All things considered, driving in Slovenia is a joy. Despite the country's high level of car ownership, Slovenia's well-surfaced roads often seem blissfully traffic-free, and you'll be endlessly distracted by the scenery. Neither is driving likely to tire you out, such are the (very short) distances between destinations. If driving in the mountainous regions, bear in mind that some of the higher passes, such as the Vršič Pass in the Julian Alps, often close for days or weeks at a time during periods of heavy snowfall. To drive in Slovenia you'll need your **driving licence** and **third-party insurance.**

Hitchhiking is widely practised by Slovenes, and you'll often see queues of students lining roadsides on the outskirts of Ljubljana and other towns on a Friday evening in a quest to get home. Avoid these places at these times and you shouldn't have too much of a problem getting a ride with someone. As anywhere, however, it's not a foolproof pursuit, so caution should be exercised.

Roads and services

The country is crossed by two **motorway** corridors (*avtocesta*), the A1 which runs in an east–west direction from Šentilj, just north of Maribor, down to the Koper on the coast (there's also a short stretch from Postojna up to Nova Gorica, the H4), and the A2 which runs north-south from the Karavanke Tunnel on the Austrian border to Obrežje on the Croatian border (and continuing down to Zagreb) – both these motorways pass through Ljubljana. However, sections of both are still under construction, and it's unlikely that either will be fully completed before the end of 2005. **Tolls** are payable (in tolars or euros) on each stretch: some typical costs are: on the A1, Ljubljana to Postojna 500SIT, and Ljubljana to Kozina or Sežana 900SIT; and on the A2, Ljubljana to Torovo (en route to Jesenice and Austria), 360SIT. Lesser **highways**, linking the major centres of population, are numbered with a single digit link, whilst **secondary** or **tertiary** roads are identified by two or three digit numbers.

Petrol stations (*Bencinska črpalka*) can be found everywhere, even in the most rural backwaters. Whilst most open from around 7am to 8 or 9pm, there are now quite a few 24-hour service stations, usually located on the outskirts of larger towns and cities, and around resort areas. At around 190SIT per litre, fuel in Slovenia is amongst the cheapest in Europe; lead-free fuel (*neosvinčen bencin*) is now the most commonly used. Credit cards are accepted at most stations.

In cities, **parking** in "white zones" (ie where you see white lines) is permitted for up to one hour (100SIT), whilst you can stay in a "blue zone" for up thirty minutes (free). *Brezplačno* means free parking. Parking in car parks normally costs around 250SIT per hour.

For information on any aspect of driving within Slovenia, you can contact the Automobile Association of Slovenia (Avto-moto zveza Slovenije or AMZS), based in Ljubljana at Dunajska 128 (Ⓣ01/530-5100). Their information centre (daily 5.30am–11pm; Ⓣ01/530-5300) provides information and assistance, whilst their excellent website (Ⓦwww.amzs.si) tells you all you need to know about driving in Slovenia, as well as providing up-to-the-minute information on road traffic conditions. They also publish a 1:270,000 tourist road map of Slovenia (1600SIT).

Rules & regulations

Traffic drives on the right: **speed limits** for vehicles are 130kph on motorways, 100kph on second and tertiary roads, and 50kph in built-up areas. Otherwise, the most important **rules** are the prohibitions against sounding the horn in a built-up area (unless to avert accidents); and using a hand-held mobile whilst driving. It is also compulsory for driver and passengers to wear seatbelts; to use dipped headlights when travelling on all roads at all times of the day; and to keep a triangular breakdown sign in the car.

If you're stopped by the police – and you'll see plenty of them on approaches to villages and built-up areas – you'll be required to show all your documents, so make sure you have them in the car at all times. Any road traffic violations (speeding, not wearing a seatbelt, illegal parking, etc) are subject to on-the-spot **fines**, which can be anything between 5000SIT and 45,000SIT, depending upon the offence. It goes without saying that **drinking and driving** do not go hand in hand; the permitted blood-alcohol level for drivers is 0.05mg per 100ml of blood, although you may still be liable to a 20,000SIT fine if caught with this amount. Any amount over this means a fine of anything up to 90,000SIT and the confiscation of your licence.

Accidents and emergencies

In the event of a **breakdown**, call AMZS's Assistance-Information Service (SPI) on the

24-hour emergency number ⓣ1987. There are 24-hour **technical centres** in Celje, Koper, Kranj, Ljubljana, Maribor, Otočec and Postojna, with technical units (open 7am–8pm) in the other major towns; the addresses and telephone numbers of all centres can be found on the AMZS website. All accidents should be reported to the police on ⓣ113.

Car rental

Renting a car is simple enough, provided you are 21 or older, and hold a valid national driving licence. You can order a car through rental agencies in your own country (see below), which sometimes works out cheaper. Once in Slovenia, the most convenient place to rent a car is at Brnik airport, where all the major companies have an outlet, or in downtown Ljubljana (see "Listings" in the Ljubljana chapter, p.85); some companies have branches in other major towns and cities.

Car rental **costs** are not especially cheap; expect to pay around 12,000SIT/€50 upwards for a day's hire (unlimited mileage) and 60,000SIT/€260 upwards for a week. As anywhere, it becomes cheaper the longer the hire period. There's little difference in price amongst the major companies, but you may find that local companies, such as ABC Cars in Ljubljana (see p.85), offer better deals, so it's worth looking around before deciding upon which company to use. Credit cards are usually required for a deposit. Before signing, check on any mileage limits or other restrictions, extras, and what you're covered for in the event of an accident. You should normally be able to take the car into neighbouring countries, although some companies may balk (or just charge you a little more) at the thought of you driving into Hungary or Croatia; in any case, should you have any intention of leaving the country, check with the car rental company first.

Car rental agencies

In Britain

Avis ⓣ0870/606 0100, ⓦwww.avis.co.uk.
Budget ⓣ0800/181 181, ⓦwww.budget.co.uk.
Europcar ⓣ0845/722 2525, ⓦwww.europcar.co.uk.
National ⓣ0870/536 5365, ⓦwww.nationalcar.co.uk.
Hertz ⓣ0870/844 8844, ⓦwww.hertz.co.uk.
Holiday Autos ⓣ0870/400 0099, ⓦwww.holidayautos.co.uk.
Suncars ⓣ0870/500 5566, ⓦwww.suncars.com.
Thrifty ⓣ01494/751 600, ⓦwww.thrifty.co.uk.

In Ireland

Avis Northern Ireland ⓣ028/9024 0404, Republic of Ireland ⓣ01/605 7500, ⓦwww.avis.ie.
Budget Republic of Ireland ⓣ0903/277 11, ⓦwww.budget.ie.
Cosmo Thrifty Northern Ireland ⓣ028/9445 2565, ⓦwww.thrifty.co.uk.
Europcar Northern Ireland ⓣ028/9442 3444, Republic of Ireland ⓣ01/614 2888, ⓦwww.europcar.ie.
Hertz Republic of Ireland ⓣ01/676 7476, ⓦwww.hertz.ie.
Holiday Autos Republic of Ireland ⓣ01/872 9366, ⓦwww.holidayautos.ie.
SIXT Republic of Ireland ⓣ1850/206 088, ⓦwww.irishcarrentals.ie.
Thrifty Republic of Ireland ⓣ1800/515 800, ⓦwww.thrifty.ie.

In North America

Avis US ⓣ1-800/331-1084, Canada ⓣ1-800/272-5871, ⓦwww.avis.com.
Budget US ⓣ1-800/527-0700, ⓦwww.budgetrentacar.com.
Dollar US ⓣ1-800/800-4000, ⓦwww.dollar.com.
Europcar US & Canada ⓣ1-877/940 6900, ⓦwww.europcar.com.
Hertz US ⓣ1-800/654-3001, Canada ⓣ1-800/263-0600, ⓦwww.hertz.com.
Holiday Autos US ⓣ1-800/422-7737, ⓦwww.holidayautos.com.
National ⓣ1-800/227-7368, ⓦwww.nationalcar.com.
Thrifty ⓣ1-800/367-2277, ⓦwww.thrifty.com.

In Australia

Avis ⓣ13 63 33 or 02/9353 9000, ⓦwww.avis.com.au
Budget ⓣ1300/362 848, ⓦwww.budget.com.au
Dollar ⓣ02/9223 1444, ⓦwww.dollarcar.com.au.
Europcar ⓣ1300/131 390, ⓦwww.deltaeuropcar.com.au.
Hertz ⓣ13 30 39 or 03/9698 2555, ⓦwww.hertz.com.au.

Holiday Autos ⓣ1300/554 432, ⓦwww.holidayautos.com.au.
National ⓣ13 10 45, ⓦwww.nationalcar.com.au.
Thrifty ⓣ1300/367 227, ⓦwww.thrifty.com.au.

In New Zealand

Avis ⓣ09/526 2847 or 0800/655 111, ⓦwww.avis.co.nz.
Budget ⓣ09/976 2222, ⓦwww.budget.co.nz.
Hertz ⓣ0800/654 321, ⓦwww.hertz.co.nz.
Holiday Autos ⓣ0800/144 040, ⓦwww.holidayautos.co.nz.
National ⓣ0800/800 115, ⓦwww.nationalcar.co.nz.
Thrifty ⓣ09/309 0111, ⓦwww.thrifty.co.nz.

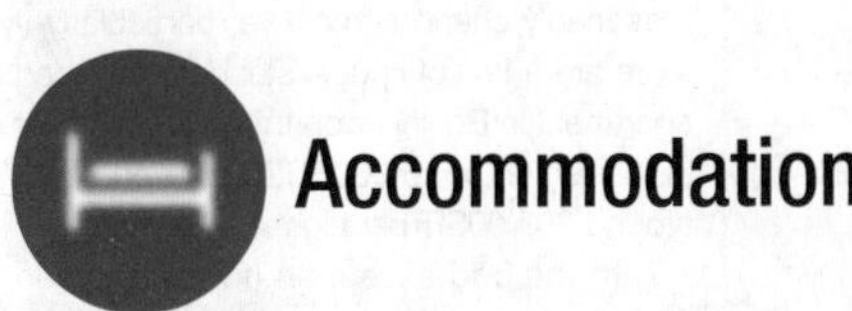

Accommodation

Finding somewhere to bed down, even in the busiest resorts during high season, is unlikely to be a problem; hotels abound and there are an increasing number of good-value pensions to choose from. For those with less cash to spend, there are plenty of private rooms to go around, particularly in the more well-touristed areas such as Bled, Bohinj and the coast, whilst a stay on a tourist farm provides an attractive, affordable, and peaceful alternative. There's a good spread of decent campsites across the country, though hostels are few and far between.

Reservations for all types of accommodation are advisable during high season in the more popular places (June to August, and December to February in the ski resorts), or if you're bound for somewhere with limited possibilities. You can do this, either through a specialist travel agent or by contacting places directly – most places now have an email address, and these are given throughout the guide where this is the case. Details of all Slovenia's hotels and campsites can be found in booklets available from the Slovenia Tourist Board; you can view the same contents online at ⓦwww.slovenia-tourism.si.

Hotels and pensions

Slovenian hotels use the traditional **five-star grading system** for classification, although in many cases this only gives a vague idea of prices, which can vary dramatically according to the locality and season. Generally speaking, prices in the capital, along the coast and in the major resorts, such as Bled, Bohinj and Kranjska Gora are higher than elsewhere, though prices (except in Ljubljana) do drop considerably outside the main tourist seasons. Moreover, the ratings are not always indicative of the quality of a place – for example, three-star places can, and do, vary appreciably from one place to another.

Unfortunately, many of Slovenia's city **hotels** are heavily geared towards the business traveller – in Ljubljana, for example, budget or medium-priced hotels are almost nonexistent, a situation common to other places like Maribor, Celje and Nova Gorica; whilst hotels in key resorts such as Bled, Bohinj or Portorož are predominantly aimed squarely at the package-tourist. That said there are a growing number of **family-run hotels** and **pensions** (*penzion*), which, in most cases, offer much better value than a hotel of a similar price. Some pensions are more commonly known as *gostišče*, not to be confused with a gostilna (which is an eating establishment only), but these are usually found in smaller towns and more rural areas.

Slovenia can count less than a handful of five-star establishments, a couple of which are in Ljubljana and Maribor, whilst the others have been incorporated into historic

Accommodation price codes

Accommodation in this guide is graded according to the price bands below. Note that prices refer to the **cheapest available double room in high season**. For hostels and dormitories, the price per bed has been given.

1 Under 5000SIT
2 5000SIT–7500SIT
3 7500SIT–10,000SIT
4 10,000SIT–13,000SIT
5 13,000SIT–16,000SIT
6 16,000SIT–19,000SIT
7 19,000SIT–22,000SIT
8 22,000SIT–26,000SIT
9 over 26,000SIT

buildings, for example at Mokrice and Otočec castles. Most four-star hotels have all the luxuries you'd expect, with modern, and in many cases, renovated, rooms, satellite TV, minibar and Internet access. The vast majority of the country's hotels are in the three-star category, and this is where standards can vary wildly. However, in most cases the rooms are reliably comfortable and come with TV and minibar. More predictably, one and two-star hotels are often tatty, soulless places (and sometimes come without private bathroom) but are usually clean and bearable. Most hotels include **breakfast** in the price, but this is not always clear and is worth checking.

Private rooms and apartments

Hostels aside, taking a **private room** (*zasebne sobe*) is the cheapest option available, particularly if there are two of you sharing. Whilst few towns and cities are well stocked with private rooms, you'll find that there are plenty to go around in the busier lake and coastal resorts. Rooms are **categorized** from one to three stars; a one-star place is very basic and comes with shared shower and toilets, a two-star usually has private shower and toilet, and a three-star comes with plusher furnishings and television.

As a rough guideline, **prices** start at around 3500SIT for a double room in a category-one place, 5000SIT for a category-two place, and 6000SIT for a category-three place. Not included in the price is tourist tax, which is usually around 300SIT per person; nor is breakfast included. Moreover, in most places, prices are subject to a thirty percent surcharge if you stay fewer than three nights. Rented out in the same way as private rooms, **apartments** (*apartmaji*) are another reasonably cheap alternative, particularly if there are a few of you. A standard four-bed apartment in Bohinj or on the coast will cost in the region of 15,000SIT, a six-bed place around 20,000SIT per night.

With the odd exception (for example in Bohinj) very few tourist offices administer **bookings** for private rooms; these are usually handled by local agencies, which can be found in most places. Larger agencies such as Kompas or Globtour have branches in several towns and resorts.

Tourist farms

Farm tourism (*turističnih kmetji*) is a thriving sector in Slovenia, and if you're looking for a more restful alternative, then these rural retreats are ideal. On the downside, their very isolation means that, unless you have your own means of transport, they can often be quite difficult to reach.

Accommodation is **graded** according to an apple classification system: four apples represent a farm with large, well-furnished rooms with television and private bathroom, down to one apple, a basic, simply furnished place with shared wash and toilet facilities. Although there are no hard and fast rules regarding **pricing**, as a guide a farm with three or four apples will cost around 3500–4000SIT, two apples around 3000SIT, and one, or unclassified, farms around 2500SIT; all these are inclusive of breakfast. Most farms offer a half-board option (approximately 1000SIT extra), which is a bargain given that the cooking is almost always exceptional. Some farms also offer additional activities, such as horse riding, cycling and tennis, whilst others allow you to help out on the farm – from preparing foodstuffs (baking bread or making jam), to milking the cows or feeding the calves.

The excellent *Countryside (Tourist Farms)* brochure, produced by the Association of Tourist Farms of Slovenia in conjunction with the Slovenian Tourist Board, lists and describes each and every tourist farm in the country. The Association is based in Celje at Trnoveljska 1 (ⓣ03/491-6480, ⓦwww.slovenia-tourism.si/touristfarms).

Mountain huts

There are over 160 **mountain huts** (*Planinarski Domovi*) scattered across Slovenia's hills and mountains, ranging from the most basic refuges with huge dorms and cold running water, to more comfortable alpine villas offering a wider range of cosier rooms, hot water and other amenities. In any case, most huts are convivial places, where hikers share a beer or two and exchange information about trails or the weather before pushing on.

The majority of huts, especially those at higher altitudes, are open between June and September, whilst some are open a month or two longer than this; if you're planning to spend any length of time in the more popular hiking areas, for example around Triglav, you'd be wise to book ahead wherever possible. Depending upon the type of hut and its location, you'll pay anything between 2000SIT and 3500SIT for a bed; UIAA-affiliated members are entitled to a discount. The useful, if a little dated, *Mountain Huts* book, published by the Slovene Alpine Association, lists every hut, together with routes and approaches to the next lodge. For more on mountain huts see the box on p.144.

Hostels and dormitories

Hostels in Slovenia are thin on the ground, whilst most of those that do exist are actually student dormitories. The four year-round hostels – in Bled, Ljubljana, Piran and Ptuj – are uniformly excellent, each with rooms sleeping between two and six people (Ljubljana also has a 14-bed dorm) and each charging around 4000SIT per person, including breakfast. All these offer discounts to HI card holders. **Student dorms** (*dijaški dom*), which are generally of a decent standard, are usually only open in July and August once the students have packed up (although some keep a few beds aside during the rest of the year, but these are usually available at weekends only); expect to pay around 2000–3000SIT for a bed. The head office of the Slovenian Hostelling Association is in Maribor, at Gosposvetska 84 (ⓣ02/234-2137, ⓦwww.gaudeamus.si/hostelling).

Youth hostel associations

In England and Wales

Youth Hostel Association (YHA) ⓣ0870/770 8868, ⓦwww.yha.org.uk.

In Scotland

Scottish Youth Hostel Association ⓣ0870/155 3255, ⓦwww.syha.org.uk.

In Ireland

Hostelling International Northern Ireland ⓣ028/9032 4733, ⓦwww.hini.org.uk.
Irish Youth Hostel Association ⓣ01/830 4555, ⓦwww.irelandyha.org.

In the US

Hostelling International-American Youth Hostels ⓣ202/783-6161, ⓦwww.hiayh.org.

In Canada

Hostelling International Canada ⓣ1-800/663 5777 or 613/237 7884, ⓦwww.hostellingintl.ca.

In Australia

Youth Hostels Association Australia ⓣ02/9261 1111, ⓦwww.yha.com.au.

In New Zealand

Youth Hostelling Association New Zealand ⓣ0800/278 299 or 03/379 9970, ⓦwww.yha.co.nz.

Camping

Slovenia has a good, if rather uneven, spread of **camping grounds** (*kampi*) across the country. Most campsites, whatever their size, are clean and well-appointed places, whilst the better ones (sites are categorized from between one and three stars), such as those in Bled and Bohinj, have excellent amenities – more often than not with restaurants, shops, sports facilities and children's play areas. Nearly all sites have hot water.

Expect to pay around 500SIT for ground rent plus 1000SIT per person per night, around twice that at the better sites. Prices are reduced slightly outside July and August. The majority of sites are open from April or May to September or October, with a handful – including the one in Ljubljana – open year-round. Note that **camping rough** is illegal.

If you're planning to do a lot of camping, an international camping carnet is a good investment. The carnet gives discounts at member sites and serves as useful identification. Many campsites will take it instead of making you surrender your passport during your stay, and it covers you for third-party insurance when camping. In the **UK and Ireland**, the carnet costs £4.50, and is available to members of the AA or the RAC (see p.12), or for members only from either of the following: the **Camping and Caravanning Club** (☎024/7669 4995, Ⓦwww.campingandcaravanningclub.co.uk; annual membership £27.50), or the foreign touring arm of the same company, the **Carefree Travel Service** (☎024/7642 2024), which provides the international camping carnet free if you take out insurance with them; they also book ferry crossings and inspect camping sites in Europe. In the **US and Canada**, the carnet is available from home motoring organizations, or from **Family Campers and RVers** (FCRV; ☎1-800/245-9755, Ⓦwww.fcrv.org). FCRV annual membership costs $25, and the carnet an additional $10.

Eating and drinking

Slovenia straddles several culinary cultures, absorbing a number of Austrian, Balkan, Mediterranean and Pannonian influences. That said, and despite the increasing internationalization of restaurants and cafés, there remains a strong native Slovene tradition, too, based on age-old peasant recipes. For a full glossary of food and drink terms, see p.343–345.

Breakfasts, snacks and sandwiches

Breakfast (*zajtrk*) in your average hotel typically consists of bread or rolls with jam or marmalade as an accompaniment, and sometimes cereal and yoghurt – only in the better hotels will you be offered a full buffet complement, with cooked food, pastries or croissants and fresh fruit. Breakfast on a tourist farm is invariably an enjoyable, wholesome affair, with everything from bread and milk to jams and cheeses prepared on the farm.

The best place for **snacks** are *okrepčevalnice* (snack bars) and street kiosks, which dole out *burek*, a flaky and often very greasy, pastry filled with cheese (*burek z sirov*) or meat (*burek z mesom*). Sausages come in various forms, most commonly hot dogs, *hrenovke* (Slovene frankfurters), or the much tastier *kranjska klobasa* (big spicy sausages). A popular light lunchtime meal is *Malica*, a quick-filling two or three-course meal with drink usually served from 11am or midday until 3pm, and costing around 600–800SIT.

Slovenia's **supermarkets** (*trgovina*) and **delicatessens** (*delikatesa*) are good places to stock up on **sandwich and picnic** ingredients, like local cheese (*sir*) and salami (*salama*). You can buy fresh fruit and vegetables here too, but if possible, try and get your produce from outdoor **markets** (*tržnica*) or roadside stalls. Bread (*kruh*) is best bought from **bakeries** (*pekarna*), most of which usually sell a decent range of croissants and sandwiches – which makes them the best place to head to if you've not been offered breakfast at your hotel or lodging. In a similar vein is the almost impossible to pronounce *slaščičarna* (patisserie), where you can indulge in all sorts of sweet-toothed delights.

Restaurants and meals

The most common type of place to eat in Slovenia is a **restavracija** (restaurant). These can be found everywhere, though the quality is often variable, from the down-at-heel to the very classy and, although there are plenty of restaurants in the larger towns and cities (Ljubljana and Maribor specifically), you'll often find that choices are extremely limited in smaller towns. Invariably more atmospheric is a **gostilna**, an inn-type place which is usually, but not always, located on the outskirts of town and in more rural areas; along the same lines, a **gostišče** is a similar establishment but which also has some accommodation available. Of course, no self-respecting town is without a **pizzeria**.

Generally speaking **menus** vary little wherever you eat, and are invariably dominated by meat dishes (*mesne jedi*), mostly schnitzels (*zrezek*), beef (*govedina*), pork (*svinjina*) and veal (*teletina*), whilst the tasty southern Balkan meats *čevapčiči* (grilled rolls of minced meat) and *sarma* (cabbage stuffed with meat and rice) frequently make their way onto menus. One particularly curious Slovene speciality is horse steak (*žrebickov zrezek*), and neither are Slovenes squeamish about offal – liver (*jetra*) and grilled or fried brains (*možgani*) are popular standbys in cheaper restaurants. The majority of menus in classier restaurants will often feature game, with Slovenes particularly partial to bear (*medved*), deer (*srna*), pheasant (*fazan*) and rabbit (*zajec*). Soup (*juha*) is a standard **starter** – in Primorska try *jota* (beans and sauerkraut), and in Štajerska, *kisla juha* (pigs' knuckles and head with sour cream); delicious dry-cured ham (*pršut*) from the Karst is another good appetizer. Two of the most traditional Slovene dishes are *žlikrofi*, ravioli filled with potato, onion and bacon; and *žganci*, once the staple diet of rural Slovenes, a buckwheat or maize porridge often served with sauerkraut.

On the coast you'll find plenty of fish dishes (*ribje jedi*), with mussels (*školjke*), shrimps (*škampi*) and squid (*lignji*) particularly prominent. If you're anywhere near the Soča Valley (and in particular Kobarid, which has three of the country's best restaurants), do try the fabulous freshwater trout (*postrvi*) from the local Soča River, the king of which is the superb, and much sought-after, marble trout (*Salmo trutta marmoratus*). Otherwise, Italian pasta dishes appear on many restaurant menus, whilst goulash (*golaž*) is found almost everywhere, though, not surprisingly, more so near the border with Hungary; *segedin* is goulash with lashings of sauerkraut.

Typical **desserts** include solid Central European favourites such as strudel (pastry filled with apple or rhubarb), and *štruklji*, dumplings with fruit filling; whilst the two most traditional Slovene sweets are *potica*, a doughy roll filled with all sorts of fillings – nuts, tarragon, honey; and, from the Prekmurje region, *gibanica*, a delicious layered pastry consisting of poppy seeds, walnuts, apple and cream. For something more straightforward you can't go wrong with *palačinke* (pancakes with a choice of fillings) or ice-cream (*sladoled*).

Inevitably, standards of **service** vary depending upon the type of establishment you are dining in, but by and large you'll find waiting staff courteous and friendly; moreover, you'll rarely have trouble making yourself understood as most waiting staff speak a good standard of English. If you think it's merited, a ten percent **tip** would be standard.

Vegetarians

Whilst the situation for **vegetarians** is no longer the disaster zone it once was, the options, except in the better restaurants, are usually both meagre and fairly predictable. Aside from the usual salads, vegetable and omelette dishes, Slovenian specialities to look out for are *štruklji* (dumplings with cheese or fruit filling), *ocvrti sir* (cheese fried in breadcrumbs) and *gobova rižota* (mushroom risotto) – the latter is usually excellent;

in the better restaurants, you'll find upmarket variations on the above plus, possibly, one or two other dishes.

Drinking

Daytime drinking takes place in small **café-bars**, or in a *kavarna*, where you might also find a range of cakes, pastries and ice cream on offer. **Coffee** (*kava*) is usually served black unless specified otherwise – ask for *mleko* (milk) or *smetana* (cream) – and often drunk alongside a glass of mineral water (*mineralna voda*), the most popular of which is *Radenci*, from the spa town of the same name. Cappucinos are usually a hit-or-miss affair, ranging from good quality to little more than a regular coffee with a dollop of whipped cream on top. **Tea** (*čaj*) drinkers are in a minority here, although its popularity is growing and there are a couple of fantastic little teahouses (*Čajna hiša*) in Ljubljana and Maribor.

Evening drinking usually goes on in small European-style bars or the more traditional *pivnica* (beer hall) or *vinarna* (wine cellar). Slovene **beer** (*pivo*) is of the Pilsner type and is not bad at all – in fact it was always considered amongst the best of the many beers brewed in any of the ex-Yugoslav republics. The two dominant breweries are Laško, based in the town of the same name and producer of *Zlatorog* (the mythical chamois), and the Ljubljana-based Union; opinion varies as to which is the best, though, on balance the more flavoursome Laško probably has the edge; both breweries also produce *temno pivo* (literally "dark beer"), a Guinness-like stout. There are also many imported varieties to choose from.

Although excellent, Slovenian **wine** (*vino*) is little known – it rarely makes it onto the shelves of Western supermarkets – but its reputation is growing. Although white wine (*belo*) predominates, particularly worth trying are *Beli Pinot* and *Šipon*, there are some fine reds (*črno*) too, notably Cabernet Sauvignon and Merlot from the Vipava Valley, and the dark, acidic *Kraški teran* from the Karst. For more on Slovenian wine, see the box on p.vii. You shouldn't leave the country without trying one of the fiery **brandies**: *slivovka* (plum brandy), *viljemovka* (pear brandy), *sadjevec*, a brandy made from various fruits, and the gin-like juniper-based *brinovec*.

Communications: post, phones and Internet

Both the Slovene postal service (Pošta Slovenije) and telecommunications service (Telekom Slovenije) are well-run, efficient organizations. Unfortunately for the traveller, there are few Internet cafes about, even in the larger towns and cities.

Mail

Post offices (*pošta*), rarely crowded, and efficient, orderly affairs, are usually open Monday to Friday 8am to 6 or 7pm and until noon or 1pm on Saturday, although in Ljubljana and some of the coastal resorts you'll find that the main post offices keep longer hours. As well as the post office, stamps (*znamke*) can be bought at newsstands.

Telephones

Public phone boxes, found just about everywhere, use **phonecards** (*telekartice*), which currently come in denominations of 700SIT, 1000SIT, 1700SIT and 3500SIT; you can buy these from post offices, newspaper kiosks and tobacco shops. If making long-distance and international calls it's usually easier to go to the post office, where you're assigned to a cabin and given the bill afterwards. All Slovenian land line numbers are seven-digit, and are preceded by two-digit regional codes – of which there are six (Ⓣ01 for Ljubljana, up to Ⓣ07, but no Ⓣ06). To make a direct call to somewhere outside the area you are in, you must use the regional code.

Calling home from abroad

One of the most convenient ways of phoning home from abroad is via a **telephone charge card** from your phone company back home. Using a PIN number, you can make calls from most hotel, public and private phones that will be charged to your account. Since most major charge cards are free to obtain, it's certainly worth getting one at least for emergencies; enquire first though whether your destination is covered, and bear in mind that rates aren't necessarily cheaper than calling from a public phone.

In **the UK and Ireland**, British Telecom (Ⓣ0800/345 144, Ⓦwww.chargecard.bt.com) will issue the BT Charge Card, which can be used in 116 countries, free to all BT customers; AT&T (dial Ⓣ0800/890 011, then 888/641-6123 when you hear the AT&T prompt to be transferred to the Florida Call Centre, free 24 hours) has the Global Calling Card; while NTL (Ⓣ0500/100 505) issues its own Global Calling Card, which can be used in more than sixty countries abroad, though the fees cannot be charged to a normal phone bill.

In the **US and Canada**, AT&T, MCI, Sprint, Canada Direct and other North American long-distance companies all enable their customers to make credit-card calls while overseas, billed to your home number. Call your company's customer service line to find out if they provide service from Slovenia, and if so, what the toll-free access code is.

To call **Australia and New Zealand** from overseas, telephone charge cards such as Telstra Telecard or Optus Calling Card in Australia, and Telecom NZ's Calling Card can be used to make calls abroad, which are charged back to a domestic account or credit card. Apply to Telstra (Ⓣ1800/038 000), Optus (Ⓣ1300/300 937), or Telecom NZ (Ⓣ04/801 9000).

Calling home from overseas

Note that the initial zero is omitted from the area code when dialling the UK, Ireland, Australia and New Zealand from abroad.

UK International access code + 44 + city code.
Republic of Ireland International access code + 353 + city code.
USA and Canada International access code + 1 + area code.
Australia International access code + 61 + city code.
New Zealand International access code + 64 + city code.

Mobile phones

The **mobile phone** is as ubiquitous in Slovenia as it is any other European country, and you'll find few Slovenes without one. There are currently four mobile phone providers, the most popular of which are Mobitel and Simobil. Slovenian mobile phone numbers have nine digits, including one of these prefixes, Ⓣ031, Ⓣ041, Ⓣ051, or Ⓣ040. Calling a mobile from a public or private phone you must dial all the numbers; when calling from abroad drop the 0.

If you want to use your mobile phone abroad, you'll need to check with your phone provider whether it will work abroad, and what the call charges are. In the UK, for all but the very top-of-the-range packages, you'll have to inform your phone provider before going abroad to get international access switched on. You may get charged extra for this depending on your existing package and where you are travelling to. You are also likely to be charged extra for incoming calls when abroad, as the people calling you will be paying the usual rate. If you want to retrieve messages while you're away, you'll have to ask your provider for a new access code, as your home one is unlikely to work. Most UK mobiles use GSM, which gives access to most places worldwide, except the US. For further information about using your phone abroad, check out Ⓦwww.telecomsadvice.org.uk/features/using_your_mobile_abroad.htm.

Unless you have a tri-band phone, it is unlikely that a mobile bought for use outside the US will work inside the States and vice versa, with many only working within the region designated by the area code in the phone number, ie 212, 415 etc. They tend to be very expensive to own in the US, too, as users are billed for both incoming and outgoing calls. Calling a US mobile, however, costs no more than making a call to a landline in that area code. For details of which mobiles will work outside the US, contact your mobile service provider. Most mobiles in Australia and New Zealand use GSM, which works well in Southeast Asia and Europe but check with your provider.

Email

One of the best ways to keep in touch while travelling is to sign up for a free Internet email address that can be accessed from anywhere, for example YahooMail or Hotmail – accessible through Ⓦwww.yahoo.com and Ⓦwww.hotmail.com. Once you've set up an account, you can use these sites to pick up and send mail from any Internet café, or hotel with Internet access. Ⓦwww.kropla.com is a useful website giving details of how to plug your laptop in when abroad, phone country codes around the world, and information about electrical systems in different countries.

Frustratingly there are very few **Internet cafés** in Slovenia, even in the larger towns and cities – Ljubljana, in particular, is poorly served. Your safest bet is the local library (although these are usually closed at weekends), most of which have a handful of terminals and charge between 100SIT and 200SIT per hour, though some are free; connections vary but more often than not are infuriatingly slow. Some of the more upmarket hotels have an ISDN line.

The media

Despite 45 years of communism, the Slovene media always had the most balanced and pluralistic coverage of the ex-Yugoslav republics. Given its size, though, it's not surprising that the country has fewer daily newspapers in circulation than just about any other European nation; its television coverage, meanwhile, differs little from that in any other central-east European country, with foreign cable and satellite television having made huge inroads in recent years.

Television

As in most countries, national TV is a rather bland, often unedifying, diet of dull movies, game shows and soaps, although many households now subscribe to satellite channels. The public service broadcaster, RTV Slovenija (Radio-Television Slovenia), transmits on two channels, whilst the chief commercial channels are Kanal A and Pop TV, both of which broadcast the standard diet of foreign movies, soaps, sit-coms and music. RTV Slovenija also broadcasts the country's three major radio channels.

Most hotels have satellite TV, though in most cases they will be German or Italian channels only, whilst the better-quality hotels will usually have English language channels such as CNN, Sky News and BBC World.

The press

Amongst the five major dailies, the most widely read by the urban population is the mildly pro-government *Delo*, which is also considered the most sophisticated read; this is followed by *Dnevnik* (daily), and the Maribor-based *Večer* (evening). Closest to western tabloids in style is *Slovenske Novice*, full of the usual sensationalist trash stories.

With the exception of some of the major bookshops and more upmarket hotels in

Mladina

Mladina (Youth), which began life as a periodical of the League of Slovene Youth in 1943, is Slovenia's foremost liberal non-party youth magazine. In the late 1970s the magazine's focus changed dramatically from a straightforward cultural-oriented rag to a highly politicized and confrontational publication, renowned for its stinging campaigns against corrupt officials, and fearless reporting of taboo subjects such as the Yugoslav Army, World War II massacres, and homosexuality. In 1988 three of the magazine's editors (and an army corporal) were put on trial, and subsequently convicted, by the Yugoslav Federal government for allegedly distributing state secrets – dubbed the "Ljubljana Four Trial" (see p.325) – an event which sparked Slovenia's final drive towards independence. Despite fewer and less obvious targets since independence, *Mladina* remains an influential and topical political journal.

Ljubljana, English dailies are difficult (if not impossible) to come by. There are, however, a couple of decent English-language publications worth seeking out: the informative weekly *Slovenia News* and, along the same lines, the less frequently published *Slovenia Times*. News and articles from both can be viewed online – see p.16. The bi-monthly *Ljubljana Life* is a more straightforward listings magazine for the capital, with a good entertainments section.

BBC (Ⓦwww.bbc.co.uk/worldservice), **Radio Canada** (Ⓦwww.rcinet.ca), and **Voice of America** (Ⓦwww.voa.gov) list all the world service frequencies around the globe.

Opening hours and public holidays

Most shops open Monday to Friday from 8am to 7pm and on Saturdays from 8am to 1pm, with some (usually the mall-type places in bigger towns and cities) open on Sundays between 11am and 5pm. There are, too, an increasing number of 24-hour food shops open throughout the country. Post offices open Monday to Friday 8am to 6 or 7pm and until noon or 1pm on Saturday; banks generally open 8.30am–12.30pm and 2–5pm weekdays, and 8.30–11am or noon on Saturdays; and pharmacies 7am to 7 or 8pm.

Inevitably, **tourist office** opening times vary greatly, depending upon both their location and the season; some keep impossibly convoluted hours, but as a rule you'll find most open between 9am and 6 or 7pm (till 8 or 9pm in more touristed areas) over summer. Similarly, tourist agencies' opening hours vary enormously, depending upon the time of year; during high season, some stay open as late as 10pm, though some are prone to closing an hour or so earlier, or later, than the scheduled time, depending upon custom.

Museums are generally open Tuesday to Sunday 10am to 6pm, with shorter hours in winter, whilst some close down altogether during this period; there are, of course, exceptions to the above but in any case all times are detailed throughout the guide.

Public holidays

Slovenia counts no less than fourteen national holidays, a number of which celebrate important milestones in the country's history. Should any of these fall on a Sunday, then the Monday becomes the holiday. Don't expect much to be open on the following days.

January 1 & 2 New Year
February 8 Day of Slovene Culture (Prešeren Day)
Easter Monday
April 27 Resistance Day
May 1 & 2 Labour Day Holidays
June 25 Day of Slovene Statehood
August 15 Assumption Day
October 31 Reformation Day
November 1 All Saints' Day
December 25 Christmas
December 26 Independence Day

Festivals

The Slovenian calendar is littered with some marvellous festivals and events, and whilst a good number of these take place in the larger cities such as Ljubljana and Maribor, there's an excellent spread of events throughout the rest of the country. Neither are these entirely confined to the summer: Slovenia has several strongly rooted seasonal traditions, none more so than the "Pust", perhaps the most uniquely Slovenian celebration.

Most cities, and many of the larger towns, stage some form of **Summer Festival**, which invariably incorporates a colourful mix of classical and contemporary music, art and theatrical performances. A great deal of fun are the **Medieval Days Festivals**, which seek to re-create life in the Middle Ages in the form of medieval crafts markets, song and dance, and knights' games; the two highest-profile ones are held in the historic towns of Kamnik and Škofja Loka in June. A number of the country's castles stage classical music concerts on summer evenings.

The country's strong wine-growing tradition is manifest in its many **wine-related events**, which occur throughout the major wine-producing centres, such as Brda and Jeruzalem, between May and September; the main collective wine celebration is St Martin's Day, on November 11. Aside from the main festivals listed below – each of which is covered in greater detail in their respective chapters – there are dozens of other, more local, events taking place across the country, some of which are also described in the guide.

February Kurentovanje Ptuj, Sunday before Shrove Tuesday and Shrove Tuesday. The most famous of Slovenia's pre-Lent carnivals, featuring riotous displays of masked revelry; the other major Pust carnivals take place in Cerkno and Cerknica.

March Ski-jumping World Championships Planica (Kranjska Gora), mid-March. The climax to the World Ski-Jumping Championship at Planica is a high-octane weekend of top-class sport, music and lots of beer.

May Druga Godba Ljubljana, end of May for one week. Alternative/world music festival with a strong line-up of both Slovene and international artists.

June Ana Desetnica Street Theatre Ljubljana, end of June. Colourful and enjoyable street theatre performances in the Old Town and surrounds.

Brežice Festival Brežice and other venues across Slovenia, end of June to the end of August. Prestigious classical music festival of ancient Baroque music, starring some of Europe's finest singers, orchestras and musicians.

Lent Festival Maribor, end of June for two weeks. Massive gathering of popular and serious music, dance and ballet, street and puppet theatre, and folkloric events down by the Drava River.

Ljubljana Jazz Festival Ljubljana, end of June. Three days of world-class musicians at Slovenia's premier jazz festival.

July Bled Days Bled, mid-July. Weekend fair and crafts stalls down by the lake, culminating in a spectacular fireworks display and thousands of candles on the lake.

Ljubljana Summer Festival Ljubljana, July to mid-September. More than two months of top-notch opera, classical music, ballet and theatre in the capital's key cultural happening.
Mediterranean Festival Izola, July. World, ethno and folk music festival on an open-air stage in Izola's Old Town.
Primorska Summer Festival Izola, Koper and Portorož, July to August. Open-air stage and street theatre performances, some of which take place in unusual locations such as a disused railway tunnel and the Sečovlje saltpans.
Rock Otočec Novo Mesto, first week of July. The country's largest rock festival, with a cool line-up of both Slovenian and international artists.
Soča Reggae Riversplash Tolmin, mid-July. Good-time international festival consistently attracting some of the biggest names in reggae.

August Knights' Tournament Predjama Castle, last Sunday in August. Jousting tournament and large doses of medieval merriment.
TrnFest Ljubljana, August. Cracking, small-scale festival with gigs, exhibitions and workshops (some for kids) organized by the KUD cultural centre.

September Kravji Bal (Cow's Ball) Lake Bohinj, second or third weekend in September. Mass booze-up to celebrate the return of the cows from the mountains.

November St Martin's Day Countrywide, November 11. Nationwide wine celebrations.

December Christmas Celebrations Countrywide. A month of yuletide celebrations kick off on December 6 (St Nicholas's Day) with the giving of gifts to children.

Sports

Given its size and resources, Slovenia's sporting pedigree is impressive, many of its sportsmen and women having achieved notable successes in a number of sports since the split with Yugoslavia in 1991. The most high-profile sporting event in the Slovenian calendar is the World Ski-Jumping Championships at Planica in March.

The country's finest moment came at the 2000 Sydney Olympics, when it captured its first ever gold medal courtesy of the **rowers** Iztok Čop and Luka Špik; indeed, rowing has been Slovenia's most prominent summer sport since the times of the former Yugoslavia, and now, as then, several major regattas are held each summer on Lake Bled. Given the country's excellent facilities, it's little surprise that Slovenia has produced a legion of fine **skiers** and **ski-jumpers** – the Yugoslav national ski team was almost always comprised exclusively of Slovenes – and there's been a healthy measure of Olympic and World Championship success over the past decade.

In popular team sports such as basketball, handball and water polo – traditionally very strong sports in the former Yugoslavia – Slovenia has been left somewhat in the slip-stream of Serbia and Croatia, but its teams still manage to perform creditably at European level. The current golden girl of Slovenian sport is the outstanding middle distance runner Jolanda Čeplak, holder of several European and world 800/1500-metre records. In spite of a weak domestic league Slovenia's **footballers** have massively overachieved in recent years, qualifying for both the European Championship Finals in Holland and Belgium in 2000, and then the 2002 World Cup in Japan – the first time it had qualified for either finals.

Outdoor activities

There are few more active nations in Europe than the Slovenes, most of whom begin trekking, climbing and skiing from a very early age. The country's mountains, forests, hills, rivers and lakes offer unlimited potential to indulge in a wide range of outdoor pursuits – hiking, skiing, rafting, horse riding and cycling – to name just a few. Moreover, just about any of these activities can be done as part of an organized group, usually with gear supplied. Before taking part in any adventure activities, check your insurance cover.

Skiing

Skiing (*smučanje*) was first popularized in Slovenia in the seventeenth century, when natives took to the broad open spaces of the Bloke Plateau in Notranjska. Slovenes today are no less enthusiastic about the sport and alpine skiing remains the nation's number one pursuit.

Uniformly well equipped, efficient and safe, Slovenian ski resorts cannot really compare with those in neighbouring Italy or Austria, although the majority of the larger resorts do possess a full complement of ski services and lodgings. Slovenia counts more than fifteen major resorts (and many more smaller ones), the best equipped and most popular of which are Kranjska Gora, a good family resort and international competition venue near the Austrian border, Krvavec, near Kranj (very popular with weekending Ljubljančani), Cerkno, in Primorska, and Pohorje, on the outskirts of Maribor – this the country's largest skiing area. Kanin, near Bovec on the Italian border, offers Slovenia's highest altitude skiing (2300m).

Generally speaking, the ski season begins in earnest in late November, running through to March or April in most places, although many slopes have been furnished with snow cannons enabling resorts to stay open longer. For more detailed information on skiing in northwestern Slovenia, see the box on p.138; elsewhere, individual resort accounts are given where relevant. Brochures are published by both the Slovenian Tourist Board and the Association Ropeways of Slovenia, the latter located in Ljubljana, at Parmova 33 (Ⓣ01/280-1813, Ⓦwww.slo-skiing.net).

Hiking and climbing

Slovene alpinists have a world-class reputation, thanks in no small part to the deeds of mountaineers Tomaž Humar and Davo Karničar, the latter the first man to ski down Everest, in 2000.

The country is traversed by over seven thousand kilometres of marked paths, and for the majority of climbers and hikers, the main destination is the Julian Alps, at the heart of which is Mount Triglav (2864m), the country's highest peak. There are dozens more peaks topping the 2500-metre mark, both in the Julians and, to the northeast of here on the Austrian border, the Karavanke Mountains and Kamniške-Savinja Alps, the latter a particularly stunning mountain range. Non-alpine tracts include the Pohorje Massif near Maribor, and the Snežnik hills south of Postojna along the Croatian border, while there's gentler rambling territory south of Triglav National Park in the subalpine hills of Cerkno and Idrija, and in the deep forests of Dolenjska. The country's longest trail (Slovene Alpine Trail) runs from Maribor to the Gulf of Trieste via the Pohorje Massif, the Kamniške-Savinja Alps and Triglav National Park, whilst two European hiking trails, the E6 and E7, also traverse Slovene territory.

The Alpine Association of Slovenia (PZS) in Ljubljana, at Dvoržakova 9 (Ⓣ01/434-3022, Ⓦwww.pzs.si) produces an extensive range of hiking **maps** (The Julian Alps, Triglav, Triglav National Park, and so on; around 1500SIT), which can be ordered directly from them, or bought in bookshops and tourist offices.

Adventure sports

Slovenia is geared up in a big way for adventure sports and activities, and in particular around its rivers, which attract enthusiasts from all over Europe each summer. The peerless Soča River in Primorska is renowned as one of the finest **white-water rafting** rivers in Europe. Here too, the waters also offer the ultimate test for **canoeists** and **kayakers**, whilst **hydrospeed** is a relatively recent addition to the burgeoning roster of adrenaline sports available. All these activities are also possible on Slovenia's other major rivers, namely, the Kolpa and Krka in Dolenjska, the Sava in Gorenjska, and the Savinja in Štajerska. **Canyoning**, **paragliding** and **bungee jumping** are three more pursuits offered by some of the larger agencies.

Cycling

From the smooth grassy plains of Prekmurje, to the gently undulating folds of Dolenjska and the gruelling mountain passes in the Alps, Slovenia presents superb opportunities for **cycling** (*kolesarjenje*). Moreover, cycling is safe, the roads are largely traffic-free, and the scenery can be superb. An increasing number of local tourist associations are developing local and regional cycle routes, complete with waymarked, and graded, paths and tracks; there are currently well-developed trails around Škofja Loka, Kranjska Gora, throughout the Karst region, across Prekmurje, and in Koroška, the last of which incorporates a specially designed mountain bike park.

Although **bike hire** is at a premium in those towns and cities off the tourist track, you can rent them pretty much everywhere else. In places like Bled, Bohinj and Kranjska Gora, you'll find many adventure sports and tourist agencies offering hire, whilst some tourist offices, hotels and campsites can also supply bikes. Only in those places where cycling routes exist are you likely to find dedicated **cycling maps**. The Slovenian Tourist Board publishes *Slovenia by Bicycle*, a brochure that gives a basic rundown of around ten of the country's key cycling areas.

Horse riding

As the home of the Lipizzaner it's perhaps not surprising that Slovenes profess a deep-rooted attachment to all things equine. Whilst the most obvious destination for riders is Lipica, there are dozens more **horse-back riding centres** throughout the country, many sited in fabulously scenic locations. Most offer some form of recreational (trail) and arena riding, and/or a range of classes and courses – some also offer carriage rides; three of the most established centres are Pristava Lepena in the gorgeous Trenta Valley (there are Lipizzaner here too), the Kaval Centre at Prestranek near Postojna, and the Brdo estate just outside Kranj. You might also find that some tourist farms offer the opportunity to participate in more informal riding. The Slovenian Tourist Board's brochure, *Riding in Slovenia*, details several of the main riding schools, whilst the Slovenian Equestrian Federation in Ljubljana, at Čelovska 25 (☎01/434-7265), has a more complete list.

Fishing

Slovenia offers some of the finest freshwater fishing (*ribolov*) in Europe, its abundant rivers, streams and lakes richly sourced with many different species of fish. The magnificent Soča river is renowned for its bountiful reserves of grayling and trout – brown trout, rainbow trout, and, above all, the highly prized marble trout. Elsewhere, the Kolpa, Krka, Sava Bohinjka and Unica rivers have healthy stocks of pike, perch, chub and eelpout. Of the lakes, fishing from boats is permitted at Lake Bohinj and the intermittent Lake Cerknica. The main fishing season lasts approximately from April to October, although this can vary slightly depending upon the water levels. Permits, which don't come cheap (expect to pay 5000–10,000SIT for a daily permit), can be obtained from local tourist associations, tourist offices, and some hotels and campsites – details are listed throughout the guide where relevant.

The Fisheries Institute in Ljubljana, at Župančičeva ulica 9 (☎01/244-3400; wwww.zzrs.si), can provide more information on licences and seasons.

Other sports and activities

Although the Slovene coast is a mere 46km long, it's possible to indulge in a number of water sports: **scuba diving** (*potapljanje*) in the waters around Piran is very popular – there are a couple of dive schools in town – whilst facilities for **sailing** (*jadranje*) and **windsurfing** (*surfanje*) are well provided for.

The coastal waters are perfectly fine for **swimming** (*plavanje*), but if you fancy something a little bit warmer you should be able to track down a local indoor pool in most towns of a reasonable size. Some of the better hotels, particularly those on the coast, have their own pools that can be used for a small fee by those not staying as guests. There are currently ten **golf** courses in Slovenia (with more in the pipeline), some of which, like those at Bled and Voljči Potok, can be played out against quite stunning alpine backdrops. You can find **tennis** courts in most places.

Crime and personal safety

With a crime rate amongst the lowest in Europe, Slovenia is one of the continent's safest countries and it's extremely unlikely that you'll have any problems; violent crime against tourists is almost nonexistent and petty crime rare. That said, the usual common sense precautions apply; watching where you walk late at night, keeping an eye on valuables, particularly in crowded buses, and locking your car at all times when unattended.

In the unlikely event of any dealings with the **police** (*policija*), you'll generally find them easy-going and approachable, and likely to speak some basic English. The only time you may be asked to provide some form of identification is if stopped whilst driving. If you do have anything stolen while in Slovenia, you'll need to go to the police and file a report, which your insurance company will require before paying out for any claims made on your policy. Should you be arrested or need legal advice, ask to contact your embassy or consulate in Ljubljana. To call the police dial ☎113.

Working and studying in Slovenia

Opportunities for working in Slovenia are few and far between. The most traditional form of work abroad, teaching English, is your best bet and, although none of the major international schools have teaching centres here, there are a number of small private schools in Ljubljana and Maribor. There is also an excellent voluntary work programme, and, for those keen to pick up a new language – or brush up on existing skills – there's a well-established language centre at Ljubljana University.

Study and work programmes

For over twenty years, the Centre for Slovene as a Second Foreign Language, at Ljubljana University's Faculty of Arts Department, has been running a **summer language course.** The courses, available at all levels from beginners to advanced, and covering a range of topics including Slovene literature and culture, business Slovene and theatre workshops, run for either two (€390) or four (€700) weeks throughout July; the course also incorporates a varied social programme, which may include, for example, a two-day mountain trip, local workshops, and evening entertainment; registration is usually required by the end of May for participation that summer. Accommodation can also be arranged if you wish. The centre also runs a number of more straightforward language courses throughout the year, lasting from two weeks up to a year. For more information contact the centre at Aškerčeva 2 (ⓣ01/241-1320; ⓦwww.ff.uni-lj.si/center-slo/).

An organization called Voluntariat, working in conjunction with local organizations, coordinates around a dozen **work camps** throughout Slovenia, with projects as varied as working with Roma in Prekmurje, to working on the saltpans near Portorož. In theory, these programmes, which can last from two weeks to several months, are available year-round, but most volunteers work in the period between May and September. The only cost involved is a participation fee (around 17,000SIT), payable upon registration; thereafter all board and lodgings are paid for, although, if you are involved in a longer-term project (ie several months), you may receive pocket money. To find out more contact Voluntariat at Breg 12, Ljubljana (ⓣ01/241-7620, ⓔplacement@zavod-voluntariat.si).

UK and Ireland

British Council ⓣ020/7930 8466. Produces a free leaflet which details study opportunities abroad. The Council's Central Management Direct Teaching (ⓣ020/7389 4931) recruits TEFL teachers for posts worldwide (check ⓦwww.britishcouncil.org/work/jobs.htm for a current list of vacancies), and its Central Bureau for International Education and Training (ⓣ020/7389 4004, ⓦwww.centralbureau.org.uk) enables those who already work as educators to find out about teacher development programmes abroad. It also publishes a book, Year Between, aimed principally at gap-year students detailing volunteer programmes, and schemes abroad.

Erasmus EU-run student exchange programme enabling students at participating universities in Britain and Ireland to study in one of 26 European countries. Mobility grants available for three months to a full academic year. Anyone interested should contact their university's international relations office, or check the Erasmus websiteⓦwww.europa.eu.int/comm/education/erasmus.html.

The US

Bernan Associates ⓣ1-800/274-4888, ⓦwww.bernan.com. Distributes UNESCO's encyclopedic Study Abroad.

Council on International Educational Exchange (CIEE) ⓣ1-800/2COUNCIL,

Ⓦ www.ciee.org. The non-profit parent organization of Council Travel, CIEE runs summer, semester and academic-year programmes, as well as volunteer projects, throughout Europe. Also publishes *Work, Study, Travel Abroad and Volunteer! The Comprehensive Guide to Voluntary Service in the US and Abroad.*

Earthwatch Institute Ⓣ 1-800/776-0188 or 978/461-0081, Ⓦ www.earthwatch.org. International non-profit organization with offices in Boston, Oxford, England, Melbourne, Australia and Tokyo, Japan. 50,000 members and supporters are spread across the US, Europe, Africa, Asia and Australia and volunteer their time and skills to work with 120 research scientists each year on Earthwatch field research projects in over 50 countries all around the world.

Harper Collins Perseus Division Ⓣ 1-800/242-7737, Ⓦ www.harpercollins.com. Publishes *International Jobs: Where They Are, How to Get Them.*

Volunteers for Peace Ⓣ 802/259-2759, Ⓦ www.vfp.org. Non-profit organization with links to a huge international network of "workcamps", two- to four-week programmes that bring volunteers together from many countries to carry out needed community projects. Most workcamps are in summer, with registration in April–May. Annual membership including directory costs $20.

Australia and New Zealand

Australians Studying Abroad Ⓣ 03/9509 1955, Ⓦ www.asatravinfo.com.au. Study tours focusing on art and culture.

Useful publications and websites

Another pre-planning strategy for working abroad, whether teaching English or otherwise, is to get hold of *Overseas Jobs Express* (Ⓣ 01273/699 611, Ⓦ www.overseasjobs.com), a fortnightly publication with a range of job vacancies, available by subscription only. *Vacation Work* also publishes books on summer jobs abroad and how to work your way around the world; call Ⓣ 01865/241 978 or visit Ⓦ www.vacationwork.co.uk for their catalogue. Travel magazines like the reliable *Wanderlust* (every two months; £3.60) have a Job Shop section which often advertises job opportunities with tour companies. Ⓦ www.studyabroad.com is a useful website with listings and links to study and work programmes worldwide.

Gay and lesbian travellers

Slovenia was always the most tolerant of the ex-Yugoslav republics, with an active gay and lesbian movement in existence since the mid-1980s, though that's not to say gays and lesbians have had an easy time of it. Although attitudes have softened slightly in recent years, the majority of the population remains largely unsympathetic towards the gay and lesbian community.

Not surprisingly, Ljubljana is the centre of the gay and lesbian scene in Slovenia, and manifestations of gay life beyond the capital are almost nonexistent. An increasing number of events and happenings are taking place in Ljubljana, the most prominent of which are the annual **Gay Pride Parade** (late June or early July) – first organized in 2001 and now an established fixture in the capital's festival calendar – and the **Gay and Lesbian Film Festival** at the beginning of December, which has been running for the best part of a decade.

Both of these events are organized by the proactive gay association **Roza Klub**, itself just one wing of the autonomous, alternative cultural society Škuc, based at Kersnikova 4 (Ⓣ01/430-4740, Ⓦwww.ljudmila.org/siqrd). Roza Klub also runs Galfon, a gay and lesbian advice line (Ⓣ01/432-4089; 7–10pm), organizes club nights, and publishes several magazines and fanzines. The group **Out in Slovenija**, at Kašeljska 121 (Ⓣ041/562-375, Ⓦwww.outinslovenija.com), organizes numerous sport and recreational activities – hiking, cycling, skiing and the like – for gays and lesbians.

Contacts for gay and lesbian travellers

In the UK

Gay Travel Ⓦwww.gaytravel.co.uk Online gay and lesbian travel agent, offering good deals on all types of holiday. Also lists gay- and lesbian-friendly hotels around the world.
Madison Travel Ⓣ01273/202 532, Ⓦwww.madisontravel.co.uk. Established travel agents specializing in packages to gay- and lesbian-friendly mainstream destinations, and also to gay/lesbian destinations. Also check out **adverts** in the weekly papers *Boyz* and *Pink Paper*, handed out free in gay venues.

In the US and Canada

Gaytravel.com Ⓣ1-800/GAY-TRAVEL, Ⓦwww.gaytravel.com. The premier site for trip planning, bookings, and general information about international gay and lesbian travel.
International Gay & Lesbian Travel Association Ⓣ1-800/448-8550 or 954/776-2626, Ⓦwww.iglta.org. Trade group that can provide a list of gay- and lesbian-owned or -friendly travel agents, accommodation and other travel businesses.

In Australia and New Zealand

Parkside Travel Ⓣ08/8274 1222, Ⓔparkside@herveyworld.com.au. Gay travel agent associated with local branch of Hervey World Travel; all aspects of gay and lesbian travel worldwide.
Silke's Travel Ⓣ1800/807 860 or 02/8347 2000, Ⓦwww.silkes.com.au. Long-established gay and lesbian specialist, with the emphasis on women's travel.
Tearaway Travel Ⓣ1800/664 440 or 03/9510 6644, Ⓦwww.tearaway.com. Gay-specific business dealing with international and domestic travel.

Travellers with disabilities

Like so many other countries, Slovenia has been dreadfully slow to acknowledge the needs of the disabled traveller, and whilst progress is being made, there remains much work to be done and you shouldn't expect much in the way of special facilities.

Few places are well equipped, or have facilities, for disabled travellers, and, aside from the better ones, access to hotels and public buildings is generally poor, even in Ljubljana. Public transport is little better, although the new Inter City Slovenije trains between Maribor and Ljubljana do have wheelchair facilities, and specially adapted toilets, whilst an increasing number of train stations provide ramps for access to platforms. Similarly, most museums are ill equipped to deal with wheelchair users. The Disabled Association (Zveza Paraplegikov Slovenije) at Štihova ulica 14 (ⓣ01/432-7138; ⓦwww.zveza-paraplegikov.si) can assist with any specific queries you may have about travelling in Slovenia.

Contacts for travellers with disabilities

In the UK and Ireland

Holiday Care 2nd floor, Imperial Building, Victoria Rd, Horley, Surrey RH6 7PZ ⓣ0845/124 9971, minicom ⓣ0845/124 9976, ⓦwww.holidaycare.org.uk. Provides free lists of accessible accommodation abroad – European, American and long-haul destinations – plus a list of accessible attractions in the UK. Information on financial help for holidays available.

Irish Wheelchair Association Blackheath Drive, Clontarf, Dublin 3 ⓣ01/818 6400, ⓦwww.iwa.ie. Useful information provided about travelling abroad with a wheelchair.

RADAR (Royal Association for Disability and Rehabilitation) 12 City Forum, 250 City Rd, London EC1V 8AF ⓣ020/7250 3222, minicom ⓣ020/7250 4119, ⓦwww.radar.org.uk. A good source of advice on holidays and travel.

Tripscope Alexandra House, Albany Rd, Brentford, Middlesex TW8 ONE ⓣ0845/7585 641, ⓦwww.tripscope.org.uk. This registered charity provides a national telephone information service offering free advice on UK and international transport for those with mobility problems.

In the US and Canada

Access-Able ⓦwww.access-able.com. Online resource for travellers with disabilities.

Directions Unlimited 123 Green Lane, Bedford Hills, NY 10507 ⓣ1-800/533-5343 or 914/241-1700. Travel agency specializing in bookings for people with disabilities.

Mobility International USA 451 Broadway, Eugene, OR 97401 ⓣ541/343-1284, ⓦwww.miusa.org. Information and referral services, access guides, tours and exchange programmes. Annual membership $35 (includes quarterly newsletter).

Society for the Advancement of Travelers with Handicaps (SATH) 347 5th Ave, New York, NY 10016 ⓣ212/447-7284, ⓦwww.sath.org. Non-profit educational organization that has actively represented travellers with disabilities since 1976.

Wheels Up! ⓣ1-888/38-WHEELS, ⓦwww.wheelsup.com. Provides discounted air fares, tour and cruise prices for disabled travellers, also publishes a free monthly newsletter and has a comprehensive website.

In Australia and New Zealand

ACROD (Australian Council for Rehabilitation of the Disabled) PO Box 60, Curtin ACT 2605; Suite 103, 1st floor, 1–5 Commercial Rd, Kings Grove 2208; ⓣ02/6282 4333, TTY ⓣ02/6282 4333, ⓦwww.acrod.org.au. Provides lists of travel agencies and tour operators for people with disabilities.

Disabled Persons Assembly 4/173–175 Victoria St, Wellington, New Zealand ⓣ04/801 9100 (also TTY), ⓦwww.dpa.org.nz. Resource centre with lists of travel agencies and tour operators for people with disabilities.

Travelling with children

From a practical point of view travelling with children in Slovenia will present no obvious problems. Most of the better-quality hotels are well disposed to catering for children, whilst most restaurants (at least those of a decent standard) should be able to provide highchairs for younger children and babies. Most car-rental firms provide child or baby seats for a small extra charge. All supermarkets, and many smaller shops, are well stocked with the requisite nappies, baby food and so on.

Your biggest challenge will be keeping the kids entertained; bar the odd zoo there are few attractions specifically targeted at children, even in Ljubljana. The most obvious destinations are the **beaches** along the coast, which, on the whole, are clean and safe (most bathing areas are roped off), whilst some have grassy areas with sporting and play facilities. Another thing that might appeal to adults as well as kids is **puppetry**, a popular and well-regarded form of entertainment in Slovenia; there are particularly good theatres in Ljubljana and Maribor, details of which are given in the relevant sections. Beyond this, you'll find that some of the country's **festivals** – enjoyable events in themselves – also incorporate elements specifically designed with children in mind, such as the excellent TrnFest, which takes place in Ljubljana in August.

Directory

Addresses Following the Slovenian address system is not difficult. The most common terms are: ***ulica*** (street), ***cesta*** (road), ***pot*** (trail), ***steza*** (path), and ***trg*** (square). The street name always comes before the number. In some smaller towns and many villages there is no street name at all, just a house number; where no street name is given in the guide, assume it's because there isn't one.

Electric Power 220 volts. Round, two-pin plugs are used. A standard continental adaptor allows the use of 13 amp, square-pin plugs.

Film Major brands of colour print are widely available, as well as instant processing facilities. A 36-exposure roll costs around 1000SIT.

Laundry There are very few self-service laundries (***pralnica***) in Slovenia, even in the larger towns and cities. Your options are, therefore, limited to hotels, some hostels and campsites.

Left Luggage Only the larger train and bus stations have a left-luggage office (***garderoba***), or, more typically, lockers, which usually have a daily charge of around 400SIT.

Museums Generally speaking, museums are open Tues–Sun 9/10am–5/6pm; these hours can and do vary slightly, however, according to the season, whilst some may close down altogether during the winter period. In any case, opening times for all museums are detailed throughout the guide. Most of Slovenia's better museums have English captioning.

Tampons Tampons and sanitary towels are cheap and easy to get hold of from department stores and supermarkets.

Time Slovenia is one hour ahead of GMT, six hours ahead of Eastern Standard Time and nine ahead of Western Standard Time, ten hours behind Australian Eastern Standard Time and twelve hours behind New Zealand.

Tipping Although not obligatory, it is polite to round the bill up to a convenient figure in restaurants.

Toilets Public toilets (***javno stranišče***), which can be found in most train and bus stations, are, on the whole, clean; most charge around 50SIT. Otherwise, pop into the nearest bar or restaurant, smile nicely, and ask to use the toilet. ***Moški*** means men and ***Ženske*** means women.

Guide

Guide

1

Ljubljana

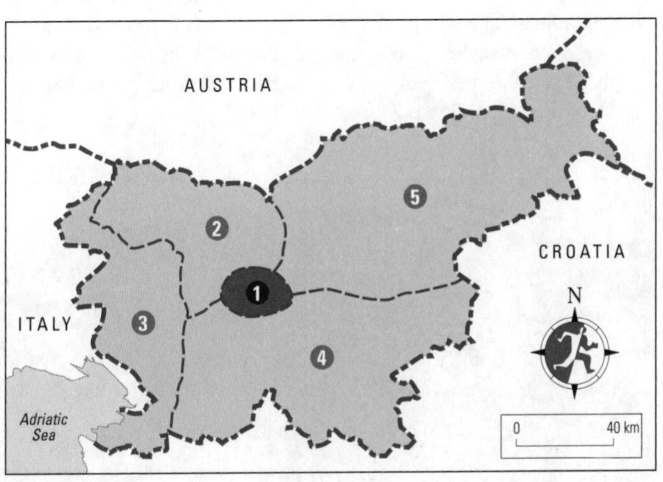

CHAPTER 1 Highlights

* **Jože Plečnik** – Stunning architecture at almost every turn from the nation's greatest architect. **See p.63**
* **Old Town** – Baroque churches, elegant townhouses and cool cafés, the Old Town has charm in spades. **See p.64**
* **Ljubljana Castle** – Looming high above the Old Town, climb the clocktower and take in the magnificent views of the Alps. **See p.68**
* **Križanke** – Take in a jazz or rock concert at the atmospheric, Plečnik designed open-air theatre. **See p.71**
* **Trnovo** – Roman ruins, Plečnik oddities and riverside cafés in this green and peaceful suburb. **See p.73**
* **Tivoli Park** – The city's green heart, affording easy promenade strolls or more exerting hillside walks. **See p.76**
* **Pri Škofu** – Understated but wonderful restaurant serving the best and most original food in town. **See p.81**
* **Drinking by the Ljubljanica** – Enjoy a beer at sundown in one of the many bars along the willow-fringed banks of the Ljubljanica River. **See p.81**

△ House front, Ljubljana

1

Ljubljana

Thrust into the spotlight in 1991 as the capital of a newly self-confident nation, **LJUBLJANA** is one of Europe's brightest and most engaging small cities. Situated in the southern part of the Ljubljana basin, at the juncture of the Alps and Dinaric mountain ranges, pretty much everything converges here: all major transport links (including Brnik, the country's only civilian airport), industry and commerce, culture, politics and power. However, with a population of less than 300,000 – which easily makes it one of Europe's smallest capital cities – the city retains a distinctly languorous and provincial air.

As the former Yugoslavia imploded in the early 1990s, Ljubljana suffered few of the traumas that befell neighbouring Zagreb, its path smoothed by a relatively sound economic and political infrastructure. A little over a decade later – as capital of one of the European Union's newest member states – Ljubljana is a prosperous, self-assured place, its slick veneer of sophistication masking a disparate number of outside influences – Austrian, Balkan and Mediterranean – subtly absorbed and tinkered with over the years. That said, it is Slovenian through and through, and one of the least ethnically diverse capitals in Europe, which perhaps explains why it suffers relatively few of the ills commonly associated with the big city.

The city's tremendously compact centre lends itself perfectly to discovery by foot and it's unlikely you'll need, or want, to use the refreshingly clean and efficient public transport system. While the city boasts a number of eminently enjoyable museums and galleries – the Museum of Modern History, City Museum, and National Gallery chief amongst them – the city's real charms lie outdoors. Its central core is a showcase of princely Baroque and Secessionist edifices, while the legacy of magnificent buildings, bridges and pathways bequeathed by Jože Plečnik, Slovenia's greatest architect, is difficult to overestimate, transforming as it did the entire fabric of the city between the two world wars. Its churches too reveal dazzling artistry, from Francesco Robba's extraordinary altar sculptures to Quaglio's resplendent frescoes.

Fundamental to the city's layout and history is the slender **River Ljubljanica**, a once navigable waterway, but now sprinkled with several fine-looking bridges. On both the left and right banks vestiges of the city's Roman and medieval past can be detected, but it's the splendid Baroque townhouses and maze-like streets of the majestic **Old Town**, lorded over by the landmark castle, which exerts the greatest pull. Furthermore, the splashes of greenery – such as **Tivoli Park** – give just a hint of what lies beyond the city's boundaries. Above all though, Ljubljana is a sociable city, a place to come and meet people, dip in and out of its enchanting riverside cafés, and engage in the nightlife.

Owing to both the country's size and the city's central location, it's perfectly feasible to do a day-trip from here to just about any of the country's principal

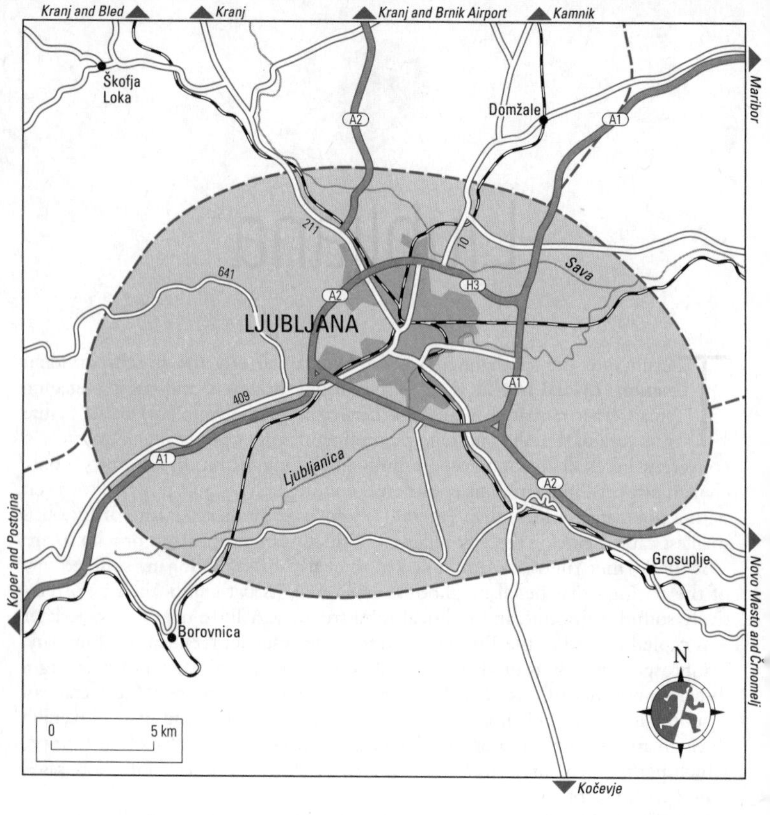

attractions, be it the mountain lakes of Bled and Bohinj to the northwest, the karst and coast to the south and west, or the castles and spas to the east.

Some history

Though sources first mention Ljubljana in 1144, the history of settlement here goes as far back as 2000 BC, when lake-dwellers inhabited the area of the marshes to the south of the city. They were closely followed by the **Illyrians** and **Celts**, though it was the **Romans** who engineered the first major commune, constructing a fortified military encampment on the left bank of the River Ljubljanica around 50 BC. It was given the name **Emona**, inhabited by some 5000 civilians working as artisans, tradesmen and retired officers; remnants of this Roman period can still be seen in the form of several sections of the city walls, as well as archeological sites contained within two gardens in the eastern and southern parts of the city. After repeated attacks by the Huns and Barbarians, Emona was eventually sacked around 450 AD.

Next up were the **Slavs**, who settled here at the tail end of the sixth century and proceeded to establish a settlement on the right bank of the Ljubljanica beneath the castle – what is now Stari trg and Mestni trg. During the twelfth century this evolved into Ljubljana's **medieval** core, and was given the German name Laibach in 1144, before assuming its Slovenian name, Luwigana, in 1146. Aside from Stari trg and Mestni trg, medieval Ljubljana also incorporated Novi trg on the left bank, and by the sixteenth century, this entire district was enclosed by city walls rearing all the way up to the castle. Following their arrival in the thirteenth century, the **Spanheim** family of **Carinthian dukes** granted the municipality city rights, and in 1243 the name **Ljubljana** first appeared; at around the same time, the city became the capital of the Carniola province, before falling under the jurisdiction of the **Habsburgs** in 1335.

A catastrophic **earthquake** in 1511, which left little of the city standing, coincided with Ljubljana becoming the leading centre of the **Reformation** in Slovenia, a period marked by significant spiritual and cultural progression, thanks largely to leading reformers such as Primož Trubar, who sought to promote literacy among the populace and who successfully published the first Slovene book – the primer, *Abecedarium* – in 1550; at this time the city also gained its first college and public library. The Reformation was successfully snuffed out at the end of the sixteenth century, a period that saw the arrival of the **Jesuits** (1597), who set about reorganizing the city's educational system, as well as establishing many religious buildings. The city's cultural pulse quickened further with the establishment of the Academia Operosorum – the first society of scholars and intellectuals – in 1693, and the Academia Philharmonicorum in 1701, one of the first musical institutions in Europe. Alongside this new Catholic order, a distinct architectural style, **Ljubljana Baroque**, emerged, expressed most sublimely in the city's four principal churches: St James's (1615); the Annunciation (1660); St Nicholas's (1706); and Ursuline (1726), as well as Robba's outstanding Fountain of the Three Rivers.

Between 1809 and 1814, Ljubljana was designated the capital of Napoleon's **Illyrian Provinces**, the city deemed a geographically convenient location for Napoleon in his attempt to prevent the Habsburgs accessing the Adriatic. A few years after his downfall Ljubljana was chosen to host the prestigious **Congress of the Holy Alliance** (in 1821), a gathering of the triumphant monarchy states that had defeated the French. During the mid-nineteenth century, and despite continued political repression, the city experienced something of an **industrial revolution** – the catalyst for which was the completion of the Vienna–Ljubljana–Trieste rail line in 1857. Having been provincialized for the greater part of the century, the city then began to emerge from its cultural and political straightjacket in the 1880s; all its elected mayors were Slovenian, while a raft of cultural institutions, including the Opera House (1892) and National House (1896), were established. In 1895, a second, and equally destructive earthquake necessitated yet more wholesale reconstruction, though this time it was Vienna and the Secessionist school which provided the inspiration – the results of which are particularly outstanding along Miklošičeva ulica.

With the creation of the **Kingdom of Serbs, Croats and Slovenes** in 1918 – recast as the Kingdom of **Yugoslavia** in 1929 – power transferred from Vienna to Belgrade, though this left Ljubljana no better off than when under Habsburg rule. Nevertheless, the founding of the National Gallery (1918), University (1919) and Academy of Sciences and Arts (1938) was confirmation of the city's continuing cultural efflorescence. During this interwar period, the city also experienced an architectural revolution, thanks to **Jože Plečnik**, Slovenia's greatest and most revered urban planner. From stunning new monuments – such as the National University Library and Žale Cemetery – to randomly scattered pillars and pyramids, the great architect completely transformed the city landscape. With every justification, the city was dubbed "Plečnik's Ljubljana". Following **World War II**, a period during which the city was occupied by both Italians and Germans before being liberated by the Partisans, it became the capital of the Republic of Slovenia, one of the six federal republics of the Federal People's Republic of Yugoslavia, and then, in 1963, the Socialist Federal Republic of Yugoslavia.

After Tito's death in 1980, relations between Ljubljana and Belgrade gradually worsened, coming to a head in 1988 with the staging of the "**Ljubljana Four Trial**" (see p.325), a case many at the time regarded as the final denouement in Slovene–Serb relations (and by implication the end of Yugoslavia). At around the same time, Ljubljana was at the forefront of Yugoslavia's intoxicating **alternative cultural scene**, thanks in no small part to the controversial and provocative arts collective Neue Slowenische Kunst (NSK), or New Slovene Art, the core of which was the anarchic rock group Laibach, one of the few bands from the former Yugoslavia to make an impact outside their own country. They, and other alternative movements – styled as New Social Movement groups – were fundamental in stimulating further debate on the social and political issues of the time, prescient given the deepening tensions between Ljubljana and Belgrade.

On June 26 1991, the day after Slovenia had officially declared its **independence**, thousands gathered on Republic Square to celebrate – somewhat prematurely as it turned out – unaware that Yugoslav Army (JNA) tank units were closing in on Brnik airport, just 23km away. However, the subsequent **ten-day war** had little direct effect on the city and on July 7 it was able, finally, to rejoice in its status as the capital of a new **republic**. As Ljubljana now settles down to life as the capital of a fully fledged EU member state, there's little doubt that the city's profile is on the increase, and deservedly so, yet the hope is that it manages to retain the low-key charm which makes it such an enjoyable destination.

Arrival, information and city transport

Ljubljana's **airport**, Letališče, is located in Brnik, 23km north of the city, and connected to the main bus station by a number of buses operated by various companies. The most frequent, but slowest, are public buses (Mon–Fri hourly 5am–8pm; Sat & Sun 7am, then every 2hr between 10am–8pm; 45min; 780SIT) which arrive at bay 28 of the bus station from where they also leave (Mon–Fri 5.20am, then hourly 6.10am–8.10pm; Sat & Sun 6.10am, then every 2hr 9.10am–7.10pm). Adria Airways operate nine buses a day from Brnik (7.40am–midnight; 30min; 1000SIT) to their terminal at the bus station, and seven in the opposite direction (6.30am–10.30pm). A quicker, but much more expensive option is to take the airport shuttle bus (4050SIT), which operates around the clock and can drop you off anywhere in the city; reservations are required if travelling from the city to the airport (Ⓣ070/887-766, Ⓔinfo@shuttlenet.com). A taxi to or from the airport will cost around 4500SIT.

The **train** (Železniška postaja) and **bus stations** (Avtobusna postaja) are located next to each other on Trg Osvobodilne fronte, from where it's a ten-minute walk south into the centre. The immaculately clean train station has some good facilities, including a tourist information office (see below), exchange desk (daily 6am–10pm) and 24-hour left-luggage lockers (400SIT per day). For details of the bus station ticket office opening times see p.85.

Information, maps and tours

The excellent new **Slovenian Tourist Information Centre (STIC)** at Krekov trg 10 (daily: June–Sept 8am–9pm, Oct–May 8am–7pm; Ⓣ01/306-4575, Ⓔstic@ljubljana-tourism.si) can assist with information on any aspect of travel within the country, including the capital. You can also purchase tickets for cultural and sporting events here. The main city **Tourist Information Centre (TIC)** is in the old town on Stritarjeva next to the Triple Bridge (June–Sept Mon–Fri 8am–8pm, Sat & Sun 10am–6pm; Oct–May Mon–Fri 8am–6pm, Sat & Sun 10am–6pm; ⓣ01/306-1215, ⓦwww.ljubljana-tourism.si). In addition there is an information office at the train station (June–Sept daily 9am–9pm; Oct–May Mon–Fri 10am–5.30pm; ⓣ01/433-9475). Both provide comprehensive information on the city (in several languages, including English) and hand out free, reasonably detailed, **maps**, while the main office on Stritarjeva can book private accommodation (see below). Worth picking up at the tourist office are the monthly *Where To?* events pamphlet, which has museum and gallery listings as well as events and performances for that month, and the quarterly *Ljubljana Life* (ⓦwww.ljubljanalife.com), which has good restaurant, bar and club listings; both are free and published in English.

The tourist office offers two-hour **sightseeing tours** of the city, starting at the Town Hall (July & Aug daily 11am & 5pm; June & Sept daily at 5pm & also Fri, Sat & Sun at 11am; Oct–May Sun 11am; 1250SIT). They can also organize longer and special interest tours, including Baroque Ljubljana, Secessionist Ljubljana and Plečnik's Ljubljana (8500SIT for a group of five, 12,100SIT for a group of ten). Tickets can be purchased on the spot or from the tourist office.

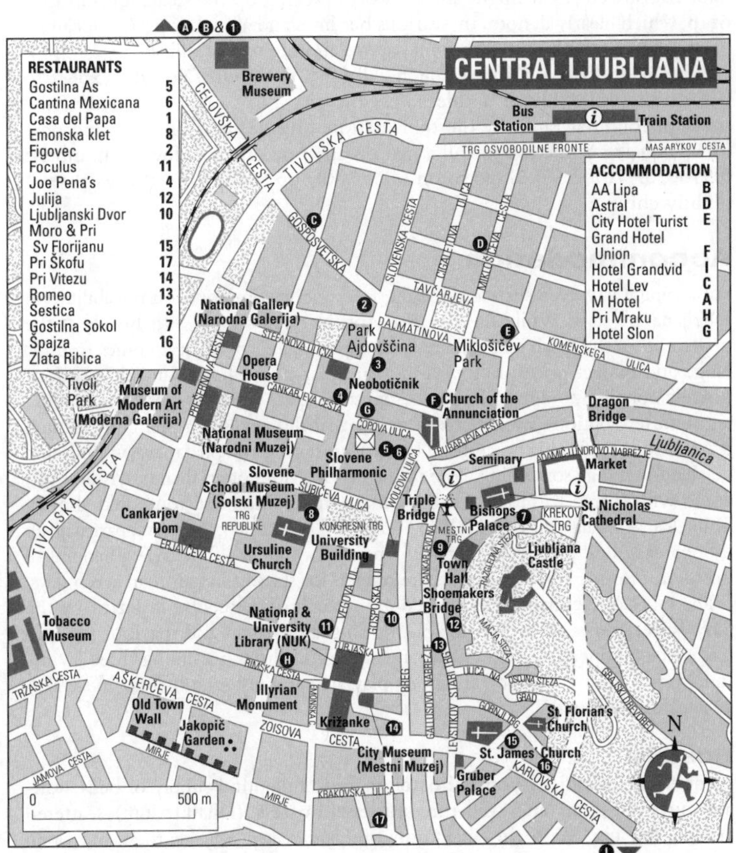

City transport

The city **buses**, run by Ljubljanski Potniški Promet (LPP), are clean, cheap and frequent; there are 22 bus lines, the majority of which operate between 5am and 10.30pm, with the most important lines (#1, #2, #3, #6 & #11) starting at 3.15am and running until midnight – each stop clearly indicates which buses stop there. Entering via the front door only, you pay in cash by depositing notes (exact amount – no coins) in the box next to the driver (a single journey costs a flat **fare** of 250SIT) or by using the slightly cheaper plastic tokens (*žetoni*; 190SIT), which are also deposited in the box and are bought in advance from post offices, newspaper kiosks and some shops and supermarkets. Each payment or token is valid for one unbroken journey only. Daily (*dnevna vozovnica*; 750SIT) and weekly (*tedenska vozovnica*; 3000SIT) tickets can be bought from the LPP kiosks at Trdinova ulica 3 and Bavarski Dvor, Slovenska cesta 55, and the main bus station. If you're planning on staying in the city for a few days, consider investing in the **Ljubljana Tourist Card** (3000SIT), which entitles you to unlimited travel on all the city's buses, and offers discounted entrance fees to selected museums, galleries, restaurants and bars; it's valid for three days and can be obtained from all of the city's tourist information centres. It might also be worth picking up the small, fold-up LPP **map**, which clearly denotes the various bus lines and all the stops. These can be obtained from the kiosks mentioned above and the tourist office.

It's unlikely that you'll have much call for a **taxi**, but if you do, expect to pay around 1500SIT for a ride across the city. They can be flagged in the street or found at ranks by the train station, outside the *Hotel Slon* and near Prešernov Trg. You can also call a taxi on any one of the following numbers: ⓣ9700, ⓣ9701, ⓣ9702, and so on, all the way up to ⓣ9709 – this works out slightly cheaper.

Accommodation

For a capital city, even such a modestly sized one, accommodation possibilities in Ljubljana are stark. While the city is reasonably well served with **hotels** at the upper end of the price range, there is an appreciable gap when it comes to mid-range and budget places, and with just one year-round hostel, and the **student hostels** opening up during July and August only, the more budget-conscious are left with few options. Even **private accommodation** is at a premium, though if this is your preferred choice, head to the tourist office on Stritarjeva, who should be able to arrange something close to the centre. More often than not, rooms (❷) come with shared bathroom facilities and without breakfast. You could also try Tour AS at Mala ulica 8 (ⓣ01/434-2660, ⓕ434-2664, ⓦwww.apartmaji.si); though they deal predominantly with apartments (❺–❼), they have a handful of private rooms too (❸) – discounts are offered for stays of longer than seven days.

The city's one **campsite** is located 4km north of the centre in Ježica, by the Sava River (buses #6 or #8 to Ježica). This large, clean and spacious site also has well-equipped bungalows (❸) and superb facilities, including three swimming pools, a bowling alley, children's play area and restaurant(ⓣ01/568-3913, ⓔacjezica@siol.net).

Hostels

Aside from the official **youth hostel**, there is a plentiful supply of beds available in four clean and well-run **student hostels** (Dijaški dom) scattered around the city. With the exception of *Dijaški dom Poljane*, these are open between mid-June and August. They are all similarly priced: excluding breakfast, expect to pay around 3000SIT per person for a dorm bed and 4000SIT for a bed in a single or double room.

Celica Youth Hostel Metelkova 9 ⓣ01/430-1890, ⓦwww.souhostel.com. Stunningly original new hostel constructed from the remnants of the barracks' former military prison. Each room, individually designed with a different theme in mind, sleeps two to five people (3750–4250 SIT); a handful of rooms have en-suite facilities and there is also one large dorm (3300SIT) sleeping fourteen. The hostel's range of facilities includes an information point, small art gallery and library, Internet access and Oriental café. Reservations essential.

Dijaški dom Bežigrad Kardeljeva ploščad 28 ⓣ01/534-2867, ⓔdd.lj-bezigrad@guest.arnes.si. Three- and four-bed rooms in three interconnected buildings, some with shower and toilet. Take bus #6 or #8 to stop Mercator, cross the road and walk back 150m then head through the small park.

Dijaški dom Ivana Cankarja Poljanska 26 ⓣ01/474-8600, ⓔdd.lj-ic@guest.arnes.si. This hostel, a short way southeast of the centre, has the largest capacity of all, with some 500 beds, including singles, doubles and multi-bedded rooms; all bathroom facilities are shared. Bus #5 to stop Ambrožev trg and it's set back 50m from the main road.

Dijaški dom Poljane Potočnikova 3 ⓣ01/300-3137, ⓔdd-poljane@guest.arnes.si. A ten-minute walk east of *dom Ivana Cankarja*, this is the smallest and cleanest of the *Dijaški doms*; four-bed rooms plus a few singles, some with shower. Open mid-June to July. Bus #5 to stop Gornje Poljane then a five-minute walk. Breakfast available.

Dijaški dom Tabor Vidovdanska 7 ⓣ01-234-8840, ⓔssljddta1s@guest.arnes.si. The most central, and busiest, of the *Dijaški doms*, located just ten minutes' walk southeast of the train and bus stations in a quiet area near the *Hotel Park*. Singles, doubles and multi-bedded rooms with shared toilet and shower facilities. Breakfast available.

Hotels

The majority of Ljubljana's **hotels** are at the upper end of the scale, patronized in the main by business people, and with prices that reflect this. Conversely, there are only a couple of places that could be termed budget, a situation unlikely to improve in the short term. Most hotels are centrally located and can easily be reached on foot from the train and bus stations. All hotels include **breakfast** in the price.

AA Lipa Celovška 264 ⓣ01/507-4822, ⓔaa-lipa@siol.net. Located in a medium-rise 4km northwest of the centre, this depressing, shabby relic, with its ubiquitous brown decor, should only be considered as a last resort. Buses #1, #15 and #16 to stop Dravlje and it's 100m ahead. ❹

Astral Miklošičeva 9 ⓣ01/308-4300, ⓦwww.astralhotel.net. Just 300m south of the bus and train stations, this hotel is aimed squarely at the business traveller. The rooms, decorated in a sunny yellow and green colour scheme, are well furnished, with stylish and comfortable beds, a little sofa, minibar, safe and Internet connection. ❾

BIT Center Hotel Litijska 57 ⓣ01/548-0055, ⓦwww.bit-center.net. Busy and lively sports hotel 2km east of the centre with clean and simple no-frills rooms; fifty-percent discount on use of sporting facilities (squash, badminton and fitness centre) and free use of the adjoining public pool in summer. Buses #5, #9, #13 and #22. ❸

City Hotel Turist Dalmatinova 15 ⓣ01/234-9130, ⓦwww.hotelturist.si. Reasonable, if somewhat overpriced downtown hotel, just a 5min walk from the stations. The refurbished rooms are pretty slick while the handful of older rooms, which have identical facilities, are rather worn and musty smelling. ❻–❼

Grand Hotel Union Miklošičeva 1 ⓣ01/308-1270, ⓦwww.gh-union.si. Housed in a splendid Art Nouveau building a few steps north of central Prešernov Trg, this is Ljubljana's most refined and characterful hotel, offering a level of comfort unmatched in the city. The generously sized, a/c rooms are magnificently furnished with the requisite first-class facilities; some have a balcony with views across to the castle. In addition to the fitness centre and sauna, it's the only hotel in town with a swimming pool (on the rooftop). It also accommodates particularly fine cellar and garden restaurants. ❾

Hotel Grandvid Dolenjska 336 ⓣ01/366-6449, ⓦwww.grandvid.com. Spanking new hotel with shiny, ultramodern rooms and facilities located 7km southeast of the city centre in the suburb of Lavrica. The hotel can arrange a taxi (2000SIT), or take any bus heading towards Grosuplje (from bay 20 at the bus station). ❼

Hotel Lev Vošnjakova 1 ⓣ01/433-2155, ⓦwww.hotel-lev.si. This gleaming glass high-rise, a 5min walk west of the bus and train stations opposite Tivoli Park, is the most expensive hotel in town, frequented in the main by business groups; the lavish, but surprisingly modestly sized rooms, have a/c, smart oak chairs and desks, and minibar. ❾

Hotel Park Tabor 9 ⓣ01/433-1306, ⓔhotel.park@siol.net. High-rise budget place located amidst a jumble of apartment buildings a few blocks east of the station. The one-star rooms, with shared toilet and shower facilities, are grim and bare; the category two rooms, with en-suite facilities and TV, are considerably better and worth paying the extra amount for. Ten percent discount for student card-holders. ❸–❹

Hotel Slon Slovenska 34 ⓣ01/470-1100, ⓦwww.hotelslon.com. The "Hotel Elephant" is so-named after Archduke Maximilian, who, with elephant in tow, allegedly stayed at an inn on the current site of the hotel en route to Vienna in 1552. Glass doors lead into bright, parquet-floored bedrooms, furnished with desks and chairs, safe, minibar and coffee-and tea-making facilities. The hotel houses two fine restaurants, a magnificent breakfast room, the *Art Café* (with confectioners) and delicatessen. ❾

M Hotel Derčeva 4 ⓣ01/513-7000, ⓦwww.m-hotel.si. Though somewhat lacking in character, this recently renovated hotel 2km northwest of the centre has modern, neat and spacious rooms painted in gentle blue tones and possesses a pleasant breakfast terrace. Triples and apartments available too. Buses #1, #3, #15 and #16 to stop Kino Šiška. ❺

Pension Tavčar Cesta v Šmartno 7 ⓣ01/541-1133, ⓦwww.penzion-tavcar.com. Neat, bright, and very reasonably priced little pension 2km northwest of the city centre. Take bus #12 to stop Hrastje, walk back 200m and take a right. ❹

Pri Mraku Rimska 4 ⓣ01/421-9600, ⓦwww.daj-dam.si. In a prime downtown location near Križanke, this perky little pension has warm, exuberantly coloured rooms with Internet access and safe; it is a little overpriced, though there is a ten-percent discount for stays of more than 3 nights. The restaurant, with its vine-covered terrace, is well regarded. ❻–❼

The City

Geographically and socially, the heart of the city is **Prešernov trg**, a small, animated square located on the left bank of the **River Ljubljanica**. Several important streets converge here while just about all the major sights and points of interest are within comfortable walking distance. With the exception of **Miklošičeva ulica** – a street rampant with extraordinary Secessionist architecture – and one or two other sights around, the commercial district north of Prešernov trg is largely devoid of worthwhile sights.

In any case, most people head straight for the magical **Old Town** on the right bank of the Ljubljanica: strewn with gorgeous Baroque townhouses and stately churches, all wrapped around a regal, **castle-topped hill**, it is easily the most appealing part of the city. The left bank too has more than its fair share of fine architecture, notably south of the main square **Kongresni trg**, beyond which are the delightful village-like suburbs of **Krakovo** and **Trnovo**.

Most of the city's key museums and galleries are concentrated within a compact area between **Slovenska cesta**, the busy main thoroughfare west of Kongresni trg, and **Tivoli Park**, the city's engaging green pocket and something of a ramblers' paradise. Beyond the central zone, and especially to the north and south, there are a handful of further sights worthy of investigation, including some fabulous churches, a castle and some splendid natural heritage.

Prešernov trg and around

Flanked on three sides by characterful buildings and busy streets, and on the other by the gently curving sweep of the River Ljubljanica, cobbled **Prešernov trg**

(Prešeren Square) is Ljubljana's major point of reference, an atmospheric space where open-air cafés do a cracking trade and street theatre performers and jazz musicians keep the punters entertained during the summer months. Presiding over all this activity, on the east side of the square, is the **monument to France Prešeren**, Slovenia's greatest poet (see box, p.123), after whom the square is named. Designed by Maks Fabiani and Ivan Zajec in 1905, the large, rather scruffy-looking bronze monument has a straight-backed Prešeren standing underneath a naked muse holding a laurel wreath – the circular plinth underneath is a traditional meeting place for locals and tourists alike.

On the north side, a three-part staircase leads up to the Baroque seventeenth-century Franciscan **Church of the Annunciation** (Frančiškanska Cerkev Marijnega oznanjenja; daily 9am–noon & 3–7pm), its striking sandy-red exterior providing a marvellous backdrop to the square. The first church on this site – this is the third – was erected in 1329 by the Augustins, but following the dissolution of the order by Emperor Joseph II in 1784, it was taken over by the Franciscans, who made several significant alterations to the structure and appearance of the church. The centrepiece of a rather gloomy and weary-looking interior is Francesco Robba's eighteenth-century marble high altar, richly adorned with spiral columns and plastic figurines. The illusionist frescoes on the nave and presbytery vaults are by Matevž Langus and Matej Sternen, while the paintings in the side altars have all but disappeared.

A few paces east of the church is the **Urbanc House**, also known as **Centromerkur**, Ljubljana's oldest department store, built in 1903 by Friedrich Sigmund of Graz. The focal points of this fine Secessionist building are the narrow clamshell-shaped glass canopy shading the entrance and the statue of Mercury, the Roman god of commerce, standing atop the narrow frontage. While the goods now on offer are unremarkable, it's worth having a look inside to view the superb Art Nouveau interior – the elegant staircase and gallery, the allegorical statue representing Craft (fabric has long been sold here), and the beautifully polished wood furnishings, most of which are original. On the opposite side of the square, a few steps down Wolfova ulica to the left of the four-storey Secessionist **Hauptman House**, you'll notice a terracotta window framing a relief of Julija Primic, gazing across to Prešeren, her life-long admirer. To the right of the Hauptman House is Čopova ulica, a lively pedestrianized shopping street, but with few shops actually worth venturing to. However, do take a look at the street's one outstanding building, the **City Savings Bank** at no. 3, featuring a fine glass and wrought-iron canopy, either side of which are allegorical statues symbolizing trade and commerce.

North of Prešernov trg

The main street spearing north from Prešernov trg, **Miklošičeva cesta**, is strewn with a raft of marvellous Secessionist buildings, all of which were designed following the earthquake in 1895. Directly behind the Franciscan church stands Ljubljana's finest hotel, the **Grand Union**, completed in 1905 by the same architect who designed the City Savings Bank, the Croatian Josip Vancaš – hence the striking similarities. Opposite the Grand Union, at no. 8, is the wildly colourful **Cooperative Bank** (Zadružna gospodarska banka). Designed in 1922 by the Slovene Ivan Vurnik, and painted by his wife Helena, the geometric folk-patterned decoration marks this building out as one of the most outstanding in the city; the interior, with a display of national motifs, is no less spectacular. Two hundred metres further on is **Miklošič Park**, laid out in 1899 by Maks Fabiani, a student of Otto Wagner and the Secessionist school

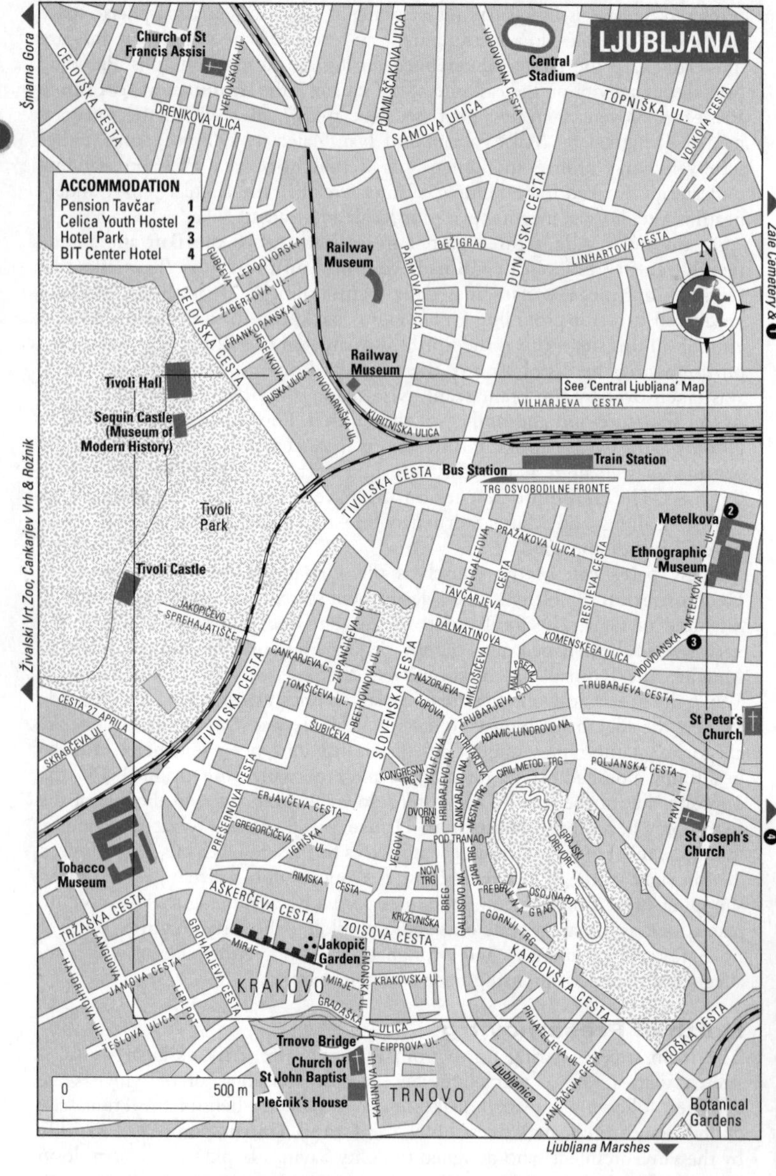

of architecture in Vienna. Immediately after the earthquake, Fabiani was assigned the task of reshaping the entire area, a task he accomplished with astonishing speed. Formerly called Slovenski trg, the square was renamed Miklošič Park in 1991 on the hundredth anniversary of the death of the philologist Fran Miklošič.

Built for the well-known Ljubljana printer Otomar Bamberg in 1907, the **Bamberg House** (Bambergova hiša) at no. 16 is one of Fabiani's more restrained pieces of work, featuring a simple, rather plain design, but worth a glance for the ceramic reliefs of several eminent printers along the top. On the opposite side of the road, at no. 20, is another, earlier Fabiani building, the **Krisper House** (Krisperjeva hiša). Built in 1901, it was the first building to be designed within his overall concept of the square, and features garland-like, botanical decoration running along the entire length of the facade and a turret under a bell-shaped roof – note how, with the exception of the Bamberg House, all the buildings standing at the corners of the square have corner turrets, another Fabiani concept. The northern side of the square is consumed by the monumental Neoclassical **Court Building**, from where it's a short walk west to the **Čuden House** (Čudnova hiša) at Cigaletova ulica 3, perhaps the most flamboyant example of Secessionist architecture in the area. Back on Miklošičeva ulica, the street winds up at **Trg Osvobodilne fronte**, a traffic-choked east–west thoroughfare and site of the train and bus stations.

Running parallel to Miklošičeva ulica is the broad slash of **Slovenska cesta**, the city's busy main north–south thoroughfare. Though there's little of note along here, there are a couple of minor landmarks worth checking out if you happen to be passing. At the corner of Slovenska cesta and Štefanova ulica is the chunky seventy-metre-high tower block, **Neobotičnik**, also known simply as "Skyscraper". Commissioned by the Slovenian Pension Fund for the purpose of housing offices and apartments – and built in response to the American Art Deco skyscrapers of that period – it was, at the time of its completion in 1933, one of the highest residential buildings in Europe, and the first multistorey building in the Balkans. The rooftop café and observation deck are both currently closed, but you can still take a peek inside at the impressive marble lobby and monumental spiral staircase. A couple of minutes further north along Slovenska, at the junction with Gosposvetska ulica, is the site of the former **Hotel Evropa**, built in 1869 by the Viennese architect Tietz and modelled on the Heinrichshof in Vienna; there is no longer a hotel here, just a rather forlorn-looking and little-frequented coffee house.

East of Prešernov trg

The area east of Prešernov trg is fairly low-key, but contains one or two sights which make its investigation worthwhile. Due east of the square is **Trubarjeva cesta**, a long, narrow, winding street accommodating a limited, yet eclectic mix of cafés, bars and shops. Midway down Trubarjeva, shortly after crossing Resljeva cesta, take a left up Vidovdanska cesta towards the *Hotel Park*, and carry on until you hit **Metelkova ulica**. Up on the right-hand side is the barracks complex of the former Yugoslav People's Army (JNA).

Metelkova's history is a fascinating one: up until the moment the JNA withdrew in the autumn of 1991, Metelkova had served as a barracks for over one hundred years, having been initially commissioned by Vienna for the Austro-Hungarian army. In December 1990, on the same day that the plebiscite for independence was held, the Network for Metelkova – an organization born out of several student and cultural movements – was established, their express aim being to convert the barracks into Ljubljana's alternative cultural mecca. However, after three years of frustrating and protracted negotiations with the city authorities, and their subsequent attempt to demolish the premises in September 1993, the Network finally carried out their threats to squat. In the event, and after further crises, various groups and societies gradually established their own territories within the complex, and there now exists among the still half-wrecked and rubble-strewn buildings a cosmopolitan gang of bars, clubs, galleries and independent societies, collectively known as Metelkova (see p.82). Located at the entrance to the site is the superb new **youth hostel** (see p.57), something of an attraction itself having been converted from the gutted remains of the former military prison. Even if you're not staying here, it's worth a look around just to see the wonderful, artistically designed "cells", which now function as dorms; there's a small gallery, neat café and cyber point here too.

At no. 2, another renovated building holds the city's **Ethnographic Museum** (Etnografski muzej; Tues–Sun 10am–6pm), currently undergoing an exhaustive two-phase restoration programme, the first fruits of which won't be seen until late 2004 at the earliest, with work continuing until at least 2007. In the meantime, part of it remains open for temporary exhibitions and special events, most of which are free.

Two hundred metres beyond the end of Trubarjeva is **St Peter's Church** (Cerkev Sv Petra), built between 1729 and 1733, according to the designs of the Trieste architect Giovanni Fusconi. Its flat, rectangular facade, with two identical bell-towers, is enlivened by several beautiful mosaics created by Ivan and Helena Vurnik, including one of St Peter above the main portal. Inside, the central cupola and vaults were beautifully frescoed by the local artisan Franc Jelovšek with scenes depicting the life of St Peter.

Triple Bridge, Marketplace and around

Linking Prešernov trg and the right bank of the **River Ljubljanica** is the enchanting **Triple Bridge** (Tromostovje), a brilliant piece of architecture and Ljubljana's most photographed landmark. In 1929, Plečnik decided to broaden the existing central bridge, which dates from 1842, with two lateral footbridges, in order to make access to the Old Town safer and more convenient for pedestrians; to top it off he added the wonderful Renaissance balustrades, based on the rising bridges of Venice's waterways, and rows of lamps, all of which gives the bridge a magical appearance at night. Once across the bridge, turn left onto Adamič-Lundrovo nabrežje and you're immediately confronted with another Plečnik masterpiece – the magnificent **Market Colonnade**, an elongated, gently curving pavilion harbouring a galaxy of excellent food shops (see p.80) and a downstairs fish market. The colonnade runs along the length of the riverbank from the Triple Bridge to the **Dragon Bridge** (Zmajski most), a quite beautiful piece of Secessionist architecture completed in 1901 by the Croatian Jurij Zaninovich, another student of the Vienna Wagner School. Sitting atop the chunky pylons located at each corner of the bridge are four beautifully carved, spitting, swirly-tailed dragons – the city symbol.

The two squares adjacent to the Colonnade, **Pogarčarjev trg** and the much larger **Vodnikov trg**, have been the site of the wonderfully brash and colourful city **market** (Mon–Sat 8am–3pm) for over a century; it's a great place to stock up on fresh produce, particularly on a Saturday morning when it seems half the city congregates here. On the southern side of Pogarčarjev trg stands the Renaissance-style **Bishop's Palace** (Škofijski dvorec), one of the oldest buildings in the city, dating back to 1512. Once a residence for distinguished guests – Napoleon stayed here in 1797, as did Tsar Alexander I in 1821 – its outstanding feature is the Baroque seventeenth-century arcaded courtyard. On the eastern side of the same square is the **Seminary** (Semenišče), built between 1708 and 1714 and still used by theology students from the dioceses of Koper and Ljubljana; the seminary houses the oldest library in the city, a quite stunning union of Baroque oak-wood furnishings and sky-blue ceiling frescoes representing Theology, Faith and Love by Giulio Quaglio. The stone

Jože Plečnik

Born on January 23, 1872 in the Ljubljana suburb of Gradišče, **Jože Plečnik** was an architect of world-class stature, transforming Ljubljana into an architectural and urban planning phenomenon, as well as completing countless other projects across the country, an immense body of work encompassing churches – and their interior furnishings, town squares and parks, public buildings, and a scattering of columns, pillars and obelisks.

After graduating in carpentry and furniture design at secondary school in Graz, Austria, Plečnik enrolled at the School of Architecture at the Vienna Academy of Fine Arts, excelling under the tutelage of his mentor **Otto Wagner**, whom he would later work with for a brief period. For the most part, though, Plečnik worked independently, renovating numerous buildings and concerning himself with interior design projects. Disillusioned with the growing tide of German nationalism, and the increasingly oppressive atmosphere in the Austrian capital – he also clashed with Archduke Franz Ferdinand, who considered Plec*nik's style too flamboyant for his own rather conservative leanings – Plečnik moved on to **Prague** in 1911, where his burgeoning reputation was further enhanced following the execution of several key projects in the Czech city, including the Sacred Heart Church in Vinohrady and the restoration of Hradčany Castle, the latter at the request of President Masaryk.

Although settled in Prague, the lure of a professorship in his home town proved too compelling and, in 1921, he accepted an offer from the newly founded **Ljubljana University** to become head of the school of architecture; moreover, his return presented him with the opportunity to map out and implement his grand vision for the city. Over the next twenty years, and with extremely limited financial resources, Plečnik married classical architectural forms with his own richly imaginative ideas to create a series of monumental new buildings (Market Colonnade, National and University Library, Žale Cemetery to name but three), bridges (Triple Bridge, Shoemaker's Bridge) and churches (St Francis in Šiška, St Michael on the Marsh). A key component of his blueprint for this new cityscape was the redesign of large segments of the city, including numerous park areas, squares and streets, as well as sections of the Ljubljanica riverbank. The design of the Križanke complex aside, the post World War II period was a difficult time for the ageing Plečnik; he received no further major contracts and many other projects conceived during the war, including plans for the new Slovene Parliament, went unrealized.

Despite his extraordinary range and output, Plečnik's work was not appreciated by everybody, not least his contemporaries, most of whom were wed to the more traditional, functionalist principles of architecture, and thus had little time for his, then unorthodox, form of modernism. Indeed it wasn't until some thirty years after his death, following a major retrospective exhibition at the Pompidou Centre in Paris in 1986, that he received the recognition his work deserved. Plečnik died on January 7, 1957 and is buried at Žale Cemetery in Ljubljana.

portal on the southern side – by the flower market – is flanked by two lumbering giants carved by Angelo Pozzo.Visits to the library can be made by contacting the tourist information centre.

St Nicholas's Cathedral

Lording it over Pogarčarjev trg, the Baroque **St Nicholas's Cathedral** (Stolnica Sv Nikolaja; daily 6am–noon & 3–6pm), easily spotted from all over town due to its enormous twin bell-towers and twenty-four-metre-high dome, is Ljubljana's most important and best-preserved ecclesiastical building. Dedicated to St Nicholas, the patron saint of fishermen and sailors – many of whom lived in the suburb of Krakovo – the present building, designed by Andrea Pozzo from Rome and completed in 1706, stands on the site of a thirteenth-century basilica. Entering through the weighty **bronze door**, designed in 1996 to commemorate the pope's visit and bearing an impressive relief portraying over a thousand years of Slovene Christianity, you're presented with a riot of fine architecture, immaculate carvings and vibrant frescoes. The cathedral really owes its reputation to the **frescoes** painted by Quaglio; these supremely colourful paintings illustrate the many sea-bound miracles of St Nicholas, such as the one depicting him steering a ship full of sailors to safety during a particularly nasty storm. Remarkably, Quaglio painted the presbytery vault, showing the scene of the Establishment of the Ljubljana bishopric, in just twelve days. The most impressive **altar** is in the northern wing of the transept, decorated by an oil painting of the Three Magi by Matevž Langus and further embellished with Robba's delightfully sculpted angels and cherubs. In the opposite, southern wing, is a copy of the *Virgin Mary of Brezje* (see p.113), held within a magnificent frame. Note too, the fine Baroque choir seats with gilded reliefs of Christ and the Apostles, and the splendid pulpit, whose author is unknown. Inevitably, Plečnik also had a hand in proceedings, designing the baptismal font and bishop's throne.

East of Vodnikov trg

The area east of Vodnikov trg is fairly nondescript, though there are a couple of buildings that might be of interest, particularly to fans of Plečnik. At the beginning of Poljanska cesta, you'll pass Plečnik's **Flat Iron Building** (Peglezen), so named after its extraordinary tapered shape; originally constructed as a municipal building in 1934, it now accommodates a shop on the ground floor, and dwellings and a winter garden on the floors above. A few minutes further on, take a right turn down Ulica Janeza Pavla II towards the huge neo-Romanesque **St Joseph's Church** (Cerkev Sv Jožefa), completed in 1922 by the Jesuits. The vast interior is remarkably bare and, aside from Plečnik's monumental semicircular altar, there is literally nothing to see – which probably explains why it was used as a film studio from the end of World War II until its return to a monastery in 1996.

The Old Town

Defined by a tangle of narrow streets, handsome orange-and-red-roofed townhouses, and neat rows of compact pavement cafés, Ljubljana's fabulous **Old Town** is for many the most enjoyable part of the city. Heavily fortified in the twelfth century by the Carinthian dukes, the Old Town – cobbled and mercifully free of traffic – extends from **Mestni trg**, across from the Triple Bridge, south down **Stari trg** to **Levstikov trg** and **Gornji trg**, the entire district wedged between the Ljubljanica to the west and the castle-topped hill to the east.

Mestni trg

After crossing the Triple Bridge and walking to the end of Stritarjeva, you enter elegant **Mestni trg** (Town Square), the first of three medieval squares that form the backbone of the Old Town. Located on the square's northern fringe is Robba's majestic Baroque **Fountain of the Three Carniolan Rivers**, indisputably his most spectacular piece of work. Allegedly modelled on Bernini's Fountain of the Four Rivers in Rome's Piazza Navona (it is strikingly similar), the fountain, completed in 1751, symbolizes the meeting of the rivers Sava, Krka and Ljubljanica, as represented by three muscular tritons grasping oval jugs, with dolphins splashing at their feet. An ongoing debate centres

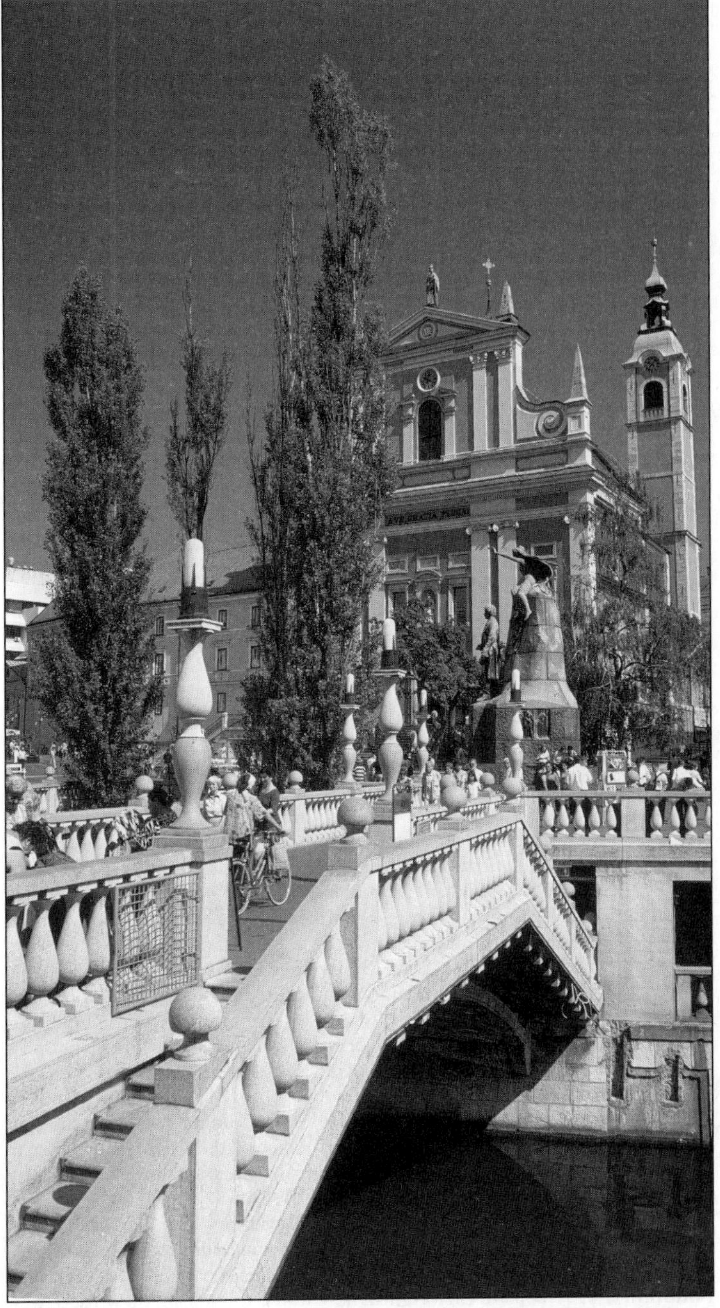

△ Plečnik's Triple Bridge, Ljubljana

around whether the fountain should be moved to the entrance hall of the National Gallery, so as to protect it from the icy winters, although it's usually encased in Perspex during the colder months anyway.

The square's most prominent and important building is the white-and grey-brick **Town Hall** (Magistrat) at no. 1, dating from 1719 and one of the most identifiably Baroque buildings in the city. Sporting a gently protruding balcony and impressive clocktower, the building's most interesting features lie within, namely the arcaded inner courtyards adorned with sgraffiti and featuring two sculptures: the fountain of Narcissus by Robba, and a statue of Hercules, which previously stood in a fountain outside the Stična Mansion on Stari trg. Of the many other fine buildings on the square, take a look at no. 24, the **Souvan House** (Souvanova hiša), whose frontage is the most beautiful example of Biedermeier to be found anywhere in the city – note the stucco reliefs under the third-floor windows representing agriculture, art and trade. Opposite the town hall a narrow passageway leads to **Ribji trg** (Fisherman's Square), a small, run-down little square, where, during the sixteenth century, the fishermen of Krakovo would bring their freshly caught haul from the Ljubljanica to sell to the local inns and houses. Points of interest here include the house at no. 2, which dates from 1528 (as indicated by its coat-of arms), making it one of the oldest residences in the city, and the Neoclassical fountain in the centre featuring a gilded statue of a girl pouring water from a pitcher. The square opens up onto cobbled **Cankarjevo nabrežje**, an engaging riverside parade quartering some of the city's busiest and most vibrant bars and cafés, and site of the terrific Sunday flea market (see p.84).

Stari trg to Levstikov trg

Mestni trg gradually tapers southwards towards **Stari trg** (Old Square), Ljubljana's oldest medieval square, a slight misnomer for this narrow, gently curving street. With a sprightly assortment of cafés, restaurants and ice cream parlours, it's the ideal place to re-energize yourself before pressing on with sightseeing.

Shortly after entering Stari trg, take a right down Pod Trančo – formerly the site of a jail ("tranča" means jail) – which opens up onto the expansive **Shoemakers Bridge** (Čevljarski most), so named after a group of local cobblers set up their trading booths here. Prior to their arrival, the bridge was settled by a group of butchers, but so troubled were the locals by the stench that the then emperor, Maximilian I, paid them all off to relocate elsewhere. Remarkably, there has been a bridge of sorts here since the thirteenth century, though this, the second of Plečnik's bridges, was built in 1932.

Back on Stari trg, at no. 11a, is the **Schweiger House**, showcasing a splendid Rococo facade. The stone telamon supporting the wrought iron balcony above the main portal has a finger raised to his lips in an apparent request for silence – Schweiger, the name of the German owner, meaning "the silent one". The house was later owned by the poet Lily Nova, a bust of whom sits to the left of the main entrance. A few doors down at no. 21 is the **Škuc Gallery** (Tues–Sun noon–8pm; free), a wing of the Škuc Cultural Society, formed in 1978 as a counterpoint to the exhibition policies of the then-dominant state cultural institutions; the gallery hosts imaginative temporary exhibitions by both local and foreign artists.

Beyond the gallery, Stari trg opens up into **Levstikov trg** (Levstik Square), considered to be the true centre of the Old Town and bounded by some notable buildings and monuments. In the centre of the square is the **Hercules Fountain**, a 1991 copy of the original, now in the town hall. A few paces west of the fountain, the **Stična Mansion** (Stiški dvorec), built as a town residence for the abbots of the Stična Monastery in 1630 (which was abolished in 1784) now houses the Academy of Music. During the Counter-Reformation period, the Jesuits settled in and around the square, acquiring a number of houses as well as introducing a grammar school and college here. Their main legacy, however, was **St James's Church** (Cerkev Sv Jakoba), the first Jesuit church in Slovenia, a bright lemon and yellow structure completed in 1615 and festooned with some magnificent sculptures. Retaining only the presbytery from the preceeding Gothic church, the present layout is unusual, comprising a Baroque nave with rows of lateral chapels either side, each adorned with colourful Venetian-style stone altars designed by the local stone-mason Luka Mislej, the author of most of the altar sculptures. The high altar, another by Robba, is a far more modest take on his other works, but no less impressive – he also made the marvellous sculptures in the Altar of St Anne, the third chapel on the left. The church's most significant addition, the octagonal chapel of St Francis Xavier, was completed in 1670, and features another marble altar with unusual statues of a "White Queen" and "Black King". The church is more often than not closed, so try and visit during daily evening mass. Next to the church stands the slender column of the Virgin Mary, erected in 1682 in honour of victory over the Turks at Monošter (now Szentgotthard) in Hungary; the pedestal with four saints, underneath the bronze figure of Mary, was added by Plečnik when he redesigned the square between the two world wars.

Across the busy main road is the custard-coloured pile of the **Gruber Palace** (Gruberjeva palača), built by the Jesuit Gabriel Gruber between 1773 and 1781 for the purposes of research into mechanics and hydraulics; it now houses the National Archives of Slovenia. However, its real architectural delights are concealed within, in particular a wonderful Baroque oval staircase with stucco flower plaits, the dome with an allegorical fresco representing trade, craft and technology, and the chapel on the second floor with oil paintings by the Austrian Kremser-Schmidt. Visits, which are free, can be arranged by appointment (Ⓣ01/241-4256).

Gornji trg

Arching eastwards from Levstikov trg is **Gornji trg** (Upper Square), a lovely, gently inclining street whose dwellings, notwithstanding the Baroque elements, have retained a number of medieval characteristics – three windows, wide with triangular gables, slightly set back from each other and separated by narrow passageways. As you walk along the street, keep your eye out for a number of interesting details, notably the rustic stone relief of St Christopher, thought to date from around 1530, on the front of the house at no. 1; the bronze plaque with a portrait of the historian Baltazar Haquet at no. 4; and, at no. 16, the sign on the portal denoting that the painter Valentin Metzinger once lived here.

Crowning the upper end of the street is **St Florian's Church**, built in 1672 following a fire twelve years earlier that wiped out the majority of houses along here – St Florian is the patron saint of firefighters and protection from fires. Above all else, the church has some intriguing external elements: in the 1930s Plečnik moved the entrance so that the statue of the Bohemian prelate St John of Nepomuk was placed in front of the original, now walled up, portal. Robba's dramatic relief, in the niche under the pedestal, is of St John being thrown from the Charles Bridge into the Vltava River in Prague. Look out too for the built-in head of an Emona citizen, thought to date from 2 AD; the two niches with badly damaged statues of Charles the Great and St Charles of Borromeo; and the fountain with a portrait of a mask from whence water spouts. Beyond the church, the building at no. 27 features a late-Baroque statue of the Virgin and

Child; at one stage it was an asylum for orphans, which earned it the rather disdainful slur, "the shitty school". If you're looking for somewhere a little bit more upmarket to dine, Gornji trg contains a handful of the city's finest restaurants (see p.80).

1 Ljubljana Castle

Peeking out above lush woodland high above the Old Town on Castle Hill, **Ljubljana Castle** (Ljubljanski Grad; daily: May–Sept 10am–9pm; Oct–April 10am–7pm; free; Ⓦwww.ljubljanskigrad.com), with its immaculate white-washed walls and silky, manicured lawns, does little to give the impression of a residence dating back to the twelfth century, although much of what remains today is actually sixteenth-century, following the earthquake in 1511. Its first inhabitants were the Spanheim family of Carinthian dukes who settled here during the twelfth century, before the provincial lords of the Carniolan province, along with the Habsburgs, took over residence in the fourteenth century. Thereafter, the castle was used as a military fortress, a provincial jail and as a refuge for the poor. Crossing the bridge into the castle, you can see, on the right, the remains of the cells where prisoners were held.

In 1905 the castle was taken over by the municipal authorities, with the intention of using it as a cultural centre, although in the event it continued to house convicts, including the writer Ivan Cankar who was imprisoned here for six weeks in 1914. Furthermore, the chronic housing shortage in the city meant that additional tenements had to be constructed, most of which remained occupied until the 1960s. Systematic development has continued ever since, including the excavation of a **lapidarium** (this can only be visited if part of an organized group) and the addition of the excellent **Virtual Museum** (Virtualni muzej; 700SIT, which includes entrance to the clock-tower); it's not a museum in the conventional sense, but an enlightening twenty-minute 3D visual presentation chronicling the city's urban and architectural development and its cultural and economic growth. Aside from the museum there's not an awful lot else to see, though the fifteenth-century Gothic **Chapel of St George** on the western side of the courtyard – one of the oldest remaining parts of the castle – is worth a look for its colourful and remarkably intact coats-of-arms, representing the Carniolan provincial governors. Most visitors, though, come here to climb the landmark **Clocktower**, built in 1848 but subsequently raised, and now affording wide and superlative views of the city and the Kamniške Alps to the north. The vast courtyard, meanwhile, stages many of the city's principal cultural happenings, including a good number of events connected to the International Summer Festival (see box p.84).

A funicular, which will eventually transport visitors from the Old Town into the heart of the castle, is currently awaiting construction; in the meantime, and if you don't have a car, you can take the **tourist train**, which leaves from Prešernov trg every hour, on the hour (8am–9pm; 500SIT return), or walk. Three paths wind up to the top, each a stiff fifteen-minute climb: south of Vodnikov trg follow the path up Študentovska ulica; on Stari trg follow Reber Way and then Osojna steza; and from St Florian's Church on Gornji trg take Ulica na Grad.

Left Bank of the Ljubljanica

The left bank of the Ljubljanica, defined here as the area between **Kongresni trg** and **Zoisova cesta** to the south, holds more magnificent architectural set-pieces, as well as vestiges from Roman Emona and some of Plečnik's greatest work. Its medieval heritage is most pronounced in **Novi trg**, the second oldest square in the city – it too was once surrounded by ramparts which extended as far south as Zoisova cesta.

Kongresni trg and around

From Prešernov trg, Wolfova ulica leads south to **Kongresni trg** (Congress Square), a popular, grassy park shaded by leafy plane trees and fringed by a number of venerable architectural gems. Also called Zvezda ("Star"), on account of its vaguely star-shaped path design, the square was laid out in 1821 for the staging of the Congress of the Holy Alliance, before which time it was the site of a Capuchin Monastery. Having been present on the site for just over two hundred years, the monastery – though never officially abolished – was converted into a barracks by the French in 1810, before being deserted and the ruins eventually cleared to make way for the congress; all that remains is the **drinking fountain** in the centre of the square. Occupying the north-western corner of the square is the **Kazina** (Casino), a lovely Classicist mansion built in 1837 by the Kazina Society for the purposes of entertaining the Ljubljana elite, largely in the form of dances, evenings of song and other prestigious social events. Among the society's more distinguished patrons was France Prešeren, who spent many an evening here with his contemporaries; the Kazina is even recalled in several of his poems. The building's present-day functions are somewhat more prosaic, housing a bookshop and dance school. Between the two world wars, the Kazina also accommodated the posh *Café Zvezda* – its rather less refined modern-day equivalent, located a little further down on the northeastern corner, serves up some of the best cakes and desserts in town (see p.82).

Recessed within a row of buildings on the western side of the square (across the road) is the **Ursuline Church of the Holy Trinity** (Uršulinska Cerkev Sv Trojice), completed in 1726 and perhaps the most original Baroque statement in Ljubljana. Its fading coffee-coloured frontage, incorporating six thick columns and a graceful triangular ridged gable containing Gothic arches, is designed in Palladian style – its curved side wings serve as the entrances. The bright, airy interior, unpainted and completely white, is rather less elaborate, the exception being Robba's dazzling high altar; made from multicoloured African marble and adorned with the allegorical figures of Faith, Hope and Charity, it ranks alongside his most distinguished work. Other notable artwork includes the side altar paintings by Metzinger, and the wooden altar of Ecce Homo with a relief of the Virgin and Child, dating from 1638. The pillar of the **Holy Trinity** opposite the church was brought here by Plečnik in 1930 from Ajdovščina, just off Slovenska cesta.

Located next to the church on the corner of Slovenska cesta and Plečnikov trg, the little known **Slovene School Museum** (Slovenski Šolski Muzej; Mon–Fri 9am–1pm; 400SIT) charts the history of Slovene schooling from the Middle Ages to the end of the twentieth century. Housed in the building of the former Ursuline school, its displays, divided by periods, include a diverse selection of educational memorabilia, ranging from books and reports to teaching aids and uniforms, as well as a couple of mock-up classrooms complete with chalkboards and desks. Alas, the absence of English captions makes what would otherwise be an engaging visit somewhat frustrating.

The square's most prepossessing building is the buttermilk-coloured **Slovene Philharmonic Hall** (Slovenska filharmonija), whose orchestra, in its various guises, has been performing on this site for over three hundred years; although this building dates only from 1892, it's one of the oldest musical institutions in Europe. Given its modest size, Slovenia's musical heritage is remarkably strong. The Academia Philharmonicorum, established in 1701, was the forerunner to today's Philharmonic, which subsequently became one of the foremost musical institutions in the Habsburg Empire. Its reputation was further enhanced by a roll call of distinguished honorary members – Haydn, Beethoven and Mozart to name just three – and it employed Gustav Mahler to conduct here for the 1881/1882 season. For more information on attending a performance, see p.83. Diagonally across from the Philharmonic, the immense neo-Renaissance **University building**, built between 1899 and 1902, has functioned as the main seat of the university since 1919, and today also houses the Faculty of Law. Busts of academic luminaries, including one of Plečnik, form a semicircular sweep around the entrance.

South of Kongresni trg

Vegova ulica, the main street darting southwards from Kongresni trg, was once the westernmost boundary of the medieval city walls. It received its present appearance during the interwar period courtesy of Plečnik, who rearranged the entire street, punctuating it with several of his greatest monuments. The first building of note, on the right-hand side at no. 4, houses the **Faculty of Engineering**, its stately neo-Romanesque facade and thrusting corner towers more than a match for the university building opposite. Across the road is the **Music School** (Glasbena Matica), distinguished by portrait reliefs on the facade, and busts of Slovene musicians – as well as a Croat and a Serb – lining the wall in front of the building; although Plečnik's idea, they were sculpted by his colleague Lojze Dolinar.

Taking five years to complete (1936–1941), the **National and University Library** (Narodna in univerzitetna knjižnica), occupying the entire block between Turjaška ulica and the Križanke, is Plečnik's most lauded piece of work. Located on the site of a former palace, its extraordinary, variegated facade, consisting of rough grey stone quarried from Vrhnika and smooth orange brick from Podpeč is one of the city's most outstanding, and conspicuous, landmarks. Upon entering the building from Turjaška ulica – note the smart bronze horse-head handles on the copper-covered wooden door – you're confronted with a dark staircase ascending to a vestibule lined with black marble columns, the walk up symbolically meant to represent the journey from darkness to light, or, from ignorance to knowledge. Beyond here, and filling the entire width of one wing of the building, is the magnificent reading room, worth visiting for its furnishings, and in particular its "catherine wheel" chandeliers and industrial-style reading lamps. Although you won't be able to access the reading room without a library card, visits are possible by appointment (Mon–Fri 8am–8pm, Sat 8am–2pm; July & Aug Mon–Sat 8am–2pm; ⓣ01/200-1110; free; ⓦwww.nuk.uni-lj.si).

Vegova ulica winds up at **Trg Francoske revolucije** (French Revolution Square), whose main point of reference is the stern, square-shaped **Illyrian Monument**, designed by Plečnik in 1929 in belated recognition of Ljubljana's short-lived stint as the capital of Napoleon's Illyrian Provinces (1809–1813). The obelisk, made from white marble from the island of Hvar in Croatia, is embellished with the Illyrian coat-of-arms – a crescent moon with three stars – and gilded bronze masks of Napoleon and Illyria. Retained within the core of the monument are the ashes of an unknown French soldier, killed in battle in 1813. The **Friedl-Rechar House**, the curved, crumbling building on the western corner of the square, was once a palace accommodating shops and apartments; its ground floor now houses *Le Petite Café*, one of Ljubljana's most frequented and atmospheric haunts (see p.82).

A few paces south of here is the majestic **Križanke**, formerly the monastic complex of the Teutonic knights but now the setting for the city's prestigious International Summer Festival and other major concerts (see box on p.84). Its present appearance dates from the mid-1950s, when Plečnik, in his last great contribution to the city – he was eighty upon its completion – set about transforming the abandoned monastery into an open-air theatre and festival space. The complex's original Gothic details were gradually usurped by Renaissance and Baroque elements, which can be most clearly seen in the main courtyard, which also features shallow archways and exuberantly coloured sgraffiti. Next door, the amphitheatre-like southern courtyard, with its vast retractable canopy, is a superb venue for classical, jazz and rock concerts. Plečnik also designed the **Devil's Courtyard** (Peklensko dvorišče), accessible through the restaurant (in itself nothing special) and spotted with neat rows of weird-looking wall lamps. On the east side of the complex is the modest **Church of Our Lady of Mercy** (Cerkev Marija Pomočnica), built between 1714 and 1715.

The City Museum

Between Križanke and the Ljubljanica the chief attraction is the **Auersperg Mansion** (Auerspergova palača), adjacent to Križanke at Gosposka ulica 15. After residing here for over three hundred years, the Turjak counts, a noble Slovene family with roots going back to the eleventh century, sold the palace to the city authorities who subsequently used the premises to house the **City Museum** (Mestni Muzej). The building has been undergoing a painstaking two-stage renovation project for the best part of a decade, but was still not ready at the time of writing; when it does open, expect to see a comprehensive account of the history of Ljubljana.

Novi trg and around

Continuing along Gosposka ulica, which runs parallel to Vegova ulica, you'll pass the eastern side of the National and University Library – and, above its second entrance, a dramatic sculpture of Moses, by Dolinar – before reaching **Novi trg** (New Square), a rectangular, sloping space extending down to the Ljubljanica. The square is framed by some wonderful seventeenth- and eighteenth-century mansions, the best example of which is the **Lontovž** on the corner at no. 3; built in 1790, it has housed the Slovenian Academy of Arts and Sciences since 1938. In its courtyard stands a beautiful fountain of Neptune, the precursor to Robba's fountain on Mestni trg (see p.64).

By taking a left turn at the bottom of Novi trg, and walking on a few paces, you'll find yourself back at the Shoemakers Bridge, which lies next to another, smaller square, Jurčičev trg. **Židovska steža** (Jewish Lane) and **Židovska ulica** (Jewish Street), immediately west of the bridge, together once comprised Ljubljana's small Jewish ghetto. Neither the synagogue, which once stood at Židovska steža 4, nor any other original tenements remain, although a new synagogue – Slovenia's third – was opened in 2003; it's located a ten-minute walk southwest of the centre at Tržaška cesta 2. Jews have played little more than a walk-on role in Slovenian history and it remains unclear as to when they first settled in the country, though it is believed that there was a Jewish presence here in the twelfth century. What is known, is that following an edict by Emperor Maximilian in 1515, all Jews

Treasures of the Ljubljanica

The languid, muddy-green waters of the Ljubljanica have for centuries concealed one of Slovenia's most unlikely, and extraordinary, archeological sites. Over the past thirty years or so a remarkable number of ancient artefacts have been retrieved from the riverbed, including Bronze Age sickles and helmets, Iron Age spearheads, 2000-year-old Hallstatt bracelets, Roman pots, and medieval swords and brooches, proof, if any were needed, that the river was a key centre of activity and movement long before its heyday in the seventeenth- and eighteenth- centuries.

Some of these items, many of which have been superbly preserved owing to centuries of submersion, are held at the National Museum (see p.75), though many more have been gathered up by amateur archeologists, and hence reside in private collections. If you fancy taking a trip along a stretch of the river, there are one-hour guided excursions during the summer, embarking from Ribji trg (July & Aug daily 10.30am & 6.30pm, Sept daily 11.30am & 4.30pm; 1500SIT).

were banished from Ljubljana, with the majority fleeing to neighbouring Italy and Hungary, and some being dispersed to Slovene villages. Today, it is estimated that around three hundred Jews live in Slovenia, most of whom are settled in Ljubljana.

Turning right at the bottom of Novi trg brings you to **Breg** (Embankment), a river wharf in the fourteenth century when the Ljubljanica was a navigable waterway. Indeed, the river remained the city's principal transport artery, with Breg as its chief port, until the end of the eighteenth century, when the widespread construction of the railways – and in particular the building of the Vienna–Trieste line – spelt its death knell. The boats and ships that used to dock here would sail up from Vrhnika, near its source 20km south of Ljubljana, laden with wood, salt and other goods from the Mediterranean.

Krakovo

A short walk south of Breg is the genteel suburb of Krakovo, reachable from either Emonska ulica – an extension of Vegova ulica – or from Breg, both routes crossing busy Zoisova cesta. During the Middle Ages Krakovo was largely settled by fishermen, many of whom supplemented their income by working as *Pelajhtarji* (light carriers), which entailed escorting the local citizens home late at night from the theatre or the inn. Horticulture is now the prime activity here and one of the first things you'll notice are the strips of magnificently tended vegetable plots, the results of which sustain the daily market on Vodnikov trg.

In parts the area still retains a wonderful, medieval village-like character and this is especially true of Krakovska ulica, with its handsome, one- and two-storey squat houses, a street which was once the haunt of prominent town artists, including the celebrated Slovenian Impressionist painter Rihard Jakopič (1869–1943) who was born at no. 11. Jakopič actually worked a short walk west of Krakovska at Mirje 4, in what is now called the **Jakopič Garden** (Jakopičev vrt), site of some Roman ruins including black and white mosaics and the remains of a complex heating system. If you wish to see the ruins close up – it's only possible to catch a glimpse of them from the gate – then contact the Cultural Information Centre of the City Museum in advance (Ⓣ01/251-4025, Ⓔmm-lj.si). West of the garden, across Barjanska cesta and spanning almost the entire length of Mirje, is a reconstructed section of the **Roman city**

wall (Rimski Zid), topped with an incongruous looking pyramid – one of Plečnik's less-inspired concepts.

Trnovo

"Trnovo, a place of miserable name", Prešeren once wrote of Krakovo's attractive neighbouring suburb. It can be reasonably assumed that the motive for this mildly apoplectic outburst was an unrequited love affair, for it was here in 1833 that Prešeren met his great love Julija Primic, who, tragically for the poet, never reciprocated his feelings. Prešeren first set eyes on Primic in the towering neo-Romanesque **Church of St John the Baptist**, built in 1855 but radically altered following the 1895 earthquake. The stark, bare interior has few highlights, though the presbytery ceiling frescoes by Matej Sternen are worth a look. The bronze relief plate to the right of the main door features portraits of Plečnik and the parish priest and writer Franc Finžgar. With the exception of Mass, the church is usually closed, so try calling at the priest's door to the right of the church if you wish to have a look. Facing the church is the Plečnik-designed **Trnovo Bridge**, completed in 1932 and incorporating several ungainly stone pyramids, a statue of St John the Baptist and rows of birch trees on either side. Leafy Eipprova ulica, the street running eastwards from the bridge along the Gradaščica canal's southern embankment, is well worth checking out for its delightfully quirky cafés and bars (see p.82).

Directly behind the church at Karunova ulica 4 is **Plečnik's House** (Plečnikova hiša; Tues & Thurs 10am–2pm; 600SIT), where the great man lived from 1921 until his death in 1957. Most of this fascinating and neatly preserved collection of equipment, books, plans and furniture is located in the cylindrical annexe which Plečnik purposely built to house his studio. The house exemplifies Plečnik's extraordinary commitment to modesty, each room practically yet creatively schemed. Among the more interesting rooms are his studio, with desks bearing numerous instruments, plans and models; the spartan-looking bathroom complete with ingenious wood-heated shower; the small reception room, where he would receive friends and colleagues – note the stove with its built-in copper kettle; and the kitchen, containing his special chair that enabled him to eat and work at the same time. Having browsed around the house, it's hard to reconcile such a modest man with the grand structures that have left such an indelible mark on this city.

West of Slovenska cesta

The neatly ordered district west of Slovenska cesta contains some of the city's most significant museums. Heading west along Cankarjeva cesta, you'll pass the horseshoe-shaped, neo-Renaissance **Opera House**, constructed in 1892 and home to the Slovenian National Opera and Ballet companies (see p.83). Within the impressive tympanum above the main entrance are the figures of Poetry and Glory, above which is a statue of Genius; in the niches in the facade either side of the main entrance stand the allegorical figures of Comedy and Tragedy.

The National Gallery

At the end of Cankarjeva ulica is the **National Gallery** (Narodna galerija; Tues–Sun 10am–6pm; 800SIT; Ⓦwww.ng-slo.si), whose modest but rewarding two-part collection makes this one of the city's more deserving visits. The collection is actually located in two buildings: the exhibition of Slovenian painting is housed in Slovenski Dom (National House), a grandiloquent, Habsburg-era pile facing Cankarjeva ulica, and initially designed to house a range of Slovene cultural institutions. The exhibition of European painting is located in the northern extension, a stark postmodernist building around the corner on Prešernova ulica. The two buildings were connected in 2001 by a walkway and glass-fronted entrance – the vacant stand in the middle of the hall is intended for Robba's fountain, currently on Mestni trg, although continued bickering has put the move on hold for the time being.

The Slovene collection, which presents Slovene art from the Middle Ages through to Impressionism, is located up the stairs and to the right. The collection kicks off with **medieval art** and a superb display of Gothic statuary and frescoes, the most interesting of which are located immediately to the left and right as you enter; the most renowned piece is the exquisite, almost porcelain-like *Standing Madonna* (minus Jesus, who was cut off) from the Ptujska gora workshop, thought to date from around 1410. Other notable pieces here include the tympanum with the relief of *Madonna on Solomon's Throne*, which once stood in Križanke, and the fragment of the fresco of *Madonna and Child*, from the late fourteenth century. From here, you enter the grand main hall containing paintings from the **Baroque** and **Neoclassical** periods. Its highlight is the *Cardplayers* by Almanach, considered to be the most important seventeenth-century group portrait in the country (this Dutch piece is included here, as opposed to in the European section, as Almanach worked extensively in the former Slovene province of Carniola). There is also an impressive clutch of paintings by Valentin Metzinger and Franc Jelovšek, two of the country's foremost exponents of eighteenth-century church painting – the former was principally concerned with oils, whereas Jelovšek was almost entirely devoted to painting wall and ceiling frescoes. Next up after a rather ordinary collection of **Biedermeiers** are the **Realists**, with a superb offering by its leading representatives, Janez and Jurij Šubic, including the fine *Before the Hunt* and the melancholic *Alone*, both by Jurij. One of the more curious pieces here is by Jožef Petkovšek, whose bleak *At Home* is notable for the missing arm and lower body of his mother – it's believed he'd gone mad by the time he painted this. There is also a wonderful collection by Ivana Kobilca (1861–1926), Slovenia's most celebrated female painter; amongst her finest works are the cheeky-looking *Woman Drinking Coffee* and the joyous *Summer*.

After passing through a room of bronze busts and statues, the exhibition finishes on a high, with an outstanding collection of work from Slovenia's highly revered **Impressionist** painters. This distinguished group of four artists was led by Ivan Grohar (1867–1911), renowned for investing great emotion in his dreamlike landscapes, such as the masterful *Sower* and *Škofja Loka in Snowstorm*. Rihard Jakopič, a close colleague of Grohar, was a painter of bolder, more expressionist works, as shown in his paintings *Memories* and *The Green Veil/Girl with Crown*. The third and fourth members of this quartet, Matej Sternen and Matija Jama, produced works of a brighter, more orthodox bent, for example in Sternen's *The Red Parasol* and Jama's *Village in Winter*.

The **European collection** is a less thrilling affair, although there are one or two notable highlights, such as another *Cardplayers* by Almanach – the players in this one considerably more worse for wear. One of the collection's most prestigious paintings is *Empress Maria Theresa* by Martin van Meytens, located in the Central European section.

Museum of Modern Art

Diagonally across from the National Gallery, the **Museum of Modern Art** (Moderna galerija; Tues–Sat 10am–6pm, Sat 10am–1pm; 500SIT; Ⓦwww.mg-lj.si) takes over from where the National Gallery left off, namely Slovene art from the 1950s onwards. However, it's a bit of a mixed bag and comes as something of a disappointment after its counterpart. It does, however, stage excellent temporary exhibitions. The highlights from the first hall are the smooth sculptures by Zdenko Kalin and Jakob Savinšek, while the second hall is the most heterogeneous – by virtue of the fact that the work on display spans the 1960s to the 1980s. The most intriguing pieces are Lojze Spacal's wooden sculpture of Downing Street and Rudolf Kotnik's series of oddly shaped canvases interwoven with metal plates and wires. Also worth taking a look at are the exhibits by the retro-avant-garde collective Irwin, who co-founded the controversial and influential Neue Slowenische Kunst or NSK (New Slovene Art) movement in the mid-1980s. The exhibition winds up with a bunch of odd, media-inspired pieces from the 1990s and a more sobering piece of work – a vase created from a mortar shell that fell on Sarajevo.

The National Museum and the Natural History Museum

A short walk southeast of the Museum of Modern Art, at Prešernova 20, lies the **National Museum** (Narodni muzej; Tues–Sun 10am–6pm, Thurs till 8pm; 700SIT; Ⓦwww.narmuz.lj.si), housed in this handsome Rudolfinum building since 1888 and graced at the entrance by four allegorical figures representing Art, History, Natural History and Labour. Inside there's a magnificent double staircase with beautiful sculptures of reclining muses, and ceiling frescoes executed by the Šubic brothers. Unfortunately, and inexplicably, the museum's rich permanent collection is currently under wraps and will remain so until 2005 at the earliest. Although the vacant space is used for temporary exhibitions – check with the tourist office to see what's currently on – you're better off saving your money until the permanent exhibition returns, or visiting another museum.

Located on the second floor of the building is the **Natural History Museum** (Prirodoslovni muzej; same hours and ticket; Ⓦwww2.pms-lj.si), featuring an almost complete 20,000-year-old skeleton of a mammoth found near Kamnik in 1938, and a 200,000,000 year-old fossilized fish skeleton found near Triglav. The museum's most impressive assemblage, and one of the most important collections of its kind in Slovenia, is the Zois Collection of Minerals, named after the eminent mineralogist Žiga Zois. To round things off, there is a small multimedia presentation of the extraordinary Proteus Anguinus (aka "The Human Fish"), the largest cave-dwelling vertebrate in the world (see box on p.217).

Trg Republike and around

South of the National Museum is the vast concrete car park of **Trg Republike** (Republic Square), the largest, and, by some distance, the ugliest square in the city, embraced by unsightly postmodern buildings. Shadowing the south side are two towering office blocks, behind which is **Cankarjev Dom**, the country's most capacious cultural and congress centre, named in honour of the great Slovene novelist Ivan Cankar; the centre's two galleries regularly host top-class exhibitions (Tues–Sat 10am–7pm, Sun 10am–2pm; Ⓦwww.cd-cc.si; free). Residing on the north side is the unexceptional **Parliament** building, worth a glance for its portal, framed by blackened statues depicting the working-class family and various industries. It was in front of here, on the night of June 26, 1991, that President Milan Kučan unfurled the new Slovene flag and pronounced "This evening dreams are allowed, tomorrow is a new day" – the thousands celebrating on the square oblivious to the fact that, in a matter of hours, they would be at war (see box on p.325).

Between the two office blocks, across Erjavčeva ulica and behind the primary school, are further **ruins** of Emona. Discovered during excavations in 1969, the finds included part of a baptistry and portico, as well as some lovely mosaics. The gate is likely to be closed but it is possible to see a reasonable amount from a distance. However, if you wish to see it close up contact the Cultural Information Centre of the City Museum (Ⓣ01/251-4025, Ⓔmm-lj.si). East along Erjavčeva cesta, on the corner of Slovenska cesta, is the muddy-green **Slovene National Theatre** (Narodno Gledališče), also known as the German Theatre – on account of the fact that it was initially intended for German-speaking audiences only, with Slovenian performances taking place in the Opera House.

A five-minute walk southwest of Erjavčeva at Tobačna ulica 5 is the **Tobacco Museum** (Tobačni muzej; first Wed and third Thurs of each month 10am–6pm; free; Ⓦwww.tobacna.si), housed in the Ljubljana Tobacco company building. Despite the absence of English captions, it's one of Ljubljana's more enlightening museums, though you'll do well to get a visit in as its rarely open. The collection, neatly presented in gleaming glass cabinets, documents the processing and use of tobacco from the factory's establishment in 1871 to the present day, as well as the lives of those who worked in the factory. Prior to the introduction of machines at the beginning of the twentieth century, the factory employed mainly women (known as *cigarice* or "cigar ladies") as they were deemed to be more dexterous, a prerequisite for the delicate task of hand-rolling hundreds of cigars each day. Aside from photographs and documents there are some wonderful tobacco products, including a superb display of beautifully crafted pipes, cigar holders and snuff boxes. The factory now churns out some three tonnes of tobacco a day, mass-producing several brands of cigarette.

Tivoli Park

If you're looking for a bit of peace and relaxation you won't have to go far. To the west of Trg Republike, beyond Tivolski cesta, is Tivoli Park, a lush expanse of greenery carved up by broad promenades and backed by dense woodland and hills; it's also a major recreation centre with the city's principal sporting facilities located here. The park is accessible from a number of routes, though the most direct is via the subway by the Museum of Modern Art. Exiting the subway, head up Jakopič Promenade, laid out by Plečnik and split down the middle by a row of shabby lampposts, towards **Tivoli Castle** (Tivolski Grad). Since being transformed into a mansion by the Jesuits in 1713, it has been used as a military hospital and barracks, and as a residence for city officials. Local rumour has it that the creator of the cast-iron dogs by the staircase, Anton Fernkorn, was so disturbed by omitting their tongues that – in what might be construed as an over-reaction – he shot himself. The mansion is now the permanent home of the **International Centre of Graphic Arts** (Mednarodni Grafični Likovni Center; Wed–Sun 11am–6pm; 400SIT; Ⓦwww.mglc-lj.org), an enterprising institution devoted to the promotion and printing of graphic art. Its chief activity, however, is the organization of the International Graphic Arts Biennial, the world's longest-running graphic-arts exhibition – a prestigious, three-month-long event taking place between June and September every odd-numbered year.

Up on the northern edge of the park is the brilliant-white Baroque mansion of the **Sequin Castle** (Cekinov grad), which, since 1951, has housed the enlightening **Museum of Modern History** (Muzej novejše zgodovine;

Tues–Sun 10am–6pm; 500SIT, free first Sun of the month; Ⓦwww.muzej-nz.si). The collection, much of it presented in multimedia form, is arranged chronologically, each room representing a period of twentieth-century Slovenia. The starting point is World War I, featuring several mock-up shelters and a remarkable display of photos and mementoes from the battlefields. The collection moves swiftly on to the interwar period, and illustrates the struggle to establish the country within the new Kingdom of Serbs, Croats and Slovenes. This first part concludes with World War II and a rapid-fire projection of 1500 photos onto the surrounding walls, accompanied by thunderous sound effects. Among the more interesting exhibits in this room, which includes uniforms from the warring sides, is a chess set made from bread and saliva by a prisoner of war. The following rooms are devoted to war damage reconstruction and daily life in socialist Yugoslavia, with particular emphasis on the Slovenian economy. Of interest to most will be the last room, which documents the events surrounding Slovenia's gaining of independence in 1991 and the accompanying Ten Days' War (see box on p.325); exhibits include the remains of a Yugoslav army helicopter shot down and items dumped by the army as they retreated.

Rožnik Hill and the Zoo

Bunched up behind Tivoli Park are a number of modest peaks, sewn together by a network of tidy, well-signposted tracks. The most popular short hike (approx 45min) is up to **Rožnik Hill**, accessible via a number of paths, the best of which begins from behind Tivoli Castle. Having made it to the top, you can take in some refreshments at the **Cankar Inn**, periodically the home of Ivan Cankar; opposite is a memorial room (April–Oct Sat & Sun 11am–6pm; free) containing a few of his personal effects and some original furniture. The **Church of St Mary's Visitation**, just down from the inn, was built in 1740 – the high altar has a particularly fine painting by Jurij Šubic (visits during Mass only; May–Sept 10.30am).

Nestling in thick woodland on the southern slope of the hill is the city **Zoo** (Živalski vrt; Tues–Sun: April–Oct 9am–7pm; Nov–March 9am–4pm; 800SIT), an impressively landscaped park, with more than a few steep paths, keeping an exhaustive range of animals, which will at least keep the kids happy. No buses head this way, though the #14 passes through the suburb of Vič, a fifteen-minute walk south (alight at Cesta XV); otherwise, from Tivoli Castle it's a thirty-minute walk around the southern rim of Tivoli Park (along Cesta 27 aprila then Večna pot).

North of the centre

Otherwise unexceptional, the area north of the centre has a few sights worthy of exploration, most of which, inevitably, bear Plečnik's unmistakeable stamp. West of the train station, at the intersection of Celovška cesta and Ruska ulica (opposite Tivoli Park) is the **Brewery Museum** (Pivovarski muzej; first Tues of the month by appointment; 400SIT; Ⓣ01/471-7340, Ⓦwww.pivo-union.si), located in the old malt-house of the sprawling Union Brewery – founded in 1864 by the cartographer Peter Kosler and one of the two largest breweries in the country. The two-part visit first takes in a tour of the filtration and bottling plants where some 60,000 bottles are filled each hour, followed by the museum proper, whose exhibits include century-old wooden barrels, carts for carrying crates and a fine collection of beer mugs and tankards. Slovenes consume on average 87 litres of beer a year, which places them in a steady mid-table position in the European league of drinkers.

Close by is the **Railway Museum** (Železniški muzej; Mon–Thurs 9am–1pm; 300SIT), which is actually split between two locations. In the roundhouse at Parmova ulica 35 is a marvellous collection of old steam locomotives and rolling stock – sure to get rail buffs misty-eyed – while 300m further south, at Kurilniška ulica 3, there is a more straightforward exhibition presenting the history and development of the Slovenian rail network.

A fifteen-minute walk north of these museums in the suburb of Šiška is the first of the city's two Plečnik-designed churches, the **Church of St Francis of Assisi** (Cerkev Sv Frančiška Asiškega), Verovškova ulica (bus #22 to Drenikova ulica), distinguished by its double-storey, cylindrical belfry topped with a cone. Completed in 1931, this is the least conventional of Ljubljana's churches, its square main hall with a high, flat wooden ceiling and rows of square windows more redolent of a school gymnasium than your average place of worship. A colonnade of chunky, circular brick pillars forms a kind of inner square, in the centre of which is a pyramid-shaped altar; both this and the chandeliers are classic Plečnik.

From the church, head eastwards along Drenikova ulica, and then Samova ulica, for twenty minutes (or take bus #22 from Drenikova) until you reach Dunajska cesta in the suburb of Bežigrad. On your left is the modestly sized **Central Stadium** (Centralni Stadion), home to both the local football team, Olimpija Ljubljana, and the national side. It's rare for sports stadiums to be given such a classy touch, but here Plečnik embellished the arena using his favoured motif of columns in both the interior (the elegant pavilion) and the exterior (the colonnade). Unless you're here to see a game – alas, there's not much in the way of quality or atmosphere in the Slovenian league – you'll only catch a glimpse of the pavilion through the gates.

One and a half kilometres east of the stadium is **Žale Cemetery** (Pokopališče Žale), announced by a magnificent entrance in the form of a bright, two-storeyed arcade split by a graceful ceremonial arch – meant to symbolize the border between the city of the living and that of the dead. In the park through the entrance there are a number of funeral chapels dedicated to patron saints, part of Plečnik's overall concept for the entire complex. The cemetery itself is beautifully ordered with lovely gravel walkways and well-tended graves – Plečnik's grave, as modest as the man himself, is to the left of the entrance in Plot 6. From the centre of town bus #2 stops outside the entrance.

Around the city centre

While it's unlikely you'll be in any hurry to escape the city centre, there are some very enjoyable visits to be had not too far away. Just under 1km south of the centre, and easily reached on foot (along busy Karlovška cesta or, more peacefully, along the banks of the Ljubljanica), are the university's **Botanical Gardens**, at Ižanska cesta 15 (Botanični vrt; daily: April–Oct 7am–7pm; Nov–March 7am–5pm; free; bus #3 to Strelišče). Established in 1810 by the Slovene botanist Franc Hladnik, these colourful gardens hold over 5000 species of plants, shrubs and trees, representing every continent.

Covering an area of over 160 square kilometres, the **Ljubljana Marshes** (Ljubljansko barje), 2km south of the Botanical Gardens, originated some two million years ago and are believed to have been the site of the first settlement in the city. The marshes are now a protected area, noted for their tremendously varied flora and fauna, with excellent opportunities for birdwatching, particularly around Kozlerjeva gošča, near the village of **Črna Vas**

(Black Village) on the eastern extremes. The marshes are also something of a fertile hunting ground for archeologists, having yielded innumerable objects since extensive research began here soon after World War II; the latest significant find, in 2002, was a wooden wheel believed to be over 5000 years old, making it the oldest such wheel ever discovered; after a thorough preservation project, it is anticipated that it will be displayed in the City Museum (see p.71). In the centre of Črna Vas is Plečnik's **Church of St Michael on the Marsh** (Cerkev Sv Mihaela na Barju), built in 1938 – some ten years later than the Church of St Francis of Assisi (see p.78) but perhaps even more bewitching. The stone-built exterior, bridge-style staircase and detached hollow belfry are all instantly recognizable as Plečnik's work, as is the extraordinary, largely wooden interior, with its cupboard-shaped altar and Turkish-style lamps. The marshy ground necessitated construction on solid eight-metre-long oak piles, while the hall was elevated to the second floor because of the dangers of flooding. To be sure of getting a look-in, try and visit during Mass (weekend mornings at 10am). To get to the church from the centre take bus #19 to the last stop, Barje, walk back across the junction, and it's 500m ahead; to return, take the same bus from the same stop.

Two kilometres east of the centre, in the suburb of Studenec, is **Fužine Castle** (Grad Fužine), a handsome, Renaissance structure dating from the mid-sixteenth century. The castle was named after the old iron foundry near Polje pri Ljubljani – Fužine means "smelter" – and was originally intended to house a glassworks and paper mill, its location on the Ljubljanica ideal for such industries. Over the centuries, and under various owners, it was rearranged, modified and tinkered with, and there is now very little of interest to see, save for the chapel interior which has some fresco remains. In one wing of the castle is the **Architectural Museum** (Arhitekturni muzej; Mon–Fri 10am–3pm; 400SIT) – a slight misnomer for what is no more than an exhibition of Plečnik's oeuvre, consisting of photos, illustrations and models of some of his projects. The display is actually a condensed edition of a larger exhibition held in 1986 at the Pompidou Centre in Paris, and, interestingly, it includes sketches and photos of his earlier works in Vienna and Prague. To get here take bus #20 to the last stop and it's a five-minute walk; return from the same stop, via the same bus.

Šmarna gora, some 10km northwest of the centre, is an extremely popular outing with Ljubljančani, many of whom come here after work to pound up and down this isolated 669-metre-high hill. At the summit, a partly preserved fifteenth-century wall is evidence that the hill was once a fortified camp providing protection from the rampaging Turks, though in the event it was never conquered. The **Pilgrimage Church of the Holy Mother**, first mentioned in 1314, was built on the old ruins in 1729 and has some lovely frescoes by Matevž Langus, though the only chance you'll get to see these is by visiting during Mass, each Sunday at 11am. Once you've reached the top, which takes around 45 minutes up one of the steep and bumpy tracks, give the bell-rope a sharp tug, partake in a sweet cup of tea, available from the hilltop hut, and take in the terrific views of the city and Sava Plain spread out below. To get to the hill take bus #8 to Brod and it's a five-minute walk to the start of the main trail.

Eating and drinking

As befits its sophisticated image, Ljubljana is able to boast a tight concentration of first-rate **restaurants**, most of which offer excellent value for money.

However, beyond the predominantly Slovene and international cuisine, there is still disappointingly little in the way of genuine ethnic food. During the summer al fresco dining is extremely popular amongst Ljubljančani, and many of the restaurants listed offer outdoor seating in the warmer summer months. Although prices here in Ljubljana are slightly higher than in most other places, you can still eat extremely well without having to break the bank: expect to pay around 2000–2500SIT for a two-course meal with a glass of wine in an average establishment, and around 4000SIT upwards in the most expensive places. Phone numbers are included where booking is advisable.

The best choice for **snacks** is the kiosks and stands near the stations and throughout town selling burek, hot dogs and the local *gorenjska* sausages. Plečnik's splendid **Market Colonnade**, curving along the east bank of the Ljubljanica between the Triple Bridge and the Dragon Bridge, houses dozens of excellent little food shops (Mon–Fri 7am–4pm, Sat 7am–1pm), selling a wide range of different breads, cheeses, sandwiches, cakes and confectionery; during the day vans near the Dragon Bridge knock-up a variety of quick-fix snacks (chicken, tuna salads, etc).

The large and colourful outdoor **market** (Mon–Sat 6am–2pm), opposite the Colonnade on Vodnikov trg, is the best place to stock up on fresh produce, and there are fish, meat and dairy products down in the basement of the Seminary building on adjacent Pogarčarjev trg. Aside from all the above, there are plenty of well-stocked **supermarkets** around town, the most central and largest of which is the one in the basement of the Maximarket shopping centre on Trg Republike (Mon–Fri 9am–7pm, Sat 8am–7pm). Also located down here is an excellent **self-service restaurant** (Samopostrežna Restavracija; Mon–Fri 9am–7pm, Sat 9am–4pm).

Restaurants

Gostilna As Čopova 5 (enter via Knafljev prehod) ☎01/425-8822. A perennial favourite amongst local politicians and bigwigs, *As* is as posh and as expensive as it gets in Ljubljana. The food's not bad either, with seafood and risotto dishes the main staples, complemented by some fine Slovene vintages. The bistro dining area offers simpler, more affordable eating (salads, pizza and pastas). Daily 9am–2pm.

Cantina Mexicana Knafljev prehod. Smart and colourful new Mexican restaurant just across from *As* in this busy courtyard area – the menu differs little from your average Mexican, but the food is well cooked and presented with style; there's a fancy cocktail bar too. Daily 11am–1am.

Casa del Papa Celovška 54a. International food in rooms decorated on an Ernest Hemingway theme (Key West room, Cuba room and so on). You can get down to Latino and salsa grooves as the evening wears on. Daily noon–midnight.

Emonska klet Plečnikov trg 1. Once the halls of the Ursuline convent, this capacious cellar restaurant serves up pizzas, salads and Slovenian dishes. Nightly live music and a cracking bar turns this into a bit of a party place in the evenings. Mon–Sat 8am–2am, Sun noon–midnight.

Figovec Gosposvetska 1. Charmingly old-fashioned downtown restaurant specializing in pony steaks, horsemeat goulash and traditional Slovene standards. Mon–Fri 9am–midnight, Sat & Sun noon–5pm.

Foculus Gregorčičeva 3. Eternally popular, flamboyantly decorated pizzeria offering an exhaustive range of pizzas in lively surroundings, including a better-than-average vegetarian selection, and a generous salad buffet. Mon–Fri 10am–midnight, Sat & Sun noon–midnight.

Joe Pena's Cankarjeva 6. Although not as flash as *Cantina Mexicana*, the food at this breezy, and justifiably popular, Mexican restaurant is no less enjoyable. Mon–Thurs 10am–1am, Fri & Sat till 2.30am, Sun till midnight.

Julija Stari trg 9. A bright, simple eatery in a lovely Old Town location, with decent salads, pastas and Mediterranean dishes. Daily 8am–midnight.

Ljubljanski Dvor Dvorni trg 1. Another of the city's impressive stock of pizzerias, *Dvor* counts some one hundred pizzas, including the best vegetarian choice in town; the expansive patio area overlooking the Ljubljanica is terrific. Mon–Sat 10am–midnight, Sun 1–11pm.

Moro & Pri Sv Florijanu Gornji trg 20 ☎01/251-2214. Two restaurants in one: the former in the cosy vaulted basement specializes in fine Moroccan cuisine, and though not an extensive menu, the food is exquisite – try the chicken and lamb tagine with couscous or the fish skewer, and top it off with a cup of mint tea; *Florijanu*, the rather more formal restaurant upstairs, offers an interesting choice of exotic dishes such as fillet of deer, beefsteak with truffles, and chicken tandoori. It has good-value daily lunch menus for under 2000SIT. Daily noon–midnight.

Pri Škofu Rečna cesta 5 ⓣ01/426-4508. Secreted away in a quiet residential street in Krakovo, this is arguably the city's best restaurant; the menu changes daily, but if you don't fancy anything on offer, ask for one of the house specialities – gnocci, black risotto (*Črna rižota*), black pepper encrusted tenderloin medallions (*Biftek Škof*) or grilled aubergine with white rice and buckwheat (*Malančani Damjana*). The simple, sunny interior, with its lovely handmade ceramic wall hangings, paintings and table decorations, rounds things off beautifully. Mon–Fri 8am–11pm, Sat & Sun noon–midnight.

Pri Vitezu Breg 18–20 ⓣ01/426-6058. *Pri Vitezu* is another of Ljubljana's top-end restaurants, a warm, classy place offering a creditably distinguished menu including, for appetizers, swordfish, scallops and snails, and for mains, duck breast and horse fillets. Mon–Sat 9am–11pm.

Romeo Stari trg 6. Located opposite *Julija*, naturally, *Romeo* offers a more wide-ranging menu, though with an obvious slant towards Mexican – tacos, burritos and the like. Good for late-night munchies. Daily 9am–1am.

Šestica Slovenska 40. Tuck into meat-heavy standards – grilled and smoked sausages, horse fillets and beefsteaks (there's lighter fare, too: pasta and risotto dishes) – under the elegant vine-trellised interior of this agreeably old-fashioned place situated on the busy main street. Mon–Sat 8am–11pm.

Gostilna Sokol Ciril Metodov trg 18. As close to a traditional countryside gostilna as you'll get in Ljubljana; the thick wooden bench seating and tables of this labyrinthine establishment provide a congenial setting for very hearty portions of Slovene food culled from the country's various regions – for example, ham and olives from the Karst, trout from Primorska, and *Gibanica* from Prekmurje. Try, too, a bottle of the domestic *Sokol pivo*, or a glass of red wine in the downstairs bar. Daily 6am–11pm.

Špajza Gornji trg 28 ⓣ01/425-3094. Completing the trio of excellent restaurants along Gornji trg, the elegant rustic trappings of this super restaurant complement the beautifully cooked Slovene food superbly. First-class selection of wines too. Moderate to expensive. Mon–Fri noon–midnight, Sat 7pm–midnight.

Zlata Ribica Cankarjevo Nabrežje 5. Occupying one of the best outdoor dining areas in the city, this modest and inexpensive fish restaurant facing the River Ljubljanica, on the corner of Ribji trg, is delightful. Daily 11am–11pm.

Drinking and nightlife

Ljubljana's **nightlife** is not exactly its strongest suit, although a drink on a warm summer's evening in one of the many convivial **cafés and bars** strung along the banks of the River Ljubljanica is one of the joys of being in this city. Alternatively, a wander up and down Mestni trg and Stari trg will yield an interesting locale every fifty yards or so, whilst the clutch of energetic bars in Knafljev prehod (the courtyard area between Wolfova ulica and Slovenska cesta) are usually packed to the rafters. Ljubljana's limited, but eclectic, bunch of **clubs** – some of which double up as multicultural, arts-type centres – are more widely dispersed throughout town, although all are within walking distance of the centre.

The city's major **gig venues** are Tivoli Hall, in Tivoli Park, the Cankarjev Dom Congress Centre on Trg republike and, best of the lot, the open-air stage at the Plečnik-designed Križanke complex on Trg francoske revolucije. The free English-language *Ljubljana Life* magazine (ⓦwww.ljubljanalife.com), available from the tourist information offices, has fairly comprehensive listings of bars and clubs.

Cafés and bars

Café Antico Stari trg 27. Bare wooden floors, high tables and stools, and pastel-vaulted ceiling give this popular Old Town hangout a pleasantly dated ambience; a couple of little coves for more solitudinous drinking.

Bi-Ko-Fe Židovska steza 1. Artsy, colourful and chilled out café with an imaginative range of coffees, as well as teas and alcoholic beverages.

Breg Breg 2. Classy, if rather posey, wine bar, set in a lovely location by the Ljubljanica; excellent selection of wines available, as well as (expensive) tasting sessions. Mon–Sat noon–midnight.

Café Gaudi Nazorjeva 10. Delightful interior and seductive range of coffees – alcoholic, iced, chocolate – makes this a terrific place for a quick coffee stop.

Čajna Hiša Stari trg 3. Bijou tea-house offering superb teas, excellent sandwiches and cakes and decent breakfasts. Deservedly one of the most popular places with the locals. Closed Sun.

Cutty Sark Knafljev prehod 1. Opposite *Cantina Mexicana*, this lively pub has a more raucous atmosphere than most places in town, and regularly features live music.

Geonavtik Kongresni trg 1. Adjoining an excellent travel map and bookshop, this mellow, nautically themed bar is conducive to a spot of contemplative drinking.

Lepa Žoga Celovžka 43. Small sports café-bar near Tivoli Park, with shirts and other paraphernalia of the good and great (ie mostly foreign sports stars) draped along the walls, and a constant diet of live TV sports, including English football on Sunday afternoons.

Le Petite Café Trg francoske revolucije 4. Eternally popular and wonderfully atmospheric street corner café opposite Križanke, perfect for a large white coffee (*bela kava*) and croissant for breakfast or a glass of wine in the evening.

Maček Krojaška 5. The most popular of the string of hip cafés on the right bank of the Ljubljanica; the place to see and be seen, and consequently always crammed. Happy hour 4–7pm.

Vinoteka Movia Mestni trg 2 ⓣ01/425-5448. This snug little wine bar next to the Town Hall on Mestni trg is the best place in town to sample Slovenian wine. The friendly, knowledgeable staff can assist with vintages from every Slovene wine-producing region, including those from their own winery in Goriška Brda (see p.171). Mon–Fri noon–11pm, Sat 6–11pm; visits outside these times can be arranged.

Patrick's Prečna 6. Up a little side street off Trubarjeva, the city's token Irish pub is not a bad place at all, though the draught beers (Guinness, Murphy's, Kilkenny) are as expensive as you'd expect.

Pr'skelet Ključavničarska 5. Devilishly original basement bar a couple of side alleys away from *Maček* – it's full of skeletons.

Ragamuffin Krojaška 4. In the first alleyway behind *Maček*, this intimate, reggae-oriented café-bar is an enjoyable chill-out haunt, by day or by night. Good tunes too.

Samsara Permanently crowded, summer-only outdoor café on Prešernov trg, offering a bewildering choice of ice creams and sundaes; another seasonal hotspot is the *Pločnik* café on the opposite side of the square – there's an ice-cream parlour here, too.

Sax Pub Eipprova 7. The colourful, spray-painted *Sax* is just one of several cool cafés and bars in this idyllic canalside street five-minute's walk south of Breg.

Zlata Ladjica Jurčičev trg 1. Fun, energetic pub next to the Shoemaker's Bridge on the left bank of the Ljubljanica; if you're here during winter, try the delicious mulled wine.

Zvezda Wolfova 14. Named after the eponymous pre-World War II café in the Kazina building further up on Kongresni trg, this is the place to come for ices and pastries.

Clubs and discos

Bacchus Kongresni trg 3. Swanky three-in-one club (Tues–Sat 9pm–4am; 500SIT), lounge bar (Mon–Sat 8am–1am) and restaurant; the banging club features different music on different nights of the week (Thurs disco, Fri hip-hop, Sat R&B), while the lounge bar suffices equally for a daytime coffee or shake, or an evening beer.

Global Slovenska (top of the Nama department store). Lots of spangly silver and gold decor in the city's most straightforward disco venue, with a different musical theme for each night of the week (Tues student night, Wed R&B, Fri House/Dance, Sat 70s disco). Access is via a glass lift on the street. Tues–Sat (1000SIT).

Jazz Club Gajo Beethovnova 8. Refined late-night jazz club with regular quality offerings by both domestic and foreign acts. Jam sessions on Mondays from 9pm. See ⓦwww.jazzclubgajo.com for programme.

K4 Kersnikova 4. Stalwart of Ljubljana's alternative scene, offering some of the best music in the city – rock, jazz, folk, techno, plus at least one gay night per week. Student parties and performance art too. Look out for flyers or check ⓦwww.klubk4.org.

KUD Prešeren Karunova 14. Superb, long-standing gig venue in the Trnovo district that also organizes regular literary events, workshops (including some for kids) and art exhibitions. Also stages the excellent *Trnfest* festival in August (see box on p.84). Daily 11am–1am.

Metelkova mesto Metelkova cesta. Ljubljana's alternative cultural mecca, consisting of a cosmopolitan gang of clubs and bars (collectively entitled

Metelkova), is located in the former army barracks near the youth hostel; venues include Gala Hala (punk/metal), Klub Monocle (lesbian only), Tiffany (gay) and Gromki (performance).

Orto Bar Grablovičeva 1. Stylish, good-time haunt a couple of blocks east of the train station, with pumping disco tunes and frequent live-rock evenings. Daily 8am–4pm.

Entertainment

For a relatively small city, Ljubljana offers a surprisingly rich diet of **classical culture**, with well-established orchestral, operatic and theatrical companies, and there's a good chance you'll catch something whatever time of the year you're here; although most of these institutions close down in July and August, by way of compensation there's plenty going on as part of the city's International Summer Festival (see box on p.84).

Classical music, ballet and opera, and drama

Cankarjev Dom, the enormous arts and convention centre on Trg Republike, is the scene of major orchestral and theatrical events, folk and jazz concerts and all manner of art exhibitions (the box office is in the nearby Maximarket shopping centre Mon–Fri 10am–2pm & 4.30–8pm, Sat 10am–1pm; also 1hr before each performance; Ⓣ01/241-7299, Ⓦwww.cd-cc.si). Ljubljana's energetic and highly regarded **symphony orchestra**, the Slovenska Filharmonija, performs at the newly renovated Philharmonic Hall on Kongresni trg (Ⓣ01/241-0800, Ⓦwww.filharmonija.si; tickets 2200–4800SIT), while the republic's **opera and ballet** companies are housed in the National Opera and Ballet Theatre, Župančičeva 1 (ticket office Mon–Fri 2–5pm, Sat 6–7pm; also 1hr before each performance; Ⓣ01/241-1702). **Theatrical** productions take place at the Slovene National Theatre (Narodno Gledališče), just off Slovenska cesta at Erjavčeva 1 (Ⓣ01/252-1511), whilst the extremely popular **puppet theatre** (Lutkovno Gledališče), Krekov trg 2 (Ⓣ01/300-0970), puts on a regular programme of shows throughout the year.

There's an outstanding programme of domestic and international classical and orchestral concerts as part of the **International Summer Festival** (see box on p.84) taking place between July and mid-September; venues include the Križanke Theatre, Cankarjev Dom and castle (the festival box office is at Križanke: Ⓣ01/241-6026, Ⓦwww.festival-lj.si). The monthly English-language *Where To?* events pamphlet, available free from the tourist information centres, has complete listings of concerts and events.

Cinema

The majority of **cinema**-(*kino*) goers now make the trek out to the **Kolosej multiplex** at the BTC shopping complex 1.5km east of the centre on Šmartinska cesta (bus #2 or #7). The best of the few remaining downtown cinemas are the excellent new art cinema, Kinodvor, near the train station at Kolodvorska 13; Kinoteka, at Miklošičeva 28, which screens premieres, cult classics and retrospectives, and Komuna, at Cankarjeva cesta 1; tickets for all cinemas cost around 1000SIT. There are occasional screenings at Cankarjev Dom (see p.75), which is also the principal venue for the two-week **Ljubljana International Film Festival** (LIFFe) in November (see box on p.84).

Festivals and events: the Ljubljana year

Ljubljana puts on a wonderfully diverse range of festivals throughout the year, many of which attract a distinguished roster of artists and performers. The festival year kicks off in Spring with **Slovenian Musical Days**, four or five days (usually at the end of March) of concerts performed principally by the Slovene Philharmonic and RTV Symphonic orchestras. One of the year's most enjoyable music events is the ethno-alternative music festival **Druga Godba** ('The Other Music'), held at the end of May in the wonderful surrounds of Križanke, and featuring a terrific line-up of both domestic and foreign musicians and bands; previous acts have included Baaba Mal and Youssou N'Dour.

The key festival months are those between June and September; taking place between July and mid-September, the **International Summer Festival** has been the city's major annual event for over fifty years, comprising orchestral and chamber music, theatre and dance – the main venues are Križanke and the Ljubljana Castle courtyard, with additional concerts at Cankarjev Dom and the Slovene Philharmonic Hall. Also staged at Križanke (at the end of June) is the **Ljubljana Jazz Festival**, three days of world-class jazz concerts. Otherwise, the end of June offers the **Ana Desetnica Festival of Street Theatre**, in which the streets of the Old Town and thereabouts are the setting for a varied programme of wonderful and often wacky street performances; and the **Viticulture and Winegrowers Fair**, staged at the Ljubljana Exhibition Grounds behind the train station, which might appeal, particularly if you're unable to get to any of Slovenia's wine regions – there's plenty of tasting to be had.

The city's foremost artistic event (albeit taking place every odd-numbered year) is the **International Biennial of Graphic Arts**, held between June and September at Tivoli Castle, a prestigious affair rated as one of the premier exhibitions of its kind in Europe. **Trnfest**, a smaller-scale summer festival organized by the KUD cultural centre takes place throughout August, with gigs, exhibitions, workshops and video screenings – there's a good programme for kids here too.

Rounding off the year is the **City of Women International Festival of Contemporary Art**, ten days of female artists' exhibitions, as well as theatre and performance, taking place in the middle of October. The **Ljubljana International Film Festival (LIFFe)** presents a wide selection of, primarily European, films for two weeks during November at Cankarjev Dom.

Christmas celebrations start in earnest at the beginning of December with a procession by Santa Claus, followed by a month of festive events for both adults and children, most of which take place in and around the Old Town and along the banks of the Ljubljanica; the month's festivities conclude with a spectacular New Year's Eve fireworks display from the castle. Advance information on all these events can be obtained from the Ljubljana tourist information centre (Ⓣ01/306-1215, Ⓦwww.ljubljana-tourism.si).

Shopping

There are few **shopping areas** of note within the city centre itself, although a wander up and down Čopova ulica, Trubarjeva cesta or Mestni trg might yield the odd find. Otherwise, most of the city folk do their shopping out at the enormous and ever-expanding BTC shopping complex (Mon–Sat 9am–8pm, Sun 9am–1pm), 1.5km east of town on Šmartinska cesta; this is also the location for the Kolosej multiplex (see p.83). A great place to browse on a Sunday morning is the **flea market** along the right bank of the Ljubljanica, between the Triple Bridge and the Shoemaker's Bridge; here you can find just about anything and everything, from old records, books and stamps, to furniture, musical instruments and Tito-era memorabilia.

There are several excellent **bookshops** in town, all of which stock a wide-ranging selection of English-language books: the two best ones are Mladinska at Slovenska 29 (Mon–Fri 9am–7.30pm, Sat 9am–1pm), and the smaller Novak at Wolfova 8 (Mon–Fri 10am–10pm, Sat 9am–1pm). For **maps**, try Kod & Kam, just down from Križanke at Trg francoske revolucije 7 (Mon–Fri 9am–7pm, Sat 8am–1pm), or Geonavtik, at Kongresni trg 1. If you're on the lookout for **music** head to Big Bang or Mueller, next to each other on Čopova ulica (both also have stores at BTC – see p.84), though Music Box, at Levstikov trg 4a (Mon–Sat 10am–10pm, Sun 4–8pm), has the best selection of music from both Slovenia and the other ex-Yugoslav republics.

Ljubljana listings

Airlines Adria, Gospsovetska 6 ⓣ01/231-3312; Aeroflot, Dunajska 21 ⓣ01/436-8566; Austrian Airlines, Dunajska 58 ⓣ/01-436-8566; British Airways, Trg Republike 3 ⓣ01/241-4000; Lufthansa, Gosposvetska 6 ⓣ01/434-7246; Swissair, World Trade Centre, Dunajska 156 ⓣ01/569-1010.

American Express Kolodvorska 16 (Mon–Fri 8am–5pm; ⓣ01/430-7720).

Banks and exchange Money can be exchanged at all banks, and the post offices (see p.86), while the exchange office in the train station is useful if arriving early or late (daily 6am–10pm). There are several exchange bureaus (*menjalnice*) throughout the city, most of which offer good rates – one of the best is on Pogarčarjev trg (Mon–Fri 7am–7pm, Sat 7am–2pm).

Bicycles From May to October the excellent "Ljubljana Cycle" programme offers free bike rental (1000SIT deposit required); bikes, which must be returned the same day, can be rented from Prešernov trg and in front of the railway station. During this same period you can also hire bikes from the Tir Bar next to the train station (200SIT per hour, 500SIT per day).

Buses The bus station ticket office on Trg Osvobodilne fronte is open daily between 4.45am and 10.30pm; information (in English) can be obtained from the touch screens or phones located inside the ticket office.

Car Rental ABC/Europcar, Miklošičeva 11 (*City Hotel Turist*) ⓣ01/438-2330, and Brnik airport ⓣ04/206-1684, are an excellent local company with very competitive rates; Avis, Čufarjeva 2 ⓣ01/430-8010, and Brnik airport ⓣ04/236-5000; Budget, Miklošičeva 3 (*Grand Hotel Union*) ⓣ01/421-7340 and airport ⓣ04/201-4300; Golftourist, Trdinova 3 ⓣ01/430-6780; Ines Rent-a-Car, Mestni trg 9 ⓣ01/422-2960; Hertz, Trg Osvobodilne fronte (next to the post office) ⓣ01/530-5380; National CarRental, Baragova 5 ⓣ01/588-4450, and airport ⓣ04/238-1020.

Embassies and consulates Australia, Trg republike 3 ⓣ425-4252; Britain, Trg republike 3/IV ⓣ01/200-3910; Canada, Miklošičeva 19 ⓣ01/430-3570; Ireland, Miklošičeva 1 (room 234 of the *Grand Hotel Union*) ⓣ01/308-1234; USA, Prešernova 31 ⓣ01/200-5500.

Emergencies Ambulance ⓣ112; police ⓣ113; fire service ⓣ112.

Hospitals The main hospital is at Bohoričeva 4 ⓣ01/232-3060, while emergency treatment is also available from the Klinični center at Zaloška cesta 2 ⓣ01/543-1408. There is also a dental clinic (Stomatološka klinika) here ⓣ01/431-3113.

Internet access The best places to access a terminal are the Slovenian Tourist Information Centre, Krekov trg 10 (daily June–Sept 8am–9pm, Oct–May til 7pm; eight terminals, 250SIT for 30min), and the British Council, Cankarjevo nabrežje 27 (Mon–Thurs 10am–6pm, Fri 10am–4pm, closed Aug; six terminals, 300SIT per hour). Otherwise, try *Čerin* café, Trubarjeva 52, which has just two terminals, but is free (Mon–Fri 9am–7pm); *Cyber Café*, Slovenska 10 (Mon–Thurs 7am–11pm, Fri 7am–midnight, Sat 11am–midnight; 600SIT per hour); *Kiber Pipa*, in the student centre at Kersnikova 6 (Mon–Fri 10am–10pm; free); three terminals inside the bus station ticket office (100SIT per hour); and the small library in the train station underpass (Mon–Fri 7am–7pm) which allows just 15 minutes surf time, but at no cost.

Laundry Chemo-express, Wolfova 12 (service washes only; Mon–Fri 7am–6pm; ⓣ01/251-4404).

Left Luggage Lockers at the train station (open 24hrs; 400SIT).

Petrol Several petrol stations open 24hrs; Celovška 226; Dunajska 130; Tivolska 43; Tržaška 130.

Pharmacies Lekarna Miklošič, Miklošičeva 24 ⓣ01/231-4558, has a 24hr duty service.

Police For accidents and emergencies go to Trdinova 10 ⓣ01/432-0341.

Post office The main office/poste restante is at Slovenska 32 (Mon–Fri 7am–8pm, Sat 7am–1pm), though the office at Trg Osvobodilne fronte, next to the train station, keeps much longer hours (Mon–Fri 7am–midnight, Sat 7am–6pm, Sun 9am–noon).

Telephones International calls can be made from any phone box on the street, or from booths inside the two post offices (see above).

Travel agencies Specializing in travel for those under 27, the friendly Erazem agency, Trubarjeva 7 (ⓣ01/433-1076, ⓦwww.erazem.net), make hotel and hostel reservations, issue ISIC and hostel cards, and sell domestic and international tickets (for all forms of transport); Mladi Turist, Salendrova 4 (ⓣ01/425-9260, ⓔcmt.mt@siol.net), also make reservations for hostels throughout the country, and issue plane and train tickets; outdoor pursuits specialists TrekTrek, Krakovski nasip 12 (ⓣ041/521-655, ⓦwww.trektrek.si), offer a wide range of adventure-sports activities in the Julian Alps.

Travel details

Trains

Ljubljana to: Bled-Lesce (hourly; 45min–1hr); Brežice (7–13 daily; 1hr 45min–2hr); Celje (every 30min–2hr; 1hr–1hr 40min); Črnomelj (4–9 daily; 2hr 10min–2hr 45min); Divača (every 40min–1hr; 1hr 30min); Kamnik (hourly; 50min); Koper (3–5 daily; 2hr–2hr 30min); Kranj (hourly; 25–35min); Litija (every 30min–2hr; 30min); Maribor (every 30min–2hr; 1hr 45min–2hr 45min); Metlika (4–9 daily; 2hr 30min–3hr); Novo Mesto (6–13 daily; 1hr 20min–2hr); Postojna (every 40min–1hr; 1hr); Sežana (hourly; 1hr 40min–2hr); Ptuj (5–9 daily; 2hr 30min–3hr); Zidani Most (every 30min–1hr; 45min–1hr).

Buses

Ljubljana to: Bled (hourly; 1hr 20min); Brežice (Mon–Fri 5 daily, Sat & Sun 3 daily; 2hr 30min); Celje (every 1–2hr; 1hr 35min); Idrija (every 2hr; 1hr 15min); Ivančna Gorica (hourly; 50min); Kamnik (every 15–30min; 35min); Kočevje (hourly; 1hr 30min); Koper (Mon–Fri 8 daily, Sat & Sun 4 daily; 2hr 20min); Kranj (every 30min–1hr; 40min); Kranjska Gora (10 daily; 2hr); Maribor (7 daily; 2hr 20min–3hr 10min); Murska Sobota (3 daily; 3hr 30min); Nova Gorica (Mon–Fri 10 daily, Sat & Sun 6 daily; 2hr 30min); Novo Mesto (Mon–Fri 10 daily, Sat & Sun 6 daily; 1hr 10min); Piran (Mon–Fri 6 daily, Sat & Sun 4 daily; 2hr 40min); Postojna (every 30min–1hr; 1hr); Ribčev Laz (Lake Bohinj) (hourly; 2hr); Škofja Loka (every 30min–1hr; 40min).

International trains

Ljubljana to: Belgrade (3 daily; 8hr 30min); Budapest (3 daily; 8hr 45min); Munich (2 daily; 6hr 30min); Rijeka (2 daily; 2hr 35min); Trieste (2 daily; 3hr); Venice (2 daily; 6hr); Vienna (1 daily; 6hr 15min); Zagreb (6 daily; 2hr 15min).

International buses

Ljubljana to: Munich (1 daily; 6hr 45min); Rijeka (1 daily; 2hr 30min); Trieste (1 daily; 2hr 30min); Zagreb (3 daily; 2hr 50min).

2

Northwest Slovenia

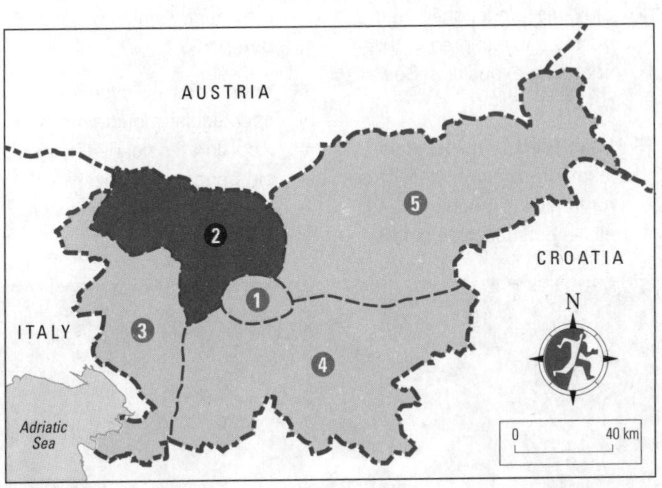

CHAPTER 2

Highlights

* **Velika Planina** – This beautiful highland plain is spotted with shepherd's huts, and offers great walking opportunities. See p.94

* **Škofja Loka** – Compact and elegant Škofja Loka is one of Slovenia's most beautifully preserved medieval towns. See p.96

* **Beekeeping Museum, Radovljica** – One of Slovenia's most cherished customs is explored in this engaging exposition. See p.111

* **Lake Bled** – This fairytale lake comes complete with a romantic island church and cliff-top castle. See p.118

* **Oldtimer Museum Train** – Enjoy the wonderful alpine countryside from the comfort of the Oldtimer. See p.127

* **Lake Bohinj** – Fish, swim, take a boat ride, or just stroll around Slovenia's most stunning lake. See p.127

* **Hiking in the Julian Alps** – Superb hiking and climbing, including, for the more adventurous, Mount Triglav, the country's highest peak. See p.133

* **Vršič Pass** – Slovenia's most spectacular mountain pass incorporates nearly fifty hairpin bends, with dozens of attractions along the way. See p.144

△ Vintgar Gorge

2

Northwest Slovenia

With by far the highest profile of any of the country's eight regions, **Gorenjska**, Slovenia's northwestern province, offers an outstanding synthesis of natural and cultural heritage, from dramatic alpine mountains, valleys and lakes to startlingly pretty medieval towns and villages. The defining feature of the region is the **Julian Alps**, a majestic limestone range packed with sawtoothed peaks, fantastically shaped gorges and ravines, deep mountain lakes, and dozens of waterfalls. Most of the Slovene part of the Julians – a small portion spills over into neighbouring Italy – fall within **Triglav National Park**, Slovenia's only designated national park, at the heart of which is **Mount Triglav**, the country's highest and most exalted peak. Bordering Austria to the north are two further mountain ranges: the slender **Karavanke** chain, and, east of here, the **Kamniške Alps**, whose gloriously tapered peaks strongly resemble the Julians in parts. The tangle of well-worn paths furrowed across these three ranges heaves with hikers during the summer, though the crowds, rarely oppressive, are easily avoided. Hiking aside, the region present stacks of opportunities for adrenaline-fuelled activities – typically, rafting, canyoning, hydrospeed and paragliding – as well as more traditional pursuits such as cycling, horse riding, fishing and swimming. Moreover, Gorenjska possesses the country's densest concentration of ski resorts, the largest of which is in **Kranjska Gora**, squeezed up against the Italian and Austrian borders in the extreme northwestern corner of the country. Located at the tail end of the Alps are Slovenia's most celebrated alpine resorts, the most known and visited of which is **Bled**, a once fashionable health resort, but whose enchanting lake now ranks as one of the most popular sites in the country. For many though, Lake Bled is surpassed by the fjord-like **Lake Bohinj**, a majestic body of water settled amidst gorgeous mountain scenery and bound by a huddle of sleepy villages.

Gorenjska is sprinkled with a few, albeit small, urban towns, too: the most engaging of these are the medieval towns of **Kamnik**, sheltered under the Kamniške Alps a short way north of Ljubljana, and **Škofja Loka**, located west of Ljubljana on the fringe of some delightful, rolling countryside; meanwhile, **Kranj**, Gorenjska's largest city and its key commercial and industrial centre, though initially uninviting, masks a surprisingly endearing old core. Pushing on towards the mountains – as most travellers are apt to do as quickly as possible – the towns of **Tržič** and **Radovljica** are both worthy of a brief stopoff, especially the latter, whose fascinating Beekeeping Museum is one of the region's best museums. Just beyond here are the exquisite villages of **Kropa** and **Begunje**, both of which also offer a couple of excellent museums, and **Brezje**, the site of Slovenia's most important pilgrimage church.

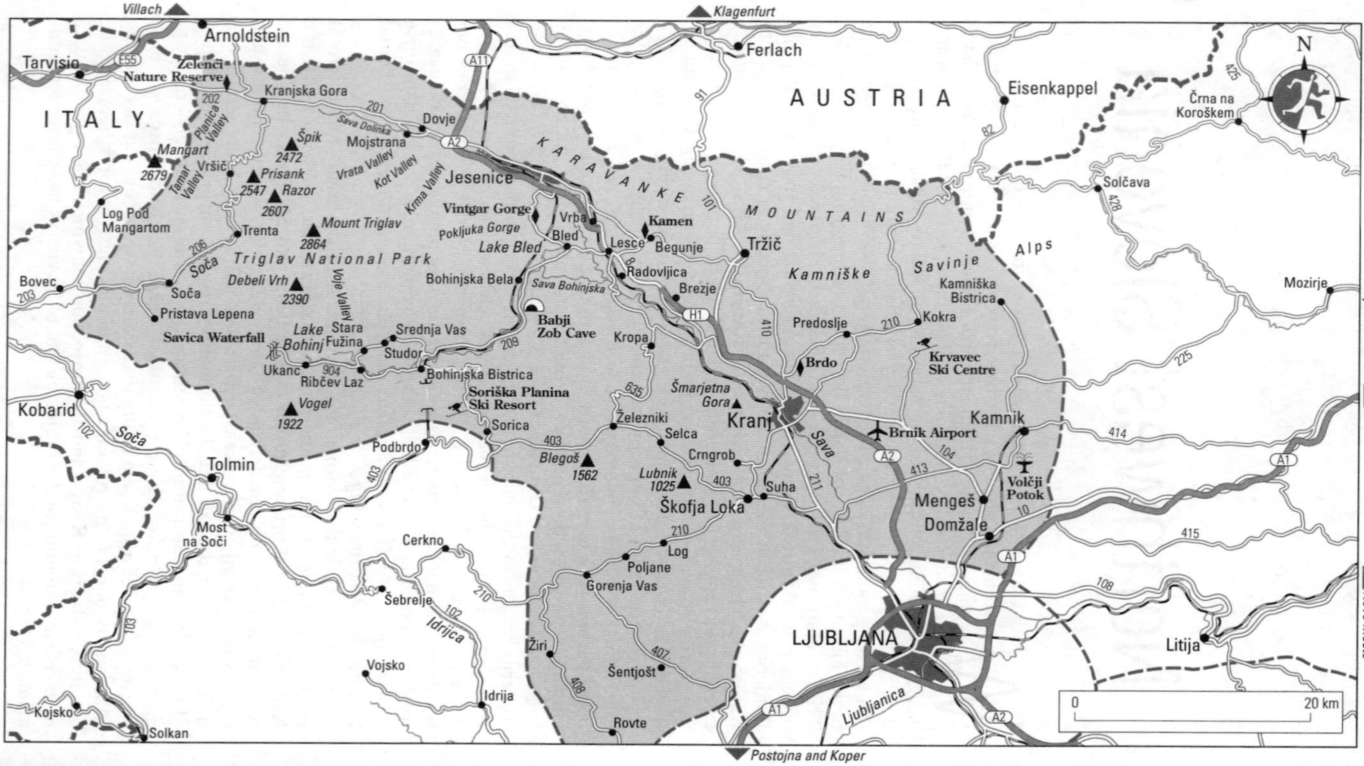

Villach
Klagenfurt
Celje and Maribor
Novo Mesto
Postojna and Koper
N
0 20 km
AUSTRIA
ITALY
Arnoldstein
Tarvisio
Ferlach
Eisenkappel
Črna na Koroškem
Solčava
Mozirje
Zelenči Nature Reserve
Kranjska Gora
Dovje
Mojstrana
Sava Dolinka
Planica Valley
Mangart 2679
Tamar Valley
Vršič
Špik 2472
Prisank 2547
Razor 2607
Vrata Valley
Kot Valley
Krma Valley
Jesenice
KARAVANKE MOUNTAINS
Log Pod Mangartom
Trenta
Mount Triglav 2864
Vintgar Gorge
Pokljuka Gorge
Lake Bled
Bled
Vrba
Kamen
Lesce
Begunje
Radovljica
Brezje
Tržič
Kamniške Savinje Alps
Kamniška Bistrica
Kokra
Predoslje
Brdo
Krvavec Ski Centre
Triglav National Park
Soča
Bovec
Debeli Vrh 2390
Voje Valley
Bohinjska Bela
Sava Bohinjska
Babji Zob Cave
Pristava Lepena
Savica Waterfall
Lake Bohinj
Stara Fužina
Srednja Vas
Studor
Ukanc
Ribčev Laz
Bohinjska Bistrica
Soriška Planina Ski Resort
Vogel 1922
Kobarid
Tolmin
Podbrdo
Sorica
Kropa
Železniki
Šmarjetna Gora
Kranj
Sava
Brnik Airport
Kamnik
Volčji Potok
Menges
Domžale
Selca
Crngrob
Blegoš 1562
Lubnik 1025
Suha
Škofja Loka
Log
Poljane
Gorenja Vas
Most na Soči
Cerkno
Šebrelje
Idrijca
Vojsko
Idrija
Žiri
Šentjošt
Rovte
Kojsko
Solkan
LJUBLJANA
Ljubljanica
Litija
E55 202 201 206 203 A11 A2 91 82 101 8 H1 410 210 225 414 A1 413 104 10 415 108 635 403 209 904 211 102 103 407 408 428 425

Just about all these places can be reached from Ljubljana with the minimum of fuss, and, with the exception of the park interior, **getting around** the region is easy. Although trains serve most places – and there is the useful **car train** (see p.127) which runs between Bohinj Bistrica and Most na Soči – you're best off sticking to buses, which offer quicker and more frequent connections. Save for a couple of key roads, most notably the serpentine **Vršič Pass**, which forges a route across the mountains between Kranjska Gora and Bovec (in the Soča Valley) – motorized access within Triglav Park is fairly limited, though you'll have few problems reaching the major attractions if you have your own transport. There are also quick and easy crossings into Italy and Austria, the former reached via the main road that bypasses Kranjska Gora, and the latter via the Karavanke tunnel, under the mountains near Jesenice, and the Ljubelj tunnel north of Tržič.

Kamnik and around

In many ways the tract of land northwest of Ljubljana is a gentle teaser for what lies beyond. It's an area of hugely varied topography, a blend of flatlands, twisting, wooded valleys and sharp mountain peaks, all of which present great opportunities for rambling, cycling, skiing and other leisurely pursuits.

Hemmed in by thick forests at the foot of the Kamniške Alps, **KAMNIK** – 23km north of Ljubljana – is one of Slovenia's prettiest medieval towns and a major staging post for hikers and skiers heading onwards to the nearby alpine resorts. A market borough in the thirteenth century, the town established itself as a key trade and crafts centre during the Middle Ages, though the later creation of alternative routes left the town somewhat out on a limb. Industrialization and the construction of the Ljubljana–Kamnik railway in the nineteenth century played a part in its revival, as did the popularity of its thermal spas, frequented by both Ljubljančani and Austrians. Nowadays, Kamnik is a sleepy, old-fashioned place which really only ever comes alive during the staging of the town's two major festivals. Nevertheless, its spruce, neatly preserved medieval core, castles and museums warrant a trip here any time.

Arrival, information and accommodation

The town's main **train station** is on Kranjska cesta, a five-minute walk south of the main street, Šutna, but you're better off alighting at the next stop, Kamnik-Mesto, a short walk west of Glavni trg (main square) on Kolodvorska ulica; Kamnik-Graben, a couple of minutes' further down the line, is the last stop. The **bus station** is located 200m east of Glavni trg at the end of Prešernova ulica, just a few paces from the **tourist office** at Tomšičeva ulica 23 (June–Sept Mon–Fri 8am–6pm, Sat 9am–1pm; Oct–May Mon–Fri 8am–4pm, Sat 9am–1pm; ⓣ01/839-1470, ⓦwww.kamnik.si). The **post office** is at Glavni trg 27 (Mon–Fri 8am–7pm, Sat 8am–noon).

Of the town's three **pensions**, the *Prenočišča Špenko*, right by the bus station at Prešernova ulica 14c (ⓣ01/831-7330; ❹), is the most ordinary, with small, heavily wood-furnished rooms; while *Pension Kamrica*, beneath Mali Grad at Trg svobode 2 (ⓣ01/831-7707; ❹), is similarly furnished but with larger rooms and in a better location; marginally more comfortable is the *Pri Cesarju*, a five-minute walk north of Glavni trg at Tunjiška cesta 1 (ⓣ01/839-2917; ⓕ839-1196; ❹), and which also has a few triples. The crowns on the doors are in tribute to the time when Emperor Franz Jozef allegedly stayed here. The very small and basic **campsite** (☎01/831-7314; May–Sept) is located on Maistrova ulica, a ten-minute walk northeast of the bus station next to the outdoor public swimming pool.

The Town

Most of Kamnik's attractions lie east and south of **Glavni trg** (Main Square), part square, part street, and the town's focal point. On the east side of the square, at no. 2, is the **Miha Maleš Gallery** (Tues–Sat 8am–1pm & 4–7pm; 500SIT), named after the celebrated graphic artist, but actually hosting temporary exhibitions by other local artists. A short walk west of Glavni trg is the **Franciscan Monastery** (Frančiškanski samostan), dating from 1495, whose library holds a fine collection of manuscripts and incunabula (contact the tourist office if you wish to visit – see p.91). Adjoining the monastery is the **Church of St Jacob** (Cerkev Sv Jakoba), also built in the fifteenth century but redesigned in Baroque style; otherwise unexceptional, the church is a must-see for Plečnik's extraordinary **Chapel of the Holy Grave**, positioned to the right of the high altar – charged with images of war, the great architect cast the altar in the shape of a bullet, lined the walls with rows of studded lights (meant to represent helmets), and shaped the door-knob into a dove's head, to symbolize peace.

Mali Grad

Occupying a hillock south of Glavni trg is **Mali Grad** (Little Castle), the town's most evocative and identifiable symbol. At the summit, on the eastern tip of the ruins, is the whitewashed, two-storey **Romanesque chapel and crypt** (daily: June–Aug 9am–7pm; 300SIT), parts of which date from the eleventh century, making it one of Slovenia's oldest and most important surviving ecclesiastical monuments. The exquisite chapel, much strengthened and remodelled, contains remnants of some superb fifteenth-century late-Gothic frescoes illustrating several venerated saints, as well as paintings by Janez Potočnik. Step outside onto the balcony and there are some fantastic views of the Alps.

Three decades of ongoing research have revealed some intriguing finds around the castle site, including the remains of a **Stone-Age settlement** and some 27 graves from an Old Slavic burial ground believed to date from the tenth century – some of the finds are on display at the Kamnik Museum (see opposite). According to local myth the castle is home to **Countess Veronika**, half-woman, half-snake, who is said to jealously guard the castle's hidden treasures. Whatever the truth, her legend lives on in the town seal, while each year she's brought back to life during the Medieval Days festival (see opposite).

Šutna and beyond

From the bottom of the castle continue south along **Šutna**, the town's attractive, crescent-shaped main street, lined with neat two-storey Baroque buildings variously housing shops, living quarters and the odd café. Midway along the street, the **Parish Church of the Annunciation**, along with its enormous detached Gothic belfry, looms into sight. Preceded by two earlier churches, this eighteenth-century building features a Renaissance-style altar by Ivan Vurnik – well known for his decorative work in Ljubljana – while the frescoes on the presbytery walls, illustrating various feast days, are by Matija Kozelj who also painted the nave and chapels. Note too the relief above the portal entrance, which depicts a lamb with vine leaves.

A little further down at no. 33 is the **Sadnikar Collection** (Sadnikarjeva muzejska zbirka), a wonderful assemblage of antique furniture, porcelain, weapons and sacral art, amassed by local veterinarian Dr Josip Nikolaj Sadnikar (1863–1952), the man who discovered the woolly mammoth skeleton now residing in Ljubljana's Natural History Museum (see p.75). Among its most priceless items are paintings by Metzinger and Tintoretto (the latter one of only two in the country), and a bust by Ivan Mestrovič, Croatia's greatest sculptor. Take a close look at the magnificent carved wooden door leading into the main room, which is inscribed with the date August 12, 1936, when the king of Yugoslavia visited the house. Visits must be arranged through the tourist office (300SIT per person).

Two hundred metres south of here, on a gently sloping hillside across the rail tracks, is the sixteenth-century **Zaprice Castle** (Grad Zaprice), later renovated into a Baroque mansion and now housing the occasionally stimulating **Kamnik Museum** (Tues–Fri 8am–1pm & 4–7pm, Sat 10am–1pm & 4–6pm, Sun 10am–1pm; 500SIT). It's particularly worth visiting for its exhibition on the recent excavations at Mali Grad (see opposite), which includes an old Slavic skeleton discovered in 1990 and various other prehistoric relics. Rather less stirring is the exhibition of Bentwood furniture, whose pioneer, Michael Thonet, was the first to use wood-bending techniques for the purpose of crafting chairs and tables, and an exhibition on Kamnik bourgeois life in the nineteenth century. On the overgrown lawn in front of the museum are four one- and two-cell *Kašče* or **granaries** – squat, thatched-roof structures which served as storehouses for alpine herdsmen as they went about their work in the mountain valleys. Although prevalent in the nearby Tuhinj Valley (from where these are taken), this particular form of peasant architecture is common throughout the country.

Atop the 585-metre-high Bergantov Hill, east of the Kamniška Bistrica river, is **Stari Grad** (Old Castle), dating from the twelfth century but abandoned in the sixteenth century. Although there's now little to see except a desolate heap of ruins, the reward for the tough little walk – which begins 100m south along the main road opposite the bus station – is some fine views of the town and Alps.

Eating, drinking and entertainment

The best **restaurant**, in a town where there are few, is *Pri Podkvi*, next to the *Pension Kamrica* at Trg Svobode 1; despite a limited menu, mostly steak and trout, the food is of a high standard and the service exemplary. Otherwise, your choices are limited to a couple of modest pizzerias: the characterful *Napoli*, on the south side of Mali Grad at Sadnikarjeva 5, and *Korobač*, near the main train station at Šutna 76. *Kavarna Veronika*, located in a fabulous spot underneath Mali Grad, on the corner of Glavni trg and Japljeva ulica, is, day or night, the town's premier meeting place, serving up the full range of **coffees** and **beers** as well as a tempting selection of cakes.

Each year the town plays host to two very colourful festivals. **Medieval Days**, taking place on the first or second weekend of June, involves a mock medieval market, trades and crafts shows and medieval sports such as sword fighting and archery. The **National Costumes Festival**, on the second weekend of September, sees groups from Slovenia's multifarious regions dress up in their most colourful finery. Naturally, there is much merriment at both.

Volčji Potok

Four kilometres south of Kamnik, near the village of Radomlje, is the **Volčji Potok Arboretum** (daily 8am–6pm, until 8pm in summer; 1000SIT, free in winter; Ⓦwww.arboretum-vp.si), Slovenia's largest and most important horticultural park. Volčji Potok, meaning "Wolf's Brook", had a number of proprietors over the centuries, before the aristocratic Souvan family bought the estate in 1882 and nurtured extensive parklands around the Baroque mansion house – which was subsequently destroyed during World War II. Following Leo Souvan's death in 1949, the estate was turned over to the government, though it was under the auspices of Ljubljana University that the park was conceived, in 1952.

The great Slovene polymath, Janez Vajkard Valvasor (see p.235) once described the park as "a great and fertile place, boasting superb meadows and most fruitful fields". It is no less appealing today, home to over three thousand species of plants, shrubs and trees, all sensitively assimilated into the surrounding woodland. However, it's the neatly manicured **French Garden** that most people make a beeline for, though just as lovely is the landscaped **English Park**, with its silky, perfectly trimmed lawns, while the **beech forests** are ideal for a gentle ramble. Although a beautiful place to visit any time of year, the best time to come is in spring, when the daffodils and tulips are in full bloom. The bizarre bus schedule has just three buses a day making the trip from Kamnik on weekdays (1.15pm, 2.45pm & 7.10pm), but only one on Saturdays (4.50pm), and Sundays (4pm). Coming back, there are also three a day on weekdays, with one on Saturdays (9.45am), and on Sunday (9.35am). The fantastically scenic **Golf Course Arboretum**, located right next to the park, is a very tight eighteen-hole course, guaranteed to satisfy even the most demanding of golfers – expect to pay around 6000SIT per round (Ⓣ01/831-8080, Ⓔigrisce@golfarboretum.si).

Velika Planina

Velika Planina, a broad alpine plateau comprising grassy slopes, sinkholes and clusters of dwarf pines, is one of Slovenia's prime dairy farming regions as well as a hugely popular destination for skiers and walkers. Touching a height of 1666m, the plain, also known as the Great Highlands, was once a heavily forested area – as evidenced by the remaining clumps of trees scattered across the terrain – but is now given over to a group of small settlements (Velika Planina, Mali Planina, Tiha Dolina and others), distinguished by dozens of silvery-grey wooden huts, unique for their conical, shingled roofs which extend like witches' hats almost all the way down to ground level. Though popular with skiers during the winter, the plateau is at its busiest during the summer months, when walkers, loaded with picnic supplies, trek the well-worn, marked paths between settlements, occasionally stopping off to buy cheese or milk from the shepherds. There are mountain huts in Velika Planina (Ⓣ050/647-523) and Mali Planina (Ⓣ041/843-172), both of which have **accommodation** in multi-bedded rooms, and are open daily between June and September, and at weekends during the rest of the year – see box on p.144 for more information on mountain huts.

The most satisfying way to visit Velika Planina is to hike up and take the **cable car** down. The cable car (*žičnica*; summer: hourly Mon–Thurs 8am–6pm, Fri–Sun 8am–8pm; winter: hourly Mon–Thurs 8am–4pm; Fri–Sun 8am–6pm; 1600SIT return) is located 11km north of Kamnik and ascends to 1407m, from where there are chairlifts up to the top of the plateau – the area known as Gradišče; alternatively, or if the chairlift is not operational, you can walk, though it is a steep and gruelling climb. You will be rewarded, however, by the presence of the *Zeleni Rob* snack bar at the top (closed Mon). The main trail begins at the village of **Stahovica**, 5km north of Kamnik (or 6km south

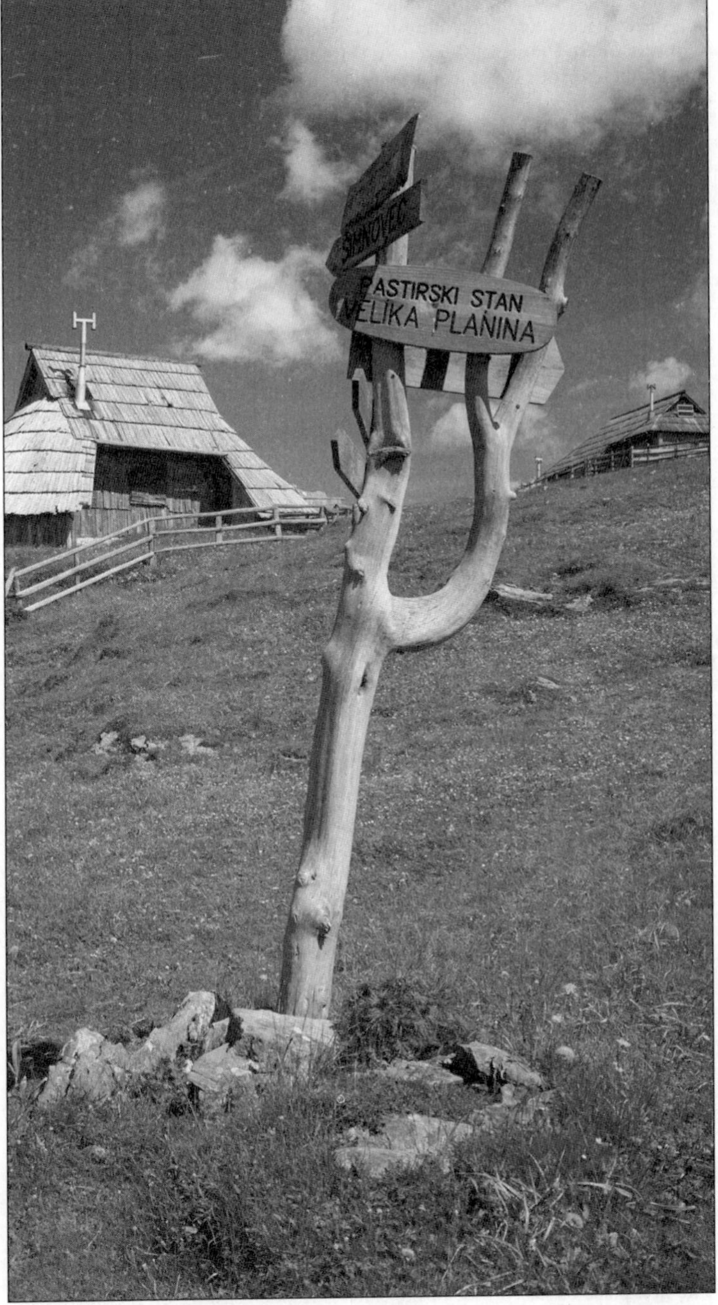

△ Signpost, Velika Planina

of the cable car station), a most enjoyable hike which takes around three hours at a steady pace; after about an hour, a sign diverts you to the fifteenth-century **Church of St Primoz** (Cerkev Sv Primoz), a convenient spot to pause and take in the glorious views, before pushing on towards Mali Planina.

Kamniška Bistrica

Three kilometres north of the cable car station is the tiny settlement of **KAMNIŠKA BISTRICA**, an idyllic recreation spot lying at the head of the Kamniške Alps and a key starting point for **hikes** up into the central tract of the mountains. Note that the following routes are all one way. The two most popular hikes from here, which should suit walkers of all abilities, are **Kamniško Sedlo** to the north (1884m; 3hr 30min) and **Kokrško Sedlo** to the northwest (1793m; 3hr 30min) – both have mountain huts open between June and mid-October. There are several longer and more demanding hikes just over a kilometre back down towards the cable car station, beginning at a track just before the stone bridge; the track, which heads eastwards up the **Kamniška Bela Valley** (you must also cross the brook, which may be tricky if there has been rain), leads to **Presedelj** (1613m; 3hr), **Korošica** (1910m; 4hr 45min) – there's a hut here open between June and September – and **Ojstrica** (2350m; 6hr). If you don't fancy one of these hikes, take the same path for about 25 minutes until you come to a fork – the rocky path to the left will shortly bring you to the **Orglice Waterfall** (*Slap Orglice*), partly concealed but still an impressive sight. Back in Kamniška Bistrica, **refreshments** can be taken at the *Dom v Kamniški Bistrici* (☎01/832-5544), which also offers dorm **accommodation** (May–Oct daily; Nov–April Sat & Sun only). From Kamnik to Kamniška Bistrica, there are three **buses** a day on weekdays and two on Saturdays and Sundays.

Škofja Loka and around

Not to be outdone by Kamnik, **ŠKOFJA LOKA** (Bishop's Meadow), 19km northwest of Ljubljana, lays fair claim to being one of the oldest and loveliest settlements in Slovenia. Lying at the confluence of the two branches of the Sora River, Škofja Loka was first documented in 973 AD, when the settlement of Stara Loka, along with the Selšča Dolina and Poljanska Dolina valleys, was conferred upon the bishops of Freising, who would oversee town rule for the next eight centuries. During the early fourteenth century the town was fortified with a five-gate wall – parts of which can still be seen – while the ancient core was "parcelled" into segments. However, despite being pillaged by both the counts of Celje and the Turks, the town layout has changed remarkably little.

For such a modestly sized town, its sights are reasonably well dispersed, from Mestni trg and the handsome-looking town castle in the centre, to Stara Loka in the north, and the suburb of Puštal to the southeast. Beyond here, in **Crngrob** and **Suha**, are two of the finest frescoed churches in Slovenia. Škofja Loka could easily be done as a half- or full-day trip from Ljubljana – accommodation is scarce and the nightlife won't detain you – or alternatively en route to Bled or Bohinj via Kranj.

The Town

The best place to start a tour of the town is Kapucinsksi trg on the north bank of the River Selščica. On this square, and a few paces west of the bus station,

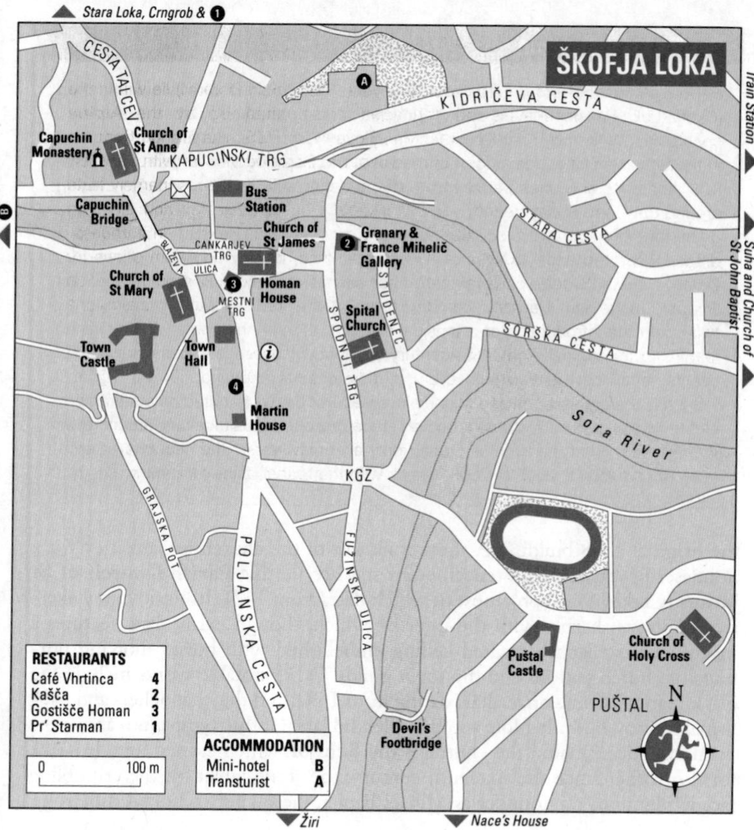

is the modest little **Church of St Anne**, consecrated in 1713. More interesting is the adjoining **Capuchin Monastery**, and its library, whose priceless collection of medieval manuscripts includes a copy of the celebrated *Škofjeloški Pasjon* (Škofja Loka Passion), the oldest written dramatic text in the Slovene language, dating from 1721 (see box p.98). If you want to see this, as well as other works in the library, contact the tourist office or the monastery (Ⓣ04/512-0970). From the monastery proceed south across the narrow **Capuchin Bridge** (Kapucinski most), whose stunning stone arch is reminiscent of the Mostar Bridge in Bosnia, which was blown up in 1993 during the Bosnian war. The bridge was built upon the orders of Bishop Leopold in the fourteenth century, making it one of the oldest of its type in Europe, and later named after the Capuchin friars who settled here in the eighteenth century. Some years later, in a cruel twist of fate, the bishop plunged headlong into the river whilst riding across the bridge on his horse – an incident which probably would not have occurred had he also erected iron balustrades of the type that now line either side of the bridge. Perched on a pedestal in the centre of the bridge is a statue of a wistful looking St John Nepomuk.

Passing through the arch that once served as the town gate, you enter the old town. The first site of note is the **Convent Church of St Mary**, whose Baroque design came about as a result of a fire in 1669 that destroyed much of

Škofja Loka Passion

Performed for the first time in over 270 years in 1999, the **Skofjeloški pasijon** (Škofja Loka Passion Play) is one of Slovenia's most remarkable, albeit rarely seen, spectacles. Written by Friar Romauld Marušič in 1721, it was the first dramatic text in the Slovenian language, a form of medieval and Baroque theatre comprising biblical stories or allegories pertaining to the suffering of Christ – hence its staging around the Good Friday period.

The tone of the play (it's actually more of a procession) is set by the Starbearer – dressed in a red habit to symbolize the impending, bloody agony – followed by Death, Hell and a total of seventeen other scenes, or tableaux, such as the Last Supper, Judgement Day and the Crucifixion. Aside from its slight contemporary twist, and the introduction of a musical element, the play has otherwise remained faithful to its original eighteenth-century production, based on a similar order of events, an almost identical text, and use of the original language.

Such is the organization and finance involved – some six hundred amateur actors, eighty horses, and carefully constructed stage sets at various locations around town are required – that the event is staged only every few years; the next one is tentatively scheduled for 2005 or 2006. Check with the tourist office for details.

the original 1358 building. A short walk east of the church is Cankarjev trg, a nondescript square partly redeemed by the late-Gothic **Parish Church of St James** (Cerkev Sv Jakob), most of which dates from 1471. Its untidy grey exterior contrasts sharply with the interior, which, though eerily dark, features a magnificent stellar rib-vaulted ceiling embellished with bosses showing portraits of church patrons and the town guilds. Other notable works include the black marble Renaissance altars dating from 1694, and the chandeliers and baptismal font by Plečnik. Note too the splendid late-Gothic tympanum above the main entrance. Behind the church is the **School**, which existed here in some form or other since the sixteenth century; the stone tablet on the crumbling facade identifies the founder as Mihael Papler, the owner of Loka Castle.

Mestni trg and Spodnji trg

From Cankarjev trg the street narrows before opening up into **Mestni trg** (Town Square), the town's old medieval market place, an atmospheric, rectangular-shaped space framed by many-coloured three-storey burgher houses, almost every other one marked with a plaque denoting its historical significance. Occupying a prime spot at the square's north end is the **Homan House** (Homanova hiša), an exceptional amalgam of Gothic and Renaissance styles, featuring a turret-like corner projection and sixteenth-century frescoes of St Christopher and the bottom half of a warrior, only discovered in 1970. Its outdoor **café**, shaded by a magnificent linden tree, is the most popular meeting place in town; Ivan Grohar, the great Impressionist painter, was a regular at the inn and completed his celebrated *Loka in Snow*, now sitting in the National Gallery in Ljubljana, from here. Further Baroque frescoes were revealed in 1972 on the facade of no. 35 – the former **Town Hall** (Rotovž) – which also possesses a fine Gothic portal and Renaissance-style arcaded courtyard. Opposite the town hall is the **Plague Pillar**, erected in 1751 by the townspeople in gratitude for their deliverance from fire and plague. Heading down through the square, other buildings worth a glance include the **Žigon House** (Žigonova hiša) at no. 15, formerly a sixteenth-century residential and trade house, and the **Martin House** (Martinova hiša), the last house on the right at no. 26, which was built on top of a section of the old town walls.

Running parallel to Mestni trg to the east is **Spodnji trg** (Lower Square), formerly a residential area for the poorer townsfolk, but now a downtrodden, traffic-filled thoroughfare. At its extreme northern end is the **Town Granary** (Kašča), a sturdy old building used during the Middle Ages for collecting taxes, which usually took the form of grain or cheese; the granary now houses a good restaurant (see p.101) and the **Mihelič France Gallery** (Galerija Franceta Miheliča; Tues–Sun noon–5pm; 400SIT), featuring a superb exhibition of the artist's work from the 1970s. His apocalyptic themes of disintegration, decay and disappearance are embodied in a series of disturbing, surrealist paintings of dismembered bodies and rotting organisms; of particular interest are his paintings of scenes from the Ptuj Kurent (see box on p.300). Midway down the street is the **Špital Church**, a shabby-looking Baroque structure rebuilt in 1720 after the previous church burnt down.

Škofja Loka Castle

Mounted on a low grassy hill to the west of Mestni trg is Škofja Loka's majestic medieval **Town Castle** (Loški Grad), first mentioned in 1215 as "castrum firnmissimum Lonca" – meaning "strongly fortified castle" – though most of what you see today dates from the beginning of the sixteenth century, following the earthquake of 1511. The main reason for visiting the castle is its **Town Museum** (Loški Muzej; April–Oct Tues–Sun 9am–6pm; Sept–March Sat & Sun 9am–5pm; 550SIT), which holds a comprehensive, and occasionally enlightening collection of local and regional exhibits. Before entering the museum proper, pop into the **castle chapel**, which holds four spectacular Baroque gilded altars rescued from the church in the village of Dražgoše, near Železniki, which was destroyed by the Germans during World War II.

The first three rooms, given over to the dominion of Škofja Loka, are unspectacular, save for a superb votive oil painting depicting the great town fire of August 19 1698. The next room charts the rise of the town craftsmen and their **guilds**, set up in and around Škofja Loka in the fifteenth century in order to protect the interests of blacksmiths, tanners, tailors and other trades from both local and foreign competition; the assemblage of deeds, chests and banners is very impressive. Guilds were eventually abolished in 1859, owing to a combination of increased free-marketing practices and the French Revolution, although many of their customs were preserved until World War II in the form of guild fraternities. Elsewhere on the ground floor, look out for some possessions of the acclaimed Slovene writer Ivan Tavčar, and painted peasant furniture belonging to the Kalan family, whom Tavčar wrote about in his celebrated novel *Visoška kronika* (Visoko Chronicle; see p.104).

Heading upstairs, bypass the dull natural history and archeological sections and make for the excellent **ethnographical collection**, which illustrates the traditional ways and means of peasant living before industrialization, with a fine display of agricultural tools and objects, models of buildings indigenous to the Loka region, and a mock-up of a typical "black" kitchen (a superb real-life example of which can be seen in Nace's House; see p.100). The remaining rooms catalogue the importance to the region of crafts such as lace-making, millinery and dyeing, many of which have long since disappeared. The last room is dedicated to the art of making honey bread using ornate wooden moulds, a practice known as "Mali Kruhek" ("Small Loaves"); on display is a collection of the types of moulds – typically made from pear or plum-tree wood and featuring motifs of a secular or figural design – used to shape the bread, traditionally baked for holidays and religious feasts. The castle is reachable via two footpaths: from Klobovsova ulica, just to the west of the Homan House, or from the path at the southern end of Mestni trg.

Stara Loka

The suburb of **Stara Loka** (Old Loka), a short walk north of Kapucinski trg, stakes its claim to be one of the oldest localities in Slovenia, with origins dating from 973 AD. In the centre of the district is the lesser-known **Old Loka Castle**, thought to have evolved from the Bishop's Palace around the beginning of the fifteenth century, but which, save for the round towers, has retained few of its original features. One part of the castle houses the **Museum of Post and Telecommunications** (Tues & Thurs 9am–1pm, Sat & Sun 10.30am–5pm; 400SIT), which, as its title implies, presents the development of the Slovene postal and telecommunications systems – though interesting enough, it would be far more enjoyable with some English captions. Opposite the castle stands the neo-Romanesque **Church of St George** (Cerkev Sv Jurij), built in 1865 and unremarkable save for some impressive sixteenth- and-seventeenth-century tombstones along the side chapels.

Puštal

Located on the right bank of the Poljanska Sora River, the peaceful suburb of **Puštal** is a lovely place for a stroll and also contains one of the town's best sights. Crossing the wooden **Hudičeva brv** (Devil's Footbridge), a ten-minute walk south of Spodnji trg, follow the road south until you arrive at Puštal 74, otherwise known as **Nace's House** (Nacetova hiša; Sat 10am–6pm & first Sun of every month; to visit outside these times, contact the owner, Tone Polenec on ⓣ04/202-1871; 350SIT; ⓦwww.nacetovahisa.com). Named after its first owner, Ignacij "Nace" Homan, this almost perfectly preserved eighteenth-century Slovene homestead is predominantly of Baroque appearance, though its stone-vaulted cellar and two "black kitchens" (see p.130) are evidence of fifteenth- and sixteenth-century elements. Its furnishings, including a fine maple-wood table, carved chairs and a ceramic heating stove featuring a motifed-tile from 1417, are all original; take a look too at the fine iron grills (gatri) adorning the windows.

From the house, head north towards the main road; on the left-hand side is **Puštal Castle** (Puštal Grad), dating from around 1220 and now housing a music school. Two hundred metres east of the castle, a gravelly path breaks off from the main road and spirals steeply up to the simple Baroque **Church of the Holy Cross** (Cerkev Sv Križ), from where there are wonderful views of the town and castle (you can get the key to the church from the house just below).

Practicalitites

The **train station** is located 3km northeast of town and connected to the centre by hourly buses (none on Sunday). Far more conveniently, the **bus station** is located on Kapucinski trg, just a few paces from the old town across the river; it has a left-luggage office (daily 6am–3pm; 200SIT). The **tourist office** (Mestni trg 7; June–Aug Mon–Fri 8.30am–7.30pm, Sat & Sun 8.30am–12.30pm & 5–7.30pm; Sept–May Mon–Fri 9am–7pm, Sat 9am–12.30pm; ⓣ04/512-0268, ⓦwww.skofjaloka.si) is little more than a souvenir shop, but they can assist in finding **private accommodation**.

The only **hotel** in town is the *Transturist*, 200m east of the bus station at Kapucinski trg 9 (ⓣ04/512-4026, ⓦwww.alpetour-thp.si; ❹), a 70s-style relic with dreary rooms and charmless service. A more uplifting alternative is the *Mini-hotel*, located 1.5km west of the centre at Vincarje 47 (ⓣ04/515-0540, ⓦwww.minihotelzorka-sp.si; ❹), with ultra-clean, comfortably furnished rooms, some of which have fabulous views of the Alps; the hotel also has tennis and squash courts (free to guests), sauna and fitness facilities. To get here from the bus station, cross the Capuchin Bridge, take a right turn and continue along the road. Another possibility, if you don't mind staying a little further out, is accommodation on a **tourist farm**; these can be booked through the tourist office – expect to pay around 2800SIT per person.

There are two particularly fine **restaurants** in town. The *Gostišče Homan*, located on the upstairs floor of the Homan House, is a good-looking restaurant with unrestrained red and orange decor, and tables partitioned by drapes; the menu is wide-ranging and the food spot-on, though the service is rather plodding (closed Mon). The downstairs café – by far the most popular in town – serves pizzas, fresh salads and other snacks. *Kašča* (closed Sun), housed in the basement of the old granary at Spodnji trg 2, is a thoroughly enjoyable place to eat, serving some tasty stews, such as *Kašča pot*, to augment its impressive stock of fish and grilled-meat dishes – this is also the place to head to for wine. Another place worth checking out is *Pr' Starman*, Škofja Loka's most typically Slovene restaurant, located just down from the old castle at Stara Loka 22.

After *Homan*, the next best **drinking** spot in town is *Café Vhrtinca* at Mestni trg 31, its lovely floral garden attracting a more youthful crowd. The **post office** is located next to the bus station (Mon–Fri 7am–7pm, Sat 7am–noon). The town's major annual happening, at the end of June, is the **Medieval Days Festival**, a week of medieval-themed events similar to those which take place in Kamnik (see p.93).

Hiking and cycling around Škofja Loka

The **Škofja Loka Hills** to the west of town present some terrific opportunities for hiking and cycling. The most popular local excursion is the two-hour **hike** to **Lubnik** (1025m), reachable via footpaths from Vincarje or from Škofja Loka Castle, passing by the castle ruins and the hamlet of Grabovo. The *Dom na Lubnik* mountain hut at the summit is open between mid-March and December (☎04/512-0501). The further west you go, the higher the peaks, culminating in **Stari Vrh**, a small ski resort, and **Blegoš**, the region's highest peak at 1562m. The 1:50,000 map *Škofjeloško in Cerkljansko Hribovje*, available from the tourist office, details all routes.

A superb network of **cycling tracks** has recently been established in the hills, with routes designed to suit riders of all abilities. The entire track covers an area of some 300km, divided up into twelve stages, with each trail clearly marked by green boards attached to posts. The excellent *Loka's Cycling Track* (1200SIT) map, available from the tourist office, details all stages, indicating elevation, degree of difficulty and sights along the way. **Bikes** can be rented from the tourist office (2000SIT for half a day; 4000SIT for a full day).

Around Škofja Loka: Suha and Crngrob

Standing anonymously in a field 2.5km east of town on the outskirts of the village of **Suha** is the diminutive **Church of St John the Baptist** (Cerkev Sv Janez Krstnik), acclaimed for its outstanding medieval paintings. Upon entering this small fifteenth-century church, you are immediately drawn to the stellar rib-vaulted presbytery, coated with stunning frescoes depicting scenes from the life of Christ and the Virgin Mary (surrounded by evangelists, angels and various Apostles peering through columns). The lower panels depict images of the wise and foolish maidens and the holy martyrs, executed by Jernej of Loka. On the inner wall of the triumphal arch is a representation of the Last

Judgement. There is no public transport to the village (and buses do not stop on the nearby main road), so if you don't have your own transport it's a long and draining walk. The key to the church can be obtained from no. 32, approximately 150m down from the church.

Crngrob and the Church of the Annunciation

Four kilometres north of Škofja Loka, in the tiny settlement of **Crngrob** (Black Grave), is the fourteenth-century pilgrimage **Church of the Annunciation** (Marijino oznanenje), regarded as one of Slovenia's most significant monuments and distinguished by some matchless frescoes. Completed in the seventeenth century, but originating in the thirteenth century, the church manifests a variety of styles – Romanesque, Gothic and Baroque – though its outward form is predominantly Gothic. The nineteenth-century neo-Gothic columned portico at the western end of the church reveals one of the finest **frescoes** in Slovenia, the partly-effaced *Holy Sunday* (Sveta Nedelja), completed around 1470 by the workshop of Janez Ljubljanski. More than forty scenes portray a series of tasks which good Christians are obliged to do on the Sabbath – pray, assist the sick, and so on; as well as what they should not be doing – gambling, drinking and the like. To the left is *The Passion of Christ*, an earlier work completed by the Friulian masters.

Though on a much larger scale, the church interior is strikingly similar to that of the parish church in Škofja Loka, its shadowy tripartite nave giving way to a sumptuously light chancel supported by six octagonal columns and featuring a delightful pale red-, yellow- and blue-painted rib-vaulted ceiling. Completed by Ljubljana craftsman Jurij Skarnos in 1652, the profoundly ornate **high altar** – the largest Baroque gilded altar in the country – is festooned with almost one hundred statuettes and pillars and rounded off with an oil painting by Leopold Layer. The fabulous organ dates from 1753, and the immense bell-tower, featuring a large fresco of St Christopher on its south wall, was raised to its present height of 62 metres in 1666. If the church is locked you can obtain the key from the house below (no. 10). The church can be reached via a monotonous, straggling road which extends northwards from Groharjevo naselje in Stara Loka (approx 1hr if walking). Alternatively, take the Kranj bus and alight at the village of **Dorfarje**, from where it's a fifteen-minute walk to the church.

The Selška and Poljanska valleys

The **Selška** and **Poljanska Valleys**, which fan out from Škofja Loka northwest and southwest respectively, are often ignored in favour of the region's more obvious attractions a short way north. This is unfortunate, as there are several lovely villages here and some of the scenery is immensely rewarding. Although there are a few buses serving most of these places, having your own transport will enable you to see a lot more, a lot quicker.

Selška Valley: Železniki and Sorica

Twisting its way north out of Škofja Loka, the narrow, flat-bottomed **Selška Dolina Valley** stretches for some 34km between the northern flank of the Škofja Loka Hills and the southern ridge of the forested Jelovica plateau. Twelve kilometres up the valley is the quaint village of **SELCA** (from where the valley took its name), distinguished by the Baroque **Church of St Peter** (Cerkev Sv Petra), rebuilt in 1767 after having been burnt down on two previous occasions; the centrepiece of the church is the high altar, featuring a fine painting by Langus, depicting Christ bestowing power upon Peter.

The road continues west for 5km to **ŽELEZNIKI**, the valley's key economic centre. This spindly three-kilometre-long town, made up of several interconnected settlements, has been shaped by its centuries-old iron-smelting industry, which reached its peak here in the seventeenth century when two blast furnaces and more than sixty workshops were operational. Technological advances throughout Europe at the end of the nineteenth century, coupled with the depletion of iron-ore stocks, brought about the demise of the industry and the last furnace was decommissioned in 1902.

The one remaining **blast furnace** (*Plavž*), dating from 1826 and the only preserved technical monument of its kind in the country, is situated at the western end of town and stands as a fitting memorial to a bygone era. The town's industrial heritage is thoroughly documented in the **Železniki Museum** (Muzej Železniki; June–Aug Tues–Sat 8am–5pm, Sun 1–5pm; Sept–May Tues–Fri 9am–2pm, Sat 8am–1pm; 500SIT), located opposite the furnace in the **Plavec house**, dating from 1637 and named after the former owner of the furnace. Despite the absence of English captions, the museum is an enjoyable affair, and includes a lovely collection of lace work from Železniki, considered to be the second largest lace centre in Slovenia after Idrija. If you want to see what all the fuss is about, visit the town in mid-July during the **Days of Lace Fair** (*Čipkarski Dnevi v Železnikih*), a week-long series of lace-related events.

Buses drop passengers off in the centre of town by the **tourist office**, at Trnje 20 (Mon–Fri 9am–noon & 2–5pm, Sat 9am–noon; ⓣ04/510-2600), which also sells a range of lace products. The only place to **stay** in Železniki is the homely *Kemperle*, located just beyond the public swimming pool in the eastern part of town at Otoki 3 (ⓣ04/514-6084, Ⓔkemperle@siol.net; ❸). There's nowhere to eat here, but if you've got your own transport it's worth stopping off at the *Pri Slavcu* (closed Tues & Wed) in **Zali Log**, the next village along.

Nine kilometres west of Železniki, the road branches off to the right and winds steeply up to the picturesque alpine village of **SORICA**, its smooth undulating pastures spotted with small clusters of houses and dozens of drying racks. Sorica is celebrated as the birthplace of the great Slovene Impressionist painter Ivan Grohar, a sculpture of whom – palette in hand – greets visitors at the entrance to the village; his **birthplace** (Groharjeva hiša; daily 3–5pm, or ask for the key at the restaurant opposite; 400SIT) is located beyond the church at Spodnja Sorica 7, and contains a limited collection of his paintings and belongings. If you fancy stopping the night, there are several **tourist farms** in the village, with two possibilities just a few paces down from Grohar's house at no. 13 (ⓣ04-519-7055; ❷) and no. 14 (ⓣ04/519-7018; ❷). The road continues onwards and upwards to the Soriška Planina ski resort and beyond to Bohinj. There are currently just two buses from Sorica to Železniki, at 5.07am and 1.17pm, Monday to Friday only.

Poljanska Valley

Flanked by the Škofja Loka Hills to the north and the slightly lower Polhov Gradec Hills to the south, the **Poljanska Valley** extends for some 35km between Škofja Loka and the small town of Žiri. Eleven kilometres southwest of Škofja Loka, in the tiny settlement of **LOG**, is the *Gostišče Premtovc*, a magnificent roadside inn accommodating one of the most distinguished restaurants in the region (Tues–Sat 4–9pm, Sun 11am–6pm; reservations are advised; ⓣ04/518-6000). The inn also has two immaculately furnished suites (❺).

Rupnik Line

Sequenced in an almost vertical chain between Soriška Planina in the north and the small town of Žiri some 50km further south are dozens of bunkers, tunnels, casemates and observation posts, built by the Yugoslavs in response to border fortifications constructed by the Italians following the **Treaty of Rapallo in 1920** (see p.320). Although proposals to fortify the border were initially submitted in the mid-1920s, construction work didn't begin until 1937, under the command of its chief architect **Leon Rupnik**, a Yugoslav army general who was later tried and shot in Ljubljana for treason. In the event, the line was neither fully completed – due to the onset of World War II – nor were its existing fortifications pressed into service.

Many of the fortifications have recently been cleaned up and it's now possible (with a guide) to visit some of them, an opportunity that will almost certainly appeal to adrenaline junkies; the descent into the bunkers and tunnels – some nearly forty metres deep – is quite exhilarating. Moreover, the **hiking** in this region is terrific. The line has been divided into three stages (each stage is roughly a 6–7hr hike, the first is also accessible to cyclists), with a number of different excursions organized by the tourist office in Škofja Loka (☎04/512-0268; see p.100) and the Impulse agency in Žiri (☎04/510-5580; see below). These range from short two-hour tours (1000SIT), to day-long hikes (2000SIT per person, 4000SIT with lunch), though tours can be tailored to suit individual or group needs.

Five hundred metres beyond the inn, across the bridge on the left, and then along the road to the right, is the **Visoko Mansion**, once the property of the celebrated writer Ivan Tavčar (1851–1923). The mansion (also known as the Tavčar Manor) is now sadly derelict and all there is to see is an enormous bronze sculpture – completed in 1957 by Jakob Savinšek – of a cross-legged Tavčar gazing across the field. Born in **Poljane**, the next village along, Tavčar, erstwhile Ljubljana mayor and politician, was considered one of the country's foremost prose writers, basing much of his work on his experiences of life in the valley. His most famous novel, *Visoška Kronika* ("Visoko Chronicle"), charted the lives of the Kalan family who lived in the same house some two hundred years before Tavčar. Beyond the mansion lie the valley's central settlements, Poljane and Gorenja Vas, both pleasant enough but neither worth stopping off for.

Žiri

Twelve kilometres south of Gorenja Vas is **ŽIRI**, a small, conservative town renowned for its lace and shoemaking industries, both of which are well covered in the **Žiri Museum** (Muzej Žiri; May–Oct Sat & Sun 2–4pm; other times by appointment, contact the Impulse Agency below; 400SIT). This is located 1km south of the centre at Tabor 2 in the dilapidated former mansion of the Freising bishops. Following World War II the town's various shoemaking industries morphed into the Alpina factory, which now employs over a thousand people who manufacture ski boots and a range of other sports footwear for some of the world's top climbers and athletes. Although Žiri is not as large a lace centre as either Idrija or Železniki, the museum's bobbin-lace collection attests to its importance in the town during the first part of the twentieth century. If you wish to have a look at, or purchase, some lace items, pop into the small **Lace Gallery** at Jobstova 29 (Mon–Fri 4.30–7pm, Sat 9am–noon).

Buses drop passengers off in the centre of town by the large information board with a useful map for getting your bearings; directly opposite here is the Impulse agency (Mon–Fri 9am–noon & 3–7pm, Sat 9am–noon; ⓣ04/510-5580, ⓔimpulse-travel@siol.net), whose helpful staff can book **accommodation** on local tourist farms (❷). The *Gostilna Županu*, at Loška 78 (ⓣ04/505-0000; ❸) in the northern part of town, is the sole central source of accommodation here, with a handful of neat, fresh-looking rooms. This is also the best place in town to **eat**, with pizzas, salads and meat dishes constituting the bulk of the menu. A good alternative is the *Lenger*, a countrified roadside restaurant 200m north of the museum at Staroširovska 11, with a Slovene and Italian-heavy menu (closed Tues).

Kranj and around

Despite its reputation as a hard-nosed and gritty industrial centre, **KRANJ**, 10km from Škofja Loka and Slovenia's fourth largest city, possesses an attractive old city centre severely at odds with its drab surrounds. Positioned on a steep, rocky promontory above the confluence of the Sava and Kokra rivers, between the foothills of the Julian Alps and the western spur of the Kamniške-Savinja Alps, Kranj has been the country's most important industrial city since the end of World War I, home to several of Slovenia's major manufacturing industries, including textiles, leather and electronics, which in total employ almost half of the city's population. However, beyond the grimescape of smoking chimneys, the old town possesses a clutch of fine late-Gothic buildings, while the city's strong associations with France Prešeren – he lived, worked and died here – are manifest in an excellent museum. Furthermore, nearby **Brdo Castle** is enjoyable side attraction.

The Town

The town's attractive medieval centre begins at **Maistrov trg**, formerly the site of the upper town gate and once enclosed by the northern section of the city walls, the most obvious legacy of which is the **Spital Tower** – one of seven defensive towers incorporated within the walls – and which now forms part of the shop at no. 3. The square, liberally sprinkled with cafés and the hub of all social activity, segues into Prešernova ulica. At no. 7, a memorial plaque above the entrance denotes **Prešeren's House** (Prešerenova hiša; Tues–Sun 10am–6pm; 500SIT). The two-storey building where Prešeren spent the last three years of his life is a fine example of a late-Gothic town-house, its arcaded gallery uniting what were once two separate dwellings. The first floor has been turned into a superb memorial museum, chronologically presenting phases of Prešeren's life, with manuscripts, diaries and letters, accompanied by excellent explanatory notes. There is also much original furniture to admire, including the bed he died in and the desk and chair he used while working as a lawyer (see box on p.123). Prešeren is buried in **Prešernov Gaj** (Prešeren Grove), a small cemetery 500m north of town, and which has only one other grave, that of another local poet, Simon Jenko.

Glavni trg

Prešernova ulica opens up into **Glavni trg** (Main Square), an elongated square framed by delightful Gothic and Renaissance buildings, the most prominent of which is the **town hall** (Mestna hiša) on the corner of Poštna ulica, and which now accommodates the enjoyable **Gorenjska Museum** (Muzej Gorenjski; Tues–Sun 10am–6pm; 500SIT). Its trio of exhibitions kicks off with an

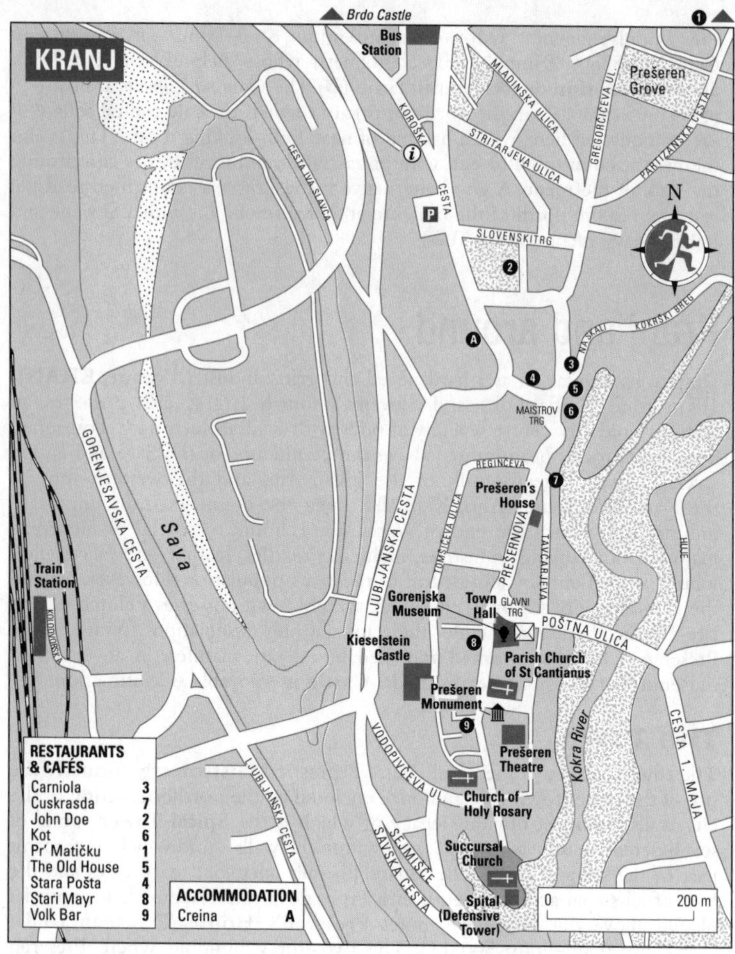

above-average collection of archeological finds, the most recent of which is a valuable hoard of Roman tools – probably from a carpenter's workshop and thought to date from 4 AD – discovered in 1996 near Radomlje. The remainder of the museum's collection comprises an interesting assortment of sculptures by Lojze Dolinar (a student of the eminent Croatian sculptor Ivan Mestrovič), and an ethnological exhibition of folk art from Gorenjska, including beautifully crafted chests and cupboards and fifteenth-century frescoes. Have a look, too, at the magnificent Renaissance Hall, sporting a coffered ceiling and two inlaid wooden portals, which is now used as a venue for wedding ceremonies.

Dominating the square – indeed the city skyline – is the glowering **Parish Church of St Cantianus** (Cerkev Sv Kancijan), the most outstanding example of a Gothic hall church in Slovenia; supported by four immense octagonal columns, its stellar-vaulted central nave is decorated with the *Star of Beautiful Angels* fresco, attributed to the workshop of Janez Ljubljanski. Other highlights are the high altar by Vurnik, and the neo-Gothic stained-glass windows by Kregar. Have a look too at the tympanum above the main entrance incorporating a relief of Christ on the Mount of Olives.

Outside the north side of the church is an early-Slavonic **ossuary**, containing thousands of neatly stacked bones and skulls of Kranj citizens, thought to have been buried here between the fourteenth and sixteenth centuries but which were only discovered in the early 1970s (you need to ask at the town hall if you want to have a look). On the church's exterior south wall is a small **lapidary** of Roman and medieval tombstones and, beneath, a **fountain** bearing a statue of St John Nepomuk, somewhat bizarrely entangled in an octopus. Across the way, next to an oversized **monument** of Prešeren, is the **Prešeren Theatre** (Prešernovo Gledališče), a bland building which not even Plečnik's arched portico can enliven.

South to Pungert

From here the square narrows into Cankarjeva ulica; halfway down is the **Church of the Holy Rosary** (Cerkev Roženvesnka), a bland Gothic structure entirely reconstructed in 1892, which once served as a Protestant sanctuary during the Reformation. Beside the church is a Plečnik-designed **staircase**; on one side is a characteristic arcade, and in the middle, an unattractive looking fountain, also both by Plečnik. Walking down the stairs brings you to Vodopivčeva ulica (aka "Mohor's Slope"), where the lower town gate once stood, and beyond to the Sava River.

Cankarjeva ulica winds up at Trubarjev trg and the southern tip of the promontory known as **Pungert**, which rises up over the confluence of the Sava and Kokra rivers; unfortunately, the **Kokra Gorge**, an inaccessible 30-metre-deep canyon, is largely obscured by trees, though there are some much better views from the Poštna ulica bridge, east of Glavni trg. The three-storey **Defensive Tower**, right on the tip, is the only entirely preserved tower within the ancient city walls; at one stage it was adapted for use as a prison and as lodgings. Next to the tower, the late fifteenth-century **Succursal Church** (also called the Plague Church) is dedicated to SS Rok, Fabian and Sebastian in thanks for their intervention against the plague. Unfortunately, Martin Kremser-Schmidt's illustrious painting *Intercessors Against the Plague* (1773) – which until recently ornamented the high altar – has been removed and is currently held within the priest's house. The church is now used for services by the local Serbian Orthodox community.

Retracing your steps back to the Church of the Holy Rosary, head north along Tomšičeva ulica, where you'll pass a restored section of the **city walls**, beyond which is the **Kieselstein Castle** (Grad Kieselstein), formerly a fifteenth-century stronghold, later a manor house and now home to several cultural organizations and occasionally used as a venue for outdoor concerts. Continuing along the street, past a series of decaying buildings, you'll eventually end up back at Maistrov trg.

Practicalities

The **train station** is on the west bank of the River Sava, a ten-minute walk from town (or bus #2; 170SIT). The **bus station** is handily located 500m north of the old town on Stošičeva ulica, from where it's 200m south to the **tourist office** at Koroška cesta 29 (Mon–Fri 8am–7pm; Ⓣ04/236-3030, Ⓔtd.kranj@siol.net); they can arrange **accommodation** on tourist farms (❶) in the villages of **Preddvor**, **Naklo** and **Jezersko**, all a short way north of

Kranj. The town's only hotel is the *Creina*, a hideous-looking brick building midway between the tourist office and the old town at Koroška cesta 5 (Ⓣ04/202-4550, Ⓦwww.hotel-creina.si; ❹); the rooms are an unsightly mix of gaudy mauve and brown decor, but decent enough and the staff try hard.

The best **restaurant** is *Pri Matičku*, albeit inconveniently located in a residential area 1km northeast of town at Jezerska cesta 41; in a building aping a hunter's lodge, the menu features a good selection of game dishes (medallions of bear, deer and pheasant, goulash and so on), alongside the more prosaic pizzas and salads. Of those places in the old town, *Kot*, tucked away in the eastern corner of Maistrov trg, is the most agreeable, serving up superb, very reasonably priced home specials; and *Stari Mayr*, down by the parish church, which, though it may not look all that much, has good Slovene food.

The area in and around Maistrov trg is crammed with **bars** and **cafés**: *The Old House*, a few paces to the north of Maistrov trg at Na Skali 5, serves all manner of drinks and is the liveliest place in town when full, while next door, *Carniola* is especially good for ice creams. The best of those on the square itself is the comfortable *Stara Pošta*, up on the fourth floor of the old post office building and sporting a groovy semicircular terrace bar that overlooks the square (open till 2am Fri & Sat). Working your way down through the old town, two more options are *Cuskrasda*, a funky, designer-furnished café at Tavčarjeva ulica 9, and the *Volk Bar*, a neat café-bar opposite the parish church. Late-night fiends, meanwhile, should head to the loud and lively *John Doe* bar, Slovenski trg 7, which motors on till 4am on Fridays and Saturdays. The **post office** is at Poštna ulica 4 (Mon–Fri 7am–7pm, Sat 7am–noon).

Around Kranj: Brdo, Šmarjetna Gora and Sv Jošt

Kranj's suburbs present some good opportunities for more solitudinous excursions, the best of which is **Brdo Castle**, while the modest peaks of **Šmarjetna Gora** and **Sv Jošt** offer good walking for those with slightly more energy to expend.

Brdo Castle

Four kilometres northeast of Kranj, near the village of **Predoslje**, is **Brdo Castle** (Grad Brdo), Slovenia's most beautiful and elite presidential residence. Surrounded by 11km of fencing, the estate is no longer reserved exclusively for visits by high-ranking politicians and statesmen – among others, its most recent distinguished guests have included Pope John Paul II, George W. Bush and Vladimir Putin – and now anyone can nose around the castle's stately rooms (groups only here), ramble through the expansive parklands, or even partake in some sporting activities.

As early as 1446, a manor house – under the proprietary of the noble Egkh family (Egkh is German for "brdo" which in English means "hillock") – existed close to, or on the site of, the present castle, though it didn't assume its present form until the sixteenth century. In the mid-eighteenth century, ownership was transferred to the munificent Zois family, who remained in custody of the estate until 1929, after which time it was owned for a short period by the Karadjordjevič Yugoslav royal family. At the end of World War II the estate was nationalized and became one of Tito's many summer retreats – he was particularly enamoured with the place as it afforded him ample opportunity to indulge in his favoured activity of hunting. In 1961 Tito himself issued a decree declaring the estate to the Republic of Slovenia. However, this hasn't stopped various members of the Karadjordjevič clan from recently trying to reclaim the property; unsurprisingly, the Slovene authorities have rejected this out of hand.

Even if you don't visit the castle itself – essentially a brief tour around a handful of rooms, including the magnificent dining room and Tito's trophy room – the grounds, which are free to enter, are most definitely worth the short trip from Kranj. Furthermore, you can participate in some horse riding (3500SIT 2hr), fishing (20,000SIT per day), or tennis (800SIT 1hr). Visits to the castle (1800SIT per person) must be booked several days in advance, as must bookings to the sumptuous *Zois* **restaurant** (unfortunately, groups only to both). If you require **information** regarding any aspect of visiting the estate, contact the reception desk at the *Hotel Kokra*, located at the park entrance (Ⓣ04/260-1000, Ⓦwww.sigov.si/brdo; ❻); this smoothly run place, with supremely comfortable rooms, is almost entirely geared up for business groups flying into nearby Brnik airport. If you wish to stay in one of the six Castle suites, then count on parting with around 140,000SIT (around €550). Bus #5 runs to the estate at five minutes to the hour between 6.55am and 3.55pm, Monday to Friday, and at twenty-five minutes past the hour between 6.25am and 1.25pm on Saturdays – there are no buses on Sunday.

Šmarjetna Gora and Sv Jošt

From Kranj's western suburb of Stražišče, several paths wend their way up to **Šmarjetna Gora** (St Margaret's Hill), a popular forty-minute walk also accessible by car. At the summit is **St Margaret's Church** (Cerkev Sv Marjete), originally dating from 1342, but heavily renovated in 1989; though there's little to see inside, if you want to have a look the key can be obtained from the *Hotel Bellevue* (Ⓣ04/270-0070, Ⓦwww.bellevue.si; ❹), across the car park. This high-class **hotel**, with large, designer-furnished rooms, each with a balcony, also has a good **restaurant** with a pleasant outdoor terrace. There are marvellous views of Kranj, the Alps, and west across to **Sv Jošt**, a higher peak at 847m, and reachable from Stražišče – it's just under two hours from Pot na Jošt. At the summit is the Baroque **Church of St Jošt** (Cerkev Sv Joštu), built between 1735 and 1740 on the site of a former Gothic church. Snacks and drinks are available from the hut a few paces away (closed Mon).

Tržič

From Kranj, hourly buses make the twenty-minute trip north to **TRŽIČ**, a small, somnolent market town holding a handful of satisfying museums and just a stone's throw away from a delightful gorge (see p.110). Although the town has a strong tradition in a number of trades and crafts dating back to the Middle Ages, it was shoemaking that put Tržič on the map, an industry which forms the centrepiece of the **Tržič Museum**, located in the upper reaches of town at Muzejska 11 (Tržiški Muzej; July & Aug Tues–Sun 9am–6pm; Jan–June Tues–Fri 9am–3pm; 400SIT). At the end of the nineteenth century, almost every second house in town accommodated a shoemakers' workshop, though the trade slowly became more industrialized, culminating in the Peko factory – once one of the most modern footwear factories in Europe – which today employs some five hundred people. Other important town crafts represented in the museum include tanners, wheelwrights, dyers and charcoal-burners.

One hundred and fifty metres south of the Tržič Museum, housed in the former Peko factory building at Koroška 9, is the entertaining **Homogea Museum** (July–Aug Tues–Sun 9am–6pm; rest of year by appointment, contact the tourist office; 500SIT). Its permanent exhibition, entitled *Mammoth*

Hunters, traces the evolution of man and his environment from four million years ago to the end of the early Stone Age in the form of fossil remains, archeological finds and life-size models. Two hundred metres southeast of the museum at Kurnikova pot 2 – walk south to the church, then along Partizanska ulica and across the bridge – is the **Kurnik House** (Kurnikova hiša; Tues–Fri & Sun 4–6pm, Sat 10am–noon; 250SIT), a beautifully preserved eighteenth-century Gorenjska peasant house named after its original owner, Vojteh Kurnik, who was born here in 1826. Although a wheelwright by profession, Kurnik's true passion was poetry, and in the memorial room (*izba*) dedicated to him, you can see a handful of wood shavings on which he wrote verses while working.

A forty-five-minute walk northeast of Tržič, beyond the tiny settlement of **Čadovlje**, is the fabulous **Dovžan Gorge** (Dovžanova soteska), a protected natural monument owing to its rich deposits of Palaeozoic fossils. Its most distinguishing features are the pyramidal limestone columns on the eastern slopes, and Borova Peč ("Pine's bluff") on the western side, though the thrashing Tržiška Bistrica River, bisecting the gorge's steeply pitched sides, is no less impressive. At the gorge entrance you'll pass through a remarkable road tunnel, built at the end of the nineteenth century by Julij Born.

There are no trains to Tržič, but the **bus station** is handily located south of town on Cankarjeva Cesta, from where it's a couple of minutes' walk north to the **tourist office** at Trg svobode 18 (Mon–Fri 9am–5pm, Sat 9am–2pm; ⓣ04/597-1536, ⓔinformacije@trzic.si). There's nowhere to sleep in town but the tourist office can book **accommodation** on local tourist farms (❷). There are two very average places to **eat** here: the *Pri Slug*, 100m west of the bus station at Predilniška 4, and the marginally better *Pizzeria Pod Gradom*, just up from the Homogea Museum at Koroška 26 (closed Mon).

Radovljica

The initial urge for most travellers upon reaching **RADOVLJICA**, an expanding little town 21km north of Kranj, is to push straight on to Bled. This is a pity, as it boasts a beautiful square stuffed with some superb Gothic and Renaissance architecture, and one of Slovenia's most surprisingly engaging museums among its attractions. Built upon a 75-metre-high outcrop above the River Sava, the town's golden period came during the early Middle Ages when feudal lords, most importantly the Ortenburgs, settled upon the town, building their vast estates here. Although Radovljica suffered a lengthy period of stagnation in the eighteenth and nineteenth centuries, the subsequent development of both the highway and railway kick-started the town back into life, and today, despite a population of little more than six thousand, it's a significant administrative and educational centre. With buses every thirty minutes from Bled, just 6km north, it makes for a simple and satisfying half-day trip.

The Town

Everything of interest in town is centred on quiet **Linhartov trg** (Linhart Square), the old medieval core framed by a raft of fine Gothic and Renaissance buildings. The square was named in honour of the Slovene dramatist-historian Anton Tomaž Linhart (1756–1795), whose **birthplace** (Bulovčeva hiša) at no. 7 bears a commemorative plaque and bas-relief of people at work and play. Linhart was regarded as Slovenia's most important enlightener, a position reinforced following the publication (in German) in 1791 of his seminal works on the history of Slovenes; moreover, he was credited with writing the first

A nation of beekeepers

Beekeeping, or apiculture, is one of Slovenia's oldest and most celebrated traditions, originating during the sixteenth century when honey was the principal sweetening agent available and wax an indispensable material for making candles. Bees, and in particular the indigenous Grey Carniolan (*Apis mellifera carniolica*) – affectionately known as the "Grizzly" owing to the lining of bright grey hair along its abdomen – have thrived in Slovenia for centuries, attracted to the rich forage afforded by the country's abundant fields of buckwheat and forests of linden, pine and fir. At the tail end of the nineteenth century **bee trading** became a hugely lucrative business, with the export of live bees and their associated products of honey, wax and royal jelly to numerous European countries; today, the country's seven thousand beekeepers produce around two thousand tonnes of honey annually, just about sufficient for domestic requirements.

Bees were traditionally kept in wooden, oblong **hives** called *kranjiči* (Carniolans), neatly stacked together in rows which, if required, could be mounted onto carts and transported; the hives were particularly celebrated for their painted **front panels** (*panjske končnice*), a Slovenian folk art which emerged during the mid-eighteenth century, reaching its acme a century later. Panels were illustrated with colourfully crafted motifs, a practice carried out by both professional and self-taught artists; older motifs typically portrayed biblical or historical happenings, while later paintings depicted moral or satirical, and occasionally profane, images, usually pertaining to peasant life. Many of these were deliciously humorous – such as the local gossip having her tongue sharpened on a grindstone by villagers, or the hunter being pursued by a gun-toting bear – many other panels feature Job, the patron of beekeepers.

Panels had practical functions too, their bright colours supposedly making orientation easier for bees, as well as enabling the beekeeper to distinguish between his many swarms. Whilst there's a good chance you'll see some of the original painted hives on your travels throughout the country – particularly around Gorenjska and the Alpine regions – it's this newer type that is more common.

Slovene plays – *Županova Micka* (Mayor's Maid Micka) in 1789, and *Matiček se ženi* (Matiček is Getting Married) in 1790.

Continuing eastwards you'll pass several more exceptional buildings – notably the **Renaissance mansion** (Vidičeva hiša) at no. 3 – before hitting upon the **Thurn Mansion** (Thurnov Grad), clearly recognizable by its thickly stuccoed facade and vast spread of coats of arms. Built by the Ortenburg counts in the early Middle Ages, the mansion underwent several reincarnations before it acquired its current Baroque appearance in the eighteenth century. Inside, a magnificent double stairway leads up to the first floor and the unlikely sounding but quite splendid **Beekeeping Museum** (Čebelarski Muzej; May–Oct Tues–Sun 10am–1pm & 3–6pm; March–April & Nov–Dec Wed, Sat & Sun 10am–noon & 3–5pm; 400SIT). Comprising a handful of slickly arranged rooms, the museum presents the development and tradition of Slovenian apiculture from the eighteenth century to the present day. It begins with a collection of hives and wax presses, and by acknowledging the debt owed to the pioneers of beekeeping, such as master apiarists Anton Janša (1734–1773), who published the first treatise on beekeeping, and Michael Ambrožič (1846–1904), the first Slovene to trade in the indigenous Grey Carniolan bee. Next up, and the undoubted high point of the museum, is its collection of over two hundred **beehive panels** (*Panjske Končnice*), wooden end panels painted with religious, satirical or humorous motifs and scenes – illustrated here in individually themed cabinets (deserters, bandits, religion and so on). Elsewhere, there is an exposition on the **biology** of the aforementioned Carniolan bee, including a live hive and a reconstructed **apiary**. For more on the panels, and beekeeping in general, see the box on p.111. The mansion also houses the **Linhart Memorial Room**, currently closed pending renovation.

A few paces east of the mansion, in a pretty, irregularly shaped courtyard, stands the **Parish Church of St Peter** (Cerkev Sv Petra), another fine Gothic hall-church, modelled on the Parish Church in Kranj. The oldest part of the church, the presbytery, dates from the fifteenth century, while the church's Romanesque nave was replaced with its present, late-Gothic one in 1495. The Baroque high altar, from 1713, incorporates beautiful sculptural decoration by Angelo Pozzo, as does the white marble altar of St Mary, its sculptures completed by local stonemason Janez Vurnik. Next to the church is the **Priest's House**, assimilated within a neat, recently renovated, late-Gothic arched courtyard (if the church is closed you can obtain the key from here).

The most outstanding building on the square is the muralled **Šivec House** (Šivčeva hiša) at no. 22, an exceptional example of a Gothic-Renaissance house, and especially noteworthy for its vaulted ground-floor hall and first-floor wood-panelled drawing room – the latter was once the living quarters of a Radovljica burgher family but is now used for weddings. The building also now plays host to an **art gallery** with rotating exhibitions (daily 10am–noon & 4–6pm; 300SIT). Leaving town en route to Bled, keep an eye out for the former **Savings Bank Building**, on your right at Gorenjska 17, an Art Nouveau edifice notable for its Secessionist-style mosaic of a flowering tree surrounding the entrance.

Practicalities

The **train station** is a couple of minutes south of the centre on Cesta svobode – head up Kolodvorska ulica to Linhartov trg. The **bus station** is smack bang in the centre of town on Kranjska cesta, just a few steps from the **tourist office** at no. 18 (Mon–Fri 8am–7pm, till 6pm in winter, Sat 8am–noon; ⓣ04/531-5300). Opposite is the *Hotel Grajski Dvor*, (ⓣ04/531-5585; ⓦwww.hotel-grajski-dvor.si; ❹), outwardly unpromising but with perfectly agreeable **rooms**, each with bath or shower. Another option, 1.5km north of the centre at Gradnikova cesta 2, is the very pleasant and restful *Sport Penzion Manca*, (ⓣ04/531-4120, ⓦwww.manca-sp.si; ❹), which has a pool and tennis court – to get here, head north along Gorenjska cesta (direction Bled), turn right at the traffic lights and walk to the end of Ulica Staneta Žagarja, which joins up with Gradnikova cesta. The small **campsite** is located just south of the *Manca* at Obla gorica (ⓣ04/531-5770; June to mid-Sept). Use of the adjoining swimming pool, one of the best in the country and used to host championship events, is free for campers.

The town is blessed with a trio of first-rate **restaurants**: housed in a 500-year-old building at Linhartov trg 2, the *Gostilna Lectar* offers an upscale take on traditional Slovenian meat dishes, as well as buckwheat, mushrooms and dumplings for vegetarians. Equally as enjoyable is the *Gostilna Avguštin*, opposite at no. 15, which serves cheaper standards as well as a more discerning menu of beef, lamb and fish; the seating towards the rear of the restaurant is more comfortable, as is the lovely garden terrace with views across to Jelovica. A pleasant, low-key alternative is *Gostilna Kunstelj*, just west of Linhartov trg at Gorenjska cesta 9, whose Slovene-oriented food is arguably the best of the three; they've got some super wines too. If you want to buy some Slovenian wine, head to *Vinoteka Sodček* at Linhartov trg 8 (Mon–Fri 9am–7pm, Sat 8am–noon).

Brezje

A cluster of souvenir stalls, snack bars and an overpriced car park welcome you to the small village of **BREZJE**, famed as Slovenia's most important place of pilgrimage, the **Basilica of the Virgin** (Marija pomagaj). Attracting some 300,000 visitors each year, the church began life as a chapel in 1800, built as an extension to the fifteenth-century **St Vitus' Church**. It first became a site of prayer during Napoleon's occupation of northern Slovenia at the beginning of the nineteenth century, but it wasn't until the French departed that rumours of miracles occurring at Brezje began to spread, fuelling the arrival of tens of thousands of pilgrims from all over Europe. So great was the influx that, in 1900, it was necessary to construct a larger church, the results of which you see today. Around the same time, the Franciscans pitched up and proceeded to build an adjoining **monastery** and have remained the guardians of the church ever since.

Save for Janez Vurnik's stunning **high altar** – adorned with beautifully sculpted cherubs and instrument-playing angels – the interior is actually rather plain; still, this doesn't bother the majority of visitors, most of whom come here to pray at the **altar** of the Blessed Virgin of Help. This much reworked altar – the fourth chapel on the right – contains the church's most renowned piece of work, Leopold Layer's painting of *Mary Help*, framed by a dazzling gold mount designed by Tone Bitenc in 1977. There's also a contribution from Ivan Grohar, who completed the paintings in the third altars on the left and right. In the niche above the southern door is a statue by Boris Kalin, which previously stood at the nearby Otoče train station, and just across the way is a statue of Pope John Paul II, built to commemorate his visit here in 1996. There are three daily buses from Bled to Brezje (7.20am, 9.20am & 11.20am), with four making the return trip (8.45am, 10.45am, 4.45pm and 6.45pm).

Begunje

It was in the tidy little village of **BEGUNJE**, 5km north of Radovljica, that thousands of hostages – including many women and children – were detained, beaten and executed during the German occupation of Gorenjska between 1941 and 1945. This grim episode in Slovenian history is vividly documented in the moving **Museum of Hostages** (Muzej in Grobišče talcev; July & Aug Tues–Sun 1–5pm; May–June & Sept–Oct Tues–Fri 9am–2pm, Sat & Sun 1–5pm; March–April & Nov–Dec Wed & Sat 9am–1pm, Sun 2–5pm; 300SIT), housed in a wing of the rather grand **Katzenstein Castle** – part of which houses a psychiatric hospital – 200m north of the main bus stop. During World War II this seventeenth-century castle was used as a Gestapo prison in which more than twelve thousand prisoners, mostly Slovenes, were held. The bare statistics reveal that 849 prisoners were either executed or died in the prison, while a further 5000 were sent away to concentration camps in Austria, Germany and Poland.

Ten authentically preserved cells illustrate the brutal experiences of the hostages confined here for months and years on end, most harrowingly in the form of farewell messages, which the Germans tried unsuccessfully to erase, etched into the walls as they awaited impending death. In one cell there are stakes onto which prisoners were tied before being shot, and in another, objects from Dachau, such as books of the murdered and keys of the guards, as well as more sobering items such as a gas sprinkler and a branch from which prisoners were hung. In the park just across from the museum is a **graveyard** where many of those executed are buried.

Two kilometres north of the village lie the impressive ruins of **Kamen Castle** (Grad Kamen; for current opening hours contact the tourist office – see below; 250SIT), established by the Ortenburg counts in the twelfth century as a means of defending the Radovljica Plain. Its most extensive period of development, however, came in the fifteenth century, when the still remarkably well-preserved tower and residential palace were constructed. In the early eighteenth century, its defensive function of protecting trade routes, warding off Turkish invaders and quelling peasant revolts was rendered obsolete and it was abandoned. The castle remained in a state of decay until 1959, when work finally began to restore it.

The **tourist office** (Tues–Sun: summer 10am–6pm; winter 11am–5pm; Ⓣ04/533-3411, Ⓦwww.begunje.si) is located directly across the road from the main **bus stop**. Upstairs is a gallery containing an arsenal of awards dedicated to local musician and celebrity Slavko Avsenik – a major star in Germany, apparently (same hours as tourist office; 150SIT). If you desire to eat in the village, there is the reasonable *Avsenik* **restaurant** next to the tourist office, though it's all rather hammed up for the tourists (closed Mon). There are hourly buses to and from Bled and Radovljica.

Kropa

Settled in a narrow valley below the Jelovica plateau, and flanked by precipitously slanting hills, **KROPA**, 10km southwest of Radovljica, is the place to aim for if you've only time for one excursion. This comely single-street village is renowned for its iron mining and forging industries, which reached their peak here during the early to mid-nineteenth century, and whose history is relayed in the **Iron Forging Museum**, housed in the **Klinar House** – owned by the eponymous iron baron – at no. 10 (Kovaški Muzej; May–Aug Tues–Sun 10am–1pm & 3–6pm; Sep & Oct Tues–Sun 10am–noon & 3–5pm; March, April, Nov & Dec Wed, Sat & Sun 10am–noon & 3–5pm; 300SIT). As impressive as the assemblage of models, bellows and spikes is (there are, incredibly, over one hundred varieties of spike), it's the work of master forger Joža Bertoncelj (1901–1976) which trumps all else here; already forging nails at the age of eleven, Bertoncelj soon graduated to the village's Plamen factory before settling upon a career as an artistic forger, resulting in a quite marvellous collection of wrought-iron gratings, chandeliers, and sepulchral monuments. The second floor illustrates the economic and social conditions under which a blacksmith lived and worked; typically, the smiths and their families would squeeze into the attic, while the first floor was given over to the owner of the foundry. Judging by the salon and its coffered ceiling in this house, it's possible to appreciate just how wealthy some of these owners were.

A few paces north of the museum, at no. 7b, is the **UKO workshop** (Umetniško kovaštvo; July & Aug Mon–Fri 7am–7pm, Sat 9am–noon; Sept–June Mon–Fri 7am–3pm, Sat 9am–noon), a decorative ironwork company set up in 1956 in order to preserve the tradition of manual forging; you can view the masters at work here and buy ironwork products from the neighbouring shop. Heading south towards **Plac**, the very small main square, have a look at the **Partisan monument**, comprised of iron figures made at the aforementioned workshop, before crossing the **Kroparica**, a rapid, thrashing mountain stream which once propelled over fifty water wheels for the bellows and sledgehammers of the foundries, most of which were decommissioned after World War I. A short way south of the bridge is the **Vice Forge** (Vigenjc), the only preserved and operative workshop in Kropa; to view a demonstration, contact the Iron Forging Museum a day or two in advance (Ⓣ04/533-6717). Just north of the forge, up the slope, is the Gothic **Parish Church of St Leonard** (Cerkev Sv Lenarta), whose cemetery contains some beautifully crafted iron headstones, including the grave of Bertoncelj; there are some lovely views of the village from the terrace. One and a half kilometres south of the village, up on the road to Železniki, stands a fourteenth-century **Smelting Furnace**, (Slovenska peč), discovered as recently as 1953 when the mountain road to Jamnik was built. Nicknamed the "wolf", it could produce 200kg of iron in one day.

The village accommodates two very welcoming **gostilna**: at the extreme northern end of the village, at Kropa 2, is the *Gostilna Pri Jarmu*, a pizzeria-style place (closed Wed); and in the centre, 50m south of Plac at Kropa 30, is the cosy *Pri Kovač*, which knocks up some superb local specialities such as Blacksmith's Plate (an assortment of meats) and sour milk and bean soup – they have some excellent wines too (closed Mon). The main **bus stop** is located near the post office, 200m south of the *Pri Jarmu*.

Bled and around

One thousand years old in 2004, **BLED** is by far the country's most popular destination, thanks to its placid fairytale lake and island, dramatically sited castle and snow-tipped mountains. The town itself, which is most densely concentrated to the east of the lake, is thoroughly unspectacular, though there's nothing specific to see here anyway. By way of contrast, the lake – created some 14,000 years ago when water flooded the depression left by a receding glacier – is a natural and spontaneous playground, deluged with skaters during the winter and bristling with rowing boats, gondolas and swimmers during the spring and summer months.

The town dates from 1004, when the German emperor Henry II bestowed the castle, and the land between the two Sava rivers, to the bishops of Brixen – who would subsequently rule for the next 800 years. The first visitors to Bled were medieval pilgrims from Carniola and Carinthia, who came to pray at the island church, although mass tourism didn't take long to find its feet thanks in no small measure to Arnold Rikli, a Swiss-born physician who opened a bathing resort and associated accommodation facilities here in 1855. Between the two World Wars the resort became a popular hideaway for politicians and royalty, with both the Yugoslav Royal family, and later, Tito, spending much time here during the summer; even today, Bled is the one place high-ranking officials and diplomats are ushered to when visiting Slovenia. Despite its status as the country's star turn, Bled rarely feels overwhelmed – indeed it can even feel a little bleak outside summer and winter – but if you do fancy a change of pace and a bit of solitude, there are some terrific attractions close by in which to immerse yourself. Furthermore, it's a good base from which to partake in any number of hikes into the eastern tranche of the Julian Alps.

Arrival and information

Bled's **bus station** is five minutes northeast of the lake at the junction of Cesta svobode and Grajska cesta. The nearest **train station** to Bled is Bled Jezero (on the Jesenice–Nova Gorica line), located on Kolodvorska cesta, a

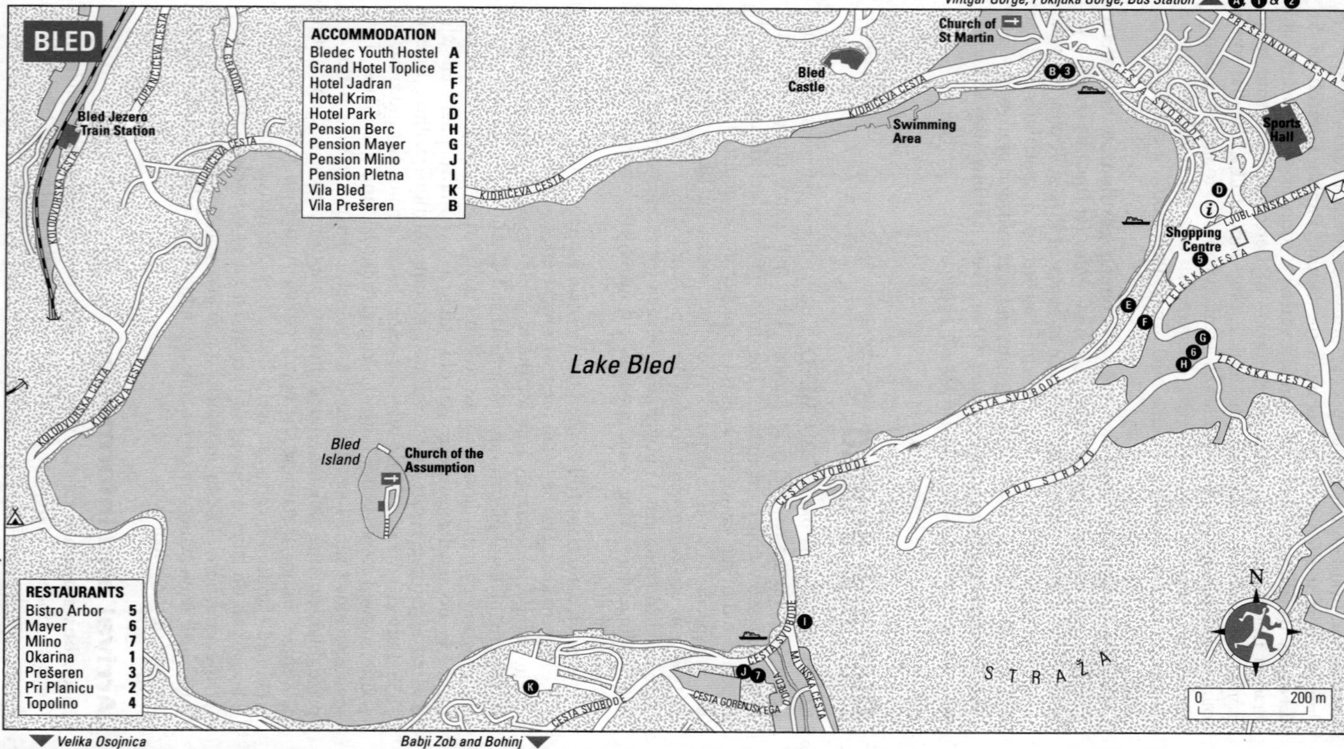
BLED
ACCOMMODATION
Bledec Youth Hostel A
Grand Hotel Toplice E
Hotel Jadran F
Hotel Krim C
Hotel Park D
Pension Berc H
Pension Mayer G
Pension Mlino J
Pension Pletna I
Vila Bled K
Vila Prešeren B
RESTAURANTS
Bistro Arbor 5
Mayer 6
Mlino 7
Okarina 1
Prešeren 3
Pri Planicu 2
Topolino 4
Vintgar Gorge, Pokljuka Gorge, Bus Station A, 1 & 2
Lesce, C & 4
Velika Osojnica
Velika Osojnica
Babji Zob and Bohinj
Church of St Martin
Bled Castle
Swimming Area
Sports Hall
Shopping Centre
Bled Jezero Train Station
Lake Bled
Bled Island
Church of the Assumption
STRAŽA
PREŠERNOVA CESTA
CESTA SVOBODE
LJUBLJANSKA CESTA
ŽELEŠKA CESTA
KIDRIČEVA CESTA
ZA GRADOM
ŽUPANČIČEVA CESTA
KOLODVORSKA CESTA
POD STRAŽO
MLINSKA CESTA
CESTA GORENJSKEGA
ODREDA
N
0
200 m

ten-minute walk northwest of the lake. However, if coming from Ljubljana, you'll alight at Bled-Lesce, 4km southeast of Bled and connected to the town by half-hourly buses. The **tourist office** is located beneath the *Hotel Park* at Cesta Svobode 15 (July & Aug Mon–Sat 8am–9pm, Sun 10am–8pm; June & Sept Mon–Sat 8am–8pm, Sun 10am–6pm; rest of year Mon–Sat 9am–6pm, Sun 11am–6pm; ⓣ04/574-1122, ⓦwww.bled.si). If you require information on any aspect of Triglav National Park, contact the park's main office, along the northern shore at Kidričeva cesta 2 (Mon–Fri 8am–4pm; ⓣ04/574-1188, ⓦwww.sigov.si). The **post office** is at Ljubljanska 14 (Mon–Fri 7am–7pm, Sat 7am–noon). There is **Internet access** available at the youth hostel (800SIT for 1hr – see below), and one terminal at the *Apropos* café in the shopping centre on Ljubljanska cesta (8am–midnight; 1000SIT per hr).

Accommodation

As befits Slovenia's premier tourist destination, there is an abundance of **accommodation** in town, and while a good number are run-of-the-mill package-type places, there are some first-rate pensions sprinkled around and beyond the lake. The well-run **Bledec Youth Hostel**, a couple of minutes' walk north of the bus station at Grajska cesta 17 (ⓣ04/574-5250; ⓔbledec@siol.net), has spotless three- four- and five-bedded rooms, all with bathrooms (4200SIT per person including breakfast); it also has laundry facilities (800SIT), Internet access (500SIT for 30min) and a commendable restaurant.

Camping Bled (ⓣ04/575-2000, ⓦwww.camping.bled.si; April to mid-Oct) – the only **campsite** in Bled itself – is located at the far western end of the lake in a lovely pine-sheltered valley (take any bus heading towards Bohinj and alight at the beginning of Kidričeva cesta). *Camping Šobec* (ⓣ04/535-3700, ⓦwww.sobec.si; mid-April–Sept) – Slovenia's largest campsite – is 2km from Bled-Lesce in the direction of Bled. The site also has half a dozen dark and dingy bungalows, each sleeping three, but without washing facilities (❷). From Bled-Lesce station just one bus a day runs to (10.55am) and from (5.10pm) the site; otherwise it's a rather convoluted twenty-minute walk: exiting the station, walk north towards the crossing, take the second left down Finžgareva ulica for 100m, left again and continue behind the industrial zone for 400m before heading down a gravel track to the right. Both sites are well equipped and maintained, each with a restaurant, market and sporting facilities; *Šobec* also has its own lake for swimming. Despite their vast capacities, both sites fill up very quickly during the summer months.

There is plentiful **private accommodation**, available from several agencies, including Globtour at Ljubljanska cesta 7 (Mon–Sat 8am–8pm, Sun 8am–noon & 4–8pm; ⓣ04/574-1821, ⓦwww.globtour.si), and Kompas, in the shopping centre at Ljubljanska cesta 4 (same times as Globtour; ⓣ04/574-1515, ⓦwww.kompas-bled.si). Furthermore, there are quite a few **tourist farms** in the vicinity, the largest concentration of which are located in the villages of **Selo** and **Zgornje Gorje**, southwest and northwest of the lake respectively; you can approach farms directly or book through the above agencies (but not the tourist office).

Hotels and Pensions

Pension Berc Željeska cesta 15 ⓣ04/574-1838, ⓦwww.berc-sp.si. Lovely, family-run place in a renovated nineteenth-century farmhouse, with spacious, cosily furnished rooms – the most restful option in town. ❹

Vila Bled Cesta svobode 26 ⓣ04/579-1500, ⓦwww.vila-bled.com. Set in its own extensive grounds on the lake's western shore, this is Bled's most characterful, and expensive, establishment. Rebuilt as yet another country retreat for Tito in 1947, the extraordinary, socialist-era rooms have remained largely untouched since the president entertained world leaders here. Has its own private beach and boats. ❾

Hotel Krim Ljubljanska cesta 7 ⓣ04/579-7000, ⓦwww.hotel-krim.si. Firmly in the category of package-tourist hotel, the rooms lack any semblance of quality, but it's one of the cheaper options in town and the jolly staff do their best to please. ❺

Pension Mayer Želeška cesta 7 ⓣ04/576-5740, ⓦwww.mayer-sp.si. Located next to the *Berc*, this fine nineteenth-century building has stylish, parquet-floored rooms with large comfy beds and spankingly clean bathrooms; minibar & safe too. ❺

Pension Mlino Cesta svobode 45 ⓣ04/574-1404, ⓦwww.mlino.si. Popular lakeside place a short walk west of *Vila Bled*; the rooms, however, are nothing special and the bathrooms are a touch dated, but there's a convivial atmosphere about the place. Reservations advised. ❺

Hotel Park Cesta svobode 15 ⓣ04/579-3000, ⓦwww.gp-hoteli.bled.si. This horrible construction blotting the southeastern corner of the lake is Bled's largest hotel; the lake-facing rooms are perfectly decent, while the older, road-facing rooms are rather careworn. ❼–❽

Pension Pletna Cesta svobode 37 ⓣ04/574-3702, ⓔpletna@bled.net. The five variously sized, neat rooms in this perky little pension just 100m west of the *Mlino* all have a balcony, but they do face the busy main road. Good value. ❹

Vila Prešeren Kidričeva cesta 1 ⓣ04/574-1608, ⓔvila.preseren@siol.net. Soothing cream and beige furnished rooms, with parquet flooring, elegant bedside lamps, wall pictures and some other neat touches. Top-quality restaurant to boot (see p.121). ❻

Grand Hotel Toplice Cesta svobode 12 ⓣ04/579-1000, ⓦwww.hotel-toplice.si. Bled's most opulent hotel has magnificently appointed rooms, with antique furniture, large, handsome beds and gold-plated trimmings; the more expensive lakeside rooms have a/c and bed pumps, for that little extra firmness. Houses a thermal pool, Jacuzzi and Finnish and Turkish saunas, all free to guests. ❾ Also owns the **Hotel Jadran** opposite (same tel no.), an old-fashioned, slightly dowdy place. ❺

Lake Bled

From a visitor's perspective, Bled is essentially the **lake** and all that happens on or around it. The best way to get your bearings is to engage in a circular walk, beginning at the *Hotel Park* and working your way round clockwise, which should take no more than two and half hours.

Bled Castle

Perched high up on a craggy bluff on the north shore is **Bled Castle** (Blejski Grad; daily 8am–7pm, until 5pm in winter; 800SIT including entrance to the museum), enclosed by a Romanesque wall and spotted with stout-looking parapets, towers and ramparts, just as a castle should be. Originally an eleventh-century fortification, the castle's present appearance dates from the seventeenth century (albeit with further renovations in the 1950s), and is characterized by a lower and upper courtyard. The outstanding feature of the neat upper courtyard is the lovely sixteenth-century **Chapel**, decorated with frescoes from around 1700, and containing a fine painting of Henry II conferring the property of Bled on Bishop Albuin.

Adjacent to the chapel is the **museum** (Grajski Muzej), a disappointing and lacklustre affair, not helped by the lack of labelling (of any description or language). However, it starts promisingly, with some fascinating archeological finds from the region, including an interesting coinage exhibition and a stack of Roman gold jewellery; thereafter, the extensive collection of Gothic, Renaissance and Baroque furniture and weaponry does little to evoke the mood of those periods. Best of all, the castle terrace offers peerless views – and great photo opportunities – of the lake and island below.

Several paths (marked "Grad") wind up to the castle, each a reasonably stiff fifteen-minute climb; one from behind the swimming area (Grajsko Kopališče) on Kidričeva Cesta, another from the youth hostel on Grajska cesta, and a third from Rikljeva ulica, near the **Parish Church of St Martin** (Cerkev Sv Martina), a neo-Gothic structure built in 1905 on the site of a previous Gothic church; it has sculptures by the ubiquitous Vurnik and frescoes by Slavko Pengov.

Activities in and around Bled

Whilst far more challenging hikes can be had in Triglav National Park (see box on p.126), there are some very enjoyable walks in the immediate vicinity of the lake. Velika Osojnica, a 756-metre-high peak at the southwestern corner of the lake, offers the stiffest walk but also the most superlative views; take either the path from Bled campsite (via Ojstrica), or from the main road, Kidričeva cesta (via Mala Osojnica) and allow three hours for a round trip. A more gentle alternative is a walk up to Straža, a 638-metre-high hill southwest of the Grand Hotel Toplice; this is also Bled's very modest ski slope, suitable for beginners only; between December and February a chairlift operates from Pod Stražo, the road above Cesta svobode, to the summit (ⓣ04/578-0530).

Although **swimming** is permitted at various points around the lake (Mlino, Velika Zaka and Mala Zaka, all at the western end), you're better off sticking to the designated, roped off, area on the north shore underneath the castle, which also has a grassy beach (*Grajsko Kopališče*; daily mid-June to Sept 8am–7pm; 1100SIT for a daily ticket, 700SIT after noon). During winter, the lake often freezes over, tempting skaters out onto the ice; however caution should be exercised if you decide to have a go yourself – although not quite as romantic, you can also try the indoor rink at the sports centre (Športna Dvorana) just to the east of the *Park Hotel* (mid-July to March Mon–Sat 10–11.30am & 4.30–6pm, Sun 4.30–6pm; 600SIT).

Licences for **fishing**, permitted on the lake between April and December, can be purchased from the tourist office (4000SIT per day). There is **horse riding** at the Hippodrome in Lesce (ⓣ041/675-482); a half-hour lesson, or a one-hour ride (either cross-country or around the track), costs around 3000SIT. Also in Lesce, the Alpine Flying Centre at Begunjska cesta 10 (Alpski Letalski Center; ⓣ04/532-0100, ⓦwww.alc-lesce.si), offers **panoramic flights** around Bled for around 11,500SIT. Slovenia's premier **golf** course, the Bled Golf and Country Club, is located 2km east of town on the Bled-Lesce road at Kidričeva cesta 10 (ⓣ04/537-7711, ⓦwww.golf-bled.si; 18-hole course 12,000SIT, 9-hole course 7500SIT). **Bikes** can be hired from both the Globtour and Kompas agencies, and Promontana (see below); all charge similar rates: 800SIT for 1hr, 1400SIT for half a day and 2000SIT per day.

Humanfish, in the shopping centre next to the *Arbor* restaurant (daily mid-June–mid-Sept 9am–7pm; rest of year 9am–noon & 3–7pm; ⓣ04/574-3000, ⓦwww.humanfish.com), offers an excellent programme of **hikes** in the Julian Alps and Karavanke mountains, including 2-day trips to Triglav (30,000SIT), as well as a number of day-hikes (eg Meadows of Bohinj, Debela Pec, 7350SIT); they also offer biking tours, horse-riding tours (both 8750SIT) and a comprehensive winter ski and snowboarding programme. Promontana, just down from the *Hotel Krim* at Ljubljanska 1 (daily: summer 8am–noon & 4–8pm; winter 8am–4pm; ⓣ04/578-0660, ⓦwww.promontana.com), organizes a number of **river-bound activities** on the nearby Sava Bohinjka River – the following prices are per person based on a group of four, participating in a 2–3hr activity (prices decrease if the group is bigger and, similarly, prices increase if there are fewer than four); rafting (4400SIT), hydrospeed and canyoning (9650SIT), and kayaking (10,500SIT; two-day course 12,100SIT, five-day 21,875SIT).

If you don't fancy walking around the lake, you can take the **tourist train**, a jump-on, jump-off train that crawls around the lake clogging up the traffic; its starting point is from the sports hall on the lake's east shore (April–Nov; 550SIT for a day ticket). Alternatively you can take a ride on one of the **horse-drawn carriages** (*fijaker*), which are parked near the Festival Hall (a thirty-minute jaunt around the lake costs 4500SIT for five people) – longer trips are available too.

Bled Island

During the day, a continual relay of stretch gondolas (*Pletnas*) glide back and forth across the water between the shore and **Bled Island** (Blejski Otok), a magically picturesque islet crowned by the exquisite **Church of the Assumption** (Cerkev Sv Marija Božja; daily 8am–dusk). Findings support the theory that there was a settlement here in prehistoric times, while further excavations have revealed the remains of a pre-Romanesque chapel, as well as a large Slavic cemetery dating from around 9 AD. The present Baroque church dates from 1698, though its most outstanding features are from the preceding Gothic church, namely the remarkably well-preserved **frescoes** on the north and south presbytery walls, depicting scenes from the life of the Virgin, and a wooden statue of the Virgin with Child. The porch on the west side of the church holds more Gothic fresco remains, discovered during the most recent excavations in 1965. The wishing bell, which seems to keep most visitors amused, was installed in 1534, though a larger bell hangs in the enormous free-standing belfry, itself a hybrid of Gothic and Baroque elements. As well as providing a home to the provost, the **Provost's House** next to the church also functioned as a guest-house, as did the **hermitage**, the smaller building behind the church.

Predictably enough, a café and souvenir stall have been squeezed onto the island, not that you'll have much time to enjoy them if you come across on a *pletna*. They depart from three locations: down below the *Hotel Park*, near the *Vila Prešeren* (both 30min to the lake) and opposite *Pension Mlino* (15min), though the price is the same whichever location you leave from (1900SIT per person); departing only when they are full – which means you may have to sit idly for a bit while the *pletnar* solicits custom – you then have thirty minutes on the island to nose around before returning. The alternative is to make your own way across: **rowing boats** can be hired from several points at the western end of the lake (2000SIT per hour for a three-person boat); it may be harder going, but you won't feel rushed once on the island. Both the pletna and rowing boats operate year-round, depending on the weather.

Eating, drinking and entertainment

Disappointingly, for such a popular destination, there is little to get excited about when it comes to nightlife. The narrow scope of dining possibilities is compounded by few decent venues in which to drink, and you'll be hard pushed to avoid going to the same places if you're here for any length of time. With the exception of one or two restaurants, the most appealing are those located in the pensions. Telephone numbers have been given where it's best to reserve.

Restaurants

Bistro Arbor Ljubljanska cesta 4 (in the shopping centre). Don't let the unattractive surrounds dissuade you – a big and varied menu, plus good cheap lunch options (700SIT) should suffice. Open 9am–11pm.

Mayer Želeška cesta 7. Refined restaurant in the pension of the same name, with a moderate to expensive menu, featuring some good starters (buckwheat, fried cheese) and impressive mains, in particular game. Mon–Fri 5pm–midnight, Sat & Sun noon–midnight. (☎04/576-5740).

Mlino Cesta svobode 45. Enjoyable and well-regarded terrace restaurant in the ***Mlino*** pension, with a commendably adventurous menu featuring horse, shark cutlets and, more teasingly, ox testicles – good veggie options too. Also has an a/c indoor restaurant. Daily 10am–10pm.

Okarina Riklijeva cesta 9. Three beautifully appointed rooms and a fabulous back terrace from which to enjoy the wonderful menu of fish, game, tandoori (knocked up by the resident Indian chef), and over a dozen superb vegetarian dishes. Highly recommended. Mon–Fri 6pm–midnight, Sat & Sun noon–midnight.

Pri Planicu Grajska cesta 8. 100m south of the ***Okarina***, this is a hugely popular and frenetic inn-style place, serving roisteringly hearty meat-heavy dishes; good for a beer too. Daily 9am–11pm.

Prešeren Kidričeva cesta 1. Fresh fish from the Adriatic is the chief inducement here, plus some splendid house delicacies, such as mushrooms and ostrich. Throw into the mix a beautiful lakeside view and unusually attentive waiting staff, and you've got a thoroughly enjoyable dining experience. Moderate to expensive. Daily 11am–11pm.

Topolino Ljubljanska cesta 26. This low-key, slow-food restaurant is Bled's most sophisticated outfit, gorgeously decorated and beautifully lit throughout, with food and wine of the highest quality. Expensive. Tues–Sun noon–11pm (Ⓣ04/574-1781).

Drinking

Rather dispiritingly, most of Bled's chief drinking venues are located in or around the sprawling, incoherent shopping centre on Ljubljanska cesta; the best of these is *Apropos*, a small cocktail bar and ice-cream parlour; and *Café Latino* just across the way, which is good for beer and wines. *Arbor* (see restaurants) is also a popular hangout. All are open till around midnight. The *Šmon* ("The Bear"), just up from the *Pri Planicu* (also a popular place for a drink) at Grajska 3, is the choice café in town, with a prodigious selection of homemade pastries (daily 7.30am–10pm).

Entertainment and festivals

Bled's key annual event is **Bled Days** (*Blejski Dnevi*) in mid-July, three days of fairs and concerts taking place along the promenade at the eastern end of the lake; the event culminates in the lighting of thousands of candles on the lake – a memorable sight – and fireworks. Bled's most interesting musical event, the **Okarina Etno Festival**, featuring performances by an eclectic group of world musicians, takes place during the first weekend of August. The **International Music Festival**, at the beginning of July, is a two-week run of classical

Rowing on Lake Bled

When the rowers Iztok Čop and Luka Špik claimed Slovenia's first ever **Olympic Gold medal** at the Sydney 2000 games – Čop also bagged Slovenia's first ever Olympic medal (bronze) at the 1992 Barcelona games – Slovenian sport, and particularly rowing, at last gained the recognition it had craved since independence in 1991. Rowing has a long and distinguished history in Slovenia, with many of its rowers having formed the core of ex-Yugoslav teams before each republic went their separate ways. Since then rowing has been a byword for Slovenian sporting achievement, its most successful rowers having been trained at the **Bled Rowing Club**, formed in 1949 and located at the western end of the lake, at Mala Zaka.

The lake is hugely popular as a practice arena with both Slovenian and international rowers, whilst its standing as a top-class international venue is manifest in the staging of three World Rowing Championships, in 1966, 1979 and 1986. Although several domestic regattas take place in Bled during Spring and Autumn, the best time to be here is in mid-June when the **Bled International Regatta** draws a world-class field. Contact the tourist office for further details.

concerts staged at various venues around the lake, including the Festival Hall and St Martin's Church – tickets cost around 1500SIT for each performance (Ⓦwww.festivalbled.com). Then there are the **rowing regattas**, which occur at various dates throughout the year (see box on p.121).

Around Bled: Vintgar Gorge, Pokljuka Gorge, Babji Zob and Vrba

Located within close proximity to Bled are three enticing excursions, each of which can be comfortably accomplished within three to four hours: to the north, there are the hugely popular **Vintgar Gorge** and the lesser-visited, but no less impressive, **Pokljuka Gorge**, while to the south, en route to Bohinj, are the fascinating **Babji Zob Caves**. To the northwest, in the village of **Vrba**, you can visit the birthplace of France Prešeren, Slovenia's greatest poet.

Vintgar Gorge

The major attraction in Bled's immediate environs is the **Vintgar Gorge** (Blejski Vintgar; daily mid-April–Oct 8am–8pm; 600SIT), an impressive 1600-metre-long and 150-metre-high defile 4km north of town. The most enjoyable way to get there is to walk, an easy and pleasant stroll along country roads and through a handful of pretty villages: from the bus station join the main road, Prešernova ulica, and head north until you come to Partizanska cesta; continue north along here and after crossing the stream take the left fork (Cesta v Vintgar), continuing towards the village of **Podhom**, from where the gorge is signposted. If the walk is beyond you, there is a daily bus to (10am) and from (noon) the gorge between mid-June and September, leaving from the bus station.

The gorge was actually chanced upon by a local mayor and his cartographer colleague in 1891. So thrilled were they with their discovery that they set up a construction committee in order to seek ways of opening the gorge up to the public, an event that duly occurred two years later. It's since been accessible via a continuous chain of wooden gantries and bridges, suspended from the precipitous rock face, and running the entire length of the gorge to the **Šum Waterfall** (Slap Šum) at its northern end; from here you can either retrace your steps and return the way you came, or take the path on the right, returning to Bled via the pilgrimage **Church of St Catherine** and the village of **Zasip**. It can get very damp in the gorge, and if it's been raining, very slippery, so you'd do well to bring some waterproofs.

Pokljuka Gorge

As an antidote to the hordes that pile up to the Vintgar Gorge, the **Pokljuka Gorge** (Pokljuška soteska), a magnificent fossilized ravine 7km west of Bled, is perfect for those seeking some solitude. Located on the northeastern margins of the **Pokljuka Plateau** – a thickly forested plain at the eastern extremes of the Julian Alps – this dry and narrow trough-like ravine was hollowed out by the former course of the Ribščica River some 10,000 years ago, the retreating glaciers leaving behind the largest fossilized gorge in the country. It's characterized by peculiar dilations – known as "vrtci" ("Garden Plots") – and a series of natural arches, although its most spectacular feature is the **Pokljuka Luknja** (Pokljuka Window), a 15-metre-high subterranean hall with three natural windows hollowed out of its ceiling. To get here take one of the regular buses from Bled to the village of **Krnica**, from where it's a 2km walk (follow signs) to the gorge entrance. If you have your own transport, it's possible to drive right to the entrance.

Babji Zob Caves

Completing this trilogy of natural wonders are the **Babji Zob Caves** (Jama Pod Babjim Zobom), near the village of **BOHINJSKA BELA**, 4km west of Bled. Located beneath **Babji Zob** ("Hags Tooth"), a formidable-looking, tooth-shaped pillar poised atop a 1128-metre peak, it couldn't be more different to your conventional cave visit – as with Postojna (see p.216) or Škocjan (see p.186) for example. The caves can only be visited on a guided tour, which entails a not inconsiderable one-hour hike up to the cave entrance; thereafter it's a further hour's trek through the complex, before the steep descent back down the hill (approximately three hours in total).

At just 300m long it's not an expansive cave system, but it does possess some unique features, not least several groupings of rarely seen helictites – contorted, sometimes horizontal, calcite deposits, which grow in random directions seemingly defying gravity. Their existence has long confounded experts and remains one of the most vexing speleological questions, though one theory suggests that their form is caused by airflow within the cave.

Tours, which cost 1600SIT, take place at 10am on Saturdays between May and September, as well as on Wednesdays and Sundays in July & August at the same time; the meeting point is in front of the *Gostilna Rot*, at Bohinjska Bela

France Prešeren

One of Slovenia's greatest nineteenth-century heroes and indisputably the country's greatest romantic poet, France Prešeren did more to advance the cause of the Slovene national consciousness in the nineteenth century than just about any other figure. Born in the village of Vrba in 1800, Prešeren was educated in Ribnica and Ljubljana, before obtaining his law degree in Vienna. Although a lawyer by profession – he spent much of his life working as a clerk in Ljubljana – Prešeren's true vocation was poetry. Underpinned by themes of unrequited love, homeland, friendships and other existential laments, Prešeren's poems combined classical, Renaissance and Romantic elements with traditional Slovene folk customs, resulting in a body of work considered to be the apotheosis of nineteenth-century Slovene language and culture. His most recognized piece of work was the epic *Krst pri Savici* (Baptism at the Savica), which explores themes of Christianization in Slovenia, though only one volume of his work, *Poezije doktorja Franceta Prešerna* (Poems of Doctor France Prešeren), was published during his lifetime, in 1845.

Through his writing, the liberal-minded Prešeren – along with his peers, and particularly his good friend and mentor Matija Čop – attempted to create an independent Slovene culture for townspeople, oriented towards classical Western traditions, whilst he also sought to stimulate national awareness amongst the emerging Slovene middle class. However, he frequently clashed with the government in Vienna over his anti-German sentiments, as well as the Catholic Church, who considered his work immoral.

Prešeren's personal life was deeply unhappy: he was a melancholy character, a drunkard and philanderer and had three children out of wedlock. He was particularly depressed by an unrequited love affair with one Julija Primič, whom he first met at the Church of St John in Trnovo, Ljubljana, and by the untimely death of the aforementioned Matija Čop.

From 1846 until his death, from cirrhosis of the liver, in 1849, Prešeren spent the last three years of his life working in his own practice in Kranj, the city in which he is also buried. His writing aside, Prešeren's legacy is very much alive in other forms – his face adorns the 1000 tolar note, whilst the seventh stanza of *Zdravljica* ("A Toast"), set to music by composer Stanko Premrl, was adopted as the national anthem of the republic in 1991.

34 in the centre of the village – incidentally, this is a good place to **eat**. For further information contact Promantana in Bled (Ⓣ04/578-0660). For the visit, take some warm clothing, waterproofs and a pair of older shoes, as it can get quite muddy.

Vrba

VRBA, a tiny village 4km northeast of Bled just off the main road to Kranjska Gora, is famed as the birthplace of France Prešeren, Slovenia's most celebrated poet. Prešeren was sufficiently enamoured with his home village to write:

O, Vrba, happy village, my old home
My father's cottage stands there to this day
The lure of learning beckoned me away
Its serpent wiles enticing me to roam

The solid whitewashed **house** (Rojstna Hiša Prešerna hiša; Tues–Sat 9am–4pm, Sun 10am–4pm; 300SIT), located on the right-hand side of the village as you enter (no. 2), was originally built in the sixteenth century, but largely destroyed by fire in 1856. Rebuilt soon after, it now contains a few original items of furniture, including the poet's cradle, numerous personal artefacts, as well as translations of some of his work. As interesting as the exhibition is, you'll learn more about the man and his work at the memorial house in Kranj (see p.105), where he lived and worked for the last few years of his life.

Once you're done with the birthplace take a walk to the eastern end of the village, site of the Gothic **Church of St Mark** (Cerkev Sv Marko), which contains sixteenth-century frescoes by the prolific Jernej of Loka, and murals by Friulian masters. From Bled, just one **bus** (7.30am) each day departs for Vrba, so you're best off taking one of the hourly buses from Lesce to Kranjska Gora, which stop at Vrba.

Bohinj and around

Some 20km long and 5km wide, **Bohinj** is the name given to the entire Sava Bohinjka basin southwest of Bled, a region of immense charm and beauty, embracing rugged valleys and mountains, alluring rustic idylls and, best of all, a magical **lake**.

Archeological finds have determined that Bohinj was settled in the late seventh century, a theory given further credence following the discovery of a handful of forges and foundries in the area. Indeed, for many centuries, the smelting of iron was the mainstay of the economy in the region, although eventually, as elsewhere in Gorenjska, competition from more sophisticated European foundries signalled an end to production. As a result, the natives turned to alpine dairy farming, and in particular the mass production of cheese, the quality of which was highly regarded throughout Central Europe. Whilst alpine farming is still practised by small pockets of the community, many more villagers are now becoming engaged in tourism as a means of subsistence.

Bohinj's two key settlements, **Bohinjska Bistrica** and **Ribčev Laz**, suffice for all things of a practical nature, including the main rail and bus connection points, and the tourist offices. By way of contrast, the group of villages northeast of the lake in the upper valley – **Stara Fužina**, **Studor** and **Srednja Vas** – are not only a restful antidote to the often crowded lakeside, but can also boast some fabulous indigenous rural architecture. More excitingly, there are

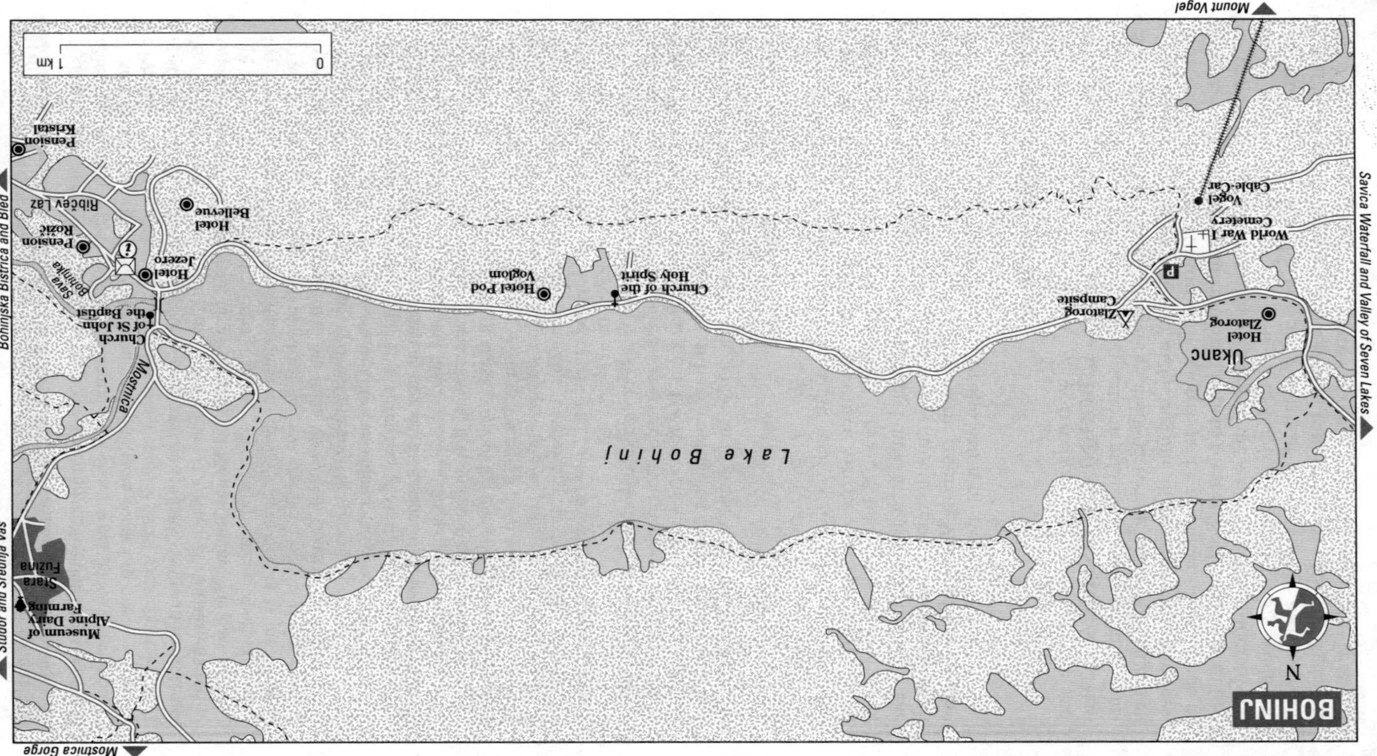
BOHINJ
N
Studor and Srednja Vas
Bohinjska Bistrica and Bled
Mostnica Gorge
Savica Waterfall and Valley of Seven Lakes
Mount Vogel
0
1 km
Museum of Alpine Dairy Farming
Stara Fužina
Mostnica
Church of St John the Baptist
Sava Bohinjka
Pension Rožič
Ribčev Laz
Pension Kristal
Hotel Jezero
Hotel Bellevue
Lake Bohinj
Hotel Pod Voglom
Church of the Holy Spirit
Zlatorog Campsite
Ukanc
Hotel Zlatorog
World War I Cemetery
Vogel Cable-Car

Triglav National Park

Abutting the Italian border to the west, within touching distance of the Austrian border to the north, and embracing almost the entire Slovene part of the Julian Alps, **Triglav National Park** (Triglavski Narodni Park) attracts some two million visitors each year. The idea for a national park was first mooted in 1908, a concept partially realized in 1924 with the creation of a "protected nature park" in the Valley of the Triglav Lakes. Proclaimed the Triglav National Park in 1961, the park assumed its present status in 1981, when it also incorporated **Mount Triglav**. The park comprises three distinct sectors: the Bohinj district – which incorporates Bohinj Lake and the greatest concentration of settlements; the Sava Dolinka district to the north, characterized by a series of glaciated valleys; and the Soča district in the west, extending southwards to Bovec and the Soča Valley (see Chapter 3), and which accommodates the only road passing directly through the park.

The park is home to a wonderful array of **flora and fauna**; the park's most revered creature is the elusive **chamois** (*Rupicapra rupicapra*), of which some two thousand are believed to roam the grassy mountain slopes; other significant species include the recently reintroduced **marmot** and **ibex**, whilst sightings of the **golden eagle**, and encounters with **brown bear** – who stray up from the southern forests – are not unknown. However, the possibility of sighting any of the above is slim, as they are all apt to steer well clear of humans. Many of the park's plant species are endemic to the mountains, such as the **Julian poppy** (*Papaver julicum*), most commonly found on scree slopes, and the purple **Zois' bellflower** (*Campanula zoysii*), named after the eighteenth-century Slovene botanist Karl Zois – be warned that most alpine flora here is protected and picking them is an offence.

The park is administered by some twenty professional, and one hundred volunteer, rangers, who are on hand to provide assistance, though there are information boards haphazardly scattered throughout the park. Otherwise, information can be obtained from the **Triglav National Park Information Centre**, located in the village of Trenta in the Trenta Valley (see p.145), and the park's headquarters in Bled (see p.117).

some wonderful excursions close at hand, such as the immensely popular **Savica Waterfall** and the beautiful **Mostnica Gorge** and **Voje Valley**, both a short way north of the aforementioned villages. Whilst a fair proportion of visitors come to Bohinj to partake in water-bound activities – on both the lake and the Sava Bohinjka River – many more come to trek the mountains, with the major southerly approach to Triglav via the stunning **Valley of the Triglav Lakes** emanating from here. Bohinj can also count on two ski resorts.

Bohinjska Bistrica

Routinely given the cold shoulder by travellers keen to reach the star attraction a few kilometres further on, **BOHINJSKA BISTRICA** – 20km southwest of Bled – is Bohinj's main settlement. In truth it is a rather nondescript place, though, that said, there's a mildly diverting museum here, as well as a sprinkling of accommodation including one of Bohinj's two campsites. Furthermore, its **train station** is the closest to the mountains on this side of the Alps, while the **car-train** runs from here to Most na Soči further south (see box opposite). Buses meet trains arriving at the station, which is located ten minutes east of the centre, and link up to Ribčev Laz (see p.128), while the main **bus stop** is located a few paces north of the post office on Triglavska cesta. You can get information at the Bohinj **tourist board office** at Triglavska cesta 30 (mid-June to mid-Sept Mon–Fri 7am–7pm, Sat & Sun 8am–7pm; rest

Bohinj Tunnel: Car and museum trains

Built between 1901 and 1906, the **Bohinj Tunnel** extends for some 6327m (6.3km) between Bohinjska Bistrica and Podbrdo, making it Slovenia's longest railway tunnel. Operational since 1999, the **car-train** transports vehicles through the tunnel in a mere ten minutes – as opposed to the one hour it takes by car across the tortuous road between Bohinj and Baška Grapa, via the village of Sorica. There are six daily trains between Bohinjska Bistrica and Podbrdo, three of which continue to Most na Soči, twenty minutes further on at the southernmost tip of the park. From Bohinjska Bistrica to Podbrdo the cost (car and passengers) is 1700SIT one-way, and 2600SIT return. The full journey (Bistrica to Most na Soči) is 2600SIT one-way, 4300SIT return – for bicycles the cost is 490SIT and 650SIT respectively (one-way).

Every Thursday between mid-June and September, the marvellous **Oldtimer Museum Train** (Muzej Vlak) puffs its way between Jesenice, some 12km north of Bled, to Most na Soči, stopping off at Bled and Bohinjska Bistrica along the way – the total journey time is 1hr 20min. It's a fantastic ride, but not cheap; a return fare costs 7000SIT, while, for an additional 5000SIT, you can partake in a full-day programme, which includes visits to Tolmin and Kobarid, and lunch. Tickets can be booked through the ABC Rent-a-Car office in Ljubljana (ⓣ01/510-4320, ⓔinfoabc@siol.net), and some of the agencies in Bled or Bohinj.

of year Mon–Fri 8am–4pm; ⓣ04/574-7590). Just across the road at Triglavska 13 is the very commendable *Pension Tripič* (ⓣ04/572-1282, ⓦwww.bohinj.si/tripic; ❹), which has great-value en-suite rooms, each with balcony. On the western fringe of the village, heading towards the lake, is the *Danica* **campsite** (ⓣ04/572-1055; May–Sept), a well-shaded site backing onto the Sava River, with restaurant and sports facilities.

If you have an hour to spare, pop into the **Tomaž Godec Museum** (Muzej Tomaža Godca; May–Oct Tues–Sun 10am–noon & 4–6pm; Jan–April Wed, Sat & Sun, same hours; 400SIT) at Zoisova 15 – it's located five minutes west of the post office, down Vodnikova cesta and across the stream. A staunch communist, Godec, a trained leather tanner and champion skier and mountaineer, was better known for his role as one of the founder members of the Slovene National Liberation Movement and as organizer of the 1941 Bohinj uprising. However, in 1942 he was captured by the Germans and carted off to Begunje (see p.113), before being transferred to Mauthausen where he was executed. The museum was also party to a rather significant piece of history: between March 15 and 18 1939, in the modest room now dedicated to Godec, the **Central Committee of the Communist Party of Yugoslavia** (CKKPJ) was formed. Fittingly, Tito, who was present at the meeting, returned to open the museum some forty years later. The remainder of the museum is given over to a reconstructed leather-tanning workshop – the only one of its kind in the country – a display of brutal-looking World War I weapons recovered from the Southern Bohinj mountains, and an eminently missable archeological display.

Lake Bohinj

The largest permanent body of water in Slovenia, **Lake Bohinj** (Bohinjsko Jezero) is utterly different from Lake Bled, its brooding, unerringly calm waters providing perfect theatre to the majestic, steeply pitched mountain faces which frame it. In his epic poem, *Baptism of the Savica*, France Prešeren eloquently described it thus:

The lake of Bohinj calm in stillness lies,
No sign of strife remains to outward sight;
Yet in the lake the fierce pike never sleep,
Nor other fell marauders of the deep.

Over 4km long, 1km wide, and reaching depths of 45m, the lake is fed by water from the Savica falls, which, in turn, feeds the Sava Bohinjka River at the southeastern corner of the lake. Mercifully, and unlike Bled, building has been forbidden along the entire lake shore, resulting in a virtually unbroken sequence of trees and grassy banks. Nevertheless, and even more so than Bled, the lake is well geared up for a number of activities, with canoeing, kayaking and windsurfing supplementing the more traditional pursuits of swimming and fishing. Moreover, it's far more likely to freeze over during winter, meaning better opportunities for skating.

Ribčev Laz and the Church of St John the Baptist

As well as containing all things of a practical nature, **RIBČEV LAZ** is the location for the lake's outstanding monument, the tiny **Church of St John the Baptist** (Cerkev Sv Janez Krstnik; July & Aug daily 9am–noon & 5–8pm; other times contact the tourist office; 100SIT), one of the most brilliantly frescoed churches in all Slovenia. Located opposite the stone bridge – invariably clogged with walkers and traffic, but offering glorious head-on views of the lake – this chunky, evocative-looking structure has origins dating back to the thirteenth century. Its exterior features a striking **wooden porch**, paved with round river stones in rhomboid style, the middle stones arranged to form the date – 1639 – when it was laid out. Most of the exterior's sixteenth-century frescoes are barely discernible, save for those to the right of the entrance, one of which depicts St John, book in hand, baptizing kneeling persons, and another of St Florian doing what he does best, dousing fires. The south exterior wall bears an oversized St Christopher with the Christ Child on his shoulder. Its Baroque **bell tower**, renovated several times over, features double windows framed with green stone from the Piračica stream, a material common to many church bell towers in the region.

Such is the sheer mass of interior **frescoes** – most of which were painted by the Master of the Bohinj – that you may desire a repeat visit just to take them all in, particularly if it's crowded. The Gothic presbytery, dating from around 1440, contains the densest concentration of frescoes; working upwards, the lower walls are painted with singing angels holding up patterned curtains, while the next belt depicts bust-length pictures of holy figures in niches bearing a random selection of items (a lamb, a dragon, a pair of breasts); next up are the Apostles, standing against a background of stage scenery carrying various items of weaponry, above which, in the vaulted compartments, are angels playing instruments. The oldest layer of frescoes – dating from the fourteenth century – are those on the north wall of the nave, featuring just about detectable fragments of scenes of St George and the Dragon, as well as St John the Evangelist blessing the poison (before drinking it and staying alive); adjacent to this, on the north exterior of the arch, are some grisly scenes entitled *St Johns Head to Herodius* and *Beheading of a Saint*, the latter featuring St John's headless corpse spewing blood.

Lake walk

The best way to get to grips with the lake is to take a leisurely, circular walk around it, which should take between four and five hours – the route outlined here follows a clockwise fashion. Generally speaking, the **south shore** – alongside which the road to the hamlet of **Ukanc** runs – contains all the historical points of interest, but it's a bit of a grind, and the path is situated away from the lake, elevated above the busy main road. By way of contrast, the rocky, undisturbed **north shore** – accessible only by foot – is far more uplifting and possesses superior views of the lake – if you're short of time take a bus to the *Hotel Zlatorog* and walk the north shore back to Ribčev Laz.

Two kilometres along the road from the stone bridge in Ribčev Laz, just beyond the *Hotel Pod Voglom*, is the **Church of the Holy Spirit** (Cerkev Sv Duh), a compact Baroque structure enclosed within a shallow wall and distinguished by its neat shingle-topped roof. On its north-facing exterior is a large fresco of St Christopher with Infant Child, completed by Matija Koželj, who also executed the interior side-altar paintings. Its bonny interior also holds some interesting decoration, including a beautiful crystal chandelier from 1743, and stucco ornaments on the nave and presbytery vaults. If the church is closed the key can be obtained from no. 62, just up the path.

Hereafter, the road continues unexcitingly towards Ukanc, the setting for one of Slovenia's more bizarre alpine festivals (see p.132). Just short of here is the turn-off for the **Vogel cable car** (daily: May to mid-Oct 8am–6pm, every half-hour; rest of year, hourly; 1100SIT single, 1600SIT return), which can accommodate up to eighty people. Cruising up to the *Ski Hotel* (1537m) in a speedy five minutes, the panorama gradually reveals itself, culminating in memorable views of the lake below and the serried peaks opposite – on cloudless days Triglav is visible. If you're feeling energetic then you can always hike up; one route starts from the *Hotel Bellevue* in Ribčev Laz, and another from Ukanc (both take around 2hr).

One hundred metres beyond the turn-off for the cable car is the Austro-Hungarian **World War I Cemetery**, containing the graves of some three hundred soldiers buried here between 1915 and 1917 following ferocious battles on nearby Mount Krn. From here, the road continues uphill for 4km towards the Savica Waterfall (see p.132); retracing your steps back to the road, follow it round to the left, past the campsite and the *Hotel Zlatorog*, and continue across the bridge spanning the Savica River. Here, the path splits – the left track heads towards the Savica Waterfall, while the other turns back towards the shore, opening up onto a pleasant grassy expanse popular with bathers and picnickers – the views across to the eastern end of the lake from here are quite splendid. The initial part of the walk along the north shore is characterized by steep slopes of scree, a dry, boulder-strewn channel and densely forested woodland, which, for the most part, meanders tightly along the course of the shoreline. It then opens up into meadowland and a curving shallow bay, one of the best locations around the lake for **bathing** – if you can find a spot. Continuing along the path will bring you back to the bridge and the Church of St John the Baptist.

Stara Fužina, Studor and Srednja Vas

One kilometre north of Ribčev Laz is **STARA FUŽINA**, the largest of the upper valley villages. Located across the bridge, thirty metres up from the *Gostilna Mihovc*, is the enjoyable **Museum of Alpine Dairy Farming** (Planšarski Muzej; Tues–Sun: July & Aug 11am–7pm, Jan–June & Oct 10am–noon & 4–6 pm; 400SIT), an ethnographic repository pertaining to the valley's rich alpine dairy-farming heritage. Thanks to its dense concentration of high-altitude alpine meadows, Bohinj was for centuries the centre of alpine dairy farming in Slovenia, reaching its high point in the late nineteenth century when the introduction of cheese cooperatives substantially increased the lot of farmers and their families. The industry continued to prosper until the 1970s, but following the opening of a modern dairy in Srednja Vas, and the exodus of younger generations to the towns and cities, dairy farming slipped into decline and today it's barely sustained by a handful of older villagers.

Among the more interesting exhibits on display in this abandoned cheese dairy are two huge copper rennet vats, a herdsman's backpack from 1961, containing all the essential items required for a season up in the mountains, and a reconstructed herder's hut. At the eastern end of the village, the **Church of St Paul** (Cerkev Sv Pavel) manifests similar external characteristics to the Church of St John, notably its paved porch, bell tower with stone windows and onion dome, and a more complete fresco of St Christopher – sadly, the frescoes by the main entrance have all but disappeared.

One and a half kilometres beyond the church is the village of **STUDOR**, well known for its splendid-looking double **hayracks**, called *toplars*. While the single stretch type of hayrack (*Kozolec*) is more common – and can be found elsewhere in Europe – the double hayrack, consisting of two parallel single hayracks connected by a double-gabled roof (used for storage), is unique to Slovenia; the ones here, dating from the eighteenth and nineteenth centuries, are perhaps the most picturesque grouping of hayracks to be seen anywhere in the country. Heading up into the village you'll pass the Bohinj Horse Centre (see box opposite), beyond which, at no. 16, is the **Oplen House** (Oplenova hiša; same hours as Alpine Museum; 400SIT), a typical nineteenth-century Bohinj farmhouse, also known as a longhouse because of its unusual arrangement, whereby the living quarters and barn are conjoined under one roof; aside from the typical living room (*hiša*) and "black" kitchen – the latter so-called because of its blackened walls from the open cooking area – the dwelling area consists of a chamber (*kamra*) – used primarily as a bedroom, as evidenced by the two impossibly small beds – and an attic. If the house is closed you can get the key from no. 14a next door. **Srednja Vas**, 1km further on, is the upper valley's central settlement, and though there's nothing specific to see, it's a pleasant enough place to stroll around, and there is a very good restaurant here (see p.132).

Lake Bohinj practicalities

Buses set passengers down just before the lake by the *Hotel Jezero* in Ribčev Laz, from where it's a few steps to the small and incredibly busy **tourist office**, located in the small complex at Ribčev Laz 48 (July & Aug daily 8am–8pm; rest of year Mon–Sat 8am–6pm, Sun 9am–3pm; ⓣ04/572-3370, ⓦwww.bohinj.si). You can change money here and in the **post office** next door (which generally offers better rates).

Accommodation

The standard of the few **hotels** here leaves much to be desired and they generally represent poor value for money (although prices drop considerably out of season). Fortunately, there is plentiful **private accommodation** around the lake, particularly in Ribčev Laz and in the villages along the upper valley (Stara Fužina, Studor and Srednja Vas). Be warned though, that, during July and August, rooms get snapped up very quickly, so it's best to book in advance, or pitch up early in the morning to be sure of finding somewhere. During the summer, expect to pay around 3000SIT per person per night for a room with bathroom; note that for stays of less than three nights you'll have to pay thirty percent more than this; outside peak season, prices are around twenty percent less. An apartment for two people will cost around 7000SIT per night.

Activities in Bohinj

As in Bled, Bohinj presents some excellent opportunities for a whole raft of activities, both land and water bound. Pac Sports, at Ribčev Laz 50 (but located in a hut just below Pension Rožič; May Sat & Sun 10am–6pm; June to mid-Sept daily 9am–8pm; ⓣ041/698-523, ⓦwww.pac-sports.com), offers a comprehensive range of activities including **rafting** (4500SIT), **canyoning** (9000SIT), **hydrospeed** (6000SIT), and **tandem paragliding** (12,000SIT for a fifteen-minute flight). They also hire out **canoes and kayaks** for use on the lake (1000SIT per hour), as do Alpin Sports by the bridge (daily: July & Aug 9am–8pm; May, June & Sept 9am–6pm; ⓣ04/572-3486, ⓦwww.alpinsport.si). **Bikes** can be rented from a number of places, including Pac Sports, Alpin Sport and the hut opposite the departure point for the excursion boats (see below); all are similarly priced (1hr 800SIT, half a day 2000SIT, full day 3500SIT). The **Bohinj Horse Centre** (Mrcina Ranč) in Studor, with its stable of Icelandic ponies, offers a varied year-round programme of local treks, with one-hour rides from around 2500SIT to half-day trips at around 10,000SIT (ⓣ041/790-297, ⓦwww.impel.bohinj.si/riding). For something a little more relaxing you can take the **excursion boat**, which shuttles up and down the lake between Ribčev Laz and the *Hotel Zlatorog* between April and October (every two hours between 10am & 6pm; 900SIT one-way, 1400SIT return). It's also possible to **fish** on the lake and in the Sava Bohinjka river, the latter well stocked with brown trout; permits begin at around 5000SIT per day up to 30,000SIT for a week for the lake, and 9000SIT (56,000SIT) for the river; licences can be obtained from the tourist office. **Swimming** is better here than in Bled due to the shallower waters close to the shore – the best areas are at the extreme western end of the lake and the bay-like area to the north-east. Bohinj has two major **ski resorts**: **Kobla**, (ⓣ04/574-7100, ⓦwww.bohinj.si/kobla), accessible from the southern part of Bohinjska Bistrica, and the larger **Vogel** ski resort, above the lake's southwestern corner, which has 26km of ski runs (ⓣ04/574-6061, ⓦwww.bohinj.si/vogel).

Bookings can be made through the tourist office or the Alpinum agency, a couple of doors along (ⓣ05/572-3441). The *Zlatorog* **campsite** is located at the southwestern corner of the lake in Ukanc (ⓣ04/572-3482; May–Sept).

Hotel Bellevue Ribčev Laz 65 ⓣ04/572-3331, ⓦwww.bohinj.si/alpinum/bellevue. Perched on a hill 800m north of the ***Hotel Jezero***, the secluded Bellevue is where Agatha Christie once stayed, the grand old lady commenting that "the lake is far too beautiful for a murder". The hotel retains a pleasant old-style atmosphere, despite the rooms being a little frayed around the edges. For a little extra, you can stay in the room Christie slept in. If you're walking, take the rocky footpath through the wood (5min) instead of the road, which is a gruelling 20-minute walk. ❻

Hotel Jezero Ribčev Laz 53 ⓣ04/572-3375, ⓦwww.bohinj.si/alpinum/jezero. Just 50m from the water, this is the lake's most prominent hotel, a slickly run place with modestly furnished rooms, each with minibar, small TV and balcony. Use of pool, sauna and fitness suite free to guests. ❼

Pension Kristal Ribčev Laz 4 ⓣ04/577-8200, ⓦwww.bohinj.si/kristal. Located at the entrance to the village, this popular pension offers a mix of newer and older rooms, all simply but smartly furnished. Two rooms for disabled persons. ❹

Hotel Pod Voglom Ribčev Laz 60 ⓣ04/572-3461, ⓦwww.bohinj.si/alpinum/podvoglom. On the southern shore, 2km along the road towards Ukanc, this place is unimaginably dull, but it's the cheapest option going. Rooms in the main building have washbasins in the room and shared shower facilities, while those in the annexe have a bathroom. No extras. ❹–❺

Pension Rožič Ribčev Laz 42 ⓣ04/572-3393, ⓦwww.bohinj.si/rozic. Located 100m east of the tourist office, the rustically styled rooms here are comfortable enough, if a little boxy. Has a reasonable restaurant too (see p.132). ❹

Hotel Zlatorog Ukanc 65 ⓣ04/572-3381, ⓦwww.bohinj.si/alpinum/zlatorog. Disappointingly average place 200m beyond the campsite; the rooms are dreary in the extreme, with uninspiring brown decor and dated furnishings. Pool is free to guests, but tennis and sauna are extra. ❼

Eating, drinking and entertainment

Aside from the hotel **restaurants**, of which the one in the *Jezero* is the best, there are precious few choices when it comes to eating around here. The *MK Pizzeria*, a few metres up from the tourist office, is the most central place, a busy and enjoyable establishment, while just up the road, the *Rožič* – in the pension of same name – has standard meats and grills. Otherwise, you'll have to head up into the villages: in Stara Fužina, the *Gostilna Mihovc*, just down from the alpine dairy museum at no. 118, has a simple setup but top-notch, homestyle Slovene food; while the *Gostilna Rupa*, situated at the eastern end of Srednja Vas at no. 87, is one of the best restaurants in the valley, with heavy emphasis on pork and fish (worth trying is the delicious Bohinj trout) – Thursday is a good day to be here during the summer as there is live music (closed Mon). The *Hotel Jezero*, and the clutch of **cafés** opposite, is where most people seem to congregate by day and night. During the summer months, there is invariably something going on at either the *Jezero* or *Zlatorog* hotels, usually folk dancing or live music – check at the tourist office.

One of the more unusual alpine festivals, taking place in the second or third weekend of September, is the **Kravji Bal**, or "Cows Ball", a mass booze-up to celebrate the return of the cattle from alpine pastures; taking place near the *Hotel Zlatorog*, happenings include folklore events, various live bands, and of course, much drinking.

Hikes and excursions around Bohinj

Beyond the confines of the lake, Bohinj has much to offer walkers of all abilities. The easiest short trek – and the only one accessible by public transport – is the **Savica Waterfall** near the western end of the lake; from here paths break off towards the **Valley of the Triglav Lakes**, a destination for the more physically inclined. To the north of the lake, and accessible from Stara Fužina, is **Mostnica Gorge**, a fabulous little beauty spot.

Savica Waterfall

Unequivocally the number-one attraction around these parts is the majestic 60-metre-high **Savica Waterfall** (Slap Savica; April–Oct; 8am–6pm), a forty-five-minute walk along the path (signposted) west of the *Hotel Zlatorog* (this hike can also be done as an extension of the circular walk – see p.128). Alternatively, you can take one of the six daily buses. Once you've reached the entrance and paid the "path maintenance fee" (400SIT), it's a heavy-going twenty-minute climb up a series of zigzagging steps to the top of the gorge and a small observation hut, invariably crammed with people angling to get a shot in. The falls themselves are undoubtedly spectacular, smooth photogenic ribbons of water tumbling into the circular pool below, before falling away to begin the long journey as the Sava River. To the left, emerging from the same fault, is the subsidiary fall, known as **Mali Savica** (Little Savica). It can get murderously busy on a summer's day, which can't help but temper its delights, so to make the most of it you're best off making an early start.

Valley of the Triglav Lakes

The car park by the entrance to the Savica Waterfall also marks the starting point for several superb hikes into the heart of the Triglav National Park – and, if desired, an assault on Triglav itself (see box on pp.136–137). One track forges westwards to the large *Dom na Komni* hut (1520m; 2hr 30min), open year-

Hiking in the Julian Alps

The Julian Alps are a hiker's wonderland, its meadows, valleys and mountains carved up by a well-worn nexus of waymarked paths and trails. There are several key **starting points**: **Bled**, furthest from the park's mountainous heart, offers easy to moderate hikes around the eastern spur of the Alps, though there are more demanding walks to be had in the heavily forested **Karavanke** chain bordering Austria to the north. From **Kranjska Gora**, trails head off up into the **Planica** and **Tamar Valleys**, as well as up the **Vršič Pass**, from where further tracks fan out in several directions. A short way east of Kranjska Gora, a trio of valleys – the most prominent being the **Vrata Valley** – provide the starting point for ascents towards Triglav itself; if you're considering tackling the great mountain, consult the box on pp.136–137. The greatest choice of hikes, however, emanate from **Bohinj** in the southeastern corner of Triglav National Park: the lush pastures of the **Fužine highlands** and the **Voje Valley** north of the lake; the **Lower Bohinj** mountains on the south side; the **Komna Plateau** to the west; and up through the **Valley of the Triglav Lakes** to the northwest (which continues towards Triglav), arguably the park's most scenically rewarding trek. Unlike in many other European countries, there is no hierarchical system of different signs and colours for **trails**; instead, all paths in Slovenia are marked by a "target", that is, a red circle with a white centre, with intersections and forks indicated by arrows; however, some of the markings are a little inconclusive in places.

The best hiking months are May, June and September, when the weather is at its most dependable and the crowds are somewhat thinner than in the peak summer months; bear in mind that the weather in the mountains can change with alarming rapidity and so the usual provisos apply – sufficient provisions and appropriate clothing and equipment – particularly if you plan to do any high-altitude hiking. If you fancy hooking up with other walkers, a number of **agencies** in Bled and Bohinj (see p.119 & p.131) offer a full range of hikes, from easy to moderate half- or full-day trips such as Debela Peč and the meadows of Bohinj, to more difficult two-day trips up to Triglav (with an overnight stay in a hut). The best up-to-date **maps** are the 1:50,000 editions of *Triglavski Narodni Park* and *Julijske Alps*, published by the Alpine Association of Slovenia (Planinska Zveza Slovenije or PZS; Ⓦwww.pzs.si). You might also like to consider Simon Brown's pocket handbook *Walking in the Alps*, which, though rather dated, outlines key hikes from Bled, Bohinj, Kranjska Gora and Bovec.

round (Ⓣ04/572-1475); while another spears northwards via the formidable Komarča cliff, a tough and very steep route, aided by iron pegs and rungs. Both then carry on northwards, meeting up at the *Koča pri Triglavskih Jezerih* (1685m; Ⓣ050/615-235; July–Sept), which marks the beginning of the magical **Valley of the Triglav Lakes** (Dolina Triglavskih jezer), also known as the **Valley of the Seven Lakes**.

Lined with white limestone cliffs, and rich in alpine and karstic flora, the valley is famed for its beautiful tarns, the lowest and warmest of which is the **Black Lake** (*Črno jezero*), just above Komarča, while the highest, the **Lake below Vršac** (*Jezero pod Vršacem*), lies at an altitude of 2000m. The largest and deepest of the seven lakes, the **Great Lake** (*Veliko jezero*), lies midway between these two. The valley is also the setting for Zlatorog, the mythical chamois with golden horns.

Mostnica Gorge and the Voje Valley

Another superb outing is the hike up through the **Mostnica Gorge** (Mostnice Korita), 1km north of Stara Fužina. Two trails – one just before the bridge and one by St Paul's Church – head towards the gorge entrance, before

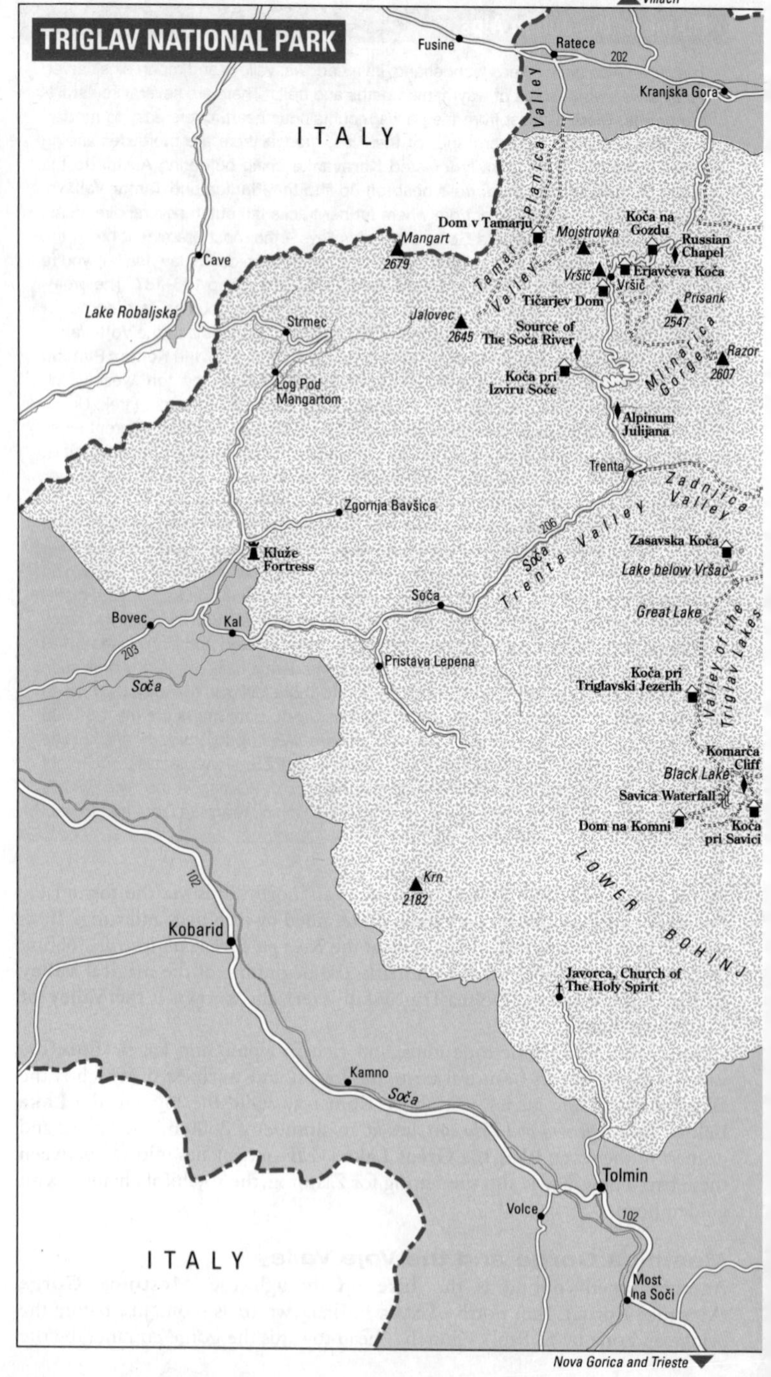
TRIGLAV NATIONAL PARK
Villach
Fusine
Ratece
202
Kranjska Gora
Planica Valley
ITALY
Dom v Tamarju
Mojstrovka
Koča na Gozdu
Russian Chapel
Mangart
2679
Cave
Tamar Valley
Vršič
Vršič
Erjavčeva Koča
Tičarjev Dom
Prisank
2547
Lake Robaljska
Strmec
Jalovec
2645
Source of The Soča River
Mlinarica Gorge
Razor
2607
Log Pod Mangartom
Koča pri Izviru Soče
Alpinum Julijana
Trenta
Zadnjica Valley
Zgornja Bavšica
206
Soča
Trenta Valley
Kluže Fortress
Zasavska Koča
Lake below Vršac
Soča
Bovec
Kal
Great Lake
203
Soča
Pristava Lepena
Koča pri Triglavski Jezerih
Valley of the Triglav Lakes
Komarča Cliff
Black Lake
Savica Waterfall
Dom na Komni
Koča pri Savici
LOWER BOHINJ
Krn
2182
102
Kobarid
Javorca, Church of The Holy Spirit
Kamno
Soča
Tolmin
Volce
102
ITALY
Most na Soči
Nova Gorica and Trieste

Klagenfurt
AUSTRIA
A11
Gozd Martuljek
201
Dovje
Mojstrana
A2
Hrušica
Špik 2472
Peričnik Waterfall
Vrata Valley
Sava Dolinka
Jesenice
Zgornja Radovna
Kot Valley
Radovna Valley
Radovna
Krma Valley
Blejska Dobrava
Kranj
Aljažev Dom
Vintgar Gorge
Debela Peč 2014
Mount Triglav 2864
Triglavski dom na Kredarici
Blejska Koča
Gorje
Bled
Dom Planika
Lake Bled
Kranj
Tržaska Koča
Kanjavec 2569
Vodnikov Dom
Pokljuka Plateau
Rudno Polje
Debeli Vrh 2390
Voje Valley
Bohinjska Bela
Mostnica Waterfall
Planinska Koča na Vojah
Kosijev Dom na Vogarju
Mostnica Gorge
Soteska
Pršivec 1761
Srednja Vas
Studor
Češnjica
Hotel Zlatorog
Lake Bohinj
Stara Fužina
Sava Bohinjska
Ukanc
904
Ribčev Laz
209
Bohinjska Bistrica
Nemški Rovt
Vogel 1922
MOUNTAINS
Sorica
Podbrdo
Zali Log
Železniki
403
N
Hudajužna
Kneža
Mountain trail
0
5 km

Climbing Triglav

It's said that every Slovene has to climb **Mount Triglav** at least once in their lifetime, but this in no sense means that it's an easy outing. In fact it remained unclimbed until 1778, when a German doctor and three local guides made it to its 2864m summit.

The **most dramatic approach** is undoubtedly from the north, as Triglav's north face is no less than 1200 metres high; its central part is for climbers only, but there are fairly tough hiking routes to either side. These involve the use of fixed cables and are not for the inexperienced or faint-hearted; most hikers prefer to stick to the south side for both ascent and descent.

A road leads up the Vrata valley to the *Aljažev Dom* hut (1015m), although purists prefer to take the two-hour hike there from Mojstrana (664m). Continue up the valley, past a monument to the partisans, and after 45 minutes take the Prag path to the left, below the cave which is the source of the Vrata. The path leads up through a ravine to a grassy ledge right at the foot of the North Face. Here the Prag or Threshold, a rock cliff, is scaled with the help of metal steps and pegs; the path winds on up on rock ledges to a small spring, after which you should fork right to reach the *Triglavski dom na Kredarici* (2515m), four or five hours from the Aljažev Dom. It's best to stay a night here and tackle the peak in the morning; from the saddle above the hut head for the huge painted marker which shows the start of the climb. This looks intimidating but has been made easier with steel cables and pegs, which will lead you to the summit in an hour or so.

The **shortest ascent** is from the east, from Rudno Polje (1340m), reached by a daily bus leaving Bled at 8.25am, arriving fifty minutes later and returning at 11.25am (with another on Fridays, Sundays and holidays at 3.45pm from Bled, returning at 4.35pm). It's about two hours' hike to the Studorski preval (1892m), and another hour to the *Vodnikov dom* (1817m), from where you continue to *Dom Planika* and the summit by the route described opposite in reverse.

However, the **most popular route** starts from the *Hotel Zlatorog* at the western end of Lake Bohinj, although it's also possible to start from Stara Fužina, walking west along the north shore of the lake. Crossing the bridge from the hotel, walk for 40 minutes, on asphalt and then gravel, to a junction 100 metres before the Savica waterfall. To the right a steep path begins the ascent of the formidable-looking Komarča Cliff, a tough climb of 700 metres but fitted with cables to make it easier and safer. It can take two hours to climb to a viewpoint at the top, from where you continue gently uphill in beech trees for a couple of minutes before finding the Črno Jezero (Black Lake; 1294m) on your left. You'll soon turn left to pass around the lake to the north; after a couple of minutes go straight ahead at a junction, continuing on a slightly rocky path in pine trees, level and then rising for an hour in all. From the top of the White Cliff (Bela Skala) it's an easy 15 minutes, walk through limestone dykes to the *Koča pri Triglavskih Jezerih* (Hut of the Triglav Lakes; 1685m), three to four hours from the Hotel Zlatorog.

A longer but easier alternative would be to start from Stara Fužina, heading north up the road towards Voje and soon turning left on a path climbing up the bank to the left, towards Planina Vogar and Pršivec. After an hour this brings you to the

which you cross the stone **Devil's Bridge** (Hudičev Most); follow the path to the right for 400m, pay at the kiosk (300SIT), then take the path to the right. The ravine, 1km long and 20 metres deep in places, has been smoothly sculpted into all manner of extraordinary shapes, while hundreds of circular hollows, known as "river mills", have been eroded into the riverbed, the result of stones spun by whirlpools in the stream; close inspection of the river is possible, as regular paths divert away from the main track, but be particularly

Vogar meadows, and a hut, the *Kosijev Dom Na Vogarju* (1054m). From the top of the meadow follow the track westwards, and when it ends take the path to the right – the path to the left leads via Pršivec (1761m), the best viewpoint over Lake Bohinj. It takes about an hour to reach the Planina Viševnik meadow (1625m), where you should swing left and go gently down to the Black Lake, about half an hour away, and about four hours from Stara Fužina, and onwards to the *Koča pri Triglavskih Jezerih* (on p.133).

In either case, from the hut you should continue north up the valley and past the Great Lake (Veliko Triglavskih Jezero), reaching the foot of an escarpment after an hour; the route leads steeply up to the right (following a red arrow to Hribarice), reaching the ridge in twenty minutes and the Yellow Lake (Želeno Jezero; 1988m) in another five minutes. Continuing up to the right, you'll pass a turning to the Prehodavici hut (visible not too far to the left), and climb up, partly on scree, for half an hour. This is a weird but wonderful plateau of bare limestone, leading in another half-hour to the Hribarice saddle (2358m), where you finally see Triglav in front of you.

From here the path is reasonably marked for a while; it descends and kinks to the left after about five minutes, then rises a little to reach the Dolič saddle (2164m) in another twenty minutes; from here the *Tržaška Koča na Doliču* is also visible just to the left. The path swings sharply to the right here, with a bit of scree, and drops a bit (with some cables); after an hour you'll reach the start of a fairly steep section with more cables, after which it takes just five minutes to reach the *Dom Planika pod Triglavom* (2401m), at the top of a scree slope, and about five hours from the *Koča pri Triglavskih Jezerih*. It's probably best to spend the night here and make your final push to the summit in the morning; the route crosses rocks, possibly snow, and scree, bringing you in thirty minutes to the foot of a cliff, where a big red and white dot marks the start of the climb. There are steel pegs for footholds, and then on the steeper sections fixed cables; a patch of scree leads to a shoulder, where a path leads left and down to the Dolič hut. The route to the summit turns right and climbs onwards, with more pegs than cables, reaching the top after another forty minutes; here you'll find the Aljazev Stolp or turret, a tiny refuge erected in 1865 that looks like a small space rocket.

Having returned to the *Dom Planika*, the easiest descent drops by good switchbacks to reach the Konsjko Sedlo (2020m) in thirty minutes. Going to the right here, you'll head south along the side of the valley (with a couple of stretches of horizontal chain), reaching the *Vodnikov dom* (1817m) in another forty minutes. The path on is rather easier; after fifteen minutes a path comes in from the right, soon after which you have to fork right; this path drops steadily to the pine forest of the Jurijavčeva vrtača. After eighty minutes it passes through a meadow and then zigzags down in beech forest, entering a field after half an hour. Here a sign points to the Mostnica waterfall (Slap Mostnice), 400m to the left. Go left, parallel to the stream, for a couple of minutes, then cross the footbridge, and take the track to the right, near a café. After twenty minutes the track crosses to the right bank, and after another fifteen minutes reaches another café. From here it takes about forty minutes down an increasingly good road to reach Stara Fužina.

careful if it has been raining. At the conclusion of the gorge (by the bridge), you can either return (via the other side), or continue northwards towards the **Voje Valley** – scramble upwards through the trees for twenty minutes before arriving at the *Koča na Vojah* hut (☎041/527-926; June–Sept), a good place to stop for refreshments; thereafter, it's a pleasant forty-minute walk through open fields and meadows to the precipitous valley headwall and the modest 21-metre-high **Mostnica Waterfall** (Slap Mostnice). From here, you can continue to Velo Polje and the *Vodnikov dom na Velo polje* hut (☎050/615-621; June–Sept) at 1817m (3hr 30min), or return via the way you came.

Kranjska Gora and around

Tucked away in the extreme northwestern corner of the country, on the doorstep of Triglav National Park, the small town of **KRANJSKA GORA** is Slovenia's number one winter playground. A remote settlement since the fourteenth century, the town merited little attention and was strategically unimportant until World War I when the nearby Vršič Pass was built to enable supplies to reach the Austrian army fighting along the Soča front. Kranjska Gora then developed into a major winter sports venue, with Slovenia's first ski jump and ski lifts constructed here in 1934 and 1950 respectively. Whilst its skiing is undoubtedly the main draw, during the summer it's an excellent base from which to embark on any number of hikes, while cyclists will

Skiing in northwest Slovenia

Given its predominantly mountainous terrain, it's not surprising that northwest Slovenia contains the greatest concentration of the country's **ski resorts**, and whilst you won't find the range of slopes that you would do in Italy or France, the spectacular alpine scenery, thinner crowds and considerably lower prices, are ample compensation. Moreover, Slovenia's ski resorts are uniformly well equipped and extremely safe, although most suffer from a lack of decent après-ski facilities.

Slovenia's largest and best-known ski resort is **Kranjska Gora**, located near the Austrian and Italian borders; however, the skiing here is not particularly exciting, its slopes best suited to beginners and intermediate skiiers, which makes it a popular base with families – it is, however, one of only two resorts in the country to host international ski (and ski-jumping) competitions. Consistently rated as one of the most complete centres in Slovenia – and the most popular resort amongst weekending *Ljubljančani* – is **Krvavec**, located some 25km due north of the capital; its extensive range of slopes are suitable for skiers of all abilities, moreover, it possesses a snowboard school, speed-skiing track and a freestyle mogul course (note that weekly passes are not available for any of these activities at Krvavec). The country's highest-altitude skiing (over 2000m) is at **Kanin**, near Bovec in the Soča Valley; both this and the centres in Bohinj – **Kobla** and **Vogel** – offer the most spectacular skiing in terms of scenery, while the latter possesses the most modern cable car in the country. The best of the rest is **Cerkno**, a short way north of Idrija, which has some of the most challenging pistes in the country.

The **season** lasts between December and March, though skiing on the higher pistes, such as Kanin, is often possible until the end of April or beginning of May. Expect to **pay** in the region of 3500–4800SIT for a day ski pass and 18,000–25,000SIT for a weekly pass, the latter figure representing the sort of price you'd expect to pay at the more developed resorts. The **Ski Pass Julijske Alps** covers several centres. Most centres have **ski schools** with English instruction (around 3500SIT for a one-hour individual lesson, and 12,000SIT for five, two-hour lessons as part of a group), and offer **ski rental** (around 3000SIT for skis, boots and poles). Telephone numbers for individual centres are given where relevant throughout the guide. For more **information** on skiing in Slovenia contact the Association Ropeways of Slovenia (*Združenje Slovenskih Žičničarjev*) at Parmova 33, Ljubljana (☎01/436-6400; ⓦwww.slo-skiing.net or ⓦwww.slovenia-tourism.si/skiing). Latest ski conditions can be obtained from the Snow Hotline (☎041/182-500).

appreciate the extensive network of recently established, and very well-marked, cycle paths.

Arrival and information

The low-key **bus station** is just five minutes' walk north of the centre on Koroška ulica – head down Kolodvorska ulica to Borovška cesta, the town's main street. The **tourist office** is in the centre of town at Tičarjeva 2 (July to mid-Sept & mid-Dec to mid-March Mon–Sat 8am–8pm, Sun 9am–6pm; other times Mon–Fri 8am–3pm, Sat 9am–6pm, Sun 9am–1pm; ⓣ04/588-1768, ⓦwww.kranjska-gora.si), 200m west of which is the **post office** (Mon–Fri 8am–7pm, Sat 8am–noon). **Internet access** is available at the *Gostilna Frida*, next to the bus station (Tues–Sun 10am–11pm; 300SIT for 30min).

Accommodation

As you'd expect from Slovenia's largest ski resort, there's a healthy stock of **hotels** in town, though the **pensions** here offer a superior level of comfort and better value for money. Accommodation in **private rooms** (❶) or **apartments** (❷) in the town centre and surrounding villages is another alternative and can be arranged through either the tourist office, or the Globtour agency, 50m west of the tourist office at Borovška cesta 90 (July to mid-Sept & mid-Dec to mid-March Mon–Sat 8.30am–6pm, Sun 9am–noon; other times of the year Mon–Fri 9am–4pm, Sat 9am–noon; ⓣ04/588-1055). There are also numerous apartments advertised in the streets east of the bus station.

Hotel Alpina Vitranška 12 ⓣ04/588-1761, ⓦwww.hotel-alpina.si. Ignore the portentous exterior, the rooms are tastefully decorated, though some are a little boxy. It's well worth paying the minimal extra for the renovated rooms. Free use of pool in the ***Hotel Kompas***. ❻

Hotel Kompas Borovška cesta 100 ⓣ04/588-1661, ⓦwww.hoteli-kompas.si. This sprawling complex on the western edge of town accommodates two categories of room; those in the main building are bright and well furnished, while those in the chalet-type annexe across the way are cheaper, but very dated. Smart indoor pool. ❻–❽

Hotel Kotnik Borovška cesta 75 ⓣ04/588-1564, ⓔkotnik@siol.net. Housed in a luminous yellow building, this classy, family-run hotel accommodates fifteen large and beautifully designed rooms – the best-value place in town. ❺

Hotel Lek Vršiška 38 ⓣ04/588-1520, ⓦwww.hotel-lek.si. Out near the ***Alpinum***, this polished hotel harbours all the requisite four-star facilities, including a beautiful indoor pool, gym and sauna. ❼

Pension Lipa Koroška cesta 14 ⓣ04/582-0000, ⓔperkolic@g-kabel.si. Attractive, comfortable pension right next to the bus station, and which possesses a wonderful restaurant (see p.140). ❺

Pension Miklič Vitranška 13 ⓣ04/588-1635, ⓔgregor.miklic@G-kabel.si. Surrounded by baize-like lawns and neatly arranged flowerbeds, this pristine pension, between the ***Alpina*** and ***Lek*** hotels, has immaculate rooms. ❻

Hotel Prisank Borovška cesta 93 ⓣ04/588-4477, ⓦwww.htp-gorenjka.si. Occupying a central location a few steps west of the tourist office, this rather down-at-heel hotel has antiquated rooms with chipped furniture and grubby, stone-floor bathrooms, but it's the cheapest place going. ❹

The Town

The one key site in town is the **Liznjek House** (Liznjekova hiša; Tues–Fri 10am–5pm, Sat & Sun 10am–4pm; closed April and Nov; 500SIT) located 200m east of the *Hotel Kotnik* at Borovška cesta 63. This superbly preserved alpine homestead – once the property of a wealthy local farmer and the largest farm in the village – mostly dates from the late eighteenth century, though its stone ground floor is of seventeenth-century origin. Its interior furnishings are particularly outstanding; in one nameless room sits a lovely selection of folk-painted trousseau chests, while in the *hiša* – the main living room – there is a beautiful corner stove and a lovely, slender grandfather clock. Upstairs is a typically modest *kamra* (bedroom), and a vast attic, once used as storage space and still chock-full with farmer's tools. Opposite the house is the capacious barn, built in 1796 and originally used for storing food and housing livestock; it's now mostly empty, save for some battered old horse carts and grand-looking sleds.

Three hundred metres west of the Liznjek House, sited on the attractive, square-like portion of Borovška cesta, is the squat, late-Gothic **Church of the Assumption** (Cerkev Sv vnebovzetje). The only surviving part of the original church is the stocky, Romanesque bell-tower, while the church itself dates from 1510. There's not an awful lot to see inside, though its exquisite interior does contain one of the most impressive vaulted ceilings in the region and a particularly fine organ, one of the oldest in Gorenjska. West beyond the church are most of the town's hotels and other key facilities, and further west still the ski slopes (see opposite).

Eating and drinking

The town is blessed with a handful of first-rate **restaurants**, the best of which are located within several of the pensions and hotels. Conversely, decent **drinking** establishments are conspicuous by their absence – disappointing, given the town's status as one of the country's premier ski resorts. Most of these restaurants are open daily till 11pm.

Gostilna Cvitar Borovška cesta 83. Housed in a delightful 200-year-old building next to the church, this characterful tavern has some of the best Slovene dishes in town; its stylish interior has smoking and nonsmoking rooms, while the informal terrace is also an enjoyable place to eat; reasonably priced and top-class service to boot.

Kotnik Borovška cesta 15. Inventively styled place in the ***Hotel Kotnik***, with a highly creditable menu featuring fish, game and, unusually, lamb. Also houses a small, rather frenetic, pizzeria.

Lipa Koroška cesta 14. Located in the pension of the same name, this restaurant offers an outstanding international and Slovene kitchen, as well as a superb pizza menu. The beautiful winter garden, with its soft green decor and wicker chairs, is the most atmospheric place in town to dine.

Miklič Vitranška 13. As accomplished as the pension it's housed in, this beautiful and classy restaurant offers a more upscale and expensive take on standard beef and fish dishes, as well as a colourful salad bar. The covered outdoor terrace is a delightful place to eat.

Pri Martinu Borovška cesta 61. Enjoyable, vaguely medievally themed restaurant next to the Liznjek House, rustling up healthy portions of solid meat dishes – such as veal stew with buckwheat mush – and some sound veggie options, including dumplings and polenta.

Drinking and entertainment

The town's central watering hole is *Papa Joe Razor*, located in a corner of the once elegant but now defunct *Razor Hotel* at Borovška 83 (daily 9am–5am) – it has live music at the weekends and is also a good place for hot snacks, including horse goulash. *Pri Bedanc*, 200m west of the *Hotel Kompas* out by the slopes, is a better après-ski place (Fri & Sat till 1am). Otherwise, the *Gostilna Cvitar* is a pleasant spot for coffee or beer, while there are a smattering of other, albeit rather uninspiring, cafés along Borovška cesta. If you fancy chancing your arm, as hundreds of neighbouring Italians do each night, then head to the 24-hour Casino adjoining the *Hotel Casino Kranjska Gora*, located to the south of town at Vršiška cesta 23. Entrance costs 1750SIT, bring some ID and make sure you dress the part.

Cycling and other activities around Kranjska Gora

The area around Kranjska Gora offers some of the best **cycling** in the region. The excellent cycling map (*Kolesarski izleti*; 400SIT), available from the tourist office, details some twelve excursions, ranging from gentle (Rateče), to very demanding (Vršič Pass, Belca) routes; paths are clearly signposted at regular intervals, each one indicating relevant turn-off points, distances and length of time to the next destination.

Bikes can be rented from the Julijana agency, located in a small hut a few paces west of the *Hotel Prisank* (daily: mid-June to mid-Sept 9am–noon & 3–9pm; mid-Dec to mid-March, same times except till 7pm; ⓣ04/588-1325, ⓦwww.sednjek.si); and Šport Bernik, at Borovška 88a (daily: 8am–7pm; winter till 6pm; ⓣ04/588-1470, ⓦwww.kranjska-gora.si/sportbernik); both charge around 700SIT for one hour, 1500SIT for half a day and 2000SIT for a full day. Julijana also organizes **rafting** (5000SIT) on the Sava and Soča rivers, **canyoning** (5500SIT) and **hiking** (4000SIT), so long as there are sufficient numbers (between four and six). During July and August the tourist office organizes free, guided hikes once a week.

Skiing in Kranjska Gora

The slopes of **Vitranc** and **Podkoren**, just west of the town centre, offer some 30km of ski runs (with five chairlifts and numerous towbars), accommodating skiers of all abilities. Between late December and early January, the town welcomes international skiers for the men's World Cup Slalom and Giant Slalom races. **Ski passes** are available from the ticket office at the Alpine Ski Club (*Alpski Smučarski Klub*), Borovška 99 (daily in winter 8.30am–3.30pm; ⓣ04/588-5300, ⓦwww.kranjska-gora.si/ask/club); expect to pay around 5300SIT for a day pass, and 29,000SIT for a weekly pass. The club's school (*Smučarska šola*) offers **ski lessons** (around 6000SIT for a 2hr individual lesson, and around 14,000SIT for five, two-hour lessons as part of a group); and **snowboarding** lessons (5500SIT 1hr). There is **ski rental** from Šport Bernik (skis, 1700SIT for one day; boots, 900SIT; snowboard, 2200SIT). Between December and April (depending on the weather) the Julijana agency offers **tobogganing** (2800SIT) and **Motor Sleigh** (5000SIT for 15min on track, 12,000SIT for panoramic ride).

West of Kranjska Gora: Zelenci, Planica Valley and Tamar Valley

To the west of Kranjska Gora is the small but beautiful Zelenci Nature Reserve, beyond which is the Planica Valley – with its head-spinning ski jumps – and the Tamar Valley, from where a number of paths lead to more challenging peaks.

Zelenci Nature Reserve

Three kilometres west of Kranjska Gora, sandwiched between the ski slopes of Podkoren and the main road to Italy, is the **Zelenci Nature Reserve**, home to an exceptional range of flora and fauna. Located within the reserve is a marsh, which consists of a brilliant emerald-blue, crystal clear lake, below which cool springs spurt, volcano-like, from limestone sediment called "kreda" – a unique phenomenon in Slovenia. The lake – which is also the source of the Sava Dolinka River, though technically this begins at the Nadiža karst spring up in the Tamar Valley (see p.142) – can be accessed via a series of carefully constructed walkways from either side of the reserve, while the observation tower provides some lovely overhead views.

As well as harbouring a dense concentration of vegetation – pygmy willows, alder trees and common cottongrass – the reserve supports some unusual

The incredible flying men

Situated at the mouth of the picturesque Planica Valley, 2km west of Kranjska Gora, are the world-renowned **Planica ski jumps**, site of the world's largest ski jump and venue for the longest jump in history. The first of the three jumps located here was built in 1934, upon the initiative of **Stanko Bloudek**, engineer, figure-skating champion and the man widely credited with bringing winter sports to a wider Slovenian audience. Not long after its construction (a mere 90 metres, the longest is a breathtaking 190 metres), the first record at Planica fell, as the Austrian, **Sepp Bradl**, became the first man to jump beyond the magical 100-metre mark, in 1936. To this day, Planica proudly boasts of holding more ski-jump records than any other venue in the world, not least the current **world record**, held by the Finn **Matti Hautamaeki**, who jumped an astonishing 231 metres here in 2003.

Slovenes too have a fine pedigree in the sport, gaining their first Olympic medal (a team bronze) in the 2002 Salt Lake City games, while their record-holder is **Robert Kranjec**, who leapt 222.5 metres at Planica in 2000. If you've got the energy, take a hike up the stairs located to the side of the jumps and enjoy the extraordinary views. Better still, if you're around at the end of March, then you shouldn't miss the annual World Cup event – celebrated as much for its drinking and music as for its sporting theatrics.

fauna, such as the whiskered bat, sand lizard, the common viper snake, and a rare bird species, the scarlet grosbeak, all of which have been placed on the "Red List" – a list of Slovenia's most endangered species.

The Planica and Tamar valleys

The most enjoyable hike from Kranjska Gora is up the **Planica Valley**, and beyond to the **Tamar Valley** (route no. 3 on the cycling map – see p.140). Just under 1km beyond the Zelenci Nature Reserve, you come to the grassy lower part of the Planica Valley, the most westerly access point into the Alps. From here, the road ascends steeply up towards the extraordinary **Planica ski jumps** (see box above); a short way north of the last ski jump, you re-enter the National Park, at which point the road gives way to an untidy mess of gravel workings, before continuing as a stony, gently inclining track (used as a cross-country ski track in winter) for about 3.5km up to a lush grassy glade and the *Dom v Tamarju* at 1108m (☎04/587-6055; open all year). The walk up to this point is tremendous, largely for the views of the mighty, razor-sharp peak of **Jalovec** (2645m), due south, and **Mojstrovka** (2366m) to the east. A ten-minute walk west of the hut is the **source of the Nadiža stream**, a powerful karstic spring which squirts through a small fissure in the rock face before disappearing into underground channels and re-emerging in Zelenci at the base of the valley (see p.141). From the hut, one path heads south up the Tamar Valley to **Jalovec** (2645m; 6hr), and another east to **Vršič** (1611m; 3hr); both contain some very exposed and difficult sections.

East of Kranjska Gora: Mojstrana and the valleys

The small village of **Gozd-Martuljek**, 3km east of Kranjska Gora, is the starting point for hikes into the **Martuljek** group of mountains, a fierce, spectacular range which counts the imperious **Mount Špik** (2472m) among its number, regarded as one of the toughest climbs in the Alps. From the village of

Mojstrana, a further 10km east, three parallel valleys fan out southwards into the core of the Park, each furrowed with mountain paths heading towards Triglav itself. Adjoining the easternmost of these valleys is the hamlet of **Zgornja Radovna**, which marks the northwestern extremes of the **Radovna Valley**.

Mojstrana and the Vrata Valley

Thirteen kilometres east of Kranjska Gora, just off the fast main road towards Jesenice, is the village of **MOJSTRANA**, the starting point for hikers attempting Triglav's north face (see box pp.136–137). The most direct road from the village heads southwest up into the **Vrata Valley** ("Gateway Valley"), the largest glacial valley in the northern tract of the Julian Alps and the most direct route to Triglav – consequently, it's often overflowing with hikers and motorists.

Nearing the southern end of the village, the **Triglav Museum Collection** (Triglavska Muzejska Zbirka; May–Oct Tues–Sun 10am–5pm; 500SIT) at Triglavska cesta 50 has some illuminating exhibits pertaining to the National Park and those who have shaped it. One of the park's foremost pioneers was Jakob Aljaž (1845–1927) – parish priest, composer and mountaineer – and after whom both the hut at the end of the valley and the rocket-shaped turret (Aljažev stolp) at the top of Triglav are named. In 1895, as competing claims from Germany and Austria for Triglav intensified, Aljaž, a staunch Slovene patriot, purchased the peak for the sum of 1 Florin, thus ensuring the mountain remained Slovene property. Other rooms document the work of the Slovenian Mountain Association, the Mountain Rescue Service and the first mountain guides.

Six kilometres beyond the village, two paths branch off up a forest slope (10min) to the **Peričnik Waterfall** (Slap Peričnik), which actually comprises an upper (16m) and lower (52m) fall. Unusually, the falls can be circled – via the narrow, sandy ledge – but wherever you view it from you're likely to get a good soaking from the itinerant spray. The best time to see the falls is in winter when the water freezes into thick curtains of ice.

Six kilometres further north, up an increasingly steep and rugged track (accessible by car) is *Aljažev Dom* (ⓣ04/589-1030; May–Oct), named after the eponymous mountaineer, and the key lodge for hikers en route to Triglav. Ten minutes' walk north of the hut is a **memorial to World War II Partisan fighters**, which takes the form of a karibaner and piton. From here, a couple of paths lead off towards the summit. On a clear day, the views of Triglav's indomitable 1200-metre-high and 3km-wide north face are nothing short of spectacular.

Kot and Krma valleys and Zgornja Radovna

From Mojstrana another road cuts south towards the second and third of the glens which forge into the belly of the National Park. Three kilometres beyond the Kosma Pass (847m), one road branches off into the secluded **Kot Valley**, while the main road continues through the tiny hamlet of **ZGORNJA RADOVNA** and on to the **Krma Valley**, which, at 7km in length, is the longest of the glacial valleys in the Julian Alps. In Zgornja Radovna, at no. 25, is the **Pocar Farmhouse** (Pocarjeva Domačija; Fri–Sun 10am–5pm; 300SIT), one of six farms believed to have existed in the hamlet during feudal times. This unusually large seventeenth-century farmhouse consists of a main living area (*hiša*), bedroom (*kamra hiša*) – note the date, 1775, inscribed onto the ceiling beam – a "black" kitchen (see p.130) and, upstairs, the attic and granary room. The entire furnishings and contents of the house are all original. The

Mountain huts

Nearly a third of Slovenia's 160 **mountain huts** (Planinarski Domovi) lie within the National Park's boundaries, all managed and maintained by the **Alpine Association of Slovenia** (Planinska Zveza Slovenije or PZS). Huts range from the most basic of refuges (*zavetišče*), often without accommodation or with very few beds and sometimes no running water, to more comfortable places, namely **huts** (*koča*) or **houses** (*dom*), which vary considerably in size, quality and sleeping capacity; expect to pay around 2000SIT for a dorm bed, 2750SIT in a four-to-eight-bed room, and 3400SIT for a twin-bed – these are the maximum prices for category I huts (classified as a hut more than one hour's walk away from motorized transport) – and typically those around Triglav. A thirty-percent discount is available to UIAA-affiliated members.

Food, available at just about all huts, is usually wholesome, filling and cheap; typical staples include vegetable soup (*zelenjavna juha*; 600SIT), goulash (*golaž*; 1000SIT), and tea with lemon (*čaj z limono*; 300SIT). Owing to their high-altitude location, the majority of the park's huts are **open** between June and September, though most of those along the Vršič Pass are open year-round. However, these months aren't fixed and may deviate by a month either side depending on the weather. All huts take bookings.

two-storey, part-stone, part-wooden **outbuilding**, previously used for housing livestock and storing hay, now houses a display of farmer's implements and long wooden carts. From the farmhouse, the road east continues down through the **Radovna Valley** towards Bled, some 15km away.

There are two **campsites** (both open year-round) along the road between Kranjska Gora and Mojstrana; the larger of the two is *Camping Špik* (ⓣ04/588-0120), located at the eastern edge of Gozd Martuljek – buses stop in the centre of the village, from where it's a 400m walk east across the river; the small *Kamne* campsite (ⓣ04/589-1105) is located in **Dovje**, a small village settled on the slopes just above the main road 1km east of Mojstrana (buses stop on the main road just outside the site) – it also has two-to-five-bed bungalows (❷–❹). At the road junction is a **monument to Jakob Aljaž**, which has the local hero pointing towards Triglav.

South to the Soča Valley

Linking the Upper Sava and Soča Valleys, the **Vršič Pass** – the highest mountain pass in Slovenia – is one of the most spectacular and scenically rewarding trips anywhere in the country. Constituting the stretch of road between Kranjska Gora and Trenta – a total of some 25km – the pass is defined by some fifty hairpin bends, twenty-four on the Kranjska Gora side, twenty-six on the Trenta side (each bend is numbered and the altitude recorded). Between June and September, four daily buses haul themselves up and over the pass and down to Bovec (44km south of Kranjska Gora), and while there are regular stops at all the huts and villages along the way, this limited service makes it extremely difficult to see much in one day. Hence, it's really only feasible to see many of the places described here if you have your own transport (the road is not suitable for caravans or trailers). The other alternative, of course, is to hike to or between various points. Due to snow drifts and the threat of avalanches, the pass is periodically closed between November and April.

From Kranjska Gora to Vršič

Two kilometres south of Kranjska Gora, in the centre of a large gravel flood plain, is the artificial **Lake Jasna**, a popular excursion spot with the locals but not worth stopping off for. The road then climbs steadily up past the 1000-metre point, reaching, at turn eight (1129m), the **Russian Chapel** (Ruska kapelica), probably the most poignant sight along the pass. Set back 100m from the road, the tiny wood-latticed chapel (which cannot be entered) was built between 1916 and 1917 to commemorate the deaths of over three hundred Russian prisoners of war buried by an avalanche as they constructed the road; thousands more prisoners died from fatigue, starvation and torture during its construction, a few of whom are buried in the small **military cemetery**, set back forty metres from the road just after turn twenty-one.

Beyond this point the road becomes ever more sinuous, passing a couple of mountain huts – *Koča na Gozdu* (Ⓣ05/062-6641) and *Erjavčeva koča* (Ⓣ05/061-0031) – before arriving at **Vršič**, the highest point along the pass at 1611m; if you wish to park, you'll have to pay (300SIT). There's another hut here – *Tičarjev Dom* (Ⓣ05/063-4171; May–Oct) – and it's a good starting point for hikes into the surrounding mountains, including **Tamar**, via Vratca (1108m; 3hr 30min), and **Prisank** (2547m; 4hr 30min), though both are hikes of some difficulty.

Vršič to Trenta

The descent from Vršič to the **Trenta Valley** is every bit as dramatic as the ascent, with many an unscheduled diversion almost guaranteed – if you have wheels that is. Stationed on an exposed ledge just after turn forty-eight is a fine-looking **monument to Julius Kugy**, the esteemed mountaineer and botanist who pioneered many new routes across the Alps, and whose biography *Alpine Pilgrimage* extolled the virtues of both the mountains and those who climbed them. At the next bend, a road branches off towards the *Koča pri Izviru Soče* (Ⓣ04/586-6070; May–Oct), 2km away, and the **source of the Soča River** (Izvir Soče). From the hut it's a short, twenty-minute climb up a very rocky and partially secured path to the source – care should be taken on approaching the latter part as it can get slippery; fed by an underground lake, the water emerges from a dark cave before streaking away on its long and eventful journey to the Adriatic, some 136km downriver. Secreted away in perfect rural isolation just ten minutes' walk west of the hut (signposted) is the wonderful *Kekčeva domacija* pension and restaurant (Ⓣ05/381-1088, Ⓔkekec@siol.net; ❺), named after the legendary Slovenian children's character *Kekec*, the clever shepherd boy, created by the Kranjska Gora-born writer Josip Vandot (1883–1940) – the film, *Good luck, Kekec*, was shot here in 1963. The pension has four beautifully appointed apartments, each with an upstairs bedroom and a downstairs living area and bathroom.

Back on the main road, 400m south of the junction, is the **Mlinarica Gorge**, another magical masterpiece of nature, which takes the form of immense, overhanging rock faces and an impenetrable ravine, at the head of which is another waterfall; to get here, cross the suspension bridge and follow the footpath to the right around to the gorge entrance. Grafted onto a picturesque hillside location 2km south of the gorge is the **Alpinum Juliana** (daily May–Sept 8.30am–6.30pm; 500SIT), Slovenia's only alpine botanical garden. Founded in 1926 by Albert Bois de Chesne, a Trieste merchant and close colleague of Kugy, the garden has a fine collection of flora from the country's various alpine regions, as well as samples from the Pyrenees and Caucasus. The best time to visit is in May following the winter thaws.

Two kilometres further down the road is *Camping Trenta* (☎041/615-966), the first of several campsites between here and Bovec, all of which are open between May and October. The road continues down the narrow valley and into the village of **TRENTA**, which marks the border of the upper part of the Trenta Valley. The major point of interest here is the **Trenta Lodge** (Dom Trenta), at no. 34, which houses both the **Triglav National Park Information Centre** and the **Trenta Museum** (both daily April–Oct 10am–6pm; ☎05/388-9330; 700SIT for museum). When the centre is closed, information can be obtained from the **tourist office** just around the corner (daily 8–10am & 5–8pm). Beginning with an insightful fifteen-minute multi-vision presentation on the National Park, the museum goes on to explore, in excellent and detailed fashion, the geology and geomorphology of the park, together with displays on its indigenous flora and fauna. The exhibition then peters out somewhat with a rather flat ethnological collection, though there's a reasonably faithful attempt at a mock-up of a Trenta homestead and shepherd's dwelling. The lodge also accommodates a handful of apartments, each sleeping up to five people, with a kitchen and living space downstairs and a bedroom upstairs (❻); the lodge can also arrange private rooms in a house some 300m away (❷). Trenta is also the starting off point for assaults on Triglav's massive west face, via the **Zadnjica Valley**.

Trenta to Bovec

Ten kilometres on from Trenta is the village of **SOČA**, consisting of little more than a string of roadside houses and the **Church of St Joseph** (Cerkev Sv Jozef), renowned for Tone Kralj's 1944 painting of the devil, which here bears an uncanny resemblance to Mussolini. There are also a couple of places to stay here; the dowdy *Pension Julius* at no. 31 (☎05/388-9355; ❷), and the marginally more comfortable *Pension Lovec*, 400m further along the road at no. 19 (☎05/388-9305; ❷). Below the village, the powerful current of the Soča river has hollowed out spectacular erosion and abrasion potholes in the limestone rock, creating the fantastic 750-metre-long, fifteen-metre-deep **Velika Korita Gorge** (also called the Soča Ravine), the best views of which can be had from the swing bridge at its upper end. Here, a road branches off left towards the *Klin* **campsite** (☎05/388-9513; April–Sept) and the **Lepena Valley**; the road winds up to *Pristava Lepena* (☎05/388-9900, ⓦwww.levant.si), a self-contained complex incorporating a handful of wooden, cottage-style apartments (❼) at the edge of the forest, a riding school (2600SIT for 50min in riding ring, 3500SIT trail riding on Lipizzaners), and an expensive, but first-rate, restaurant (daily 8am–10pm); guests receive free use of the swimming pool and tennis court. *Pristava Lepena* is open between mid-March and October.

The last point of interest before exiting the park is the **Golobar Telpher Line** (Žicnica Golobar), an odd-looking, but immensely powerful, roadside contraption which was once used to transport heavy goods via overhead cables. Although this one was built in 1931 – one of the few remaining in Slovenia – telpher lines first appeared throughout the region during World War I as a means of supplying the front lines. They were later put to good use by farmers and foresters who used them to transport timber back and forth across the valley. The road descends through the lower Trenta valley and exits the park just prior to Bovec, covered in the next chapter.

Travel Details

Trains

Bled Jezero to: Bohinjska Bistrica (Mon–Fri 6 daily, Sat & Sun 4 daily; 20min); Most na Soči (Mon–Fri 6 daily, Sat & Sun 4 daily; 55min); Nova Gorica (Mon–Fri 6 daily, Sat & Sun 4 daily; 1hr 45min).
Bled Lesce to: Jesenice (every 1–3hr; 15min); Kranj (every 1–3hr; 25min); Ljubljana (every 1–3hr; 1hr); Radovljica (every 1–3hr; 5min); Škofja Loka (every 1–3hr; 35min).
Bohinjska Bistrica to: Bled Jezero (Mon–Fri 7 daily, Sat & Sun 4 daily; 20min); Most na Soči (Mon–Fri 8 daily, Sat & Sun 5 daily; 35min); Nova Gorica (Mon–Fri 8 daily, Sat & Sun 5 daily; 1hr 20min).
Kamnik to: Ljubljana (hourly; 50min).
Kranj to: Bled Lesce (every 1–3hr; 25min); Ljubljana (every 1–3hr; 35min); Radovljica (every 1–3hr; 20min); Škofja Loka (every 1–3hr; 10min).
Radovljica to: Bled Lesce (every 1–3hr; 5 min); Kranj (every 1–3hr; 20min); Ljubljana (every 1–3hr; 55min); Škofja Loka (every 1–3hr; 30min).
Škofja Loka to: Bled Lesce (every 1–3hr; 35min); Kranj (every 1–3hr; 10min); Ljubljana (every 1–3hr; 25min); Radovljica (every 1–3hr; 30min).

Buses

Bled to: Kranj (every 30min; 40min); Kranjska Gora (7 daily; 1hr 15min); Ljubljana (hourly; 1hr 15min); Radovljica (every 30min; 15min); Ribčev Laz for Lake Bohinj (hourly; 40min).
Bohinjska Bistrica to: Ribčev Laz, for Lake Bohinj (hourly; 15min).
Kamnik to: Ljubljana (Mon–Fri every 20–30min, Sat & Sun every 45min–hourly; 40–50min).
Kranj to: Bled (hourly; 40min); Ljubljana (every 30min; 50min); Radovljica (every 30min; 30min); Škofja Loka (hourly; 20min); Tržič (hourly; 20min).
Kranjska Gora to: Bled (Mon–Fri hourly; Sat & Sun 8 daily; 1hr 15min); Bovec (July & Aug 4 daily; 1hr 45min); Ljubljana (Mon–Fri hourly; Sat & Sun 8 daily; 2hr 30min) Radovljica (Mon–Fri hourly; Sat & Sun 8 daily; 1hr 25min); international bus to Tarvisio in Italy (Mon–Sat at 9.35am).
Kropa to: Radovljica (7–8 daily; 20min).
Radovljica to: Bled (every 30min; 15min); Kranjska Gora (hourly; 1hr 25min); Kropa (8 daily Mon–Fri; 20min); Ljubljana (every 30min; 1hr 15min); Ribčev Laz, for Lake Bohinj (hourly; 45min).
Ribčev Laz (Lake Bohinj) to: Bled (hourly; 40min); Bohinjska Bistrica (hourly; 15min); Ljubljana (8 daily; 1hr 45min); Stara Fužina (Mon–Fri 5 daily; 10min); Studor (Mon–Fri 5 daily; 10min).
Selca to: Škofja Loka (7 daily; 20min); Železniki (9 daily; 10min).
Stara Fužina to: Bohinjska Bistrica (Mon–Fri 6 daily; 15min); Ribčev Laz, for Lake Bohinj (Mon–Fri 5 daily; 10min).
Škofja Loka to: Cerkno (1 daily; 45min); Kranj (hourly; 20min); Ljubljana (hourly; 30min); Železniki (12 daily; 30min); Žiri (11 daily; 45min).
Tržič to: Kranj (hourly; 20min).

3

The Soča valley to the Istrian coast

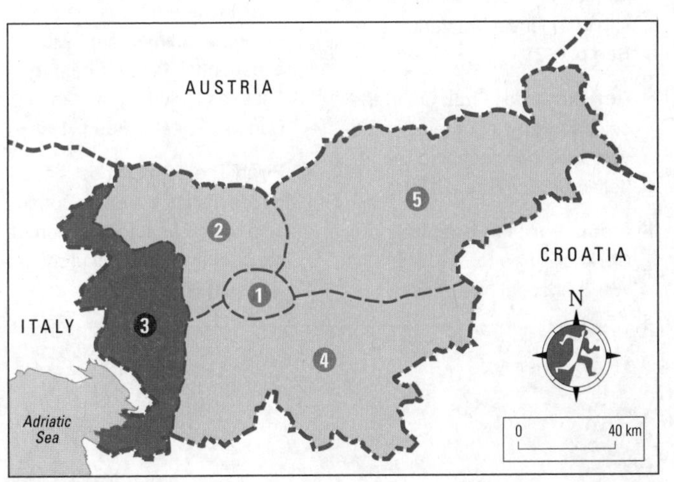

CHAPTER 3 Highlights

* **White-water rafting on the Soča** – This magical alpine river affords some of the best rafting, kayaking and canoeing in Europe. See p.155
* **Kobarid Museum** – A former European Museum of the Year winner, this compelling museum documents this region's World War I mountain battles. See p.160
* **Franko, Kobarid** – Enjoy top-rank comfort and food in this sublime pension/restaurant. See p.162
* **Goriška Brda** – Trek down the cellars of these gorgeous, vineyard-clad hills touching the Italian border. See p.172
* **Franja Partisan Hospital, Cerkno** – This former World War II hospital has been converted into a moving memorial museum. See p.181
* **Lipica Stud Farm** – Marvel at the elegant displays of the world famous Lipizzaner horses. See p.185
* **Škocjan Caves** – Take a trip through this breathtaking cave system, which features the world's largest subterranean canyon. See p.186
* **Church of the Holy Trinity, Hrastovlje** – A romanesque monument, smothered with exceptional fifteenth-century frescoes including the famous Dance of Death. See p.190
* **Piran** The coast's most beautiful resort has Venetian Gothic inspired architecture, Italianate squares and pretty churches. See p.199

△ Seventeenth-century Karst house

3

The Soča Valley to the Istrian coast

Whilst northwest Slovenia may possess the lion's share of the country's primary attractions, the thin wedge of land skirting the Italian border – known as **Primorska** – is unquestionably the country's most diverse region, constituting four geographically distinct areas, namely, from north to south, the Soča Valley, Central Primorska, the Karst, and the Coast.

Crossing over from the Julian Alps or Triglav National Park, your first encounter with this region is likely to be the imperious **Soča Valley**, whose magisterial peaks were the setting for a sustained period of crushing mountain warfare between Italian forces and the Central Powers during World War I – events which are superbly relayed in the museum in **Kobarid**, itself situated close to many of the battle sites. The valley now ranks as the country's premier adventure-sports centre, thanks both to its mountains, which embrace a continuous stream of hikers and skiers all year round, and the amazing **Soča River**, one of Europe's most scenic rivers, chock-full of rafters, canoeists and kayakers during the warmer months.

The valley's alpine peaks eventually give way to the more uniform topography of **Central Primorska**, a region defined primarily by its fertile wine and fruit-growing regions – specifically the **Vipava** and **Brda** hills, located east and west respectively of the bland, modern town of **Nova Gorica**. Central Primorska also incorporates an attractive belt of subalpine countryside (but with peaks still exceeding 1200m), sheltering the relatively little-known and under-visited towns of **Idrija** and **Cerkno**, themselves handy bases from which to take in any number of local sights, chief amongst which is the superb **Franja Partisan Hospital**. Nature asserts itself in spectacular fashion a short way south of here with the **Karst** region, whose star attractions are the jaw-dropping **Škocjan Caves** and the world-famous **Lipica Stud Farm**.

Whilst the **Slovene coast** (all 46km of it) might lack some of the glamour of its more well-heeled Croatian cousin to the south – its beaches are, for the most part, rocky, concrete or grass affairs – there is still much to enjoy. Nearly five centuries of Venetian rule have endowed its towns with some fabulous architecture, not least in its prettiest and most popular resort, **Piran**, although both **Izola** and the coast's largest town and major port, **Koper**, possess a fine kernel of medieval buildings. Those seeking more self-indulgent fare should

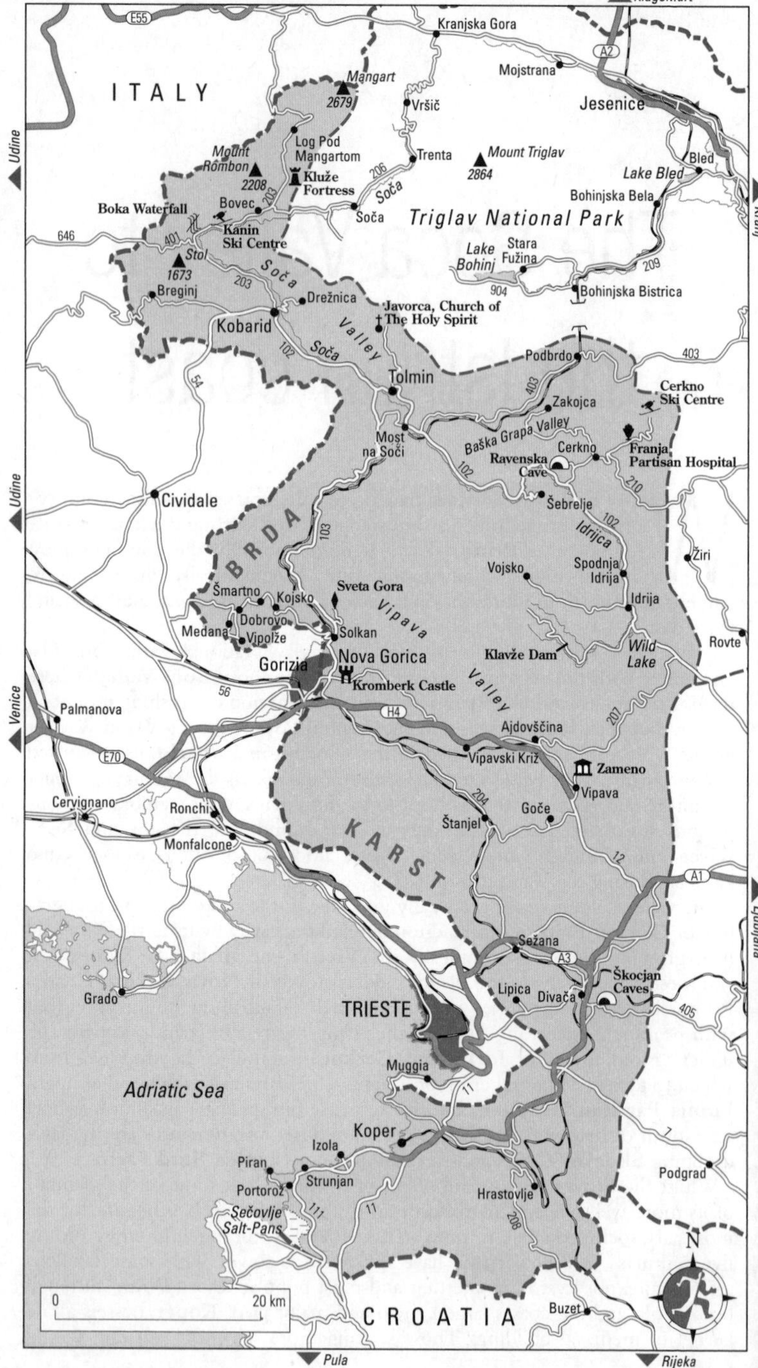
ITALY
CROATIA
Klagenfurt
Udine
Venice
Pula
Rijeka
Ljubljana
Kranj
Kranjska Gora
Mojstrana
Jesenice
Mangart
2679
Vršič
Log Pod Mangartom
Mount Rombon
2208
Kluže Fortress
Trenta
Mount Triglav
2864
Bled
Lake Bled
Bohinjska Bela
Boka Waterfall
Bovec
Kanin Ski Centre
Soča
Triglav National Park
Stol
1673
Lake Bohinj
Stara Fužina
Bohinjska Bistrica
Breginj
Drežnica
Javorca, Church of The Holy Spirit
Kobarid
Soča Valley
Tolmin
Podbrdo
Zakojca
Cerkno Ski Centre
Baška Grapa Valley
Most na Soči
Cerkno
Ravenska Cave
Franja Partisan Hospital
Šebrelje
Idrijca
Cividale
BRDA
Spodnja Idrija
Žiri
Vojsko
Idrija
Šmartno
Kojsko
Sveta Gora
Vipava
Dobrovo
Medana
Vipolže
Solkan
Rovte
Klavže Dam
Wild Lake
Gorizia
Nova Gorica
Kromberk Castle
Valley
Palmanova
Ajdovščina
Vipavski Križ
Zameno
Vipava
Cervignano
Ronchi
Goče
Štanjel
Monfalcone
KARST
Sežana
Lipica
Divača
Škocjan Caves
Grado
TRIESTE
Muggia
Adriatic Sea
Koper
Izola
Piran
Strunjan
Portorož
Hrastovlje
Podgrad
Sečovlje Salt-Pans
Buzet
0
20 km
N
E55
A2
E70
H4
A1
A3
646
401
203
206
102
54
403
209
904
210
103
56
207
204
12
405
11
7
111
208

find **Portorož**, a stone's throw from Piran and the coast's brashest resort, more to their liking. Crowds in this part of Slovenia are rarely an inconvenience, although the major coastal spots can get uncomfortably congested during August; even then, as in other parts of the region, finding accommodation should present few problems.

Getting around here shouldn't present any problems either; a healthy stream of **trains** and **buses** serve both the Karst and coast, though access up and down the Soča Valley is patchy, the rail line going no further than Most na Soči (midway between Nova Gorica and Kobarid), and bus services sporadic.

The Soča Valley

Richly textured by history and nature, the **Soča Valley**, skirting Triglav National Park's western boundary and extending all the way down to the flatlands of Nova Gorica, is one of Slovenia's most captivating regions. Although not an immediately obvious destination, the valley has few peers when it comes to sheer, stark beauty; moreover, it boasts one of Europe's most dramatic alpine rivers, the **Soča**, which commands thousands of rafters, canoeists and kayakers to its milky blue-green waters.

During World War I the valley marked the front line – known as the **Soča Front** (or Isonzo Front) – between the Italian and Austro-Hungarian armies who, for two years, engaged in some of the most savage and relentless fighting in the history of mountain warfare, leaving lands ravaged, villages wasted and an estimated one million soldiers and civilians dead. Consequently, the valley is strewn with memorial chapels, abandoned fortifications and dignified military cemeteries.

There are several key settlements sequenced in vertical fashion down the valley's spine: both **Bovec** and **Kobarid**, located in the upper part of the valley (Gornje Posočje), are important tourist hubs, the former, one of the major adventure-sports centres in the country, the latter replete with poignant reminders from the battle front, as attested to in its memorable museum. Further down the valley, the small town of **Tolmin** is worth investigating, not least because of its proximity to the fantastic **Tolminska Gorge** and stunningly located **Church of the Holy Spirit** on Javorca, while a few kilometres further south, **Most na Soči** holds some of Slovenia's most significant archeological sites. **Access** up and down the valley is, however, patchy; the closest rail line passes through Most na Soči, while infrequent buses ply the route between Tolmin and Bovec.

Bovec and around

Situated in a broad basin in the shadow of the Kanin mountain range and the mighty Mount Rombon, the small, rather faceless, alpine town of **BOVEC** is one of Slovenia's premier adventure-sports centres, its proximity to the Soča River luring rafters, kayakers and canoeists from all over Europe in their thousands –

activities so popular that they have supplanted skiing as the main source of tourist income in Bovec in recent years. For centuries, however, the town and its surrounds was an important centre for animal husbandry, its lofty alpine plateaus ideally suited for high-level pasturing, while the broad valley floor was used for growing hay. The last century was particularly unkind to Bovec: burnt down in 1903; massive destruction followed during World War I, when the town was razed and much of the population deported; and more recently, Bovec was struck by two powerful earthquakes – the first in 1976, and a second one on Easter Sunday 1998. There are several interesting attractions within close proximity to Bovec, including the magnificent **Boka Waterfall**, the **Kluže Fortress**, and, right up towards the Italian border, the pretty village of **Log Pod Mangrtom**.

The Town

As a result of the 1998 earthquake over sixty percent of the buildings in town were seriously damaged, and while most have been repaired or rebuilt, many remain in a perilous state. Walking around you'll notice a number of buildings with either a red or a yellow circle painted on them – no. 1 next to the *Letni Vrt* restaurant is a good example. Red circles indicate a building deemed to be too unsafe to be inhabited, while yellow ones denote a building requiring reconstruction.

One of those buildings seriously damaged, and one of the first to be repaired, was the **Parish Church of St Ulric** (Cerkev Sv Urh), situated 200m up the hill from the tourist office. Originally a Gothic construction, this present church was rebuilt in neo-Romanesque style in 1734, but underwent substantial reconstruction following heavy World War I damage. Although the interior retains the odd Gothic flourish, notably the portals and triumphal arch, the highlight is the reddish-brown Baroque high altar, made from marble hewn from Mount Rombon, and framed either side by sculptures of St John Nepomuk and St Paul. Unusual features of the church are the niches on the front exterior, containing statues of SS Peter, Paul and Ulric, and the headstones in the surrounding walls, which would indicate that this was the old cemetery – the current one is now located behind the church.

For those keen to learn more about the Soča Front (see box on p.160), it's possible to view a **private collection** of World War I weaponry and other objects retrieved from the battle sites. Amassed by a member of the **1313 Association** (Društvo 13-13) – an ardent group of local historians committed to honouring the men who fought on the Front – this extraordinary collection consists of a stash of weapons (grenades, shells, knives and so on), personal effects (flasks, combs and toothbrushes), and illuminating photographs of some of the battle scenes; to arrange a visit contact the tourist office. If you want to see where part of the action took place, a signposted path 1km south of Bovec (500m before the turning towards Trenta) leads towards a string of **huts**, **caverns** and **trenches**, abandoned following the cessation of fighting; many have been cleaned up and partly reconstructed but are, nevertheless, fascinating to look around. Two kilometres east of Bovec, at the crossroads of the Predel and Vršič roads, is the **Bovec military cemetery** (Vojaško Pokopališče), containing over five hundred headstones of Austrian soldiers killed near Bovec and on Mount Rombon between 1915 and 1917.

Practicalities

All **buses** terminate outside the *Letni Vrt* restaurant on the main square, Trg Golobarskih Žrtev. Just around the corner, in the community centre at no. 8, is the **tourist office** (Jan–June Mon–Fri 9am–5pm; July–Aug daily 9am–8pm; Sept–Dec Sat & Sun 9am–noon; ⓣ05/384-1919, ⓦwww.bovec.si), which has a good stock of information and maps on the Soča Valley. The **post office** is just up from the tourist office at Slomškov trg 10 (Mon–Fri 8am–7pm, Sat 8am–noon).

The best agency for private **accommodation** is Avrigo Tours, on the square at no. 47 (June–Sept Mon & Wed–Sat 8.30–11.30am & 4.30–8pm, Sun 9am–noon & 3–5pm; Oct & Nov daily 8.30am–noon & 1–4pm; Dec–May 8.30am–noon & 3.30–5pm; ⓣ05/384-1150, ⓔavrigotours.bovec@avrigo.si); they have a stack of rooms (❶) as well as apartments sleeping between two and ten people (❸–❼). Go Tours, located through the passageway next to the Mercator supermarket, is a useful backup (Mon–Fri 9am–1pm & 1.30–5pm, Sat 9am–1pm; ⓣ05/389-6366, ⓔgotour.bovec@siol.net).

The large *Alp Hotel*, located on the south side of the square, is a well-run three-star place, with neat, agreeable rooms (ⓣ05/388-6040, ⓦwww.alp-chandler.si; ❻). Barely distinguishable, but in quieter surrounds and with a pool, is the *Hotel Kanin* (ⓣ05/388-6021, ⓔhoteli.bovec@siol.net; ❻), 200m

Activities in and around Bovec

Between April and October, the **Soča River** draws water-sports enthusiasts from many countries keen to test out one of the most beautiful and challenging white-water rivers in Europe. Sections of the river are graded according to the level of difficulty – from one, the easiest, up to six, the most difficult (which is open only to experienced competition rafters); most trips depart from Boka, 6km west of Bovec, and finish at Trnovo ob Soči, 10km further downriver. A number of agencies located in Bovec and Kobarid offer rafting and a plethora of other river activities, the best of which is X-Point, based in Kobarid at Stresova 1 (ⓣ05/388-5308, ⓔx.point@siol.net). In Bovec, take your pick from: Bovec Rafting Team, located in a small hut a few paces west of the main square (ⓣ05/388-6128, ⓔbovec.rafting.team@siol.net); Soča Rafting, 100m up the hill from the tourist office (ⓣ05/389-6200, ⓦwww.arctur.si/soca.rafting); and Sport Mix, on the square at no. 18 (ⓣ05/389-6160, ⓦwww.sportmix.traftbovec.si). Each raft can take up to nine people including one instructor; whoever you go with, expect to pay around 7000SIT per person, which also covers transfers to and from the river and all equipment – just make sure you have swimming gear and a towel. Most of the agencies also offer **kayak** and **canoe** courses (around 13,000SIT for one day); alternatively, you can rent kayaks (4500SIT half-day, 5500SIT full day) and Canadian canoes, which seat two (4400SIT half-day, 6600SIT full day). Most also offer **hydrospeed** (8000SIT) and **canyoning** (9000SIT). All agencies have similar opening times (July–Sept daily 9am–7/8pm; April, May & Oct weekends only, same times).

Between April and October, the river becomes prime **fishing** territory, richly sourced with brown trout, rainbow trout, the famous marble trout (*Salmo trutta marmoratus*) and grayling. There are two types of licence; the regular one (1 day 10,150SIT, 3 days 25,200SIT, 1 week 50,925SIT), valid for the upper section of the Soča and its tributaries, and the Trophy licence (13,300SIT, 32,550SIT, 65,800SIT), which covers a three-kilometre stretch of the river in the middle part; these can be obtained from the *Alp Hotel* and the *Klin* campsite in Lepena (see p.146).

At weekends between April and October, Top Rafting offer **bungee-jumping** over the Soča (8000SIT), although this is located in Nova Gorica, some 70km away. Depending on where you fly, a twenty-minute **Tandem paragliding** flight with X-point will cost 14,000–17,000SIT. **Bikes** (700SIT 1hr, 2000SIT half-day, 2800Sit full day) and **scooters** (2200SIT 1hr, 6000SIT half-day, 7700SIT full day) can be rented from Bovec Rafting team.

north of the *Alp*. Another option, if you can get in, is the *Stari Kovač*, west of the *Alp* at Rupa 3 (ⓣ05/388-6699, ⓦwww.starikovac.com; ❺), which possesses four very comfortable and well-furnished apartments. There are, somewhat excessively, four **campsites** located on the edge of town, all of which are open between April and October. The closest, and smallest, is the grubby *Polovnik* (ⓣ05/288-6069), 500m southwest of the *Kanin Hotel*. Two kilometres further south, there are three sites bunched together: the first is *Vodenca* (ⓣ041/620-885); 200m down the hill is *Kayak Kamp Toni* (ⓣ05/388-6454), the best equipped of the sites and frequented almost exclusively by kayakers due to its proximity to the water; behind here is the smaller *Liza* site (ⓣ05/389-6370).

Bovec is woefully bereft of **places to eat**; the best food is to be had at *Sovdat*, 50m west of the square at no. 24, which does a reasonably varied choice of moderately priced steak and fish dishes, as well as a smattering of veggie options. Of the two pizzerias, *Stari Kovač*, at Rupa 3, and *Letni Vrt*, on the main square (closed Tues), the former does better pizzas and is a touch more atmospheric.

Similarly, there are few **drinking** venues of note, though the *Pink Panter* (daily 5pm–1am) up the hill from the church at Kaninska Vas 7, is the most enjoyable place to sup a beer, while *Café Plec* opposite the tourist office (daily 5pm–1am), draws a slightly younger clientele. The *Alp Hotel's* terrace café is also worth stopping off at and there's a delicious ice-cream parlour here too. If you're looking for an unusual **souvenir** gift the Galerija Čopi (Mon–Sat 10am–2pm & 5–8pm), on the western side of the square at no. 47, sells a superb range of framed and painted beehive panels.

Skiing and hiking around Bovec

Not only do the Kanin mountains offer the highest-altitude skiing in Slovenia (around 2300m), but there are slopes here for skiers of all abilities. The **Kanin ski centre** is based in the hamlet of **Dvor**, 1km southwest of Bovec (ⓣ05/389-9310, ⓔkanin@siol.net). The modern, four-seater **cable cars** transport passengers to the upper station (station D; 2200m) in thirty minutes (daily: winter 8am–4pm; nonstop; July & Aug same times, every 2hr; 2300SIT return); be warned, this ride is not for the jittery. In summer, the sun-bleached rocks and boulders make for a rather bleak scene, but the views on a cloudless day are sensational – there's a basic restaurant at the top too.

If you're not here to ski, or have just come up to have a look around, then there are a number of excellent **hikes** to consider; one of the easiest, though not particularly well-marked, paths is to **Prestreljenik** (2499m; 1hr 30min), with more demanding paths to **Visoki Kanin** (2587m; 3hr 30min) – on a clear day it's possible to see the Adriatic from here – and **Rombon** (2208m; 5hr). The one hut in these mountains is the *Dom Petra Skalarja na Kaninu*, a short walk south of the upper station (mid-July to Aug weekends only; ⓣ05/388-6139). All the above hikes are doable from Bovec itself, but, with the exception of Rombon (5hr from Bovec), you should count on an additional four hours at least for each. The excellent 1:50,000 map *Posočje*, available from the tourist office, will help you get your bearings. The X-Point agency (see p.155) organizes a number of guided hikes and walks, beginning at the *Alp Hotel* in Bovec – by way of example, a typical full-day hike (8hr) to Krn Lake (including transfers) costs around 7000SIT.

Boka Waterfall

The most popular local attraction is the thundering 106-metre-high and thirty-metre-wide **Boka Waterfall** (Slap Boka), located 6km southwest of Bovec just prior to the village of **Žaga**. While it's possible to see the waterfall from the main road (albeit at quite some distance), close-up views can be obtained by scrambling along two trails located by the **Boka Bridge** (Most Boka), each offering very different perspectives of Slovenia's highest permanent waterfall: the trail beginning at the west side of the bridge – which provides a head-on view – is the shorter and easier of the two paths, but does involve a fair amount of clambering over boulders; the far more difficult second route, beginning at the east side of the bridge, ascends to a spot above the head of the falls. Emanating from a deep karst spring in the Kanin mountains, the Boka is a stupendous sight, highly dependent upon precipitation and snow-melt from the Kanin plateaus for its massive volume of water – hence the best time to view it is in late spring.

Kluže Fortress

Four kilometres north of Bovec, back inside Triglav National Park on the road towards Log pod Mangrtom and the Predel Pass, stands the formidable-looking **Kluže Fortress** (Trdnjava Kluže; July & Aug 9am–1pm & 4–7pm). Strategically positioned on a steep rock face overlooking the impressive sixty-metre deep Koritnica gorge, this chunky grey fortress is now little more than a desolate, crumbling shell, though it has seen more than its fair share of action over the years.

Although a wooden fortification was built here in the fifteenth century, it's believed that some kind of fortress existed on this site during Roman times, a theory predicated on the fact that a Roman road ran through the nearby Predel Pass, connecting the northern and southern parts of the Empire. The wooden fortification was supplanted by a stone construction in 1613, during which time it successfully repelled repeated Turkish attacks, before Napoleon's French marauders razed it in 1797. Its current appearance dates from 1882, though the upper part – named Fort Hermann after the hero of the 1809 Battle of Predel – was demolished by heavy and sustained shelling during World War I. Although there's now nothing of substance to see inside, the fortress does stage periodic exhibitions and it's also used as a summer venue for classical and rock concerts, as well as for re-enactments of battle scenes performed by the 1313 Association; check with the tourist office in Bovec for events (see p.155).

Log pod Mangrtom and Mangart Mountain

Nestling under the Mangart mountain range 6km north of Kluže is the pretty village of **LOG POD MANGRTOM**, which actually comprises the two adjoining settlements of **Spodnji Log** (Lower Log) and **Gorenji Log** (Upper Log). As if the 1998 earthquake wasn't enough, the village had to contend with an even greater catastrophe during the night of 16–17 November 2000, when a crushing **landslide** – believed to have been caused by a combination of torrential rainfall and significant seismological activity in the area – struck. The landslide began some 1000m further up in the Mangartski mountains and coursed down the valley slopes and along the bed of the Predelnica River in a matter of seconds, before smashing into the upper settlement. The impact was such that seven people lost their lives – one person was never found – and a number of houses and farm buildings were wiped out or irreparably damaged.

At the reconstructed metal bridge, where the devastation is still very much in evidence, the aftermath of the event is documented by several photos pinned to a board. If you have your own transport, you can drive up to the top of the pass, and another reconstructed bridge, to see where the slide began. Just beyond the bridge, the main road continues onwards to Italy, while another –

the country's highest mountain road – branches off towards the **Mangart Saddle** (2072m), below which is the *Koča na Mangartskem sedlu* (Ⓣ050/630-863; July–Sept). Two hours' walk from the hut is the magnificent **Mount Mangart** (2679m), Slovenia's third highest peak and known for its reddish-coloured sandstone.

Back in Gorenji Log, the **Parish Church of St Stephen** contains a ceiling fresco by Ivan Grohar, entitled *The Stoning of St Stephen*, and a wooden Gothic statue of Queen Mary dating from the end of the fifteenth century. Midway between the two settlements, just behind the small civilian cemetery, lies a **World War I military cemetery** – one of the few in the region preserved in its original form – with neat rows of black iron crosses on mounds denoting the final resting places of nearly nine hundred Austrian soldiers killed on Mount Rombon and Mount Čuklja. The monument in the centre of the cemetery features two soldiers, one an Austrian, the other a Bosnian, gazing up to the summit of Rombon. Just to the west of the cemetery is a now disused **mining tunnel**, over 4km long, which villagers used to travel through in order to reach the lead and zinc mines at Cave del Predil in Italy; it was also used to supply the army with materials during the war.

There are a couple of **places to stay** in the village: in the lower settlement, the *Motel Encijan* at no. 31 (Ⓣ05/384-5130, Ⓕ384-5131) has basic but pleasant rooms (❷) and apartments (❹), as well as a tennis court; in the upper settlement, the *Gostišče Mangrt* at no. 57 has just three rooms (Ⓣ05/388-6024; ❷) – its comely little **restaurant** offers excellent home-style Slovenian cooking, such as the local speciality *Čompe*, a delicious combination of potato, hard cheese and cottage cheese (July & Aug daily 10am–10pm; Sept–June Mon & Wed–Sun 10am–10pm). Unfortunately, there is no public transport from Bovec to Log pod Mangrtom, so you'll have to cycle, hitch or walk.

Kobarid and around

"A little white town with a campanile in a valley", was how American writer Ernest Hemingway described **KOBARID** in *Farewell to Arms* in 1929, and though it has retained its pleasantly relaxed air, this good-looking town 21km south of Bovec has had a pretty rum time of it over the years. In October 1917, the nearby Krn mountain range was the chief battleground for one of the war's most decisive military engagements – otherwise known as the twelfth offensive – in which the Italians were routed by the combined Central Powers of Germany and Austria, an event superbly documented in the town's gripping museum. The interwar years were defined by nationalist struggles on both sides, but Kobarid (then Caporetto) remained, as did much of the region, under Italian control until the end of World War II.

Although it retains a strong Italianate flavour – the border is just 9km to the west – much of the town's present appearance dates from 1976 following the massive earthquake. Aside from its museum, and a superb selection of restaurants, its proximity to the Soča River and a stack of other historical and natural sights means that Kobarid could quite easily detain you for a day or two.

Arrival, information and accommodation

All **buses** stop opposite the church on Trg svobode. The **post office** is located next to the *Hotel Hvala* on the south side of the square (Mon–Fri 8am–6pm, Sat 8am–noon). There's no **tourist office** in Kobarid but the staff in the

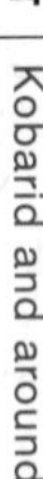

museum can assist with any enquiries as well as provide literature and maps (same opening times as museum; ⓣ05/389-9200, ⓦwww.kobarid.si). They can also book **rooms** (❷) both in the town and the villages of Drežnica (see p.163) and Trnovo ob Soči, 5km north. The town's single **hotel** is the beautifully appointed, family-run *Hotel Hvala*, on the main square at no. 1 (ⓣ05/389-9300, ⓦwww.topli-val-sp.si; ❺), whose rooms are remarkably good value. In addition, there are two first-class pension-style places; on the east side of the square at no. 11, the *Kotlar* (ⓣ05/389-1110; ❺) has six simple, but exquisitely furnished, rooms, each with sumptuous designer beds – it also houses a kidney-shaped top-floor pool which is free to guests. Located 3km west of town in the settlement of **Staro Selo**, *Hiša Franko*, at Staro Selo 1 (ⓣ05/389-4120, ⓦwww.hisafranko.com; ❻), simply oozes class; the highly original and idiosyncratic rooms are furnished with finely cut drapes, bamboo and other such exotic materials, and each has a safe, minibar and stereo (TV if desired); there are also a handful of older rooms in the building opposite (❸).

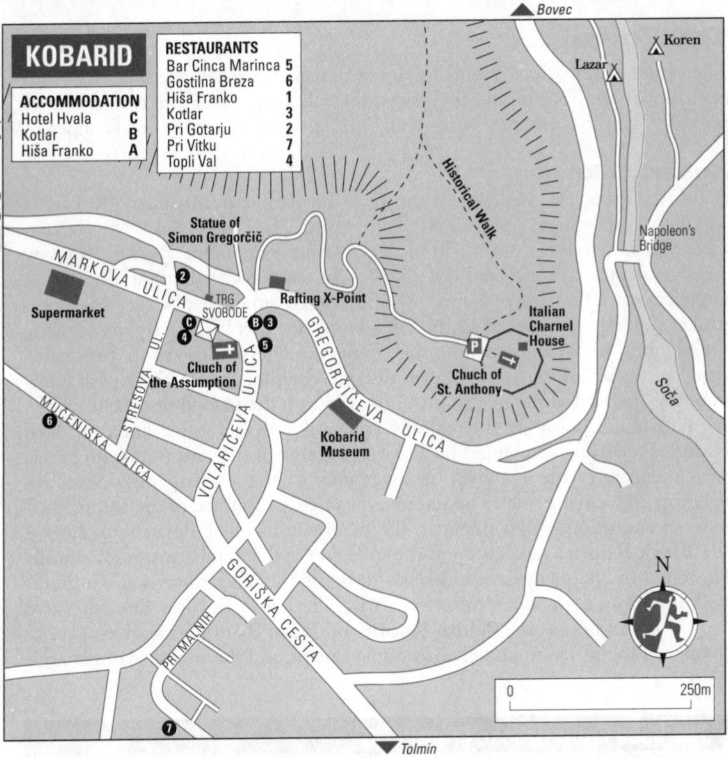

The town's two **campsites** (both open March–Oct) are located down by the Soča River, 500m east of town on the road towards Drežnica; *Camp Lazar* (ⓣ05/388-5333), on the west bank of the river, is a small site with good, clean facilities and a ranch-style bar, while the larger *Camp Koren* (ⓣ05/389-1311), across Napoleon's Bridge on the opposite bank, has similar facilities as well as a market.

The Town

The centre of Kobarid is essentially the small main square, where the main roads from Bovec and Tolmin, and the road from Italy, converge. From the square, it's no more than five minutes' walk to any of the town's attractions or facilities.

Kobarid Museum

A former European Museum of the Year, the **Kobarid Museum** (Kobariški Muzej; April–Sept Mon–Fri 9am–6pm, Sat & Sun 9am–7pm, Oct–March Mon–Fri 10am–5pm, Sat & Sun 9am–6pm; 700SIT, ⓦwww.kobariski-muzej.si), situated in the lovely two-storey Baroque house at Gregorčičeva 10 – once owned by the naval commander Sergej Mašera – evokes superbly the horrors of the Soča Front (see box below). Before viewing the exhibits, it's worth watching the twenty-minute **multi-vision presentation** on the Soča Front (in the form of rapid-fire slides and with English commentary), located in the first room to the right on the second floor. Otherwise, the remaining rooms are thematically arranged: up on the first floor, the **Krn Range Room** is represented by a vast map-relief of the Krn mountain range, which illustrates the complex arrangements of the military positions confronting the warring sides. The photographs here, as in most of the rooms, provide an exceptional supplement to the main exhibits. The next room along – the **Black Room** – reflects upon the suffering of the combatant, as graphically illustrated by the pictures of hideously disfigured soldiers; there is also a graffitied door from the military prison in Smast village near Kobarid. The other two rooms on this floor – the **White Room** and **Rear Room** – are given over to themes of mobilization and civilian displacement, and the nightmarish struggle

The Soča Front (Izonso Front)

When the Italians declared war on the Central Powers in May 1915, the Great War assumed a new and altogether more brutal dimension. This fresh battlefield, part of which extended for some 90km from Mount Rombon, north of Bovec, through Kobarid to a position a short way north of Trieste (Trst) on the Adriatic coast, was known as the **Soča Front** (Izonso Front).

Although the Austro-Hungarians, under the command of the "Soča Lion", General Svetozar Borojevič von Bojna, had already fortified the front, the Italians secured immediate success, capturing Kobarid and the nearby Krn range. More than two years and eleven debilitating and futile offensives later, the two heavily entrenched sides prepared for the denouement. With severely depleted troop numbers, Austrian Emperor Charles I approached the German Kaiser Wilhelm II for reinforcements, and together, they formed the fourteenth Austro-German army. Their breakthrough plan, "Faith in Arms", was based on swiftly coordinated lightning strikes and the element of surprise; in this case, thousands of troops and armoury were quickly repositioned between Bovec and Tolmin.

Effected on October 24, 1917, this **twelfth offensive** – the first counteroffensive by the Central Powers – resulted in the Italian army being pressed all the way back to the Friulian Plain and the Piave River, an episode acknowledged as the greatest single breakthrough of the war and the first successful "blitzkrieg" in the history of European warfare. Fighting continued around the Piave River for another year, the outcome of which was victory for the Italians. With an estimated million fatalities on all sides, a significant number of whom were women and children, the human cost was catastrophic; moreover many thousands more were forced to flee the region, only a fraction of whom returned at the war's end.

for survival in the mountains during the ferociously cold winter months. As an interesting aside, the two rooms behind the Krn room hold a collection of local archeological finds, the most fascinating exhibits being some delicate bronze statuettes unearthed from Gradič Hill.

On the second floor, the room with the **map-relief** of the Upper Soča region clearly identifies both the positions of the warring troops throughout the valley prior to the twelfth offensive, and the awesome volume of military machinery required for this attack; this room leads through to a mock-up **cavern**, in which a wistful young soldier pens one last letter to his father. The central **Breakthrough Room** considers the events pertaining to the critical breakthrough operation of 24–27 October 1917, featuring a hoard of hellish-looking weaponry.

Parish Church of the Assumption

On the south side of Trg Svobode, the ordered **Parish Church of the Assumption** (Cerkev Marijino vnebovzetje) is bestowed with some terrific artwork. The striking red and white marble high altar, designed by Lazzarini in 1716, features a handful of sculpted saints and angels, but is more interesting for what you can't see. Concealed behind the altar picture is a late fifteenth-century statue of the Holy Mother, which is only revealed on special religious occasions or, if you're lucky, upon request; ask at the priest's house opposite the church entrance. To commemorate the pope's visit to Slovenia in 1996 (although he didn't actually visit Kobarid) the balcony was blanketed with a beautiful canvas, and is notable for its paintings of several eminent historical characters, including the pope himself. The stained-glass windows were installed as recently as 1995 in order to lighten the church interior. Opposite the church is an oversized **sculpture of Simon Gregorčič** (1844–1906), the beloved Slovenian priest and poet who hailed from nearby **Vrsno**.

Kobarid historical walk

For a real flavour of Kobarid's historical, cultural and natural heritage, you should participate in the **Kobarid Historical Walk** (Kobariška Zgodovinska Pot), an enjoyable five-kilometre stroll taking in wartime monuments, abandoned fortifications, bridges and waterfalls. A free leaflet outlining the route, and the key sights along the way, is available from the museum – a gently paced walk, including stops for viewing, should take between three and four hours.

Beginning on the north side of the main square, Trg svobode, a winding road lined with the stations of the cross ascends to Gradič Hill and the **Italian Charnel House**, perhaps the valley's most evocative monument, especially when viewed from afar (note that it's possible to drive up to this point, but no further). The Charnel House – opened in 1938 with Mussolini in attendance – consists of three-tiered octagons tapering upwards towards the **Church of St Anthony**, in itself nothing outstanding. Inside the huge ossuary lie the remains of more than seven thousand Italian soldiers killed during fighting on the Soča Front, the names of whom are engraved onto the slabs of greenish serpentine inside the large niches. From the Charnel House, take the path to the left which forks off into the woods – hereafter, the route is marked with red arrows and the museum logo – and onwards to the remains of the ancient fort of **Tonočov Grad**, unique in that it was occupied continuously from the middle Stone Age, through Antiquity to the Middle Ages; there was also once a significant settlement of some twenty houses and several churches located here. The site is currently a bit of a mess due to ongoing research projects.

From the fort, the path continues down towards the main road, which you should cross carefully, before a knee-jarring descent down to the Soča River – en route you'll pass a section of the **Italian Line of Defence**, one of three constructed by the Italians on the Soča Front during World War I; the trail then continues along a track in the direction of the *Koren* campsite, but you should take the path to the left which opens up into the **Soča Gorge** and a sturdy swing bridge, this one having replaced the original from World War I. From the bridge – where there are terrific views of the gorge and river – it's a twenty-minute walk to most people's favourite part of the circuit, the **Kozjak waterfall** (Slap Kozjak), a graceful, fifteen-metre-high waterfall less impressive for its height than its atmospheric cave-like hall carved out of the surrounding rock. From here, retrace your steps and take the path that forks left up to a **small fortress** and another **line of defence**, scattered with yet more caverns, shelters and observation posts.

The path then cuts inland, passing the campsite and winding up at the **Napoleon Bridge** (Napoleonov Most), an elegant, stone-arched structure connecting the two banks of the river at one of the narrowest and most spectacular points of the gorge. The original bridge was built in 1750 and later named after the eponymous French leader after he marched across it en route to the Predel Pass. The day after World War I was declared, the bridge was blown up by retreating Austrians, though this didn't deter the Italians who first built a wooden, then an iron bridge, while this one was completed after the war.

Eating and drinking

Few places in the country, of any size, can boast such a surfeit of distinguished **restaurants** as Kobarid, which may explain why the town is so popular with neighbouring Italians. With one budget exception, the restaurants listed here offer first-class cuisine, exemplary service and an enjoyable atmosphere, though they don't come cheap. More predictably, the drinking options in such a small place are very limited, though there are one or two pleasant cafes around the centre.

Gostilna Breza Mučeniška ulica 17. Secreted away 300m south of the main square, this restful place serves up the most traditional Slovene food in town; the interior's subtle green colour scheme, wood-beamed ceiling and ceramic stove is complemented by the smart summery terrace. Mon–Wed & Fri–Sun 11am–10pm.

Franko Staro Selo 1. Come here if you only have the time to eat in one place in Kobarid: a breathtakingly imaginative menu features dishes such as trout sushi in leek for starters, and, for mains, thorn rabbit meat with couscous or blueberry pasta with fine bear ragout. Also available is a tasting menu for 8000SIT. Wine buffs will be in their element with some 600 bottles to select from. The restaurant itself, with bright orange painted walls, looks fantastic. March–Oct & Dec–Jan Tues–Sun noon–3pm & 7–11pm; also closed Tues throughout Nov & Feb.

Kotlar Trg svobode 11 ☎05/389-1110. Along with the *Topli Val*, this is one of the country's finest fish restaurants, with a menu almost exclusively devoted to seafood; the beautifully lit interior features a curvaceous, nautically themed bar with blue drapings – all in all, a divine eating experience. Reservations advised. Mon & Wed–Sun noon–11pm, until midnight Fri & Sat; closed Wed also in summer.

Pri Vitku Pri Malnik 41. For those on a somewhat tighter budget, this small, rather downbeat pizzeria, located in a residential area south of town (follow the signs), should suffice. Mon–Fri 9.30am–midnight, Sat & Sun noon–midnight.

Topli Val Trg svobode 1. Despite now having a serious rival in the *Kotlar*, the classy "Warm Wave" restaurant (in the *Hotel Hvala*) is the town's most established place, with a fish menu regarded as one of the country's finest – Soča trout and mussels are just two of its specialities. Daily noon–10pm.

Drinking

The best place for a **coffee** is the *Bar Cinca Marinca*, located on the west side of the square next to the *Kotlar*, while the rather arrogantly staffed *Okrepčevalnica Soča*, opposite the *Hotel Hvala*, is a popular café with a good **ice-cream** parlour. For more vigorous drinking make your way to *Pri Gotarju*, a cosy **bar** opposite the Mercator supermarket (daily 6am–11pm, until midnight Fri & Sat). If you don't mind a little walk, then you could always head down to the lively bar at *Camp Lazar* (see p.159).

Around Kobarid: Drežnica and Breginj

Dramatically situated under the sunny slopes of the Krn mountain range 6km north of Kobarid, the peaceful little village of **DREŽNICA** is renowned for its **Shrovetide Carnival**, one of the most enjoyable local events in Slovenia. Taking place at the end of February, it's a kind of mini-Kurent (see box on p.300), starring a procession of masked figures (known as *psti*), who cut a dash through town, visiting houses and causing much good-natured mayhem; the day concludes with much drinking and dancing.

Towering over the village is the oversized neo-Romanesque **Church of the Sacred Heart**, which, despite its prominent position, survived remarkably unscathed during the fighting in these parts during World War I. Dating from 1911, this church replaced one pulled down a few years earlier and features a capacious, pastel-coloured tripartite nave smothered in frescoes, the most celebrated of which is *The Sacred Heart*, a dual effort by Avgust Černigoj and Zoran Mušič. Note too, above the main entrance, the mosaic representing the Good Shepherd, completed by Kokalj in 1981. The village has some good **accommodation** possibilities – enquire either at the museum in Kobarid (see p.160), or wander the narrow streets in search of signs. From the village it's a four-hour hike up to **Mount Krn** (2244m). To get to Drežnica from Kobarid, you'll have to cycle, walk or hitch.

Until the earthquake in 1976, the village of **BREGINJ**, 15km west of Kobarid, was unique for its highly unorthodox street layout, whereby houses were conjoined in oval fashion, joined to a stable and hayloft and connected by wooden galleries known as *gank*. The one building left standing, or at least not so badly damaged that it couldn't be reconstructed, has been converted into a nameless **museum** (no set times; the key can be obtained from no. 119 behind the museum; 300SIT), located in the centre of the village and sign-posted from the main road. This building, fairly representative of most of the village before the earthquake, comprises three separate, but interconnected, dwellings, each with four, almost identically sized rooms. Although it's not clear when these Mediterranean-style buildings date from exactly, it's believed that they were first inhabited around the beginning of the eighteenth century. The exhibition room has some superb aerial photos, depicting the village as it was both before and after the earthquake – you could easily be forgiven for thinking that these were two different places. Ongoing restoration should eventually see the inclusion of a restaurant and possibly some apartments. There is public transport, albeit limited, from Kobarid, with three **buses** on Mondays, Wednesdays and Fridays.

Tolmin and around

Travelling south from Kobarid, the valley flattens out markedly before reaching **TOLMIN** some 14km further on. As the valley's administrative centre it's not an especially appealing place – most people come here to catch or change buses – but it does conceal a handful of worthwhile sights, whilst it also serves as an excellent jumping-off point for a couple of attractions just inside Triglav National Park a short way north, namely the fabulous **Tolmin Gorge**, and the **Church of the Holy Spirit** in Javorca. Furthermore, it's home to one of the country's most exciting and colourful music festivals, the **Soča Reggae Riversplash**.

The Town

Wedged between the *Hotel Krn* and *Pension Rutar* on Mestni trg is the **Tolmin Museum** (Tolminski Muzej; Tues–Fri 10am–4pm, Sat & Sun 1–5pm; 500SIT; ⓦwww.tol-muzej.si), housed in the Coronini Mansion, formerly the home of the noble sixteenth-century Coronini family. The museum's centrepiece is its treasure-trove of **archeological finds**, excavated from a grave in Most na Soči between 1999 and 2001 (see p.166); the most extraordinary discovery was a clay greek owl skyphos (a drinking cup) from Attica, an exquisite piece featuring one horizontal and one vertical handle, to the side of which is a painted owl, now the museum symbol. Look out too for the bronze handle of a patera in the form of a ram's head, the ornamented clay pythos (a pottery urn) – which, when discovered, contained charred human remains – and a necklace composed of glass and bronze beads. The remainder of the museum is given over to a modest **art history** collection, the most notable exhibit being the wall painting of *Our Lady of Mercy* (1886), rescued from a house in Breginj following the earthquake in 1976 (see p.163); and some lovely **folk art** exhibits, including painted chests, cradles and beehive panels, and masks from the Drežnica (see p.163) and Laufarji (see p.181) carnivals.

Two kilometres south of town, down by the Soča River, is the tiny and undistinguished-looking **German Charnel House** (Nemška kostnica), completed in 1936 from German materials and containing the remains of over one thousand German soldiers killed during the twelfth offensive (see box, p.160). Beyond the forged grill that divides the space inside, the names of the dead are beautifully engraved mosaic-style on three walls – the key to the house can be obtained from the museum. To get here follow the tarmac road to its conclusion, then take a right turn along the asphalt track.

If you've got further energy to expend, then you might consider tackling **Kozlov Rob**, a 426-metre-high mound located 1km northwest of town, atop of which are the substantial remains of a Middle Ages fort. To get to the base of the hill it's a fifteen-minute walk along Brunov drevored, the road which forks left by the Church of St Ulric, located a short way north of Mestni trg; from here it's a pleasantly exhausting forty-minute, zigzagging climb to the top, which comes as a bit of a disappointment owing to the thicket of shrubs and weeds smothering the fort – even the views of the town and Soča River are heavily obscured by the shield of trees. Once fortified by four gigantic towers, Kozlov Rob (meaning "Goat's Edge") is believed to originate from around the twelfth century, when it was fought over by various factions, including the Venetian and then the Habsburg monarchies. The fort underwent several restoration projects thereafter, the last of which occurred under the auspices of the Dornberg family at the beginning of the seventeenth century, after which time the Corinni family took control and the fort fell into a long-term state of dilapidation; despite periodic excavation works, it has pretty much remained that way ever since.

Practicalities

The **bus station** is located in the centre of town on the main through road, Trg maršala Tita. Three hundred metres southwest of here, just beyond Mestni trg at Petra Skalarja 4, is the **tourist office** (Mon–Fri 9am–noon & 2–7.30pm, Sat & Sun 9am–noon & 5–8pm; ⓣ05/381-0084, ⓦwww.lto-sotocje-tolmin.si); they've also got one screen for Internet access (free) and can book **private accommodation** (❶) in town and the surrounding villages. They also sell the excellent 1:50,000 *Turistični Zemljevid Kobarid Tolmin* map (1500SIT). The **post office** is 100m west of the bus station (Mon–Fri 8am–7pm, Sat 8am–noon).

The two places to **stay** are located opposite each other on Mestni trg; the friendly *Hotel Krn* (ⓣ05/388-1911, ⓦwww.hotel-krn.com) has spacious, tidy rooms (❺), as well as a stock of older, rather careworn rooms (❹). More agreeable is the lovely lime-green *Pension Rutar* opposite (ⓣ05/380-0500, ⓦwww.pension-rutar.com; ❺), which has eight supremely comfortable, air-conditioned rooms, all of which can sleep three; it also houses the best **restaurant** in town, offering fresh Italian cuisine and first-class service, all at a very affordable price – it's quite small though, and very popular, so get in early (closed Thurs); otherwise the restaurant in the *Krn* should suffice, or alternatively, try the more down-at-heel *Pri Kranjcu* at Trg 1 maja 3, 200m east of the tourist office. The choice **drinking** venues are the fairly pumping *Paradiso*, next to the post office, and the more restful *M Bar*, opposite the tourist office.

The Maya sports agency, 100m west of Mestni trg at Ulica Padlih borcev 1 (April–Oct July & Aug daily 8am–8pm; ⓣ05/381-0060, ⓦwww.maya-bn.si), offer a welter of **activities**, including the usual water sports plus mountain bike trips (4800SIT one day), and excursions to Dante's Cave (5500SIT; see below) – for water-bound activities, expect to pay the same prices as you would do at those agencies in Bovec (see box on p.155). One of the country's more internationally oriented music events, featuring an impressive line-up of both domestic and international artists – recent performers have included Buju Banton and Lee Scratch Perry – is the four-day **Soča Reggae Riversplash Festival**, which takes place in mid-July down by the banks of the Soča, 3km south of town. Four-day tickets can be bought in advance through ⓦwww.vinylmaniarecords.si, and cost 9000SIT, or on the day for 10,000SIT (from the stage only); day tickets cost 3000SIT, but can only be purchased on the day. It's possible to camp here during the festival, but not at any other time of the year.

Tolminska Gorge and Church of the Holy Spirit

If you have the time and inclination, there are two wonderful excursions in the vicinity of Tolmin to consider, both of which are easily reached by car or foot. Forty-five minutes' walk north of town (it's all signposted), the **Tolminska Gorge** (Tolminska Korita) – the lowest point of Triglav National Park (180m) and its southernmost entry point – is as wild and spectacular as anything else the park has to offer. From the entrance, just up from the snack bar, there are several rather confusing signs pointing to various sections of the gorge. However, the best way forward is to head straight along the road and through the tunnel to the vertiginous **Hudičev Most** (Devil's Bridge), looming some 60m above the magnificent ravine. Approximately 500m on from the bridge, just after the bend in the road, is the **Zadlaška Cave**, also known as **Dante's Cave**, for it was here that the poet supposedly found the inspiration for his terrifying inferno images in the *Divine Comedy* – the caves are closed but can be visited on a guided tour through the Maya agency in Tolmin (see above).

Backtracking 200m or so down the road, steps lead down to a couple of paths which fork – take the left path down the **Zadlascica gorge** and after 400m, where the path ends, you'll chance upon the gorge's most bizarre feature,

Glava Medved ("Bear's Head"), a huge triangular-shaped boulder wedged between two rock faces. Caution should be exercised here as the paths can get very slippery. Retracing your steps back to the fork, a couple of paths head down to the river; at this point you'll probably get lost among the twisting paths, secret tunnels and swing bridges, but it's all good fun and you're never far from the nearest path out.

From the gorge it's a twenty-minute drive (or a 2hr walk) up a mainly asphalt track that ascends to Javorca (571m) – if coming by car, you'll have to walk the last 500m or so, as the road is too narrow and rocky. Nestled on a panoramic terrace, with resplendent views across the Tolmin Valley, the half-stone, half-wooden **Church of the Holy Spirit** (Cerkev Sv Duha; June–Aug daily 10am–5pm; May & Sept Sat & Sun 10am–5pm; 300SIT) was built in 1916 by soldiers of the Austro-Hungarian army. Approaching via the stone staircase – which replaced the previous one damaged in the 1998 earthquake – the first thing you'll notice is the remarkably well-preserved coats-of-arms (22 in all), representing the various regions of the Austro-Hungarian Empire. The interior, meanwhile, is striking for its bold Secessionist-style decoration, painted in just four colours, black, blue, white and gold, and the wall-covered wooden panels, onto which the names of more than three thousand soldiers have been scorched. There is also a small collection of rusting World War I weaponry just inside the church entrance.

Most na Soči

Located on a rocky ledge at the confluence of the Soča and Idrijca rivers 5km south of Tolmin, **MOST NA SOČI** (formerly St Lucija) was once one of the most important prehistoric settlements in Slovenia, as evidenced by its exceptional hoard of archeological finds from the Bronze and Iron Ages through to the early Middle Ages. Since the former rector of St Lucija, Tomaž Rutar, began excavations in the mid-nineteenth century, some seven thousand graves and architectural remains including 35 Hallstatt dwellings have been discovered in the surrounding area; further recent digs have unearthed yet more finds, such as, in 2002, forty Roman Graves (5 BC–2 AD). You can see a selection of these finds on display at the Tolmin Museum (see p.164), while other items are kept in Nova Gorica, Trieste and Vienna. A partial reconstruction of one of the Hallstatt dwellings, discovered during the 1970s and 1980s, is housed in the small **Archeological Museum** (Halštatska hiša; July & Aug Sat & Sun 1–5pm, other times call the tourist information centre or museum in Tolmin; 300SIT), located in one room of a school at no. 18, in the centre of town. Disappointingly, neither this nor the remainder of the exhibits have English labelling.

Next to the museum, the former Gothic, but now Baroque, **Parish Church of St Lucy** (Cerkev Sv Lucija) is worth a glimpse for its exceptional range of artwork by Tone Kralj. Not only did he paint the allegory of St Lucy and the Apostles on the ceiling, but also the eight paintings in the presbytery representing the life and martyrdom of the same saint; and the fantastically colourful oil pictures of the Way of the Cross in the nave. For good measure he completed the four wall statues. Much like the private collection in Bovec (see p.154), the **Soča Front Museum** (Mali Muzej Soške Fronte), a few paces west of the petrol station at no. 53, harbours a comprehensive stash of weaponry from both the Italian and Austrian armies – these items were retrieved from the Tolmin region. To arrange a visit call ⓣ05/388-7045, or contact the tourist office in Tolmin (see p.165).

Most na Soči is on the rail line between Jesenice and Nova Gorica, and is the last stop for the **car-train** from Bohinjska Bistrica; the station is located 1.5km southeast of town, across the bridge.

Baška Grapa Valley

If you have your own transport, and an hour or two to spare, take a ride through the lovely **Baška Grapa Valley**, which meanders eastwards from Most na Soči joining up with the **Selščica Valley** some 30km distant. Incised with deeply cut slopes onto which dozens of picturesque hamlets and lush vegetation have been neatly grafted, the road snakes along the valley floor in tow with the Bača stream and the scenic rail line.

At the narrow upper end of the valley, the village of **PODBRDO** was once an important frontier post, but is now significant as the southern entrance of the Bohinj tunnel and one of the stopping stations for the car-train (see box on p.126). A few kilometres east of Podbrdo is **PETROVO BRDO**, a tiny hamlet on the mountain-top pass linking the two valleys. The owner of the roadside hut *Planinski Dom Petrovo Brdo* (Ⓣ05/380-8101), which serves limited refreshments and has a few beds, organizes local excursions along the **Rapallo Border Trail**, the one-time border between Yugoslavia and Italy. Established in 1918, and confirmed by the Treaty of Rapallo in 1920 – which effectively annexed the Primorska region to Italy – the border is riddled with deserted fortifications, overgrown bunkers (there's one just yards from the hut) and bomb shelters constructed by the Italians between the two World Wars. Walks, which take in a number of these extraordinary defences (many of which are in the process of being cleaned up), can be improvised to suit whatever time you have, from a short trip (2hr) to a full-day excursion. If you want to know more about visiting the trail, contact the hut or the tourist office in Tolmin (see p.165). Petrovo Brdo is also an excellent starting point for ascents up into the Lower Bohinj mountains; trails lead to **Kobla** (1498m; 90min) and **Črna Prst** (1844; 4hr), where there's the *Dom Zorka Jelinčiča na Črni prsti* – and **Porezen** (1630m; 2hr 30min), and the *Dom Andreja Žvana* (both huts are open June to mid-Sept).

Central Primorska

Central Primorska – which roughly covers the block of territory between the southern reaches of the Soča Valley and the Karst region, and the area inland from here – offers a number of exciting and wide-ranging things to see and do. At the tail end of the valley, the bland casino town of **Nova Gorica** offers little more than the opportunity to make or lose a quick buck, though it does serve as a handy base from which to explore the lovely wine regions of **Goriška Brda** and the **Vipava Valley**. Northeast of here, sheltered amid the deep-sided valleys of the Idrija and Cerklje Hills, the towns of **Idrija** – famed nationwide for its mining and lace – and **Cerkno** – a popular ski town – can both count on enough attractions and activities, particularly in their outlying areas, to make a visit worthwhile.

Nova Gorica and around

Thirty-nine kilometres south of Tolmin, **NOVA GORICA** was built little more than half a century ago following Gorica's (Gorizia) annexation to Italy at the end of World War II. Until this point in time, and despite having been placed under Italian jurisdiction as part of the 1920 Treaty of Rapallo, it had been a predominantly Slovene-speaking community, but following the Paris Peace Treaty of 1947, the city was assigned to Italy leaving the Slovenes without a centre of their own. Undeterred, the local authorities pressed on with the construction of a nascent Slovene Gorica, based upon plans drawn up by the prominent Slovene architect Edo Ravnikar, a keen disciple of Le Corbusier.

Although vestiges of antiquity remain, most notably in the northern suburb of Solkan, as well as in the form of one or two other historic structures, its central hub is ultimately too modern to be anything other than charmless. With only its casinos – upon which the local economy is almost entirely dependent – and the odd splash of greenery to possibly detain you, it's not a place to linger. That said, there are some wonderful attractions close by, most obviously the enchanting **Goriška Brda** wine region northwest of town and, slightly closer, the twin attractions of **Sveta Gora** and **Kostanjevica Monastery**, both of which should satisfy those in search of ecclesiastical excitement, and **Kromberk Castle,** out in the suburbs.

As well as being an important **transport** hub for destinations north into the Soča Valley and south towards the Karst and coast, Nova Gorica is also a key crossing point into Italy, so there's a good chance you'll wind up here at some point.

Arrival and information

The **train station**, a lovely Secessionist pile built in 1906, is located 1.5km west of town on Kolodvorska ulica abutting the Italian border; upon exiting the station turn left and walk for ten minutes, before turning left again at the local border crossing – a further fifteen minutes' walk along Erjavčeva and you're in the centre. Note that neither this crossing nor the one in Solkan, north of town, are open to non-Slovenes or non-Italians; the international border crossing is 3km south of town in Rožna Dolina. The **bus station** is smack bang in the centre of town on Kidričeva ulica, from where it's a five-minute walk north to the **tourist office**, housed in the Cultural Centre on Bevkov trg (July & Aug Mon–Fri 8am–8pm, Sat & Sun 9am–1pm; rest of the year Mon–Fri 8am–6pm, Sat & Sun 9am–1pm; ⓣ05/330-4600, ⓔtzticng@siol.net). The **post office** is across the road from the bus station at

Nova Gorica's Casinos

As Slovenia's gaming capital, Nova Gorica panders unashamedly to the pretensions of its Italian neighbours, with both the **Perla** and **Park** hotels offering the stock American and French Roulette, Black Jack and Draw Poker games, not to mention a combined total of over one thousand slot machines. Open round the clock, **admission** (you must be 18) to either casino is €2 (Mon–Thurs) and €5 (Fri–Sun); you should hold on to the admission ticket until you leave the gaming floor. Once inside, you play with tokens (chips) – which can be obtained from the cashier or from automated machines – or cash (€). If you fancy something a little more relaxing, there's bingo twice a night, each card costing €5. Dress code is smart.

Kidričeva ulica 19 (Mon–Fri 7am–7pm, Sat 7am–1pm). There's free **internet access** at the Cyberia student club, located in the town hall on Trg Edvarda Kardelija; if it's full there, try Go.Net, adjoining the post office at Kidričeva Ulica 19 (daily 8am–10pm; 500SIT for 1hr).

Accommodation

There's not much here in the way of **private accommodation**, but the Turist Biro (Mon–Fri 8am–noon & 12.30–4pm; ⓣ04/333-4400), inside the train station, or the tourist office, may be able to help out. The town's premier **hotel** is the *HIT Casino Perla* (ⓣ05/336-3000, ⓔhotel.perla@hit.si; ❽), a flash glass and steel behemoth located, rather jarringly, opposite several blocks of flats at Kidričeva 7; concealing disappointingly modest rooms, it's patronized in the main by businessmen and Italians, as is its sister hotel, the *HIT Casino Park*, 100m west of the bus station at Delpinova 5 (ⓣ05/336-2000, ⓔhotel.park@hit.si; ❽); guests of both receive free entrance to the casino. By some distance, the city's most affordable place is the *HIT Sabotin*, a comfortable and decently furnished hotel 2km north of town in the suburb of Solkan at Cesta IX. korpusa 35 (ⓣ05/336-5000, ⓔhotel.sabotin@hit.si; ❻).

Kostanjevica Monastery

Fifteen minutes' walk south of town (walk down Erjavčeva ulica and follow the signs), situated atop a small, green hill overlooking Gorizia is **Kostanjevica Monastery** (Kostanjevica Samostan; Mon–Sat 9am–noon & 3–5pm; free). Built in 1624, its first custodians were the Carmelites, but following their expulsion in 1781 and a brief period of closure, the monastery was entrusted to the Franciscans, who have remained its guardians ever since.

Most visitors come here to view the tombs of the **French Bourbons**. Exiled from France following the 1830 Revolution in Paris, Charles X sought refuge in various countries, before eventually finding sanctuary in Gorizia under the protection of Count Coronini. His stay, however, was a short-lived one, for barely three weeks after his arrival he died of cholera. The **crypt**, located along a narrow whitewashed passageway under the central aisle of the church, holds the sarcophagi of Charles X and five other members of the Bourbons, including Marie Thérèse Charlotte, daughter of Marie-Antoinette (who was the granddaughter of Austrian Empress Maria Theresa).

Although usually only open to groups, it's worth enquiring about visits to the monastery's beautiful sixteenth-century completely renovated **library**, named after Stanislav Škrabec, one of Slovenia's greatest linguists and grammarians, who lived here for more than forty years. The library's most priceless work is Adam Bohorič's delightful pocket-sized book, *Arcticae horulae* (*Winter Hours*), the first Slovene grammar book, written in 1584. The monastery's small, single-nave **church**, which was almost completely destroyed during World War II, is worth a glimpse for its fabulous stuccowork.

Kromberk Castle

Three kilometres east of town in the suburban village of **KROMBERK** is **Kromberk Castle** (Mon–Fri 8am–2pm, Sun 1–5pm; 300SIT), a northern-Italian inspired construction that replaced the original thirteenth-century castle in the early seventeenth century. Despite several reincarnations since – most markedly an almost complete reconstruction in the late 1970s following the 1976 earthquake, and a thorough restoration of the interior in the 1990s –

the castle has retained its Renaissance appearance. Its **museum collection** is fairly uninspiring, comprising a gallery of old art (Middle Ages to Baroque), and a dour assemblage of period furniture, gloomy portraits and a few abstract pieces by the likes of Spacal and Kralj. Of more interest is the ethnographic section located upstairs on the second floor, which offers temporary thematic exhibitions related to the Goriško region; there's also a small lapidarium on the ground floor.

A much better reason for coming to the castle is to dine in the fine *Grajska Klet* **restaurant** on the ground floor (see opposite). If you don't fancy the hike, a couple of buses a day (1.45pm and 3.25pm) stop off en route to Ajdovščina.

Sveta Gora

Positioned atop the 681-metre-high **Sveta Gora** (Holy Mountain), just over 5km north of Nova Gorica, the **Basilica of the Assumption** has been an important place of pilgrimage for centuries. Local legend has it that in 1539 a local shepherd girl, Urška Ferligoj, was visited on several occasions by apparitions of the Virgin Mary, an occurrence that precipitated the building of the basilica two years later. A stone slab unearthed during its construction indicated that some form of religious centre had been present on this site possibly as early as the eleventh century, but which was most probably destroyed by the Turks in the late fifteenth century.

Having been reduced to a pile of rubble during World War I, church authorities initially considered employing Jože Plečnik to redesign the church, but because the project was ostensibly an Italian concern, the task fell to Silvano Barich from Gorizia. The stained-glass windows aside, the church's high, dark and capacious interior betrays little in the way of ornamentation or colour – the high altar, too, is very simple, its only distinguishing feature a picture of the Virgin Mary; originally donated to the church in 1544, the painting (believed to be of Venetian origin) was taken to Gorizia during World War II, later found at the Vatican and returned to the basilica in 1951. Miraculously, the **Chapel of Appearance** – located to the rear of the high altar and containing the original gold wooden statue dating from 1541 – survived the bombing almost completely unscathed. The basilica's **museum** (visits by appointment only) holds fragments from the bombed out church, and the usual stock of church reliquaries.

A few steps down from the church, in the building housing a rather dull restaurant, is the **Soča Front Museum** (Sat & Sun 11am–6pm; 300SIT; if it's closed ask at the restaurant for the key), displaying a rather tired assortment of artefacts pertaining to the nearby battles fought during World War I – you're best off saving your time and money for the museum in Kobarid (see p.160). Unfortunately, there are no buses to Sveta Gora so, unless you have your own transport, it's a very steep and exacting walk (approx 1hr): after passing through Solkan, take the road marked Trnovo/Čepovan (it's a sharp right – the road straight ahead is the Tolmin road) for about 3km, before branching off up the steep and twisting road towards Sveta Gora. From the summit, there are superlative views south across to the Gulf of Trieste and the snow-tipped mountains of the Soča Valley to the north. On the way from Nova Gorica, you'll see the magnificent **Solkan Railway Bridge**, which was, at the time of its construction in 1906, the largest stone arch bridge in Europe, some 85-metres high.

Eating and drinking

There are depressingly few **places to eat** in town, so you're best off heading to a couple of terrific places on the outskirts. Located 3km east of town, on the ground floor of Kromberk Castle, is the outstanding *Grajska Klet* (☎05/302-7160; closed Wed & Thurs): tall-backed wooden chairs, lush red carpets and cast-iron chandeliers provide a classy setting for a distinguished and unusual menu, typically featuring *mešani narezek* (homemade cold cuts of ham), *jota* (a local vegetable soup) and *oves sčrno trobento* (oatgrain with black trumpet mushrooms); there's a fine wine selection too, but reserve ahead. Not quite in the same league, but very enjoyable and a good deal cheaper, is *Pri Hrastu*, a one-hundred-year-old inn located at Kromberška cesta 2, just fifteen minutes' walk from the centre on the main road towards Kromberk Castle. For those on a somewhat tighter budget, try the *Vrtnica* self-service restaurant at Kidričeva 11, or *Pecivo*, opposite the *Hotel Park* at Delpinova 16.

The liveliest place in town to **drink** is the *Cyberia* student club (see p.169), which also runs an interesting programme of film, and music.

Goriška Brda

Goriška Brda (often just referred to as Brda, which means "hill"), a small nub of land around 5km northwest of Nova Gorica, is a beautiful region of low, smoothly rounded hills, scattered villages and little white churches, best known for producing some of the country's finest red and white wines. The hills are perfect for fruit growing, too, with the harvesting of cherries, peaches and apricots a major seasonal activity. From the wine aficionado's point of view, the most interesting villages are concentrated in the southernmost part of Brda, namely **Dobrovo** and **Medana**, while the villages of **Šmartno** and **Vipolže** attest to the region's position as an important frontier zone during the Venetian/Habsburg wars.

But whether you're here for the wine or not, Goriška Brda is a wonderful place to explore and, should you choose to stay longer, there's a smattering of accommodation available in several villages. However long you decide to stay, you'll get a lot more out of the region with your own transport, as there is only a very limited, and not very well-coordinated, bus service between Nova Gorica and Dobrovo (Mon–Fri at 12.24pm, 2.10pm & 3.20pm, returning at 7.06am, & 1.40pm).

Kojsko and Šmartno

The first major stop en route from Nova Gorica is **KOJSKO**, a comely little wayside settlement worth a brief stop to view the **Church of the Holy Cross on Tabor** (Sveta Križna Taboru), stationed just above the village. One of the four watchtowers (the other three were burnt down) which once formed part of an ancient fortification here was later rearranged into the church belltower, a feature common to many churches in these parts. The interior stars a beautifully preserved late-Gothic winged high altar from around 1500.

A couple of kilometres west of Kojsko, a monumentally ugly twenty-three-metre-high **viewing tower** (Razgledni stolp) provides a commanding sweep of the surrounding hills, including quite splendid views of **ŠMARTNO**, a superb-looking, fortified village some 2km away. Girdled by partially preserved white-stone walls and watchtowers erected during the sixteenth century, the village is an attractive jumble of crooked, unevenly paved streets lined with crumbling stone houses. In the centre stands the **Church of St Martin** whose fourteenth-century belltower is another that was converted from a watchtower; take a look inside at the contemporary, and very colourful, frescoes by Tone Kralj.

Dobrovo

Three kilometres west of Šmartno, **DOBROVO** is Goriška Brda's largest and most heavily populated settlement, as well as the region's principal wine centre. Here, too, you will find Goriška Brda's only **tourist office** (Mon–Thurs 7am–3pm; ⓣ05/395-9594, ⓔobcina.brda@guest.arnes.si), located in the centre of the village at Trg 25. maja 2, just 100m from where buses stop; the office can assist with enquiries on any aspect of the Brda region, from wine tours and tasting to private accommodation.

Two hundred metres south of the tourist office on Grajska cesta stands **Dobrovo Castle** (Grad Dobrovo; Tues–Fri 8am–4pm, Sat & Sun noon–4pm; 300SIT), a Renaissance-style structure erected around 1600 on the site of an older castle, and not dissimilar to Kromberk Castle near Nova Gorica (see p.169); its cultural history collection is not particularly stimulating, though the gallery of graphic prints up on the second floor by internationally renowned local artist Zoran Mušič is worth a look. In any case, the chances are that you'll soon end up sampling wine in the Vinoteka (Tues–Sun 11.30am–9pm), a magnificent stone-vault cellar located in the castle's handsome courtyard.

Alternatively, you could try the **Goriška Brda** winery, a short way north of the castle at Zadružna cesta 9 (ⓦwww.klet-brda.com), one of the largest wine production cellars in Slovenia. A visit to the winery includes some informative spiel about the region's wines, a tour of the cellar – where you'll get the chance to see stunning four-hundred-year-old oak barrels from Bosnia – and a tasting session with snacks (1100SIT per person). Wines can be purchased from their on-site shop (daily: Jan–March 8am–5pm, April–Dec 8am–7pm).

Whilst there are several wine-related events occurring in many of the villages throughout the year, the biggest and brashest festival in Brda is the **Cherry Fest**, which takes place in Dobrovo during the second weekend of June. Marking the beginning of the cherry season this lively spectacle entails concerts, tastings and much general merriment, climaxing with the parade of the "Cherry Girl".

The wines of Goriška Brda

Goriška Brda is the northernmost of the four wine-growing districts that constitute Slovenia's **Primorje** (coastal) wine-growing region. Thanks to its favourable geographical location and Mediterranean climate and soil, Goriška Brda consistently yields a superlative range of both **red** and **white wines** – one of the few regions in Slovenia to harvest both. Among the former, Cabernet Sauvignon and the lighter Merlot are pre-eminent, whilst of the latter, the ubiquitous Chardonnay (produced all over Slovenia), Beli Pinot, and the dry Briski Tokaj (as opposed to the famous sweet Hungarian variety) prevail. The most distinctive white, though, is the golden-yellow Rebula, a widely cultivated, indigenous grape used in the production of *slamno vino* (straw wine). Local **vintners** to look out for include Simčič and Movia, both in Ceglo, and Prinčič, in Kozana.

If you fancy a spot of **tasting**, there are dozens of cellars in a number of villages to choose from; expect to pay around 1000–1500SIT per person for four or five wines, with bread and cheese or a small cold buffet (depending on how many of you there are). You can either contact the cellars directly, or call the tourist office in Dobrovo for further information (ⓣ05/395-9594).

Medana and Ceglo

If you've got time, two further villages worth checking out are **MEDANA** and **VIPOLŽE**, 1.5km and 3.5km south of Dobrovo respectively, the former one of Brda's most prolific winegrowing villages. One of the most highly regarded wineries here is the **Klinec** tourist farm at no. 20 (Ⓣ05/304-5092, Ⓔklinec-medana@s5.net), which has been producing vintages since 1918; there's good food and accommodation available here too (❸). The owners of the farm also organize the **Days of Poetry and Wine Festival** in late August, an international gathering of poets complemented by the requisite quantities of wine.

From Medana, the road continues south towards the Italian border; after passing through the village of **CEGLO**, veer eastwards (continuing south will bring you to the local border crossing) and continue up the hill towards Vipolže. Located in the upper reaches of this quaint little village is **Vipolže Castle**, originally an eleventh-century fortification, but later transformed into a handsome Renaissance-style manor house following its appropriation by the Venetians in the seventeenth century. The oaks and cypresses of this once lovely park still flourish, but otherwise it's a wretched site, the castle's bricked-up windows and tumbledown walls the result of heavy bomb damage during World War I when it was used as a military hospital, and years of subsequent neglect. As some compensation, there are marvellous views across the Friulian Plain. From Vipolže, you can return to Dobrovo via the road running parallel to Medana, or take the northeasterly road towards Šmartno.

The Vipava Valley

If the Brda region hasn't sated your thirst for wine, you might like to venture in the opposite direction towards the **Vipava Valley** (Vipavska dolina), the second and largest of Primorje's winegrowing regions. Sandwiched between the thickly forested Trnovo Plateau to the north and the low lying Karst region to the south, this flat-bottomed valley is raked by lush rolling vineyards which, like Goriška Brda, yield a superb quota of both reds, notably Cabernet Sauvignon and Merlot, and whites; check out the autochthonous varieties, Zelen and Pinela.

The valley's continental climate is epitomized by the **burja** (bora), a fiendishly cold and dry wind that whips down from the northern mountain peaks and batters its way through the valley, across the Karst, and down towards the Adriatic. For this reason many of the two dozen or so **wine villages** dispersed throughout the Vipava hills were built in relatively sheltered, south-facing locations, with neither windows nor doors positioned on sides exposed to the wind. The only centres of any meaningful size in the valley are **Ajdovščina** and **Vipava**, unspectacular little towns, but both useful as jumping off points if the villages are your intended target.

The handy little *Vipava Wine Road* leaflet (available from the tourist office in Ajdovščina – see p.174) outlines a number of villages and cellars you can visit. However, having your own **transport** is pretty much essential here, as public transport is virtually nonexistent.

Ajdovščina

The only centre of any significant size in the Vipava Valley is **AJDOVŠČINA**, a small, plain sort of town, with little to hold your attention save for some extant Roman remains. The compact ancient core of present-day Ajdovščina was once a military encampment called **Castra ad Fluvium Frigidum** (Fortress by the Cold River), built by the Romans around 270 AD as an important link in the defence line of the Empire. Its four-metre-thick defence walls were perforated with fourteen circular towers, of which seven, either whole or partial, remain; the most tangible remnants, including an almost complete tower, lie east of the main square Lavričev trg – other portions of the wall can be detected on the western side of the ancient quarter.

Arriving at the **bus** or **train** station, located opposite each other on Goriška cesta, it's a five-minute walk northeast to the centre of town and the **tourist office**, housed in a section of a Roman tower at Lokarjev drevored 8b (Mon–Fri 9am–5pm, Sat 10am–2pm; ⓣ05/366-3900, ⓔtic-ajdika@siol.net); they can arrange accommodation on local tourist farms and visits to local wine cellars. Should you desire to stay here, there's the dreary-looking but decent enough *Hotel Planika* 200m east of the stations at Goriška cesta 25 (ⓣ05/364-4700, ⓔplanika@pigal.si; ❹).

Vipava and Zemono

From Ajdovščina hourly buses continue southeast to **VIPAVA**, the valley's second centre some 6km distant. This somnolent little market town, nestled under the towering slopes of the Nanos Plateau, somewhat misguidedly styles itself as the Slovene Venice – for no good reason other than that it developed alongside the many karstic springs of the Vipava River. Of course, it's nothing like Venice and, though endowed with a modicum of charm thanks to its generous spread of Baroque architecture and picturesque stone-block bridges, you're unlikely to stay long, if you stop at all.

That said, the **Vipava Winery** at Vinarska cesta 5 (ⓣ05/367-1200, ⓦwww.vipava1894.si), 500m east of the main square where buses drop passengers off, is another of Primorje's major wine cooperatives, and is worth considering if you're unable to reach any of the villages. Its barrique (harvested in barrels) red wines – in particular Merlot and Cabernet Sauvignon – are rated as some of the best in the country. Guided tours and tasting are possible, and there's also a good wine shop on site.

Occupying a solitary location less than 2km west ofVipava (just off the main road), the Palladian-style **Zemono Mansion** (Grad Zemono; Mon–Fri noon–7pm, Sat 9am–2pm; free) is one of Slovenia's best-preserved Renaissance buildings. Formerly a seventeenth-century hunting lodge, the cross-shaped ground floor, whose walls are blanketed with pastel-coloured landscape murals, is now used principally as a concert venue, and occasionally for weddings. The upper floor, meanwhile, has been rather crudely turned into a home furnishings showroom. More appropriately, the cellar has been converted into the high-class and very expensive *Gostilna Pri Lojzetu* **restaurant**, which features an innovative menu using specially prepared vegetables, mushrooms and the freshest seafood (Wed–Sun noon–10pm).

Vipavski Križ and Goče

Rising out of the flat plain just 2km west of Ajdovščina, the scenic fortified medieval village of **VIPAVSKI KRIŽ** is one of the few settlements in the valley whose historical importance is greater than its viticultural significance. Its focal point is the **Capuchin Monastery**, built in 1637 and whose **Church of the Holy Cross** harbours a quite beautifully carved dark-wooden high altar, together with a sublime painting of the Holy Trinity, one of the largest Baroque canvases in the country and dating from 1668. Its **library** contains an extensive assortment of books from the fifteenth century onwards. Visits to the monastery are best arranged through the tourist office in Ajdovščina (see p.174). Adjacent to the monastery, on the eastern tip of the village, is the magnificent shell of the ruined fifteenth-century **castle**, erected on the orders of the bishop of Gorica so as to protect the village from Turkish and Venetian raids.

If just one wine village is your limit then make a beeline for **GOČE**, some 5km west of the main trunk road in the southeastern Vipava hills. With streets barely wide enough to squeeze a car through, the village is distinguished by its knot of tightly clustered eighteenth-century sandstone houses, ornamented with Karst-style courtyards (*borjači*) and hewn stone portals. You'll have little difficulty tracking down somewhere to try some sampling; there are over sixty **cellars** here, which amounts to one for almost every house. A couple of good ones are Fajdiga at no. 4a and Ferjančič at no. 9.

Idrija and around

The history and development of **IDRIJA**, a town of some 7000 inhabitants 36km north of Vipava, has been inextricably linked to its mines ever since the discovery of mercury here in 1490. During the eighteenth century, the growth and success of the **mines** – which are now in the process of being closed down for good – spawned a number of other local industries, most importantly forestry and medicine, a period during which the town could justifiably claim to rival Ljubljana as a centre of scientific and technological advancement. **Lace-making**, too, has played a significant part in shaping the town's identity; originally a seventeenth-century cottage industry, the craft grew to such an extent that the town received Slovenia's first lace school in the late nineteenth century, an institution that still functions today.

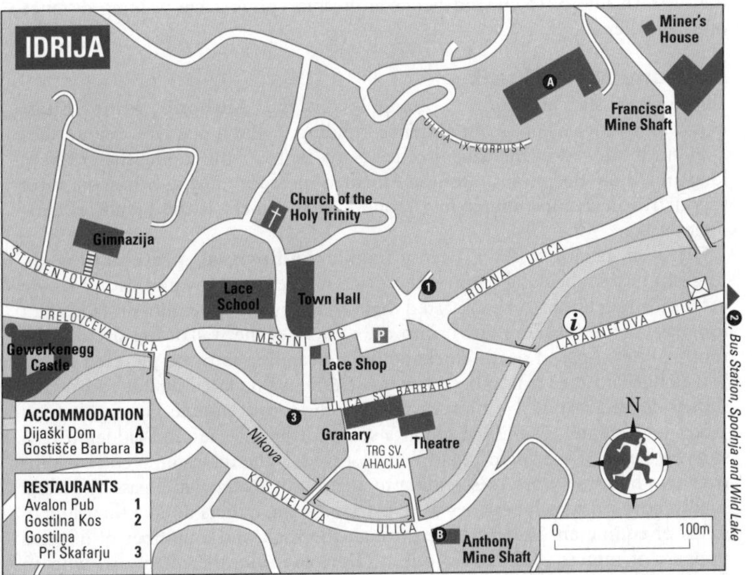

Despite its modest size, Idrija can comfortably summon up enough attractions to rate a full day's sightseeing, more if you're looking to explore the surrounding countryside. Within walking distance of town is the wonderful **Wild Lake**, while further afield, the immense **Klavže** water barriers and the fascinating **Partisan Printworks** are no less deserving of a visit.

Arrival, information and accommodation

The **bus station** is centrally located on Lapajnetova ulica, from where it's just a couple of minutes walk to the **tourist office** at Lapajnetova ulica 7 (summer daily 9am–6pm; winter Mon–Fri 9am–4pm; ⓣ05/377-3898, ⓦwww.rzs-idrija.si). The **post office** (Mon–Fri 8am–7pm, Sat 8am–noon) is directly opposite the bus station.

There's precious little **accommodation** in town: the small *Dijaški Dom*, up on the hill at Ulica IX Korpusa 6 (just behind the Francisca Mine Shaft), has beds available in summer for around 2000SIT (ⓣ05/377-1052). Otherwise, the only other place to sleep is at the *Gostišče Barbara*, which occupies the second floor of the Anthony Mine Shaft building at Kosovelova ulica 3 (ⓣ05/377-1142); it has two categories of room – four en-suite double rooms with TV and minibar (❺), and two hostel-style rooms sleeping two to four people, with shared wash/shower facilities (❷). Another option, albeit a very expensive one, is the five-star *Hotel Kendov Dvorec*, a splendidly renovated fourteenth-century manor house 4km north of town in **Spodnja Idrija**, at Na griču 2 (ⓣ05/372-5100, ⓦwww.kendov-dvorec.com; ❾); the immaculate rooms come with antique furniture and linen made from Idrija lace.

The Town

Idrija's handful of terrific sites – all, more or less, associated with the mining and lace industries, such as the **Mine Shaft**, **Gewerkenegg castle** and **Lace School** – are broadly contained within the attractive and compact old core on the western side of town, and hence all within comfortable walking distance of each other.

Anthony Mine Shaft

The town's star attraction is undoubtedly the **Anthony Mine Shaft** (Antonijev Rov) whose main entrance building (Šelštev) is at Kosovelova ulica 3, 200m southwest of the tourist office. Sunk in 1500, the tunnel shaft (1.5km long and 400m deep), was, after the Almaden mercury mine in Spain, the most productive in Europe, employing around 1300 miners at the height of production.

The visit begins with a twenty-minute **audiovisual presentation** (in English) in the checking room – the place where miners would gather in the early morning hours to be allocated their duties by the Obergutman (a kind of foreman) before heading down into the mine. On the wall at the back of the room is the so-called death clock: before descending into the pit, each miner was obliged to take a number plate which, if not replaced at the end of the shift, indicated that he'd got lost or was in some sort of trouble. Having donned jacket and helmet, you're led along a series of lit galleries and laddered passageways, part of the Main Road which served as the main mine entrance for over two hundred years. Descending to a depth of 100m, you'll pass by several small alcoves in which benches were placed for the miners to take their lunch, items of equipment used to bore through the rock, and a number of life-size puppets of miners – including one of **Berkmandlc**, the pit dwarf, who in return for parcels of food, would tap the walls to indicate to the miners where the richest sources of mercury lay.

The tour winds up at the tiny underground **Chapel of the Holy Trinity**, where miners would pray before the statues of SS Barbara and Acacius (patron saints of miners) for a safe return from their day's work. Scheduled tours, which last around one hour thirty minutes, take place daily at 10am and 4pm, with an extra tour at 3pm at weekends (1200SIT; Ⓦwww.rzs-idrija.si).

Gewerkenegg Castle and the Lace School

Sited atop a small hill on the western fringe of town, and discernible from some distance thanks to its two cylindrical corner towers and an oddly protruding central clock tower, **Gewerkenegg Castle** (Grad Gewerkenegg) was built by the Acacius Society of Mining Entrepreneurs around 1530 to house the mine administration and other official bodies. Though prevailingly Renaissance in form, the castle was embellished with Baroque appendages in the eighteenth century – including the arcaded courtyard and its rather lurid foliage-style frescoes.

It now plays host to the **Town Museum** (Mestni muzej; daily 9am–6pm; 500SIT), which, not surprisingly, dotes almost exclusively upon the town's **mining** heritage. An absorbing exhibition begins with an introduction to the Idrija mine, including a depiction of the local tub-maker who kick-started the whole thing. The next three rooms are devoted to all matters geological, and while most people are drawn to the steel ball floating in a bowl of mercury, don't let that detract you from the fine assemblage of fossils, minerals and cinnabar ore deposits on display. Similarly enlightening is the collection of mine maps, land registers, flasks and other objects gathered in the northern Rondel Tower, while the staircase in the southern Mercury Tower has been designed to symbolize the descent down the pit. At the bottom is a Plexiglas cube filled with droplets of mercury.

Inevitably, the town's rich **lace** tradition is well documented with, among other exhibits, a display of work by the winners of the annual bobbin lace competition; the most interesting piece is a sprawling tablecloth, originally made for President Tito's wife, Jovanka Broz, but retained by the museum following his death, and her banishment from political life, in 1980.

The Old Town and the Lace School

Just below the castle, the old town core showcases a couple of significant buildings, including, on Trg Svetega Ahacija, the former mine **Granary** (Magazin), which was used to store grain and wheat but which now functions as a gallery and library; next to this stands the oldest **theatre** in Slovenia, built in 1769 but now a cinema.

The most impressive building, however, is the lovely Neoclassical Old School (Stara šola) at Prelovčeva ulica 2, which has been home to the town's **Lace school** (Čipkarska šola; Mon–Fri 8am–3pm; 400SIT) since 1876 (see box on p.178). The items on display here were completed by students of the school, all of whom attend voluntarily and are mostly aged between six and fourteen; if you ask, you may be allowed to see a lesson in progress. You can also buy lace here, or at one of several **lace shops** dotted around town; the best of these is the Galerija Idrijske Čipke, opposite the school at Mestni trg 16 (Mon–Fri 10am–noon & 4–7pm, Sat 10am–noon). Idrija's major annual event is the **Lace Festival** (Čipkarski Festival) during the last week of August, entailing lace-making competitions, arts and crafts exhibitions and evening entertainment.

Lace-making in Idrija

The art of bobbin **lace-making** first took off in Slovenia in the seventeenth century and, despite having been practised in many towns and rural areas throughout the country, its roots have remained strongest in Idrija, where the craft has been taught in the town's **lace school** since 1876.

Traditionally, lace-making was practised by most women as a means of supplementing a miner's often very meagre wage – a state of affairs that became even more pressing following the decline of this and other traditional industries (such as iron smelting) in the late nineteenth and early twentieth centuries. The lace-making industry continued apace, with its products sold mainly to the Church, until World War II. After this, however, its popularity waned, only to be revived in the 1980s. Today's lace products are primarily made as gifts and souvenirs.

Idrija Lace (*Idrijska čipka*) takes many forms, from simple flower-based patterns to intricately weaved cloths featuring folk or peasant motifs, many of which are technically superb pieces; you can view, and purchase, many such specimens in several of the region's museums and shops. Moreover, the **Lace Festival** in Idrija, and the **Days of Lace Fair** in Železniki (another important regional lace centre), attest to this exquisite handicraft's ongoing importance and enduring popularity.

Francisca Mine Shaft, Miner's House and Kamšt

Up the hill on Bazoviška ulica, a few hundred metres due north of the post office is the **Francisca Mine Shaft** (Jašek Frančiške), whose former workshops now house a marvellous collection of beautifully restored, nineteenth-century steam-driven pumps, boilers and compressors, most of which were taken out of operation in the 1950s following the introduction of more modern working practices; if you wish to visit, ask at the Town Museum in the castle.

Set against a gentle slope just behind the mine shaft is a typically striking, albeit heavily renovated, example of an eighteenth-century **miner's house** (Rudarska hiša). Defined by a high, slender frontage, a sharply pointed roof and neat rows of small, square windows, these houses were traditionally constructed from wood and stone, the external walls made of thick boards daubed with lime-wash, and the rooftops protected with wooden shingles (*šinkln*). A miner's house usually comprised three or four floors, in order that several families could be accommodated in the same building – an important consideration during times of overpopulation; moreover, miners could rarely afford their own houses. Today, sadly, you'll do well to spot more than half a dozen such dwellings around Idrija.

There's yet another reminder of Idrija's industrial pedigree 1km southeast of the bus station at the end of Vodnikova ulica. Concealed within the chunky stone-block building is the beautifully preserved **Kamšt**, held to be the largest wooden waterwheel in Europe, measuring 13.6m in diameter. For more than 150 years, it pumped pit water from a depth of over 200m from the Joseph Shaft (daily 9am–4pm; 300SIT). If it's closed you can get the key from no. 22. From the Kamšt you can continue to the Wild Lake (see opposite).

Eating and drinking

Disappointingly, Idrija is bereft of decent places to **eat**, though the two gostilna here are reasonable enough and both serve up the Idrija speciality, *Žlikrofi* – spiced potato balls wrapped in thin pastry. *Gostilna Pri Škafarju*, 50m east of the former granary at Ulica Svete Barbare 9 (closed Tues), is fairly plain-looking but there's a decent menu to choose from, including a handful of horse-meat dishes (including, somewhat disconcertingly, grilled colt); while *Gostilna Kos*, 200m east of the bus station at Tomšičeva ulica 4, veers more towards Italian fare (closed Sun). The studenty *Avalon Pub*, at Mestni trg 7, is just about the only place in town to **drink**.

Around Idrija: The Wild Lake and Klavže Dams

From the Kamšt a three-kilometre-long trail (Pot ob Rakah) leads south to the brilliant blue-green **Wild Lake** (Divje Jezero), an apposite name for this small body of water that has claimed the lives of several divers attempting to locate the lake's as yet undiscovered source – to date 156m is the deepest anyone has got. What is known is that water flows into the lake from an underground passage, or siphon, reckoned to measure approximately 200m long. The lake itself measures about 65m in length and 30m in width, taking barely fifteen minutes to circle, unless, that is, you happen to be here following snow melt or extremely heavy rainfall, when massive volumes of water are discharged from its depths, flooding the lake to 3m above its normal level. Emanating from the lake is Slovenia's shortest river, the Jezernica, which discharges into the Idrijca after only 55m.

Just as impressive are the precipitous, hundred-metre-high cliffs encircling the lake, whose crevices and ledges shelter a galaxy of alpine **flora**, including several endemic species, such as the Carniolan primrose and hacquetia, the latter named after eminent local surgeon Baltazar hacquet. Lurking in the lake's depths, and something you won't see, is Proteus Anguinus, the human-fish (see p.217). If you have your own car, take the Ljubljana road south and the lake is signposted after about 1.5km.

Twelve kilometres upstream from the Wild Lake on the Belca River (accessible via an increasingly rutted forest road), is the first of two remaining **dams** (Klavže). Known locally as the "Slovene Pyramids", these superb technical monuments were originally constructed from wood in the sixteenth century, but were replaced by sturdier stone structures in 1770. Their function was to accumulate enough water to enable vast quantities of timber to be floated downriver to Idrija, whereupon the logs would gather in front of a 412-metre-long dam (rake), at which point they would be carted off to the mines (where they were used as supporting structures for the galleries) and smelting plants (for fuel for burning iron ore). The rake remained operational until 1926, when road transportation was deemed more efficient, while the Klavže gradually fell into a state of disrepair. Restored in the 1980s, they now stand as a fitting memorial to a bygone era. There's another dam, also accessible by road, on the Idrijca River, which runs roughly parallel to the Belca.

Partisan Printing Works

Secreted away in an almost impenetrable forest ravine below the Vojsko plateau, 2km north of the tiny hamlet of **Planina** (itself 14km west of Idrija), are several modestly sized wooden cabins which, for a brief period during World War II, functioned as the **Partisan Printing Works** (Partizanska tiskarna; April–Oct 9am–4pm; 400SIT). Operational between September 1944 and May 1945, the clandestinely run printworks rolled out some 1000 copies of *Partizanski Dnevnik* (*Partisan Daily*) per hour (or around 7000–9000 per day), the only daily newspaper to be published by a resistance movement in occupied Europe during the war; over the eight months more than a million copies of the paper were published, as well as stacks of other printed matter.

During the visit, you'll get to see the typesetting room (complete with printing moulds and dozens of original papers), the bindery, kitchen and dining room, the power plant, and the printing room. Purchased for a million lira, the still-functioning printing press was smuggled across from Milan, via Gorica, before being transported, piece by piece, to Vojsko; a demonstration is usually given. Despite numerous German offensives in the vicinity – including one final major assault during the Spring of 1945 in which over 300 Partisans were killed – the printworks were never rumbled. Owing to its extremely remote location, a visit to the printworks requires a little organization and a degree of physical exertion; in the first instance, you should contact the tourist office in Idrija or the Town Museum at Gewerkenegg Castle (see p.177).

Cerkno and around

Located somewhat out on a limb 19km north of Idrija (and 4km off the main Idrija–Tolmin road), **CERKNO** was a key centre of Partisan activity during World War II, when a number of military and political bodies, workshops and schools were stationed hereabouts. Life in Cerkno today is played out at a rather more languid pace, and unless you're here for the **skiing** (see box on p.138) or to see the **Laufarija carnival** in February (see box opposite), there's little inducement to linger. That said, it's a good jumping-off spot if you're planning to visit any of the outlying sights, and it also makes a good base for walks into the **Cerkno Hills** (Cerkljansko Hribovje).

If you do find yourself with a bit of time to spare, it's worth a browse around the **Cerkno Museum** (Cerkljanski muzej; Tues–Sun 10am–1pm & 2–6pm; 400SIT), just off the small main square (Glavni trg) at Bevkova 12, where you can see the masks used during the Laufarija (see opposite), as well as a handful of local archeological exhibits.

Practicalities

Buses arrive and depart from Glavni trg, the small main square around which everything in town revolves. Amenities in Cerkno, however, are negligible; there's no tourist office here, though the staff at the *Hotel Cerkno* can furnish you with **information** and help to arrange visits to some of the outlying attractions. The **post office** is 100m west of Glavni trg (Mon–Fri 8–9.30am, 10am–3pm & 4–6pm, Sat 8am–noon). The only **accommodation** in town is the aforementioned hotel, a comfortable, clean and roomy place located a two-minute walk away from the main square at Sedejev trg 8 (Ⓣ05/374-3400, Ⓦwww.hotel-cerkno.si; ❺); it's got a large pool too.

If you don't mind staying a little way outside town, there are a couple of excellent possibilities: back out on the Idrija–Tolmin road (at the junction of the Cerkno turn-off) in **Straža**, the (excellent) *Želinc* tourist farm (Ⓣ05/372-4020, Ⓦwww.zelinc.com; ❸) offers very comfortable rooms, with good food to boot; in the other direction, 6km along the road towards the ski centre in the wayside hamlet of **Log**, the great-value *Gostilna Na Logu* (Ⓣ05/372-4005; ❸) is a cosy, family-run tavern (with good discounts for kids); its modern **restaurant** offers a wide choice of exotic game (stag's back, chamois, boar, etc), Serbian meats (*Čevapi* and *Sarma*), and the local Idrijan speciality (*Žlikrofi*). In Cerkno itself, the restaurant in the *Hotel Cerkno* is pretty much the best place to dine. The only other option is the rather downbeat *Pri Štruklu* (closed Mon) just up from the museum at Platiševa 1, which offers little more than the stock

The Laufarija

One of Slovenia's more enjoyable Pust (Shrovetide) festivals is the **Laufarija**, staged each year on the Sunday before Ash Wednesday and on Shrove Tuesday in Cerkno's small town square. The central character is the horned **Pust**, made up in a costume of straw, moss and pine branches; as the personification of winter, the Pust is hauled up in front of a court and charged with a litany of barmy crimes – a poor harvest, inclement weather, dodgy roads and so on – before being found guilty and sentenced to summary execution.

The two dozen or so other members of the Laufarija family – each of whom wears one of the distinctive **masks** (larfe) carved from soft lime tree wood – represent either a local trade or craft (baker, butcher, cobbler, etc), or display certain character traits or afflictions, such as the drunk and his wife, the scabby one, and the sick man with his accordion.

To be honest it's debatable whether even the locals know what's going on, but it's a great deal of fun all the same. If you don't manage to get here for the festival, there's a fine display of the masks worn in the Cerkno Museum (see p.180).

pizzas and grills. The place to **drink** is *Pri Gabrielju* just off the square at Mučnikova 5 (open until 1am).

Around Cerkno

If there's little to excite in Cerkno itself, then the surrounding countryside is well invested with terrific sites, although unless you have your own wheels or aren't disposed to a reasonable amount of walking, reaching them will prove problematic. Best of all is the wonderful **Franja Partisan Hospital**, an evocative reminder of Slovenia's Partisan heritage, while less well known, and hence rarely visited, are the **Divje Babe** and **Ravenska Caves**, both a little way southwest of town; and in **Zakojca** to the north, the writer France Bevk's house. Embracing most of the above, the **Cerkno hills** themselves offer some good hikes.

Franja Partisan Hospital

Dramatically sited in the heart of the spectacular **Pasica gorge** 7km northeast of Cerkno, the **Franja Partisan Hospital** (Partizanska Bolnišnica Franja; April–Sept daily 9am–6pm; March, Oct & Nov daily 9am–4pm; Dec–Feb Sat & Sun 9am–4pm; 600SIT) was built in December 1943 for wounded soldiers of the Ninth Corps of the Slovene Partisan Army. Named after its chief physician Franja Bojc-Bidovec, the hospital remained operational until May 1945, a period during which it treated more than five hundred Partisans, as well as soldiers from Italy, Russia and America.

Comprising thirteen camouflaged **wooden cabins** that housed an operating room, isolation ward, recovery room, X-ray room and so on, the complex was protected by bunkers, minefields and machine gun nests pressed into the cliffs above. However, despite the area being shelled by Germans on several occasions, it was never captured. Indeed, its secrecy was such that the wounded were blindfolded before being admitted, food was lowered down the cliff face by neighbouring farmers, and medical supplies were air-dropped in by allied forces; note the picture of Winston Churchill in the Invalids Room. Supplies notwithstanding, the hospital was remarkably self-reliant throughout the period of its operation, making its own orthopaedic accessories, organizing cultural and educational activities for the wounded and even managing to publish its own bulletin, *Bolniški list* (*Patient's Bulletin*).

Despite its relatively remote location, and unlike the Partisan Printworks in Vojsko (see p.179), getting to the hospital is not especially difficult, particularly if you have your own transport; the only buses that pass this way are the ski buses from Cerkno in the winter. Seven kilometres along the road east of Cerkno, a road branches north just beyond the tiny hamlet of **Log**; 1km on you come to a car park. From here, a secured trail (10min) inclines up the forested gorge, bisected by the babbling Čerinščica stream and hemmed in by overhanging boulders.

The Divje Babe and Ravenska Caves

Two hundred metres above the Idrija–Tolmin road and the Idrijca river, near the village of **Šebrelje**, some 12km west of Cerkno, is **Divje Babe Cave**, one of the most important Palaeolithic sites in Slovenia. Whilst digging near the cave entrance in 1995, excavators stumbled across the femur of a young cave bear – nothing particularly revelatory in itself – but this one had been perforated with four holes (two complete, two partially worn away), giving it a flute-like appearance. Researchers in Canada calculated the four-inch bone to be around 45,000 years old, possibly more, thus dating from the Mousterian period, time of Neanderthal man. On the assumption that the holes were made by human hands – the most plausible explanation given that no teeth marks were detected on the bone – it can lay fair claim to being the oldest known **musical instrument** in Europe. Getting here really does entail having your own transport; otherwise, you can take a Cerkno–Tolmin bus and alight at the roadside hamlet of Stopnik; however, from there, you've still got a long (about 3km) and steep walk along the road up to Šebrelje.

Chanced upon by a local farmer in 1832, the **Ravenska Cave** (Ravenska jama), high up in the village of **Ravne Pri Cerkne**, 7km southwest of Cerkno, is known for its clusters of brilliant white aragonite crystals, spidery-like formations that owe their shape and colour to the high levels of magnesium present in the soil. The crystals here are amongst some of the finest specimens of aragonite to be found anywhere in Europe. The cave itself is something of a minnow in Slovene terms, measuring just over 350m in length, of which you'll get to see about 100m; there's no need for sensible shoes, as walkways have been constructed, but bring a jumper as the temperature is around just eight or nine degrees.

In theory, the cave is not officially open, though in practice visits can be arranged if you show enough interest – contact the *Hotel Cerkno*. If you don't have transport and are considering walking, there's a very satisfying circular hike from Cerkno to the cave, via the village of **Zakriž** (4hr). To arrange a visit contact the *Hotel Cerkno*, in Cerkno (see p.180), or the Polak family in Šebrelje, at no. 34a (ⓣ05/374-4500).

Zakojca and the Cerkno Hills

Approximately 20km north of the Ravenska Cave, and rather more difficult to reach (but still accessible by road or several marked paths), is the tiny village of **ZAKOJCA**, birthplace of children's novelist France Bevk (1870–1970). The immaculately restored **homestead** (Domačija Franceta Bevka; no set times; 300SIT) where Bevk also spent much of his youth is a fairly simple dwelling; the downstairs space comprises a living room (*hiša*), two small bedrooms, a "black" kitchen (see p.130) and a small stable for livestock, while the first floor attic, where he wrote his earliest works, has been transformed into an exhibition space, with family photos, books and personal effects.

The house is a ten-minute walk from the Pri Flandru tourist farm (where you'll have to go first to get the key) in the centre of the village at no. 1 (Ⓣ05/377-9800, Ⓦwww.kmetija-flander.si; ❷) – this is a good place to **stay** if you're planning to spend a day or two hiking in the surrounding hills. From Zakojca, you could tackle the highland area's highest peak, **Porezen**, which tops a very respectable 1632m; just below the summit is the *Koča na Poreznu* mountain hut, which has beds available between June and mid-September (Ⓣ05/377-6275). Porezen can also be attempted from the Franja Partisan Hospital (3hr). If you're considering any sort of hiking in the hills, consider buying the 1:50,000 *Idrijsko In Cerkljansko* map.

The Karst

A dry, rocky, and thickly forested limestone plateau, scattered with ancient stone villages, the Karst is famed for its subterranean wonderland of rivers and streams, hollows, depressions and caves, which have fired the imagination of travellers for centuries – none more so than those at **Škocjan**. Just a few kilometres west of Škocjan is the Karst's second major draw, the world-famous **Lipica Stud Farm**, home of the magnificent Lipizzaner horses. Of the villages, the obvious draw is **Štanjel**, whose bleached-white stone houses and wonderfully disparate range of sights are a delight.

Whilst here take the opportunity to sample the local culinary delights, in particular the delicious air-dried *pršut* ham, which combines perfectly with **Kraški Teran**, a spiky, cherry-red wine that acquires its deep aroma and colour from the iron-rich *terra rosa* soil peculiar to this region.

Štanjel

Contender for most picturesque village in the Karst, if not Slovenia, the medieval hilltop settlement of **ŠTANJEL**, situated 28km southeast of Nova Gorica, is the archetypal Karst village. Most probably the site of a Halstatt settlement, the prominent limestone hill was fortified around the twelfth century, gradually evolving across several gently curving, south-facing terraces, a layout modelled on the plans of the ancient Etruscan towns. Its textbook stone houses are delightful, and there's more than enough to see to warrant a few hours' exploration.

The Village

The best place to start exploring the village's disproportionate number of sights is the **Castle** (Grad Štanjel), located through the main **entrance tower**, itself sited just below the **tourist office** (see p.185). Erected by the counts of Koblenz in the sixteenth century, upon the foundations of an older, medieval castle, there is now little to see except for a battered shell, the result of heavy pounding during World War II. There's redemption, however, in the renovated residential wing of the castle, which houses the **Lojze Spacal Gallery** (Galerija Lojzeta Spacala; no set times, contact the castle café; 300SIT, which includes entry to the Karst House – see below), a brilliant collection of abstract paintings, prints, woodcuts and tapestries by the eponymous, Trieste-born artist. Spacal was profoundly influenced by the surrounding landscape, as is evident in his extensive use of Karst motifs and colours – greys and whites representing stone, and reds representing the soil.

Štanjel's most visible symbol, courtesy of its smooth, cone-like steeple shaped like a bishop's hat, is the **Church of St Daniel**, just down from the tourist office. Its most interesting interior features are a marble tomb etched with a relief of Daniel and the lions, a relief of the castle as it once supposedly looked, and paintings of interlocking crosses on the presbytery walls; if the church is locked contact the tourist office just across the way.

From the church it's a few paces east to the six-hundred-year-old **Karst House** (Kraška Hiša), a superb example of vernacular architecture, constructed entirely from stone, including the roof and gutters. The downstairs space would have been used for keeping livestock, with the living quarters located upstairs, into which a family of typically five or six members would squeeze; both floors now hold a modest ethnological collection. The key can be obtained from the café in the castle (see p.180).

In the southeastern corner of the village, a few hundred metres and a couple of terraces below the Karst house, is the **Ferrari Garden**, designed by internationally renowned architect and town planner (and former mayor of Štanjel) Max Fabiani, but named after his brother-in-law, Enrico Ferrari. The centrepiece of this winsome little park is an artificial pond, in the centre of which is a tiny oval island, reached via a delicate, balustraded stone bridge – the inspiration for which was undoubtedly the author's earlier work in Vienna. From the garden you can survey the expansive views across the Karst towards Italy, or follow a marked footpath (Fabiani Path; 1hr) south towards the village of **Kobdilj**, Fabiani's birthplace.

The Karst

Derived from a pre-Indo-European word meaning stone, the term Karst stems from the Slovene Kras and Italian Carso areas, the gently sloping limestone plateau running northwest from Divača and Lokev to the Trieste hinterland in Italy. For this reason the Slovenian Karst is regarded as the classical, or true, Karst, and the only such region in the world which uses the capital 'K'. The word has since become an internationally applied term denoting any landscape with permeable limestone features. Interestingly, it was the German version of the word, "Karst", that was used as opposed to the Slovene word, "Kras", owing to the popularity of the German language amongst travellers in the nineteenth century.

The Karst is commonly, if a little erroneously, represented as a barren, stony wasteland, though in fact much of it is heavily wooded with dense vegetation thanks to intensive afforestation in recent decades. The special characteristics of Karst landscapes are the result of millions of years of erosion and corrosion of the soluble limestone rock by rainwater (limestone has an extremely high calcium carbonate content), as well as other factors, such as fracturing and climate. The results are rarely anything other than spectacular: weird and wonderfully formed caves and tunnels, often with fantastically shaped and richly coloured stalactites and stalagmites, such as those at Postojna (see p.216); subterranean streams and rivers; and deep-sided depressions (also known as collapse dolines), the best examples of which can be seen at the amazing **Škocjan Caves**. As well as in Slovenia, karst scenery can also be found throughout other parts of the former Yugoslavia, including along the Dalmatian coastline, in Croatia, and in Montenegro.

Should you wish to stay here, the **tourist office**, located just below the castle entrance (April–Oct Wed–Sun 10am–6pm, Nov–March Tues–Sat 10am–5pm; ⓣ05/769-0056, ⓔtic.stanjel@komen.si), can arrange **private accommodation** in apartments in Štanjel, and on tourist farms in nearby villages.

Sežana and Divača

If you're heading to Lipica or the Škocjan Caves, there's a good chance you'll pass through either **Sežana** or **Divača** at some point, as both towns are on the rail line from Ljubljana and buses pass through here en route to the coast or Trieste. Whilst neither has anything particularly interesting to see, both have accommodation as well as a handful of other practical facilities. If you do find yourself waiting for a connection in **SEŽANA** (5km north of Lipica), you could make the fifteen-minute walk north along Partizanska ulica to view the well-turned-out **Botanical Gardens** (Botanični Park). Alongside the gardens (behind the civilian cemetery) is a World War I **cemetery**, holding some fifty neatly tended graves from soldiers lost in battle between 1915 and 1917.

The **train** and **bus** stations are situated just 200m apart on Kolodvorska ulica; inside the bus station building the small and helpful **tourist office** (Mon–Fri 8am–4pm; ⓣ05/731-0128, ⓔtic.sezana@siol.net) can advise on private **accommodation** and other aspects of visits to Lipica or the Škocjan caves. Conveniently situated between the two stations is the bright and clean *Hotel Tabor*, at Kolodvorska 4 (ⓣ05/734-1551; ❺).

DIVAČA, 6km east of Lipica, is a less-enticing option but has cheaper accommodation and a couple of decent places to eat. From the **train** station on Trg 15 Aprila (buses stop here too), it's a five-minute walk up the road to the grim and gloomy *Pension Risnik* (ⓣ05/763-0008; ❷) located opposite the petrol station; a better option is the *Malovec* (ⓣ05/763-1225; ❸), 200m north of the *Risnik* along Kraška cesta at no. 30a. The *Divaški Hr'm*, next to the *Malovec* at Kraška cesta 32 (closed Tues), is a delightful little cellar **restaurant** serving up steaming plates of gnocchi and pasta; they have some good wines too (closed Tues).

Lipica

After Postojna and Lake Bled, Slovenia's most emblematic tourist draw is **Lipica**, 6km south of Sežana and just 2km from the Italian border. Having acquired the Lipica estates in 1580, Austrian Archduke Karl (son of Emperor Ferdinand I) established this stud in order to breed horses for the Spanish Riding School in Vienna, as well as the Royal Court stables in Graz. That the Lipizzaner has survived at all is remarkable, having been evacuated to southern Hungary during Napoleon's occupation in the late eighteenth century, divided by the Italians and Austrians during World War I, and then seized by the Germans during World War II. Today the horse is bred at half a dozen European stud farms and widely throughout the United States. Here at Lipica there are around three hundred horses divided between show, competition and riding horses, and an estimated three hundred more around Slovenia in private hands.

Practicalities

A tour of the **stud farm**, which entails little more than a visit to the stables and riding halls, is not in itself that enthralling, though you do get the opportunity to

The Lipizzaner

Despite competing claims from Austria and Italy over the geographical origin and lineage of the **Lipizzaner** (Lipicanec), the original stud was established here at Lipica in 1580 by the then governor of the Slovene territories, Habsburg Archduke Karl. Horses of Spanish, Arabian and Berber stock were bred with the tough and muscular local Karst horse, thus creating the Lipizzaner strain. As a result of such fastidious breeding, Lipizzaner are comparatively small in stature – 14.3 to 15.2 hands – with a long back, short, thick neck, and a powerful build. Born dark or bay coloured they do not turn white until the age of five or six, though their coat is in fact grey, a colour that only manifests itself when the horse sweats. These distinctive physical traits are complemented by a beautiful sense of balance and rhythm, a lively, high stepping-gait and even temperament. With such qualities, it's little wonder that the Lipizzaner have for centuries excelled at both **carriage driving** and as **show horses** – performing the bows, pirouettes and other manoeuvres that delight dressage cognoscenti as well as the average punter.

see these magnificent creatures close up. **Tours** take place throughout the year (daily: Jan–March & Nov–Dec 11am, 1pm, 2pm and 3pm; April–June & Sept–Oct 10am, 11am, 1pm then hourly until 5pm; July & Aug hourly 9am–6pm, except noon; 1400SIT). To really make your coming here worthwhile, try and coincide a visit with a presentation of the **Classical Riding School** (May–Oct Tues, Fri & Sun at 3pm; April Fri & Sun at 3pm; 2600SIT); whilst nothing as grand as the shows put on at the Spanish Riding School in Vienna, it's still quite something to see, the riders all toffed up in period costume while the horses go about performing their well-crafted exercises.

The school offers a number of **riding** programmes (all 50min long), from rides out in a guided group (3800SIT), to group or individual classes with an instructor (5200SIT/8900SIT), and dressage (14,000SIT). For real enthusiasts, there are a host of week-long riding courses. Reservations are required for all lessons. Between May and September it's also possible to go **carriage-riding** (Fri–Sun 3.30pm and 4.30pm; 8900SIT per carriage for 1hr, maximum 4 people; Ⓦwww.lipica.org).

If you don't have your own **transport**, getting here will be difficult; the only buses which head this way are the school ones (Mon–Fri term-time only) – otherwise you'll have to hitch or take a taxi (1500SIT), which can be booked through the tourist office in Sežana (see p.185).

Neither of the two **hotels** located within the complex, the spacious and comfortable *Maestoso* (Ⓣ05/739-1580, Ⓔlipica@siol.net; ❼), or the extremely shabby *Klub* (same number and email; ❻), are likely to appeal, or are particularly good value for money – in any case they're more interested in catering to groups. If you do plan to stick around the area, you're best off staying in Sežana or Divača (see p.185). Within the Lipica estate there are several sporting and leisure amenities available, including tennis (1750SIT per court; free to hotel guests), a casino, and a nine-hole golf course, Slovenia's only year-round course (Ⓣ05/734-6373; 5500SIT for nine holes/8000SIT for eighteen holes).

Škocjan Regional Park

Located 5km south of Divača in the belly of the **Škocjan Regional Park**, the **Škocjan Caves** are the country's most memorable natural attraction, a breathtaking complex of passages, chambers, collapsed valleys and, reputedly, the world's largest subterranean canyon. Measuring around 5800m in length, the caves were formed by the **Reka River** (literally, "River River"), which begins its journey from springs deep below Snežnik mountain 50km southeast of the cave near the Croatian border. At the village of Škocjan, not far from the cave entrance, the river sinks underground for the first time, briefly reappearing at the bottom of two collapsed dolines, before vanishing again into the mouth of the cave. It re-emerges some 40km later at the Timavo springs north of Trieste. The park also embraces three tiny villages, **Škocjan**, **Betanja** and **Matavun**, the last of which is where the cave reception is located.

Little was known about the caves until the sixteenth century, when the first maps of the system were printed, before more thoroughgoing accounts were offered in several seminal seventeenth- and eighteenth- century works, most notably Valvasor's *Glory of the Duchy of Carniola* and Gruber's *Hydrological Letters from the Carniola.*

Although parts of the cave had already been discovered, and several paths cut, during the early nineteenth century, it wasn't until around 1840 that the first systematic explorations of the main cave took place, when Giovanni Svetina from Trieste managed to penetrate some 150m downstream. Other pioneering explorers followed, but the most important explorations were left to **Anton Hanke**, a Czech mining engineer, and two colleagues who, between 1884 and 1890 progressed to the fourteenth waterfall along what is now known as the Hanke Canal – in the process stumbling upon several more chambers. A few years later four locals entered the Silent Cave for the first time. Electricity was finally installed in 1959 and the caves were given UNESCO World Heritage status in 1986.

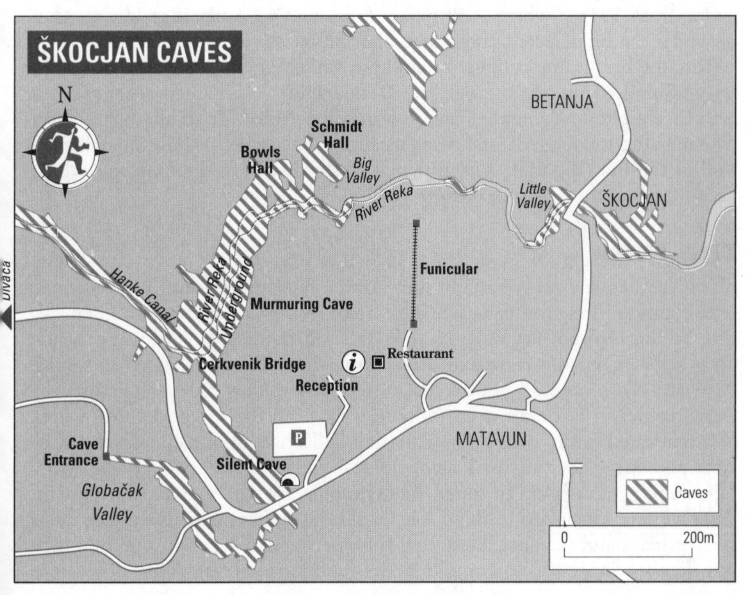

The Caves

After purchasing your ticket from the booth in the reception area (tours daily June & Sept 10am, 11.30am, and hourly 1pm–5pm; Oct–May 10am, 1pm and 3pm; 2100SIT, tours last approx 1hr 30min), join the crowd milling around by the tables and wait for the guides to appear. From here, you'll be escorted to the cave entrance down in the **Globočak Valley** (Dolina Globočak), some ten minutes' walk away. Heading along the one hundred and thirty-metre-long, artificially created tunnel, you enter the cave proper, the first part of which is called the **Silent Cave** (Tiha jama); at this point, you'll break off into different groups, depending on which language you speak.

Discovered around 1904, and totalling some 500m, the Silent Cave is comprised of several smaller chambers, each modestly decorated with stalagmites and stalactites, though neither the first, the **Paradise Cave**, nor the second, the **Calvary**, is particularly well endowed, having been subjected to earthquakes and floods aeons ago. More impressive is the one hundred and thirty-metre-long and thirty-metre-high **Great Hall** (Velika dvorana), whose most celebrated formations are the 250,000-year-old Giant stalagmite, and a ribbed dripstone stalactite dubbed the Organ, because of its resemblance to a pipe organ and the sounds it emits when tapped.

Beyond here the cave widens, the temperature drops and the low rumbling of the **Reka River** can be heard; this marks your entry into the magnificent **Murmuring Cave** (Šumeča jama), a three hundred-metre-long, sixty-metre-wide and one hundred-metre-high subterranean gorge carved out by the Reka – it is, quite simply, the most fantastic creation imaginable. From here you walk along a narrow ledge incised into the great shafts of limestone rock, towards the vertiginous forty-five-metre-high **Cerkvenik Bridge** (Cerkvenikov most), under which the Reka flows before continuing its course along the **Hanke Canal** towards further, larger chambers (accessible only to speleologists). The bridge was rebuilt in 2003, replacing the original Hanke Bridge – dating from 1933 – which itself replaced the **Cat's Footbridge**, the remains of which can be detected 20m higher, just below the ceiling.

From the bridge, the path continues upstream along the side of the gorge for several hundred metres, through the **Bowls Hall** – so-named because of its circular limestone troughs – and towards the **Schmidt Hall** (Schmidlova dvorana), the yawning, natural cave entrance which emerges into the collapsed **Velika Dolina** (Big Valley); from here it's a short walk to the funicular, which transports you the 150m back to the top.

The Park

If you've still got time, you might want to trek the **Educational Trail**, a scenic two-kilometre-long footpath, which more or less circles the two collapsed valleys, **Velika Dolina** (Big Valley) and **Mala Dolina** (Little Valley); you can pick up a leaflet from the reception area, from where the trail begins and ends. Alternatively, you could just do part of the walk taking you as far as the tiny Karst hamlet of **Škocjan**, a ten-minute walk from the reception area, where two renovated stone barns house a modest collection of implements and artefacts pertaining to the park's archeological and ethnological heritage (daily June–Sept 11am–4pm, at other times enquire at the information booth; entrance fee is included in the ticket for the cave). The most interesting items are the maps and sketches illustrating the discovery of the cave, one of which was drawn by Valvasor, and an old ladder used for lowering cavers down into the depths. The 1:6000 *Regijski park Škocjanske jame* map outlines further walks in the park.

Practicalities

Without your own **transport**, getting to the caves will entail a fair bit of walking: the nearest train station is in Divača, some 5km to the northwest by road (see p.185), but 3km (45min) if walking from the station – the caves are signposted from here. If travelling by bus, you may be able to get the driver to set you down by the access road (just off the Ljubljana–Koper highway), from where it's a more manageable walk 1.5km to the caves.

Next to the ticket booth is a café-cum-**restaurant**, where you can get drinks and simple meals.

Hrastovlje

Thirty-one kilometres south of Divača, in the upper Rižana River Valley – which roughly separates the Karst plateau from the coastal hinterland – **HRASTOVLJE** would be just another pretty, yet inconsequential, Istrian village, were it not for the Romanesque **Church of the Holy Trinity** (Svėta Trojica), whose exceptional spread of late-medieval frescoes mark it out as a cultural monument of the highest rank.

The Church

Sited on an exposed, shallow rise, and concealed within a thick, ten-metre-high, grey-stone wall, the **Church of the Holy Trinity** was built some time between the twelfth and fourteenth centuries, although the wall was a sixteenth-century addition, erected to provide a place of refuge for the locals against marauding Turks. Constructed from stone-cut square blocks, with a typical Istrian stone-slab roof, this beautifully compact church is even smaller than you might have imagined from outside the wall. The inside, comprising a simple tripartite nave, is completely unfurnished.

Taking almost ten years to complete, the **frescoes** were executed by the master Istrian painter Johannes de Castua (Janez Kastav) at the end of the fifteenth century, although they weren't discovered until the 1950s, concealed under several layers of whitewash. Far and away the most celebrated and complete painting is the *Dance of Death*, or *Dance Macabre* (see box on p.190), on the lower half of the south wall; with its powerful images alluding to the inevitability of death, this fresco pretty much surpasses any other specimen of medieval iconography in Slovenia. Cast your eye downwards and you'll see some decorative **Glagolitic inscriptions**, an ancient Slav script which originated in the ninth century as a means of converting Slavs to Christianity.

The remaining frescoes depicting numerous biblical scenes take some digesting, so it's worth focusing your attention on a select few: represented in fifteen scenes immediately above the *Dance of Death* is the cycle of Christ's Passion, while, on the opposite, north wall, the Three Kings come bearing gifts for Mary, who is seated upon a gold throne with Infant Child. On the ceilings of the north and south aisles, the calendar year is represented by scenes (note there are fourteen) of seasonal activities – hunting, harvesting and so on – and local customs, and is unique in that it is believed to be the only case of a secular cycle in a Slovene Gothic church. The apses are decorated with portraits of the Apostles, and scenes from the Crucifixion and the crowning of Mary.

The Dance of Death

The **Dance of Death** is not unique to Hrastovlje and can be found in many countries throughout Europe, from England to Estonia, although the only other one in Istria is in the village of Beram, in Croatia. Thought to have derived from a thirteenth-century literary genre called Vado Mori ("I prepare myself to die"), the artistic genre of the Dance of Death originated as **La Danse Macabre** at the Cemetery of the Innocents in Paris around 1424. More often than not painted (or carved) on the outside walls of cloisters and ossuaries, or church interiors, the composition of the dance, and the number of characters involved, varied from place to place.

In this one in Hrastovlje, a cast of eleven characters – which include the pope, a king and queen, bishop, burgher, cripple, and a child – are escorted by skeletons towards the narrator (the twelfth skeleton), who sits on a stone throne, waiting with shovel and pick at his feet, and hand poised on the coffin lid. There's some wonderful detail to admire, such as the painting of the usurer who – deciding it's not his time to go – tries to bribe the skeleton by offering a purse, seemingly impervious to the idea that not even the rich can circumvent a fate that awaits us all.

To help you negotiate your way around this tangle of paintings, there's a taped commentary available in English. If the church is locked, as it most probably will be, go to house no. 30, a five-minute walk away in the village, whereupon the old lady will dodder back up to the church with you; there's a small entrance fee to pay (500SIT).

Practicalities

Getting to Hrastovlje is not easy. The closest that **buses** get is 6km north, in the village of **Črni Val** just off the main highway to Koper. The alternative is **train**, though, rather hopelessly, there's just one train stopping here each day; the 6am from Ljubljana (7.45am from Divača), arriving in Hrastovlje at 8.16am, with the one return train to Divača/Ljubljana departing from Hrastovlje at 7.30pm. The station is actually located in the village of **Dol**, 1.5km southeast of Hrastovlje; exiting the station, take a left down the path towards the main road, from where it's around a twenty-minute walk to the church.

The Istrian Coast

Sandwiched between the Gulf of Trieste and the Croatian coast, the Slovenian seaboard packs a surprisingly large amount into its short 46km stretch, harbouring a rich complement of historical sights amongst the more traditional beach-related pursuits. Whilst its proximity to Italy ensures that it receives a healthy number of vacationing Italians, this also means that certain places can get a little mobbed at the height of summer. By way of contrast it's largely avoided by Slovenes, most of whom prefer to holiday along Croatia's Dalmatian coast. That said, in places, it possesses an abundance of charm, not least in **Piran**, a protected cultural monument and the coast's most seductive spot. **Koper**, too, possesses a fabulously appealing old town, much at odds with its prevailingly industrial backdrop; edging down the coast, the pretty little fishing town of **Izola** is worth a minor diversion, while **Portorož** – the coast's main beach resort, just a stone's throw from Piran – will appeal to those seeking more hedonistic fare. More generally, the beaches along the coast, such as they are, are invariably rocky or concrete affairs, though you might find the odd sandy spot if you're lucky.

The basis for much of the coast's fabulous cultural legacy is overwhelmingly Italian – indeed, its handful of towns wouldn't look out of place on the other side of the Adriatic – thanks to nearly 500 years of **Venetian rule** that preceded the region's incorporation into the Austro-Hungarian Empire, and, eventually, the Yugoslav Federation.

This northern part of Istria didn't actually become a part of Yugoslavia until the **1954 London Agreement**, which finally resolved the problem of post-World War II territorial boundaries between Italy and Yugoslavia. Until then, this bitterly disputed area of the Adriatic had been divided into two zones, known as the Free Territory of Trieste – Zone A, (which included Trieste), and Zone B (which included Koper); the agreement subsequently assigned Zone A to Italy and Zone B to Yugoslavia. However, neither side was entirely appeased, as both lost what they considered to be historic pieces of territory, a fact recognized by the Italians who refused to ratify the agreement, at least until the 1975 Treaty of Osimo, which did little more than review and reaffirm the original agreement. Although many Italians resettled in their homeland following the 1954 Agreement, many towns have retained significant communities.

Getting around is simple enough, with buses and ferries shuttling up and down the coast, and, if you're looking to push on to Trieste or the Croatian Istrian towns, there are frequent bus connections.

Koper

Easily reached by train from Ljubljana, and just 20km from Trieste, **KOPER** (Capodistria in Italian) is the first major stop along the coast. At first glance it's an unenticing spectacle, little more than a messy jumble of cranes, tower blocks and wasteland. However, within this gritty outer shell lies a beautifully preserved medieval core, embracing an attractive lattice of paved alleys, Italianate squares and a stack of fine cultural monuments.

Believed to have originated as Aegida in around 3 BC, the town – at that time an island – acquired several identities before the Venetians assumed control in the late thirteenth century. Thanks to its maritime industries, the town's economy remained in rude health until the beginning of the eighteenth century, when both Trieste and Rijeka (in Croatia) were proclaimed free ports and an already bleak situation was further compounded by the opening of the Vienna–Trieste rail line in 1857. Following the 1954 London Agreement, the town experienced a surge of development, with the advancement of a new port and an extension of the rail line to Koper, thus reaffirming the town's status as the coast's most important economic and political centre. Today, not only is it Slovenia's largest coastal town and chief maritime port, but it also services the shipping needs of Austria and Hungary.

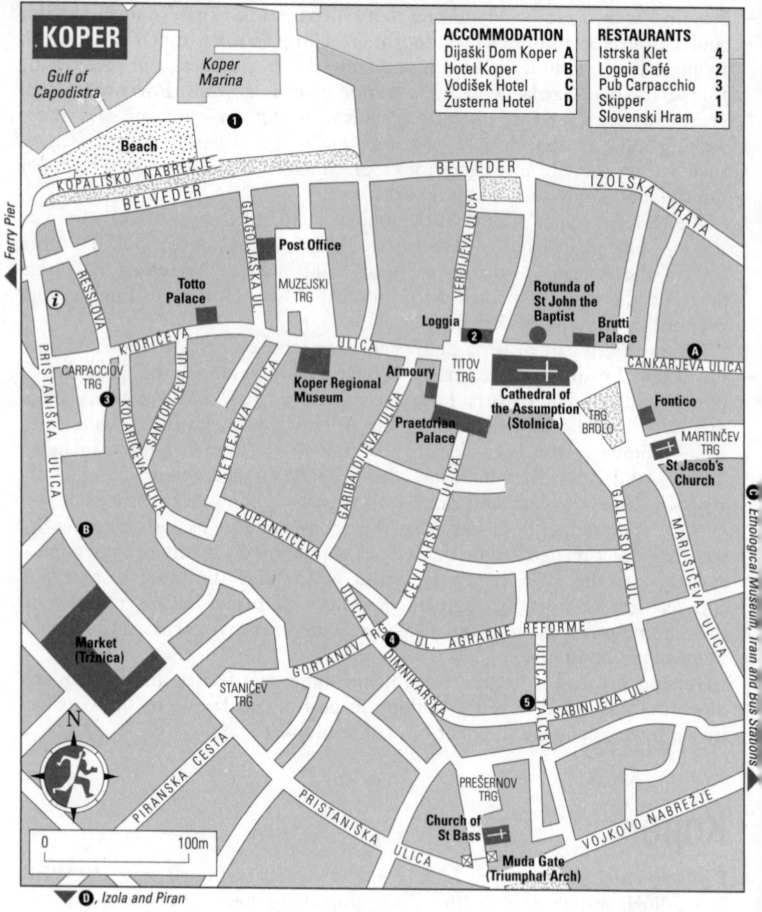

Arrival and information

The **train** and **bus** stations are located next to each other in a wasteland 1.5km southeast of town, from where it's a dull walk along Kolodvorska Cesta to the centre. The **tourist office** is located on the northwestern edge of the old town opposite the marina at Ukmarjev trg 7 (June–Aug Mon–Sat 9am–8pm, Sun 9am–noon; Sept–May Mon–Fri 9am–5pm, Sat 9am–1pm; ⓣ05/663-1010, ⓔtic@koper.si). Although the main **post office** is located next to the train station, there is another in the old town on Muzejski trg (both Mon–Fri 8am–7pm, Sat 8am–noon). There's free **Internet access** at the *Net Bar*, next to the Ethnological museum at Gramšijev trg 7 (daily 8am–10.30pm).

Four times a day between June and September, *Big Red*, a shuttle **catamaran**, sails back and forth between Ankaran (10km north of Koper by road) and Portorož, stopping at all places in between (Koper, Izola, Strunjan and Piran). A standard fare between Koper and Portorož is 1400SIT single and

1900SIT return; see ⓦwww.slo-istra.com/aquamarine for the timetable. The pier is located in the marina opposite the tourist office.

Accommodation

The tourist office can arrange **private accommodation**, although Kompas, 300m south of here at Pristaniška ulica 17 (Mon–Fri 8am–7.30pm, Sat 8am–1pm; ⓣ05/663-0582, ⓔkompas.koper@siol.net) has a far better stock of rooms (❶) and apartments (❸–❺) – note that there is a surcharge for stays of less than three nights with any private accommodation. There are no **campsites** in Koper, though there are several elsewhere along the coast; these are detailed in the relevant sections.

Those on a budget should head to the student **hostel** *Dijaški Dom Koper* at Cankarjeva 5 (ⓣ05/627-3250, ⓔddkoper@guest.arnes.si; ❶), located 100m east of the cathedral; it has one-, two- and three-bed rooms (all with shared wash and shower facilities) available during July and August, and a handful at weekends during the rest of the year. None of the town's **hotels** represent particularly good value for money, though the *Žusterna*, located out on the road to Portorož at Istrska 67 (ⓣ05/663-8000, ⓔzusterna@terme-catez.si; ❻), is a colourful, frenetic place with slick, air-conditioned rooms, some of which have a balcony; all guests receive free use of the seven pools in the adjoining Aquapark. Buses stop by the swimming pool opposite. Otherwise, the *Hotel Koper*, smack bang in the centre at Pristaniška 3 (ⓣ05/610-0500, ⓔinfo@terme-catez.si; ❻), is a stylish – albeit rather self-important – place, frequented in the main by busloads of package tourists; whilst the *Vodišek*, located in a barren spot midway between the stations and the town centre at Kolodvorska 2 (ⓣ05/639-2468, ⓦwww.hotel-vodisek.com; ❻), has neat and functional rooms, all with air-conditioning.

Carpaccio trg and Kidričeva ulica

As good a place as any to start your exploration of the old town is **Carpaccio trg**, just behind the old **salt warehouse** a short way south of the tourist office. In the centre of this peaceful little square named after the Venetian painter is the spindly **Column of St Justin**, erected to commemorate the famous naval victory against the Turks at Lepanto in 1571, in which a Koper galley participated. From here, Kidričeva ulica inclines gently eastwards past the redundant churches of **St Nicholas** (1594) and the **Holy Trinity** (1735). A little further up on the right is a splendid **Venetian-Gothic townhouse** – one of several such buildings in town – this one sporting a protruding upper floor and check-painted facade. Opposite here is the **Totto Palace**, whose facade bears a relief of a lion with an open book; traditionally, this was meant to symbolize peace, as opposed to a closed book which symbolized war; similar reliefs adorn many other prominent buildings along the coast.

A few paces along at no. 19 is the fine, sixteenth-century Mannerist-Baroque **Belgramoni-Tacco Palace**, whose interior is palpably more interesting than the **Regional Museum** housed within (Pokrajinski Muzej; Mon–Fri 8am–1pm & 6–8pm, Sat 8am–1pm; 350SIT). This insipid collection of art and cultural history merits only the briefest of visits, though it's partially redeemed by a decent archeological collection, the highlight of which is a collection of animal reliefs, and a copy of the *Dance of Death* fresco from Hrastovlje (see p.190). Housed in the pavilion next to the lapidarium, containing sculptures of Apostles and prophets, is a marginally more interesting exhibition of contemporary history, which pertains to Slovene Istria's role before, during and after the two World Wars. The most illuminating aspect of this exhibition, however, is Tone Kralj's gruesome painting, *Rapallo*, in which a woman is savaged by hideous looking creatures.

Titov trg and around

Continuing eastwards, Kidričeva ulica opens up into **Titov trg** (Tito Square), laid out in the fifteenth century and once the fulcrum of the old city. The square's stunning synthesis of Gothic, Renaissance and Baroque styles is superbly encapsulated in the **Praetorian Palace** (Pretorska palača), Koper's most enduring symbol, whose battlements look like a stage backdrop for a Renaissance drama. Equally as impressive is its facade, randomly plastered with reliefs and busts – the most striking of which is the black bust of Nicola Donato, praetor of Koper between 1579 and 1580. Although there was a building here in the thirteenth century (which was subsequently destroyed), the foundations for the current palace were laid down in the fifteenth century, when the Gothic left wing and the Renaissance right wing were constructed; its Baroque elements were added during further seventeenth-century renovations. Following the downfall of the Venetian Republic in 1797, whose governors had used the palace as their main headquarters, the palace fell into a state of long-term decline; first the Austrians moved into the adjacent **Armoury** building (previously an arms dump), then successive town authorities snubbed it in favour of alternative buildings. Its handsomely restored interior is now used almost exclusively for council and mayoral functions, and weddings; free guided tours are possible, though really there's not a whole lot to see.

Opposite the palace, the fifteenth-century town **Loggia** (Loža), with its striking Gothic-style lancet arches, has been the town's most popular meeting place ever since philosophers and artists gathered here for chinwags in the seventeenth century – its first coffee house, *Caffe della Loggia*, established in 1846, is now the *Loggia*, which remains the most swish **café** in town; the statue of the Madonna in the corner pillar was placed there to commemorate the 1554 plague. The Loggia's upper floor houses a **gallery**, which holds different exhibitions each month (Galerija Loža; Tues–Sat 3–10pm, Sun 8–10pm; 400SIT).

The **Cathedral of the Assumption** (Stolnica Marija vnebovzetja; 7am–noon & 3–7pm) on the east side of the square is believed to be the fifth or sixth church on this site, though much of this present one has eighteenth-century origins. Its exterior is an odd amalgam of Gothic lower storey and Lombardy-style upper storey, the latter part completed a century later than the lower part. By way of contrast, its vast interior, endowed with some glorious works of art and furnishings, is mostly of Baroque appearance; particularly worth paying attention to is the central nave's magnificent Rococo pulpit, designed by Lorenzo Ferolli in 1758, and, in the presbytery, the finely carved olive-wood choir pews and the gold-plate-encrusted bishop's throne, dating from 1730. The major works of art were completed by Vittore Carpaccio, the most outstanding of which is *The Enthroned Madonna with Child and Saints* from 1516. Pressed into the cathedral's south side is the formidable **city belltower** (Mon–Sat 9am–12.30pm & 4.30–7.30pm, Sun 3.30–7.30pm), a fifteenth-century structure which once doubled as a lookout; climb the 43m to the top and you'll understand why – the views of the town, coast and hinterland are tremendous. Situated on the cathedral's north side is one of the coast's oldest sacral monuments, the twelfth-century Romanesque **Rotunda of John the Baptist**.

Trg Brolo, a leafy, triangular square just east of the cathedral, showcases some terrific Venetian-Baroque architecture, the most eye-catching of which is the **Brutti Palace** on the north side, whose facade is attractively ornamented with relief images from the Old Testament – the building now functions as the town library. On the east side of the square at no. 4 is the several-times rebuilt **Fontico**, a former grain warehouse studded with rich heraldic decoration completed by Lombardian stonemasons. Tucked in just behind the Fontico is the crumbling, fourteenth-century Gothic Church of St Jacob (Cerkev Sv Jakob), which cannot be entered.

South and east of Titov trg

Back on Titov trg, pass through the portico under the Praetor's Palace and take a stroll down Čevljarska ulica (Shoemaker's Street), which took its name from the profession which was practised here for several centuries. Probably the prettiest single street in the town, Čevljarska ulica preserves a happy ensemble of two- and three-storey shuttered buildings, variously housing tenements, shops and galleries. At the end of the street cross Župančičeva ulica, continue down the steps into Gortanov trg, passing the Almerigogna Palace, whose delightful pink-chequered facade now conceals a beer hall. Gortanov trg segues into Staničev trg, which in turn brings you out to the main road ringing the old town, a rather sobering return to the twenty-first century.

By taking a left turn at the junction of Čevljarska ulica and Župančičeva ulica, you'll wind up at Prešernov trg (Prešeren Square), a pleasant, elongated space, in the centre of which stands Ponte's Fountain; built in 1666, the fountain is furnished with a small, Plečnik-style bridge – "*ponte*" is Italian for bridge – and, at the bottom, four masks from whence water spouted until 1898. South of the fountain is the triumphal arch-style Muda Gate (Vrata Muda), built in 1516 and the last of the city's twelve town gates; note, on the inner arches, two reliefs of a blazing sun with the shape of a face, which is the city coat-of-arms.

Housed in another exceptional Venetian-Gothic house east of town at Gramšijev trg 4, is the **Ethnological Museum** (Etnološki Muzej; March–Oct; Mon–Fri 8am–1pm & 6–8pm, Sat 8am–1pm; 350SIT), one of the most enjoyable museums on the coast, though it's sadly little visited due to its rather isolated location. For the most part, the collection focuses on the Istrian cultural landscape, with particular emphasis on the art of stonecutting and stonedressing, industries which first took wing in the region during the seventeenth century. The pick of the museum's collection is its assemblage of skilfully hewn stone-cut **portals**, commonly found at entrances to courtyards and houses; many portals were traditionally ornamented with floral patterns, sacral symbols and other motifs and reliefs, though few have been preserved. More superb stonemasonry can be seen in a partial reconstruction of a **shepherd's hut**, typically used to store farming tools and arable crops but also useful as a form of shelter during extremes in temperature; and a portion of a **dry-stone wall**, a prevalent feature of the Istrian landscape. To round off this engaging collection, there is a presentation of a Koper **kitchen**, at the centre of which is a hearth, surrounded by some exquisite copper, glass and china food-preparation items garnered from the Veneto and Friuli regions, and which date from the nineteenth and twentieth centuries.

Eating and drinking

Disappointingly, Koper has a meagre selection of **restaurants**. A very congenial place is *Slovenski Hram*, located a short walk northeast of Prešernov trg at

Ulica Talcev 8, which serves up salads, pasta, meat and fish, as well as a very strong veggie menu (closed Sun). Almost as good is *Istrska Klet* at Župančičeva ulica 39, which has filling domestic fare and wines straight from the barrel (closed Sat). Far more straightforward and clinical is the fish restaurant, *Skipper*, located 100m north along the road running behind the beach at Kopališko Nabrežje 3, though it does have some fine views overlooking the water. Otherwise, you can pick up goods from the lively **market** by the shopping centre (Tržnica) on Pristaniška, which also has a couple of very tempting ice-cream parlours.

Similarly, **drinking** venues are thin on the ground. The grooviest spot around is *Pub Carpaccio* (daily 5pm–1am), on the square of the same name, an English-style place with split-level flooring and a good selection of beers. Both its setting, on Titov trg, and its choice of drinks, mark the *Loggia Café* out as the place to indulge in coffee (see p.194).

Festivals and Activities

The **Primorsko Summer Festival**, a two-month-long series of open-air theatrical performances (and occasionally dance and music), takes place in several towns along the coast, but principally here and in Izola and Portorož. Some of the more unusual venues include a catamaran, a disused railway tunnel and the Sečovlje saltpans (see p.206). Otherwise, the main summer event is **Koper Nights** at the end of July, a weekend of theatrical and musical performances, culminating in an epic fireworks display.

The town's small, tidy beach is located between the pier and the Marina on Kopališko Nabrežje (daily 8am–8pm; 450SIT), while further fun can be had at the Aquapark, located in the *Žusterna* (see p.193); it has a total of seven indoor and outdoor pools (daily 9am–9pm; 1050SIT for 3hr; 2200SIT all day).

Izola and around

Jutting out to sea on a rounded promontory 6km south of Koper, **IZOLA** is a busy little fishing town and one of the country's fastest-growing tourist destinations. Though most visitors come here for the beaches, Izola possesses an endearing old town core, whose narrow, sloping streets and pastel-coloured tenements delight in all their crumbling charm.

Numerous local ruins bear testament to the long-standing presence of the Romans hereabouts, not least in Simon's Bay, where the ancient port of Heliaetum was located – it's said that, at very low tide, parts of the ancient pier are still visible. First mentioned in historical sources in 972 AD as Insula, the town enjoyed a brief period of autonomy before becoming a satellite of Venice in 1280, which it remained until the Republic's downfall in 1797; around the same time, both the town wall and its two gates were pulled down, and the town (hitherto an island) was finally connected to the mainland. Thereafter, the town acquired the northern Adriatic's largest fishing fleet, as well as a number of fish canneries, the first of which opened in 1879. While tourism has since supplanted the industry as the main source of income, the town's fishing tradition remains alive and kicking.

Arrival and information

The town's main **bus stop** is on Trg Republike, from where it's a 50m walk west to the small and helpful **tourist office** at Sončno nabrežje 2 (June to mid-Sept daily 8am–9pm; mid-Sept–May Mon–Fri 8am–7pm, Sat 8am–noon; ⓣ05/640-1050). The *Big Red* **catamaran** docks at the pier by the fishing port, opposite Veliki trg. Between April and October, the *Prince of Venice* catamaran offers day-trips across to Venice and back; tickets (the schedule changes monthly; 15,000SIT) can be purchased from the Kompas agency in Portorož, Obala 41 (ⓣ05/617-8000). Trg Republike is also where the **post office** is located (Mon–Fri 8am–7pm, Sat 8am–noon).

Accommodation

Several agencies can arrange **private accommodation**, the most convenient of which is Bele Skale (daily: June–Aug 6am–7pm; Sept–May Mon–Fri 6am–6pm, Sat 6am–noon; ⓣ05/640-3555, ⓔbeleskale@siol.net), right next to the bus stop. The cheapest place to **stay** in town is the *Hotel Riviera* (ⓣ05/641-7159; ❶), a somewhat misleading name for this large student dorm located on the waterfront, 200m south of the tourist office at Prekmorskih brigad 7; the rooms, available in summer only, come with or without shower facilities; the *Hotel Marina* in the centre of town on Veliki trg (ⓣ06/660-4100; ❻), is a considerable step up in class, with variously sized air-conditioned rooms, some of which have large balconies with sea views. Located amidst a pine grove atop a bluff 2.5km west of town is the *Belvedere Hotel* (ⓣ05/660-5100, ⓦwww.belvedere.si), which has good-looking rooms (❻) and apartments (❻–❼) housed within several brightly coloured villas; within the grounds, there is a **campsite** (April–Oct); buses doing the Koper–Portorož route stop outside the entrance. Izola's other campsite, the *Jadranka*, is wedged between the noisy main road and its own bit of beach 1km east of town (ⓣ05/640-2300; April–Oct). Conveniently, buses to and from Koper pass by here.

The Town

Everything of interest in Izola is located within the confines of the old town. From **Trg Republike** head north to Kristinov trg, past the small market, and then left up Smrekarjeva ulica for about 100m before taking a right turn down Alme Vivode. Just before the church, a passageway leads to the **Railway Museum** (Tues–Sun 10am–5pm; 500SIT), which contains a staggering assortment of model trains assembled from all over the world. Its chief exhibit, however, is a model replica of the Parenzana Line, once the most important transport link between Central Europe and Istria; built in 1902 by the Austrians, the line ran between Trieste and Poreč (in Croatia), passing through Koper, Izola and Portorož along the way, until 1937 when Mussolini pulled the plug and closed it. The locomotive that used to chug up and down the line is stationed at the town's eastern entrance by the Jadranka campsite. Meanwhile, the line – passing through settlements, hills, vineyards and all the old tunnels – has recently been transformed into a **cycle** and **recreation track**; ask at the tourist office for more information.

From the church, take a left, and then another left, onto Gregorčičeva ulica; after about 300m you come to the town's most important architectural set piece, the **Besenghi degli Ughi Palace**, distinguished by its pale blue, stucco-ornamented wrought-iron grilles. Its interior, too, is festooned with stuccowork, but is especially worth viewing for its first-floor salon, furnished with a fine wooden balcony and illusionist ceiling piece – the palace is now home to a music school. The street to the side of the building, Bruna ulica, slopes upwards to the much remodelled sixteenth-century **Church of St Maurus** (Cerkev Sv Mavricij), whose dark yet impressive clutch of paintings do little to lift the air of gloom; the mighty **belltower**, visible from all over town, was built in 1585.

From the church, head down Garibadjeva, then Krpanova, which brings you to Veliki trg and the waterfront. From Veliki trg walk south past the **Municipal Palace**, whose Gothic frontage bears another relief of a lion with an open book, and round to Manzioli trg, a bright little square on which stands the **Church of St Mary** (Cerkev Sv Marija), whose oldest parts date from the ninth century. Directly opposite the church is the recently restored Venetian late-Gothic **Manzioli Palace**, which now houses the town's Italian centre. Walking down Koprska ulica and Ljubljanska ulica, two pleasant streets that curl southwards towards Trg Republike, you'll notice a disproportionate number of **artists' workshops and galleries**; these were set up a few years ago on the initiative of the town authorities, who decided to rent out these previously empty buildings for free in the hope of rejuvenating the area – evidently, this was a highly successful strategy.

Izola has a couple of good **beaches**, both of which are free: one of the best along the coast is at **Simon's Bay**, a blue flag beach 1.5km west of the centre. The rocky beach north of Veliki trg, which also has a grassy area, is less developed.

Eating, drinking and entertainment

The most convivial **place to eat** is *Gušt*, just south of Trg Republike at Drevored 1 Maja, serving up over thirty varieties of pizza, steaming plates of pasta and spaghetti, soups and salads (open until 1am Fri & Sat) – it's also a good place to drink. Of those restaurants along the waterfront, the best is *Parangal* at Sončno nabrežje 20, a refined, beautifully decorated place, with a spot-on fish menu. Next door, the *Wall Pub* is the liveliest spot for a beer (open until midnight). Izola can also boast two of the coast's better **clubs**: *Gavioli* (Fri & Sat; entrance 2500–4000SIT) out in the industrial zone east of town, and the cheaper *Club Belvedere* (daily; entrance 1000SIT) in the grounds of the *Hotel Belvedere*. One of the best events along the coast is the **Mediterranean Festival**, which features a quality line-up of musicians from all genres including rock, ethno and brass. Performances take place every weekend during July and August on Manzioli trg.

Strunjan

A few kilometres along the coast from Izola is **STRUNJAN**, a small, yet widely dispersed, settlement, part of which has been turned into a **nature reserve**. All Koper–Piran buses stop just off the main road, from where it's a three-hundred-metre walk west towards the pleasant Strunjan **campsite** (Ⓣ05/678-2076). Five hundred metres further on, in a wonderfully secluded spot facing the bay, is the *Salinera complex*, which has **accommodation** in the form of a rather tatty hotel (❹), and in more comfortable bungalows (❹) – both are open between April and September (Ⓣ05/676-3100); there's also a decent bathing area here (800SIT). Retracing your steps back to the abandoned saltpans, where the brackish water now supports a wide range of fauna, walk north along the narrow path to another, busier, beach (500SIT), to the west of which is **Giuseppe Tartini's Villa**, once the Tartini family home (see p.201) but now off-limits to visitors.

North of the large **Stjuža lagoon**, which backs onto the beach, a path trundles up to the top of the cliffs, passing the Church of St Mary and a small snack bar along the way. Unique along the Adriatic for its distinctive layers of Flysch sediment – composed of sandstone, marl and turbidite – the most prominent feature of this stretch of coastline is **Cape Ronek** (Rtič Ronek) at its northernmost point, which harbours what few sub-Mediterranean species exist in the region, such as myrtle and strawberry trees. Below, in the **Bay of St Cross** (Zaliv Sv Križa), the large bed of seaweed shelters fan-mussels, sea dates and crabs. From the cliff top several paths wind down to the rocky beaches below, popular with naturists.

Piran

Located on the tip of a long, tapering peninsula that projects like a lizard's tail into the Adriatic, **PIRAN** – the most Italianate of the coastal towns – is simply delightful. Having retained its compact medieval shape and character, the town is a tangle of arched alleys and tightly packed ranks of houses, fantastic Venetian-inspired architecture and exquisite little churches.

Major urban development first occurred during the seventh century following the fall of the Roman Empire, when Piran became a heavily fortified "castrum". Under Venetian rule, which began here in 1283, the town's physical appearance changed considerably, as further town walls were erected to supplement the existing ones – which at that time encompassed the western Punta district at the end of the promontory. Economically too, the town was in good shape, thanks in no small measure to its three **saltworks** – in Sečovlje, Strunjan and Lucija, of which only the first is still operational. A prolonged period of decline ensued thereafter, first under the Habsburgs, and

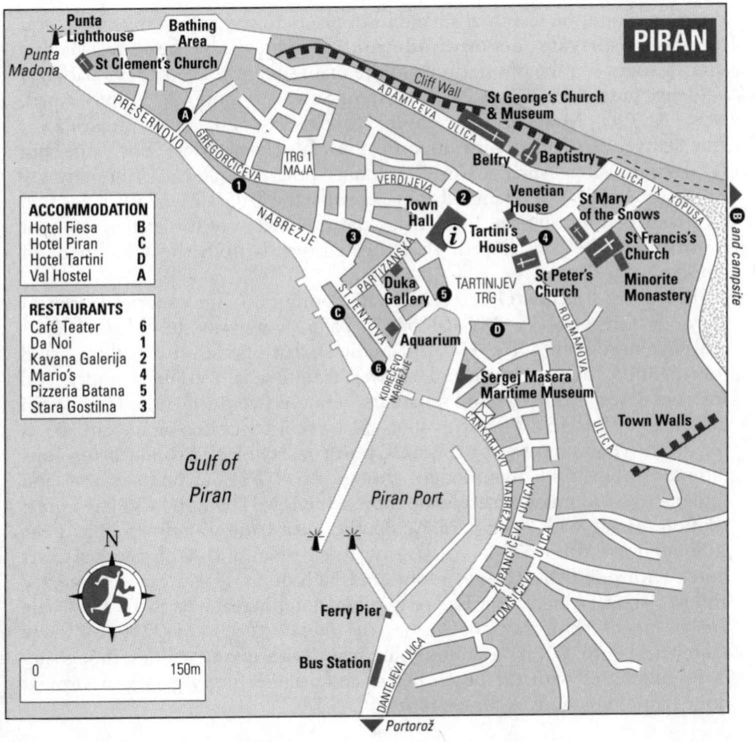

then, between the two World Wars, the Italians. However, the development of nearby Portorož as a popular health resort, and the construction of the Lucija–Piran rail line, last operational in 1956, lead to an increase in visitors to the town. Whilst relations with Italy are today on a somewhat better footing, ongoing disputes with Croatia over fishing rights in the Bay of Piran are doing little to ameliorate an already bitter relationship between the two countries.

Arrival and information

The **bus station** is located on Dantejeva ulica, from where it's a pleasant 400m walk past the bustling little fishing harbour to Tartinjev trg, the main square. Located on the square's west side, by the town hall, is the **tourist office** (July & Aug 9am–1.30pm & 3–9pm; rest of year Mon–Fri 9am–4pm, Sat 10am–2pm; ⓣ05/673-0220, ⓦwww.portoroz.si). The **post office** is located on Cankarjevo nabrežje (Mon–Fri 8am–7pm, Sat 8am–noon). There is **Internet access** on the third floor of the student centre at Župančičeva 14 (daily 1–9pm; 1000SIT). The *Big Red* **catamaran** docks at the south side of the marina near the bus station. There are other companies hereabouts offering **boat trips** up and down the coast, such as the **Marconi**, which offers cruises down to Rovinj (6000SIT) and Brioni (12,000SIT) in Croatia – your best bet, however, is to contact one of the agencies here (such as Maona) or in Portorož.

Accommodation

Piran can count on less than a handful of places to stay, which may force you to opt for **private accommodation**, in which case head to Maona, midway between the bus station and the main square at Cankarjevo nabrežje 7 (daily: June–Sept Mon–Sat 9am–8pm, Sun 9am–noon & 5–8pm; April, May & Oct Mon–Fri 9am–5pm; ⓣ05/673-4520, ⓦwww.maona.si). Alternatively, try Turist Biro opposite the *Hotel Piran* (May–Sept 9am–1pm & 4–8pm; Oct–April Mon–Fri 9am–1pm; ⓣ05/673-2509, ⓦwww.turistbiro-ag.si). The cramped Fiesa **campsite** (ⓣ05/674-6230) is located 1km east of Piran by the Fiesa Lake; the quickest way to get here by foot is to follow the coastal path that runs eastwards from the Church of St George.

The superb *Val* **hostel**, secreted away amongst an atmospheric warren of alleys at Gregorčičeva 38a (ⓣ05/673-2555, ⓦwww.hostel-val.com; ❶ – ten-percent discount for HI card-holders), has spotless two- three- and four-bedded rooms and shared shower facilities; it also has laundry and Internet access. There's a good restaurant here too (see p.203). The *Hotel Tartini* on Tartinjev trg 15 (ⓣ05/671-1666, ⓦwww.hotel-tartini-piran.com; ❼) is one of the coast's most elegant **hotels**, featuring stylish and colourful air-conditioned rooms with ultramodern fittings, small TV and minibar; sea- and square-facing rooms are marginally more expensive. The hotel also has a great rooftop terrace with small pool. Across the square, the waterfront *Hotel Piran* at Stjenkova 1 (ⓣ05/676-2100, ⓦwww.hoteli-piran.si; ❻-❼) is another smart hotel, with polished, spacious rooms and bathrooms; if you can get one, try and bag a sea-facing room. The only other hotel hereabouts is the beachside *Hotel Fiesa*, 1km east of town in Fiesa (ⓣ05/671-2200, ⓦwww.hotel-fiesa.com; ❺); it's a comfortable place with good facilities, though it's not a quiet area with the beach below and a rather noisy games room next door (same directions as for campsite).

Tartinjev trg

The town's most obvious point of reference is **Tartinjev trg** (Tartini Square), whose striking, marble-surfaced oval interior features a bronze statue of the acclaimed violinist Giuseppe Tartini (1692–1770), after whom the square is named. At its entrance, on the southeastern corner, are two fifteenth-century **stone flagpoles** bearing several Latin inscriptions and reliefs of St Mark with the lion symbol, and St George, the town patron.

The building on the square's west side is the old **court house**, adjacent to which is the **town hall**, dating from the late nineteenth century and distinguished by four graceful pillars, the lower parts of which are beautifully ornamented; in the central axis is the ubiquitous lion relief with an open book (see p.193). Continuing in a clockwise fashion, the stunning ruby-red Gothic **Venetian House** (Benečanke hiša) at no. 10 is the oldest preserved building on the square, a fifteenth-century edifice showcasing some outstanding stonemasonry, exemplified by its superb corner balcony. The relief under the windows on the second floor bears the inscription "Lassa pur dir" ("Let them talk"), a retort to gossiping townsfolk disapproving of a wealthy merchant's romantic liaisons with a local girl. A few paces further south, up the small flight of steps, is **Tartini's House** (Tartinijeva Hiša; daily: June–Aug 9am–noon & 6–9pm; rest of year 11am–noon & 5–6pm; 250SIT), where the musician was born in 1692. After being schooled in Koper, Tartini left Piran for Padua, in Italy, and remained there for the greater part of his life, composing, teaching and performing, before later devoting himself to theoretical and pedagogical issues. He is buried alongside his wife in Padua. One room of the birthplace has been converted into a small memorial room containing one of his four violins – the whereabouts of the other three are unknown – his death mask, and scores of books, diaries and letters.

Opposite Tartini's house is **St Peter's Church** (Cerkev Sv Petra), unremarkable save for the **Crucifix from Piran**, one of three such medieval masterpieces on the eastern Adriatic (the others are in Split, in Croatia, and Kotor, in Montenegro). This much-restored polychrome sculpture, a beautifully mournful Christ nailed to a tree-shaped cross, is believed to have been completed some time in the fourteenth century, though its creator is unknown.

West of Tartinjev trg

Heading west from Tartinjev trg through the dense lattice of arched alleys, you'll wind up at **Trg 1 Maja** (First of May Square), once the heart of the town but now a pleasantly scruffy space framed by peeling Baroque edifices. Located under the square's vast elevated deck and guarded by allegorical stone statues of law and justice is a stone rainwater cistern, built in 1776 following a drought in order to conserve water; at the rear, the two statues of babies – one holding a pot, the other a fish – once connected surrounding gutters with the cistern. Classical concerts are regularly held here during the summer.

Picking your way west through the maze of streets will eventually bring you out at the very tip of the peninsula and the **Punta lighthouse**, behind which is the sadly decrepit **Church of St Clement** (Cerkev Sv Zdravja), also known as the Church of Our Lady of Health on account of the role it played during the plague which swept across Istria in the seventeenth century; the interior can only be seen through the grilles or by attending mass. The lively promenade east of here is the location for the town's main (concrete) **bathing area** and a handful of places to eat. It is also one of the coast's best **diving** areas – if you fancy a spot of diving (which doesn't come cheap), Sub-net, along the promenade at no. 24 (Ⓣ05/673-2218, Ⓦwww.sub-net.si), offers a comprehensive programme. En route back to the square take a look at the fine Gothic **Dolphin Gate** (Dolfinova vrata) in Savudrijska ulica, and, if you've time, pop into the **Duka Gallery**, close by at Partizanska 2 (Atelje Duka; May–Sept 9am–1pm & 7–10pm; Oct–April 9am–1pm & 4–7pm; Ⓦwww.ateljeduka-sp.si), which has a marvellous display of pottery and ceramic art; you can even see items being made, many of which are for sale.

Church of St George and around

Crowning a commanding spot on a steep rise to the north of town is the temple-like **Church of St George** (Cerkev Sv Jurji), originally built some time around the twelfth century, but whose present appearance dates from 1637. It's a classic example of a simple Baroque hall-church, lined with seven mighty altars, each laden with paintings by Venetian and Dutch artists; the second altar on the left also incorporates a large sculpture of St George slaying the dragon. Take a look too at the cream and gold church organ, a magnificent specimen designed in 1746 by the Venetian master organ builder Peter Nakič. At the time of writing, the church was undergoing a major restoration programme, and it'll be several years before this is completed. The unusually long and deep presbytery, which can still be viewed during the period of closure, boasts the largest oil on canvas painting in the country, a colourful depiction of the martyrdom of St George (1844); by way of contrast, the other two paintings here, *Mass of Bolsensa* and *The Miracle of St George*, are rather dull.

Displayed within the small **church museum** (Župnijski Muzej; Mon & Wed–Fri 10am–1pm & 5–8pm, Sat & Sun 10am–8pm; 200SIT), which is actually more interesting than it sounds, is a glittering hoard of church treasures, including bejewelled chalices, reliquaries and staffs, though the most memorable piece is a marvellous silver-coated sculpture of St George and the dragon. One floor below are some well-preserved archeological remains from an eighth-century Roman temple and a section of the church as it was in the fourteenth century; look out for the protruding bones in the corner. The lapidary, held in the basement, is especially interesting for its superb pictures illustrating the restoration process of the Crucifix from Piran, now in St Peter's Church (see p.201), and a four hundred-year-old wooden model of St George's Church thought to be the oldest model of its type in the country. Between the church and **Baptistry** – where a large Roman sarcophagus can be viewed – is the monumental **belfry** (100SIT), a fine-looking structure built in 1609 and modelled on the campanile in St Mark's Square, Venice. If you thought the views from the church terrace were impressive, then you'll be wowed by the sensational vista of the Adriatic atop the 46-metre-high tower.

South of here, amongst the tightly knit web of streets are a cluster of beautiful little churches. At the corner of Istrska and Bolniška, the delightfully named **Church of St Mary of the Snows** (Cerkev Marija Snežna) features a marvellous Baroque altar and two broad canvases depicting the Annunciation and other scenes from the life of the Virgin Mary. Opposite here is the fourteenth-century, but much remodelled, **Church of St Francis**, whose impressive gallery of paintings would be even more valuable had the most important one – *Mary with all the Saints* by Vittore Carpaccio – not been taken to Italy in 1940. It's an issue that still rankles with Slovenes, many of whom insist that this and other valuable Renaissance works be returned to Slovenia (these are collectively known as "Istria's Jewels", some of which are currently on display in Rome); not surprisingly, the Italians have steadfastly resolved to keep them. The adjoining **Minorite Monastery** incorporates a bright atrium (*Križni Hodnik*, or *Passage of the Cross*), entered via a lovely stone-carved portal; the acoustics in the atrium are splendid, so try and catch a concert here if you can. Unfortunately, owing to previous incidents of theft and vandalism, most of Piran's churches are closed, or can only be viewed through metal grilles. However, if you wish to visit any of them contact the tourist office.

From Korpusa ulica (back up by St George's Church), one path heads down towards a rocky beach and onwards to the small bay at **Fiesa** 1km away (mind out for falling rock and debris from the cliff face, which strangely isn't protected), the other uphill towards Mogorn Hill – which is also accessible from Tartinijev trg via Rožmanova ulica. Ranged across the top of the hill is a two-hundred-metre stretch of the old **town walls**, completed between the late fifteenth and early sixteenth centuries and perforated with seven inspiring-looking towers; at the southern end of the wall stands the Gothic **Rašpor Gate** (Rašporska vrata). The walls, now connected by specially constructed walkways and stairs, offer the best photo opportunities in town.

South of Tartinjev trg

Housed in the battered old building to the west of the marina is the **aquarium** (Akvarij; mid-June to Aug daily 9am–10pm; April to mid-June & Sept 10am–noon & 2–7pm; 500SIT), which accommodates a rather desperate assortment of marine life in its depressing tanks.

Occupying the splendid nineteenth-century **Gabrielli Palace** on the opposite side of the marina, is the **Sergej Mašera Maritime Museum** (Pomorski Muzej Sergej Mašera; Tues–Sun: July & Aug 9am–noon & 6–9pm; Sept–June 9am–noon & 3–6pm; 500SIT), named after the naval commander, whose destroyer, *Zagreb*, was blown up off the Croatian coast during World War II. The highlight of this eminently enjoyable collection, which charts Slovenia's seafaring exploits, is its outstanding ensemble of eighteenth-century model ships – originally built as teaching aids for future naval officers and nautical engineers – made in the Gruber workshop in Ljubljana; one model in particular to look out for is the Austrian warship, *Emperor Charles VI*. On the ground floor there is a fine, and cleverly presented, display of underwater archeological finds from the Slovene Istrian coast, consisting mainly of Roman amphorae, fragments of earthen vessels and lead tiles and hoops; there's also an informative ethnological saltworks collection, which will especially appeal if you're thinking of visiting the saltpans in Sečovlje (see p.206).

Eating and drinking

Best avoided is the row of uninspiring, rather samey and very expensive **restaurants** lining the waterfront promenade west of the *Hotel Piran*. Instead, there are a brace of enjoyable alternatives nearby, such as the very comfortable restaurant in the *Hostel Val*, which has a colourful salad bar and good domestic wines to complement its accomplished menu. *Stara Gostilna*, 50m north of the *Hotel Piran* at Savudrijska 2, is a secluded place with a pleasant little conservatory restaurant and pavement dining – the menu is limited but the food is decent. *Pizzeria Batana*, housed in the old courthouse by the marina front, is a standard pizzeria but its agreeably tatty terrace is an enjoyable place to eat. *Mario's*, across the square by Tartini's house, is a more traditional gostilna which does a good line in moderately priced meats and grills.

The town's most popular **drinking** spot is *Café Teater*, next to the theatre by the waterfront; as lively a place as this can be – the views are excellent too –

the beer is ridiculously expensive and the staff rather ill-mannered. A far better bet is *Da Noi*, on Prešeren nabrežje; its neat outdoor drinking terrace is complemented by a cool, indoor cellar-style bar (both of these open until midnight). For a decent cup of coffee in relaxing surrounds, head to *Kavana Galerija*, just off Tartinjev trg.

Portorož and around

Situated in its own sunny sheltered bay just 2km south of Piran, **PORTOROŽ** (Port of Roses) is Slovenia's major beach resort. While it may feel like stepping into a cold shower after Piran's charm, it's a likeable enough place, and despite possessing all the customary trappings of your average seaside resort, it's by no means a brash place; moreover, the beaches are clean, safe and well maintained, and there's enough going on here to keep activity-seekers happy.

The town's modern appearance belies a history dating back to the thirteenth century, when Benedictine monks from the nearby monastery of St Lawrence cured a range of diseases using the local mineral-rich brine and mud from the saltpans, the same health-inducing properties that led to the development of Portorož as a popular resort in the nineteenth century. The resort's first hotel – originally intended to accommodate the military – went up in 1830, followed by the once magnificent *Palace Hotel* in 1912, built in expectation of a visit by Emperor Franz Jozef. Whilst the town remains a popular health and treatment centre, most visitors to Portorož today come here for the more traditional **beach** diversions.

Arrival and information

From Piran it's a thirty-minute **walk**, via the Bernadin Complex, to Portorož. The main **bus stop** is located midway along Obala, the main coastal strip, though buses doing the loop between Piran and Koper stop at regular intervals along here. The **tourist office** is housed in the large building opposite the bus stop at Obala 16 (July & Aug 9am–1.30pm & 3–9pm; Sept–June 10am–5pm; ⓣ05/674-8260, ⓦwww.portoroz.si). The **post office** is at K Stari cesta 1, just down from the *Hoteli Palace* (Mon–Fri 8am–7pm, Sat 8am–noon). There is expensive **Internet access** at the Student Dom Portorož, west of town at Obala 11 (June–Aug daily 3–11pm; Sept–May Mon–Fri 1–9pm; 1000SIT for 1hr). The beaches aside, everything of interest is located along Obala.

Accommodation

As befits Slovenia's major beach resort, Portorož is awash with **hotels**, though most are managed by small groups of companies, resulting in a characterless uniformity to the majority; furthermore, there is nothing which could remotely be termed budget. This being the case, your best bet is **private accommodation**, for which the most efficient agency is Tourist Service Portorož, conveniently located by the main bus stop (July & Aug daily 8am–10pm; Sept to mid-Oct daily 9am–9pm; mid-Oct to June Mon–Fri 9am–5pm; ⓣ05/674-0360, ⓦwww.tourist-portoroz-sp.si); they have the best stock of both rooms (❶–❷) and apartments (❷–❼), all of which are priced according to category and distance from the sea. Otherwise, Maona, just around the corner at Obala 53, is a useful backup (daily June–Aug Mon–Sat 9am–8pm, Sun 10am–1pm & 5–8pm; Sept–May Mon–Fri 9am–5pm; Ⓣ05/674-0363, Ⓦwww.maona.si). With any agency, it's almost always assumed that you'll be staying for at least three days, so if you aren't, expect to pay thirty percent more. Out of season, prices drop considerably. The town's large **campsite** is located 2km south of the main bus stop in the small suburb of Lucija (Ⓣ05/690-6000; May–Sept).

Hotels

The village-like **Bernadin complex** on the western edge of town (midway between Portorož and Piran) incorporates three contrasting places: the *Emona* (Ⓣ05/695-0000, Ⓦwww.h-bernadin.si; ❾), a monstrous-looking building sloping down to the sea, but which has quite spectacular rooms and sea views and all the attendant facilities of a five-star hotel; the very well-appointed *Histrion* (same tel. as *Emona*; ❽); and the unfortunately named *Vile Park* (same tel. as *Emona*; ❺; closed April–Oct), the cheapest hotel in town – guests of all three receive free entry to the Waterpark located in the complex (see below).

The almost identical *Riviera* (Ⓣ05/692-0000, Ⓦwww.hoteli-morje.si; ❼) and *Slovenija* (same contact details as *Riviera*) at Obala 33 are two of the better-value hotels along the main strip; the former has an authentic Thai Massage Centre. Of the cluster of Metropol-owned hotels at Obala 77 (towards Lucija), the roadside *Lucija* (Ⓣ05/690-3000, Ⓦwww.metropolgroup.si; ❻), and the *Roža* (Ⓣ05/690-2000; ❽), behind, are the only ones possessing any semblance of character – guests of these hotels receive free use of the tennis courts and the swimming pool, both of which are located opposite the *Lucija*. At some point, you're bound to pass the gutted **Hotel Palace** on Obala, a once grand establishment but now stripped of its dignity and awaiting its fate.

The beaches

The main **beach** (8am–8pm; 500SIT, 400SIT after 1pm, free after 5pm), an incongruous mix of sand, grass and concrete, is clean and well maintained, with lifeguards dispersed along the shore and a wide range of facilities available. Parasols and sunbeds can be rented (600SIT), as well as cabins and safes (same price plus 1100SIT deposit). For those intending to spend some time here, beach passes are available (3200SIT for 7 days, 4200SIT for 10 days and 5900SIT for 15 days). Inevitably, it can get tremendously crowded when it's hot, though there's usually enough space to go around; otherwise you could head to one of several **private beaches** – in effect those owned by the hotels – the best of which are those in front of the *Hotel Emona* (1300SIT) and the *Hotel Slovenija* (600SIT). All these designated beaches are roped off and it is forbidden to swim outside the boundary. There are other spots along the beachfront (essentially concrete banks) where you can bathe for free and without restriction.

There are activities aplenty to be had on the main beach. The **water sports centre** in the central kiosk offers, among other activities, water-skiing (6000SIT) and jet-skiing (11,000SIT for 30min). The Laguna Waterpark in the Bernadin Complex has a beautiful **swimming pool** (900SIT), with a great section for kids, and Turkish and Finnish saunas (1800SIT). There's also a good pool opposite the *Metropol Hotel* (daily 8am–7pm; 900SIT), next door to which are **tennis** courts (1500SIT for 1hr). The Terme Palace **spa**, located within the *Hoteli Palace* at Obala 43 (Ⓣ05/696-9001, Ⓦwww.hoteli-palace.si), houses some five different centres, each offering a bewildering range of treatments and therapies – the centre also accommodates two thermal pools and two whirlpools. From the main pier, a number of boat companies solicit custom for **excursions** around the bay and to other destinations along the coast, including Poreč in Croatia and Trieste in Italy.

Seča

If you want to leave the crowds behind, take a stroll over to **Seča**, 2km south of town. Dispersed throughout the western end of this knobbly peninsula is the **Former Viva Sculpture Park** (April–Sept 9am–9pm; Oct–March until 4pm – accessible via the road behind the campsite or via a set of steps partway through the campsite), one of several such sculpture parks in Slovenia (each park demonstrates works of art made from a different material). This particular grouping, opened in 1961, consists of over one hundred greying, weather-worn pieces carved from stone; though the odd piece might interest, a better reason for coming here is for the views back to Portorož and the sea. On the other side of the peninsula are the famous Sečovlje saltpans (see below).

Eating, drinking and entertainment

Obala is lined with an endless succession of indistinguishable **restaurants**, pizzerias and snack joints, few of which stand out. One restaurant worth trying, however, is *Zlato Sidro*, 100m east of the Maona agency at no. 55; it's a restful, rather old-fashioned place, but its fish, the mainstay of a reasonably pricey menu, comes highly recommended. Away from here, there are a couple of decent places worth venturing to, the best of which is *Tomi*, 500m north of the main bus stop, just by the bend in the road at Letoviška 1; this smart place, with a vast canopied terrace, has a strong menu, featuring fish – including exotic starters such as truffles and crab – and stomach-busting, meat-heavy Serbian dishes. Halfway up the hill towards Piran, at Vilfanova 10, is *Miranda*, a low-key place with a tidy, straw-covered terrace from which to enjoy the sea views; the food, a good mix of fish and meat dishes, is not bad either. The best place to stock up on provisions is the Market Lucija (daily 6am–midnight) by the *Metropol Hotel*.

By the standards of your average coastal resort, nightlife in Portorož is pretty tame. Cruising Obala is your best bet for **drinking** spots, though again, there's nowhere particularly outstanding. You could also try the Bernadin complex to the west of town, where there are a reasonable selection of eateries and bars. Also look out for happenings – usually films and concerts – at the **open-air theatre** (Portorož Avditorjia), behind the bus station at Senčna pot 12.

Sečovlje saltpans

Located right along the border with Croatia, some 3km south of Portorož, are the **Sečovlje saltpans** (Sečoveljske soline), once the most extensive saltpans in Slovenia, but now a designated Regional Park. Although salt is still harvested in the northern section of the park (Lera), this larger southern part (Fontanigga) – traversed by vast grids of canals, dykes and pools – has been out of commission since the late 1960s.

From the main road (for how to get here see opposite), a long, dusty track runs alongside the Dragonje River, which marks the border between Slovenia and Croatia. After the first kilometre or so – by which point you'll probably have despaired at the monotony of the walk – dozens of deserted saltpanners' houses inch into view. It makes for an eerie sight, dozens of stark, crumbling, grey-stone houses randomly strewn across the pancake-flat landscape. A further 3km down the track, it comes as some relief to see the **Saltworks Museum** (Muzej Solinarstva; daily 9am–1pm & 2–7pm; 500SIT), easily spotted as this comprises the only two intact buildings in the park, having been completely renovated for the purposes of housing the museum. As interesting as the exhibits are, including a store of salt-making equipment and techniques and, upstairs, a mock-up of a saltpanners' living quarters, more fascinating is the detailed explanation of the salt-making process given by the helpful guide (see box below).

Amongst the most important heritage sites in the country – it is, along with the Škocjan Caves, on the Ramsar List of internationally protected wetlands – the rich, salt-impregnated soil supports a wide variety of saltwater (halophytic) **flora**, sheltering over forty species of plant, many of which feature on the "Red List" (Slovenia's list of endangered plant and animal species), and a range of land vertebrates, including *Suncus etruscus*, a tiny shrew alleged to be the smallest mammal in the world. **Bird-life**, too, is prominent, the warm, sub-Mediterranean climate and abundance of food in the basins attracting large numbers of migratory birds, such as the common coot and great cormorant, while herons, gulls and egrets have established themselves as permanent residents.

If you haven't got your own transport, **getting here** is tricky and time-consuming: your best bet is to take the *Solinarka* boat (July and August only), which departs from the Bernadin Complex (see p.205) at 9.15am, Portorož at 9.30am and Piran at 9.45am every day except Sunday; the trip, which includes entrance to the museum, lasts around four hours (Ⓣ05/677-2383, Ⓔaltair@siol.net; 2500SIT). Otherwise, the nearest you can get by bus (there are none direct to the pans) is the village of Sečovlje itself, some 1.5km before the border crossing, though you could also jump on a Croatia-bound bus and get off at the border crossing; either way, take your passport as a precaution, as you will have to pass through Slovenian customs. One hundred metres beyond the crossing (but before the Croatian border – you are now in "no-man's-land"), a sign on your right points to the museum.

Salt of the earth

Salt harvesting has been practised along the Slovenian coast since the first saltpans were introduced in Piran some time in the thirteenth century. Although the pans remain at Strunjan, Sečovlje is now the only place where harvesting still takes place, albeit on a much smaller scale than in its heyday during the first half of the last century, when over 40,000 tonnes of salt were yielded annually – today it's barely a tenth of that.

The **saltpans** are supplied by seawater funnelled along several large channels, before settling in dammed crystallization basins lined with "petola" (artificially grown crust consisting of algae, gypsum and clay), a method used so as to prevent the salt mixing with sea mud and other sediments. The water is then slowly removed with the aid of large wind-powered pumps, while the remainder evaporates in the sun as the salt crystallizes. After being drained and washed, the salt would – in days of yore – be carted off to large warehouses (*skladišča soli*) sited along the coast, before being distributed; there's a good example of one of these (now disused) warehouses in Portorož, near the Bernadin complex.

A saltpanners' (*solinarji*) dwellings – inhabited by the entire family, but only during the harvesting season (April to September) – were extremely modest, comprising a large downstairs storage room and, upstairs, living quarters, divided into a couple of bedrooms and a joint living and kitchen area; the most important aspects of the building, however, were the windows and doors, positioned on both sides of the house so that changes in the weather could be carefully observed.

Travel details

Trains

Divača to: Koper (4–7 daily; 50min); Ljubljana (5–8 daily; 1hr 30min); Postojna (4–7 daily; 35min); Sežana (13 daily; 10min).
Koper to: Divača (5–7 daily; 50min); Ljubljana (5–7 daily; 2hr 30min); Postojna (5–7 daily; 1hr 30min).
Most na Soči to: Bled Jezero (4–7 daily; 1hr); Bohinjska Bistrica (4–7 daily; 50min); Jesenice (4–7 daily; 1hr 15min); Nova Gorica (4–7 daily; 40min).
Nova Gorica to: Ajdovščina (2 daily; 40min); Bled Jezero (4–7 daily; 1hr 30min); Bohinjska Bistrica (4–7 daily; 1hr 15min); Jesenice (4–7 daily; 1hr 50min); Most na Soči (4–7 daily; 40min); Sežana (3–5 daily; 1hr)
Sežana to: Divača (13 daily; 10min); Ljubljana (7 daily; 1hr 35min–2hr); Nova Gorica (4–6 daily; 1hr).

Buses

Ajdovščina to: Idrija (Mon–Fri 3 daily; 45min); Ljubljana (Mon–Fri 9 daily, Sat & Sun 4 daily; 1hr 20min); Nova Gorica (Mon–Fri hourly, Sat & Sun 5 daily; 40min); Postojna (Mon–Sat hourly, Sun 4; 40min); Vipava (Mon–Sat hourly, Sun 3; 10min).
Bovec to: Kranjska Gora (June & Aug 4 daily; 1hr 45min).
Cerkno to: Bovec (2 daily; 1hr 15min); Idrija (hourly; 25min); Ljubljana (Mon–Fri 4 daily, Sat & Sun 2 daily; 1hr 25min); Tolmin (Mon–Fri 5 daily; Sat & Sun 2 daily; 40min).
Idrija to: Bovec (1 daily; 1hr 30min); Cerkno (hourly; 25min); Ljubljana (Mon–Fri 10 daily, Sat & Sun 3 daily; 1hr 15min); Tolmin (2 daily; 1hr).
Koper to: Ljubljana (2hr 20min); Piran (every 20–30min; 25min); Postojna (1hr 20min).
Nova Gorica to: Ajdovščina (Mon–Fri 19 daily, Sat & Sun 9 daily; 40min); Bovec (Mon–Fri 4 daily, Sat & Sun 2 daily; 1hr 15min); Kobarid (Mon–Fri 4 daily, Sat & Sun 2 daily; 50min); Ljubljana (Mon–Fri 10 daily, Sat & Sun 6 daily; 2hr 30min); Postojna (Mon–Fri 13 daily, Sat & Sun 9 daily; 1hr 10min); Tolmin (Mon–Fri 8 daily, Sat & Sun 4 daily; 40min); Vipava (Mon–Fri 16 daily, Sat & Sun 8 daily; 45min).
Piran to: Koper (every 20–30min; 25min); Ljubljana (2hr 40min); Postojna (1hr 40min).
Sežana to: Ajdovščina (Mon–Sat 1 daily; 40min); Divača (Mon–Sat 1 daily; 15min); Ljubljana (Mon–Fri 3 daily, Sat & Sun 2 daily; 1hr 40min); Nova Gorica (Mon–Fri 4 daily, Sat & Sun 2 daily; 1hr 10min); Štanjel (Mon–Fri 4 daily; 30min); Postojna (Mon–Fri 3 daily; 40min).

International trains

Divača to: Pula (2 daily; 2hr 40min–3hr); Trieste (2 daily; 1hr 30min–2hr).

International buses

Sežana to: Trieste (Mon–Sat 1 daily; 30min).

Southern Slovenia

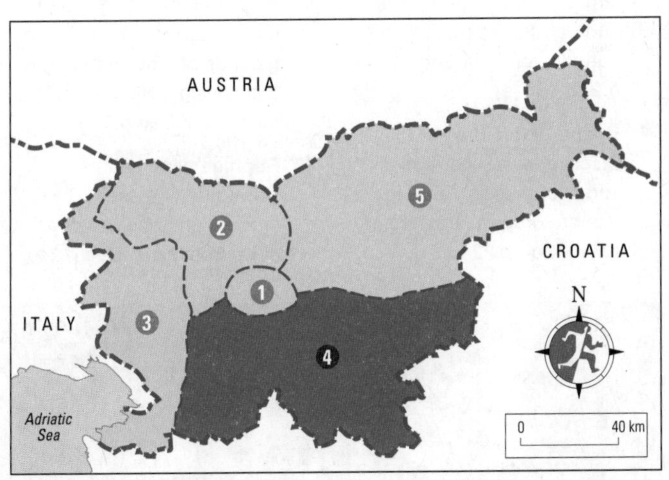

CHAPTER 4 Highlights

* **Postojna Caves** – Vast chambers and dazzling formations in one of the world's truly great cave systems. **See p.216**

* **Predjama Castle** – Visit Slovenia's most dramatically sited castle, and discover the legend of Erasmus Lueger. **See p.218**

* **Lake Cerknica** – Europe's largest intermittent lake is another of Slovenia's great natural wonders. **See p.223**

* **Križna Water Cave** – Discover cave-bear bones and over a dozen lakes in one of Europe's finest water caves. **See p.224**

* **Walking in Kočevjski Rog** – Explore Slovenia's finest expanse of forest, and catch some wildlife along the way – mind the bears though! **See p.229**

* **Kayaking on the Kolpa River** – The beautiful, twisting, Kolpa River is a great spot for kayaking and other water sports. **See p.232**

* **Pleterje Monastery** – Visit the atmospheric church and grounds of Slovenia's only functioning Carthusian monastery. **See p.243**

* **Repnice wine cellars** – Down a few glasses of wine in these amazing cellars hewn from sand. **See p.249**

△ Otočec castle

4

Southern Slovenia

The three regions comprising southern Slovenia, Notranjska, Dolenjska and Bela Krajina, offer a deeply attractive mix of darkly forested hills, karstic rock formations, river valleys, castles, monasteries and spas, not to mention several outstanding wine-producing regions. Moreover, and with very few major centres of population in the region, there are opportunities aplenty for hiking, cycling and other leisurely pursuits.

The province of **Notranjska** encompasses an expanse of terrain extending south from the Ljubljana Marshes to the Croatian border, and bound by Primorska and the Karst to the west, and by the Velika Gora hills to the east. Characterized by karst fields (called *poljes*), underground rivers and thickly forested limestone hills and plateaus pocked by innumerable cave systems, its most celebrated attractions are the astonishing **Postojna Caves** and the majestically sited **Predjama Castle**. Largely ignored by most travellers, Notranjska's lesser-known sites include **Lake Cerknica**, Europe's largest intermittent lake, and the wonderful **Križna Water Cave**. Pressed up hard against the Croatian border, the **Snežnik Mountains** offer some of the country's best non-alpine hiking.

The thick forests of Notranjska extend eastwards into the neighbouring province of **Dolenjska**, the largest of the three regions and the one possessed of the lion's share of southern Slovenia's historical sites. Its westernmost flank centres around the towns of **Ribnica** and **Kočevje**, close to both the massive forests of Velika Gora and Kočevski Rog, and the **Kolpa River Valley** on the Croatian border, the latter offering an exciting complement of fantastic scenery and superb walking, cycling and adrenaline-fuelled sports.

The only town of any real size is **Novo Mesto**, a handy base from which to take in any number of local attractions, foremost of which is the beautiful **Krka River Valley**, which extends northwest to the village of **Muljava**, itself just a few kilometres from the ancient **Stična Monastery**. Following the course of the Krka River eastwards from Novo Mesto brings you to **Otočec Castle**, the secluded **Pleterje Monastery** and the sleepy island town of **Kostanjevica na Krki**. Beyond here the road and river continue to **Brežice**, setting for one of the country's most celebrated classical music festivals; **Čatež**, the country's largest spa centre; and the **Bizeljsko wine region**, perhaps the most appealing of Posavje's four winegrowing centres.

Quietly tucked away in the far southeastern corner of the country, bound by the forests of Kočevjski Rog to the west and the Croatian border to the south and east, **Bela Krajina** is easily the smallest of southern Slovenia's regions, a gentle landscape where hilly slopes raked with lush vineyards descend to flatlands strewn with the region's famous white birch trees.

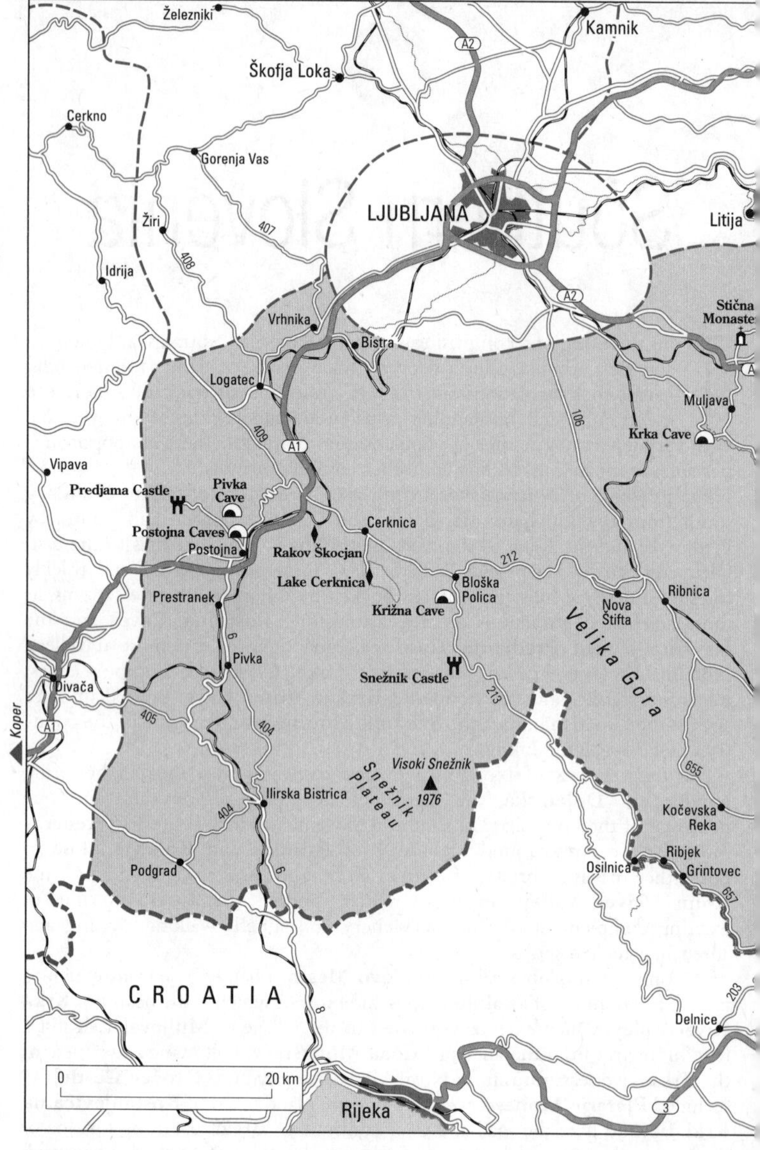

Today, viticulture and fruit growing are the main agricultural activities, and it's these, along with the region's strong folk traditions, which entice what relatively few visitors the region receives. Of the province's two main towns, **Črnomelj** and **Metlika**, the latter is more appealing, by dint of its architecture and museums, as well as its proximity to the fabulous Gothic pilgrimage shrine of **Tri Fare** (Three Parishes) and some lovely **wine villages**.

Getting around by **public transport** is perhaps more difficult here than in any other part of the country, and it's the one region where having your own wheels is particularly advantageous; trains serve less than a handful of places outlined in this chapter, whilst local bus services are patchy at best.

Notranjska and Western Dolenjska

Most visitors to **Notranjska** head straight to Slovenia's number one tourist attraction, the **Postojna Caves**, and follow that with a visit to the nearby **Predjama Castle**, perched miraculously halfway up a cliff. However, the region contains other, less-visited subterranean delights in the form of the **Pivka and Black Caves**, a mere stone's throw from their more famous counterparts. To the north of the caves, a worthwhile diversion en route to or from Postojna/Ljubljana is the **Bistra Technical Museum**; containing a massive collection of agricultural and industrial machines, trams, carriages and cars, this is a must for any vehicle enthusiast.

South of Postojna, the **Snežnik mountains** offer both tremendous hiking and the opportunity to spot some of Slovenia's most spectacular, and aggressive, wildlife, whilst, further east, the **Rakov Škocjan Regional Park** presents further rambling possibilities. Close by is one of Slovenia's most unusual landmarks, the extraordinary **Lake Cerknica** – by winter a lake by summer a field – while permanent, though underwater, lakes can be explored at **Križna Water Cave**, where skeletons of prehistoric cave-bears have been discovered. For a less energetic time, **Snežnik Castle** has lovely landscaped gardens and a fine art collection.

Although the main towns in **Western Dolenjska** are nothing special in themselves, they are useful jumping-off points for **Velika Gora** and the stunning virgin forests of **Kočevjski Rog**. They are not totally devoid of attractions, however: **Ribnica** has a fine woodenware tradition in evidence in the town's museum and at the annual fair, and in nearby Nova Štifta lies one of Slovenia's main pilgrimage churches; **Kočevje**, once home to the country's German-speaking minority, contains Slovenia's first parliament building. Straddling the Croatian border south of Kočevje, the beautiful **Kolpa Valley** is the region's centre for river-based activities, all of which can be organized from the valley's main village, **Osilnica**.

Postojna and around

The town of **POSTOJNA**, 66km south of Ljubljana, would be the most forgettable place imaginable were it not the location for one of Slovenia's most popular tourist attractions, the amazing **Postojna Caves**, whose vast chambers and dazzling formations have been pulling in the punters for nearly two centuries. Despite its role as Notranjska's administrative and economic centre, the town itself is utterly devoid of character and you'll not want to hang around once you've visited the caves and the **Predjama Castle** (see p.218), just a few kilometres away. Indeed, just about the only other "distinction" the town has is that it's home to one of the country's largest army barracks, acquired in 1945 following the annexation of Primorska to Italy. Located on the main road and rail routes to the coast, the caves are easily managed as a half-day trip from Ljubljana, or as a stopoff en route to the coast itself.

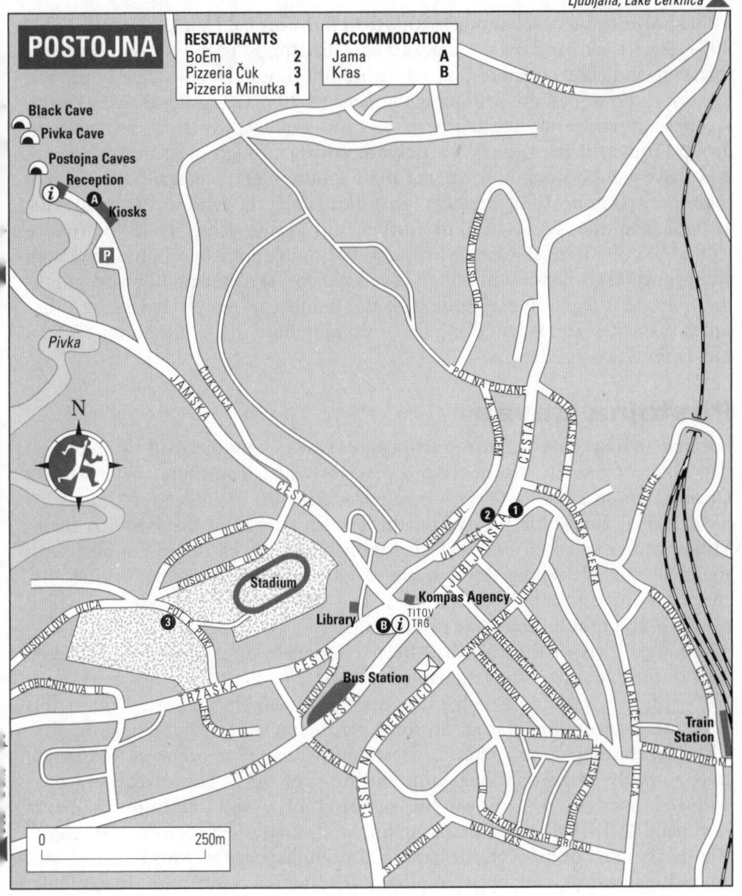

Arrival, information and accommodation

From the **bus station** on Titova cesta, it's an easy five-minute walk to the main square, Titov trg, while the **train station** is less conveniently located 1km southeast of town on Kolodvorska cesta – from the station exit, take the stairs down to Pod Kolodvorom, then walk along Ulica 1 Maja until you reach the main square. The **tourist office**, housed in a small kiosk on the main square, is a temporary affair, opening during the summer months only (daily: May–Sept 9am–8pm, until 9pm in July & Aug; ⓣ040/594-894, ⓔzzt@postojna.si). Alternatively, the Kompas agency, across the road at Titov trg 2a (April–Sept Mon–Fri 8am–8pm, Sat 9am–1pm; Oct–March Mon–Fri 8am–5pm, Sat 9am–1pm; ⓣ05/721-1480, ⓔinfo@kompas-postojna.si), can provide all the information you need. There's **Internet access** in the library, 100m behind the *Hotel Kras* on Trg Padlih borcev (free), and the **post office** is at Ulica 1 Maja 2a, a few paces south of the main square (Mon–Fri 8am–7pm, Sat 8am–noon).

The only central hotel **accommodation** is the dismal *Hotel Kras* (Ⓣ05/726-4071; ❺), smack bang on the main square; its depressing rooms, with battered furniture and cold, concrete-floored bathrooms should be considered only as a last resort. Postojna's other hotel is the *Jama* (Ⓣ/05/728-2400; ❹; May–Sept), a concrete monstrosity located near the cave entrance, which caters mainly to groups. Your best bet is to take a **private room** through the Kompas agency, who have a good stock in town and the surrounds (❷). Scenically located in a pine forest 4km north of the cave (go 1.5km along the road to Predjama, take a right and the site is 2.5km further on) is the large *Pivka* **campsite** (Ⓣ05/720-3993; April–Oct), which also has simple four-bed bungalows with bathrooms (❺), a handful of which have kitchens (❻). During July and August the full rate is applicable, regardless of the number of people staying; at other times, it's half-price. If you don't fancy walking here (there are no buses), you can order a taxi at Kompas.

Postojna Caves

Located an easy walk (1.5km) northwest of town along the road to Predjama, the 19km of tunnels, chambers and passages which constitute the **Postojna Caves** (Postojnska jama; Ⓦwww.postojna-cave.com) lie under the slopes of a broad karstic limestone plateau on the eastern fringes of the Postojna basin. Millions of years of erosion and corrosion by the Pivka River, coupled with abundant rainfall seeping through the cave's permeable limestone ceilings, has created a fantastic jungle of stalactites and stalagmites, Gothic-like chiselled columns, and translucent stone draperies.

Although parts of the cave had been continually visited since the Middle Ages – the oldest of many signatures etched into the rock walls dates from 1213 – it was Valvasor (see p.235), inevitably, who first reported upon this immense grotto, commenting, "in some places you see terrifying heights, elsewhere everything is in columns so strangely shaped as to seem like some creepy-crawly, snake or other animal in front of one". The caves were pronounced open to tourists on the occasion of a visit by Emperor Franz Ferdinand in 1819, the first in a long line of distinguished visitors to Postojna. Within six years of his visit, the caves had been illuminated with oil lamps and professional guides had been employed. The famous cave train, meanwhile, entered service in 1872, a rather crude model in which tourists were shunted along in hand-pushed wagons. These carriages were superseded by gas operated trains in 1914, themselves replaced by the electric version (used today) in 1959.

The Cave Tour

Tours take place throughout the year (May–Sept hourly 9am–6pm, March, April & Oct every 2hr 10am–4pm plus hourly 10am–5pm on Sun in Oct; Jan, Feb, Nov & Dec daily 10am & 2pm plus noon & 4pm on Sun; 2700SIT), but to get the most out of your visit, particularly if you're here in the summer months when the place can get swamped with groups, try and make one of the first or last tours of the day. Dress warmly, as it can get quite chilly.

After purchasing your ticket, assemble with everybody else by the entrance and wait for the signal to board the **cave train**, which whisks you along 2km of preliminary systems before the tour proper begins. As the train hurtles forth keep an eye out for several interesting features: a shaft of blackened walls, the result of a Nazi fuel dump blown up by Partisan saboteurs during World War II; the **Congress Hall**, a beautifully lit chamber so-named following the

Proteus Anguinus – the Human Fish

There are an estimated two hundred or so animal species in these caves, but none is as enigmatic, or has been such a source of fascination, as **Proteus Anguinus**, aka the Human Fish. Believed to be the whelp of the dragon when it was first discovered by local inhabitants several centuries ago, this peculiar looking creature was officially announced to the world as Proteus Anguinus by Viennese zoologist Laurenti in 1768, taking its name partly from the Greek sea-god (Proteus), and partly from the Latin word for snake (Anguinus). Locally it is known as **mocheril**, etymologically speaking "that which burrows into wetness".

A member of the Proteidae amphibian family, Proteus measures around 25cm in length and is possessed of pigmentless skin and atrophied eyes, the latter detectable only at the foetal stage. True to its Latin name, it is snake-like in appearance, but has two tiny pairs of legs (the front ones have three digits, the rear two – hence the "human" part of its name) and a flat, pointed fin to help propel itself through water. It spends almost all of its one hundred years' existence entirely in the dark and, although blind, can detect light through the surface of its body. The two bright-red gills located on the back of its head are its breathing apparatus, though when out of water it's able to breathe through its skin.

Its eating habits are no less bizarre: known to consume small animals such as cave shrimps, insect larvae and amphipods, it's not uncommon for Proteus to indulge in a spot of cannibalism, while, conversely, it can go years without food. The most vexing questions, however, concern its habits of reproduction, as this has yet to be witnessed in captivity, although it is believed to reproduce in its late teens. Although normally always associated with Postojna, Proteus can be found in other caves throughout the Slovenian Karst, as well as the Dinaric karst regions of Bosnia and Croatia.

staging of a Speleological Congress here in 1965; and the **Curtain**, a transparent, wafer-thin formation precariously angled on a sloping wall.

Alighting at the **Great Mountain** (Velika Gora), you'll break off into the group of your chosen language before the guided tour begins, which amounts to around one hour of walking. The most impressive formations in this vast hall – a forty-five-metre-high stone-block mound formed when the ceiling collapsed and which, in time, became smothered in calcite – are the so-called **Natural Curtains**, whose shape and colour is akin to that of dried tobacco leaves. Crossing the **Russian Bridge**, built in 1916 by Russian prisoners of war, you enter the most enchanting part of the system, a series of chambers collectively known as the **Beautiful Caves** (Lepe jame), whose names are suggestive of some of the lustrous formations and colours on display, such as the **Spaghetti Hall**, with its dripping, needle-like formations, the calcium-rich **White Hall**, and the **Red Room**, stained a rich ochre by iron oxides. Continuing in a circuitous route, you pass back under the Russian Bridge through several more chambers, one of which, the **Winter Chamber** (Zimska dvorana), is home to the two formations that have become the cave symbols: one called the **Pillar**, and another dubbed **Brilliant**, the latter on account of its dazzling snow-white colour and peculiar shape, which resembles something like a stack of giant cauliflowers.

The main attraction in the next gallery has less to do with the formations on display and more to do with the contents of the large tank located in the centre, which contains **Proteus Anguinus**, the largest permanent cave-dwelling vertebrate known to man (see box above). The tour concludes a little further on in the **Concert Hall** (Koncertna dvorana), the largest open space in the system, and which, you are told, can hold some 10,000 people – the odd concert is still held here. From here you return to the entrance by train.

Pivka and Black Caves

If you'd rather see some caves minus the crowds, then more low-key alternatives are the **Pivka Cave** (Pivka jama) and **Black Cave** (Črna jama). The entrance to the former is via a sixty-metre-deep collapsed chasm near the Pivka camping ground, some 4km north of the main Postojna entrance (follow the signs to the camp). Descending nearly three hundred steps, the route then follows a specially constructed walkway cut into the wall just above the level of the Pivka River. Beyond an iron door and a short tunnel is the Black Cave (also known as the Magdalena Cave), a modestly sized, dry gallery, which takes its name from the large amount of black calcite present. From here, another, much longer, man-made tunnel links the cave with one of the main chambers in Postojna; this last part is generally not accessible to tourists, though it might be worth asking. If you wish to visit these caves, you should contact the ticket office at the Postojna Caves two or three days in advance (1400SIT).

Eating and drinking

Eating options are somewhat limited: by some distance the best place is *Pizzeria Minutka*, a five-minute walk northwest of the main square at Ljubljanska cesta 14, a simple but colourful place which, aside from the usual range of pizzas and fresh salads, offers a superb choice of grills, the tastiest of which are its Serbian specialities such as *Čevapi* and *Pljeskavica* – the service is good too; otherwise, *Pizzeria Čuk*, slightly out of the way near the sports park at Pot k Pivki 4 (head along Tržaška cesta for 200m then turn right), is decent, if more straightforward. If you're out by the cave there is a cluster of typically tacky tourist eateries to choose from. Opposite *Minutka*, the café-cum-bar *BoEm* is about as exciting as it gets for **drinking**.

Predjama Castle

Second only to Postojna as the region's main tourist attraction is the fabulously dramatic **Predjama Castle** (Predjamski grad; Jan, Feb, Nov & Dec Tues–Fri 10am–4pm, Sat & Sun 10am–5pm; March, April & Oct daily 10am–5pm; May daily 9am–6pm; June–Sept daily 9am–7pm; 800SIT), 9km north of the caves in the village of the same name. Pressed into a huge cavern, hollowed out of the high, flat rock face over the karstic swallow hole of the Lokva stream, its setting is as unforgettable as it is improbable. Stopping here in 1802 en route to Italy, the German architect Karl Schinkel recalled "it was with the wildest bravery that man was ordered to settle in this place. There is nothing more stirring than to look upon the castle, wondrously composed of tower-like structures which, built under the dark vault of the cavern, need not their own ramparts, as the dark cavern's huge bulk hangs far beyond them."

Amongst its many aristocratic residents, the most infamous was the castle's last owner, knight and brigand **Erasmus Lueger** (see box opposite), who inhabited the castle during the second half of the fifteenth century, and whose life – in particular the manner of his death – has intrigued historians for centuries.

With origins dating back to around the twelfth century, the castle manifests a number of styles, from Romanesque through to Gothic, although its predominant form is Renaissance following heavy renovation in the sixteenth century. With a total of some fifteen rooms, as well as numerous passageways, galleries and alcoves, all condensed into five floors, there's much to see, though

Erasmus Lueger

The beginning of what proved to be a rather sticky ending for **Erasmus** began after he killed one of the Austrian emperor Frederick III's kinsmen. Hot on his heels as he fled to Predjama was the governor of Trieste, Caspar Ravbar, whose mission it was to capture Erasmus. For more than a year Ravbar and his men laid siege to Predjama, attempting to starve out its defenders. However, he hadn't reckoned on a **secret natural passage**, located beyond the castle walls and which was constantly supplied with fresh food that Erasmus would occasionally hurl down into the valley to taunt his besiegers. Betrayed by a double-dealing servant, Erasmus's **death**, when it finally came, was an ignoble one, the poor fellow blasted to bits by a large projectile while settling down to answer nature's call. Local legend has it that he is buried under the linden tree, supposedly planted by his girlfriend, next to the **Church of Our Lady of Sorrows**, just down from the castle.

little of what's on display is original. Before you start, take one of the useful accompanying leaflets to guide you through the numbered rooms. On the second floor, keep an eye out for a portrait of the suitably gruff Erasmus (one of the few pictures of him known to exist), and the cupboard in the dining room – made by an inmate who spent four years in a local prison using just his pocket-knife. Located on the same (third) floor where Erasmus came to grief (room no. 13, but there's nothing there now) is the tiny castle **chapel**, containing a fifteenth-century Gothic pietà. Next door is the chaplain's room, from where he could witness the punishments being meted out in the torture chamber one floor below. From the natural apertures on each floor there are fine panoramas of the flower-speckled Vipava Valley ahead.

At the very top of the castle – across the drawbridge and up some uneven steps – lie the ruins of the Cave Castle, beyond which is the **secret natural passage**; tours of the latter are possible during the summer, but you should call a couple of days in advance. Easier to visit is the **cave under the Castle** (Jama pod Predjamskim gradom), which extends for some 13km (much of it still unexplored) to the Vipava Valley, though only around 700m of walking is possible for the casual visitor. Bar the odd stalactite, there's not an awful lot to see, but it's one of the few caves around that hasn't been artificially lit, so it's quite good fun wandering around with torches. Scheduled tours take place between May and September (11am, 1pm, 3pm & 5pm; 900SIT); contact the ticket office in the castle. If you're around in August try and make it for the annual **jousting tournament**, which takes place on the narrow strip of grass just below the castle on the last, or second to last, Sunday of that month.

Bistra Technical Museum

Twenty-two kilometres southwest of Ljubljana, close to the small settlement of Vrhnika in the tiny hamlet of Bistra, is the former **Bistra Monastery**, a large complex that is now home to the **Technical Museum of Slovenia** (Muzej Tehniški Slovenije; March–Nov Tues–Fri 9am–5pm, Sat & Sun 9am–6pm; 700SIT). The museum is divided up into several departments, though such is the size of the place you're best off making a beeline for a select few, particularly if time is short. As interesting as the voluminous displays of textiles, forestry, agriculture and engineering are, it's the massive road vehicle department – comprising a magnificent collection of pre-World War II automobiles, carriages (including a fine Ljubljana tram from 1901), bicycles and tractors – which demands greatest attention.

The highlight of the collection is some two dozen cars given as gifts to Tito by various government offices and heads of state, and which were used for his many travels throughout Yugoslavia and abroad, including India and Burma; there are some splendid models on display, notably a magnificent Rolls Royce Silver Wraith, a Mercedes Benz (from the Croatian Home Office), and an armour-plated 1937 Packard Twelve, presented to Tito by Stalin in 1945 – ironically, just three years before Yugoslavia's expulsion from Cominform. There's also a 1953 Fiat Zastava, just one of Tito's many hunting vehicles. Before making the trek back you may wish to partake in some refreshments from the gostilna next door.

Although undoubtedly worth a special visit from Ljubljana, visiting the museum is more conveniently done as a trip en route to Postojna. Moreover, without your own transport, getting here is fairly time-consuming; take one of the regular buses from Ljubljana (stand 29 at the bus station) to Vrhnika, and alight by the *Hotel Mantova* in the centre; from here, it's a signposted three-kilometre walk along a winding country road to the museum – however, many cars travel this road, so there's a good chance of hitching a lift.

South of Postojna: the Snežnik Mountains

Thirty-three kilometres south of Postojna, and just 11km from the Croatian border, the nondescript market town of **ILIRSKA BISTRICA** holds no specific appeal, but it's a good place from which to strike out into the wonderful **Snežnik Mountains**, a densely forested karst plateau cloaked in spruce, beech, fir and dwarf pine, and traversed by a number of well-marked trails, including a section of the European footpath E-6. From Ilirska Bistrica, it's a good three-hour walk to **Sviščaki** (1242m), where the *Dom na Sviščakih* (Ⓣ050/613-601) has a handful of beds available between June and mid-September as well as at weekends throughout the rest of the year; from here it's a further two-hour trek to the cone-like **Mount Snežnik**, where there are more beds at the *Zavetišče na Velikem Snežniku* (Ⓣ050/615-356; mid-June to mid-Oct). Usually topped with snow until late spring, Slovenia's highest non-Alpine mountain (1796m) offers fantastic views of the Alps to the north, and the Croatian seaboard, dotted with its many islands, to the south. From Mount Snežnik, the path continues to **Mašun** (1024m; 4hr), where there's good food served (daily 8am–10pm), and down through the Leskova Valley towards Snežnik Castle (see p.225). If you have a car, you could drive to Sviščaki and walk to Snežnik from there – from Sviščaki, the deteriorating mountain road continues to Mašun (13km), before descending to Snežnik Castle. If you're doing this route in reverse (ie from Snežnik Castle), you could drive to Mašun and walk to Snežnik from there. The plateau also shelters numerous large mammals, including lynx, wolf and a growing bear population – sightings of all three are not uncommon.

In Ilirska Bistrica, the **tourist office**, just 100m northeast of the bus station (itself located 400m south of the train station) at Gregorčičeva cesta 2 (Mon–Thurs 8am–4pm, Fri 9am–5pm, plus Sat in summer 9am–noon; Ⓣ05/710-1384, Ⓔrazvojni.center@siol.net), can organize **private accommodation** if you wish to stick around. One bus (daily Mon–Fri 12:45pm) passes through Ilirska Bistrica en route to Rijeka, in Croatia.

East of Postojna

The area east of Postojna is blessed with several first-rate attractions. The first of these is the **Rakov Škocjan Regional Park**, an enjoyable walking spot from where it's a short distance to the small town of **Cerknica**, of little interest itself but which is close to one of the counry's most extraordinary geographical features, the intermittent **Lake Cerknica**, sometimes lake, sometimes field. East and south of here respectively is the must-see **Križna Water Cave** and **Snežnik Castle**, the latter tucked away under the shadow of the Snežnik Mountains. Unfortunately, public transport around this relative backwater is extremely limited, and so, without your own transport, careful planning is required, particularly if you wish to see more than one of these places in the same day.

Rakov Škocjan Regional Park

A couple of kilometres north of Postojna, the secondary road running parallel to the main E70/E61 Ljubljana–Koper highway, breaks off sharply to the right in the direction of Cerknica. After a further 5km, the road passes the **Rakov Škocjan Regional Park**, a small, lush karst valley popular with local walkers, where there's an easy, well-marked, circular trail around the park, which should take no more than a couple of hours to complete.

The park's focal point is the short, yet well-defined, **Rak Gorge**, which begins at the **Small Natural Bridge** (Mali Naravni Most) – the first of two stunning natural rock bridges sited at either end of the gorge – just below which lurks the **Zelške Cave** (Zelške Jama) and the Rak Spring, from whence the babbling **Rak River** emerges. The river, which carries water from Cerknica Polje to the Planina Polje, winds its way down the gorge to the immaculately cut arch of the **Great Natural Bridge** (Veliki Naravni Most), underneath which is the **Tkalca Cave** (Tkalca Jama). On the far side of the bridge a crumbling heap of stone ruins, including parts of a stone altar, are all that remain of the **Church of St Kancijan**. During periods when the river is low, or completely dry, it is possible to explore both cave entrances, but caution should be exercised as it's likely to be slippery.

Cerknica and Lake Cerknica

Approximately 4km kilometres east of Rakov Škocjan, the town of **Cerknica** (see below) is the jumping off point for **Lake Cerknica** (Cerkniško Jezero), an enormous karst *polje* (or field) that is also Europe's largest intermittent lake.

Cerknica and Slivnica Plateau

CERKNICA town is a drab place, enlivened only during the **Pust Festival** each February – one of Slovenia's better organized carnivals – but it does offer a smattering of accommodation, useful if you're planning to spend a day or two anywhere in the vicinity of the lake. There is a **train station** 4km northwest of Cerknica in **Rakek**, which may be a more feasible option if you don't mind walking or hitching the rest of the way, given the paucity of buses to Cerknica. The **bus station** is on Čabranska ulica, from where it's a short walk to the **tourist association office**, located next to the post office at Cesta 4 maja 51 (Ⓣ01/709-3636, Ⓔzzt@postojna.si). *TeliCo*, 500m east of the tourist office up the hill at Brestova 9 (Ⓣ01/709-7090; ❷), has a couple of **rooms** (shared bathroom) with great views out towards the lake. The tourist association can also point you in the direction of private rooms. Pretty much the only place in town to eat is the *Valvasorjev hram* **restaurant** opposite the tourist office, which knocks up cheap, good food in a roomy, if rather unatmospheric, cellar bar.

Cerknica is also the starting point for trails to the **Slivnica Plateau**, ranged across the lake's northern shore. If the lake looks impressive from ground level,

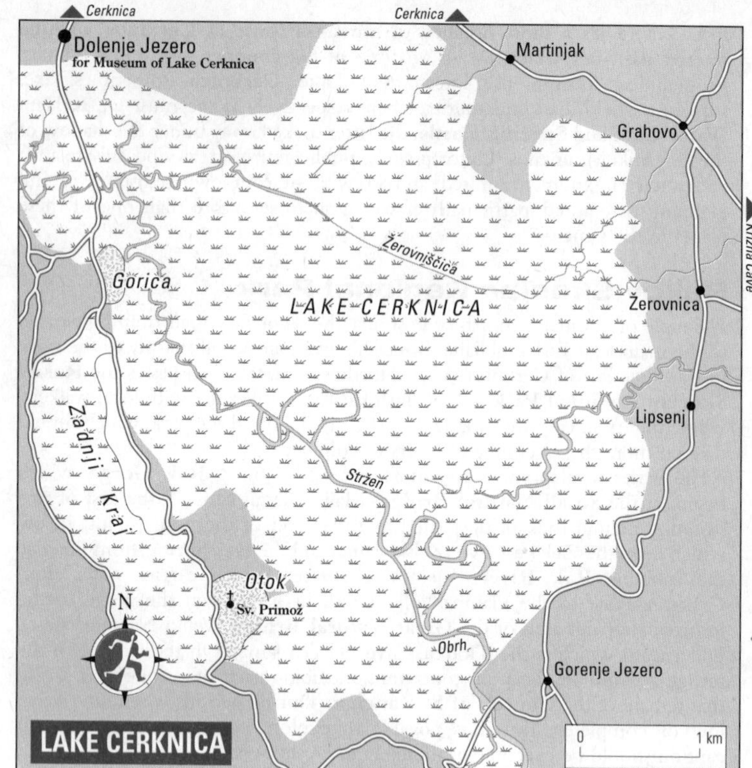

the views from atop its highest peak, **Velika Slivnica** (1114m; 2hr from Cerknica), are superlative; Velika Slivnica is also known as "witch mountain", owing to its associations with witchcraft hereabouts in the Middle Ages. Once at the top, you can partake in some refreshments at the *Dom na Slivnici* (Ⓣ01/709-4140) just below the summit, which also has beds available year-round (Nov–Feb Sat & Sun only).

Lake practicalities

There are several ways to approach a visit to Lake Cerknica, but what you see, and how you see it, will largely be determined by which time of the year you visit, and which mode of transport, if any, you use. The most direct route across the lake (or field) is via an unsurfaced north–south road that shaves the lake's western shore. Beginning at **Dolenje Jezero**, a small village 2km south of Cerknica, the road bisects a group of sink holes, before passing by the small wooded island of Gorica and continuing southwards to **Otok** ("Island") which, when the lake is full, magically becomes the country's sole inhabited island. From Otok you can either head back in a northerly direction via the forest road which skirts the western shore of the **Zadnji kraj inlet**, or take the longer route along the lake's eastern shore through the settlements of Laze, Gorenje Jezero, Lipsenj and Žerovnica, winding up at Grahovo on the main road.

The disappearing lake

Although the so-called "**disappearing lake**", located about 2.5km south of Cerknica, had been the subject of much postulation and fascination on the part of researchers and explorers long before Valvasor's time, it was left to the great polymath himself to unravel the lake's eccentricities, concluding as he did: "I think there is no lake so remarkable either in Europe or in any other of the three corners of the world...no lake has as many exceptional features". As a result of his efforts, which included the publication of a map of the lake in 1689, Valvasor was granted honorary membership of the Royal Society in London. There were other significant contributions too, most notably from the botanist Balthazar Haquet and the Jesuit Tobijas Gruber, both of whom offered thoroughgoing accounts of the lake's extraordinary hydrological functions.

The lake functions thus: once water from the Slivnica and Bloke Plateaus to the east, and the Javornik mountains to the west, enters the permeable limestone surface of the lakebed, it begins to percolate through the lake's many sink holes, into the subterranean area, and when more water enters the lake than can be depleted, the waters of the main channel, the Stržen (itself fed by a number of tributaries and streams), overflow and the shallow lake is created, sometimes in a matter of days. At its fullest, the lake can extend for some 10km in length and nearly 5km in width – that's roughly three to four times the size of Lake Bohinj, Slovenia's largest permanent body of water. The disappearing act takes a little longer, usually between three and four weeks. There have been numerous, hitherto unsuccessful, attempts at human intervention over the years – either to prevent the lake filling (in order to grow more hay for livestock), or, conversely, to preserve a permanent body of water (in order to prolong the fishing season and encourage tourism).

As a rule the lake is usually present between October and June, and at its most voluminous during spring, following snowmelt from both the Snežnik and Slivnica plateaus. During this period, the lake becomes a vast playground for a multitude of **activities**, the most popular of which is fishing – pike, tench and chub are the main stock here – as well as swimming, rowing, windsurfing, and even skiing and skating when it's cold enough. With over two hundred species of bird either migrating or nesting amongst the wide expanse of reeds, including corncrake, lapwing and field lark, the lake is also something of a haven for birdwatchers.

The most enjoyable way to see the lake is by **bike**, which can be rented from *TeliCo* in Cerknica (☎01/709-7090; see p.221) and from Čeho Bike (☎070/427-747) in Postojna; expect to pay around 1000SIT for half a day's hire and 2000SIT for a full day. Alternatively, the family at Dolenjske Jezero 50a organize jollies around the lake by **horse and cart** (45min; 350SIT per person in a small group). If you plan to spend any length of time around the lake, arm yourself with a copy of the 1:25,000 *Notranjska Cerkniško jezero* map, which outlines a good range of walks and cycle routes in the area.

Museum of Lake Cerknica

For a better understanding of the lake's peculiarities, you should pay a visit to the **Museum of Lake Cerknica** (Muzej Cerkniškega Jezera; 750SIT) in **Dolenje Jezero** (no. 1e). The centrepiece of this family-run museum is an enormous 1:2500-scale **map-relief** of the lake and its surrounding features, constructed by the museum's indefatigable owner over the course of three years. By way of the lake's most salient features – tributaries, springs, sink holes, as well as settlements and roads, and complemented by live recordings of bird and other animal sounds – the map illustrates how the lake performs and what it looks like during both dry and wet periods.

There's also a twenty-five-minute slide show, featuring some beautifully shot images of the lake in its various guises, and a collection of tools and implements traditionally used by local fishermen – wooden skates, nets, baskets and suchlike – as well as models of the Drevak, long wooden canoes that were used, until the 1970s, for transporting cattle and other livestock across the lake. In theory the museum is only open to visitors at 3pm on Saturdays, but if you call in advance a visit should be possible at other times (ⓣ01/709-4053, ⓦwww.jezerski-hram.si). However, the adjoining café-cum-bar (open daily except Tues; 10am–7pm) is a useful place to stop off for **refreshments** en route to, or coming back from, the lake.

Križna Water Cave

Utterly different from Postojna and that ilk of cave, the eight-kilometre-long **Križna Water Cave** (Križna jama), 12km southeast of Cerknica, is one of the world's great lake caves, and *the* cave to visit in Slovenia if it's a more authentic caving experience you're after. Entering the cave via a small aperture hollowed out of the rock face, you immediately descend into a rocky, dry gallery, also known as the **Bear's Corridor** (Medvedji rov) owing to the many cave-bear (*ursus spelaeus*) that sheltered here thousands of years ago. The first cave-bear excavations – carried out some 130 years ago – uncovered around two thousand fossil remains from over one hundred animals, mainly mandibles, skulls and other bone fragments; there are still many fragments, typically part of a jaw or a tooth, embedded within the rock, some of which you'll see as you walk around. There's also an almost-complete cave-bear skull on display, next to a much smaller skull of a brown bear; the difference in size is striking, though this will be of little comfort should you have the misfortune to encounter one in the surrounding forests, which is by no means improbable. Less alarmingly, the cave is home to a large number of bats, drawn here by the relatively warm temperature of around 8°C.

First explored in 1926, the chain of 22 lakes that comprise the **Lakes and Stream Passages** (Jezerski rov) is, should you decide to go this far, the undoubted high point of a visit to Križna. Separated by calcite barriers, the lakes are fed with water from the nearby Bloke Plateau, via a number of springs in the eastern part of Lake Cerknica; a group in excess of four persons cannot go any further than the first lake, but, smaller groups can venture to the thirteenth and most decorative of all the lakes, the **Calvary** (Kalvarija), a wonderful grotto comprising a huge mound of collapsed material and a shimmering array of stalactites and stalagmites, many of which lie submerged under water. Beyond the Calvary the cave splits, one branch leading to **Mud Passage** (Blata rov), the other to the **Coloured Passage** (Pisani rov), both of which can only be visited by professional cavers.

Visits to the cave take place at 3pm on Sundays between May and September, and should be arranged at least two or three days in advance; trips just to the dry part (including a paddle on the first lake) cost 1000SIT per person, whereas a trip across the lakes to the Calvary – which you should allow around four hours for – costs 6500SIT per person if there are two of you, 5500SIT each if there are three, and 5000SIT each if there are four people. Bear in mind, though, that after a period of heavy rainfall it's usually not possible to advance beyond the first lake. All equipment – helmet, flashlight and boots – is supplied by the **cave guide**, Alojz Troha, who lives in the tiny village of Bloška Polica (no.7) (T 041-632-153; W www.kovinoplastika.si/gsk/krizna-jama), approximately 1km north of the turning off the main road towards the track which leads to the cave (it's signposted).

Snežnik Castle

Sitting in the middle of a luscious landscaped park of chestnut trees and silky lawns, some 7km south of Križna Jama, just beyond the village of **Kozarišče**, is **Snežnik Castle** (Snežnik Grad; mid-April to Oct Wed–Fri 10am–noon & 3–6pm, Sat & Sun 10am–6pm; 700SIT), a handsome, three-storey Renaissance building impressively girdled by ramparts, towers and a high grey wall.

Entranced via a graceful stone-arch bridge spanning a small brook, the castle was originally the thirteenth-century domain of the Aquileian patriarchs, and their subjects the Snežniški lords, after which time the castle changed hands on many occasions. As a result of a court assessment in 1832 the castle was recovered from the heavily in debt Lichtenberg family and declared a lottery prize; however, its winner, a Hungarian blacksmith, opted for a cash prize instead, leaving the entire estate up for grabs. Snapped up by Prince Oton Schönburg at an auction in 1853, the castle remained under the ownership of the family until World War I, when it was appropriated by the state. Although there's not a great deal to see inside, the castle was fortunate enough – unlike many other castles in Slovenia during World War II – to retain most of its original nineteenth-century bourgeois furnishings and other works of art, the pick of which is an exotic hoard of deities, sphinxes and pharaohs in the Egyptian Room.

Without your own transport getting here is awkward: the closest you can get by one of the few buses heading this way is the village of **Stari Trg**, 4km north of Kozarišče – from here there's little option but to hitch a ride or walk. The castle is also the main starting point for **hiking trails** and **cycle routes** up into the Snežnik plateau (see p.220), while those with a car can take the mountain road, which winds its way across the plateau to Ilirska Bistrica.

From Lake Cerknica to Ribnica

From Lake Cerknica the road heads eastwards across the **Bloke Plateau** – a flat, wide, and largely featureless karst plateau whose abundant streams feed Lake Cerknica and Križna Cave to the southwest. The name of the plateau gave rise to one of Slovenia's most enduring cultural symbols, the **Bloke skis**; these short, fat skis, made of beech or birch wood and bound to the foot by a leather strap, were used principally as a means of transportation across the snowy plateau during winter. Valvasor, for one, was suitably impressed, proclaiming: "they descend into the valley with incredible speed…one such strip of wood is strapped under each foot, they take a stout cudgel into their hands and push it into their armpit, and use it as if it were some sort of a rudder to slide off…no less swift than those who use skates in Holland to glide on ice". Whilst skiing as a sport all but died out here after World War I, the plateau is now a popular cross-country skiing venue. Some 25km beyond the plateau's unremarkable main settlement, Nova vas, is Ribnica.

Ribnica and around

Pitched in the centre of a lovely flat-bottomed river valley, between the pine-beech covered ridges of Velika Gora and Mala Gora some 40km south of

Ljubljana, **RIBNICA** is an idyllic, diminutive town known throughout Slovenia for its woodenware, pottery and witchcraft. Like many other towns and villages in the Dolenjska region, Ribnica suffered mercilessly at the hands of the Turks during the fifteenth century: records recount some 27 raids in all, though, ironically, it was as a result of these incursions that the town's woodenware, or *suha roba* (dry goods), industry flourished. In order to kick-start the local economy back into life, Emperor Frederick III issued a decree allowing peddlers from Ribnica, Kočevje and surrounding areas to trade freely throughout the Austrian territories. Such was their aptitude for a good sell, however, that these indomitable characters began to trade as far afield as Africa and Asia. Ribnica is a good place to break up a journey en route to the forests of Kočevje and other attractions further south.

The Town

Pretty much everything of interest (and of a practical nature) lies along, or just off, the town's main street, **Škrabčev trg**, a fetching thoroughfare preserving a neat ensemble of grey, cream and white two-storey tenements. Running parallel to the main street is the slender Bistrica River, spanned by three exquisite stone bridges, each of which crosses over to **Ribnica Castle** on the left bank. Originally built around the tenth or eleventh century, it later assumed a Renaissance form, though all that remains now – two defensive towers linked by a residential passageway – is the result of the building having been occupied, and subsequently wrecked, during Word War II. More commonly known as the **Cultural Activists' Park**, the surrounding grounds feature busts and memorial stones of prominent local achievers such as Jakob Gallus (composer) and Stanislav Škrabec (linguist; see opposite).

Now a cultural centre, the castle holds the collection of the **Ribnica Town Museum** (June–Sept 10am–noon & 4–6pm; 300SIT), a hit-and-miss affair, but worth a visit to view its Woodenware Collection. This activity was traditionally split into nine or ten branches, each branch – for example, frame making, vessel making, wickerwork and sieve making – linked to a particular household, village, or type of wood (typically pine, beech or lime-tree wood). Although somewhat haphazardly arranged, there's much to admire here, from wicker baskets, drinking vessels and farm tools, to less orthodox items such as mousetraps, ski-shoes and backpacks, plus all the appliances used for making these items, every single one of which was hand made. There's also a tidy little collection of ceramic goods from nearby Dolenja Vas, the valley's principal pottery centre. The best time to see the full array of products is at the **Ribnica Fair**, held each year on the first Sunday in September, and which entails much buying and selling of wares along the main street.

The museum's other exhibitions merit just a brief look: the first documents the lives of those emigrants who left Dolenjska, mainly for North America, during the late nineteenth and early twentieth centuries in search of a more fruitful life; while the second features a group of mock-up implements and nasty looking contraptions – gallows, spiked chairs and suchlike – used in the torture and killing of witches in these parts between the fifteenth and eighteenth centuries.

A short walk east of the castle, across the river and midway along Škrabčev trg, stands the **Parish Church of St Stephen** (Cerkev Sv Štefan), the third church on this site, built in 1868. Its drab exterior was given a sharp contemporary twist shortly after World War II by Slovene architect Jože Plečnik (see p.63), who designed the crown-like steeples atop the twin bell-towers – an odd, but effective, amalgamation of triangular arches, spiked cones and pillars.

Originally designed for an unnamed cathedral, this was Plečnik's last ever project, though it was actually completed by one of his students after his death. Its interior stars a ceiling painting of the Holy Trinity, a couple of sculptures of St Peter and St Paul, and some terrific paintings by the likes of Langus and Koželj, although, unfortunately, Ivan Grohar's wonderful painting *St Stephen the Pope*, which once adorned the high altar, is no longer on show; however, you will get to see it if you're here at Easter when it's brought out specially. If the church is closed, call in at the priest's house next door (no. 15). The **Šteklíček House**, opposite the church at no. 26, is where Slovenia's most esteemed poet, France Prešeren (see box on p.123), was schooled between 1810 and 1812.

Located 1km south of town in Hrovača (no. 42), is the town's most enjoyable diversion, the **Škrabec Homestead** (Škrabčeva Domačija; 400SIT), ancestral home of the Škrabec family for more than two centuries. Widely regarded as the country's premier nineteenth-century linguist, Stanislav Škrabec (1844–1918) published his first work in 1870 – a text on the vocal properties and dialect of Slovene literary language and writing – followed by a number of other important treatises, critiques and religious texts. Moreover, he taught several languages at a monastic school in Gorizia. Renovated in 1998 the house comprises the traditional setup of "black" kitchen, living room and bedroom, each room having retained its outstanding original furnishings. The thoroughly modern-looking barn, formerly used for threshing wheat and millet, displays a number of objects made from glass, clay, and, of course, wood. The house has no set opening times, so contact the tourist office if you wish to visit.

Practicalities

Although there is a rail station at Ribnica, this line nowadays carries only freight traffic. All **buses** stop outside the church on Škrabčev trg, from where it's a two-minute walk to the **tourist office**, on the same street at no. 40 (Mon–Fri 9am–3pm; ⓣ01/836-9335, ⓦwww.ribnica.si).

There's no **accommodation** in town, but a couple of possibilities exist just outside: 4km south of town in the village of Prigorica, *Pension Izlaty* at no. 115 (ⓣ01/836-4515; ❸), has six boxy rooms sleeping between one and three persons; buses en route to Kočevje stop 50m from the pension opposite the church. A more rural alternative is the *Boletni* tourist farm (ⓣ01/836-0208; ❷), located on the edge of a forest in the tiny village of Dane (no. 9) 4km west of town, and hence only really accessible by car.

You'll fare marginally better if you're looking for somewhere to **eat**: *Gostilna Mihelič*, opposite the church at Škrabčev trg 22 (closed Mon), can sustain you with a decent range of fish, grills and salads, as well as dumplings and cottage cheese dishes for vegetarians. Simpler fare can be had at *Pizzeria Harlekin*, 200m north of the *Mihelič* at Gorenjska cesta 4. Across the road from here, the oddly named *Pub Hotel* (there is no hotel) is a surprisingly lively place, equally good for a daytime coffee or late-night beer (open until midnight, Fri & Sun until 2am). The **post office** is at Kolodvorska ulica 2, a few metres from the *Pub Hotel*.

Nova Štifta

Six kilometres west of Ribnica in the tiny hamlet of **Nova Štifta**, at the foothills of Velika Gora, the **Church of the Assumption** (Vnebovzetje Device Marije) is one of Slovenia's foremost pilgrimage churches, a fine-looking Baroque structure built between 1641 and 1671 and noteworthy for its unorthodox octagonal form and unusual arcaded portico embracing the south and east facades.

Its interior, meanwhile, would ordinarily be considered unremarkable were it not for the blisteringly colourful, gold, red and green wood-carved altars, ornamented with dazzling spiral columns. Around a century after the church was built, the **Holy Steps** (Sancta Sanctorum) were constructed on the north side in order to allow greater numbers of pilgrims into the church; unfortunately, the steps are now out of bounds, though you can just catch a glimpse of them, and the frescoes lining the side walls, through the windows. As the church is usually kept locked, it's best to call before you set off (Ⓣ01/836-9943), although there should be someone with the key in the monastery building adjacent. Without your own **transport**, the only way to get here is to hitch or walk, neither of which are especially appealing options.

Kočevje and around

From Ribnica, hourly buses trundle south to **KOČEVJE**, (some 16km distant), whose first inhabitants were German settlers way back in the fourteenth century, the result of a policy of systematic colonization introduced by the then ruling Ortenburgs – the name Kočevje is actually derived from the German word Gottschee, the name of the region (and the German-language speaking, Slovene, minority) during the interwar years. Historically, Kočevjska (the name of the region) has always been a sparsely populated area, the legacy of poor transportation links, a programme of mass resettlement of the majority ethnic German population towards the end of World War II, and the closure of a large part of the region for military purposes following the end of the same war – a regulation that was lifted following independence in 1991. Although the town itself is not particularly appetizing, its proximity to **Kočevjski Rog**, the country's finest uninterrupted expanse of forest, and the **Kolpa Valley** on the Croatian border, means that there's a good chance you'll pass through here if either of these places are your intended destination.

The Town

As hard as it is to imagine, a castle stood on the site of the present main square, Trg Zbora Odposlancev until as recently as World War II, when it was obliterated and its remains removed. From the **World War II monument to freedom** in the centre of this same square, it's a short walk to the enormous Neo-Gothic **Parish Church of St Fabian and St Sebastian**, completed in 1903 and announced by two searing sixty-five-metre-high spires. Inside, the bright and beautiful paintings of the Holy Trinity on the presbytery ceiling, the twenty-four old men of Israel underneath, and the kings and angels to the side, were executed by Slavko Pengov in 1932, while the large wooden statue of Saint Jernej next to the high altar was completed by popular local sculptor, Stane Jarm, a native of Osilnica (see p.232).

If you've got some time to pass, then head to the **Kočevje Regional Museum** (Pokrajinski Muzej Kočevje; Mon–Sat 9am–noon, plus Wed 4–6pm; 200SIT), a ten-minute walk east of the main square at Prešernova 11. Of particular interest – indeed of some historical importance for Slovenes – is the building itself: built in 1937, the **Šeškov House** (Šeškov Dom) staged the Assembly of the Delegates of the Slovene Nation in October 1943, the first elected parliament in Slovenia's history. The only remaining original feature of the hall is the heavily pockmarked bright red insignia above the stage, which reads "Narod si bo pisal Sodbo Sam" ("The people will make their own judgement"). The walls of the hall are now framed with a fine selection of sketches and drawings by Dolenjska native **Božidar Jakac**, an artist whose work you'll come across time and again in this region; completed during the sessions of the 1943 assembly, his drawings depict local landscapes, portraits and the lives of the Rog inhabitants – notably the Partisans, for whom he was their pictorial chronicler.

The museum's core exhibition deals with the plight of the **Kočevje Germans**, who, until the Italian occupation during the winter of 1941–42, had been the region's majority population for some 600 years. The effect of the occupation was catastrophic; most of the population was relocated into homes of previously deported Slovenes in the lower Posavje region (which was then under German control), more than half of the 170 or so German-speaking settlements in the region were abandoned, demolished or renamed, whilst nearly one hundred churches were razed. The absence of English captioning, however, makes this part of the museum a frustrating, and frankly, rather dull experience.

Practicalities

The **bus station** is 200m south of the main square, Trg Zbora Odposlancev, location for pretty much everything else of a practical nature, including the **tourist office** at no. 18b (April–Aug daily 7am–7pm; Sept–March Mon–Fri 8am–3pm; Ⓣ01/895-4979, Ⓔinfo@kocevje.si). Opposite is the town's sole **hotel**, the recently renovated and, despite the grim exterior, quite fine *Valentin* (Ⓣ01/895-1286; ❺). Less conveniently located out by the Rudnik Lake, 1km northeast of town, the rather downbeat *Pension Jezero* (Ⓣ01/895-2230; ❸) is a cheaper alternative.

Eating options are both limited and uninspiring: the *Lorella Grill*, across from the tourist office at no. 59, is about as good as it gets, offering hearty, meat-heavy dishes. Otherwise, *Pizzeria Luigi*, on the top floor of the Nama department store, does decent-sized pizzas, though the venue is bland. Drinking options are marginally better: just along from the Nama store on the main square, the *Pav* (Peacock) bar gets pretty cramped but it's fairly lively and there's outdoor space, while the much larger *Melody Bar*, behind the Nama store at no. 50, has regular disco nights to crank things up a bit.

Kočevjski Rog

One of the country's most secluded karst landscapes, **Kočevjski Rog** is a massively forested thirty-five-kilometre-long mountain range bordering Kočevje to the east, and extending in a northwest–southeast direction (a typical Dinaric range) towards the Kolpa River and Croatian border. During World War II Kočevjski Rog offered perfect sanctuary for Partisan activities, sheltering military and political offices, workshops, hospitals, printing presses and schools. The centre of operations was **Baza 20** (Base 20), which consisted of some 26 wooden shacks occupied by members of both the Central Committee of the Communist Party of Slovenia, and the Executive Committee of the Liberation Front. At the height of operations, nearly two hundred people were ensconced here, including twenty senior commanders, although Tito only visited once, when the war was over.

As an attraction it can't compare with the Franja Partisan Hospital near Cerkno (see p.181), but if you want to see inside a couple of the huts (save for some bunk beds and a small exhibition there's not much to see), contact the tourist offices either in Kočevje (see above) or Dolenjske Toplice (see p.238). Baza 20 is sited on the eastern ridge of Kočevjski Rog, and is actually easier to get to from the small town of Dolenjske Toplice (see p.238) at the foot of Rog, than it is Kočevje. From Dolenjske Toplice take the road south for 1km to Podturn, then head up the mountain road to the car park, a further 7km

Hiking in Kočevjski Rog and the virgin forests

Kočevjski Rog offers some of the best non-alpine hiking in the country, and though not especially demanding, the walks here are no less enjoyable. You'd do well, however, to stick closely to the trails; not only are you likely to get completely lost if you stray, but it's not inconceivable that you'll encounter brown bear, a large number of whom inhabit these parts – as do lynx, wolf, boar and red deer. Not surprisingly, Kočevjksi Rog is a popular destination with functionaries and hunters. The circular **Rog Footpath** (Roška Pešpot) – the trail is somewhat ominously marked out by bear paws – totals some 60km, though it's unlikely you'd want to tackle the whole thing as this would take around three days; one possibility is to drive to the highest point, **Veliki Rog** (1099m), where's there's a viewing tower, and partake in a section of the trail from there.

Three kilometres south of Veliki Rog is **Rajhenavski Rog**, one of Kočevjska's six **virgin forests** – there are a total of fourteen in the country. The trees here are manifestly higher, thicker, and older (four and five hundred-year-old trees are not uncommon) than those of your average forest, whilst strictly administered rules forbid the cutting or removal of any trees, dead or alive; moreover, as protected and preserved areas, virgin forests are strictly off-limits to the general public, though trails are laid out around the periphery. The best known of the forests' trees, and the symbol of Kočevjski Rog, is the **Queen of Rog**, a magnificent fifty-metre-high, five hundred-year-old fir sited 2km south of Rajhenavski Rog. There are sleeping possibilities at two **forest huts**; Luža at the northernmost point of the path (approx 16km from the start in Kočevje), and at Podstene, 2km south of the Queen of Rog.

An excellent alternative to the above is the Stojna Highland south and west of town, and in particular the popular trail which leads up to **Mestni Vrh** (1034m; 1hr) and the ruins of **Friedrichstein Castle** (970m), built in the early fifteenth century but abandoned around 1650. The dated but still useful 1:50,000 *Kočevsko* map, available from the tourist office, is an essential aid if you plan to undertake any hikes in these forests.

distant; from here it's a fifteen-minute walk through the forest to Baza 20. There's also a small **restaurant** by the car park.

It was in these forests, too, that several thousand anti-communist forces – mostly members of the notorious Slovene Home Guard (Domobranci) returned by British military authorities at the war's conclusion – were summarily executed and dumped into limestone pits. The existence of these **mass graves** remained a secret until 1975, when the dissident writer and politician, Edvard Kocbek, revealed the grim details in an interview to a Trieste newspaper. It was only recently, however, that the victims of these "silent killings" were acknowledged, with the passing of the 2003 War Graves Act, which effectively made provision for the management and marking of burial sites at the appropriate spots.

The Kolpa Valley

The main Ljubljana–Ribnica–Kočevje road continues south towards the stunning **Kolpa Valley**, a contorted, gorge-like river valley named after the beautiful 120-kilometre-long **Kolpa River** (Kupa in Croatian) which forms the border with Croatia. For the most part, the valley remains well off the main tourist track, thanks both to the popularity of more-established destinations further north and the paucity of public transport hereabouts. This is, though, wonderful driving and cycling country, and if you have wheels or are prepared to hitch then you could do a lot worse than spend a day taking in the scenery, partaking in any number of water-bound activities, or just resting up at one of the many delightful riverside picnic spots. Although quite different in character and temperament to the Soča River, the Kolpa, with its picturesque rapids and dams, is a big draw for adventure-sports enthusiasts, while swimmers and bathers flock to its warm waters in the summer months.

Before you reach the border, it's worth taking a minor detour to the dramatically sited ruins of the thirteenth-century **Kostel Castle**, perched atop a lofty promontory about 20km south of Kočevje, and just 6km shy of the Petrina border crossing. The castle is currently undergoing extensive renovation works (and hence, partly closed off), but you can scramble up to the entrance, a great spot from which to soak up the magnificent views. A good time to visit is at the end of August, when the **Tamburanje Festival**, a showpiece for local folk bands, is staged in and around the castle's grounds.

The Upper Kolpa Valley

The valley is at its most imperious between the tiny hamlet of **Dol** – some 26km east of the Petrina border crossing – and the village of Osilnica, 20km west of the same crossing, a stretch known as the **Upper Kolpa Valley** (Zgornja Kolpska Dolina).

Approximately 10km west of the border crossing, just beyond the village of Srobotnik (stop off at the small parking bay), a short gravel path sneaks its way up to the redundant **Church of Saint Anne** (Cerkev Sv Ana); the church is closed but the stupendous views are more than ample compensation. Back on the road, shortly after the church, the entrance to the uppermost part of the valley – **Osilnica Valley** (Osilniška Dolina) – is marked by a hulk-sized **wooden statue** of the local mythological folk hero **Peter Klepec**, whose feats of strength and daring against the Turks are the stuff of legend in these parts. A further 4km on from here, the village of **GRINTOVEC PRI OSILNICI** is the starting point for an energetic hike up to the formidable bluff of **Loška stena** (875m; 5hr).

The first building you see upon entering the village of **RIBJEK**, some 2km on from Grintovec and sited almost directly beneath Loška stena, is the preposterously pretty roadside **Church of St Egidius** (Cerkev Sv Egidija), the valley's most important historical monument. Built around 1680 but substantially renovated a few years ago, this dinky Renaissance structure manifests some absorbing detail: whitewashed walls, painted window frames, shingled gable roof and portico, and a flat bell-tower. Its interior, meanwhile, stars a wood-coffered ceiling and elaborately carved wooden altars dating from around the same time. If the church is locked the key can be obtained from no. 2, just a few paces away.

Osilnica

Sited at the confluence of the Kolpa and Čabranka rivers, 3km beyond Ribjek, **OSILNICA** is the valley's largest settlement, and pretty much the end of the line so far as things to see and do are concerned. Aside from harbouring most of the valley's practical facilities, the reason you're most likely to wind up here is to have a crack at one of the many adventure activities on offer.

The helpful little **tourist office** is located on the small main square at no. 16 (Mon–Fri 8am–2pm plus occasionally at weekends; ⓣ01/894-1594, ⓦwww.osilnica.si); if it's closed head to Kovač Tourism and Sports, a large family-run affair five minutes' walk away at Sela 5 (ⓣ01/894-1508,

Ⓦwww.kovac-kolpa.com) – it's quite likely you'll end up here anyway, as this is virtually where everything in the village happens. **Accommodation** is present in the form of two Kovač-run hotels: the larger, brand-new three-star (❹); and, across the road, the hostel-like but reasonable enough two-star (❸). There's also a small area for **camping** near the new hotel. They also rent out apartments (located next to the tourist office) sleeping between four and six people (❷). Their **restaurant** offers superb home-style cooking and the terrace is a splendid place to eat in the summer months.

As far as **activities** go, there's just about everything on offer here, most of which is available between April and September: rafting, kayaking, hydrospeed and canyoning, each costing around 4000SIT per person for a three- to four-hour trip; in addition, there's archery (2800SIT for 1hr), paintballing (3700SIT for 3–4hr) and tennis (1400SIT 1hr). Guided hikes are also possible upon request. For any of the above, it's best to call the Kovač centre at least a day in advance. If you've got your passport, you could also hike to the **source of the Kolpa** in Croatia, which should take around five hours there and back.

A short walk uphill from the tourist office, at no. 19, is the **Stane Jarm Gallery**, named after the sculptor who was born here in 1931. Using wood as his principal medium (see also his dramatic sculpture of Saint Jernej in the Parish Church in Kočevje, p.228), the small gallery is chock-full of the master sculptor's haunting, rigidly cut faces; contact the tourist office if you wish to visit. A good time to be in the village is on the last Saturday in July (**St Peter's Day**), a day of live music, food and drink in honour of the local hero, Peter Klepec.

Eastern Dolenjska and Bela Krajina

The Eastern half of Dolenjska holds the majority of its sights. These are by and large ranged along the **Krka River**, which emanates from a cave near the village of the same name and flows eastwards towards the Croatian border, joining up with the mighty Sava River near Brežice. Although fairly tricky to get to, it's well worth the endeavour required to see **Stična Monastery** and **Bogenšperk Castle**, both of which are approximately midway between Ljubljana and the beginning of the Krka.

From its source, the Krka, continues downriver towards the ruins of **Žužemberk Castle** and **Soteska Manor**, before turning upwards just prior to the atmospheric little spa town of **Dolenjske Toplice**. A little further on, **Novo Mesto** hoves into view; comfortably southern Slovenia's largest town, it retains enough points of interest for a leisurely half-day visit. East of Novo Mesto, the river continues a course past the beautifully set **Otočec Castle**, and the delightfully slumberous town of **Kostanjevica na Krki**, itself close to another of

Slovenia's ancient monasteries, **Pleterje**. The region's easternmost attractions are the small market town of **Brežice**, and the country's largest spa centre in **Čatež**.

Bela Krajina acquired its name – meaning "White Carniola", derived partially from the ubiquitous birch tree, and the white costumes worn by its inhabitants, the **Bela Kranjci** ("White Carniolans") – during the fifteenth century, when the lands were incorporated into the province of Carniola. Its frontline position ensured that, around the same time, the region's towns and villages suffered a fair battering at the hands of the Turks, whose unremitting drive up through the Balkans also led to an influx of Croat and Serb refugees and renegades (Uskoks) from Bosnia. A period of cultural and economic efflorescence eventually gave way to regional decline, as the closure of many important industrial plants was compounded by a catastrophic bout of Phylloxera at the end of the nineteenth century, which destroyed almost all the region's vineyards. Much of the local population was forced to emigrate, mainly to North America, whilst those that remained continued to engage in traditional cottage industries as a means of eking out a living. Its two main towns, **Črnomelj** and **Metlika**, are fairly low-key places but are convenient for the more interesting sites close at hand.

Stična Monastery

Some thirty kilometres southeast of Ljubljana, just off the Ljubljana–Novo Mesto highway near the village of **Ivančna Gorica**, stands **Stična Monastery**. Slovenia's oldest monastery, it was established in 1136 as part of the European network of Cistercian monasteries. Within a few years of its foundation Stična had assumed the role of Dolenjska's chief centre of culture and learning, with several important religious manuscripts having been drawn up in the monastery's scriptorium; these are now kept at the NUK library in Ljubljana and the Austrian National Library in Vienna.

The thick walls and towers you see today were erected as a result of repeated Turkish raids during the fifteenth century, a period of otherwise relative prosperity for Stična. Dissolved by Emperor Joseph II in 1784 as part of his sweeping reforms, the monastery remained defunct until 1898, at which point it was revived by Cistercians from the monastery at Bodensee (Lake Constance). It is currently home to thirteen monks (including the abbot), and whilst not as asocial as Pleterje Monastery (see p.243), the monks at Stična remain strictly governed by the motto of Saint Benedict, "*Ora et labora*" ("Pray and Work"), and so must devote themselves to between six and eight hours of prayer each day, whilst all meals are taken in complete silence. A trip to Stična entails a visit to the monastery's religious museum, the church and cloister.

Practicalities

The nearest **train station** is in Ivančna Gorica (on the Ljubljana–Novo Mesto line), 2km south of the monastery, whilst buses can set you down on the highway running parallel to the rail track. It is possible to sleep at the monastery (ⓣ01/787-7100), though you'll have to be on the premises by 6pm, and remain on site until the morning. More practically, there's **accommodation** close by at the *Grofija* Tourist Farm, about 1.5km southeast of the monastery in the village of Vir pri Stični, at no. 30 (ⓣ01/787-8141; ❷).

The Slovene Religious Museum

On the north side of the courtyard (to the right as you enter), the two-storeyed, Renaissance-era **Old Prelature**, formerly the monastery's administrative centre, now houses the **Slovene Religious Museum**; its first floor is a treasure trove of monastic riches – antique furniture, liturgical vessels, vestments and so on – while the second floor (entitled Christianity in Slovenia) chronicles the many disparate groups and movements that have shaped the development of the Slovene Church throughout the centuries, including Protestants, Jesuits, Capuchins and Ursulines. The museum's impressive art and cultural history section has fresco remains by the renowned fifteenth-century artist Janez Ljubljanski, paintings by Langus and Metzinger, and a typically exuberant chalice designed by architect Jože Plečnik as a gift for Simon Ašič, a former abbot who also happened to be one of Slovenia's most eminent herbalists; you can purchase some of his medicinal herbs and teas from the shop by the entrance.

The Abbey Church and Cloister

Adjacent to the Prelature, the twelfth-century **Abbey Church** betrays few signs of its Romanesque origins, having been extensively reworked in Baroque style during the seventeenth and eighteenth centuries. Its vast, white tripartite nave is fairly naked, save for a larger than usual number of side altars – one for each priest to pray to – although there are some fine artistic treasures to admire, most notably the fourteen Stations of the Cross painted by Fortunat Bregant in 1766; a marble tabernacle by Plečnik; and some beautifully worked tombstones – look out for the red stone tombstone of Abbot Jacob Reinprecht, the chief architect of the church's present Baroque appearance.

Abutting the church at the heart of the complex is the thirteenth-century Gothic **cloister**, a splendid rib-vaulted space complete with lancet windows and several layers of just about discernible frescoes, the best of which are those by master painter Janez Ljubljanski in the north wing. Elsewhere, look out for the figural keystones in the western wing depicting human faces, and the two superbly restored bifora (double-arched windows), the cloister's most obvious Romanesque remains. On the south side of the cloister, the **refectory's** pink vaulted ceiling is decorated with some marvellous stuccowork (it's not possible to enter, but you can see it from the doorway), as is the ceiling of the **Upper Tower**, located on the opposite side of the Prelature; the compositions on the latter depict scenes from the Crucifixion and Last Judgement, as well as images of the four Church Fathers. Visits to the monastery can only be made as part of a **guided tour** (Tues–Sat 8.30am, 10am, 2pm & 4pm, Sun 2pm & 4pm; 600SIT).

Bogenšperk Castle

Surrounded by the densely forested Dolenjska hills some 20km north of Stična, close to the large village of Šmartno pri Litiji, **Bogenšperk Castle** (March–Oct Fri 9am–5pm, Sat & Sun 10am–5pm; Nov–Feb Sat & Sun 9am–5pm; 200SIT) is a descendant of a twelfth-century medieval fortification, though the present structure dates from around 1511. Built by the lords of Wagen (Wagensperg is German for Bogenšperk), the castle is synonymous with the great polymath Janez Vajkard Valvasor (see box opposite), who lived and worked here between 1672 and 1692, during which time he compiled his immense opus *The Glory of the Duchy of Carniola*.

The building is a classic Renaissance-era chateau featuring three cylindrical towers and a partly arcaded inner courtyard. The interior, meanwhile, has been refurbished – the castle's entire contents were plundered at the end of World War II – so as to evoke the atmosphere of Valvasor's day. His **library** (at least

Janez Vajkard Valvasor

Arguably Slovenia's greatest scholar, **Janez Vajkard Valvasor** – historian, topographer and ethnologist – was born in Ljubljana in 1641 of a noble family from Bergamo in Italy. Following extensive travels throughout Europe and North Africa, Valvasor purchased Bogenšperk in 1672, assembling a rich library and establishing important graphics and printing workshops within the castle. Having devoted his entire life to research, he spent the next fifteen years compiling and writing his monumental baroque topography *The Glory of the Duchy of Carniola*, four illustrated encyclopaedic volumes weighing in at 3532 pages. In it, Valvasor offered the first thoroughgoing presentation of the then province of Carniola, as well as several neighbouring provinces, expounding upon the region's extraordinary natural phenomena, such as the caves at Postojna and Škocjan, and the disappearing Lake Cerknica, as well as extolling the virtues of the people who shaped these lands. Following the book's publication, Valvasor lectured to the Royal Society in London on the miraculous workings of the lake, an occasion that saw him rewarded with a fellowship from the society. However, such was the debt accumulated by Valvasor during the process of compiling and publishing the book, that he was eventually forced to sell both the castle and all its contents. He died, destitute, in the town of Krško in 1693.

that's the assumption, based on the fact that it's the largest room in the castle) is now used as a wedding venue, while the old hunting room contains an odd, and rather mundane, mishmash of exhibits: hunting trophies, geological and folk-costume displays, and an exposition on seventeenth-century witch trials, a subject Valvasor wrote about in his aforementioned work. Of greater interest are the two rooms packed with fascinating maps and sketches, including original works by Valvasor and eminent Slovene cartographer Peter Kosler, and a cylinder printing press of the type Valvasor used – the original is in Mainz, Germany. Valvasor's **study**, which we know to be his because of the four marble pillars to which he referred in his writings, contains the museum's principal exhibit, an original copy of *The Glory of the Duchy of Carniola*. Indeed, the castle retains just four of Valvasor's books: one other is kept in Zagreb, whilst the whereabouts of the other two is unknown.

Bogenšperk is not the easiest place to get to; if you're coming from Ivančna Gora, you'll have to get here under your own steam, be it by bike or car. By **public transport** you must take a bus or train from Ljubljana as far as Litija, though from here it's still another 6km slog uphill to the castle.

Trebnje

Back on the main Ljubljana–Zagreb E70 highway, 18km east of Stična (it's also on the Ljubljana–Novo Mesto rail line), it's worth stopping off at the small town of **TREBNJE** to visit the **Gallery of Naïve Artists** (Galerija Likovnih Samorastnikov; Mon–Fri 2–4pm; 500SIT), the only museum of its kind in the country. Modelled on the famous Hlebine school in northern Croatia, the gallery presents an outstanding collection of naïve art garnered from Slovenia and other countries of the former Yugoslavia, as well as Africa, Asia and Latin America. The origins of self-taught painting in Slovenia can be traced back to the popular nineteenth-century folk art of beehive panel painting (see p.111), itself believed to have derived from the widely practised discipline of painting farm furniture and glass. These wonderfully authentic expressions of indigenous peasant culture later manifest themselves in the colourful world of the naïve painters during the 1930s and 1940s.

The pictures here – painted on wood, canvas or glass – are typically fresh and vibrant, occasionally kitsch or sometimes just plain bizarre, but in nearly all cases touch upon themes pertaining to everyday village life; there are also some wonderfully bucolic landscape paintings, such as *Eve* by the Bosnian Sekula Dugandič, and *Two Blooms*, by eminent Croatian village painter Ivan Rabuzin. Works by Slovenian artists to look out for include scenes from the Kurent by Boris Žohar, and several portraits by Irena Polanec.

If you're here at the end of June there's a week-long festival starring international artists working live inside the gallery. The museum is in the centre of town on Baragov trg, just across from the **bus station** next to the church. From the **train station** on Kolodvorska ulica, walk up to the main road, turn left and continue towards the church.

The Krka River Valley

The **Krka River Valley** is one of the country's most picturesque valley regions, yet it's little visited by tourists, many of whom inadvertently bypass it travelling on the main road or rail routes just to the north. The valley's defining feature is its wide, languid river richly stocked with brown trout, pike perch and grayling; issuing forth from a spring in the Krka Cave, it continues beyond the valley's lower reaches to Novo Mesto, and then onwards to Brežice where it discharges into the Sava River. The Krka is also known for its attractive calc-tufa falls and rapids, step-like waterfalls composed of porous rock formed from calcium carbonate, which you can see at regular intervals along the entire stretch of the river. Natural attractions aside, there's much of historical importance to see within the valley, including castle remains at **Žužemberk** and **Soteska**, the village of **Muljava** – birthplace of one of Slovenia's great writers – and, at the tail end of the valley, the delightful spa town, **Dolenjske Toplice**.

Muljava and the source of the Krka

Due south of Ivančna Gorica, on the other side of the highway, **MULJAVA** is an attractive little village known throughout the country as the birthplace of popular Slovene novelist and journalist Josip Jurčič (1844–1881), the man credited with writing Slovenia's first full-length novel *Deseti Brat* ("The Tenth Brother"), in 1866. The house in which he was born (Jurčičeva Domačija; Tues–Sat 9am–noon & 1–4pm, Sun 1–4pm; 450SIT), and lived in until the age of twelve, was built by his grandfather in 1826 and is as interesting for its architectural detail – a traditional "black" kitchen, living room, bedroom and cellar – as it is for the memorabilia on display pertaining to Jurčič's life. In the garden stands a beehive, furnished with the traditional painted panels, while to the rear of the house there's a storehouse, or granary (kašča), and a Krjavelj Hut, a timber shack dwelling usually inhabited by a *bajtar* – a poor villager. The house, at no. 11, is signposted from the main square.

Each year, on two or three consecutive weekends at the end of June/beginning of July several of Jurčič's works are staged in the fabulous natural amphitheatre located at the edge of woodland behind the house; tickets (1500SIT) can be purchased one hour before each performance. Muljava also marks the start and finish point for the very scenic and very popular **Jurčičeva Pot walk;** named after Jurčič, the walk (3–4hr) winds up at Višnja Gora (550m) some 15km further north.

One section of the walk takes in the village of **Krka**, 2km south of Muljava, and the **source of the Krka River** (Pri Izviru), another 2km further on. The source (a seventeen-metre-deep siphon lake) is actually located inside the small, 200-metre-long **Krka Cave** (Krška jama), an unexciting spectacle with none of the spectacular formations you'd find in Slovenia's better-known caves; it does, however, hold a specimen of Proteus Anguinus (the "Human Fish" – see box on p.217). To visit you should head to the kiosk located 200m before the entrance, from where you will be escorted to the cave and given a short guided tour; the cave is usually open daily between 9am and 6pm (4 or 5pm in winter), but it's best to call in advance to make sure (ⓣ01/780-6333; 250SIT).

Žužemberk Castle and Soteska Manor

The valley's major settlement is the market town of **ŽUŽEMBERK**, which is dominated by the formidable bulk of **Žužemberk Castle**, much of which was razed during World War II; although a programme of renovation has been ongoing for years, the restoration of the five huge towers and bastions aside, you'd hardly think so. Dramatically sited on a steep bank high above the Krka River and buffered by a thick clump of trees which slope down to the water, the original castle dates from the thirteenth century, with piecemeal development over the ensuing centuries, including the aforementioned towers, as well as defensive walls, arcades and vaulted cellars, most of which you can still see.

Today, the castle's large inner courtyard is the atmospheric venue for summer concerts and plays; tickets (around 1000SIT) can be purchased from the castle one hour prior to each performance. To find out what's on, contact the municipal building (Občina) opposite the castle at Grajska trg 33 (ⓣ07/388-5180). In the centre of this main square is a fine little cast-iron fountain, forged at the ironworks in the nearby village of Dvor and worth a look for its splendidly crafted animal heads from whence water spouts. For the best views of the castle, walk down to the river and across to the opposite bank; standing on the bridge gives you head-on views of the calc-tufa falls.

The town's position on the Krka allowed for the extensive development of water-powered installations during the sixteenth and seventeenth centuries, most commonly iron foundries and sawmills. At one stage there were around forty of the latter lining this stretch of river, though by the end of the twentieth century most had ceased functioning. The Zajčev Mill, located a little way upstream near Prapreče, is the only mill still in operation and can be visited if you contact the municipal building (see above). The Krka River is also popular with water-sports enthusiasts; the *Koren* tourist farm, down by the river at Dolga Vas 5 (ⓣ07/308-7260, ⓔturizem-koren@volja.net; ❷), has one- to four-bed **rooms**, and rents canoes and kayaks (500SIT per hour).

Some 9km downriver from Žužemberk are the less complete ruins of **Soteska Manor** (Dvorec Soteska), built between 1664 and 1689 by Duke Jurij Gallenberg but which, for the greater part of its existence, was the domicile of the Auersperg counts. Today, a fairly unbroken outer shell incorporating two of the four original corner towers and the entrance gate are all that remain of the manor following its destruction in 1943 by Partisan units, an act of deliberate sabotage carried out in order to prevent German troops from appropriating it.

From the former entrance to the manor, a path cuts across the main road towards a field (formerly a walled-in park), in the centre of which stands the park pavilion, otherwise known as the **Devils Tower** (Hudičev turn); its empty interior is illuminated with murals of mythological figures, pillared architecture and other fantastical compositions painted by the Almanach workshop in the seventeenth century. Before the manor's destruction, the path was lined with three stone portals, one of which – and it's a particularly fine piece of craftsmanship – marks the entrance to the field. If you wish to see inside the tower, contact the tourist office in Dolenjske Toplice (see below).

Dolenjske Toplice

Just where the river turns sharply in the direction of Novo Mesto, is **DOLENJSKE TOPLICE**, a classic, neat and orderly spa town, whose elegant Habsburg-era buildings give it an authentic *fin-de-siècle* ambience. Exploited since medieval times for curative purposes, the town's springs were first channelled into a bathhouse by Ivan Vajkard, a member of the Auersperg family, in the seventeenth century, although it wasn't until the late nineteenth century that Dolenjske Toplice (then called Strascha Toplitz) prospered as a fashionable, modern spa resort, utilized to treat a wide range of disorders and illnesses. During both World Wars the resort was pressed into action as an emergency military treatment centre and hospital.

The modern complex inside the *Kristal/Vital* hotels (see below) houses three **pools** (1400SIT for three hours, free to hotel guests). If you fancy doing something a little more energetic than wallowing, pop into the K2M agency, 100m south of the tourist office at Pionirska cesta 3 (Mon–Fri 9am–4pm, Sat 9am–1pm; ⓣ07/306-6830; ⓦwww.k2m.si); they organize rafting (3300SIT per person for 2hr) and kayaking (4900SIT per person for 2hr) on the Krka, and you can also rent canoes (7500SIT per day) and bikes (300SIT per hour, 1500SIT per day).

Practicalities

Buses stop off along Zdraviliški trg, the town's main street and from where nothing is more than a ten-minute walk away. From the bus stop it's just metres to the **tourist office** at no. 8 (Mon–Fri 10am–5pm, Sat 10am–noon & 3–6pm, Sun 10am–noon; ⓣ07/384-5190, ⓔobcina.dtoplice@siol.net), and the **post office** at no. 3 (Mon–Fri 8–9.30am & 10am–5pm).

Facing each other across Zdraviliški trg's southern, square-like portion, are the town's two, almost identical spa **hotels**, the lime-green *Kristal* and the pink *Vital* (ⓣ07/391-9500, ⓔbooking.dolenjske@krka-zdravilisca.si; reception for both is in the *Vital*; ❻); each possesses the comforts you'd expect from a four-star spa hotel. Aside from the two hotels there's more than enough accommodation to go around: 200m east of Zdraviliški trg at Ulica Maksa Henigmana 15, the *Gostišče Račka* (ⓣ07/306-5510; ❸) has a handful of perfectly decent rooms plus a couple of apartments or, alternatively, take your pick from one of the many private rooms (❷) advertised throughout town, such as at the *Pri Tomljetu* guesthouse (Zdraviliški trg 24; ⓣ07/306-5023), located up along the road behind the pool; either the tourist office or the K2M agency should be able to help out if you're struggling to find a place. The town's small and tidy **campsite** is nicely located at the northern end of Zdraviliški trg at the foot of the wooded slopes by the Sušica stream (ⓣ07/391-9400; May–Sept).

For eating, the town's main **restaurant** is the vaguely countrified *Gostilna Rog* at Zdraviliški trg 22, though for a similar menu and at similar prices you can dine under the huge chandeliers of the rather more refined *Kristal Hotel* restaurant; there's also the *Gostišče Račka*, which serves stock pizza and pasta dishes. Coffee is best taken at the *Bistro Rožek*, the small circular building in between the *Kristal* and *Vital* hotels, while the *Illy Pub* next to the K2M agency is a more heads-down drinking venue.

Novo Mesto

As Dolenjska's cultural and religious centre since the Middle Ages, **NOVO MESTO** ("New Town") is quite comfortably the largest town in southeastern Slovenia. Continuously settled since the Bronze Age – as attested to by the numerous archeological sites hereabouts – Novo Mesto was granted city rights in 1365, thereafter evolving into a prosperous market town and trade centre, and, following the establishment of a collegiate chapter around the same time, a centre of ecclesiastical importance too. In recent times, Novo Mesto has established itself as one of the country's leading industrial heartlands, home to the major pharmaceutical enterprise Krka, and the vehicle manufacturer Revoz (a subsidiary of Renault), formerly the largest plant in Yugoslavia.

The town's sights are few, but its personable old core, attractively sited on a rocky promontory in a hairpin bend of the Krka River, does possess a couple of noteworthy monuments, while its museum keeps a first-rate collection of archeological treasures; moreover, it's handy as a springboard for the many attractions – rivers, castles, spas and monasteries – lying close at hand.

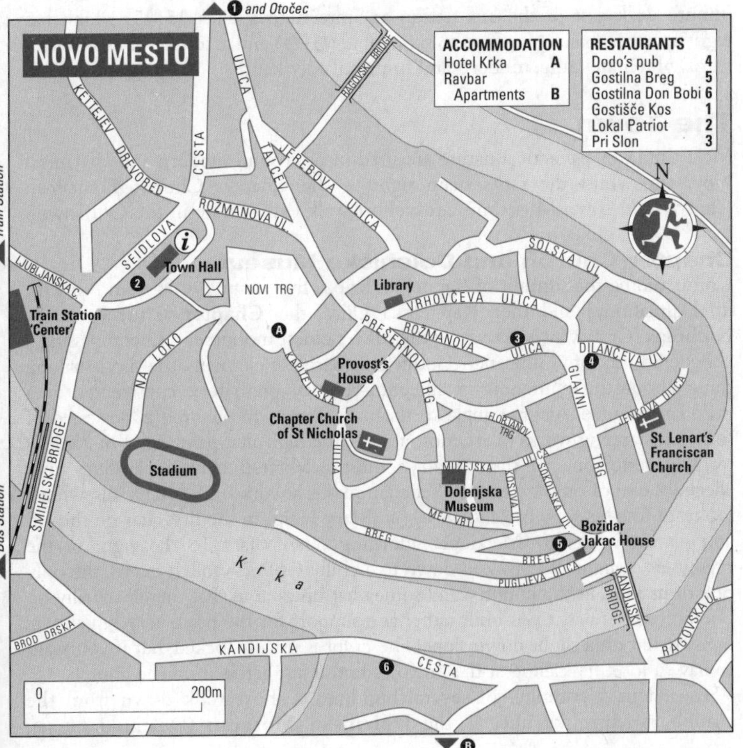

Most of the out-of-town sights are situated along the E216 (west from Novo Mesto) and E419 (east from Novo Mesto) roads, both of which run south of and parallel to the main E70 Ljubljana–Zagreb highway. However, without your own transport, you will have to rely on a modest bus service in order to reach them, as most buses travel the highway; moreover, the rail line from Ljubljana follows the same course as the highway, although only as far as Novo Mesto, before continuing south into Bela Krajina.

Arrival, information and accommodation

The **bus station** is on Topliška Cesta, a ten-minute walk southwest of the town centre, whilst there are two **train stations** to the west of town – the main one, Novo Mesto, and, some 800m south of here, Center, the latter just five minutes' walk into town; all trains stop at both stations, so alight at Center. The **tourist office** (June–Sept Mon–Fri 9am–6pm, Sat 9am–noon; Oct–May Mon–Fri 8am–3pm; ⓣ07/393-9263, ⓦwww.novomesto.si) is presently secreted away by the side of the Občina (municipal) building at Novi trg 6, though plans are afoot for a move to the Old Town. The **post office** (Mon–Fri 7am–8pm, Sat 7am–1pm) is on Novi trg across from the *Hotel Krka*, and there's **Internet access** at the library (Mon–Fri 8.30am–7pm) just up from *Pri Slon* at Rozmanova ulica 26.

The town's sole **hotel** is the *Krka* on Novi trg (ⓣ07/394-2100, ⓔhotel.krka@krka.si; ❼), a self-styled business hotel with well-turned-out rooms including minibar, safe and air-conditioning. A better alternative is the family-run *Ravbar apartments* (ⓣ07/373-0680, ⓦww.ravbar.net), a fifteen-minute walk east of the bus station at Smrečnikova ulica 15–17, which has eight apartments sleeping two to six people (❸–❻) and a couple of rooms (❷), all of which are large, modern and immaculately kept.

The Town

Most things of a practical nature are sited in or around modern and charmless Novi trg, whilst the city's main sights – the Chapter Church, Franciscan Church, and Town Museum – are a short walk east of here in the Old Town.

Chapter Church and Dolenjska Museum

Commanding the summit of Kapiteljski hrib, a five-minute walk from Novi trg up Dalmatinova and then Kapiteljska Ulica, the **Chapter Church of St Nicholas** (Cerkev sv Miklavza) is the town's oldest monument. Encompassing a chequered mix of Gothic, neo-Gothic and Baroque elements, the most striking thing about the church is its fifteenth-century presbytery, constructed at a peculiar seventeen-degree angle to the nave. Inside, the church is possessed of some outstanding works of art, most notably the high altar painting of *St Nicholas* by Tintoretto, one of the country's most celebrated church paintings and, allegedly, one of only two of the Venetian master's works in Slovenia. Elsewhere, look out for the copy of *Maria Pomagaj* (Mary Help) in the first altar on the left and several works by Metzinger adorning other altars. To the right of the presbytery a flight of steps lead down to a chilly, Gothic-vaulted **crypt**, the only one of its kind in the country and somewhat unusual in that there's actually no one buried here as it was built rather as a support for the presbytery which was constructed on a slight down slope. The crypt is usually locked, but if you want to have a look try calling at the provost's house just across from the church.

Housed in a complex of several buildings a short walk down from the church at Muzejska ulica 7, the **Dolenjska Museum** (Dolenjski muzej;

April–Oct Tues–Fri 8am–5pm, Sat 10am–5pm, Sun 10am–1pm; Nov–March Tues–Fri 8am–4pm, Sat 9am–1pm, Sun 9am–noon; 600SIT) keeps arguably the finest stockpile of archeological treasures in Slovenia. The core of the collection comprises grave finds unearthed from hundreds of burial sites on the slopes of Marof and Mestne njive, two modest rises located a short way north of the town centre. The earliest artefacts, from the late Bronze Age (the so-called Urnfield culture), comprise a superb display of large ceramic urns, into which the remains of the deceased, together with their personal belongings – bronze needles, jewellery, beads and the like – were placed.

The **Hallstatt** period (aka the early Iron or late Bronze Age, approximately 8th–4th BC) is represented by more vessels and jewellery, including earrings, bracelets and anklets, as well as several pieces of armour – the star exhibit a beautifully well-preserved Bronze Age helmet. The most impressive items, however, are the specimens of **Situla Art**, bronze buckets, or pails, ornately embossed with festive or hunting scenes. The larger grave urns from the Celtic period were somewhat more sophisticated, suggesting that the deceased were from a higher social rank. Rounding off this veritable treasure trove is a hoard of Roman grave goods: tableware, wine pitchers, oil lamps, cups and so on. The remainder of the museum, comprising ethnological and modern history collections is, by comparison, distinctly underwhelming.

Glavni trg and around

From the museum a number of narrow alleyways descend through town to cobbled **Glavni Trg** (Main Square). Actually more street than square, this is the city's focal point, once the haunt of merchants and craftsmen but today profiled with two rows of handsome townhouses, variously accommodating public buildings, shops and the odd café or bar. The square's most striking feature is its elegant arcades, although its most prominent building, located midway down the left-hand side at no. 6, is the grey, mock-Renaissance **Town Hall** (Rotovž), built in 1905.

Lurking just behind the Town Hall on Frančišk trg (accessed via Jenkova ulica) stands **St Leonard's Franciscan Church** (Frančiškanska cerkev sv Lenarta), whose elegant, mustard-coloured neo-Gothic gabled facade dating from around 1880 was just one of the church's many piecemeal additions following a fire in 1664. From the original church, built in 1472 as a place of refuge for Franciscan monks from Bosnia (who had initially sheltered at the Tri Fare Parish in Metlika, see p.255), only the Gothic presbytery was retained, although its wooden altars were lost and replaced with the current neo-Gothic editions. The adjoining **monastery** boasts a fine library with some superb incunabula, a tiny prayer book from 1450, and a psalm book made from animal skin and featuring Gothic and Baroque text dating from 1418 (visits to the monastery are possible by prior arrangement only; contact the tourist office).

At the square's southern end, just above the picturesque **Breg** embankment (turn right just before the bridge), the **Božidar Jakac House** (Jačkev Dom; Tues–Fri 10am–4pm, Sat 9am–1pm, Sun 9am–noon; 200SIT) holds the eponymous artist's largest collection of sketches and drawings outside Kostanjevica (see p.245); there's also a terrific selection of watercolours and oils depicting town scenes and local landscapes. Formerly a hotel, this building was actually the house of his father – Jakac was born 100m further up the street in what is now the *Breg* restaurant (see p.242). Crossing the **Kandijski Bridge** (Kandijski Most) gives you some lovely views back to Breg and the bright orange-tiled rooftops of the Old Town.

Cviček

Whilst in Novo Mesto, it would be remiss not to try the local speciality, **Cviček** (pronounced "tsveechek"), one of the country's most distinctive and unusual wines. Cultivated only here in southeast Dolenjska, Cviček is produced from a blend of red and white grapes – said to be more than a dozen, but this is considered an exaggeration – giving it a cranberry-juice-like appearance. Despite its dry, rather sour taste, it's a surprisingly refreshing wine, made all the more drinkable thanks to its low alcoholic content of around nine percent. Whilst most Cviček is produced for home consumption, it's the first drink you'll be offered in the local restaurants and bars.

Eating, drinking and entertainment

The town is severely lacking in decent places to **eat**: your best bet is the cosy, cellar-like cavern *Gostilna Don Bobi*, out on the busy main road Kandijska cesta (no. 14), which knocks up steaming plates of pastas; otherwise, there's the very average and fairly downbeat *Gostilna Breg*, 100m along from the Jakac House at Cvelbarjeva ulica 9; or the restaurant in the *Hotel Krka* which has simple, good-value lunchtime specials. The town's best restaurant, however, is *Gostišče Kos*, albeit somewhat inconveniently located 1km out on the road towards Otočec at Šmarješka cesta 26; its stylish interior is complemented by a high-quality menu, featuring a selection of mushroom, steak and fish dishes and, for vegetarians, a decent choice of buckwheat and *štruklji* (fruit dumplings) dishes; with the exception of the hotel restaurant, all the above are closed on Sundays.

The most atmospheric place to **drink** is the Old Town, the location for a couple of cafês and bars, the best of which are *Dodo's Pub* at the top end of Glavni trg, and *Pri Slon* ("At the Elephant"), a short walk away at Rozmanova ulica 22, an old-style café good for coffee; otherwise, there's an indistinguishable spread of cafés on Novi trg. The student club, *Lokal Patriot*, in the Občina building (on the opposite side to the tourist office), offers a great mix of club nights, film showings, and rock and jazz concerts featuring many of Slovenia's top names; pick up a flyer or check out the website (Mon–Fri 7am–midnight, Sat 5pm–2am; Ⓦ www.lokalpatriot.si).

The first week of July sees Novo Mesto host **Rock Otočec** (Ⓦ www.rock-otocec.com), the country's largest rock festival, and which has in recent years featured international acts such as Asian Dub Foundation and Morcheeba, alongside Slovenia's premier bands; the venue has no permanent site but for the past few years has been held at the airfield in Prečna, 4km northwest of town. During the festival there are free buses to/from Novo Mesto.

Otočec Castle

Picturesquely sited on an elongated, tree-covered island in the middle of another attractive stretch of the Krka river, 7km east of Novo Mesto, is **Otočec Castle**. Surrounded by dozens of tiny islets and the Krka's distinctive calc-tufa falls, the country's only island castle was originally occupied by the knights of Otočec during the thirteenth century, thereafter passing through the hands of various noble families. Fortified with walls and four chunky towers during persistent fifteenth-century Turkish raids, the castle was purchased in 1560 by Ivan Lenkovič, commander of the Austrian Empire's Vojna Krajina region, during which time it acquired its present, largely Renaissance appearance, albeit heavily renovated following extensive World War II damage.

The castle now functions as one of Slovenia's few five-star **hotels**, the *Hotel Grad Otočec* (ⓣ07/307-5165, ⓔbooking.otocec@krka-zdravilisca.si; ❾), whose apartment-style rooms are fitted out with extravagant period furniture and enormous bathrooms with oversized baths. The hotel's understatedly elegant **restaurant**, complete with waiters in rather daft medieval get-up, offers superb fish (red trout and pikeperch), as well as more exotic dishes such as ostrich steak, and avocado dumplings with octopus; suffice to say, it doesn't come cheap. If your wallet can't stretch to a meal, then take a coffee in the courtyard café.

There's more accommodation back across the main road (next to the highway) in the shape of the *Hotel Šport* (same contact details as the *Grad Otočec*; ❺), whose ugly exterior belies some good-looking and comfortable rooms; they've also got cheaper, en-suite bungalows opposite (❹). Guests of both hotels receive complimentary use of the thermal pools in Šmarješke Toplice (see below), and there's an adjoining **tennis centre** with indoor and outdoor courts (3000SIT & 1000SIT respectively). The small and grubby **campsite** (ⓣ07/307-5168; May–Sept) is located a few hundred metres east of the castle on the river's south bank.

There's a smattering of other accommodation hereabouts, the best of which is the fabulous *Šeruga* tourist farm, located in perfect rural isolation some 3km south of Otočec (just off the main road to Kostanjevica) at Sela pri Ratežu 15 (ⓣ07/334-6900, ⓔturist.kmetija.seruga@siol.net; ❷). Back on the main road, 2km further east at Ratež 48, the roadside inn *Gostilna Vovko* also has a handful of good-value rooms (ⓣ07/308-5603; ❸), but if you're heading this way anyway don't pass up the opportunity to try out its terrific **restaurant** (closed Mon), which specializes in fantastically tasty and filling grilled meat dishes.

Šmarješke Toplice

From Otočec, five daily buses (Mon–Fri) make the short trip to **ŠMARJEŠKE TOPLICE** some 5km to the northeast. Although far smaller and more low-key than Dolenjske Toplice (see p.238), Šmarješke Toplice has been a spa centre of sorts since the eighteenth century, but only developed into a serious resort after World War II, when it served the needs of ailing Communist Party members. It now counts five thermal pools – two indoor and three outdoor, averaging 32°C (1400SIT). Even if you don't plan on taking a dip, the park is a good place for a gentle stroll or a picnic.

Accommodation comes in the form of three conjoined hotels located at the heart of the complex, itself a short way north of the village (ⓣ07/384-3400, ⓔbooking.smarjeske@krka-zdravilisca.si); the *Krka I* and *Krka II* (both ❹) – *Krka II* is usually reserved for longer-term medical patients – and the more modern *Šmarjeta* (❺), easily the nicest of the three; although the hotels are primarily concerned with serious therapy treatments, they also offer all manner of health and fitness facilities. In addition to the regular pools (free of charge to hotel guests) there are steam baths, saunas and massage pools. A much cheaper alternative is the *Domen Pension* (ⓣ07/307-3051; ❸), located 1.5km southeast of Šmarješke Toplice in Družinska Vas (no. 1).

Pleterje Monastery and Skansen

Beautifully set in a secluded valley at the foot of the Gorjanci forests, **Pleterje Monastery** is Europe's easternmost Carthusian monastery, and the only one of Slovenia's four Charterhouses still functioning. Shut off from the outside world by a formidable 2600-metre-long, three-metre-high enclosure wall, the monastery has endured a chequered history, one not that dissimilar to that of Stična (see p.233). Founded in 1407 by Count Herman II of Celje, Pleterje was fortified during the fifteenth century in advance of Turkish raids, before its dissolution, and subsequent appropriation by the Jesuits at the end of the sixteenth century. Following the reforms of Emperor Joseph II, the monastery was disbanded again in 1784, only to be repurchased and rebuilt by the Carthusian order in 1899.

While the main church is open to visitors, the rest of the monastery (cloisters, courtyards, the New Monastery Church, orchards and meadows) is strictly out of bounds, and it's unlikely that you'll get to see one of the sixteen monks that live here. Rooted in the anchorite traditions of Early Christianity, the Pleterje monks live according to a precisely defined schedule, completely devoted to prayer (liturgy and meditation) and work (both study and manual labour). While here, make time to visit the **Skansen**, located just down from the monastery.

Church of the Holy Trinity

Rated as one of the best-preserved examples of early French Gothic in Central Europe, the single nave **Church of the Holy Trinity** (built in 1420) is astonishingly simple, and, though almost completely devoid of furniture or ornamentation, is possessed of some wonderfully subtle detail. Entering through the low, stone rood screen which separates the nave and chancel, have a look up at the splendid cross rib-vaulted ceiling, embellished with numerous bosses bearing a range of motifs, and the seventy or so clay vessels (also known as "acoustical pottery") spotted along the walls. You can't really miss the high altar, a smooth slab of grey stone placed upon two stone stools. On the exterior the badly pockmarked wall was the result of heavy shelling during World War II.

You can learn more about the Carthusian order by watching the informative, twenty-five-minute **presentation**, set up in the sacristy to the side of the church. The monastery **shop** (Mon–Sat 7.30am–5.30pm), located at the entrance to the main building, has a terrific stock of wines and brandies produced at its own distillery – take your pick from juniper (*brinovec*), pear (*hruška*), and plum (*slivovka*) – as well as cheese, honey and propolis (another bee-produced substance).

The Skansen

Spread out across a lovely green field at the bottom of the road leading up to the monastery is a fabulous little **Skansen**, or open-air museum (Pleterje Skansen; April–Oct daily 9am–6pm, Nov–March 10am–4pm; 450SIT including the monastery; 300SIT for museum only), whose handful of buildings, representing a typical farmyard from this region, were relocated here partly in order to draw visitors away from the monastery itself. As well as its classic thatched wooden houses, fully equipped with authentic domestic furniture, the complex includes a threshing floor, fruit and flax dryer, and a superb double hayrack; you can also buy pottery and ceramics.

Time and energy permitting, you can partake in the **Pleterje Way**, a circular footpath that skirts the hills above the monastery, and which affords views of the complex you wouldn't normally get to see; allow around ninety minutes to complete it. Unless you've got your own transport, getting here entails taking a bus to Šentjernej (6km west of Kostanjevica along the road to Novo Mesto), from where it's a 3km walk south to the monastery.

Kostanjevica na Krki

Compacted into a tight loop of the Krka River, the island settlement is one of the country's smallest towns, a once thriving commercial centre with its own mint but now a rural backwater, possessed of a ghostly, slumberous charm. From the bus station on Ljubljanska cesta, it's a five-minute walk north to the bridge, which in turn leads you onto the tranquil, palette-shaped island, comprised of two main streets that join to form a circle around a cluster of buildings in an advanced state of decay. Aside from a couple of small Gothic churches sited at either end, there's actually very little to see or do in this part of town, but if you've got an hour to spare following a visit to the out-of-town attractions, it's definitely worth taking a leisurely stroll around.

The Božidar Jakac and Jože Gorjup galleries

A fifteen-minute walk southwest of town (head down Ljubljanska Cesta and follow the signs) is the former **Cistercian Monastery**, founded in 1234, disbanded in 1784 and largely destroyed during World War II. All but completely renovated now, there are some interesting masonry fragments – vaulted ribs, keystones and so on – from the previously damaged church in the **lapidarium**, located in the eastern arcaded passage of the monastery's immense three-sided cloister. The cloister's numerous rooms now accommodate the **Božidar Jakac Gallery** (Galerija Božidar Jakac; April–Oct Tues–Sun 9am–6pm, Nov–March 9am–4pm; 600SIT) which, with the works of no less than eight of Slovenia's most prominent artists to plough through, requires no little stamina.

The most obvious place to start is the collection by the versatile Jakac, whose prolific stock of prints and graphics, many of which document his time spent with the Partisans, are complemented by some exquisite pastels and oils, featuring land or townscapes from both Slovenia (*Hayrack*) and Prague, where he studied – keep an eye out for the lovely *Midnight Mass on Hradčani*. After Jakac, make a beeline for the rooms holding the extensive collections of the Kralj brothers, France and Tone, both key figures in the interwar Slovene avant-garde but whose later works veered towards the realm of Socialist Realism. Tone's later work, in particular, is biased towards themes of war, revolt and daily peasant life (*Black Gold*). Family portraits feature heavily too, such as the disturbing *My Mother*, which has their mother standing over his dead pilot brother's body.

Of the other artists, try not to miss the fabulously creative bronze sculptures of Janez Boljka, whose work evolved from sculpting simple motifs from Ribnica, to more adventurous subject matter, such as the animal kingdom (*Bull*, *Chimpanzee*) and the human form, and in particular, eminent Slovenes (*Ivan Cankar and his Muse*, *Rihard Jakopič Seated*); there are further sculptures (and oils) by France Gorše and Jože Gorjup – Gorše also specialized in portraits of noteworthy Slovenes, such as Primož Trubar. Worth a peek, too, is a rather dusty collection of Old European Masters (German, Italian and Flemish) from Pleterje Monastery. The monastery's gardens are used to exhibit some one hundred oak-wood sculptures, otherwise known as the **Former Viva** (Living Form), one of several such sculpture parks around Slovenia, each of which demonstrates works of art made from a different material.

If you've still got the appetite, there's more work by some of the same artists at the **Jože Gorjup Gallery**, housed in the primary school of the same name at Gorjanska ulica 2200m east of the bridge. Take a look at the wall on the side of the school's gym building, which features a brilliant mosaic of the 1573 Battle on Krško Plain, in which the counts do battle with peasants amidst a fierce snowstorm.

Kostanjevica Cave

One and a half kilometres southeast of town, in a small wooded area bound by a stream, is **Kostanjevica Cave** (Kostanjeviška Jama), the largest and most impressive of Dolenjska's cave systems. Speleologists were first drawn to the possibility of the cave's existence following a flood in 1937, after which time systematic exploration uncovered numerous other shafts, chambers and lakes. Fifty-minute guided tours of the old part of the cave take in approximately 250m of the 1800m discovered to date, beginning at the sixty-metre-long entrance tunnel. Beyond here a series of tight passages and staircases wend their way through several chambers, past two lakes, the **Watershed Cavern** (Razvodna dvorana) and the **Intermittent Lake** (Presihajoče jezero – see p.223), and up to the **Cross Cavern** (Križna dvorana). The tour winds up at the **Stalactite Cavern** (Kapniška dvorana), a relatively narrow hall that, true to its name, is replete with dozens of shimmering stalactites, the tallest of which, the pillar, stands twelve metres high. The remainder of the cave is accessible only to experienced cavers. There are bats here, too, lots of them, including the southern horseshoe bat, which is found only in this cave. **Visits** (1000SIT) take place every two hours between 10am and 6pm each day in July and August, and at the same times but only at weekends between April and June, and September and October.

Practicalities

The main **bus stop** is opposite the *Green Bar* on Ljubljanska cesta, from where it's a five-minute walk to the island and the **tourist office** at Talcev ulica 20 (Ⓣ07/498-7108); however, the office is often closed for no apparent reason, so you may or may not get lucky. The *Gostilna Žolnir*, 500m north of St James Church at Krška cesta 4 (Ⓣ07/498-7133, Ⓦwww.zolnir-sp.si; ❸), doubles up as the only place in town to **sleep** and the best place to **eat**. Otherwise, your other choices are limited to the rustically styled *Kmečki Hram* (closed Thurs) and *Pizzeria Otok*, both on Oražnova ulica.

Brežice

The town of **BREŽICE**, a moderately important regional economic and cultural centre, sits at the confluence of the Krka and Sava rivers in the middle of the hill-fringed Krško Plain 15km east of Kostanjevica na Krki. Granted its town charter in 1354, Brežice retains a distinctive, small-town atmosphere, it's single concession to grandeur a fine Renaissance Castle now housing a very good museum. Beyond this one major sight there's little else to see or do here, but if you want to make good use of a night's stopover you have the option of several not too distant trips; the **Čatež Spa** and **Mokrice Castle** a few kilometres to the south, and the **Bizeljkso wine region** to the north, though the latter is served by just a few buses.

Arrival, information and accommodation

From the **bus station**, around 800m east of town on Cesta Svobode, it's a ten-minute walk to the centre: head south along Cesta Svobode, then right down Bizeljska Ulica, past the Water Tower to the main street Cesta prvih borcev. Less conveniently, the **train station** is located 2.5km north of town on Trg Vstaje, in the village of Šentlenart; buses depart from the station forecourt every thirty minutes on weekdays. If walking, exit the station, turn left, and follow the road around, and you'll eventually end up on Cesta prvih borcev. The town's **tourist office** (summer 9am–7pm, winter 9am–5pm; Ⓣ07/493-6777,

Ⓔturizem-brezice@siol.net) is actually at the Čatež spa complex, 3km southeast of town (see p.248).

There's a reasonable stock of **accommodation** in town, the best of which is the very comfortable *Splavar* at Cesta prvih borcev 40a (Ⓣ07/499-0630; ❹). For those on a tighter budget, there are four hostel-style rooms (shared bathrooms) at the *Gostilna Berdnik* (Ⓣ07/496-1161; ❶), just up from the *Debeluk Hram* restaurant on Trg Izgnancev. Just south of town, across the bridge and near the traffic lights, *Gostilna Les* (Ⓣ07/496-1100; ❷) is a bit gloomy but basically fine.

Brežice Castle and the Posavje Museum

Prominently positioned at the extreme southern end of the town's long and attractive main street, Cesta prvih borcev, the foundations of present-day **Brežice Castle** were laid in 1529, when it was also fortified with robust, red-tiled conical towers. Following its purchase by the counts of Attems in the seventeenth century, the castle underwent a major style renovation – the courtyard was arcaded with Tuscan columns and several of its most important spaces, such as the stairway, chapel and, most famously, the Knight's Hall, were decorated with splendid Baroque frescoes.

The castle is now home to the **Posavje Museum** (Posavski Muzej; Mon–Sat 8am–1pm, Sun 9am–noon; 300SIT), as comprehensive a regional museum as you'll come across; there are useful information sheets in each room to guide you. The first ten of the museum's twenty or so rooms are given over to archeological and ethnological collections: the former is crammed with ancient skeletons, weapons, jewellery, and equine equipment extricated from over four hundred Celtic graves at Dobova on the Croatian border, whilst the latter documents life in the Posavje region, with due prominence given to wine-making, featuring a weighty display of viticultural implements including two large wine presses.

Located in two small vaulted rooms in the northeastern tower is a small medieval history section documenting the Slovene and Croatian peasant struggles of the sixteenth century, as well as items and literature related to the Reformation in Dolenjska; the key exhibit, and the museum's most precious item, is the Dalmatin Bible from 1584, the first complete translation of the Bible from German into Slovene. Of the 1500 copies originally printed, only around eighty survive. The several rooms constituting the Baroque Art collection are taken up with portraits of the aristocracy, some fine sacral art (paintings by Metzinger and wooden sculptures), and best of all, a magnificent eighteenth-century wooden sled, made in Vienna and donated to Brežice by Empress Maria Theresa.

The Brežice Festival

One of the country's most celebrated musical and cultural events, the **Brežice Festival** (mid-June to mid-Aug) is an outstanding series of ancient and Baroque music concerts, featuring some of Europe's finest musicians. Whilst the majority of concerts are staged here in Brežice – many in the superb Knight's Hall – many other concerts take place in other locations throughout Slovenia, mostly in first-rate venues such as Bogenšperk Castle, the Monastery Church in Kostanjevica na Krki, and Fužine Castle in Ljubljana. Tickets (2500–5000SIT), available from the Festival Box Office at Cesta prvih borcev 5 (Ⓣ07/499-1050), usually go on sale from around mid-May; for more information consult the website Ⓦwww.festivalbrezice.com, which has full programme details.

The museum's centrepiece is the **Knight's Hall** (Viteška dvorana), awash with typically florid Italian Baroque paintings featuring scenes from classical myth and legend, the arts and sciences, and portraits of the Attems family; the hall is now used for weddings, high-level state functions, and as one of the principal venues for concerts of the Brežice Festival.

Eating and drinking

Given its modest size, the town has a surprisingly healthy number of places to **eat and drink**; the most popular eatery is the *Santa Lucia* at Cesta prvih borcev 15, whose bright walls are a bit much, but the Italian food on offer is good (daily until 1am). Otherwise, there's the *Ošterija Debeluk Hram* at Trg Izgnancev 7 (closed Sun), a cool restaurant (specializing in Balkan grills) and bar, with a good selection of wines from the local Bizeljsko region – see opposite page. The two most popular drinking venues in town are the *Jazz Club*, opposite the post office at Trg Izgnancev 2 (daily until midnight), and *Rafters*, part of the *Splavar* pension (see p.247). The most original drinking venue is *Aquarium* with four small circular floors inside the enormous pink Water Tower on Bizeljska ulica. The bright *Kavarna*, just down from the castle at Cesta prvih borcev 14, has a good selection of **coffees and teas** to indulge in, alongside some delicious cakes (Mon–Fri 7am–8pm, Sat 7am–2pm).

Čatež

From Brežice, hourly buses (five on Saturdays) run the 3km southeast (across the Sava) to **ČATEŽ**, Slovenia's largest and most popular **spa centre** (Terme Čatež; Ⓦwww.terme-catez.si). Hot springs were first discovered at Čatež in 1797, only to be flooded by the Sava, then rediscovered again some fifty years later, around which time the first private spa – a basic wood cabin and pool – was built by Father Edvard Zagorc. A fledgling resort in the 1920s, offering numerous therapies and treatments to a wide variety of disorders, Čatež only really began to develop as a serious spa centre in the 1960s, with the construction of the first large pools and hotels. Today this more or less self-contained village, incorporating restaurants, shops, a bank and post office, is as much a recreational park as it is a therapeutic and treatment centre.

Water and sauna parks

The huge **water park** (daily April to mid-Oct 9am–8pm; weekdays 1700SIT, weekends 1900SIT) comprises some nine thermal pools and bathing areas (average temperature 30°C), some with wave machines, waterfalls and slides. If it gets a bit cool, there's indoor action at the *Toplice's* modern Thermal Riviera (daily 9am–9pm; weekdays 1900SIT, weekends 2300SIT), which has a multitude of slides, wave pools, whirlpools and water massage machines; guests of the *Toplice* have unlimited free use of this pool, while guests of the other two hotels have free usage once a day.

If you fancy sweating off a few pounds, then the **sauna park** (weekdays 1900SIT, weekends 2300SIT), also inside the *Toplice*, incorporates eight different saunas – the Indian sauna, Salt sauna and Finnish Aroma sauna, to name but three. There are more activities in the shape of indoor and outdoor tennis (1200–2300SIT per hour), badminton (1200SIT per hour) and squash (1600SIT for 45min).

Practicalities

Unless you're here for more than a few days, it's unlikely you'll need or want to stay on site. If you do, the complex incorporates three **hotels**, the *Toplice* and *Terme* (ⓣ07/493-5000; ❺–❻), both of which are typically slick and fairly expensive spa hotels; and, in between these two, the *Zdravilišče* (same ⓣ; ❹), frequented in the main by patients receiving treatments; they've also got some very dated bungalows (❷). At the eastern end of the complex, alongside the clean and well-equipped **campsite** (ⓣ07/493-6000; March–Oct), is the holiday village, which has dozens of large, two-and four-bed apartments (❻–❼).

The only places to **eat** are the hotel restaurants, but there are several cafes sprinkled around the complex, where you can grab a snack.

Mokrice Castle

At the end of the secondary road which runs parallel with the E70 highway to Zagreb, 8km southeast of Čatež, stands **Mokrice Castle**, a beautifully proportioned Renaissance chateau which once functioned as a defensive outpost against the Turks. Today, and like Otočec Castle (see p.242), it has been converted into a luxury **hotel**, the *Golf Grad Mokrice* (ⓣ07/493-5000; ❾), and very posh **restaurant**; those staying longer than one night receive free use of the pools at Čatež.

Both the restaurant and the hilly eighteen-hole **golf course** (ⓣ07/457-4260; 8300SIT 18 holes, 5900SIT 9 holes, plus 2400SIT for club hire) are popular with the moneyed middle classes, a good number of whom make the short trip up from Zagreb. For those with neither the time nor wallet for a meal or a round of golf, you can take a stroll around the impressively manicured lawns of the stately landscaped English Park, whose pear-tree orchards provide the fruits for the fiery local brandy, *Viljamovka*. There's more affordable **accommodation** out along the road between Čatež and Mokrice at the super-modern and very smart *Penzion Dvorec* (ⓣ07/499-4870; ❺), which has good discounts for kids – there's a decent **restaurant** here too.

Bizeljsko-Sremič wine wegion and Podsreda Castle

Tracking the Croatian border, the road heading north out of Brežice heads up through the **Bizeljsko-Sremič wine region**, renowned for its characteristic blended wines, such as the dry whites *Bizeljčan* and *Sremičan*. Although the odd **bus** trundles this way (4 daily Mon–Fri), it's difficult to get the most out of the region unless you've got your own wheels. Wine can be sampled anywhere where you see the sign *vinska klet* (wine cellar) of which there are many; however, to be sure of getting a visit in, it's best to call in advance – reckon on paying around 1000SIT for three or four wines, a little more for sparkling wine.

The wine road doesn't really begin until the village of **Stari Vas**, some 10km north of Brežice, where you can sample sparkling wines at the *Istenič* cellar at no. 7 (ⓣ60/851-647); they've also got a comfortable little pension on site (❸). Two kilometres further up the road, there's more tasting and nicer accommodation at the countrified roadside inn *Pri Peču* (ⓣ07/452-0103; ❸).

The most interesting cellars, however, are those in the village of **BREZOVICA**, several kilometres on from Stari Vas. These unique cellars, known as *repnice*, are small sand caves hewn from the surrounding flint-stone hills, their walls and ceilings wonderfully patterned with obliquely laid layers of sand. *Repnice* were traditionally used for the storage of turnips (*repa* means turnip) and other produce, before local vintners discovered that the caves' climatic conditions (a constant 7–11°C) and humidity (around 95°C) were ideal for the ripening and storage of wine. There are currently six *repnice* open in the village; three worth trying are *Kovačič* at no. 29 (ⓣ07/495-1091), *Najger* at no. 32 (ⓣ07/495-1115), and *Kelhar* at no. 31 (ⓣ07/495-1551), the last of which was dug out in 1825 – all three are located approximately 1.5km from the main road up the hill.

The next village along is **Bizeljsko** itself, the region's main settlement, where's there's one excellent cellar, the *Klet Pinterič*, at no. 115 (ⓣ07/495-1266). Beyond here, the road gently ascends to **Bistrica ob Sotli**, whereupon a branch road cuts west to the village of **PODSREDA**, above which looms the resplendent-looking **Podsreda Castle** (Tues–Sun April–Oct 10am–6pm 600SIT). Originally a thirteenth-century fortification, its fine Romanesque core remains splendidly intact, although systematic and comprehensive renovation work on the interior has left few visible traces of its former state, with just the old medieval kitchen and single-cell gaol remaining from the original building. Its empty rooms are now used almost exclusively as exhibition and gallery spaces, and there are currently collections devoted to glassworks and prints.

The castle can be reached by road (5km from Podsreda) or, if you're walking, via a steep trail (45min) beginning south of the village – look for the signs to Levstikov Mlin (Levstikov Mill) and the trail starts there.

Bela Krajina

Of the region's two towns, **Črnomelj** and **Metlika**, the latter, with its fetching architecture and two fine museums, is more deserving of a visit. The best of Bela Krajina, however, is to be found in the surrounding countryside, amidst the birch trees and vineyards: history and culture buffs can get their kicks at the **Mithraeum shrine** at Rožanec, near Črnomelj, and the fabulous **Three Parishes Pilgrimage Centre** at Rosalnice, near Metlika; those seeking more relaxing fare should make a beeline for the **Lahinja Landscape Park** or the numerous wine villages sprinkled around the region. To combine a wine-tasting session with an overnight stay, head for **Drašiči** with its pleasant vineyard-clad surrounds.

Črnomelj and around

Sitting plum in the geographical centre of Bela Krajina, 45km east of Kočevje, **ČRNOMELJ** is both the capital, and the largest, of the province's towns. Frankly, though, there's not much to get excited about, and the only reason you might contemplate a visit here is to indulge in the town's marvellous folklore **festival** in June, or to use it as a springboard for visits to surrounding attractions (see p.253).

Unlike many settlements in the region, Črnomelj was spared widespread devastation by the Turks, owing to its naturally strong fortifications, although its strategic importance was stripped away in the mid-sixteenth century following the erection of a fort and the relocation of the command of the military frontier across the border in Karlovac, Croatia. Its decline continued for several centuries thereafter, though its fortunes were partially revived following the opening of the Novo Mesto–Karlovac rail line in 1914.

If Črnomelj is bereft of sights, there's enough a short drive away to keep you occupied for a few hours: north of town in the village of Rožanec is the **Mithraeum**, one of the country's most outstanding Roman monuments; to the south, en route to the Kolpa River, the **Lahinja Landscape Park** and the border village of **Vinica** are each worth taking the trouble to visit.

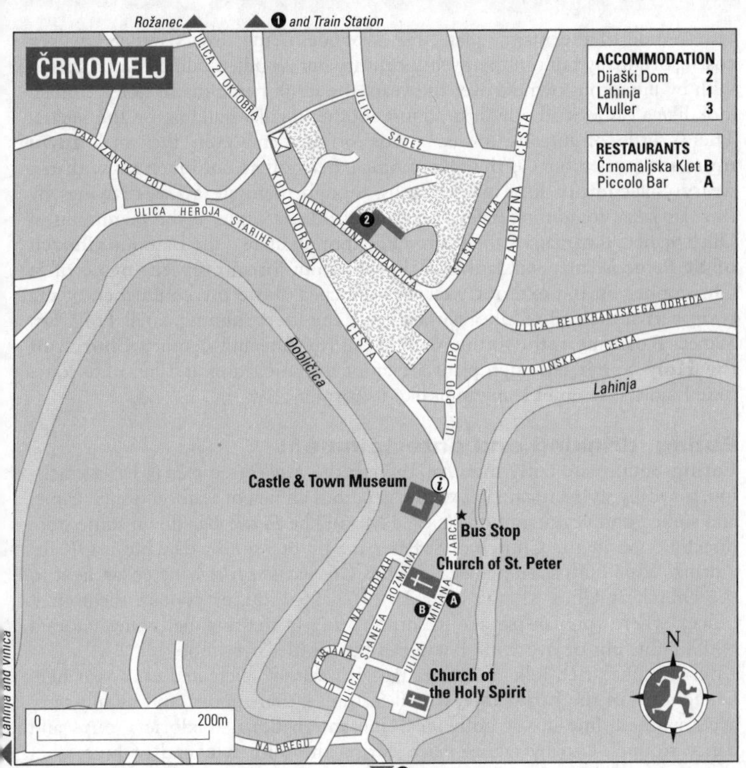

Arrival, information and accommodation

The town's **train station** is located 1km due north of the centre on Železničarska cesta, from where it's a twenty-minute walk due south to the Old Town core. More conveniently, all **buses** stop on the main square, Trg Svobode, from where it's a quick hop across the road to the **tourist office**, located inside the castle building at no. 3 (Mon–Fri 9am–3pm, Thurs until 5pm, Sat 8am–noon plus Sun 8am–noon in summer; ⓣ07/306-1142, ⓔturizem@crnomelj.si); they can advise on private accommodation and local tourist farms.

Town **accommodation** is scant: there are dorm beds available in July and August in the *Dijaški Dom*, 400m north of the tourist office at Otona Župančičeva 7 (ⓣ07/306-2160); *Gostišče Muller*, south of the main square, and along the road below the bridge at Ločka cesta 6 (ⓣ07/356-7200, ⓦwww.gostilna-muller.si; ④), has four large, modern, spotless and reasonably priced rooms; whilst the town's only hotel, the *Lahinja* (ⓣ07/306-1650; ③), 200m from the train station on the main road Kolodvorska cesta, is old, tired and only recommended as a last resort.

The Town

What little there is of interest is centred on an elongated promontory in a tight loop of the Dobličica and Lahinja rivers to the south of town. Consuming the eastern side of the main square, Trg Svobode, is the town's rather low-key **castle**, originally built in the twelfth century but rebuilt, modified and tinkered with by numerous owners over the years, the result being that it doesn't much look like a castle at all now, instead just another regular building on the square. There's little of interest to see, inside or out, and even the small **town museum** (same hours as the tourist office; free), offers not much more than a weary collection of local photographs, though there are a few drawings by Božidar Jakac to admire. A few paces south of the castle, at the beginning of Ulica Staneta Rozmana – the main traffic thoroughfare – the Baroque **Church of St Peter** is fairly standard issue, but look out for an oversized fresco of St Christopher on the exterior west wall. Perched above the confluence of the two rivers at the end of Ulica Mirana Jarca, the street running parallel to Ulica Staneta Rozmana, is the rotting shell of the late-fifteenth-century **Church of the Holy Spirit**; although plans are afoot for renovation, it'll be quite some time before it resembles anything like its former glory.

Eating, drinking and entertainment

Eating options are fairly minimal, though the *Muller* (see p.251) has a cracking, rustically styled restaurant, with a generous choice of seafood dishes, game, and some good veggie options (closed Mon). The *Piccolo Bar*, down some steps directly opposite the Church of St Peter, is a bit of a smoky den, but is OK for a drink. Wine buffs should check out the *Črnomaljska Klet* wine cellar, next to the church at Ulica Mirana Jarca 2 (☎07/306-1100, or contact the tourist office), where you can partake in some tasting of the regional wines (around 800SIT for four or five wines); you can buy bottles here too.

Bela Krajina's rich folk-music heritage is joyously celebrated each year here in the form of the **Jurjevanje**, which features a tremendous, and usually very accomplished, line-up of both local and international folkloric groups and dance troupes. Usually taking place during the third weekend of June, it's a great opportunity to see rarely used folk instruments – such as the *tamburica*, *bisernica* (lute) and *berdo* (contrabass) – being played live.

Rožanec and the Mithraeum

Just after the village of Lokve, beyond a couple of Romany settlements, a left turn takes you up to the smaller village of **Rožanec**; from the parking place, a signposted path leads you across the rail track, and up into a chestnut forest, at the edge of which is a small, picturesque hollow. Hewn into the rock face of one wall is the **Mithraeum** (Mitrej), a second-century Roman shrine dedicated to the invincible sun god Mithras.

The centrepiece of the rock-cut relief (first excavated in 1921) is the sacrifice of the bull, which has Mithras kneeling on, and plunging a dagger into, its back. The spilling of the bull's blood supposedly gave rise to the plant kingdom, while its semen gave rise to the animal kingdom, the latter represented here by the presence of a dog, a snake and a scorpion. The sacrificial scene is accompanied by personifications of the sun and the moon (light and darkness), as well as two priests, Cautopates and Cautes. The inscription, meanwhile, is an address to Mithras from three brothers (Nepos, Prokulus and Firminus), appealing for health and prosperity. The Mithraeum's presence at this particular site is unsurprising given that a Roman road once ran from Črnomelj to Semič, a small town some 5km further north, at which point it divided with one road continuing to Emona (Ljubljana), the other towards present-day Novo Mesto. A copy of the relief is held in the Bela Krajina Museum in Metlika (see p.254). For more on Mithraism, see the box on p.301.

Lahinja Landscape Park

A couple of kilometres south of Črnomelj – along the road to Vinica and the Kolpa River – you'll pass another Romany settlement, 7km beyond which is the **Lahinja Landscape Park**, a protected area of fields, marshy groves, streams and karstic springs. The park can be accessed from any one of several hamlets clustered in or around its boundary, though the best and most convenient point of entry is at **Pusti Gradac**, the park's northernmost settlement, located up a minor (gravel-track) road 1.5km beyond the village of **Dragatuš** (see below); if you're travelling by bus get the driver to set you down on the main road, from where it's a fifteen-minute walk.

Pusti Gradac also happens to be the park's most culturally well-endowed patch: not only have several extremely important archeological finds been unearthed here – including a remarkable gold coin featuring an imprint of Hungarian King Matthias Corvinus (which dates from around the fifteenth century) – but it's also the site of one of the country's few remaining working **water mills** (mlinske kamne). Dating from the late twentieth century, the mill still operates according to traditional methods, its grinders powered by an impressively large water wheel, itself propelled by waters from the nearby Lahinja River. Demonstrations of the mill are organized by the Klepec family, who live in the house next door at no. 10 (☎07/305-7660, ⓦwww.infotehna.si/klepec). They can also provide information and assistance on the park and its facilities, as well as arrange two- to four-hour-long **guided tours** of the park (500SIT); in theory these tours are only available to groups, but arrangements can be made for individuals as long as you contact the family at least a day or two in advance. There's also **accommodation** here in the renovated family house near the mill, which can sleep between three and six people (❶–❷). A leisurely circular walk around the park takes around three hours.

Vinica

There's more comfortable, accommodation in Dragatuš, at the *Pri Štefaniču* tourist farm (☎07/305-7347; ❸), which also possesses a very accomplished restaurant – the *Župančičev Hram* – named after the poet, playwright and essayist Oton Župančič, who was born in the small fishing village of **VINICA**, 10km further south. Along with Ivan Cankar, Župančič (1878–1949) was regarded as the principal exponent of the so-called *Moderna* movement, a Slovene literary trend which appeared at the end of the nineteenth century, and which was closely aligned to the tenets of Slovene national and sociohistorical identity; his principal contribution was a collection of poetry entitled *Čaša opojnosti* (*Intoxicating Cup*). A prolific wordsmith, Župančič also wrote and translated numerous plays (including Shakespeare), composed poems for the Partisan press, and wrote many children's stories; above all he is known to every Slovene as the creator of the children's character, *Ciciban*. His **birthplace** is located on the main road in the centre of the village at no. 9 (get the key from no. 6, opposite; 300SIT); on display, albeit in Slovene only, are copies of his work, his death mask and a beautiful sketch portrait completed by Božidar Jakac just two years before Župančič's death. He is buried at Žale cemetery in Ljubljana. A short way beyond the house is the derelict sixteenth-century **castle**, which now offers little more than terrific views across the Kolpa towards Croatia.

There are two beautifully located **campsites** down by the river on the southern fringe of the village, close to the border crossing: by far the better of the two is the clean, green and spacious *Katra* (☎07/364-6034; katra@siol.net), but if that's full, you might have to settle for the grubby *Kolpa-Vinica* (☎07/306-4018) right next door; both are open between May and September.

Metlika and around

Pressed up hard against the Croatian border just 15km northeast of Črnomelj, **METLIKA** is Bela Krajina's second centre of population. It's a mellow town, but palpably more interesting than its neighbour, thanks to a couple of fine museums, some good-looking architecture, and a strong viticultural tradition.

Founded in the thirteenth century when the province (then an important frontier region) was known as Metlika March, it acquired its town rights and developed into a prosperous medieval centre the following century. However, as one of Austria's border strongholds it found itself at the sharp end of Hungarian, then Turkish, attacks – it was razed no less than sixteen times. Almost entirely gutted by fire in 1705, its historic centre was swiftly rebuilt, although it received another battering at the hands of its Italian occupiers during World War II, which makes the survival of its attractive old core all the more remarkable.

Arrival, information and accommodation

The **bus station** is located by the main crossroads at the southern entrance to town, from where it's a fifteen-minute walk to the Old Town; the **train station**, meanwhile, is 1km southeast of the same crossroads, on the road towards the Croatian border crossing on Kolodvorska ulica. The small, and very helpful, **tourist office** is located in the Old Town at Mestni Trg 1 (March–April & Sept–Nov Mon–Fri 8am–3pm, Sat 9am–noon; May–Aug Mon–Fri 9am–4pm, Sat 9am–noon; Ⓣ07/363-5470, Ⓔtdvigred.metlika@siol.net). The **post office** (Mon–Fri 7am–7pm, Sat 7am–noon) is located in the ultra-sterile shopping complex across the road from the bus station.

The town's only **hotel** is the *Bela Krajina*, an awful place with depressing, dishevelled rooms, located just down from the old town on the main through road, Cesta Bratstva in Enotnosti (Ⓣ07/305-8123; ❸). The nearest **campsite**, *Podzemelj ob Kolpi* (Ⓣ07/306-9572; May–Sept), is 7km southwest of town, just off the main Črnomelj–Metlika road down by the Kolpa River – the waters are good for swimming here; buses heading in either direction can drop off on the main road, from where it's about 1km to the site. Five hundred metres prior to the campsite, at Podzemelj 17, the *Gostilna Veselič* has a handful of simply furnished rooms available (Ⓣ07/306-9156; ❷), and a pretty accomplished **restaurant** too.

The Town

Everything of interest in Metlika is located within the confines of the **Old Town**, sited on a low elevation between the main thoroughfare, Cesta Bratstva in Enotnosti and the River Obrh, and reached via Ulica na Trg, opposite the *Hotel Bela Krajina*. On the north side of **Trg Svobode**, the largest and most central of the three irregularly shaped squares which form the backbone of the Old Town, stands the neat, triangular-shaped **Metlika Castle**, whose vaulted tracts house the **Bela Krajina Museum** (Belokranjski muzej; Mon–Sat 9am–4pm, Sun 9am–noon; 500SIT), one of Slovenia's finest regional museums. The collection kicks off with an impressive haul of Bronze and Iron Age artefacts – vessels, armour, jewellery and the like – and a stash of Roman finds, many of which were unearthed from Pusti Gradac south of Črnomelj (see p.253); there's also a copy of the Mithraic relief at Rožanec on display (see p.252). The most enjoyable part is the section devoted to the region's inhabitants, Bela Kranjci, and features a fine display of homespun attire, as well as items and artefacts pertaining to the traditional cottage industries practised hereabouts, typically, pottery, spinning, weaving, cart-and barrel-making, and an exhibition of one of the more delicate Slovenian folk-arts, "Pisanice" (egg-painting).

The development of viticulture – as important to the local economy today as agriculture was prior to World War II – is also given due prominence, as is the role of local societies and associations in Bela Krajina during the nineteenth and twentieth centuries. Foremost amongst these was the Metlika Fire Brigade, whose heroics are documented in the **Firefighting Museum** (Slovenski gasilski muzej; Mon–Sat 9am–1pm, Sun 9am–noon; free), in the building next to the castle. Opened upon the occasion of the Metlika fire-fighting brigade's centenary anniversary in 1969, the museum proudly displays an assortment of photographs, awards, helmets and uniforms, klaxons and other memorabilia. Best of all, though, are the old fire-fighting machines – the oldest of which is a model from Cerknica dating from 1836 – located in both this building and the pavilion opposite.

Trg Svobode segues into **Mestni Trg**, an elongated square bound by an attractive blend of beige, cream and mint-coloured buildings, the most distinguished being the neo-Gothic **Town Hall** at no. 24. Positioned atop the building is a slightly askew town coat-of-arms, featuring two ravens perched either side of a castle tower – no doubt on the look-out for rampaging Turks. The bottom end of the square is consumed by the box-like **Church of St Nicholas** (Cerkev Sv Nikolaj), a uniform Baroque structure resurrected in 1759 following a fire some fifty years earlier. The statues of St Nicholas and the pope adorning the high altar were carved by an unknown author, while the frescoes were executed by the Friulian Domenico Fabrio. Just behind the church stands the **Commandery** (Komenda), the one-time residence of the knights of the Teutonic Order, but which is now an old people's home its impressive size is best appreciated from below the Old Town.

Eating and drinking

Eating options in Metlika are thin on the ground, to say the least, and you may well spend more time drinking in the local wine cellars than you initially thought – the Old Town, in particular, is disappointingly devoid of much life. Instead, you'll have to make the trek to *Gostilna Budački*, awkwardly located in a residential area out near the train station at Ulica Belokranjskega odreda 14; the food's good though, featuring a decent grill menu and fish from the nearby Kolpa. As for **drinking**, the rather naff *Saloon Bar*, opposite the *Hotel Bela Krajina*, is as happening as it gets, while *Vinoteka Pinot*, a few paces along from the tourist office at Trg Svobode 28, is a cramped cellar bar where you can sample a few of the local wines (closed Sun).

For a more sophisticated bout of **wine-drinking**, *Vinska Klet Metlika*, across the road from the bus station, arranges organized visits of their extensive cellars with a tasting session to boot; they are, though, heavily inclined towards groups, so you may end up having to pay the group rate (around 10,000SIT) even there are only a couple of you (Ⓣ07/363-7000). The town's principal annual happening is the **Spring Wine Festival** (Vinska Vigred) at the end of May, a booze-fuelled three days of wine-related events taking place throughout the Old Town's three squares.

The Three Parishes Pilgrimage Centre

Two kilometres east of Metlika in the village of **ROSALNICE**, the **Three Parishes Pilgrimage Centre** (Tri Fare) – comprising three fourteenth- and fifteenth-century Gothic churches – is the region's most outstanding ecclesiastical monument. From the few historical documents that existed, it was ascertained that the original churches were likely to have been built by the Knights Templar some time during the twelfth century. Following the arrival of a group of refugee Franciscan monks from Bosnia shortly after the completion of the middle church in the fifteenth century, the complex evolved into an important pilgrimage site, reaching its apogee a century or two later when faiths of many kinds, including Orthodox, journeyed here on a regular basis.

The largest and oldest of the three churches, the **Lady of Our Sorrows** (Žalostna Mati božja), features a superb Gothic interior with Baroque appendages, decorated with a splendid array of frescoes: the presbytery is covered with scenes from the New Testament, the side walls with images of the Apostles and, on the triumphal arch, scenes representing the Ten Commandments. The main altar is ornamented with a fine statuette of Mary with Seven Swords (aka the Seven Sorrows), the story of which is relayed in the middle church, while the Rococo side altars – dedicated to St John Nepomuk and St Francis of Paola – are no less impressive. Of the three churches this is the only one where Mass is still held.

Next to Our Sorrows, the **Ecce Homo Church** (Glej človek) is the smallest of the three and the only one possessed of a bell-tower. It, too, boasts a marvellous Gothic presbytery and high altar, but the show-stealer is its cupola ceiling, painted with wildly colourful frescoes depicting the story of Mary's Seven Sorrows. Completing the trilogy is the poorly preserved **Church of Our Lady of Lourdes** (Lurška Devica Marija), almost completely devoid of colour or ornamentation. Its singular highlight is the neo-Gothic high altar featuring a statue of Mary of Lourdes, whilst it's just about possible to detect the fragments of a fresco of the Crucifixion, from around 1500.

There is a **train station** in Rosalnice, one stop along the line from Metlika, but you're just as well off walking: the most direct route is along Cankarjeva cesta, which begins from a point some 100m north of the main crossroads in the south of town (on Cesta Bratstva in Enotnosti), and winds its way to the village. If you plan to visit the churches, make sure you call the tourist office in Metlika in advance (see p.254), so that arrangements for the keys can be made.

Drašiči, Vinomer and Radovica

The triangle of land between Metlika and the pretty wine villages of **DRAŠIČI**, **VINOMER** and **RADOVICA** to the northeast, is classic Krajina countryside, swathes of copse-like *steljniki* – birch tree and fern – set against the backdrop of soft, gently sloping vineyards. The majority of wines cultivated here are blends, the trademark one being *Metliška Črnina*, a rich, velvety and very dark red; others worth trying include the lighter reds, *Modra Portugalka* and *Modri Pinot* and, if you're prepared to spend that little extra, the sparkling white *Metliška Penina*.

Of the aforementioned villages, Drašiči (6km northeast of Metlika) offers most to the wine connoisseur, with a number of cellars providing tasting: a good one for starters is the *Simonič* tourist farm at no. 56 (Ⓣ07/305-8185); otherwise, take your pick from the many cellars advertised – these can be approached direct or, alternatively, contact the tourist office in Metlika, who will happily fix something up for you. The 1:50,000 *Bela Krajina* map, available from either of the tourist offices, should help you navigate your way around the villages.

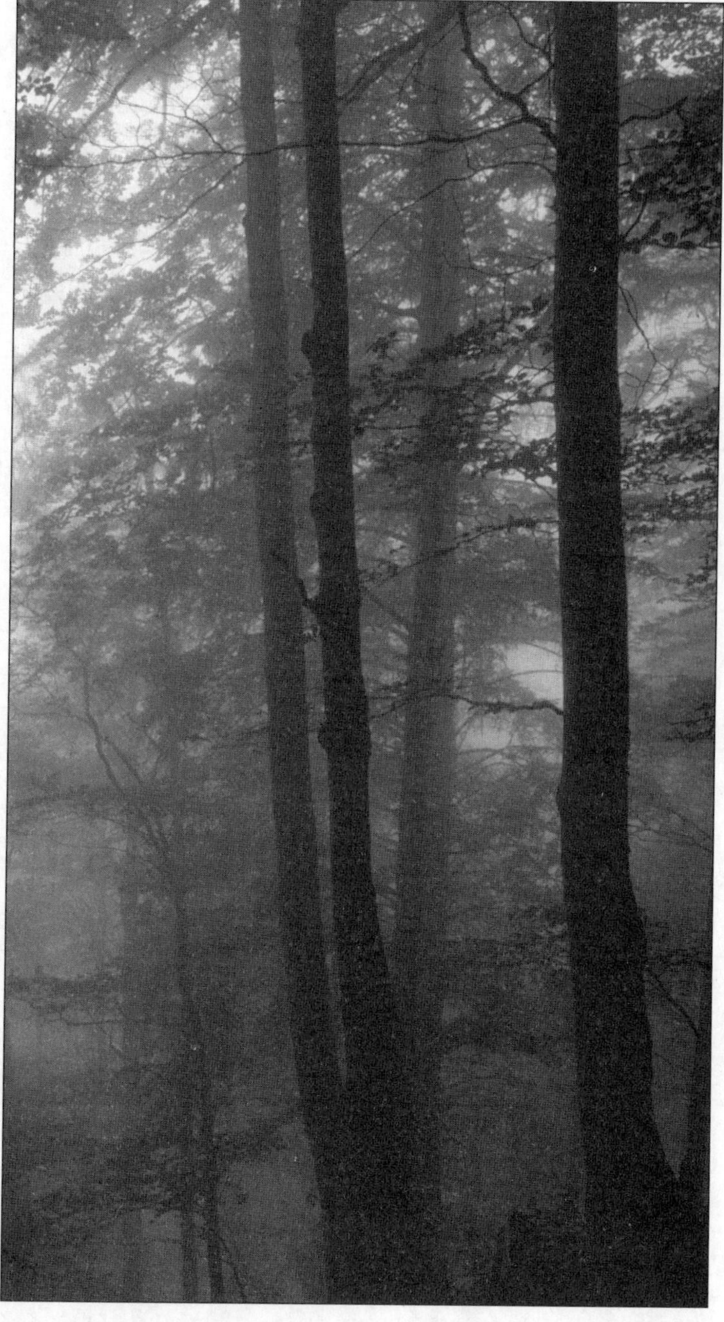

△ Kočevjski forest

Travel details

Trains

Brežice to: Ljubljana (7–13 daily; 1hr 45min–2hr).
Črnomelj to: Ljubljana (5–10 daily; 2hr 10min–2hr 45min); Metlika (5–10 daily; 20min); Novo Mesto (5–10 daily; 45min–1hr).
Metlika to: Črnomelj (5–10 daily; 20min); Ljubljana (5–10 daily; 2hr 30min–3hr); Novo Mesto (5–10 daily; 1hr–1hr 15min).
Novo Mesto to: Črnomelj (5–10 daily; 45min–1hr); Ljubljana (6–13 daily; 1hr 20min–2hr); Metlika (5–10 daily: 1hr–1hr 15min); Trebnje (6–13 daily; 20min).
Postojna to: Divača (every 40min–1hr 30min; 30min); Koper (5–7 daily; 1hr 30min); Ljubljana (every 40min–1hr 30min; 1hr); Sežana (hourly–1hr 30min; 45min).

Buses

Brežice to: Bizeljsko (Mon–Fri 4 daily; 30min); Ljubljana (Mon–Fri 5 daily, Sat & Sun 3 daily; 2hr 30min); Novo Mesto (Mon–Fri 7 daily, Sat & Sun 3 daily; 50min).
Cerknica to: Ljubljana (Mon–Fri 6 daily; 1hr 15min); Postojna (Mon–Fri 3 daily; 25min); Stari Trg (Mon–Fri 5 daily; 25min).
Črnomelj to: Metlika (Mon–Fri 4 daily; 25min); Novo Mesto (Mon–Fri 4 daily; 50min); Vinica (10 daily; 35min).
Dolenjske Toplice to: Novo Mesto (Mon–Fri 10 daily, Sat 5 daily; 25min); Žužemberk (Mon–Fri 3 daily; 30min).
Kostanjevica na Krki to: Brežice (Mon–Fri 7 daily, Sat & Sun 2 daily; 25min); Ljubljana (Mon–Fri 4 daily, Sat & Sun 2 daily; 2hr 30min); Novo Mesto (Mon–Fri 8 daily, Sat & Sun 2 daily; 35min).
Metlika to: Črnomelj (Mon–Fri 5 daily; 25min); Novo Mesto (Mon–Fri 2 daily; 25min).
Novo Mesto to: Brežice (Mon–Fri 7 daily, Sat & Sun 3 daily; 50min); Črnomelj (Mon–Fri 1 daily; 50min); Dolenjske Toplice (Mon–Fri 12 daily, Sat & Sun 3 daily; 25min); Kostanjevica na krki (Mon–Fri 7 daily, Sat & Sun 3 daily; 40min); Ljubljana (Mon–Fri 7 daily, Sat & Sun 5 daily; 2hr 10min); Metlika (Mon–Fri 3 daily; 25min); Otočec (Mon–Fri 8 daily, Sat & Sun 3 daily; 15min); Šmarjeske Toplice (Mon–Fri 6 daily, Sat & Sun 3 daily; 15min); Trebnje (Mon–Fri 6 daily, Sat & Sun 3 daily; 30min); Žužemberk (Mon–Fri 1 daily; 40min).
Postojna to: Ajdovščina (Mon–Fri 11 daily, Sat & Sun 5 daily; 40min); Cerknica (Mon–Fri 4 daily; 25min); Ilirska Bistrica (Mon–Fri 6 daily; 40min); Koper (6 daily; 1hr 15min); Ljubljana (Mon–Fri 14 daily, Sat & Sun 8 daily; 1hr); Nova Gorica (Mon–Fri 10 daily, Sat & Sun 5 daily; 1hr 10min); Piran (6 daily; 1hr 40min; Sežana (Mon–Fri 2 daily; 40min).

International trains

Postojna to: Rijeka (2 daily; 1hr 35min).

International buses

Novo Mesto to: Zagreb (2 daily; 1hr 20min).
Postojna to Rijeka (1 daily; 1hr 40min).

Eastern Slovenia

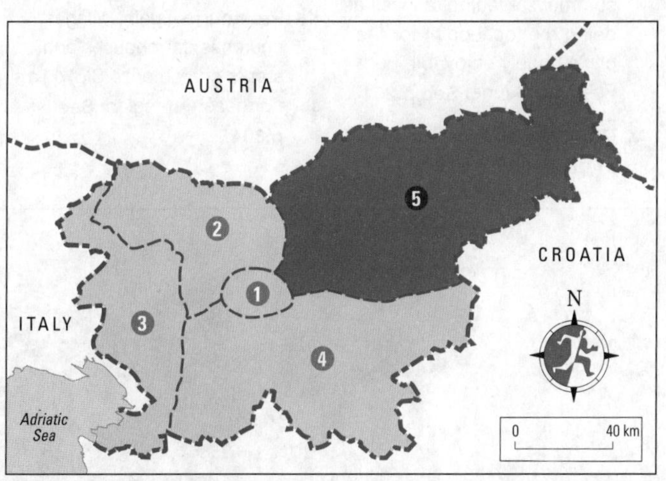

CHAPTER 5

Highlights

* **Logar Valley** An idyllic alpine valley in the heart of the Kamniške-Savinja Alps, ideal for a number of leisurely pursuits. See p.276

* **Rogaška Slatina** Wallow in temperatures of thirty degrees plus in one of the country's most fashionable spa resorts. See p.277

* **Lent, Maribor** This lively waterfront area is the perfect spot for a beer on a warm summer's evening, as well as being the focal point for the city's hugely enjoyable Lent Festival in June. See p.291

* **Ptuj** Slovenia's oldest and prettiest town, stuffed with remnants of its Roman and medieval past. See p.294

* **Church of the Virgin Mary, Ptujska Gora** Sublime Gothic church featuring the masterful *Virgin with Mantle* misericordia. See p.302

* **Ormož–Ljutomer Wine Road** Spend the day cycling through the rolling, stepped vineyards of this beautiful wine road. See p.303

* **Prekmurje** Quaint villages, churches, farmhouses and storks characterize Slovenia's northeastern region. See p.304

△ Wine press, Jeruzalem vineyards

5

Eastern Slovenia

Taken as a whole, eastern Slovenia receives relatively few visitors, as most people are content to stick to the more celebrated attractions west of Ljubljana. This is a shame, as there's some enticing countryside and a wealth of interesting sites to explore, whilst many towns and villages host excellent spring and summer festivals of classical music, drama, folk music and dancing, as well as carnivals. The region's history is certainly writ large: **Štajerska**, the country's largest province, was formerly part of Austrian Styria prior to World War I, whilst **Koroška** was once the centre of the oldest Slovene state, Karantanija, from the seventh century, and later part of the former Habsburg duchy of Carinthia. This was divided amongst Austria, Italy and Yugoslavia following the collapse of the Austro-Hungarian Empire in the early twentieth century – indeed, it's still sometimes referred to as Carinthia. Whereas Koroška and Štajerska came under the sway of the Austrians, **Prekmurje**, in many ways the country's most distinctive region – if only for its flatness – was subject to around a thousand years of Hungarian rule, before being divided between Hungary and the new Yugoslav state in 1920.

Beyond the smattering of small-scale industrial settlements of central Štajerska lie **Maribor** and **Celje**, the second- and third-largest cities in Slovenia respectively. Whilst both offer a smattering of culture, neither can match the historic resonance of **Ptuj**, Slovenia's oldest and most appealing town, which is also a short ride away from the stunning Gothic Church of the Virgin Mary in **Ptujska Gora**. As much as anything else, though, eastern Slovenia is known for its spas, notably **Rogaška Slatina**, the country's oldest and most quintessential spa town, and its wine. Štajerska harbours the largest of the country's three wine-growing regions, **Podravje**, which comprises six districts, each yielding a superb range of predominantly white wines. The one route to seek out if you're being selective is the beautiful **Ormož–Ljutomer wine road** ranged along the Croatian border. The region's main activity centre, however, is the **Pohorje Massif**, a broad, arcing plateau which extends for some 50km west from the foothills of Maribor, and which offers plentiful opportunities for recreational pursuits, including two of the country's largest and best-equipped ski resorts.

Lying to the west of the Massif and bordering Austria to the north, Koroška, Slovenia's smallest region, marks a return to the alpine peaks of the Karavanke and Kamniške-Savinja Alps to the west. The mining and iron-working towns of the region, which for years sustained the region's economy, are now largely redundant and offer little in the way of specific appeal, although they do make useful bases for forays into the surrounding hills and mountains, which are

mapped out with an excellent series of hiking and cycling routes. The one town here that merits a visit, however, is the region's economic and cultural centre, **Slovenj Gradec**.

Spread across the edge of the Pannonian basin, bordering Austria, Croatia and Hungary, **Prekmurje** is the country's easternmost province and the polar opposite of mountainous western Slovenia. It's also the least visited, yet its

mellow tranquillity offers a surprisingly enchanting mix of neat, flower bedecked villages, such as **Bogojina**, **Filovci** and **Beltinci**, ancient churches, as at **Martjanci** and **Selo**, and lush, green countryside, whose flat, wide open spaces provide the ideal terrain for cyclists with an aversion to hills. Although sparsely populated – the only settlements of any conspicuous size are **Murska Sobota** and **Lendava** – Prekmurje is one of the most multifarious regions in

Slovenia, populated with a large Hungarian minority as well as the country's largest Roma community.

Transport links in this part of the country are pretty good: the main rail line to Budapest serves quite a few places, with many destinations easily reached from the capital and a well-integrated system of buses and trains linking remoter towns and villages.

Celje and around

From Ljubljana, several main roads – the fastest of which is the still partially incomplete A1 highway – head eastwards to **CELJE**, which lies at the heart of the **Lower Savinja Valley** (Spodnja Savinjska Dolina), a predominantly flat, fairly densely populated landscape raked with vast hop plantations and wheat fields, punctuated by the occasional industrial enterprise.

Slovenia's third-largest city after Ljubljana and Maribor, though with a population that still just barely tops the fifty thousand mark, Celje derives its name from the Roman settlement, Celeia, a key administrative centre of the Roman province of Noricum. Economically and culturally the town peaked in the Middle Ages under its overlords, the counts of Celje, who, for three centuries, staked their claim as one of Central Europe's foremost ruling dynasties – one of their last acts before the Habsburgs assumed control was to award Celje its town rights in 1451. As in much of the Štajerska region, Celje faced formidable Germanizing pressures during the late nineteenth and early twentieth centuries, culminating in German occupation during World War II, during which time the town was heavily bombed by Allied planes. Despite its heavy industry, modern-day Celje is not an unattractive place, and worthy of a full day's sightseeing thanks to its clutch of impressive churches and buildings, and one of the largest castles in the country.

Aside from Celje, the area's sites are relatively few, though there's an impressive **Roman necropolis** west of Celje, in Šempeter, whilst you could spend an entertaining couple of hours in the towns of **Velenje** and **Laško**, located a short way north and south of Celje respectively.

Arrival and information

Both the **train** and **bus stations** are smack-bang in the centre of town, the former just across the road from Krekov trg, the latter 400m north of here; you'll also find left-luggage facilities at the bus station (Mon–Fri 6am–8pm, Sat 7am–2pm; around 400SIT). Buses for Šempeter and other local destinations depart from the stands just south of the train station. The **tourist office** is at Trg Celjskih Knezov 9 (April–Oct Mon–Fri 8am–6pm, Sat & Sun 11am–5pm; Nov–March Mon–Fri 9am–5pm, Sat 9am–1pm; ⓣ03/492-5080, ⓔtic@celje.si). The **post office** (Mon–Fri 7am–8pm, Sat 7am–1pm) is on Krekov trg, and the library, which has **Internet access** (Mon–Fri 8am–7pm, Sat 8am–noon; 100SIT per hour), is next to the regional museum on Muzejski trg.

Accommodation

There is a limited stock of **private accommodation** in town, which can be booked through the tourist office, and a **student dorm** (Dijaški Dom) just 300m west of the tourist office at Ljubljanska 21 (ⓣ03/426-6600; ❶), which

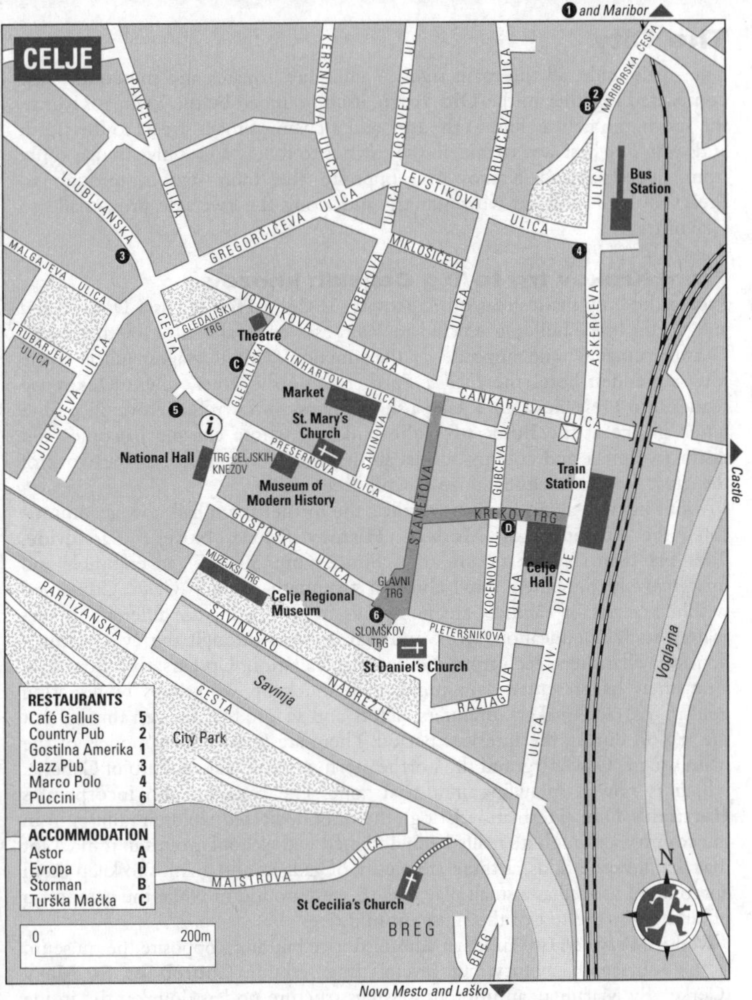

has beds available in July and August. The city's four **hotels** are fairly indistinguishable, although they're all reasonably priced.

The well-located *Hotel Evropa* at Krekov trg 4 ⓣ03/426-9000, ⓦwww.hotel-evropa.si; ❺) has clean, modern and comfy rooms, as does the *Hotel Štorman*, a nine-storey block opposite the bus station at Mariborska cesta 3 ⓣ03/426-0426, ⓔhotel-celje@storman-gos.si; ❺), which is more popular with visiting business folk. Built on the site of an inn of the same name, the town's cheapest hotel is the *Turška Mačka* (the "Turkish Cat") at Gledališka ulica 7 ⓣ03/548-4611, ⓦwww.majolka.si; ❹), which, though a little dark and gloomy, has reasonable rooms. Located 1km north of the centre on the road to Šempeter, the *Hotel Astor* at Ljubljanska 39 (ⓣ03/545-2350, ⓦwww.astor-hotel.net; ❹) is a low, unattractive two-storey building but does conceal decent rooms with tiny bathrooms.

The City

The castle aside, all the main sights – churches, squares and museums – are compacted together in the **Old Town**, itself bounded by the Savinja River to the south, the railway line to the east, and a chain of main streets to the north and west. The best way to take in the town is to follow a roughly circular route from pedestrianized Krekov trg, opposite the train station, through to Prešernova ulica, down Muzejski trg and along the riverside promenade to Glavni trg.

From Krekov trg to Trg Celjskih knezov

Facing the busy main street on Krekov trg is **Celje Hall** (Celjski Dom), a red and cream brick building erected in 1906 as a cultural centre for the town's German citizens, and opposite, at the junction with Razlagova ulica, is the town's grandest hotel, the *Evropa*. Further along the street, where Krekov trg segues into Prešernova ulica, take a short diversion down Stanetova ulica for a quick glance at the **Bank of Celje** building, whose curving balconies and distinctive pillar and column motifs are instantly recognizable as the work of the great Slovene architect, Jože Plečnik (see p.63).

About halfway along Prešernova ulica, the former town hall now accommodates the **Museum of Modern History** (Muzej Novejše Zgodovine; Tues–Fri 10am–5pm, Sat 9am–noon, Sun 2–6pm; 500SIT), an enjoyable and imaginatively presented trawl through twentieth-century Celje. Contained within a series of cabinets are numerous items relating to different subject matter, such as education, work and war, as seen through the eyes of three fictitious characters, each from a different generation. Upstairs, the "Streets of Craftsmen" is presented as a number of mock-up workshops representing goldsmiths, clockmakers, milliners, tailors and so on, that thrived throughout the region during the interwar period. There are further such models of the main square, Glavni trg, and the northeastern working-class suburb of Gaberje, which is now a sprawling industrial zone. The museum also incorporates **Herman's Den** (Hermanov Brlog), the only dedicated children's museum in the country, although it's really been designed with school groups in mind. Not that that'll bother kids, as there are plenty of gadgets and gizmos to keep them entertained, as well as a small play area to mess around in while the parents go off and enjoy the rest of the museum in peace.

Wedged between two modern administrative buildings opposite the museum is the fourteenth-century, but several times rebuilt, **Church of St Mary** (Cerkev Sv Marijina), an unprepossessing structure no less dour on the inside than it is on the outside. The church chapel once kept the tombs of the counts of Celje, whose skulls are now on display in the Regional Museum (see below). The street continues up to the grandly named **Trg Celjskih knezov** (Dukes of Celje Square), a large irregularly shaped space dominated by the late nineteenth-century, neo-Renaissance **Narodni Dom** building (National House), now the headquarters of the town council.

Celje Regional Museum

From the square's southern end, take the second left onto Muzejski trg, and partway along you come to the arcaded Old Manor House, now home to the **Celje Regional Museum** (Pokrajinksi Muzej Celje; Tues–Fri 10am–6pm, Sat 9am–noon, Sun 2–6pm; 800SIT). If you only see one thing in this museum (though, quite frankly, there's not much else really worth seeing), make it the **Celje Ceiling**, a dramatic, illusionist tempera painting discovered under

> **The counts of Celje**
>
> For more than three hundred years the **counts of Celje** ranked amongst the great Central European ruling dynasties. The dynastic line began with Gebhard I de Saun in 1130, before it morphed into the lords of Žovnek in the thirteenth century, and the counts of Celje in 1341. As their status and wealth grew, the counts established their own court system, minted their own money and built castles and churches around the Savinja region. They reached the zenith of their powers under the reign of Hermann II around the end of the fourteenth century, a period during which they extended their sphere of control outside Slovenia into neighbouring lands, at the same time establishing important ties with other European ruling aristocratic houses. Raised to the rank of dukes of the province in 1436, the counts were, for a short period, the equal of their great adversaries and former feudal overlords, the Habsburgs. Their sudden demise followed Ulrich II's assassination by his long-time Hungarian adversary, Laszlo Hunyadi, in Belgrade in 1456.

another wooden ceiling in 1926. Completed around 1600 by an unknown author (the piece has been attributed to Almanac, although this is disputed), this splendid Renaissance composition features eleven fields or panels, featuring the four seasons, four gods, two battle scenes, and, in the central panel, a tangle of pillars and columns rising upwards to an imaginary sky. As a measure of protection, the room is kept in a permanent state of near darkness.

The remainder of the museum is taken up with several rooms of not very exciting furniture garnered from all over Slovenia, including Biedermeier, Baroque, Rococo, the odd painting and a bit of sculpture. The one minor saving grace is the room given over to the deeds of the counts of Celje, its star exhibit a glass cabinet holding eighteen of the counts' grisly skulls, including that of its last ruler Ulrich II, easily identifiable as it's the one with the jaw missing. To the rear of the museum, on a small grassy patch by the riverfront, is an open-air **lapidarium** featuring a few weatherbeaten Roman stone blocks.

Slomškov trg, Glavni trg and the City Park

From the Celje Regional Museum, continue along the promenade, past a section of medieval walls, to cobbled **Slomškov trg**, a small square named in honour of the saint, Anton Slomšek – there is statue of him nearby. Standing in the middle, the fourteenth-century **Abbey Church of St Daniel** (Cerkev Sv Danijel) is the town's most impressive ecclesiastical monument. Invested with some outstanding Gothic architecture, including a fine rib-vaulted ceiling and a towering arch at the entrance to the presbytery, the church also features numerous high-quality wall frescoes, most notably in the **Chapel of Our Lady of the Sorrows**, which also keeps a fifteenth-century pietà of the Sad Madonna. The chapel dedicated to Slomšek was added in 2000, one year after his beatification in Maribor (see box, p.290).

From Slomškov trg a narrow path leads through to **Glavni trg**, a lovely square flush with Baroque and Renaissance buildings, and a convivial place to enjoy a drink during the warmer summer months. In the centre stands **St Mary's Column**, adorned with statues of SS. Rok, Joseph and Florian. Heading north out of the square brings you to the intersection with Krekov trg and Prešernova ulica.

For a bit of peace and quiet, head across the river to the **City Park** (Mestni Park), a tranquil green expanse where you can ramble, play tennis or skate (in winter) in the recreation centre. Also on this side of the river is the **Church of**

St Cecilia (Cerkev Sv Cecilija), reached via a long covered walkway (though it's often closed), and, further up the hill, the **Church of St Nicholas** (Cerkev Sv Miklavž); although this, too, is almost always closed, there are some superlative **views** of the castle opposite.

The Old Castle and around

Once the largest fortification in the country, the windswept ruin of Celje's **Old Castle** (Stari Grad; free) sits atop a four-hundred-metre rise 2km southeast of town. Originally a twelfth-century structure, the castle acquired its present layout in the fourteenth century during the rule of the counts of Celje, who reinforced the walls and invested the interior with residential quarters; ad-hoc additions followed, before its eventual demise and descent into ruin during the seventeenth century. Although there are vestigial Romanesque and Gothic remains, years of systematic and extensive renovation have quashed much of its historical charm; nevertheless it remains an impressive site, particularly when viewed from afar. Whilst here it would be remiss not to climb the enormous **Friedrich Tower** (Friderikov Stolp), originally a four-storey defence tower built by the counts in the fourteenth century but now a roofless structure offering stupendous **views** of the rust-red and orange tiled town rooftops, and the hump-backed hills of the Lower Savinja Valley. The castle stages a regular programme of medieval themed events throughout the summer; check with the tourist office (see p.264). To reach the castle, head through the underpass by the train station and follow the signs; beyond the football stadium, the quickest route by foot is to cut through the woods and rejoin the road at the top, from where it's a further 1km or so (40 min).

The castle is also a good starting point for several short to medium length **hikes** in the area, with signposted trails to Celjska koča (651m; 2hr 30min or 1hr 30min), Svebotnik (700m; 2hr) and the delightful little hill village of Svetina (679m; 2hr 30min). If you are planning to do some walking, pick up a copy of the 1:50,000 *Celjska Kotlina* **map**, available from the tourist office (see p.264). At the last of these, just above the beautiful Gothic Church of Mary of the Snows, there's an excellent mountain chalet, the *Almin Dom* (Ⓣ03/780-3000, Ⓔsvetina@almindom.com), which has spotless and very comfortable pension-style **rooms** (❹), as well as dorm beds (❶). There's a very accomplished **restaurant** here too, worth visiting even if you're not planning to sleep over. The chalet can also be reached by car (or bicycle) from Celje; heading east out of town, look for signs to the industrial zone of Store, and follow the road south from there up to Svetina. On a good day, there are views as far as the Zagrebačka Gora mountains in Croatia.

Eating and drinking

The town's best **restaurant** is *Puccini* (closed Sun), an informal, stylish gostilna located at the southern end of Glavni trg; the menu runs the entire gamut of pastas and risottos, while the piano functions as a neat little salad bar. Despite its terribly noisy location on a junction opposite the bus station, the *Marco Polo* pizzeria is a sprightly little place with a lengthy menu of soups, salads and sandwiches – there's live music here, too, at weekends. Although a bit dowdy-looking, *Istrska Konoba*, in the *Turška Mačka* hotel, is a decent seafood restaurant, and has fresh fish flown in daily from Dalmatia, in Croatia. A little way north of the centre at Mariborska cesta 79, opposite the huge Interspar building, the oddly named *Gostilna Amerika* serves up huge portions of southern Balkan specialities such as bean stews, *čevapi* (rolls of minced meat) and *ražnjiči* (a combination of meats on a skewer).

There's little to get worked up about when it comes to **nightlife** in Celje. Your best bet is the energetic *Country Pub*, attached to the *Hotel Štorman*, and which has a good selection of draught beers, or the *Jazz Pub*, midway between the tourist office and the student dorms at Ljubljanska cesta 7, just one of a number of student hangouts in this area. *Café Gallus*, secreted away just behind the tourist office, is ideal for a daytime coffee, as is the pavement café of the *Hotel Evropa*.

Entertainment

The **Slovenian People's Theatre** (Slovenski Ljudsko Gledališče), just behind the *Turška Mačka* hotel at Gledališka ulica 5 (box office Mon–Fri 9–11am & 5–7pm, plus 60min prior to each performance), is one of the best professional theatres in Slovenia; bear in mind, though, that it shuts down for most of July and August – ask at the tourist office for a monthly programme. The theatre is also the venue for the **Days of Comedy** festival in February, though surmounting the language barrier might prove a little tricky. The town puts on a couple of other festivals, foremost of which is **Summer in Celje**, a two-month programme of small concerts and gigs at various venues around town, while **medieval-themed events** (markets, jousting and the like) take place on a regular basis up at the castle during the summer months; enquire at the tourist office for information on any of the above.

Šempeter and the Roman Necropolis

Approximately 12km west of Celje along the main road running parallel to the A1 highway, the small urban settlement of **ŠEMPETER** is the setting for a **Roman Necropolis** (April–Sept Tues–Sun 10am–6pm; 700SIT). One of the most important archeological sites in this part of Europe, the necropolis, excavated and reconstructed over a fifteen year period during the 1950s and 1960s, served as a burial ground for the nobles of Celeia (Roman Celje) until it was swamped by floodwaters from the Savinja River around 270 AD. Four marble mausolea, emblazoned with relief portraits of the families they commemorate, as well as scenes from classical mythology, were re-erected, and dozens more plinths, columns and fragments were unearthed.

The largest and grandest of the four monuments is the **Spectatii** family tomb, its members represented by three headless statues; the funerary plinths are arrayed with mythical figures and various seasonal scenes, whilst the head of Medusa juts out over the gable. The most arresting tomb is that of the **Ennii** family, depicted here by three shallow relief portraits of the mother, father and daughter, Kalendina, though curiously there's not one of the son, Vitulus. On the front-facing plinth there's a fine relief of *Europa Riding the Bull*, and, on the Baldachin ceiling, sculpted caskets bursting with rosettes. By way of contrast, the other two mausolea are less fanciful creations: the altar-shaped tomb of **Vindonius** – understood to be the oldest of the four – features reliefs of *Hercules and Alcestis*, and, on the side panels, two hunters, one with a hare draped around his neck, the other carrying a shepherd's staff and a basket of birds. Built in the form of a chapel, the tomb of **Secundinii** is largely devoid of ornamentation. More detailed information about the site can be obtained from the tourist office (see below).

To get here take one of the hourly **buses** from Celje, alight in the centre, and backtrack 100m to the traffic lights; from here walk up Ob rimski nekropoli towards the church, opposite which is both the necropolis and the small **tourist association office** (April–Sept Tues–Sun 10am–6pm; ⓣ03/700-2056,

Ⓦwww.td-sempeter.si). From Šempeter, buses continue west along the main road, stopping after 2km at the road which branches south to the village of **Dolenja Vas** (which is actually part of **Prebold**). At no. 147 the tidy little *Dolina* **campsite** (Ⓣ03/572-4378; open year-round) also has a few rooms (❷) and apartments (❺).

Hell's Cave

If you don't manage to get down to the Karst region, you can content yourself with a visit to the **Pekel (Hell's) Cave** (Jama Pekel), the only one open to tourists in the Štajerska region. Located 5km north of Šempeter, across the main A1 highway near the tiny hamlet of **Podlog**, this atmospheric little cave takes its name from the devilish looking figure carved into the rock face above the entrance. Inside, it's split between two levels; the first, lower gallery tracks the Peklenščica (Hell Stream) past several lakes towards a small subterranean waterfall. Thereafter it's a steady climb to the stalactite-infested upper gallery, and then onwards to the exit, located some 40m higher than the entrance. Fifty-minute **tours** of the cave (1200SIT) take place hourly from 9am to 6pm between April and September, and at weekends only in March and October till 4pm; however, check with the tourist office in Šempeter first (see p.269); they can also advise on how to reach the cave if you're not sure. If you don't have your own transport, **bikes** (1000SIT per day) can be hired from the *Dolina* campsite (see above).

Laško and Tabor Castle

Eleven kilometres south of Celje, the small spa town of **LAŠKO** has been brewing beer since 1825, and is today one of the two largest breweries in the country – the Union brewery in Ljubljana is the other – and formerly one of the largest in Yugoslavia. Visits to the **brewery** (*pivovarna*), which take in the filtration and bottling plants, a modest museum and a spot of sampling, are usually only available for groups, but if you call well in advance it should be possible to arrange a tour (Ⓣ03/734-8413 or contact the tourist office).

However, there's more to Laško than just beer. Known to have existed since Roman times, the town's thermal springs have been attracting a more contemporary crowd since 1854 when the first formal baths were built. Today the **Laško spa** (Zdravlišče Laško), a ten-minute walk north of the tourist office at Zdravališče cesta 4 (Ⓣ03/734-5111, Ⓦwww.zdravilisce-lasko.si), is a thoroughly modern complex with superb indoor and outdoor thermal pools (daily 9.30am–10pm; 1500SIT); in addition there's a sauna centre and whirlpool and massage facilities.

The town's **train** and **bus stations** are positioned side by side on Trg Svobode on the west bank of the Savinja River, and just a few paces from the friendly **tourist office** (Mon–Fri 8am–5pm, Sat 8am–1pm; Ⓣ03/733-8950), housed in a flashy, modern glass building by the bridge. The spa complex boasts two very accomplished, albeit identical, **hotels** (❺) – ask for a riverside room. Better still, the cracking *Hotel Savinja*, across the river in the old part of town at Valvasorjev trg 1 (Ⓣ03/734-3030; ❻), has nine huge and fantastically luxurious rooms. Alternatively, there's the more down-at-heel, but perfectly acceptable, *Hotel Hum* opposite the tourist office (Ⓣ03/573-1321; ❹).

Beautifully set on the slopes of Mount Hum (583m) 1km north of town is **Tabor Castle** (Grad Tabor), whose two renovated towers – one round, one square – now accommodate a wedding hall and **restaurant** (daily noon–11pm, Sun till 8pm; closed Mon) respectively. The latter is seriously posh and expensive, but the food is exemplary, featuring an exotic menu of meats and fish (deer, duck, cuttlefish and lobster), alongside some intriguing local specialities such as beer soup and beer mousse. More affordably, the very enjoyable *Pivnica Pačnik* (closed Sun), housed in a lovely sky-blue building 200m north of the *Hotel Savinja* on Aškerčev trg, offers delicious beer sausages; and in the basement of the *Hotel Savinja* there's a traditional *pivnica* (daily 6–11pm, till 1am Fri & Sat, closed Sun) serving up beer and snacks. The town's **Beer and Flowers Festival** (*Pivo-Cvetje*) in early/mid-July is one of the most enjoyable provincial events in the Slovene calendar, four manic days of music, sports and games, flower displays and, of course, lots of beer.

Velenje

Opened with great ceremonial pomp in 1959, **VELENJE**, 24km northwest of Celje and well connected by both bus and train, is Slovenia's youngest town. Formerly known as Titov Velenje – the Yugoslav president Tito visited here no less than four times, on one occasion with Brezhnev – modern-day Velenje was designed as a model industrial workers' town, characterized by a uniform series of grim high-rise apartments and wide streets broken up by the odd splash of greenery. Amidst this Socialist-Realist aesthetic, however, are two worthwhile attractions: the town castle and museum, and the coal mining museum.

Velenje Castle and the Coal Mining Museum

Sited on a high, rounded hill above Velenje's small, almost forgotten, Old Town quarter is the beautifully renovated **Velenje Castle** (Velenjski Grad), most of which dates from the sixteenth century. The castle now houses the **town museum** (Tues–Sun 9am–5pm, 400SIT), which comprises several disparate but interesting exhibitions: the first traces the history and development of Velenje from its beginnings as a provincial market town, through to the boom period of the Velenje coal mine after World War II. For the most part, though, it's little more than a shrine to socialist-era figureheads such as Tito and Edvard Kardelj, busts and pictures of whom adorn several of the rooms. The most exciting section of the museum is the collection of African art donated to the museum by Czech-born sculptor František Foit, who spent more than twenty years living in and travelling around the continent. During this time he accumulated some terrific stuff, most of which is on display here, including jewellery, furniture, musical instruments, masks and puppets, as well as some of his own wood-carved sculptures. There's also a collection of Mastodon remains, some Baroque art, and reconstructions of a general town store and inn. The castle can be reached via a path just across from the bus station and by road from the old part of town.

Coal has been excavated at the **Velenje Coal Mine** in Škale, 1.5km north of town, since the mid-eighteenth century, although it was the drilling of the main lignite layer around a century later that really put the town on the map. Although the mine remains operational, it's possible to visit certain parts of it as part of an organized **tour** (daily 9.30am–5pm; 1800SIT). The ninety-minute visit – enlivened by audiovisual presentations and puppets of assorted mine characters – takes in sections of both the old and new mine shafts, the latter first used after World War II; you also get to partake in a hearty miner's lunch in the underground canteen.

Unless you have your own transport, it's a good thirty-minute walk to the mine; from the Old Town, head north up Cesta Talcev, cross the rail tracks and continue along Kidričeva cesta, which loops round and becomes Koroška cesta. However, in order for an ad-hoc visit to take place, there needs to be a minimum of six people, so you should ring in advance to see when tours are scheduled (Ⓣ03/587-0997).

Practicalities

The **bus station** is located to the south of town on Šaleška cesta, at the intersection of the Celje and Slovenj Gradec roads, whilst the **train station** is 1km northeast of here, just off Cesta Talcev near the industrial zone. A small kiosk stationed in the car park across from the bus station constitutes the **tourist office** (Mon–Fri 9am–noon & 3–6pm; Ⓣ03/897-6466). There are two **places to stay** in town: the clinical yet pleasant *Hotel Paka* (Ⓣ03/898-0700, Ⓦwww.hotelpaka.com; ⑥), 100m north of the bus station at Rudarska 1, and the more upmarket, nineteenth-century *Vila Herberstein* (Ⓣ03/896-1400, Ⓔvila.herberstein@siol.net; ⑦), 400m to the east of the bus station at Kopališka cesta 1. The only **eating** options are at the hotels.

Koroška

From Velenje, two roads forge their way into the heart of **Koroška**, a mountainous, heavily forested region abutting the Austrian border, crossed by three river valleys and scattered with isolated highland farmsteads and small valley settlements. One road heads north up the Mislinja Valley to the pretty town of **Slovenj Gradec**, and beyond to **Dravograd**, whilst the other (partly unsurfaced) road straggles across a mountain pass northwest to the ex-mining towns of **Črna na Koroškem** and **Mežica**; the former is also a key starting point for forays into the heart of the Koroška mountains themselves.

Slovenj Gradec

In stark contrast to Velenje, the spruce little town of **SLOVENJ GRADEC**, 27km further north in the Mislinja Valley and the largest settlement in Koroška, preserves a delightful Medieval core, one not that dissimilar to Kamnik (see p.91) or Škofja Loka (see p.96). The town is renowned for its rich cultural heritage, thanks to the likes of prominent Slovene artists, Bogdan Borčič and Jože Tisnikar, and the Austrian composer Hugo Wolf, all of whom were born here.

The Town

Everything of interest is located along **Glavni trg**, a wide, smoothly curving street that forms the heart of the town's beautifully preserved historic medieval core. The town's two principal sites are located inside the former town hall building at no. 24; on the first floor, the **Koroška Gallery of Fine Arts** (Koroška Galeriji Likovnih Umetnosti; Tues–Fri 9am–6pm, Sat & Sun 9am–noon & 3–6pm; 500SIT) – one of the largest exhibition spaces in the country – dotes almost exclusively on the works of artists from Koroška. These include Franc Berneker, the first modern Slovene sculptor, Bogdan Borčič, painter of brightly coloured abstract pieces, and, by way of contrast, Jože Tisnikar, whose bleak and moody paintings, defined as "dark modernism", undoubtedly owe much to the time he spent in a hospital pathology department. The gallery is also an important venue for guest exhibitors.

Installed in the cells of the former town prison (last used during World War II by the Germans) across the courtyard is a fine little **archeological**

collection (Arheologija Krajine; same times; 400SIT), whose finds, from the Mislinja, Mežica and Drava valleys, span several periods: the earliest exhibits include cave-bear remains, a bone harpoon, and Stone and Iron Age tools, whilst from the Roman and Slavic period there is a stack of grave goods (signet rings and bronze fibula brooches), and, from the Middle Ages, tiles and clay pots; further treasures – ceramics, coins and jewellery – were unearthed in 2000 during the building of a new school.

Situated in a recess directly opposite the town hall, the thirteenth-century, but several times rebuilt, **Parish Church of St Elizabeth** was built in honour of the Hungarian princess Elizabeth. The interior showcases an abundance of Baroque extravagances, most notably a sumptuously overblown high altar – the central painting of Elizabeth was executed by the Baroque workshop of Franz Strauss – and a richly gilded pulpit. Also keep your eye out for numerous liturgical items, Gothic knight's tombstones, and, to the right as you enter, a painting of St Anton Slomšek (see p.290), completed in 2000. The interior of the neighbouring **Church of the Holy Spirit** is beautifully ornamented with a fine array of fifteenth-century frescoes.

Practicalities

The town's **bus station** is on Pohorska cesta, from where it's a ten-minute walk south to Glavni trg. The helpful **tourist office** (Mon–Fri 9am–6pm, Sat & Sun 9am–noon & 3–6pm; ⓣ02/881-2116, ⓦwww.slovenj-gradec.si) is located on the ground floor of the old town hall halfway along Glavni trg at no. 24; they can also arrange private **accommodation**, which may be your preferred choice given that the town is possessed of just one hotel, the very ordinary *Slovenj Gradec* (ⓣ02/884-5285; ❹), a short walk up from the tourist office at no. 43. Save for the rather dingy hotel **restaurant**, there's nowhere else to eat in the centre of town, so you'll have to head to *Gostilna Murko* on the northern outskirts of town at Francetova cesta 24 (on the main road to Dravograd). There's a very appealing **coffee house**, the *Mestna kavarna*, opposite the tourist office.

Dravograd and Šentanel

Eleven kilometres north of Slovenj Gradec and just 4km shy of the Austrian border, the old market town of **DRAVOGRAD** sits at the junction of Koroška's three valleys – the Drava, the Meža and the Mislinja – as well as several key road routes and the Maribor–Klagenfurt rail line. Although it's likely that the only reason you might end up here is to take an onward connection, there are a couple of minor sights worth checking out if you've got an hour or so to spare, both of which lie across the river in the old town core.

Some 50m along the main street, Trg 4 julija, in the basement of the municipal town building at no. 7, is a World War II **Gestapo prison** (Muzej Zbirka Gestapovski; daily 8am–2pm; free), whose half a dozen dingy, cobwebbed cells now display a dusty collection of uniforms and artefacts belonging to both the captives and their captors. The Gestapo controlled the prison on two occasions, the first time between the beginning of the occupation and July 1941, and the second time, between January 1944 and the end of the war. Five minutes' walk further along the street stands the attractive twelfth-century **Church of St Vitus** (Cerkev Sv Vid) one of the few Carinthian-style Romanesque structures remaining in this region, and unusual in that it features a bell tower at its eastern end.

The **train** and **bus stations** are just 200m apart, on the south bank of the river near the bridge. The town's one **hotel** (and just about the only place to eat) is the *Hesper* at Koroška cesta 48 (Ⓣ02/878-4440, Ⓦwww.hesper.si; ❺), just 50m from the **tourist office** (Mon-Fri 10am-5pm; Ⓣ02/871-0285, Ⓔinfo@dravograd.si), itself located across the road from the Church of St Vitus in a vaulted underpass at Trg 4 julija 57.

From Dravograd, one road (and the rail line) threads its way through the scenic Drava Valley eastwards to Maribor some 60km away, whilst the road west passes through the uninteresting towns of **Ravne na Koroškem** (the "capital" of Koroška) and **Prevalje**. About 2km beyond Prevalje, a road branches off up towards the village of **ŠENTANEL**, a picturesque little settlement, 4km distant, known for its abundance of **tourist farms**: two of the best are *Ploder* at no. 3 (Ⓣ02/823-1104; ❷), and *Marin Miler* at no. 8 (Ⓣ02/824-0550, Ⓦwww.marin.koroska.org; ❷) – the latter has a terrific gostilna too.

Mežica and Črna na Koroškem

A short way south of Prevalje is the town of **MEŽICA**, where, up until a few years ago, lead and zinc had been mined for over three hundred years. Although organized mining began here way back in 1665, it wasn't until Napoleon's arrival in 1809 – and his subsequent occupation of the nearby Austrian mine areas, which forced the Austrians to look elsewhere for new sources of ore – that intensive, heavy-duty production took place. Further modernization of the mine during the early twentieth century saw the introduction of electricity in addition to pneumatic drilling methods, though the gradual depletion of ore reserves after World War II led to a decline in production and the mine finally closed in 2000. Part of it however, was kept open for **tours** (Tues–Sun: April–Oct 11am & 3pm; Nov–March 11am; Ⓣ02/870-0180, Ⓦwww.podzemljepece.com; 1500SIT). Kitted out with jacket, helmet and light, you clamber aboard the very small and rickety mine train (not for the claustrophobic), which transports you 3.5km along a shaft into the heart of the mine complex, the area known as Moring. During the one-hour tour, you walk through numerous large galleries on two levels (there are twenty in total, each approximately 30m apart), where you'll get to see the calling room, where miners would gather at the beginning of the shift before dispersing to their stations, various mining equipment and machinery preserved *in situ*, and a series of audiovisual demonstrations.

After resurfacing, head to the adjacent **mine museum** (Tues–Sun: April–Oct 9am–5pm, Nov–March 9am–3pm; price included in the mine ticket), where you can view a fine display of minerals and fossils, mine survey maps and mapping instruments, and a mock-up miner's home, a typically cramped living space which would be expected to accommodate up to eight members of the same family.

For something a little more adventurous, you can participate in **underground bike rides** through a section of the mine; the first part of the ride, which totals 5km and takes around two hours, is outdoors, before the descent into the mine and through tunnels constructed for the transportation of lead ore and waste materials. For more information contact the *Hotel Club Krnes* in the old mining settlement of **ČRNA NA KOROŠKEM** (see opposite), where the trips begin.

During the mine's heyday, most of the population of this sedate little town, 7km south of Mežica in the Upper Meža Valley, were also employed at Mežica, as well as in the local ironworking, forestry and timber industries. For the visitor, Črna is chiefly of interest as a springboard for onward ventures into the mountains, whilst there are also several tourist facilities here. If you've got some

Cycling and hiking around Črna na Koroškem

The mountains encircling Črna na Koroškem, also known as King Matjaž Park in all the tourist bumph, offer some of the best **cycling** in the country, with some 500km of marked trails; at present there are five circular routes – with a further five in the pipeline – each of which is marked out by yellow animal footprints. Everything you need to know about cycling in the region can be obtained from the *Hotel Club Krnes* (see below), where you can also **rent bikes** (3750SIT per day) and get repairs done. As well as organising guided mountain bike tours, the hotel also arranges climbing and kayaking excursions – check out Ⓦwww.mtbpark.com for more details on all the above activities.

From Črna there are a number of good **hiking** possibilities, the most popular of which is the trek northwest up to **Mala Peca** (1731m; 3hr 15min), just below which is the *Dom na Peci* hut (May–Oct; Ⓣ02/823-8406); fifteen minutes' walk from the hut is the **cave of King Matjaž** (Matjaževa jama), the alleged sleeping place of the mythological folk hero named after the Hungarian king, Matthias Corvinus – there's a bronze statue of Matjaž inside the cave entrance. From the hut, you can continue via one of two paths towards Kordeževa glava (2125m) and the Austrian border. From Črna there are shorter hikes, too, including one trail north to the *Koča na Pikovem* hut (992m; ninety minutes), and another trail south to **Najevska Lipa** (1hr 45min), the site of an enormous Linden tree, alleged to be one of the largest trees in Slovenia. Whatever activity you plan to undertake, you'll find the 1;50,000 *Koroška* **map**, available from the tourist office, a useful aid.

time to kill, there are a couple of minor collections to nose around: across from the bus station, the **ethnological museum** comprises a modest assortment of everyday household items and farming implements used by local peasants; hewn into the rock face a few metres from the bus station, the **mining museum** presents mine trucks, drilling equipment and tools used in the Mežica mine before its closure.

To view either collection contact the very helpful **tourist office** (June–Sept Mon–Fri 8am–5pm, Sat 9am–1pm; Oct–May Mon–Fri 8am–3pm, Sat 9am–1pm; Ⓣ02/870-3066, Ⓔpkm@siol.net), right next to the **bus station** at Center 100. The town's one **hotel**, which is a five-minute walk south of the tourist office at Center 153, is the *Hotel Club Krnes* (Ⓣ02/870-3060, ❷); this self-styled cyclists' hotel offers very basic, but perfectly acceptable, hostel-style accommodation in singles, doubles and apartments. There are also several gostilna dotted around town, the most central of which is *Rešer*, just around the corner from the tourist office at Center 102.

The Upper Savinja Valley

Named after the **Savinja River**, which flows from the heart of the Kamniške-Savinja Alps, down through Celje and beyond to Zidani Most, where it joins the Sava River, the **Upper Savinja Valley** (Zgornja Savinjska Dolina) is a pristine landscape of towering alpine peaks, river valleys and undulating slopes. The territory it covers extends roughly from between the aforementioned Alps, to Letuš, a small village just north of Šempeter.

The region's settlements are mainly large villages and a couple of small towns, although, as picturesque as some of them are, such as the administrative centre of **Mozirje**, they're not really worth a special visit. In any case, the chances are that you'll be keen to push on to the wonderful **Logar Valley** and the surrounding hills and mountains, where there are ample opportunities for hiking, climbing, cycling and other activities.

The Logar Valley

The region's siren draw is the extraordinarily beautiful **Logar Valley** (Logarska dolina), a seven-kilometre-long alpine valley situated along the western margins of the Upper Savinja in the cradle of the Kamniške-Savinja Alps. Formed during the Ice Age, the U-shaped glaciated valley manifests a level, green valley floor covered with flower-speckled meadows and beech woods, enclosed by step-like cliff sides riddled with glacial boulders, waterfalls, springs and streams, and a majestic wreath of jagged grey peaks, most of which top 2000m.

From the entrance to the valley (between April and Oct there's a 1000SIT charge for cars), it's about 2km to a cluster of tourist facilities, including an information hut and a couple of hotels (see below), beyond which point the road continues for a further five kilometres up to the head of the valley and Logarska's most popular site, the ninety-metre-high **Rinka Waterfall** (Slap Rinka); if you're walking, there's a trail (6km long) to the waterfall beginning approximately 1km along the road after you've entered the valley. Although the mountains look formidable, they can be traversed via a trail which starts at Rinka and climbs to **Okrešelj** (1396m), before continuing to **Kamniško Sedlo** (1864m), where there's a hut (June to mid-Oct); from here the trail continues down to Kamniška Bistrica (see p.96).

The valley's small **information hut** (May–Oct daily 8am–7pm; ⓣ03/838-9004, ⓦwww.logarska-dolina.si), located 2km along the valley road from the point of entry, has a mine of information on the valley and its surrounds, and can book private accommodation in the region. Also on offer here are three-hour guided walks of the valley (6000SIT for a group of up to ten people), as well as a number of other activities, including **horse-riding** (2600SIT for a 1hr guided tour), **rock climbing** (2500SIT for 2hr), and **archery** (1500SIT); there are also **bikes** for hire (500SIT for 1hr, 2000SIT for 4hrs plus).

Out of season, you can get information at the *Hotel Plesnik* (ⓣ03/839-2300, ⓦwww.plesnik.si; ❽) across the road; this very comfortable, and rather overpriced, place also has a pool and sauna, but it's not as homely as the neighbouring *Vila Palenk* (same tel as *Plesnik*; ❼), which has some rooms with a fireplace, lovely if you're here during the winter. Otherwise, there's cheaper accommodation 500m along the road at the *Plesnik* tourist farm (ⓣ03/838-9009; ❷), and, another 500m further on from here, the smart *Pension Na Razpotju* (ⓣ03/839-1650; ❻).

The one major approach to Logarska is via the road from **Ljubno ob Savinji**, a small town located 34km east of Kamnik and 26km northwest of the Ljubljana–Celje highway. Logarska can also be reached from Črna na Koroškem (see p.274), via a relatively short (20km), but mostly unsurfaced, mountain road – the road actually emerges in Solčava (see opposite), from where it's a short drive to Logarska. Indeed, unless you've got your own **transport**, getting to Logarska will prove difficult; although there are a handful of (weekday) buses from Celje and Velenje to Ljubno ob Savinji, Luče and Solčava (the nearest settlements to Logarska, see opposite), only one of these continues to Logarska, and even then, that's only between April and October (10.45am from Luče & 11.06am from Solčava).

Around the Logar Valley

Whilst most cars and buses pile into Logarska, the two glaciated valleys flanking Logarska Dolina, **Robanov Kot** to the east, and **Matkov Kot** to the west (and just a couple of kilometres from the Austrian border), are no less magnificent, and should appeal to those seeking more solitudinous recreation. The only accommodation in either valley is the *Govc-Vršnik* tourist farm in Robanov Kot, at no. 34 (Ⓣ03/839-5016; ❷).

The nearest settlements to Logarska are the villages of **Solčava**, 4km to the east, where there's a tourist office (May–Oct daily 8am–7pm; Ⓣ03/839-0710), and **LUČE**, 10km further along the same road, which also has a tourist office (May–Oct daily 8am–7pm; Ⓣ03/839-3555). Luče is the best place to stock up on provisions (there are a few shops and a bank here) prior to heading on to Logarska; there's **accommodation** in the form of the *Pension Raduha* at no. 67 (Ⓣ03/838-4000; ❹), which also has a good **restaurant**, and the beautifully sited *Spodnji Jerovčnik* tourist farm (Ⓣ03/584-4087; ❷), located 1.5km south of Luče in the hillside hamlet of Krnica – follow the signs for Podvolovljek. The only **campsite** in the area, *Camp Smiča* (Ⓣ03/584-4330, May–Sept), is located 1km back out along the road towards Solčava by the Savinja River.

East of Celje

The region east of Celje is dominated by spas, the best known of which are **Rogaška Slatina** and **Olimia**, the former once one of Europe's grandest resorts, the latter a relatively recent addition to the scene. There are also a brace of cultural diversions to enjoy – the Skansen-like **Rogatec open-air museum** near Rogaška Slatina, and **Olimje monastery**, not far from the Olimia spa.

Rogaška Slatina

Thirty kilometres east of Celje, **ROGAŠKA SLATINA** was built around several mineral-rich springs (Donat, Styria and Tempel) discovered during the sixteenth century, and was once one of the most fashionable spa resorts in Central Europe – some of its more illustrious visitors included the Habsburg ruler Franz Jozef, the French Bonapartes, and King Karad*ord*evič of Serbia.

Arrival, information and accommodation

The town's **train station** is on Kidričeva ulica, some 500m south of town, while the **bus station** is closer to the centre on Celjska cesta, from where it's a five-minute walk to Zdraviliški trg. The **tourist office** (April–Oct Mon–Fri 9am–7pm, Sat 9am–noon & 4–7pm; Nov–March Mon–Fri 9am–4pm, Sat 9am–noon; Ⓣ03/581-4414, Ⓦwww.tic.rogaska@siol.net), located opposite the *Strossmayer Hotel*, can arrange private **accommodation** if you can't afford, or don't fancy, one of the many hotels in town. Located at the northern end of Zdraviliški trg are two modern and unsightly hotels; the rather ordinary *Sava* (Ⓣ03/811-4000, Ⓦwww.hotel-sava-rogaska.si; ❼) and the super-slick *Donat* (Ⓣ03/811-3000, Ⓦwww.terme-rogaska.si; ❽) – the latter also has a new thermal pool (2000SIT for non-hotel guests). At the time of writing, the hotels *Grand*, *Styria* and *Strossmayer*, along from the *Donat* on Zdraviliški trg, were undergoing extensive renovation; when complete expect to see three of the most luxurious places in town; for details of these hotels contact the *Hotel Donat*. There are more options on Celjska cesta, the town's other main street, running adjacent to Zdraviliški trg; the *Slovenija* (☎03/811-5000; ❻), a large yellow building 100m north of the tourist office (ask for one of the newer rooms), and the very-good-value *Slatina* (☎03/818-4100; ❹), a short walk further along, which also has some apartments (❺).

If you so wish, you can jump on one of the **tourist trains** (*turistični vlak*), one of which runs to Rogatec (Tues, Thurs & Sat; 1000SIT return; 30min), the other to the Olimia spa and onwards to Olimije monastery (Wed, Fri & Sun; 1000SIT; 1 hour); both depart from outside the tourist office. **Bikes** can be rented from the *Sava* and *Donat* hotels (1000SIT 3hr, 1500SIT for the day).

The Town

Despite the addition of a couple of beastly looking hotels, the town has managed to preserve its quintessential spa ambience, particularly around its central square, **Zdraviliški trg**, a broad, immaculately kept landscaped park neatly framed by gravel walkways and grand buildings, the pick of which is the stately **Zdraviliški Dom** (now the *Grand Hotel Rogaška*), one of the finest Neoclassical buildings in the country.

Although its curative properties have long been used to treat a wide range of disorders – typically for those with gastrointestinal complaints and metabolic problems – the water is tapped first and foremost for commercial purposes, and you'll find many bottled waters from Rogaška in bars and restaurants throughout the country; in its purest form, however, it is incredibly metallic, and hence barely drinkable. You can sample the magnesium-laden Donat mg, the spa's most famous water, and others, in the large **pump room** (daily 7am–1pm & 3–7pm; free) located at the northern end of Zdraviliški trg near the **Temple**, an oval pavilion sitting on top of the spa's main spring; head towards reception, grab a cup and away you go.

The main therapeutic baths, as well as all the treatment centres, are located in the Terapija building adjoining the pump room, though casual visitors tend to make a beeline for the **Riviera swimming complex** (Termalna Riviera; daily 9am–8pm, Sat till 11pm; 1100SIT for 3hr, 1500SIT for the day), indoor and outdoor pools located halfway along Celjska cesta; guests of some hotels receive free entry to these pools so check with yours.

The lovely, mint-coloured building at the southern end of Zdraviliški trg, dating from 1904, houses a **glass showroom** where you can buy, or just view, some beautiful cut-glass and lead crystal pieces (Mon–Fri 9am–7pm, Sat 9am–5pm, Sun 10am–4pm). There's another shop (Mon–Fri 8am–7pm, Sat 8am–noon) out by the **Glass Factory** (Steklarska šola) 2km south of town; tours of the factory are possible by prior arrangement – contact the tourist office.

Eating and drinking

Eating options are not bad in town; the *Sonce* restaurant, a short walk beyond the Riviera pool complex on Celjska cesta, is the best place in town, with a menu heavily skewed towards fish and poultry, but which also features other, rarely found delicacies such as horsemeat and ostrich – they've got a fine stock of wines here too; back down the street at no. 6, the cute little cellar pizzeria, *La Gondola*, also has some good salads and pasta dishes; or there's *Bohor*, near the bus station on Kidričeva ulica, a good old-fashioned place serving standard grills. The cool *Café Attems*, housed in the building at the bottom of Zdraviliški trg (see above), is the place to take a coffee, or, at night, a beer (open till 1am).

Rogatec

Regular buses, and some trains, make the short trip east to the ancient little market village of **ROGATEC**, known for its delightful **Open-Air-Museum** (Muzej na Prostem Rogatec; Tues–Sun noon–7pm; 500SIT), a modest gathering of vernacular architecture from Štajerska's sub-Pannonian plain. Standing either side of the entrance gate are the **forge** and **general store** (*Lodn*), the former a single room building built from sandstone in 1930, and stuffed with tools and semi-finished products, the latter a typical Rogatec grocer's store, furnished with a counter surrounded by weighing and measuring machines, containers and jars full of goodies. The museum's central space is taken up by the early nineteenth-century, wooden **house** (*hiša*), which once belonged to the local poet Jože Šmit from the nearby village of Tlake. Comprising a traditional setup of *lojpa* (entrance hall), *kuhna* ("black" kitchen) and *hiša* (living room), the sleeping arrangements were particularly interesting; whilst young, the children would sleep with their parents in the larger bedroom (*štiblic*), but once grown up, the girls would move to another bedroom (*hiška*), which had smaller windows barred with an iron cross, in case of any unwanted male visitors; the boys, meanwhile, had to make do with the barn.

The double **hayrack** (*toplar*) is of the type found all over Slovenia, though, curiously, this one was taken from the village of Prišlin in Croatia. There's also a working well (*štepih na čapljo*), a beehive, and a thatched-roof pigsty (*štalunci*), which doubles up as a storage rack (*rante*) for turnip and carrot leaves, used as fodder for the swine during winter months. To the rear of the museum the old **winegrowers house** now serves as a catering centre. Regular workshops are held here during the summer, whereby you can watch, or participate in, such pursuits as bread-making, corn braiding and nail forging. Next door to the museum is the Strmol **riding centre** (Ⓣ070/279-249), offering trail riding and regular lessons (2500SIT per hour for either).

The museum is a little awkward to get to; from the train station, head due north using the church as a marker; at the main road turn right and walk to another road junction, where you should then turn left following the signs for Ptuj. The museum is about 1km along the road from here. Buses from Rogaška usually stop at the *Gostilna Jelša*, from where you must backtrack until you reach the road junction – again, from here, follow signs to Ptuj.

Podčetrtek and around

A somewhat more contemporary spa resort than Rogatec is **Olimia** (daily 8am–8pm, Fri until 9pm, Sat until midnight; 1300SIT for 3 hours, 1800SIT for day ticket; Ⓦwww.terme-olimia.com) in the border village of **PODČETRTEK**, 15km south of Rogaška Slatina. From a distance, the much-remodelled twelfth-century **Podčetrtek Castle** high above it, looks very impressive, but on closer inspection, it is, sadly, nothing of the sort. Ravaged by looters and now littered with debris and crumbling masonry, it's a depressing site and you're best off just viewing it from afar. The village itself holds little of interest.

The resort, 800m northeast of Podčetrtek, is essentially geared up for longer-stay and package tourists, whilst most day-trippers head to the water park a short way to the north. The spa's **information office** (Mon–Sat 9am–5pm, Sun 9am–noon; Ⓣ03/829-7896; Ⓔtic@podcetrtek.si) is just inside the entrance to the pool complex. If you're wishing to stay, there's plenty of

accommodation here, all of which is of a uniformly high standard: the super-slick *Breza* (☎03/829-7000; ❺) – which has its own pool – the *Rosa* apartments (❻–❼; same tel as *Breza*); and the *Vas Lipa* tourist village, comprising two dozen apartment buildings holding four separate units each, and sleeping two to five people (❺–❻; same tel number); there's a restaurant, supermarket, hairdressers and so on here too; guests of all three receive free entrance to the pools.

There are more thrills and spills less than 1km further north of the spa at the large **Water Park Aqualuna** (daily May–Sept; 1800SIT). Spread across a field next door is the large *Natura* **campsite** (☎03/829-7833; mid-April to mid-Oct), guests of which receive free entry to the waterpark. For **eating** try the *Gostilna Ciril*, a simple place opposite the campsite on the main road; they've also got some very basic rooms for rent (☎03/582-9109; ❸); indeed there are several places offering private rooms along this stretch of road.

If you're coming by **train** (Podčetrtek is on the Celje–Imeno line), then make sure you get off at the appropriate stop: for Podčetrtek get off at the station of the same name; for the spa it's "Atomske Toplice" (this is the old name for the spa); and for the campsite and water park, it's "Podčetrtek Toplice". **Buses** also stop in these places.

Olimje Monastery

From Podčetrtek, a smooth, winding valley road snakes through some gorgeous countryside to **Olimje Monastery**, 3km to the southwest. Originally built as a castle in 1550, on the site of a former fortification possibly dating from the eleventh century, the building was acquired by Pauline monks from Lepoglava, in Croatia, in 1663. They proceeded to convert it into a monastery, enlarging the premises and augmenting it with a church. Modifications continued apace up until the order's dissolution in 1782, when the monks were re-dispersed to various monasteries throughout Croatia. The Minorite order returned here in 1990.

Tacked on to the left-hand side of the monastery, the **Church of the Assumption** was completed in 1675 by the monks as part of the monastery's rebuilding programme. Preceded by two jet-black and gold marble altars – the one to the left holds a painting of Christ's Passion, the one to the right honours St Paul the Hermit, regarded as the founding father of the monastery – the small presbytery is almost entirely filled by an immense three-tiered golden altar, finished with several paintings and a dozen statues of saints. The side chapel, dedicated to St Francis Xavier and featuring a majestic, caramel-coloured late Baroque altar, was a later addition (1766) to the church. Note, too, the fine upright organ in the choir loft.

Reputedly the third-oldest preserved pharmacy in Europe, after ones in Paris and Dubrovnik, the Pauline **pharmacy** (daily 10am–6pm, but closed between noon and 1pm; 200SIT), located on the ground floor of the left round tower as you face the monastery, was founded some time in the mid-eighteenth century, functioning until 1782 when the monastery was disbanded. There's now little left in the way of fittings and fixtures or pharmaceutical goods (these were all removed when the monastery was dissolved), but its frescoes, executed around 1789 by local painter Anton Lerchinger, and depicting SS Cosmas and Damian, patron saints of physicians and pharmacists, eminent physicians Asculapius and Paracelsus, and scenes of Christ healing – are worth the small entrance fee. If it's not open, ring the bell on the door a few paces along the cloister.

Just behind the monastery is the most fantastic **chocolateria** (daily 10am–5pm) where you can indulge your wildest sweet-toothed fantasies with an eye-popping selection of the finest chocolates, all of which are produced in the factory to the rear of the shop.

There are a couple of places to **sleep** and **eat** along the road between Podčetrtek and the monastery; approximately midway between these two points, the roadside *Gostišče Haler* pub and brewery (Pivovarna Haler) brews its own beer (*Haler Pivo*) on the premises, the perfect foil for its bistro, which features a selection of beer dishes alongside a more sophisticated à la carte menu (both daily until 11pm). Located in a separate building just to the rear of the pub, the *Pension Katja* (Ⓣ03/812-1202; ❸) has some very smart, modern rooms and apartments; there's also a small basement swimming pool, sauna and gym.

The *Gostišče Amon* (Ⓣ03/818-2480; Ⓦwww.amon.si), 1.5km further on, was one of the first private **wineries** in the country and is renowned for its Laški Rizling and Chardonnay; tasting costs around 800SIT for four or five wines. The **restaurant** is of the highest order – almost all the fittings and fixtures have been recycled from old wine presses, hence the chunky oak tables and chairs. They've also got four great-value rooms (❸), each of which overlooks the nine-hole golf course (Ⓣ03/810-9066; 4700SIT for 18 holes). Aside from golf, there's a stable here, with horse-riding available (trail riding, lessons and, for kids, ponies) between April and October.

If you don't have your own wheels, you'll have to walk, which is no great hardship as it's a very enjoyable short trek. If you'd like to do more extensive **walking**, pick up a copy of the 1:18,000 *Podčetrtek* map from the information office, which maps out several local walks between one and four hours long, one of which is the walk to Olimje.

From Celje to Maribor

There are several worthwhile sites between Celje and Maribor, most of which are easily reached by public transport. Just off the main highway, the charming little town of **Slovenske Konjice** lies close to the enchanting ruins of **Žiče Monastery**, whilst, a few kilometres further on, the small spa town of **Zreče** is the jumping off point for the ski and sports resort of **Rogla**, which nestles at the heart of the **Pohorje Massif** mountain range.

Slovenske Konjice

Nineteen kilometres northeast of Celje, just off the main highway to Maribor, is **SLOVENSKE KONJICE**, the self-styled town of "Wine and Flowers", owing to recent, triumphant efforts in Europe-wide floral competitions and a strong tradition of wine-making. The centre of town is shaped by Stari trg, a lovely, gently inclining street framed by a neat kernel of yellow, apricot and lime-green townhouses, and bisected by the Gospodična ("Miss") stream, itself straddled by a series of tiny wooden bridges.

At no. 15, the **Riemer Gallery** (Mestna Galerija Riemer; Mon–Fri 10am–6pm, Sat 10am–noon; 300SIT) is a private collection of art and period furniture amassed by wealthy local businessman Franc Riemer. As impressive as his collection of Old Masters, paintings by Ivana Kobilica, and sketches by Rihard Jakopič are, the show stealer is a fourteenth-century fresco of the Crucifixion, retrieved from Žiče Monastery in 1996, and held to be the only fresco from the monastery still in existence. Fifty metres further up the street on the opposite side is a **wine shop** (*vinoteka*), where you can partake in some tasting (around 600SIT for three wines) – contact the tourist office (see below) first.

There's tasting of a very different kind further north at the **Trebnik Manor House** (Dvorec Trebnik; Mon–Fri 8am–6pm, Sat 10am–6pm), located just beyond the **Church of St George** (Cerkev Sv Jurij). The one renovated part of this otherwise dilapidated building has been transformed into a herbal shop and gallery, displaying and selling a range of herbal products such as honey, oils, creams, shampoos and brandies, all of which have been cultivated from the beautifully tended herb garden to the rear of the manor. A brandy-tasting session – an acquired palette is most definitely required – costs 700SIT, and includes herbal bread. In the barn next door to the shop sits a fine, but poorly maintained, collection of old carriages; ask at the shop if you wish to have a look. From behind the manor house, it's a two-hour walk up a marked path to **Konjiška Gora**, from where there is a superlative panorama of the town and vineyards below, and the Pohorje Massif in the distance.

Practicalities

The **bus station** is located on Liptovska cesta, from where it's just a couple of minutes' walk north to Mestni trg and beyond (across the bridge) to the centre of town, which is essentially the main street Stari trg. About two-thirds of the way along Stari trg, at no. 29, is the **tourist office** (Mon, Tues & Thurs 7am–3pm, Wed 7am–4pm, Fri 7am–2pm, Sat 9am–1pm; ⓣ05/759-3110), a friendly little place, although there's scant information available. The town's one **hotel** is the rather plain and not particularly good-value *Dravinja* (ⓣ05/759-3110, ⓦwww.hotel-dravinja@siol.net ❺), though its location by the bridge and river on Mestni trg does compensate somewhat.

The town's one truly outstanding **restaurant**, the *Zlati Grič*, is a fifteen-minute walk north of the centre, planted amongst the impossibly lush Škalce vineyards; the Slovene food and wine on offer is of a high standard, but really it's a place to come and enjoy the setting. To get here from Mestni trg, walk through the small park-like area to the traffic lights, cross the road and walk up Škalska cesta, from where it's a further ten minutes. There are few other places to **eat or drink** in this quiet town, but the *Beli Konj* (White Horse) at the lower end of Stari trg (no. 6) is a colourful and energetic pub; whilst the smart little *Patriot* bar, in the **Youth Club** (Mladinski Center) north of Stari trg behind the fire station at Žička 4, occasionally has live music at weekends; they've also got **Internet access** (free) upstairs in the club proper. A more laid-back alternative is the elegant *Tattenbach* coffee house next to the Riemer Gallery (Mon–Sat 7am–10pm, Sun 8am–4pm).

Žiče Monastery

Fringed by ancient woodland in the isolated splendour of the Valley of St John, some 12km southwest of Slovenske Konjice, lie the mist-swathed ruins of **Žiče Monastery** (Žička Kartuzija; March–Nov Mon–Fri 10am–6pm, Sat & Sun 9am–7pm; 350SIT). Founded around 1160 by Otakar III of Traungau, the margrave of Styria, Žiče was the first of four Carthusian monasteries to be chartered on Slovenian territory, and fairly prospered until its dissolution under the reforms of Joseph II in 1782. Although part of the complex has been renovated, the rest is pretty much as it was, including the twelfth-century Romanesque **Church of St John the Baptist**, now hollowed out – its vaults and roof collapsed around 1840 – but still exuding a befitting sense of authority. A healing place of repute during the thirteenth century, Žiče remained an important medicinal centre for locals and travellers alike until the monastery's dissolution, and there's now a reconstructed **apothecary** on the site of the old one, offering the opportunity to sample some powerful homemade herbal brandies. The small, grass-covered mounds just behind the pharmacy were the former monks' cells.

Standing at the entrance to the monastery is the *Gostišče Gastuž*, dating from 1464 and reputedly one of the oldest guesthouses in Central Europe; it's now a very good **restaurant**, which also has excellent wines (Wed–Fri 10am–7pm, Sat & Sun 10am–8pm). Getting to Žiče entails taking a local bus from Slovenske Konjice to the village of **Špitalič**, 2km shy of the monastery, and then it's a gentle walk from here.

Zreče

From Slovenske Konjice hourly buses make the short five-kilometre journey north to **ZREČE**, a relatively recent addition to the country's growing number of spa resorts. The spa aside, there's nothing else of interest in town, though you may find yourself passing through if Rogla and the Pohorje Massif are your intended destinations. The **Terme Zreče spa** has an excellent complement of facilities, including classy indoor and outdoor pools (daily 9am–9pm, Sat until 10pm; 1400SIT for 3hr, 1700SIT for a day ticket), with temperatures ranging between 28 and 36°C, sauna and solarium facilities, gym and a Thai massage centre (Mon–Sat 10am–noon & 3–9pm).

The spa's **hotel**, the *Dobrava* (ⓣ03/757-6000; ❺), is a thoroughly modern, slickly run place; they've also got apartments (❺–❻) sleeping two to four people. Aside from the *Dobrava*, there are a couple of places opposite the **bus station**, itself located adjacent to the spa: the pension-like *Zvon* (ⓣ03/757-3600; ❻), and the almost identical *Smogavc* next door (ⓣ03/757-6600; ❺); both offer good-looking rooms with all mod cons. The *Gostišče Jančič* in front of these two hotels has a good daily *Malica* menu. There's a small **tourist office** two minutes' walk from the bus station inside the small shopping mall at Cesta na Roglo 11j (Mon–Fri 7am–3pm, Wed until 5pm, Thurs until 2pm, Sat 9am–noon; ⓣ03/759-0470).

The two best **places to stay**, however, are located out of town, hence really only worth considering if you've got your own transport; 3km north of Zreče on the road up to Rogla, in the tiny hamlet of **Loška Gora**, the *Hotel Pod Roglo* (ⓣ03/757-6800, ⓔhotel.podroglo@siol.net; ❺), has beautifully warm, colourful rooms fitted with plush carpets and large beds; what's more, they brew their own beer on the premises, which complements the large pizzeria superbly – at weekends there's live music. A couple of kilometres southwest of town in **Križevec**, the *Urška* tourist farm at 11a (ⓣ03/576-2180, ⓦwww.tk.urska@siol.net; ❷) is a lovely rural retreat, and the home cooking is delicious. There are several other tourist farms scattered around the hills between Zreče and Rogla.

Rogla and the Pohorje Massif

From Zreče the road zigzags steeply for 16km to **Rogla** (1517m), one of Slovenia's premier ski and sports resorts sited on the eastern margins of the

Pohorje Massif, a fifty-kilometre-long, sparsely populated back, arcing between Dravograd in the west and Maribor in the east. Geologically, the massif is an extension of the Alps, although physically it's quite different, a series of gently rounded ridges – few peaks top 1500m – riddled with peat marshes and small swampy lakes, and where the only settlements are isolated farmsteads and tiny upland churches. Once where the massif was home to sawmills, forges and *glažute* (glass-making workshops), it is tourism that now rules the roost, with ski runs, hiking paths and other recreational facilities complemented by a good number of mountain huts and tourist farms.

Rogla's extensive **sports facilities** – an outdoor stadium, huge sports hall and swimming pool – are frequently used by Slovenian and Croatian Olympic teams, but all are available for use by the general public when they're not in residence; some sample prices (hourly rates) include: badminton 2300SIT; tennis 3200SIT; squash 1500SIT (45min); gym 1200SIT; and swimming 600SIT. For all these facilities, though, it's **skiing** that dominates, for more on which see the box below. The resort's one **hotel** is the comfortable *Planja* (ⓣ03/757-7100; ❺), a decent place that also has cheaper rooms in an annexe, as well as modern chalets (❹) sleeping up to four. Its comely little restaurant, the *Stara Koča*, serves up wholesome, filling meals, and there's also good food at the *Koča na Jurgovem* mountain hut, sited at the top of the Jugovo chairlift a few kilometres east of the *Planja*. In winter there's a **ski bus** from Zreče to Rogla (and return) six times a day.

Hiking and skiing in Pohorje

Rogla, in the heart of the Pohorje Massif, and **Mariborsko Pohorje**, further east on the doorstep of Maribor, are consistently rated two of the best **ski and snowboard** resorts in the country. Rogla has around 12km of ski trails, most of which are suited to intermediate skiers, though there are a few slopes for the less experienced. You can also hire **snowmobiles** (with a guide) here. At 1347m, Mariborsko Pohorje is a slightly lower mountain range, but has one of the largest capacities of all Slovenia's ski resorts, with more than 60km of trails, almost half of which are beginners' slopes. It also claims to have the longest night-time (floodlit) slope in Europe. Moreover, it possesses far more tourist facilities, particularly accommodation, than Rogla. The ski season at both resorts usually runs from December to March, though the presence of snow cannons along the main runs ensures that it's possible to ski throughout this period, regardless of snowfall. **Day passes** at both cost around 4800SIT and **weekly passes** around 22,000SIT. The main piste at Mariborsko Pohorje is also the venue for the women's World Cup slalom race, the "Golden Fox", at the end of January, an event not to be missed if you're in the region around this time.

Skiing aside, the massif also has some excellent **hiking**. The trails on Rogla are numbered from PP1 to PP7, and range in distance from just a few kilometres to more than thirty. If you're short on time, there's a nice and easy 45-minute walk north from the *Planja* hotel to the *Koča na Pesku* mountain hut (1386m), which has accommodation and food available year-round (ⓣ03/759-2761). From here you can either continue northwest to the beautiful **Lovrenc Marsh Lakes** (Lovrenška jezera; 1hr), and then further onwards to *Ribniška Koča* hut (1507m; 2hr), where there's more accommodation; or east to **Osankarica** (1193m) and the *Dom na Osankarica*, where there are refreshments only – the trail continues east to the **Black Lake** (Črno jezero), one of the largest lakes in the massif. The 1:25,000 *Zreče* map, available from the tourist office in Zreče (see p.283), marks out a number of hiking and cycle routes around both Zreče and Rogla.

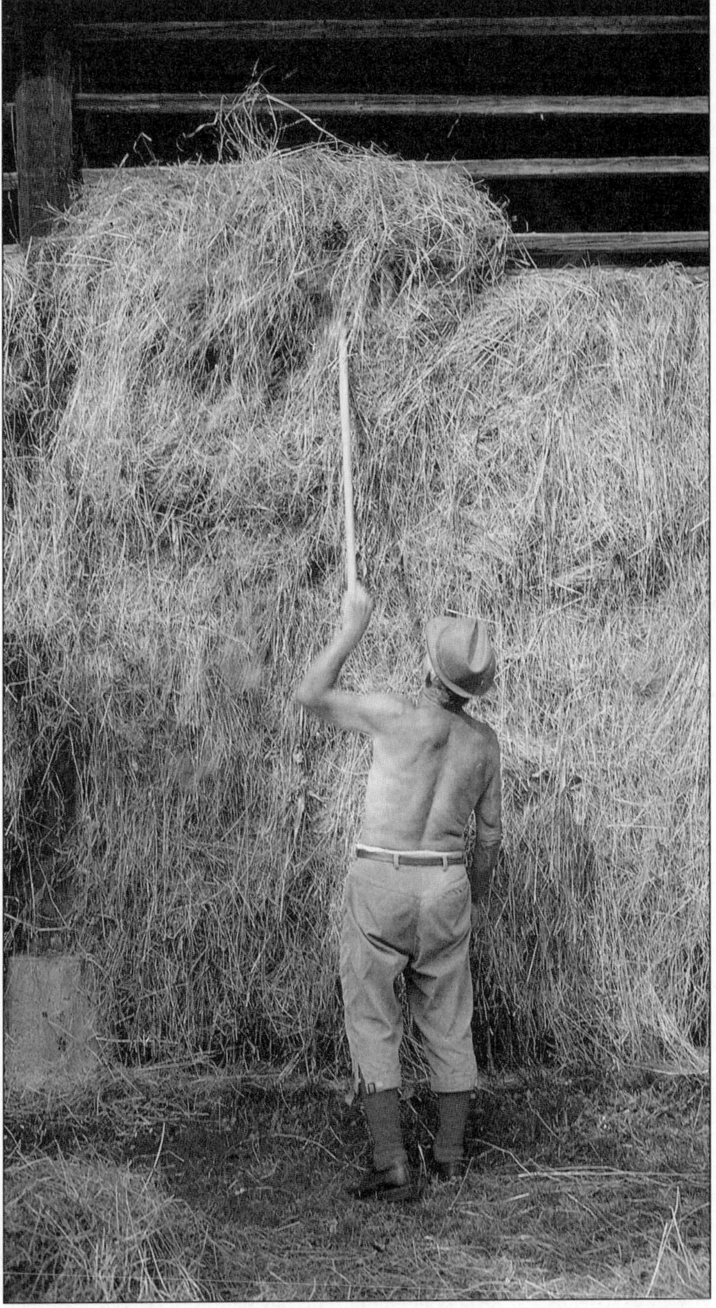

△ Taking hay from a hayrack

Maribor and around

Located at the easternmost foothills of the Pohorje Massif, **MARIBOR** is Slovenia's second city of culture, commerce and education, but with a still modest population of around 100,000, about a third that of the capital. Despite lacking Ljubljana's sophistication and cultural appeal, there's still much to enjoy here, and the city's prevailing industrial sprawl is countered by an incoherent, yet appealing, Austrianate old core, patchworked with an elegant confection of architectural styles, colourful squares and streets, monuments and churches. But if you tire of the city, there's plenty to see and do on the outskirts, including a couple of enjoyable wine roads to the north, and the Pohorje Massif to the south, where it's possible to partake in any number of activities.

Some history

Populated with smaller settlements in the **Bronze Age**, the seeds of present-day Maribor were sown around the **twelfth century**, when the Carinthian duke, Spanheim, instructed a fort to be built (known as Marchburg, later Marburg and eventually Maribor) on Piramida, a low hill to the north of town, in order to protect it from Hungarian raiders from Pannonia. During the **fourteenth century**, a large and diligent Jewish population established important commercial ties with major European cities, Milan, Prague and Dubrovnik, though their **fifteenth-century** expulsion from the city, in 1497, in addition to Hungarian and Turkish sieges, fires and recurrent plague epidemics, led to a sudden and long-term decline in the city's fortunes. The key to the city's next major revival in the **nineteenth century** was the arrival of the rail line from Vienna in 1846 (which would later be extended to Ljubljana and Trieste), together with the relocation of the seat of the Lavantine diocese from St Andraz in Austria to Maribor, and the establishment of a raft of important cultural and financial institutions.

Ongoing nationalist struggles between the city's German and Slovene populations towards the end of the nineteenth century culminated in outright warfare at the tail end of **World War I** following German attempts to incorporate the city into Austrian lands. However, a resounding defeat for the Germans at the hands of the Slovenes, led by General Rudolf Maister, resulted in the incorporation of Slovenian Styria into Slovene lands, and thereby the establishment of the present-day border with Austria. Despite Maribor's assimilation into the **Kingdom of Yugoslavia**, German expansionist tendencies continued and the city eventually succumbed to German forces in **World War II** in 1941, with the mass expulsion of thousands of Slovenes and the demolition of nearly half of the city's buildings. As one of the most industrialized cities in the former Yugoslavia, Maribor was amongst the hardest hit by the **break-up of the federation** in 1991, the sudden loss of important inter-republic trade resulting in tremendous economic hardship and high levels of unemployment. The city is today more or less back on track again, thanks largely to a booming local wine trade and its proximity to one of the largest ski resorts in the country.

Arrival and information

The **bus** and **train** stations are handily located just 400m apart on Partizanska cesta, from where it's just a ten-minute walk into the city centre. The latter has a useful information centre (Mon–Sat 6.15am–6.15pm, Sun 8.30am–6.15pm), as well as left-luggage lockers (400SIT). The bus station ticket office is open Monday to Friday 8am–7pm, and Saturday 8am–2pm.

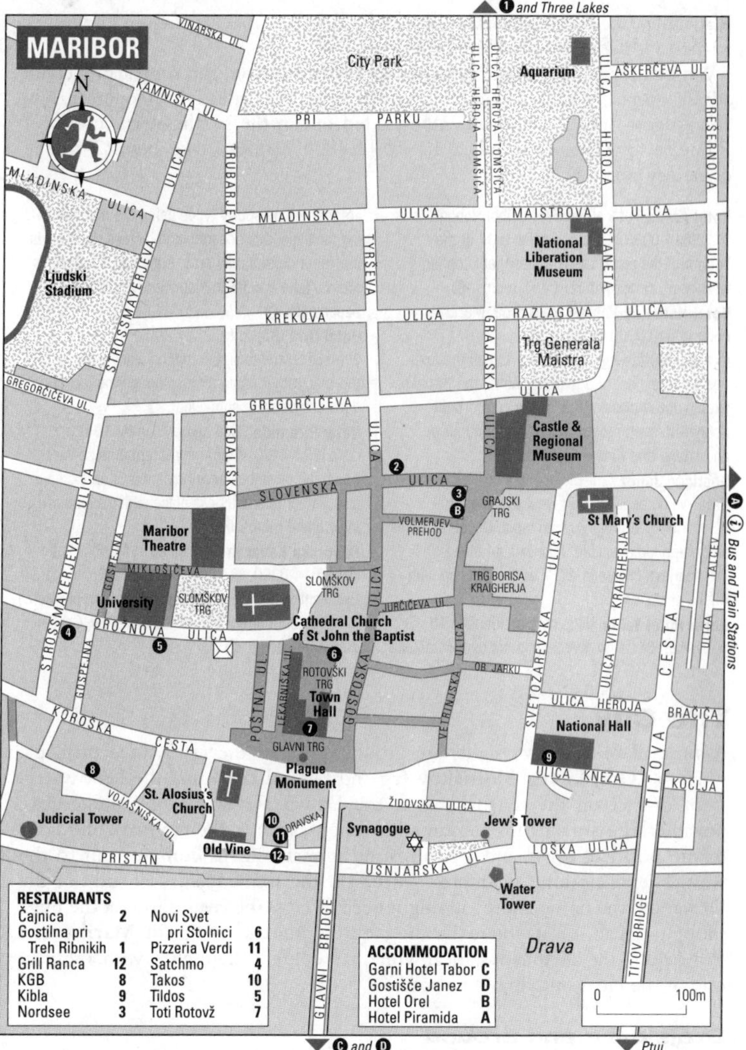

The **tourist office** is located directly opposite the train station at Partizanska cesta 47 (Mon–Fri 9am–6pm, Sat 9am–1pm; ⓣ02/234-6611, ⓦwww.maribor-tourism.si). The main city **post office** is at Slomškov trg 10 (Mon–Fri 8am–7pm, Sat 8am–1pm), whilst there's another at the rail station.

Accommodation

There's not a great selection of **places to stay** in the city itself, but there are further possibilities in Zgornje Radvanje, at the foot of the **Maribor Pohorje** ski resort 7km southwest of town; for purposes of convenience these are included along with the city hotels here. To get to any of the places in Zgornje

Radvanje, take bus #6 to its last stop, which is the cable car station. The hotels at the top of Pohorje itself are listed on p.294.

Whilst they cannot book **private accommodation**, the tourist office can advise on places to stay. The city's **youth hostel** (Dijaški Dom), open in July and August only, is inconveniently located out in the southeastern suburb of Pobrežje at Železnikova ulica 12 (ⓣ02/480-1710; ❷); take bus #3 to the cemetery stop.

Hotel Arena Pot k Mlinu 57, Maribor Pohorje ⓣ02/614-0950. A great location right at the bottom of the piste, this is a reasonable option with large, perfectly fine, if dull, rooms. ❺

Hotel Habakuk Pohorska cesta 59, Maribor Pohorje ⓣ02/300-8100, ⓔhabakuk.@termemb.si. Featuring all the luxuries you'd expect of a five-star hotel, the *Habakuk* simply oozes class; fantastically comfortable, richly furnished rooms, indoor and outdoor pools, and sauna and fitness facilities. ❾

Gostišče Janez Ciril-Metodova 4 ⓣ02/420-4404. Great-value pension 1km west of the centre across the river near Koroški most. Doubles, triples and one quad available. Take bus #4 along Valvasorjeva ulica and alight at the junction with Ruška cesta. ❹

Garni Hotel Tabor Ulica heroja Zidanška 18 ⓣ02/421-6410, ⓦwww.hoteltabor.podhostnik.si. Frequented by sporty types using the neighbouring facilities, this decent place, across the river in the Tabor district, has boxy, but clean, modern rooms. Take bus #6 to stop Tabor (direction Uzpenjača). ❹

Hotel Orel Grajski trg 3 ⓣ02/250-6700, ⓔorel@termemb.si. Overpriced place with run-of-the-mill, rather dank, rooms, though the location does compensate somewhat. ❻

Hotel Piramida Ulica heroja Šlandra 10 ⓣ02/234-4400, ⓔpiramida@termemb.si. Very much the city's business hotel, this is an expensive, rather characterless place with disappointingly bland rooms. ❼

Pohorska Kavarna Ob Ribniku 1, Maribor Pohorje ⓣ02/614-0200, ⓔpohorska.kavarna@potocnik.si. Excellent-value, clean, bright and modern pension located about 500m before the cable car. Good coffee house too. ❸

The City

Almost all of the city's sights are grouped around the city's three principal squares – **Grajski trg**, **Slomškov trg** and **Glavni trg** – and the Lent waterfront district on the north bank of the **Drava River**. Beyond these areas, possibilities exist for more leisurely diversions, such as the city park and lakes to the north of town, and a small island retreat and spa complex out to the west. There's nothing of interest to see on the residential, south side of the Drava, and the only reason you might need to cross the river is to visit the huge shopping mall, or if you're heading out to the ski resort in **Mariborska Pohorje**. Wine aficionados, meanwhile, can content themselves with a visit to one of the city's outlying wine roads.

Grajski trg and around

Although not especially interesting itself, the best place to start a walking tour of the city is **Grajski trg** (Castle Square), so-named after the fifteenth-century town **castle** on the square's northeastern corner. Inside the entrance to the castle (and the museum – see below), on Grajska ulica, is a wonderfully fanciful Rococo staircase, ornamented with sculptures by Jožef Straub, more of whose work is contained within, whilst the ceiling is strewn with stuccoed swirls and vines.

Most of the castle's rooms are now taken up with the **Maribor Regional Museum** (Muzej Pokrajinski; Tues–Sun 10am–5pm; 500SIT); there are excellent guiding handouts in English in each room. Following the standard display of archeological bits and bobs, the ethnological section presents some fine rafts and cargo boats – of the type that used to dock along the Drava waterfront in the nineteenth century – beautifully painted chests and wardrobes, beehive panels, and the famous *pust* masks from Ptuj. No less absorbing is the cultural history section, and in particular its voluminous collection of costumes representing the multifarious regions of Slovenia – the most celebrated piece of attire, however, is a military uniform belonging to Tito.

The upper floor is mostly given over to the history of Maribor, and although much of it is not that stimulating, the displays of locally produced wrought ironwork and glassware are worth a lengthy pause. There's some impressive artwork here too, the best of which is the group of smooth humanist sculptures by Jožef Straub (1721–1783), Slovenia's leading exponent of Baroque sculpture. Facing the square, the **castle chapel** (Grajski kapeli), built some time around 1660, is a copy of the Santa Casa church in Loreto, its blackened interior so small it barely seats twenty people.

Looming large over the square to the east is the massive red-brick **Franciscan Church of St Mary** (Cerkev Sv Marija; daily 6am–noon & 3–7.45pm), commissioned by Viennese architect Richard Jordan in 1903 and built at the same time as the Franciscan monastery complex behind. The only concession to grandeur inside the capacious and gloomy interior is the high altar, featuring four statues in niches and some contemporary, almost cartoonish, wall paintings, completed by Catholic priest and artist Stane Kregar, one of Slovenia's foremost post-World War II church painters.

Heading south, Grajski trg funnels down to Vetrinjska ulica, a busy pedestrianized thoroughfare whose houses are now mainly ramshackle and medieval, occasionally slicked up as shops and stores but mainly dark and crumbling – memories of an earlier, more fanciful past, when the street served as a major route for traffic en route from Vienna to Ljubljana; the standout building is the richly stuccoed, mint-coloured Vetrinje Mansion at no. 16, dating from 1725.

Back on the square, Grajski trg merges into Trg Svobode, a large, nondescript space containing little of note save for an ugly, bulbous-shaped bronze memorial to Partisans killed during World War II, and the Vinag wine cellar on the east side, at no. 3 (see p.294). Trg Svobode segues into grassy Maistrov trg, from where it's another five-minute walk to the **National Liberation Museum** (Muzej Narodne Osvoboditve; Mon–Fri 8am–6pm, Sat 9am–noon; 300SIT), housed in a handsome late nineteenth-century terracotta and grey villa at Ulica heroja Tomšiča 5. The most interesting exhibits, of what is otherwise a slapdash offering, are those items pertaining to Slovenia's struggle for independence in 1991, including objects left by the retreating Yugoslav army and the jacket worn by Igor Bavčar, head of police during the Ten-Day war.

The City Park

The broad, lamp-lined promenade across the road from the museum marks the entrance to the **City Park** (Mestni Park), a large, well-groomed expanse of greenery laid out in 1872 and carved up by concrete strips of pathway. For kids, there's a rather downbeat **aquarium-terrarium** (Akvarij; Mon–Fri 8am–7pm, Sat & Sun 9am–noon & 2–7pm; 550SIT) located on the park's east side, its tanks filled with the usual suspects, including fish, snakes, lizards, turtles and spiders. Beyond here the park tapers towards the slender chain of the **Three Lakes** (Trije Ribniki). If you fancy a slightly more strenuous walk, take the path that peels off of Ribniška ulica (the road skirting the park's eastern side), and continue uphill through the almost vertically pitched vineyard to **Piramida** (386m), at the top of which is a tiny chapel; from here there are fine views of the bright red and terracotta-coloured rooftops of the city, and the broad slopes of the Pohorje mountains in the distance.

Slomškov trg

Named after St Anton Slomšek (see box, below), **Slomškov trg** is the largest, greenest and grandest of the city's three squares, endowed with some venerable old buildings and site of Maribor's premier ecclesiastical monument. The lumpish **Cathedral Church of St John the Baptist** (Cerkev Sv Janez Krstnik) was originally built as a single-naved Romanesque structure in the twelfth century, though later modifications gave it its present, predominantly Gothic and Baroque appearance. The highlight of what is otherwise a rather plain interior is the splendid Gothic presbytery, featuring exquisitely carved choir stalls inlaid with reliefs showing scenes from the life of the patron saint; take a look up, too, at the splendid arch. The north side **Chapel of the Holy Cross** holds the tomb of the recently beatified Slomšek, while the stained-glass windows depicting images of Pope John Paul II were crafted on occasion of his second visit to Maribor, in 1999 – his first visit was in 1996. There's further homage to Slomšek in front of the church, in the form of a large bronze statue.

The neo-Renaissance bulk at the square's western end is the former City Savings Bank, now the **university building**. Of a similar ilk, but appreciably smaller, is the splendid, pea-green-coloured **post office** (Pošta Slovenije) building at no. 10 on the square's south side. Although aesthetically less pleasing, the one other building of note is the **National Theatre**, adjacent to the university on the north side. From the square's southeastern corner, a narrow path leads into the lovely arcaded courtyard, Rotovški trg, and then into Glavni trg.

Glavni trg and around

Bounded on one side by a sweep of elegant buildings, and on the other by one of the city's busiest thoroughfares, cobbled **Glavni trg** (Main Square) is a fine-looking Renaissance square that functioned as the city's market area during the Middle Ages. Standing in the centre of the square, and arguably one of the finest monuments of its type in Central Europe, the **Plague Monument** was originally raised in 1681 as a memorial to the thousands that perished during the great plague. This second version was erected in 1743, its smooth column topped with a gold-leaf statue of Mary, and its base with six saintly intercessors, the entire project masterfully sculpted by Straub.

Opposite, at no. 9, the Renaissance **town hall** (Mestna hiša) was originally built in 1515, though reworked several times over before it attained its present

Anton Slomšek

Bishop, poet and scribe, **Anton Martin Slomšek** was born in the small parish of Ponikva, near Celje, in 1800. Ordained in 1824, just three years into his theological studies, Slomšek took his first Mass in Olimje that same year, before returning to his studies in Celovec. He spent the next few years devoting his time to the development of Slovene schooling – in particular Sunday schools – in rural areas, and writing prayer and hymn books; by the time of his death, Slomšek had had some fifty books published.

His greatest achievement, however, was to transfer the seat of the Lavantine diocese from St Andraz in Austria, to Maribor, thus uniting all Styrian Slovenes in one diocese, as well as effecting an upgrade in the status of the parish church to a cathedral. Slomšek was also instrumental in setting up the Catholic Society of St Hermagoras (Družba Sv Mohorja), a publishing house established in 1851 in order to help Slovenes read and write. His second great contribution was the establishment of Maribor's Theological High School in 1859, the forerunner to today's university. Slomšek died in 1862, and was beatified by the pope in September 1999.

appearance, featuring an exquisite Venetian stone balcony emblazoned with a two lion relief and the city coat of arms; underneath and to the right of the town hall is *Toti Rotovž*, one of the city's best restaurants. Recessed between two buildings on the opposite side of the road is the former Jesuit **Church of St Aloysius**.

A short walk east of Glavni trg, **Židovska ulica** (Jewish street) was the centre of the Jewish ghetto during the Middle Ages, its focal point the now beautifully restored **synagogue** (Sinagoga; Mon–Fri 7.30am–2.30pm) at no. 4. The first Jewish presence in the city was recorded around 1290, at around the same time the synagogue was built, but, following a decree in 1496 banishing Jews from Maribor, the synagogue was converted into a Catholic Church. It operated as such until it was closed down under the reforms of Emperor Joseph II at the end of the eighteenth century; thereafter it functioned variously as a factory, warehouse and residential quarters. A decade-long renovation programme, during which four wooden boxes containing the remains of ancient skeletons were unearthed, has restored the synagogue to something like its former glory, and it's now used as a cultural centre and exhibition venue.

Erected in 1465, the **Jews' Tower** (Židovski stolp), just across from the synagogue, was once an integral part of the city's defence walls, as was the immaculately restored sixteenth-century **Water Tower** (Vodni stolp) down by the river. The former is now a photographic gallery (Mon–Fri 10am–7pm, Sat 10am–1pm), the latter an excellent *vinoteka* (see p.294).

Lent

Across the busy main street, Koroška ulica, several alleyways slope down to the **Drava River** and the **Pristan** (Pier) district, or, as it's more commonly known, **Lent** (Port). Until the construction of the railways in the 1860s, the Drava was the city's principal transport artery, and Lent the main docking station for the hundreds of rafts and small cargo vessels (*šajka*) that would stop here en route to the Danube and the Black Sea. Today, it's a bustling promenade and *the* place to kick back with a beer on summer evenings.

Lent's star attraction, and the city's most celebrated symbol, is the 400-year-old **Vine** (Stara Trta), reputedly the world's oldest. The vine still yields the evocatively titled *Žametna Črnina* (Black Velvet), thirty-five litres of which are harvested each year, although, unfortunately, this is usually bottled up for visiting dignitaries. Two of the city's main events, the pruning of the vine, and its ceremonial harvesting, take place here in March and October respectively.

A five-minute walk further along the embankment stands the rotund, white-washed **Judicial Tower** (Sodni stolp), though this name is something of a misnomer given that it was erected as a defensive bastion in 1310; this present structure dates from 1830. Up behind the tower, Vojašniški ulica (Army Street) and Vojašniški trg (Army Square) – essentially one and the same – are scattered with a shabby fusion of half-wrecked buildings, one of which, the former **Minorite Church and Monastery**, once functioned as a barracks and warehouse, though it's now defunct and decaying. Just beyond here is Vodnikov trg and the city's open-air marketplace. The best views of Lent can be garnered from **Glavni most** (Main Bridge), an elegant, rich-red structure completed in 1913.

Terme Fontana and Maribor Island

About 3km west of the centre (bus #15), the **Terme Fontana** spa and recreation complex at Koroška cesta 172 (daily 9am–10pm; ⓣ02/234-4100; 1900SIT for 3hr, 2400SIT for the day), offers a raft of activities – swimming, sauna and solarium, gym facilities and aerobics. A further 1.5km along the road, a left turning leads to **Maribor island** (Mariborski Otok), a pleasant rambling and bathing spot in the summer; if you don't fancy taking to the Drava, there's a large outdoor pool in the centre of the island (daily June–Sept 9am–8pm; 800SIT).

Eating and drinking

What Maribor's **restaurant** scene may lack in quantity, it makes up for in quality, with a select core of excellent and diverse places to eat. On summer evenings, the **cafés and bars** of the Lent waterfront area spill out onto the street with the hectic atmosphere of a mass open-air bar. Otherwise, there are several excellent bar-cum-club places scattered elsewhere throughout town.

Restaurants

Nordsee Slovenska cesta 1. Cheap sit-down/take-away seafood place ideal for a lunchtime snack; portions, including none-too authentic fish and chips, from around 600SIT. Mon–Fri 9am–8pm, Sat 9am–2pm.

Novi Svet pri Stolnici Slomškov trg 5. In the style of a Dalmatian *konoba* (pub), this superb, homely restaurant – with fishing regalia strung along the walls – has fresh fish flown in daily from the Adriatic. They've a fine wine list too. Located on the corner of Slomškov trg and Rotovški trg. Mon–Sat 9am–midnight, Sun 9am–9pm.

Gostilna pri Treh Ribnikih Ribniška 3. Though not quite in the same league as *Novi Svet*, this inn-style restaurant out by the Three Lakes is, nevertheless, an enjoyable place to sample fish dishes. Good set menus (1500–4000SIT), including one for vegetarians. Daily 11am–10pm, Sun 11am–8pm.

Grill Ranca Dravska 10. Fast-food Balkan style, with a menu exclusively devoted to Serbian-style meats, such as Čevapčiči and Pljeskavica, all for less than 1000SIT. Very popular, so you may have to wait for a table. Mon–Sat 8am–11pm.

Takos Mesarski prehod 3. Cool, understated Mexican restaurant-cum-bar that takes on a clubby feel as the evening wears on. Located down a narrow passage on the south side of Glavni trg. Mon–Thurs 11am–midnight, Fri & Sat till 2am, Sun noon–5pm.

Toti Rotovž Rotovžski trg 9. Wonderfully original, top-class restaurant boasting three separate kitchens; Slovene (Pohorje steak, boar, chamois and pheasant); Japanese (sushi, vegetable tempura), and Thai (red/green curry, steamed shrimps, fish with coconut milk or chilli). The fantastic cellar bar (where you can also eat) rocks to live music at weekends. Mon–Fri 9am–midnight, Sat 9am–2am.

Pizzeria Verdi Dravska 8. Simple place, good pizzas in this small joint just around the corner from *Ranca*. Daily 10am–midnight.

Cafés, bars and clubs

Čajnica Slovenska 4. Charming and cosy tea-house with the full range of teas from around the world – you even get given a timer to tell you when your brew is ready. Mon–Fri 7am–10pm, Sat 9am–2pm & 5–10pm.

KGB Vojašniški trg. Located opposite the Minorite church on a ramshackle square just west of Lent, this brilliant underground cellar bar/club (check out the fantastic door as you enter) is the funkiest place in town, with occasional live music to boot. A guaranteed good time.

Kibla Ulica Kneza Kozlja 9 (inside the Narodni Dom). Cool and relaxing Internet café, bookshop and gallery all rolled into one (Mon–Fri 9am–10pm, Sat 4–10pm); there's also a more office-like centre (KIT) at Glavni trg 14, with printing and scanning facilities available (same times except Sat 9am–2pm).

Satchmo Strossmayerjeva ulica 6. Good-time jazz club with a top-class rota of gigs, though the summer programme is irregular – count on around one gig every two weeks during this period; otherwise, ideal for a bout of mellow drinking. ⓦwww.satchmo-klub.slon.net. Daily 7am–1am.

Tildos Slomškov trg. Energetic, youthful place just across from the university building; just a few paces along from *Tildos* is *Toto Café*, another good little drinking spot, though rather less raucous. Both open till 2am Fri & Sat.

Entertainment

The highly regarded **Slovenian National Theatre** (Slovensko Narodno Gledališče; SNG) on Slomškov trg stages a regular top-class diet of plays, opera and ballet; theatre tickets cost around 1500SIT, operatic and ballet performances around 2500–3000SIT (box office Mon–Fri 10am–3pm, Sat 10am–1pm and 1hr before each performance; Ⓦwww.sng-mb.si). The **Puppet Theatre** (Lutkovno gledališče) at Rotovški trg 1 (Ⓣ02/228-1970, Ⓦwww.lg-mb.si), puts on performances, in Slovene, every Sunday at 11am (600SIT; not in July & Aug).

Maribor Pohorje

From Maribor regular buses (#6; 780SIT) run to Zgornje Radvanje, 7km southwest of town at the foot of the popular ski resort, **Maribor Pohorje**. The last stop is at the **cable car** station (vzpenjača; April–Nov hourly 7am–9pm, Dec–March nonstop 7am–10pm; 1400SIT return), from where the small four-seater cabins transport skiers and hikers to the upper station (1040m) on **Bolfenk** in fifteen minutes. A short walk from the station, inside the completely renovated Church of St Bolfenk, which burnt down in 1952, is a small **tourist office** (Wed–Sun: May–Oct 9.30am–4.30pm, Nov–April 9.30am–3pm; Ⓣ02/603-4211, Ⓔbolfenk@siol.net). A couple of rooms in the church have been given over to exhibitions, one on the geology of the mountain, the other on the history of skiing on Pohorje.

Aside from **skiing** (see box, p.284), there are plenty more exciting activities on offer at the **Adrenaline Park** (Adrenalinski Park), which is not a park as such, but rather the collective name for a range of **activities** taking place at different locations around the mountain. Take your pick from mountain biking (1400SIT one hour, 4000SIT all day), summer tobogganing (1750SIT per hour), paintballing (3250SIT per person – minimum group of eight required), and horse-riding (2200SIT one hour, 9000SIT five hours). For more information on the park and the activities on offer, contact the Sports Centre (Športni

Maribor festivals

Maribor puts on a great range of festivals and events throughout the year, the biggest and best of which is the **Lent Festival** at the end of June/beginning of July. Second only to Ljubljana's Summer Festival in size, the festival kicks off with the colourful **Baptism of the Rafts** on the Drava River, followed by two weeks of street theatre, dance and ballet, and popular and serious music along the waterfront and in the squares and streets around town. The Lent Vine is the site of the **Pruning of the Vine** at the beginning of March, and the **Embrace of the Vine** in October, the latter entailing the harvesting of the grapes, though both are actually little more than excuses for a good old jolly-up.

Musically, there's the **National and International Choir Competition**, staged in the Maribor Union Hall in April, and at the end of August the **No Border Jam Festival**, a gathering of international punk acts, with performances in the Pekarna complex. For kids (and adults too), the **International Puppet Festival** in July features acts from all over Europe.

The **Golden Fox** (Zlata Lisica) slalom race on the slopes of Maribor Pohorje at the end of January is one of the country's major sporting occasions, attracting the world's top women skiers, not to mention some 25,000 spectators, for a weekend of top-class sporting action and lots of drinking. For more details of these events contact the Maribor tourist office (see p.287).

Maribor's wine roads

Maribor is one of the **Podravje** wine region's six wine-producing areas, and counts two **wine roads** with the **Kamnica** road to the west, and the more-visited **Malečnik** road to the east. Although a couple of reds are produced here (Žametna Črnina and Modri Pinot), this is overwhelmingly white wine territory – Laški and Renski Rizling, Chardonnay and Sauvignon, as well as the blended Mariborčan. One of the region's best wineries is at the *Joannes* tourist farm (the Protner winery) in the small hamlet of **Vodole** (no. 34), in Malečnik (Ⓣ02/473-2100), where you can also sample grilled blood sausages with sauerkraut. Although having your own wheels is certainly an advantage, it is feasible to walk at least part of these routes from Maribor. The 1:50,000 *Podravje* **map**, available from the tourist office in Maribor (see p.287), should help you negotiate your way around.

If you have neither the time nor the means to head out into the countryside, make your way to the **Vinag Wine Cellar** in Maribor at Trg Svobode 3, one of the largest cellars in Central Europe; its 2.5km of tunnels hold some 150 wooden, concrete and aluminium barrels, with a storage capacity of some seven million litres. For a **tour** of the cellar and a **tasting** session (1250SIT for four wines), you should contact them a day or two in advance (Ⓣ02/220-8111, Ⓔvinag@vinag.si). You can also try wines at their *vinoteka* (June–Sept Mon–Fri 4–10pm, Sat 10am–4pm, rest of year Mon–Fri noon–6pm, Sat same times), located in the Water Tower down by the river (see p.291). There's also a shop at the cellar (Mon–Fri 7.30am–7pm, Sat till 2pm).

Centre Pohorje) in Maribor, at Mladinska ulica 29 (Ⓣ02/220-8825; Ⓦwww.pohorje.org), or the tourist office at Bolfenk (see p.293). If you're planning on doing any hikes on Pohorje arm yourself with the 1:50,000 *Pohorje* **map**.

There's stacks of **accommodation** on top of the mountain: beside the cable car station the *Hotel Bellevue* (Ⓣ02/603-6506; ❷) is a grubby, hostel-style place, though just behind here the *Bolfenk Apartments* (Ⓣ02/603-6500; ❺) offer considerably more comfort; of a similar standard is the *Pension Martin* (Ⓣ02/603-6510), 500m southwest of the *Bolfenk*, which has both rooms (❷) and apartments (❻). Approximately 2km along the road to **Areh**, the *Aparthotel Pohorje* (Ⓣ02/603-6700, Ⓦwww.aparthotel-pohorje.com) offers a range of excellent apartments sleeping two to four people (❸–❺) – the restaurant here is by far the best place to eat; whilst, in Areh itself, a further 4km distant, there's the very basic *Hotel Areh* (Ⓣ02/603-5040; ❸), and the *Ruška koča* **mountain hut** (Ⓣ02/603-5046; ❶) just across the field and open all year. There's another hut, the *Mariborska koča* (Ⓣ02/603-2731), forty-five-minutes' walk from the church at Bolfenk (or one hour from *Ruška koča*).

Across from the mountain hut is the **Church of St Areh**, a simple, late seventeenth-century Baroque building, but which is now in a rather sad state of decrepitude; if it's closed, get the key from the hut. Hourly **buses** (9am–4pm; 370SIT) from Bolfenk to Areh depart from the car park next to the cable car station. Note that the road goes no further than Areh.

Ptuj and around

If you've only got time to visit one place in eastern Slovenia, make it **PTUJ**. Set 26km southeast of Maribor on the broad, flat Drava Plain between the Slovenske Gorice and Haloze hills, Ptuj is the oldest continuously settled site in Slovenia and is historically the most important settlement outside Ljubljana. The town and its surrounds are run through with two thousand years of history, its squares, streets and buildings rampant with architectural and archeological riches – Romanesque and medieval townhouses, built-in Roman monuments and tombstones, and ancient Mithra shrines. Moreover, Ptuj is home to the wonderful Shrovetide **Kurent Carnival**, Slovenia's most famous, and entertaining, folkloric event. Though not the easiest to reach without your own transport, two further places worth venturing to are the beautiful Church of the Holy Virgin in **Ptujska Gora**, and the **Haloze wine region**, bordering Croatia to the south.

Some history

Settled as far back as the late **Stone Age**, and later populated by the **Celts**, Ptuj began life around 69 AD, when a **Roman** legionary camp was established on the south bank of the Drava River. The result of expansion across the river was the creation of a self-governing, civilian entity called Poetovio, which functioned as a major staging post linking the Roman provinces of Pannonia and Noricum. Occupied successively by **Avars**, **Magyars** and then **Slavs**, Ptuj received its town rights in 977 AD, at which point it passed into the hands of the **Salzburg** archdiocese, whose members grew rich from the trade between Pannonia and the Italian peninsula. During the **Middle Ages**, the town developed around the solidly fortified castle, and established itself as a commercial centre of some considerable importance. Until the death of **Frederick XI** in 1438, the town remained under the jurisdiction of the Ptuj nobility, vassals of the Salzburg archdiocese, though subsequent incursions by the Turks, and wars

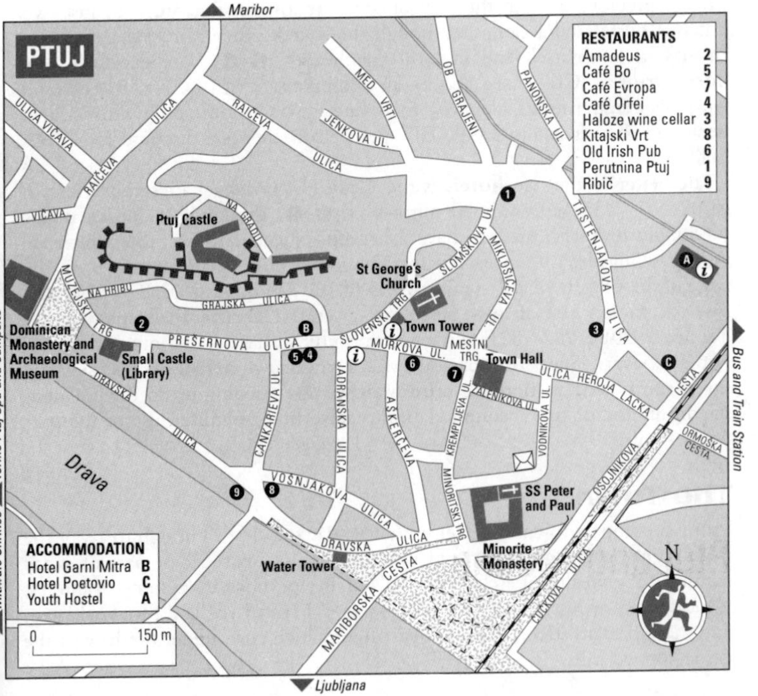

with the Hungarians, undermined the town's development. It recovered sufficiently to re-establish itself as a small provincial town, which it remains to this day.

Arrival and information

Ptuj's **train station** is 500m northeast of the centre on Osojnikova cesta, the **bus station** 200m nearer town on the same road. From both stations, continue down Osojnikova to the junction with ulica Heroja Lacka: a right turn here lands you straight in the centre. The distinctly unhelpful **tourist office** is at Slovenski trg 14 (Mon–Fri 9am–5pm, Sat 8am–noon; ⓣ02/779-6011, ⓦwww.ptuj-tourism.si), just across from the clocktower, which is where the office transfers to between June and September (same times). You're much better off heading to the welcoming **Centre for Free Time Activities** (CID), located just across from the bus station in the new, modern building at Osojnikova 9 (Mon–Thurs 8am– 8pm, Fri till 11pm, Sat 10am–1pm; ⓣ02/780-5540, ⓦwww.cid.si); they also offer **Internet access** (free), as does the town library at Prešernova ulica 35 (Mon–Fri 8am–7pm, Sat 8am–noon, 100SIT per hour). The **post office** is opposite the Minorite church at Vodnikova ulica 12 (Mon–Fri 7am–7pm, Sat 7am–1pm). **Bikes** can be hired (300SIT for one hour, 1600SIT for the day) from Terme Ptuj (see below), worth considering if you're without wheels and you'd like to visit either the Mithra Shrines (see p.301) or the Haloze wine region (see p.302).

Accommodation

There's precious little in the way of town **accommodation**, with just two hotels, a hostel and a campsite, though the tourist office can arrange **private rooms** in town itself and in local farmhouses (❷–❸). The excellent new **hostel** (run by CID – see above), at Osojnikova 9 (ⓣ02/780-5540, ⓔcsod.yhptuj@guest.arnes.si), has two-, four- and six-bed rooms, each with its own wash and shower facilities (4000SIT per person; there's a discount for IYHA holders).

The better of the two **hotels** is the *Garni Hotel Mitra* at Prešernova ulica 6 (ⓣ02/787-7455, ⓦwww.hotel-mitra-fm.si; ❺–❻), though its rooms are disappointingly ordinary; they do have a handful of larger rooms, too, which are worth paying the minimal extra for. The rather dour *Hotel Poetovio* is on the edge of the Old Town at Trstenjakova 13 (ⓣ02/779-8201, ⓕ02/779-8241; ❹). Two kilometres east of town across the river, the **Terme Ptuj spa** at Pot v Toplice 9 (ⓣ02/782-7821, ⓦwww.terme-ptuj.si) has an adjoining **campsite** (same tel. April–Sept) and spacious, well-furnished **apartments** (❻) sleeping up to six, as well as more basic **bungalows** (❸) sleeping up to three. Guests staying in any of this accommodation receive free, unlimited use of the spa's pools.

The Town

Ptuj is a compact town and a leisurely half-day should be enough to cover the main sights, although you could quite easily use up the best part of a day admiring the wealth of architectural detail. Pretty much everything of interest is located on or just off the two main squares, **Mestni trg** and **Slovenski trg**, and the old main street, **Prešernova ulica**, which curls under the base of the castle-topped hill.

Mestni trg and around

The ideal place to start is fourteenth-century **Mestni trg** (Town Square), a charming little square ringed by several stately buildings, the most prominent of which is the muddy-green **Town Hall**, a large neo-Gothic German pile raised in 1907 on the site of a late-Renaissance structure built by the Dominicans in 1571. Remnants of this earlier building are still just about visible in the form of a pair of dragon reliefs and a reclining nude on one of the corner prominences. The colourful, heavily stuccoed eighteenth-century **corner house**, opposite at no. 2, is now the popular *Café Evropa* (see p.300); above the entrance is a slender corner niche holding a statue of Mary with Child. At the heart of the square, the regulation **plague column** featuring a posturing St Florian dressed in military attire, is a copy, erected in 1993.

There's more architecture to admire along Krempljeva ulica – the street heading south from Mestni trg – notably at no. 1, whose peeling and cracked paintwork can't detract from some marvellous stuccowork, and in particular, the beehive relief between the windows on the prominence. At no. 7, the entrance to the old **Court House** is framed by a superb sixteenth-century Renaissance portal, either side of which sit a pair of lions holding escutcheons. West from Mestni trg, up Murkova ulica, check out the portal with griffins at no. 2, and the Patrician Mansion, opposite at no. 1. At its top end, Murkova ulica opens up into Slovenski trg.

The Minorite Church

Krempljeva ulica segues into Minoritski trg, site of the late thirteenth-century **Minorite Monastery** (Minoritski Samostan), which, unlike the majority of Slovenia's monasteries, wasn't closed down under the reforms of Emperor Joseph II at the end of the eighteenth century. Instead, it continued to prosper as a centre of learning until World War II, when it was confiscated by the Germans, then bombed by the Allies. The most feted part of the complex is the first-floor **summer refectory**, thanks to its thickly stuccoed ceiling, decorated by Italians Quadrio and Bettini, and oval and rectangular panels depicting scenes from the lives of the monastery's patrons, SS Peter and Paul. The prize exhibit in the monastery's richly stocked **library** is one of three original copies of the New Testament translated into Slovene by Primož Trubar in 1561 – the other two reside in the National Library in Ljubljana, and in Vienna.

Now in the final stages of a massive reconstruction programme, the **Church of St Peter and St Paul** was one of Slovenia's greatest ecclesiastical losses during World War II. The only part of the church to survive the raids was the presbytery (until the church is finished, probably by the end of 2005, the entrance is via the cloister inside the monastery), slightly shortened after the war in order to accommodate, rather insensitively, a post office on the site of the bombed out nave. Look out for the beautifully worked relief of a lamb on a keystone by the high altar, and the gargoyle-like animal heads on the exterior buttresses. The fifteen panels depicting Christ's Passion, and the stained-glass windows, were completed in 1989. If you wish to visit the monastery, contact the tourist office.

A short walk east along Dravska ulica – the street running parallel to the river – brings you to the bulky **Drava Water Tower** (Drava stolp), the largest of six former defensive towers that once formed the core of the town's fortification system; contrary to popular legend the stone balls built into the upper section of the walls were not those fired by Turks, but rather were placed there by local enthusiasts who had a penchant for this kind of architecture. The tower's two floors now function as the **France Mihelič Gallery** (Miheličeva galerija;

Tues–Sun 10am–1pm & 4–7pm; 200SIT), holding a selection of works by the graphic artist as well as other rotating exhibitions. During the Middle Ages Dravska ulica was known for its butcher's shops and tanneries, as indicated by the numerous portals embedded with the traditional tanners' symbols of a bucket with two crossed scrapers.

Slovesnki trg: the Town Tower and St George's Church

The centre of triangular-shaped **Slovenski trg** is dominated by the chunky, five-storey **Town Tower** (Mestni stolp), originally a sixteenth-century bell tower, then a seventeenth-century watchtower, before retiring gracefully in the eighteenth, when it was embellished with an onion bulb spire. Unfortunately, there are no plans as yet to open the tower up for viewing; elsewhere, though, the ground floor functions as the town's tourist office during the summer, whilst, to the rear, there's a small **gallery** with temporary exhibitions (Mon–Fri 10am–1pm & 4–6pm, Sat 9am–noon).

Embedded within the tower's lower reaches are numerous civil and military tombstones, relief votive slabs and sacrificial altars, though the most impressive tombstone is the freestanding **Orpheus Monument** in front of the tower (it's covered up in winter). Cut from Pohorje marble, the thick rectangular column commemorates Marcus Verus, former mayor of Poetovio, although during the Middle Ages it was used as a pillory, whereby petty criminals were chained to iron rings fastened to the bottom of the block – the poor state of the inscriptions is down to the wear and tear caused by the chains.

Outwardly austere, the twelfth-century Gothic **Church of St George** (Cerkev Sv Jurij) conceals some exceptional works of art. The first thing you see as you enter is a small glass cabinet on the left, containing a fragile and rather foppish-looking fourteenth-century wooden **sculpture of St George** nonchalantly slaying a dragon. From here proceed into the central nave, arranged with incongruously placed frescoes, altars and chapels, such as the **Crucifixion**, framed with an elaborately decorated banner, immediately to the left, and opposite, the **Altar of the Three Kings**, featuring a relief of the Coronation of St Mary inside a Baroque casing. The church's most renowned piece of work, **Laib's winged altar**, is positioned to the rear of the south aisle; dating from around 1460, the gilded paintings depict, in the centre, Mary's death, and to the left and right respectively, St Hieronymous with a church model in one hand and a book in the other, and St Mark writing the Gospel held by a lion. Of the several chapels dotted around the church, the most important is the **Chapel of Our Lady of Sorrows** at the end of the north aisle, the centerpiece of which is a fifteenth-century stone pietà sculpture. Just to the right of the chapel, a splendid, high lancet-arch fronts the bright fourteenth-century cross-vaulted presbytery, and a magnificent long choir, lined either side by two long rows of oak-wood pews ornamented with figures of animals.

Prešernova ulica

The Old Town's central artery, **Prešernova ulica**, is an attractive, peaceful thoroughfare, lined with tightly packed ranks of medieval townhouses, almost every single one furnished with a Renaissance stone portal or some other beautifully crafted feature. For starters take a look at house no. 1, whose corner prominence is supported by a so-called Parlerian mask, a black painted head of a grinning, curly-haired man; and, opposite, at no. 4, the Romanesque Bratonič house, the oldest tenement along the street. Just beyond here, take a quick look down **Jadranska ulica**, and in particular nos. 4 and 6, the facades of which are decorated with *Kurent*-style masks worked in flat relief (see box p.300).

Back on Prešernova, beyond the colourful neo-Baroque *Garni Hotel Mitra* at no. 6, the house at no. 16 is notable for some marble fragments jutting out of the passageway wall, which, on closer inspection, reveal themselves to be parts of dedication blocks or tombstones – there are more complete blocks embedded into the back wall of the run-down courtyard. On the opposite side of the road, at no. 27, take a peek inside the courtyard, where there's another black marble relief, this one of a prostrate, headless lion. The building on the corner of Prešernova and Cafova ulica used to be the **Small Castle** (Mali Grad), and the seat of the lords of Ptuj who held their court here; it now functions as the town library.

The Dominican monastery

A few paces on from the Small Castle, the **Dominican monastery** (Dominikanski Samostan) stands in a small park-like area on Muzejski trg, a mustardy building hung with spidery stuccowork and pocked with five niches containing statues of saints. Unlike the Minorite monastery less than 500m away, the Dominican monastery, founded in 1230, was forced to disband as part of Joseph II's reforms in 1786, after which time it was used alternately as a barracks and a residential building, before eventually falling into a state of disrepair.

The monastery is now home to the town's **Archeological Museum** (daily: May to mid-Oct 9am–6pm; July & Aug 9am–6pm plus Sat & Sun 9am–8pm; mid-Oct to Nov 9am–5pm; 600SIT), an impressive hoard of archeological treasures held within several separate areas of the building. Begin with the monastery's gloriously dishevelled **cloisters** – painted with early fourteenth-century frescoes (restored during the interwar period) and vaulted around a century later – and which are now cluttered with an array of statuary and fragments, some of which were brought across from the demolished Minorite church after World War II. The **small archeological collection** on the upper floor comprises a fabulous store of Celtic and Roman grave finds, mostly urns and vessels, but also gold jewellery, exquisite bronze and clay statuettes, and oil lamps. The **lapidarium**, meanwhile, contains a matchless collection of marble and sandstone sarcophagi, statues and busts, mosaic floors and beautiful votive altars dedicated to various deities. There are also memorials from Mithra shrines II (in the church crypt) and IV (see box, p.301). The **old refectory** now keeps a modest collection of Celtic and Roman coins (also look out for the clay piggy banks), but is more interesting for its gorgeous vaulted and stuccoed ceiling – not dissimilar to that of the summer refectory in the Minorite monastery, and similarly painted with venerated saints.

Ptuj Castle

Lording it over the flutter of red roofs and cobbled streets below, **Ptuj Castle** (Grad Ptuj) is the town's showpiece attraction. It began life around 69 AD when the inhabitants of Roman Poetovio built a fortress and temple atop this very hill, though the oldest archives date the present structure to some time in the twelfth century, when the castle was owned by the archbishops of Salzburg, who in turn leased it to the lords of Ptuj. Fortified ahead of anticipated Turkish raids in the sixteenth century, the castle was further modified in Baroque fashion during the seventeenth century.

Whether approaching from the path opposite the monastery, or via Grajska ulica, a narrow street just off Prešernova ulica near the *Garni Hotel Mitra*, you enter the castle grounds through the thick-set **Charles portal**, which opens up into the lower courtyard, once the location for the castle stables and military outbuildings, but now empty save for a weatherbeaten statue of a one-armed St Florian dousing yet another fire – the views from this platform, however, are fantastic. Walk on up through the fine Renaissance **Peruzzi portal** into the immaculate inner courtyard, enclosed by a horseshoe-shaped, three-tiered **residential palace**. Before entering the museum (see below) take a look at the splendid, red Salzburg marble tombstone of Frederick IX, the last lord of Ptuj, embedded into the wall on the left-hand side of the courtyard.

The castle's **regional museum collection** (daily: May to mid-Oct 9am–6pm; July & Aug 9am–6pm, plus Sat & Sun 9am–8pm; mid-Oct to April 9am–5pm; 600SIT) – rooms stuffed full of period furnishings, tapestries and paintings, and musical instruments – is interminably dull, a state of affairs not helped by the complete absence of captions in any language. However, the displays of *Kurenti* masks and associated carnival paraphernalia (see box, below) do at least inject a bit of colour and energy into proceedings. Your time is better off spent savouring the marvellous views of the Drava River, and Haloze Hills beyond, or partaking in a coffee in the small courtyard café.

Eating and drinking

The town counts on just two really decent **restaurants**: *Ribič* (Mon–Thurs 10am–10pm, Fri & Sat 10am–midnight, Sun noon–6pm), down by the river at Dravska ulica 9, has a menu almost exclusively devoted to fish, but it doesn't come cheap – the riverside terrace is a wonderful place to dine in summer. The other is *Amadeus* (Mon–Sat 11am–11pm, Sun noon–4pm) at the end of Prešernova (opposite the library), a warm, classy place, offering an upscale take on Slovene standards, and at slightly more affordable prices. Otherwise, there's *Kitajski Vrt*, a reasonable, if not wholly authentic, Chinese place opposite *Ribič*, and *Perutnina Ptuj* (*PP*) on Novi trg, which knocks up fast, filling and cheap daily specials for under 1000SIT.

Ptuj's **nightlife** is, predictably, fairly tame, and you'll struggle to avoid going to the same places if you're here for more than a day or two. Indisputably the number one hangout is *Café Evropa* on Mestni trg: by day a fairly relaxed place for coffee, by night a noisy, frenetic bar. If it's too busy, head up to the *Old Irish Pub* (open till 1am) on Murkova ulica. More sedate options, but equally good

The Kurent

One of the oldest, most unusual and celebrated folklore events in the Slovene calendar is the **Kurent**, a kind of fertility rite and celebration of the awakening of Spring confused together, which takes place in the ten days up to Shrove Tuesday (late February/early March). Wearing spooky masks made of sheepskin and feathers with a coloured beak for a nose, white beads for teeth and long, bright red tongues, the *Kurenti* proceed from house to house, warding off evil spirits with the incessant din from the cowbells and other instruments tied to their weighty costumes. Leading the procession is the Devil (Hudič), pitchfork in hand and wrapped in a net to symbolize his capture: behind the *Kurenti*, the ploughers (Orači) pull a small wooden plough, scattering sand around to represent the sowing of seed, whilst the other participants smash clay pots at their feet in return for good luck and health.

Although several similar carnivals, known as *pust*, take place in other towns throughout Slovenia – most famously in Cerkno and Cerknica – and in neighbouring countries such as Hungary and Croatia, most are pale imitations of the events that take place here in Ptuj.

places for a daytime or evening drink, are *Café Bo* and *Café Orfei*, just a few paces apart from each other on Prešernova. It's also worth checking out what's going on at the Centre for Free Time Activities (see p.296), as it occasionally stages the odd gig in its basement bar.

If you haven't time to visit the Haloze winegrowing region (see p.302), the next best option is to call in at the **Haloze wine cellar** at Trstenjakova 6 (Ⓣ02/787-9810); although it's usually full of tour parties, individual visits (600SIT) are possible so long as you call in advance – this incorporates a fifteen-minute multi-vision presentation, a tour of the labyrinthine cellars (complete with sound and light effects), and a sampling session. There's also a shop here (Mon–Fri 7am–7pm & Sat 7am–noon).

Mithra Shrines

Approximately 1km west of town, across the river in **Zgornji Breg**, the **Mithra III Shrine** is one of four shrines in Ptuj dedicated to the sun god and warrior Mithra (see box, below). The Mithras III shrine, housed in a small pavilion just off Mariborska cesta (it's signposted), dates from 3 AD and comprises the remains of a three-naved temple, around which are scattered sacrificial altars carved with votive inscriptions. The plate on the far wall is a copy of an altar relief of the sacrificial bull from the Mithraeum in Osterburken, in Germany, though there are a few surviving fragments from the original in the right-hand corner. The rest of the room is neatly arranged with dedication blocks, chunky slabs of marble carved with reliefs from the Mithras cult – his birth from a rock, his slaying of a bull, and another that depicts him shooting water from a rock with an arrow. The most impressive stone, however, is the one positioned in front of the main altar, which depicts two figures taking an oath over the fire on the sacrificial altar.

A twenty-minute walk southwest of Mithra III, across a dusty field in the tiny settlement of **Spodnja Hajdina**, a smaller building holds the remains of the **Mithra I Shrine**, discovered in 1898 and considered to be the oldest of the

Mithraism

Mithraism, the ancient religion of Mithras the sun god, is believed to have originated in Persia, before spreading west during the time of the Roman Empire. However, it was never officially recognized as a Roman religion, in all probability because the Romans believed that Mithraism consisted of elements of the religion of their bitter enemies, the Persians. For this reason the first Mithras shrines, such as those in Ptuj, were built outside town boundaries. By the second half of the third century, however, Mithraism – with Ptuj as one of its leading centres – had almost established itself as the state religion, rivalling Christianity as the dominant faith. However, with Emperor Constantine's ascension to the throne in the fourth century, Mithraism, along with other pagan religions, was outlawed and most of its temples destroyed.

Little is known of its rituals and believers, although it's likely that meetings took place within confined religious communities, dominated exclusively by male members, typically, imperial administrators, slaves of the customs administration or soldiers, and whose initiates would number around one hundred. These members would be grouped and divided into several ranks, ranks that were depicted in relief. Although stone dedication blocks and relief depictions of Mithras were widely distributed throughout the Roman Empire, few match the calibre of those in Ptuj. There's another excellent Mithraeum shrine in Rožanec, near Črnomelj (see p.252).

Mithra temples located in the Roman Empire's northern province; this one dates from around the second half of the second century. The most interesting of the dozen or so haphazardly arranged stone dedication blocks are statues of Mithras dragging the sacrifical bull, and a snake coiled around a torso emerging from a rock mass. Both temples are usually closed, but the keys can easily be obtained from the neighbouring houses, the numbers of which are given on the respective doors.

Church of the Virgin Mary

Twelve kilometres southwest of Ptuj along the road to Rogatec, in the village of Ptujska Gora, the Gothic **Church of the Virgin Mary** (Cerkev Sv Marija) ranks alongside the churches at Brezje, near Bled, and Sveta Gora, near Nova Gorica, as one of the country's premier pilgrimage destinations. Built some time around 1400, the church's beautifully cool interior manifests some outstanding Gothic architecture, most notably in the form of the three arches which presage the tripartite nave, whose aisles are separated by smooth slender columns. But nothing in this, or any other church in Slovenia, comes close to the splendour of the **high altar**, a majestic, towering work of art whose focal point is the *Virgin Mary with Mantle* relief, which features seven angels lifting a dusky green cloak to reveal ranks of some eighty figures, each carved in remarkable life-like detail; mingling amongst the cast of the rich and the poor are several of the counts of Celje. So compelling is this piece that it somewhat detracts from the rest of the altar's ornamentation, most notably some extraordinary sculptural work.

To the right of the high altar, in the southern aisle, the canopied **Celje Altar** pays further homage to the vounts of Celje, its baldachin ceiling and pillars beautifully ornamented with sculpted flowers, animal figures and the counts' coats-of-arms. Also worthy of close inspection are the frescoes depicting scenes from Christ's Passion by John Bruneck, located under the organ loft, and a fine statue of St James standing on the console of a pillar in the southern aisle. To get here take one of the seven daily buses heading to **Majšperk**, and alight on the main road just below the church, from where it's a five-minute walk.

Haloze Hills

Rearing up from the iron-flat Drava Plain south of Ptuj, the **Haloze hills** present further opportunities to sample more of Slovenia's fine wines. Extending for some 30km east, from the village of Makole (just beyond Ptujska Gora), along the Croatian border to Zavrč, the Haloze are divided into two diverse landscapes – the Vinorodne (winegrowing) region to the east, and the Gozdnate (forested) region to the south and west, both regions spotted with solitary farms, orchards and hamlets.

Although the many cellars here can be visited independently – the clearly visible brown and yellow signs denote what each cellar has to offer – you can, alternatively, head to the friendly and accommodating Halo Agency (Ⓣ02/795-3200, Ⓦwww.halo.si) in the village of **Cirkulane**, situated a couple of kilometres south of **Borl Castle**, now a neglected station perched high above the Drava 12km southwest of Ptuj. Located in the centre of the village across from the church, the agency can provide information on the region, arrange accommodation in holiday homes (❺), and organize guided visits to a selection of the cellars, some of which also offer domestic goat's cheese, bread and pastries, and other homemade treats. There's no public transport around these parts, so you'll need your own wheels.

Ormož

Pressed up hard against the Croatian border 23km east of Ptuj, **ORMOŽ** was the setting for some of the heaviest fighting between Slovene units of the Territorial Defence and Yugoslav Federal forces during the Ten-Day War of Independence in 1991. Nothing quite so animated happens here these days and, in truth, the town has very little to commend it, but it is the starting point for ventures up into the Ormož hills winegrowing region (see below). If you do find yourself with half an hour to spare, the recently renovated town **castle** (Mon–Fri noon–3pm, Sat 10am–2pm; free), a short walk up from the bus station, showcases a few rooms containing a selection of items and furniture, as well as a sprinkling of frescoes, whilst there's a modest gallery of local art.

The **bus station** is smack bang in the centre of town, and the **train station** about 500m beyond the castle right on the border crossing point. There is a **hotel** here, the dreadfully ordinary *Ormož* (Ⓣ02/740-1121; ❸) opposite the bus station, which is also the only source of information on the town and the surrounding area.

The Ormož–Ljutomer wine road

Extending from Ormož in the south to Ljutomer in the north (see p.304), the eponymous **wine road** is the smallest of Podravje's six winegrowing districts, yet it possesses a high density of viticultural sites. Vying with the Goriška Brda region in Primorje for the title of Slovenia's most beautiful wine-producing region, this fabulously picturesque and sunny landscape is shaped by horizontal rows of curving, terraced vineyards set against the backdrop of *Klopotec*, wooden wind-powered rattles designed to scare off birds and, according to local superstition, to drive snakes out of the vineyards. Of the predominatly white wines harvested here, the smooth and slightly sweet Beli Pinot is regarded as the finest, followed by Laški Rizling – one of the few wines to find its way into British supermarkets – Šipon and Traminec, whilst the blended wines, Jeruzalemčan and Ljutomerčan are popular alternatives. The numerous **cellars** lining the route are marked by brown and cream signposts.

The midway point of the route is the delightful little hilltop village of **JERUZALEM**, so-named after crusaders visiting here in the thirteenth century became so enamoured with the wine and the people that they decided to name the settlement after the holy city. At the centre of the village is the Baroque **Church of Our Lady of Sorrows**, whose painting of the Our Lady of Sorrows on the high altar is a late seventeenth-century copy of the original, which was brought here by the aforementioned crusaders, but later stolen. Look out, too, for the imprint of a horse hoof, which, according to local legend, was left here by one of the marauding Turks during seventeenth-century raids. Just across from the church is the **tourist office** (summer 9am–10pm daily, winter 10am–4pm), which is a more than useful source of advice on the best cellars to visit. Just beyond the village, heading towards Ljutomer, there's an **observation tower**, from where there are superlative views of the surrounding hills – on a clear day it's possible to see as far as Lake Balaton in Hungary.

The route is made for **cycling**, and you may not have much choice anyway, as what buses that do travel between Ormož and Ljutomer, and vice versa, take the main road running parallel to the east, passing through Ivanjkovci. If you're planning to cycle the entire route, you should allow for around four to five hours, a little more if cellar hopping is on the agenda. The stretch between Jeruzalem and Ljutomer is slightly tougher going than the stretch between Jeruzalem and Ormož, which flattens out markedly after Vinski Vir. **Bikes** can be hired at both the tourist offices in Jeruzalem and Ljutomer (see p.304).

Ljutomer

LJUTOMER, the economic and cultural centre of the region, is the last town before you cross the Mura River into Prekmurje. Although it's unlikely you will need, or should want to stay here, there are a couple of interesting diversions, whilst it also has excellent rail connections, including the Budapest–Venice InterCity train, which passes through here once a day. The wine connections aside, the town is best known for its horse racing, having staged trotting races since 1874. Today, the **hippodrome** – located around 500m northwest of the town's main square, Glavni trg – stages some ten **horse-trotting races** a year. These usually take place on Sundays and public holidays between April and September (approx 1000SIT), but check with the tourist office (see below) first for schedules. If you can't manage to get here for a race day, you can still visit the track and stables, whilst you may also get to see the horses in training; the tourist office should be able to fix something up for you.

Otherwise fairly limited, the small **town museum**, located in the town hall on Glavni trg, is worth visiting to view some original footage of the first ever films to be produced in Slovenia, *People Leaving the Church* and *The Fair at Ljutomer*, which were shot by Karol Grossmann in 1905. There's also an interesting exhibition on the so-called "Tabor Movement"; between 1868 and 1870, numerous groups of young intellectuals living in Slovene ethnic territories initiated regular mass open-air forums (*tabors*) to publicize and rally support for a united Slovenia, whose very existence as a national group around that time appeared seriously threatened. Although they were subsequently banned by Vienna, the influence of the *tabors* continued to be felt in later years whenever questions concerning the Slovene national movement were raised.

Practicalities

All the town's practical facilities are located within fairly close proximity to each other: Ljutomer has two **train stations**, Ljutomer, and the smaller Ljutomer Mesto, where you should alight for the town centre. This is located on Rajh nade ulica, from where it's a ten-minute walk south to the **bus station** and the town centre. The **tourist office** is about 400m west of the bus station at Jureša Cirila 4 (Mon–Fri 8am–4pm; ⓣ02/584-8333, ⓦwww.lto-prlekija.si), though it's actually located inside the courtyard of the town hall building on Glavni trg. As well as supplying information on the Ormož–Ljutomer wine road (see p.303), the helpful staff here can arrange private **accommodation** along the route, and rent out **bikes** (1250SIT per day). Glavni trg is also the site for the town's only **hotel**, the very grey and really rather depressing *Hotel Jeruzalem* (ⓣ02/581-1211; ❸).

Prekmurje

Cut off by the fast-flowing Mura River to the south, and bounded on the remaining three sides by the Austrian, Hungarian and Croatian borders, **Prekmurje** (Pomurje to Slovenes) is a region quite apart from the rest of the country. Known as Slovenia's breadbasket, it is, for the most part, a relentlessly flat landscape, carved up by grids of smooth green fields, picturesque villages and little white churches. Prekmurje's relative isolation is rooted in over a thousand years of Magyar rule, a situation that changed only after World War I when it was incorporated into Yugoslav lands, although there was another brief period of Hungarian imposition during World War II. Physically, economically and culturally distanced from the rest of the country prior to World War I – there was no bridge crossing the Mura until 1924 – Prekmurje is still regarded by many Slovenes as something of a backwater. However, thanks largely to Hungary's long-term rule, Prekmurje remains one of Slovenia's most ethnically diverse regions, embracing a sizeable Hungarian minority, as well as the country's largest Roma community. Prior to World War II it also accounted for over half of the country's Jewish population.

Prekmurje also has one of the richest culinary traditions in Slovenia, and you shouldn't leave without trying *bograč*, a steaming goulash pot of mixed meats, onions and potatoes, or its most famous product, *gibanica*, a delicious sweet pie stuffed with cottage cheese, poppy seeds, walnut and apple.

Whilst there's a fairly regular **bus service** linking the region's only two towns, **Murska Sobota** and **Lendava**, and most of the villages in between, such as **Martjanci**, **Bogojina** and **Beltinci**, services are dramatically reduced at weekends, so try and coincide a visit with a weekday. Alternatively, and if you've got the time and inclination, the best way to explore the region is by bike (see box, p.307).

Murska Sobota

Located in the geographical centre of Prekmurje, **MURSKA SOBOTA** is the largest settlement in the province, a one-horse town where nothing very much ever happens. However, it is the region's main road and rail hub, so there's a good chance you'll wind up here if you're planning to explore the surrounding countryside. The town developed alongside the Ledava River, in the plains north of the Mura River, during the eleventh century, and was almost immediately incorporated into the Hungarian state, under whose administration it remained until 1920. Another, brief period of Hungarian control during World War II was ended by the Red Army, who liberated the town in April 1945.

With the reopening, in 2001, of the rail line between Puconci, a few kilometres north of Murska Sobota, and Hodoš, on the Hungarian border, the town once again found itself the first major stop, in Slovenia, for intercity trains travelling from Budapest to Ljubljana. If you do have an hour or two to spare while waiting for buses to the outlying villages, there's a very worthwhile museum, as well as a pleasant park to laze around in.

Arrival, information and accommodation

Both the **bus** and **train stations** are centrally located, the former on Slomškova ulica, the latter to the east at the end of Ulica Arhiteka Novaka. The **tourist office** (Mon–Fri 9am–5pm, Sat 8am–noon; ⓣ02/534-1130), located inside a roadside booth, is midway along Slovenska ulica, near the junction with Trg Zmage, though it's of limited help, and you'll get far more out of the tourist office in Moravske Toplice, 7km northeast of town (see p.307). The **post office** is on the south side of Trg Zmage (Mon–Fri 7am–7pm, Sat 7am–1pm). The town's one **hotel** is the pricey *Diana* at Slovenska ulica 52 (ⓣ02/514-1200, ⓕ02/532-1097; ❻), which has slick rooms with cool blue furnishings and large beds; the hotel also possesses a pool, sauna and solarium, and gym.

The Town

The town's only real point of interest, and its saving grace, is the **Regional Museum** (Pokrajinksi muzej; Tues–Sat 10am–5pm, Sun 10am–1pm; 500SIT), housed inside an eighteenth-century Renaissance mansion in the centre of the leafy **City Park** (Mestni Park), west of the town's main square Trg Zmage (Victory Square). The museum's fifteen or so rooms (there are comprehensive English captions) offer an impressive and thorough narrative of life in the town and the wider Prekmurje region from prehistory to the present. Selected highlights from the earliest periods include Roman burial mounds and the remnants of a medieval forge discovered in Grad na Goričkem in 1990. The medieval period is further represented by some superb Gothic architecture, including a stone tabernacle and other sculptural pieces, as well as some fresco fragments. Trades and crafts, such as shoemaking, milling and wheel-making, all make an appearance, though the greatest emphasis is on pottery, one of the region's most important nineteenth-century cottage industries, and a tradition that just about survives to this day in old potters' settlements such as Filovci (see p.308). The last few rooms document the town's liberation by the Red Army in 1945, including a short film of the unveiling of the Liberation Monument on Trg Zmage, erected on August 12 1945, less than two months after the Red Army left Murska Sobota; the exhibiton concludes with a slightly tacky presentation pertaining to contemporary life in the region.

On the opposite side of City Park stands the slender, whitewashed neo-Gothic **Evangelical Church**. Although there's little in the way of traditional church ornamentation, its paintwork is striking, the cream-coloured walls splattered with geometric patterns of burgundy, green and blue; note the presbytery, too, which, unusually, is carpeted.

Eating and drinking

There's not much choice here when it comes to **eating and drinking**, though the lively *Zvezda* on the southeastern corner of Trg Zmage doubles up nicely as a restaurant and pub; worth trying is the game (particularly the chamois) and goulash (food is not served after 3pm Sun), whilst there's a good selection of light and dark beers on tap (open until 1am Fri & Sat) – before you enter, take a look at the stuccoed reliefs of moustachioed men on the facade. Otherwise, a couple of places worth considering northeast of Trg Zmage are *Rajh no 1* (closed Mon) located on the bottom floor of an apartment block on the corner of Lendavska ulica and Cvetkova ulica, and which offers deliciously simple spaghetti, salad and pasta dishes at rock-bottom prices; and, 200m east of here, the *Kitajska* (*Chinese*) restaurant at Lendavska ulica 39.

If you're prepared to travel for your food, then make tracks for the *Rajh* restaurant (Tues–Sat 10am–11pm, Sun 10am–4pm), 5km south of town in the village of **Bakovci**; neither the building nor the interior particularly flatter, but the food here, including pheasant, lamb and goose, as well as Serbian specialities such as *Sarma* (minced meat wrapped inside cabbage leaves), is exceptional. It's located at the very beginning of the village, at Soboška ulica 32.

Martjanci

Heading north out of Murska Sobota along the road to Moravske Toplice, it's worth taking a moment to stop off at the roadside **Parish Church of St Martin** in the village of **MARTJANCI**. Distinguished by an elegant high belfry, the church was designed and painted by Janez Aquila, a frequent contributor to religious monuments in the Prekmurje region. Arguably the most beautifully frescoed church in Prekmurje, its gorgeous, cross-ribbed vaulted presbytery is smothered with some fine paintings – Apostles (including the *Masters of the Apostles*), saints and prophets, as well as a painting of the author himself, supposedly one of the oldest self-portraits known to exist in European art. On the inner wall of the triumphal arch there's a fabulous fresco of George and the Dragon. The simple high altar, meanwhile, featuring a statue of St Martin, is the work of Jože Plečnik, a modest contribution by the architect in comparison to his work at Bogojina (see p.308).

Moravske Toplice

From Martjanci, buses continue for a further 3km to **Moravske Toplice**, dominated by the **Terme 3000 Spa** (Ⓦwww.terme3000.si), a sprawling, ultra-modern complex incorporating one of the largest recreational centres in the country. Starting out in the 1960s, when thermal springs were discovered during a search for oil, the spa now comprises some twenty separate indoor and outdoor bathing areas featuring water and air massage pools, geysers and waterfalls, a diving pool, wave machines, and enormous water slides (daily 9am–9pm; daily ticket 2100SIT, after 3pm 1500SIT).

There's plenty of accommodation on site, though neither of the (spa's) two **hotels** are particularly inspiring: the shiny four-star *Ajda* (Ⓣ02/512-2100; ❺) and the slightly cheaper *Termal* (Ⓣ02/512-1100; ❹). A far more pleasant alternative is the lovely thatched-roof, Prekmurje-style **bungalows** (❹) sheltered amongst trees on the opposite side of the complex (reception is in the *Ajda* hotel); or the huge *Prekmurska Vas* complex adjacent, which has newer **apartments** sleeping between two and five people (❺–❼) – reception is across the road. There's an excellent year-round **campsite** here too (Ⓣ02/512-1200). Guests of all the above accommodation receive free access to the spa pools.

Bikes can be rented from the Bike Center (2500SIT per day; daily 7am–8pm; Ⓣ02/512-2186), located in a small wooden hut near the campsite entrance. There's also **tennis** (1200SIT for 1hr) available, as well as a nine-hole **golf course**; green fees (4900SIT 9 holes, 6900SIT 18 holes) must be paid at the reception in the *Ajda* Hotel.

Cycling In Prekmurje

Given the region's predominantly flat terrain, **cycling** around Prekmurje is a joy, and there's an excellent network of well-marked and well-maintained cycle paths to choose from. Moreover, with no two villages more than a few kilometres apart, there are plenty of opportunities to rest up before pushing on to the next destination. If you do plan to do some cycling, there's plenty of information and materials to assist. The best place to start is the excellent Bike Center (Ⓣ02/512-2186; Ⓦwww.pomurjeonbike.com), whose shop is located within the grounds of the Terme 3000 spa in Moravske Toplice (see above); as well as **renting bikes** (2500SIT per day), they also organize bicycle excursions – the website outlines ten possible routes throughout the region. The *Cycling Around Prekmurje* pamphlet, available from the tourist office in Moravske Toplice (see p.308), details eight, each one indicating sights of interest, places to sleep and eat, as well as bike rental and repair shops; the useful 1:75,000 *Pomurje* **map** (900SIT) is also a useful aid. Bikes can also be rented (1750SIT for one day) from the tourist office, though these are not as good as those at the Bike Center.

There's a small **tourist office** at Kranjčeva 3 (May–Oct Mon–Sat 7am–8pm, Sun 8am–2pm, Nov–April; ⓣ02/538-1520, ⓦwww.info.moravske-toplice.si), to the side of the small complex of shops as you enter the village (if coming by bus backtrack 200m from the bus stop at the entrance to the spa); they can also assist in finding **private accommodation** (❷) in the area, of which there is plenty. They too rent bikes (300SIT 1 hour, 1750SIT for the day). The *Flisar* tourist farm, 4km northwest of Moravske Toplice at Dolga ulica 216 (ⓣ02/538-1320, ⓔtur.kmetija-flisar@siol.net; ❷), is a terrific rural retreat, combining homely accommodation with fabulous domestic cooking.

Around Moravske Toplice

Three of Prekmurje's most interesting villages – **Bogojina**, **Filovci** and **Beltinci** – are located between Moravske Toplice and Lendava, whilst another, **Selo**, is sited a short way to the north of Moravske Toplice near the Hungarian border. If you don't have your own transport, it's not difficult to hop from one village to the next using local bus services, although this possibility is rendered more difficult at weekends due to drastically reduced services.

Selo

From the village of **Tešanovci**, a kilometre or so east of Moravske Toplice, a road breaks left and climbs slowly up to the scattered settlement of **SELO**, some 10km distant. Standing in a field below the main road is the pinkish **Chapel of St Nicholas** (Rotunda Sv Nikolaj), a superb Romanesque rotunda built in the mid-thirteenth century. Its interior is adorned with some exceptional, albeit badly effaced, wall paintings, the upper half covered in scenes from the Adoration of the Magi and the Passion Cycle, and the dome smothered with evangelical symbols. To gain entrance to the church, you will need to call in at the roadside **information hut** (daily 9am–5pm), whereupon someone with the key will escort you. Located 1km back along the road (before the church), the roadside gostilna, *K Rotundi* (Mon–Sat 11am–10pm, Sun 10am–4pm), is one of the region's best **restaurants**; as well as the standard Prekmurje specialities, it's known for its game and roast goat dishes.

Bogojina, Filovci and Beltinci

BOGOJINA, the next village beyond Tešanovci, is the location for what is perhaps Prekmurje's best-known church, the **Church of the Ascension** (Cerkev Vnebovhod). Visible from miles around – owing to its slight elevation above the rest of the village – the church was redesigned by Slovenia's greatest architect, Jože Plečnik (see box on p.63), between 1925 and 1927, and clearly manifests his trademark characteristics, from the high cylindrical tower, to the columns, pillars and fanciful oddments gracing the interior. At the heart of this bright, single-nave hall church is a monumental black marble column, from which four equally striking vaults emanate, built to help support the beautiful oak timber ceiling. In typically idiosyncratic fashion, Plečnik furnished the church with numerous flamboyant accessories, such as the ceramic plates and jugs ornamenting the ceiling and high altar. The village itself is exceptionally pretty, and it's an enjoyable fifteen-minute walk from the bus stop on the main road to the church, past rows of colourful Prekmurje-style farmhouses – L-shaped homesteads built on narrow strips of land perpendicular to the traffic routes.

The so-called *črna keramika*, or **black pottery**, industry, flourished in several villages hereabouts from the late eighteenth century onwards, and especially in **FILOVCI**, 2km further along the road from Bogojina. In the centre of the village, at no. 29 – walk across the small bridge and beyond the church – the Bojnec family offers pottery demonstrations in their workshop; they've also got a shop selling a wide range of earthenware. To arrange a visit, which is free, contact the tourist office in Moravske Toplice (see opposite).

If you're around during the last weekend of July, then don't miss the **Beltinci International Folklore Festival**, which takes place in the large village of **BELTINCI**, about 10km south of Bogojina – it is actually easier to reach the village via the faster road from Murska Sobota to Lendava. For over thirty years this superb festival has consistently attracted a high-calibre roster of both domestic and foreign folk groups, musicians and dance troupes, who perform over four days on several stages in the village's large and leafy manor park – Saturday is generally reckoned to be the best day. It's also a great opportunity to try out some traditional Prekmurje dishes at the many stalls spread out around the grounds.

Lendava and around

Wedged into the southeastern corner of Prekmurje, 31km from Murska Sobota and just a stone's throw from the Croatian and Hungarian borders, **LENDAVA** (Lendva in Hungarian) is Slovenia's easternmost town and also one of the largest bilingual settlements in the country, its sizeable Hungarian minority accounting for around a third of the town's population. Despite this harmonized ethnic union, it's a fairly low-key place, its relative isolation ensuring that few visitors make it to this remote little corner of the country.

The Town

The town's major attraction is the **castle**, reached via a steep path next to the **Parish Church of St Catherine**, midway along the main thoroughfare, Glavna ulica. Although a fortification of sorts stood here as early as the twelfth century, the present castle was rebuilt by the noble Hungarian Esterházy family between 1712 and 1717, remaining within their possession until the beginning of World War II. It now houses a modest **museum** (Mon–Sat 9am–5pm, Sun 10am–2pm; 300SIT), containing a rather ordinary collection of Bronze Age artifacts, weaponry from battles with the Turks, and a small ethnographic collection.

The only other two sites of note are located on the opposite side of Glavna ulica near the town park. Built in 1866, the **synagogue** on Župančičeva ulica was cleared out, along with the town's several-hundred-strong Jewish population, during World War II. Thanks to the recent completion of a decade-long rebuilding programme, it has been restored to something like its former self, and now accommodates a few exhibits – mainly photo documentation and religious items – from the pre-World War II period. Today, the community is sustained by less than a handful of Jews. Co-financed by the Hungarian and Slovenian communities, the extraordinary building in the park opposite – designed by the renowned, and controversial, Hungarian architect **Imre Makovecz** – was supposed to have housed the town's cultural centre, though protracted wrangling over finances has seen the project put on hold for the time being.

Nestled amongst the winegrowing **Lendava Hills** (Lendavske Gorice), less than 1km southeast of town, is the **Church of the Holy Trinity** (Cerkev Sv Trojian), a standard Baroque issue built in 1728. The church is notable, however, for holding the grisly, mummified body of local warrior Mihael Hladik, slain by the Turks in 1603, but whose immaculately preserved body was miraculously discovered in a casket during construction of the castle chapel in 1728. If you wish to visit the church contact the tourist office, and a member of staff will accompany you.

Practicalities

Arriving at the **bus station** on Kolodvorska ulica, make your way across the ugly concrete square towards the *Hotel Elizabeta*, through the small complex of shops to the park; take a right here, up past the Ljubljanska bank to the triangle in the middle of the road. At this point turn right and you'll find the **tourist office** 100m along the road at Kranjčeva 4 (Mon–Fri 8am–7pm, Sat & Sun 8am–1pm & 4–7pm; Ⓣ02/578-8390, Ⓦwww.lendava.si), whose helpful staff are able to organize visits to several of the outlying attractions; you can also **rent bikes** here (600SIT half a day, 1000SIT full day).

Aimed at nonexistent business travellers, the **hotel** *Elizabeta* (Ⓣ02/577-4600, Ⓕ02/577-4625; ❻) is a gleaming glass block at Mlinska ulica 5 (though it's actually sited on the aforementioned square) – the rooms are perfectly fine and comfortable, albeit pricey. The only other hotel hereabouts is the *Lipa* (Ⓣ02/577-4440; ❼), an unattractive and absurdly overpriced place 1km south of town at Tomšičeva 2; it is actually part of the small Lendava spa complex.

The *Domačija* **restaurant**, opposite the *Hotel Elizabeta* on Mlinksa ulica, is pretty much the only place to eat in town, but really only suffices for a cheap and filling lunch. **Wine** buffs may care to visit the Cuk Wine Cellar at Lendavske Gorice 248 (Ⓣ02/577-1286), a lovely little hillside cellar 1km southeast of town on the fringe of the Lendava Hills; contact the tourist office if you're interested in some tasting (approx 1250SIT for five wines). They've also got three rooms (❺) if you wish to stop over.

Velika Polana and Črenšovci

If you've got your own transport, there are two villages of interest a short way from Lendava. **VELIKA POLANA**, around 10km west of Lendava, is one of Europe's officially designated **stork villages** (classified as a settlement with ten or more storks' nests), thanks to the dozen or so storks that pitch up here and in some of the neighbouring villages each spring. Attracted by the abundance of food, especially frogs and toads, to be found in the nearby marshes and swamplands, the storks usually return to the same nest (improbably bulky constructions perched atop telegraph poles or chimneys) they occupied the previous year. The female will usually lay between three and five eggs, then incubate them for around five weeks before they hatch in July or August. The offspring normally fledge at around eight or nine weeks. Whether kicking back in their nests, or skulking around the local fields foraging for food, these birds offer irresistible photo opportunities.

Around five kilometres further west of Velika Polana, the dusty little community of **Kamenci**, actually an adjunct of the village of **ČRENŠOVCI**, is home to one of the largest **Roma settlements** in Prekmurje. A few members of this community of around one hundred have joined forces with the tourist office in Lendava (see above) to offer organized visits, which include a programme of entertainment featuring traditional Roma music and dance. There is also a small **Gypsy Museum** here, the first and only one of its kind in the country. For more on Slovenia's Roma, see the box opposite.

Slovenia's Roma

Most of Slovenia's estimated seven thousand Gypsies, or Roma, many of whom settled in the country following the wars in Croatia and Bosnia, live in small, scattered settlements throughout Prekmurje, such as Črenšovci, near Lendava, and Pušča, on the western outskirts of Murska Sobota. The majority of the remainder of the Roma community live in southeast Dolenjska and Bela Krajina. Although the lot of the Roma in Slovenia is considerably better than that of those in many other countries of the former Eastern Bloc – Slovenia is one of few European countries that have included the Roma in the constitution – discrimination is still commonplace. Moreover, living conditions remain, on the whole, substandard, with many settlements still lacking basic infrastructure, whilst standards of education are low and unemployment remains unacceptably high.

However, and though their rights are not nearly as well protected as those of the country's Hungarian and Italian minorities, important steps have been made in recent years, and the state has made concerted attempts to integrate the Roma community into the majority culture. The most significant piece of legislation, adopted in 2002, allowed for Romany community representatives to be elected to local councils in more than twenty municipalities. The Roma community, too, have made concentrated efforts to organize themselves into coherent groups, such as the Union of Roma of Slovenia (the country's major Roma organization), which was formed in 1991 following Slovene independence. Amongst its many activities, it publishes the magazine, *Romano Them* (*Romany News*), as well as producing Roma plays and numerous other publishing and theatrical initiatives.

Travel details

Trains

Celje to: Laško (every 45min–2hr; 15min); Ljubljana (every 45min–2hr; 1hr–1hr 40min); Maribor (every 45min–2hr; 45min–1hr 10min); Podčetrtek (3–6 daily; 45min); Rogaška Slatina (3–7 daily; 45min); Velenje (Mon–Fri 8 daily; 50min).
Dravograd to: Maribor (Mon–Fri 5 daily; 1hr 40min).
Ljutomer to: Ljubljana (3–6 daily; 3hr 10min); Murska Sobota (5–9 daily; 20min); Ormož (5–9 daily; 25min).
Maribor to: Celje (every 45min–2hr; 45min–1hr 10min); Dravograd (Mon–Fri 4 daily; 1hr 40min); Ljubljana (every 45min–2hr; 1hr 45min–2hr 45min).
Murska Sobota to: Ljubljana (3–6 daily; 3hr 30min); Ljutomer (5–9 daily; 20min); Ormož (5–9 daily; 45min); Ptuj (6–8 daily; 50min–1hr 10min).
Ormož to: Ljubljana (3–6 daily; 2hr 50min): Ljutomer (5–9 daily; 25min); Maribor (6–12 daily; 1hr 20min); Murska Sobota (5–9 daily; 45min); Ptuj (6–12 daily; 25min).
Podčetrtek to: Celje (3–7 daily; 45min).
Ptuj to: Ljubljana (4–7 daily; 2hr 30min–3hr); Murska Sobota (6–8 daily; 50min–1hr 10min); Ormož (6–12 daily; 25min).
Rogaška Slatina to: Celje (3–6 daily; 45min).
Velenje to: Celje (Mon–Fri 8 daily; 50min).

Buses

Celje to: Laško (Mon–Fri 9 daily, Sat & Sun 7 daily; 15min); Ljubljana (Mon–Fri 13 daily, Sat & Sun 7 daily; 1hr 30min); Maribor (Mon–Fri 11 daily, Sat & Sun 6 daily; 1hr 15min); Murska Sobota (3 daily; 2hr 30min); Rogaška Slatina (Mon–Fri 10 daily, Sat & Sun 4 daily; 40min); Slovenske Konjice (Mon–Fri hourly, Sat & Sun 8 daily; 25min); Velenje (Mon–Sat hourly, Sun 3; 25min); Zreče (Mon–Fri 8 daily, Sat & Sun 2 daily; 25min).
Črna na Koroškem to: Celje (2 daily; 1hr 15min); Dravograd (Mon–Fri every 30min–hourly, Sat & Sun 6 daily; 45min); Maribor (4 daily; 1hr 50min); Slovenj Gradec (Mon–Fri 12 daily, Sat & Sun 7 daily; 50min); Velenje (Mon–Fri 8 daily, Sat & Sun 5 daily; 50min).
Dravograd to: Celje (2 daily; 1hr 10min); Črna na Koroškem (Mon–Fri every 30min–hourly, Sat & Sun 6 daily; 45min); Maribor (Mon–Fri 10 daily, Sat & Sun 6 daily; 1hr 15min); Slovenj Gradec (every 30min–hourly; 20min); Velenje (every 45min–hourly, Sat & Sun 7 daily; 40min).

Lendava to: Črenšovci (Mon–Fri 10 daily; 25min); Maribor (Mon–Fri 4 daily, Sat 2; 1hr 40min); Murska Sobota (Mon–Fri hourly, Sat 2; 40min); Moravske Toplice (Mon–Fri 6 daily, Sat 1; 15min).
Ljutomer to: Murska Sobota (Mon–Fri 10 daily, Sat & Sun 3 daily; 40min); Ormož (Mon–Fri 6 daily; 30min).
Maribor to: Celje (Mon–Fri 10 daily, Sat & Sun 5 daily; 1hr 15min); Dravograd (Mon–Fri hourly, Sat & Sun 7 daily; 1hr 15min); Ljubljana (Mon–Fri 9 daily, Sat & Sun 4 daily; 2hr 30min–3hr); Ljutomer (Mon–Fri 4 daily, Sat & Sun 1 daily; 1hr 20min); Murska Sobota (Mon–Fri every 30mins, Sat & Sun 6 daily; 1hr 10min); Ormož (Mon–Fri 4 daily, Sat & Sun 1 daily; 50min); Ptuj (Mon–Fri every 30mins, Sat hourly, Sun 7; 30min) Radenci (Mon–Sat every 30mins, Sat & Sun 6 daily; 1hr); Slovenske Konjice (Mon–Fri 9 daily, Sat & Sun 5 daily; 50min).
Moravske Toplice to: Bogojina & Filovci (en route to Dubrovnik) (Mon–Fri 8 daily; 10min); Lendava (Mon–Fri 3 daily; 30min); Murska Sobota (Mon–Fri 10 daily; 10min).
Murska Sobota to: Bakovci Mon–Fri hourly; 15min) Beltinci (Mon–Fri every 20–30min, Sat & Sun 3 daily; 15min); Bogojina (Mon–Fri 9 daily; 20min); Filovci (Mon–Fri 9 daily; 25min); Lendava (Mon–Fri hourly, Sat & Sun 3 daily; 40min); Ljubljana (Mon–Fri 3 daily, Sat & Sun 2 daily; 4hr); Ljutomer (Mon–Fri hourly; 40min); Maribor (Mon–Fri hourly Sat & Sun 5 daily; 1hr 10min); Moravske Toplice (9 daily; 10min); Radenci (Mon–Fri every 20–30mins, Sat & Sun 7 daily; 15min).
Ormož to: Ljutomer (Mon–Fri 6 daily; 30min); Maribor (2–3 daily; 50min); Ptuj (Mon–Fri 8 daily, Sat & Sun 2 daily; 30min).
Podčetrtek to: Bistrica ob Sotli (Mon–Fri 6 daily; 25min); Celje (Mon–Fri 5 daily; 45min); Rogaška Slatina (Mon–Fri hourly, Sat & Sun 4 daily; 20min).
Ptuj to: Ljutomer (2 daily; 1hr 10min); Maribor (Mon–Sat every 30min, Sat & Sun 7 daily; 30min); Ormož (Mon–Fri hourly, Sat & Sun 2 daily; 30min); Ptujska Gora (7 daily; 20min); Rogaška Slatina (Mon–Fri 1 daily; 1hr 5min).
Rogaška Slatina to: Celje (Mon–Fri 8 daily, Sat & Sun 3 daily; 40min); Ljubljana (1 daily; 2hr 30min); Maribor (Mon–Fri 4 daily, Sat & Sun 1 daily; 1hr 10min); Podčetrtek (Mon–Fri hourly, Sat & Sun 4 daily; 20min); Ptuj (Mon–Fri 1 daily; 1hr 5min); Rogatec (Mon–Fri 10 daily, Sat & Sun 1 daily; 15min).
Rogatec to: Celje (Mon–Fri 6 daily, Sat & Sun 2 daily; 50min); Ptuj (Mon–Fri 1 daily; 1hr 20min); Rogaška Slatina (Mon–Fri 4 daily, Sat & Sun 2 daily; 15min).
Slovenj Gradec to: Celje (2 daily; 45min); Dravograd (7 daily; 20min); Ljubljana (2 daily; 2hr); Maribor (3 daily; 1hr 20min); Velenje (every 45min–hourly, Sat & Sun 7 daily; 25min).
Slovenske Konjice to: Celje (Mon–Fri hourly, Sat & Sun 6 daily; 25min); Ljubljana (Mon–Fri 8 daily, Sat & Sun 5 daily; 2hr 15min); Maribor (Mon–Fri 9 daily, Sat & Sun 5 daily; 50min); Zreče (Mon–Fri hourly, Sat & Sun 4 daily; 10min).
Velenje to: Celje (Mon–Sat hourly, Sun 3; 25min); Črna na Koroškem (2 daily; 50min); Dravograd (7 daily; 40min); Ljubljana (Mon–Fri 3 daily, Sat & Sun 2 daily; 1hr 30min); Slovenj Gradec (hourly; 25min).
Zreče to: Celje (Mon–Fri 8 daily, Sat & Sun 1 daily; 25min); Slovenske Konjice (Mon–Fri hourly, Sat & Sun 4 daily; 10min).

International trains

Maribor to: Graz (3 daily; 1hr); Vienna (2 daily; 3hr 40min).
Murska Sobota to: Budapest (2 daily; 5hr 15min).

International buses

Lendava to: Čakovec (Croatia) (Mon–Sat 1 at 10.50am).
Ptuj to: Zagreb (Mon–Sat 1 daily + one more Fri).
Maribor to: Graz (Mon–Fri 1 daily at 7.30am).

Contexts

Contexts

The historical framework

Although recorded history of the area now covered by Slovenia begins with the arrival of the Romans, archeological finds suggest that this territory was already settled in the **Paleolithic** and **Neolithic** eras. The most intriguing discovery from the Paleolithic era was a bone flute unearthed from a cave in Šebrelje near Cerkno in 1995, whilst the most compelling evidence of the existence of a Neolithic culture comes from the Ljubljana Marshes south of the capital. Here, the inhabitants built wooden huts on stilts, made coarse pottery and raised livestock.

The early Iron Age, or **Halstatt**, period (eighth to fourth centuries BC) coincided with the arrival of the region's first identifiable peoples – Illyrian-speaking tribes, possibly called Veneti, who settled in the Alpine region. The major Hallstatt settlements were located in Most na Soči and throughout the region of Dolenjska, as indicated by some superb archeological finds in these areas, such as armour, jewellery and situlae (ornately embossed pails, or buckets). More generally, this was a period of great economic and cultural advancement. Around the third century BC the Halstatt cultures were superseded by the **Celts** who, led by the Norics, established a protostate called Noricum, the centre of which was located in the eastern Alps, whilst a second centre was established in the area of present-day Celje, then called Celeia.

The Romans

Noricum was subsumed into the Roman Empire around 10 BC, which more or less marked the beginning of **Roman occupation** on this territory. Settled by colonists from Aquileia (a small town in the Gulf of Trieste established by the Romans in 181 BC), Emona (Ljubljana) was the first Roman town to develop on the territory of present-day Slovenia, followed by Poetovio (Ptuj) and Celeia (Celje). Trade, administration and culture grew up around these garrison towns and spread along the roads constructed to link the imperial heartland with Pannonia and beyond. Some of the country's best-preserved Roman remains are still to be found in and around these towns, including vestigial ruins in Ljubljana, a wealth of monuments in Ptuj, and a superb Roman necropolis in Šempeter, just outside Celje. The most significant legacy of the Roman occupation was the partition of the Byzantine and Roman spheres – the Eastern and Western empires respectively – into separate civilizations, a division that would later result in a critical split between the Eastern Orthodox and Roman Catholic churches. The disintegration of the Roman Empire in the fifth century corresponded with a series of incursions into the region by a multitude of warring tribes, such as the Huns, Ostrogoths and Lombards, and the all-powerful **Avars**, a Turkic people from Central Asia whose empire survived well into the eighth century, before it was crushed by the Franks.

From the first Slav state to Habsburg rule

Although there is no definitive record as to when, or from where, the ancestors of today's Slovenes first entered the territory of present-day Slovenia, the most widespread theory is that migrating Slav tribes (loosely divided into two different, but related, groups, Slaveni and Antes) arrived from the Carpathian Basin in the middle of the sixth century. As Avar power waned, these tribes, along with others (including the great Kingdom of Samo), united into a loose confederation, resulting in the first Slav political entity, the **Duchy of Karantanija**, whose centre was located somewhere near present-day Klagenfurt just across the border in Austria. This brief period of autonomy lasted until 745 AD, when the Duchy was subsumed into the Carolingian Empire of the Franks, thus subjecting the Karantanian Slav population to a Germanic domination that would continue for several centuries more. Around the same time, an influx of western missionaries and the establishment of a formal church paved the way for the **Christianization of the Slovenes**.

In the tenth century, the Magyars, led by the feared Arpad clan, invaded and settled in the Slovenian regions of Pannonia. Before they were able to advance any further, however, they ran into the imperial forces of the German king, Otto I, who promptly routed them in a counter-offensive just outside Augsburg in 955 AD. German victory instigated the reorganization of Karantanian territory into frontier marches, namely, Carinthia (Koroška), Carniola (Kranjska), Styria (Štajerska), Gorica (Goriška) and Bela Krajina, the boundaries of which would essentially remain the same for the next thousand years.

The first chartered towns on Slovene territory – Kamnik, Piran, Ptuj, Škofja Loka, and the capital Ljubljana – began to develop a short while thereafter, around the beginning of the twelfth century. By the fourteenth century there would be some 27 towns and countless other market towns in Slovene lands, many of which developed trade and crafts industries as an adjunct to agricultural activity. Cultural life during this period, meanwhile, was mostly centred around the newly established monasteries, such as the Carthusian orders at Pleterje and Žiče, and the Cistercian orders at Kostanjevica and Stična. Although primarily schools for the education of the clergy, they also served a wider educational purpose, functioning as key centres of learning for intellectuals, musicians and so on. Meanwhile, the prominent ruling entities of this time – the Bamberg, Spanheim and Premysl dynasties – were confronted with the spectre of the Habsburgs who, by 1270, had already established a stronghold in the eastern Alps and would soon rule across most of the Slovene lands.

Habsburg rule, Turkish invasions and the Reformation

The **Habsburg dynasty** established its first feudal holdings in Slovene lands (the provinces of Carniola, Gorizia, Istria, Carinthia and Styria) in 1282, holding sway across most of the territory until the end of World War I, whilst small geographical areas in the eastern and western peripheries were governed by Hungary and Venice respectively. The only serious political rivals to the Habsburgs at this time were the **counts of Celje**, an aristocratic dynasty who, through a combination of fortuitous politics and skilfully arranged marriages into distinguished European feudal houses, managed to acquire great swathes of territory and wield tremendous influence across Slovene lands. Whilst the assassination of Count Ulrik II in Belgrade in 1456 nullified this particular threat, the Habsburgs now had to contend with other problems.

Having already conquered much of the Balkan peninsula in the first half of the fifteenth century, the **Ottoman Turks** resumed their advance north towards Slovene lands around 1470. Despite repeated raids, which reached their peak during the reign of Sultan Suleyman I "the Magnificent" (1520–1566), the defining moment was the **Battle of Sisak** in 1593, where the Turks were crushed by combined Habsburg-Croatian forces, an episode which effectively put the lid on Turkish aspirations in Habsburg-occupied lands.

The economic pressures engendered as a result of these assaults, coupled with the transformation of the old feudal tax system into less favourable forms, precipitated a series of violent and widespread **peasant revolts** throughout Slovene lands. The most famous of these was the 1573 uprising, during which some ten thousand Slovene and Croatian peasants (*puntarji*) participated – in the event, the rebellion was crushed, its leader, Matija Gubec, met a somewhat ignominious fate (crowned with a red-hot metal rod in Zagreb Cathedral), and the peasants were bound to perpetual serfdom. The prevalence of serfdom and other local agricultural policies meant that there was little other economic activity to speak of around this time, though pockets of proto-industrialization existed in parts of the country, for example, the Idrija Mercury Mine and the forges in Kropa.

The **Germanization** of culture, education and administration had been a key policy of Habsburg rule since the tenth century, yet despite this, Slovenes managed to preserve both their language and cultural identity. This was largely down to **Protestant reformers** such as **Primož Trubar** (the "Slovene Luther"), who wrote and published the first book in the Slovene language, and **Adam Bohorič**, who compiled the first Slovene grammar book, which was also the first grammar book in a Slav language. It would, however, be another two centuries before written Slovene would be appropriated for secular use. Having seen off the Turks, the Austrians, under Archduke Ferdinand, turned their attention to the religious revolts taking place throughout Habsburg lands, and by the end of the century the **Counter-Reformation** was in full swing. The ensuing period of recatholicization and absolutism resulted in a lengthy spell of political, economic and cultural regression for Slovenes.

The eighteenth century: reform and the Enlightenment

Prospects looked decidedly brighter at the turn of the eighteenth century owing to strong economic growth and modernization, manifest in the development of manufacturing industries – forges in Bohinj and Jesenice, textile mills in Ljubljana, improved transport links between Vienna and Trieste (via Maribor, Celje and Ljubljana), and the declaration of Trieste as a free port. These developments were taken a stage further under the centralized, state-building reforms of **Maria Theresa** and her son **Joseph II** during the second half of the century: judicial reforms were introduced, primary schooling was made compulsory and religious tolerance was decreed. More tendentiously, German replaced Latin as the language of government business, a move that caused some alarm amongst the emerging national groups, many of whom preferred to use their own language.

Led by the cultural innovator **Baron Žiga Zois** and a small coterie of Slovene intellectuals (the so-called "Zois Circle"), the **Slovene Enlightenment** (roughly 1760–1820) was the first sustained period of cultural advancement since the work of the sixteenth century Protestant reformers. This celebrated group featured the historian/playwright **Anton Linhart**, poet/journalist **Valentin Vodnik** – founder of the first Slovene newspaper, *Ljublanske Novice* (*The Ljubljana News*) – and the priest, **Marko Pohlin**, whose 1768 publication, *Kranjska gramatika* (Carniolan Grammar), was the forerunner to a modern Slovene literary language. In addition, theatres in Ljubljana, Maribor and Celje were built, public and private libraries became the focus for Slovene cultural life, while the establishment of assorted professional and cultural societies and institutions, including the Philharmonic Music Society (1794) and the literary and linguistic society, Academia Operosorum, affirmed Slovenia's integration into the circle of cultured European nations. It was also a time of great **Baroque** extravagance, particularly in the fields of architecture, painting and sculpture. Nowhere was this more so than in Ljubljana, which acquired several beautiful churches, church paintings and buildings. Leading Baroque contributors included the painters, Valentin Metzinger and Giulio Quaglio, architect Andrea Pozzo, and sculptor Francesco Robba, whose Fountain of the Three Carniolan Rivers in Ljubljana is one of the finest specimens of Baroque-era artwork in the country.

The nineteenth century: nationalism and reform

Following **Napoleon's** dissolution of the Venetian republic in 1797, the French were drawn into several wars against the Austrians, culminating in a hard-fought victory for the French at Wagram in 1809. Subsequent to this, Napoleon cut the Austrians off from the Adriatic and created a quasi-ethnic state, stretching from Graz in Austria down to the Bay of Kotor in Montenegro, a region known as the **Illyrian Provinces**. Over the next four years, and with Ljubljana designated as the provinces' administrative centre, Slovenes enjoyed a series of liberating French reforms, the most important of which was free use of the Slovene language in administration and schools. Following Napoleon's disastrous defeat at the hands of the Russians in 1813, and the subsequent collapse of the French Empire, Slovene territory was reincorporated into the Habsburg domain and all the old political and feudal systems were restored. Nevertheless, four years of French rule was long enough for Slovene intellectuals to be made aware of their ethno-national identities; moreover the inclusion of Croats, as well as a minority Serb population, within the same state gave rise to the notion that some form of common Slav union might one day be realized. These embryonic national sentiments were powerfully reinforced through the work of Slovenia's pre-eminent Romantic poet and greatest ever literary figure, **France Prešeren** (see box, p.123), who not only refashioned

Slovenian as a literary language but raised it to the level of other European languages. It was no surprise, therefore, when Prešeren's poem, *Zdravljica* (*A Toast*), was adopted as the Slovene national anthem in 1991.

The **1848 Revolution** was the catalyst for tremendous upheaval across continental Europe, including Austria, where the tenets of absolutism and serfdom had reigned since the demise of the Illyrian provinces in 1813. Fired by the literary brilliance of Prešeren and the pedagogic reforms of **Anton Slomšek** (the bishop of Maribor), **Slovene nationalism** became increasingly vocal around this time, culminating in calls for a **United Slovenia programme** (*Zedinjena Slovenija*), whose prime objectives were to unite all ethnic Slovene territories within one autonomous region and to promulgate the use of the Slovene language. In the event, no such programme was ever realized, though its basic tenets informed much of Slovene political life well into the next century. By and large though, most Slovenes remained committed to Austria and few envisaged a future outside the Habsburg Empire.

According to the terms of the **Compromise of 1867**, the Habsburg state became the **Dual Monarchy of Austria-Hungary**, whereby the two became constitutionally separate entities, albeit with the same Habsburg ruler, Franz Jozef – emperor in Austria and king in Hungary. In practice this meant shared common foreign and defence policies, but internally, each was governed by its own constitution. As a result of the compromise most Slovenes remained within Austria, though a small, yet significant, number were incorporated into Hungarian and Italian sectors. Around this time Slovenes began to make important strides politically, organizing themselves into distinct and identifiable political groupings, and by the turn of the century three core parties had been established: the liberal **National Progressive Party**, the conservative, or clerical **Slovene People's Party**, and the socialist **Yugoslav Democratic Party**, each of which presented alternative political philosophies, but who collectively espoused a common commitment to some form of pan-Slavism, or **Yugoslavism**, a political concept that had initially taken root earlier that century. However, despite adopting broadly nationalist agendas, which were largely premised upon the United Slovenia programme of some years earlier, all three parties remained firmly committed to their Austrian overlords, aware that they were too small and there were too few of them (even with their Slav allies) to go it alone. Instead, they concluded that **Trialism** – the notion that a third element, a South Slav component, would be created within the Habsburg Empire – could be the only possible framework for any form of Slovene self-determination. The latter part of the century was also a time of cultural efflorescence for Slovenes, manifest in the establishment of **reading societies** (*čitalnice*), the **Slovene Literary Society** (Slovenska Matica) and other gazettes, and the **Sokol** (Falcon) association, a patriotic gymnastic society which advocated the cult of the healthy body as well as Slavonic brotherhood.

In the two decades prior to World War I, Slovene political life became increasingly preoccupied with the idea of Yugoslavism, and while most Slovenes ostensibly remained loyal to Austria, there were those who felt increasingly uneasy with regard to Austria's domestic and foreign policies, and in particular its progressively cosy alliance with Germany. Championing the Yugoslav cause was the celebrated novelist **Ivan Cankar**, who posited that some form of linguistic and cultural merging was both practical and desirable. Cankar was closely associated with the avowedly anti-Austrian student organization **Preporod** (Rebirth), who, along with other South Slav groups, including the ultra-nationalist Young Bosnian movement from Sarajevo, advocated an independent Yugoslav state. Following the **assassination of Archduke Franz**

Ferdinand in Sarajevo in 1914 by Gavrilo Princip (a member of the Young Bosnians), Austria declared war on Serbia. Within a matter of days, Europe's major alliance systems had been activated – Germany joined forces with Austria, whilst their opponents, who supported Serbia, were the Entente powers of Russia, France and Britain.

World War I and the Kingdom of Serbs, Croats and Slovenes

During the formative stages of **World War I**, Slovenes fought in several arenas on behalf of the Austrian crown, including the Serbian and Russian fronts, though the prospect of fighting fellow Slavs appealed to few Slovenes and defections were common. The single most important factor affecting Slovenia during the course of the war was the **1915 London Pact**, under the terms of which Italians were persuaded to join the Entente forces in return for promises of land populated by Slovenes and Croats. Galvanized into action, Slovenes pitched in with the Austrians along the western, or **Soča**, front, which extended for some 90km from Mount Rombon, near Bovec, along the course of the Soča river down to a position just north of Trieste on the Adriatic coast. The Soča Front was one of the bloodiest battlegrounds of the entire war, with catastrophic losses on both sides, though particularly for the Italians who were routed during the famous twelfth and final offensive in the Krn mountain range above Kobarid in October 1917.

With an increasingly mutinous Slovene military, and the Habsburg Empire on the verge of collapse, a group of South Slav delegates, led by Slovene Anton Korošec, presented the **May 1917 declaration** to Vienna demanding the creation of an autonomous, democratic Slav state within the Habsburg monarchy. The demand was dismissed, but support for a unitary state continued apace and in October 1918, Serb, Croat and Slovene political leaders convened in Zagreb to form the **National Council**, at the same time declaring their independence from Budapest and Vienna. Little more than a month later, on December 1, 1918 in Belgrade, Serbian Prince Alexander Karađorđević declared the establishment of the **Kingdom of Serbs, Croats and Slovenes**, which also incorporated the territories of Bosnia, Montenegro and Macedonia.

At the end of the war, Slovenia's ethnic territory was subject to widescale dismemberment: whilst the greater part of Slovenia was incorporated into the kingdom, a significant portion of southern Carinthia was ceded to Austria and, under the terms of the **1920 Treaty of Rapallo**, almost a third of Slovene territory – which included the economically important cities of Trieste and Gorizia – was annexed to Italy. The first few years under Italian jurisdiction were bearable, but the situation worsened considerably following Mussolini's ascent to power: political and cultural institutions were banned, public use of the Slovene language was abolished (except in Catholic churches), and all Slavic geographical names were Italianized. Whilst large numbers of Slovenes chose to emigrate during this heightened period of Italian irredentism, many more established political, social and cultural organizations and underground movements, in order to fight for minority rights – some, such as the terror group, **TIRG** (Trst, Istra, Reka, Gorica), had several of its members executed.

For Slovenes living within the new kingdom, the situation was not much better than it was for those in Italy or Austria, and certainly not what they had in mind when they cast their lot with that of their fellow southern Slavs. The centralistic **1921 Vidovdan Constitution**, which established a parliamentary, constitutional monarchy for the kingdom, with Belgrade as its capital and Karađorđević as head of state, immediately buried any aspirations Slovenes (and other constituent groups within the state) may have had for political autonomy. Although traditional liberties were largely protected by the constitution, the rights of liberals and communists were frequently infringed and the king wielded almost absolute power. Years of political chaos – ineffectual governments, high-profile assassinations and persistent attempts to undermine Serb rule – culminated in the suspension of the constitution in January 1929. A **royal dictatorship** was imposed and the Kingdom of Serbs, Croats and Slovenes was recast as the **Kingdom of Yugoslavia**, ostensibly to foster Yugoslav political unitarism but which was ultimately a disaster for all non-Serbs. Increasingly violent nationalist strains began to emerge amongst the constituent groups, particularly in Croatia, where the ultranationalist, proto-fascist **Ustaše** movement were particularly prominent, and it was they who masterminded the assassination of King Alexander Karađorđević in Marseille in 1934. Authority, thereafter, passed to Prince Paul, whose regime merely escalated anti-Serb sentiment.

Another organization opposed to the unitary Yugoslav state was the **Communist Party of Yugoslavia** (CPY), which, from the time of its formation in 1919 until the mid-1930s, had remained a largely underground movement, with many of its congresses held abroad and most of its activity supervised from Moscow. With the appointment, in 1937, of **Josip Broz Tito** as its leader, the party began to reorganize itself into a federation of national units – hence the birth of the **Communist Party of Slovenia** (CPS). Of immediate concern to Slovenia was the menacing presence of Italian Fascism and German imperialism, for both Italy and Germany had territorial designs on Slovene lands.

World War II

Whereas in World War I Slovenia and the other Slav states found themselves embroiled in combat from the very start, it was over eighteen months after the start of **World War II** before Yugoslavia (and by implication, Slovenia) became involved. By this time much of continental Europe had already fallen under the sway of Germany and Italy. After initially being cowed into joining the Axis powers' orbit, Yugoslavia renounced the decision following a governmental coup, a decision they paid for on April 6, 1941, when Germany blitzed Belgrade. The king fled in exile to London and within a matter of days the country had capitulated. For its part, Slovenia was partitioned between Germany, which claimed the northern and eastern areas, Hungary, which took Prekmurje, and Italy, which annexed the rest. While the Italians were more or less sympathetic to Slovenes, allowing them a measure of cultural autonomy, those in the German and Hungarian occupied territories were subject to aggressive de-naturalizing policies – arrests, torture, execution and deportation.

In response, **resistance groups** took up arms almost immediately. Organized by the CPY, with Tito as chief military commander, a **Yugoslav Partisan**

resistance movement was established, while in Slovenia, the **Liberation Front** (OF – Osvobodilna Fronta), organized and controlled by the CPS and comprising Christian Socialists, the liberal Sokols and leftist intellectuals, as well as party members, was formed. The Liberation Front was broken up into smaller Partisan units, dispersed throughout the cities and countryside – circumstances, however, dictated that in the early stages at least, the Slovenes and Tito's Partisans were mostly detached from each other. The Slovene Partisan army continued in a fairly independent manner until 1944, when they joined forces in a wider pan-Yugoslav resistance movement, which had by now received official recognition from the Allies. By this stage Tito had already moved to establish a provisional government, the **Anti-Fascist Assembly for the National Liberation of Yugoslavia** (AVNOJ), which laid down the principles for the eventual Yugoslav state. For the most part, the terms of the programme – one of which made provision for a republic's right to self-determination (this was later dropped) – were welcomed by the Slovenes, as confirmed by their participation at the second AVNOJ meeting in Jajce, Bosnia, in 1943.

Communist resistance was complicated by conflicting political ideologies within Slovenia, which manifested itself in the emergence of several armed organizations. The most prominent of these was the **Home Guard** (Domobranci), a major anti-Communist organization formed in Ljubljana in September 1943 with the approval and assistance of the Germans. Their resistance, however, didn't last long. Faced by overwhelming Partisan force, the Guard was forced to retreat into Austrian Carinthia, where they were met by the British and disarmed as German collaborators. Following their repatriation to Slovenia and the waiting Partisans, thousands of guardists and anti-Communist civilians (estimates suggest up to ten thousand in total) were executed and thrown into pits close to the Liberation Fronts' wartime headquarters in the forests of Kočevski Rog in southern Slovenia. The grisly secrets were only revealed to the wider Slovene public some thirty years later, when politician and writer Edvard Kocbek spilled the beans in an interview with a Trieste newspaper.

Having finally driven the occupying forces from Slovene territory in May 1945, the Partisans liberated Trieste that same month, but just two months later the Western Allies issued an ultimatum requiring Yugoslav forces to leave. At the 1946 Paris Peace Conference the region was partitioned into two zones: Zone A (Trieste and hinterland), controlled by the Allies, and Zone B (Slovene coast and Istria), controlled by Yugoslavia. The **1954 London Agreement** restored Zone A to Italy, thus bringing an end to a bitter and long-standing dispute, though many Italians returned to Italy, as they had done at the end of the war.

The second Yugoslavia: Tito and socialism

Following the émigré government's recognition of Tito as *de facto* leader, **elections** were held towards the end of 1945, though these were something of a foregone conclusion, given that the only party standing was the **People's Front**, an organization dominated by the Communist Party. Following these elections, the monarchy was abolished and in November the **Federal People's**

Republic of Yugoslavia was proclaimed, comprising six federal republics – Serbia, Croatia, Bosnia, Macedonia, Montenegro and Slovenia.

Power was now incontrovertibly held in the hands of the Communists, who sought to emulate the Soviet model of control, a system shaped by central planning, nationalization of property and ideological conformity – this also included a substantial amount of **forced industrialization** throughout the entire country, although the speed with which this was done created numerous problems, not least the decline in agricultural practices, as individual and large institutional landowners were expropriated without compensation. A critical rift over political and ideological differences between the Soviet Union and Yugoslavia in 1948 resulted in the latter's **expulsion from the Cominform**, the Soviet-controlled organization of European communist countries. The split effected an almost immediate (albeit cosmetic) change in name of both the Communist Party of Yugoslavia, renamed the **League of Communists of Yugoslavia** (LCY), and the Communist Party of Slovenia, renamed the **League of Communists of Slovenia** (LCS).

More importantly it presented Tito with an opportunity to fashion his own, alternative brand of communism, one that featured a mix of socialist and capitalist ideals. The basic institution at the heart of "Titoism", as it was known, was a system of **workers' self-management** which, as the slogan, "Factories to the workers!", suggested, vested greater power in the hands of the workers. Such an approach, however, was open to the possibility of dissent, which duly occurred in the form of strikes and political criticism, particularly in Slovenia. In the international arena, meanwhile, Tito manoeuvred carefully, his policy of **nonalignment** enabling Yugoslavia to secure prestigious international endorsement. Meanwhile, those party members suspected of collaborating with Stalin (known as "Conformists") were immediately purged and packed off to concentration camps, such as the notorious Goli Otok ("Bare Island") camp in the Adriatic. With regard to this there were few dissidents on the Slovene side, the Slovene Communists well aware that supporting a federal Yugoslav republic was their only option, especially given that such a Yugoslavia would support Slovenia's claims to ethnic territory in Italy and Austria.

The 1960s and 1970s

Yugoslavia in the 1960s was characterized by strong economic growth and improved living conditions, particularly for Slovenes, many of whom could travel freely abroad, a liberty denied to citizens of most other countries in the Eastern bloc, including many within the Yugoslav federation itself. That said, Slovenes, and to a lesser degree, Croats, were becoming increasingly resentful at the federal bureau's centrally planned means of redistribution, whereby money was siphoned off to support the less wealthy republics in the federation, thereby stifling economic development for the likes of Slovenia. The so-called **Road Affair** of 1969 was indicative of such problems. Having solicited funds from the World Bank for the development of its road network – in order to better facilitate trade with neighbouring countries and increase tourism opportunities – the federal authorities redistributed the money to road projects in other republics instead, triggering widespread public protests throughout Slovenia. The federal bureau merely dismissed the protest as nothing more than the work of a bunch of renegade Slovene nationalists. In any case, the Road

Affair signalled the end of the **liberalization movement** of the 1960s, whose members had pushed for major market economic reforms throughout Yugoslavia. Fearful of losing control, the conservative Communists purged the party of its stronger liberal elements, before turning their attention to those in other institutions – universities, intellectual journals and the media.

Numerous **constitutional amendments and changes** (such as those of 1953, 1963 and 1974) repeatedly brought to the surface old arguments about decentralization and the need for greater autonomy within the federation, with Slovenia invariably at the forefront of these disputes. The **1974 constitution** went a stage further than previous ones, in that it not only gave more autonomy to the provinces of Vojvodina and Kosovo, but it also made provision for each republic to assume greater responsibility for its own internal affairs. However, the issue of centralism versus federalism, a recurring theme since the formation of the Kingdom of Serbs, Croats and Slovenes back in 1918, remained at the forefront of Slovene, and Yugoslav, political life right up to and following **Tito's death** in 1980.

The 1980s

With the death of its founding father, the federal construct began to fall apart in dramatic fashion: Yugoslavia had racked up enormous foreign debt and unemployment, inflation had reached unacceptably high levels, and **inter-republic relations** were at an all-time low. Of particular concern were the worsening relations between the Serbs and the Albanian majority in the autonomous province of Kosovo in southern Serbia, where riots in 1981 were followed by further draconian anti-Albanian measures, culminating in the annulment of the province's autonomy in 1989. On the domestic front, in 1986, Milan Kučan was elected president of the League of Communists of Slovenia, who were by now struggling to reconcile the political and ideological doctrines of the Yugoslav League of Communists with the increasingly widespread pluralistic inclinations pervading Slovenian society around this time.

In particular it was the emergence of **avant-garde and alternative movements** (also known as new social movements) – foremost amongst these were the arts collective **Neue Slowenische Kunst** (New Slovene Art), one of whose members was the legendary punk rock group Laibach, see p.333 – that paved the way for the democratization of Slovene society. No less influential were the countercultural **magazines** *Nova Revija* (New Review) and *Mladina* (Youth; see box on p.35), both of which provided broad-based platforms for cultural and intellectual expression and exchange, as well as political dialogue and debate. In *Nova Revija's* infamous issue no. 57 (February 1987), the magazine published "Contributions to a Slovene National Programme", a collection of papers that outlined provisions for Slovenian self-determination (this essentially echoed and amplified the content of *Revija 57*, a document which had appeared exactly thirty years earlier). Despite intense pressure from the federal government, the Slovene authorities refused to acquiesce to Belgrade's demands for those responsible to be prosecuted. *Mladina*, meanwhile, continued to provoke with its fearless and often humorous attacks on key organs and individuals within the Yugoslav federation, and articles on social taboos such as homosexuality and World War II massacres. In 1988, three of the magazine's members, along with an officer, were hauled up before a military court on trumped up charges of betraying state secrets (widely believed to be a plan for military intervention in Slovenia), an affair known as the **Ljubljana Four Trial**. Conducted entirely in secret and in Serbo-Croatian, the trial was considered unconstitutional by most Slovenes, and served only to radicalize political opinion towards Belgrade. The trial, and the mass rallies that it inspired, represented the last hurrah for these movements, which became increasingly marginalized thereafter.

The fall of the Berlin Wall in November 1989 set in motion a chain of events which convulsed Eastern Europe, culminating in the bloody overthrow of Ceaušescu in Romania. These events, though, had little direct effect on Yugoslavia, which was readying itself for its own, spectacular implosion.

The road to independence

At the fourteenth and final Congress of the Yugoslav League of Communists in January 1990, Slovenian calls for absolute independence for the respective communist parties were given short shrift by the Serbs. In response, the Slovene delegation walked out of the assembly, an incident that effectively spelt

The Ten-Day War

Even as Slovenes were celebrating the declaration of independence in Ljubljana on the night of June 26, the Serb-dominated **Yugoslav army** (JNA) had begun manoeuvring tank units towards Ljubljana's Brnik airport, and some thirty border posts that Slovenia had taken over following the declaration. The well-drilled Slovenian defence comprised the Territorial Defence (which itself was removed from the JNA's jurisdiction in a constitutional amendment the previous year) and the police, and orchestrated by Minister of Defence Janez Janša, ironically one of those implicated in the Ljubljana Four Trial three years earlier.

As Slovene soldiers and officers began **deserting** the Yugoslav army in droves, the first strikes took place, though the capture of Brnik and threatened assault on the capital itself never materialized. In the event, there were few major clashes, with the majority of engagements being small-scale skirmishes at key traffic points and border positions. Nevertheless, and much to the surprise of the Yugoslav army – as well as neutral observers and many Slovenes themselves – the Slovene forces proved themselves to be more than competent adversaries, forcing around 2500 JNA troops to desert or **surrender**, whilst many more were captured. Following a flurry of diplomatic activity and several attempts to mediate by European Union representatives, the ten-day conflict was brought to an end on July 7, following the brokering of the Brioni Agreement, which provided for an **immediate ceasefire** and **withdrawal** of the Yugoslav army. Moreover, it stipulated that Slovenia put its declaration of independence on hold for a further three months. In human terms, the price was relatively low: officially, 21 Slovenes (military and civilian) were killed and a further 100 wounded, whilst 39 Yugoslav troops were killed and around 160 wounded.

The reason for Belgrade's confused and rather diffident policy in Slovenia was unclear, though most analysts concurred that it was based on an (ill-founded) assumption that a short, sharp show of force would be enough to cow the Slovenes into submission – failing that, they could resort to a policy of escalation. Their humiliating climb-down, meanwhile, was attributed to the fact that Serbia had no strong territorial or ethnic claims to Slovenia.

the end of the Yugoslav Communist Party. Just three months later, in April 1990, the country's first ever multiparty elections were won by the coalition Demos Party (Democratic Opposition of Slovenia), whilst **Milan Kučan**, the reformed Communist leader of the Party of Democratic Renewal (SDP) – formerly the League of Communists of Slovenia – was sworn in as president. Immediately after the elections, a number of constitutional amendments were implemented, thus paving the way for eventual separation from the Yugoslav federation.

The one remaining obstacle was Serbia which, with Slobodan Miloševič in charge and championing a greater Serbia, now had control of four of the eight votes on the federal presidency (those of Vojvodina, Kosovo and Montenegro, in addition to its own), prompting Slovenes, somewhat mischievously, to coin the phrase "Serboslavia". Undaunted, Slovenia pressed on, and in December that year a **plebiscite for independence** was held, the result of which was an overwhelming 88 percent vote (the turn out was 93 percent) for a split with the federation. Six months later, on June 25, 1991, the Slovene Parliament passed a constitutional law declaring independence, thus triggering the **Ten-Day War** (see box, p.325). Slovene independence was formally recognized by the European Union on January 15, 1992, and the country was officially admitted into the United Nations on May 22.

The 1990s

Whilst the war continued to savage effect for another four years in Croatia and Bosnia, Slovenia was facing up to the **difficult transition** from communist to market economy. Despite possessing an already relatively sound economy – especially compared to its former federal partners – Slovenia still faced considerable problems, namely, rising unemployment, low salaries and high inflation, whilst additional strains were being placed upon the economy as a result of the influx of refugees fleeing the chaos in Croatia and Bosnia. The task of economic restructuring was further complicated by the necessary imposition of **trade barriers** with the other republics, hitherto its most important markets. Moreover, potential foreign investors were frightened off by the perceived political risks associated with the ongoing **hostilities in the region**. It was for this very same reason that tourist numbers remained well below the levels the country experienced prior to the war, when it was one of the most popular destinations in Yugoslavia. However, the introduction of a **new currency** (the *tolar*), coupled with reforms in the banking and public service sectors, and the creation of new institutions, gradually smoothed the path to economic stability.

Slovenia's first **multiparty elections** as an independent nation took place in December 1992, by which stage internal discord within the Demos coalition had seen that party disband. Of the eight parties to win seats in the ninety-member parliament, it was the reform-oriented centre-left Liberal Democratic Party, led by the introverted yet competent **Janez Drnovšek** (he was also president of the Yugoslav Federation from May 1989 to May 1990), who secured the greatest number of votes (22 percent), followed by the centre-right Slovene Christian Democrats. Drnovšek himself was elected head of the coalition government. That same month saw the popular and avuncular Kučan returned as president, thus cementing his considerable standing in Slovene politics. Four years down the line, the 1996 elections yielded similar results, with the Liberal Democrats once again topping the polls, leaving Drnovšek to form a coalition government with seven other parties, despite the clear ideological differences between them. However, as in 1992, the overriding agenda was economic and political modernization. In November the following year, the unassailable Kučan was re-elected president for a second and final term.

One of the key issues dominating the political agenda was **Europe**, and in particular Slovenia's prospective membership of both NATO and the European Union, organizations to which the country had aspired since 1994. With high hopes going into the Madrid summit in June 1997, Slovenia was somewhat dismayed to find itself omitted from the invitation list. This sense of grievance was compounded when Hungary, Poland and the Czech Republic formally joined NATO in March 1999, just as the alliance was preparing to launch strikes on Serbia following the collapse of diplomatic talks aimed at ending the escalating violence in Kosovo. Whilst relations with Serbia had more or less normalized by this stage, most Slovenes shed few tears over the country's plight, regarding the bombing campaign as just desserts for the events of 1991. Yet the bombing cast yet another long shadow over the region, precipitating, amongst other things, another alarming drop in visitor numbers to the country.

Europe and the New Millennium

Since the early 1990s, Slovenia was always regarded as one of the outstanding candidates for EU accession amongst the central and east European countries, which was in part a reflection of the country's relatively strong economic and political standing. The invitation to open accession talks following the Madrid summit went some way to making up for the NATO snub. In fact these talks were arguably of greater importance to Slovenia, given the wider opportunities, particularly from an economic perspective, that potential membership afforded. Obstacles remained, however, not least a simmering feud between Slovenia and **Italy** (one of the more influential EU members) over disputed property rights, and in particular the issue of **restitution of property** to Italian owners who had emigrated from Yugoslavia after World War II, an issue Slovenes claimed had been resolved in 1983 following the Treaty of Rome.

Relations with **Croatia** have been no less troubled in recent years, with disputes over the question of outstanding debt of the Zagreb branch of Slovenia's now defunct Ljubljanska Bank, as well as questions over the rights and responsibilities pertaining to the Krško nuclear reactor in southern Slovenia, which was built to provide energy for both republics. By far the thorniest issue concerns the long-standing dispute over **sea borders** in the Bay of Piran. The initial problem arose because no sea border ever existed during the time of Yugoslavia, and neither was one defined once the two countries had seceded from the federation. Following a series of incidents in the disputed waters, the situation reached crisis point in the summer of 2003, when Croatia unilaterally announced its intention to declare an Exclusive Economic Zone (EEZ), a move vehemently opposed by Slovenia, who argued that it would be impossible to create such a zone if the boundaries of the territorial waters hadn't been defined. Moreover, any such zone would effectively invalidate Slovenia's right to access international waters. Despite much diplomatic activity, including the issuing of various codes of conduct, and attempts at bilateral border agreements, a final solution appears to be as far away as ever. Slovenia's recent accession to the EU, which has entailed the imposition of tighter border controls between the two countries, is unlikely to do much to ameliorate this fraught relationship. By way of contrast, relations with Serbia have improved immeasurably since the conflicts of some years earlier, a fact confirmed by the resumption of bilateral relations in 2000.

The **elections** in December 2002 brought to an end the decade-long Kučan-Drnovšek union, for Kučan was obliged to stand down having served the maximum two terms allowed in the constitution. His retirement paved the way for Drnovšek as his successor, though not before a closer than expected run-off against the independent candidate, Barbara Brezigar. Drnovšek's elevation, meanwhile, opened the door for a new prime minister, a post duly taken up by finance minister and vice-president of the senior coalition party (Liberal Democrats), Anton Rop. Rop was immediately assigned the task of forming a new government from a broad-based coalition of four parties.

On the international front, final accession negotiations to both NATO and the EU were wrapped up at the tail end of 2002, with referendums held the following March. As predicted, support for the former was far from overwhelming, though a 66 percent "yes" vote was much higher than anticipated; support for the EU, meanwhile, was more or less unequivocal, with the "yes" camp accounting for almost 90 percent of the vote. **NATO membership** was finally confirmed in March 2004, and was followed just over a month later, on May 1st, by the country's **admission into the European Union** alongside nine other central-eastern European countries. With membership of the aforementioned bodies now safely in the can, allied to a strong economy and a thriving tourism sector, Slovenia has every reason to feel optimistic.

Books, film and music

There's a real dearth of books about Slovenia in the English language, in every genre. What recent titles there are, particularly travelogues and historical or political publications, have tended to revolve almost exclusively around the other countries of the former Yugoslavia. Slovenia's literary heritage, however, is strong, and whilst there's little available in translation, there are several impressive anthologies to choose from. Likewise, in film and music, Slovenia has yielded some terrific, and influential, artists and producers in recent years, though, with the exception of one or two, few are known beyond the country's borders.

Books and literature

The number of publications dedicated to the break-up of Yugoslavia is considerable, yet in most cases there is scant coverage of Slovenia's involvement in the conflict. Whilst you'll find some reference to Slovenia in the titles below, you may also find the following excellent reads in their own right, and well worth dipping into if you're travelling more widely around the region: Misha Glenny *The Fall of Yugoslavia*; John Allcock *Explaining Yugoslavia*; John Lampe *Yugoslavia as History*; Branka Magas & Ivo Žanič *The War in Croatia and Bosnia-Herzegovina 1991–1995*; and Leslie Benson *Yugoslavia: A Concise History*.

Jill Benderley and Evan Craft *Independent Slovenia* Enjoyable and wide-ranging collection of essays pertaining to the country's historical development up to and including independence. The most interesting accounts are those which chart the development of the so-called new social movements of the 1980s (trade unions, women's organizations and the local punk scene), all of which helped fashion a strong and independent civil society in the run-up to independence.

Janez Bogotaj *Handicrafts of Slovenia*. Beautifully illustrated work covering Slovenia's rich tradition of crafts, including ceramists, potters, lace-makers, weavers and glass painters.

Simon Brown *Walking in the Julian Alps*. Useful, though now rather dated, pocket-sized book detailing over thirty trails throughout the Julian Alps, with treks starting from Bled, Bohinj, Bovec and Kranjska Gora. Although essentially a guide to the French/Italian/Swiss Alps, Kev Reynolds' *Walking in the Alps* (Cicerone Press) also features a short chapter on hiking in the Julian Alps.

Aleš Debeljak *Twilight of the Idols; Recollections of a lost Yugoslavia*. Better known for fiction and poetry (see p.331), the Slovene novelist turns his attention here to politics in this critical reflection on the disintegration of Yugoslavia.

James Gow and Cathie Carmichael *Slovenia and the Slovenes*. This is the most thorough-going assessment of twentieth-century Slovenian history currently available. The introductory chapter sets the tone with an illuminating overview of the country, and is followed by very readable accounts of Slovenia's cultural, economic and political maturation; the book concludes with a revealing insight into the events surrounding the country's drive for independence and the Ten-Day War.

Andrej Hrausky and Janez Koželj *Architectural Guide to Ljubljana*. Insightful guide to one hundred of the capital's buildings, from its castles and churches to its many Baroque and Secessionist splendours, as well as most of the projects conceived by Slovenia's greatest ever urban planner, Jože Plečnik. For more on Plečnik, try the more detailed *Plečnik's Ljubljana*, and *National and University Library, Ljubljana*.

Tine Mihelič *Mountaineering in Slovenia*. Excellent and easy-to-follow guide to tackling Slovenia's most important summits, in the Julian, Kamnik and Savinja Alps, and the Karavanke mountains. Complete with diagrams and lots of shiny pictures.

Janko Prunk *A Brief History of Slovenia*. Broad historical sweep of Slovenia's land, people and culture from pre-Roman times up until the Ten-Day War, with a postscript on subsequent political developments.

David Robertson and Sarah Stewart *Landscapes of Slovenia*. Regional books with small maps and photos detailing easy to moderate walks, mostly covering the western half of Slovenia, as well as half a dozen car tours.

Literature

Although written records in Slovenian appeared as early as the tenth century, **Slovenian literature** began to systematically develop during the **sixteenth-century Reformation**, thanks to leading reformers Primož Trubar (writer of the first Slovene book, the primer *Abecedarium*, in 1550), Jurij Dalmatin (the first Slovene translation of the Bible, in 1584), and linguist Adam Bohorič, whose *Arcticae horulae* (Winter Hours) was the first Slovene Grammar book, written in Latin and published the same year as Dalmatin's Bible. Around a century later Janez Vajkard Valvasor (see box, p.235) wrote and published (in German) the *Glory of the Duchy of Carniola*, a seminal work that synthesized the country's history, sights and peoples in one encyclopedic, four-volume work; to this day it remains the single most important document written about the Slovene lands.

It was during the period of **romanticism** in the early nineteenth century that Slovene literature reached its first peak, thanks to the poet France Prešeren (see box on p.123), the most iconic literary figure in Slovenia's history. Although very little of Prešeren's work has been translated into English, the audio CD, *Sonnets of Unhappiness*, is a beautifully read collection (by Vanessa Redgrave, Katrin Cartlidge and Simon Callow) of the poet's key works. The next writers to make their mark were the **realists**, led by the playwright Josip Jurčič, whose enduringly popular *Deseti Brat* (*The Tenth Brother*) was the first ever full-length Slovene novel to be published (1866) – an abridged version is available in English. Literary trends at the turn of the twentieth century were shaped by the so-called **Moderna movement**, whose main representatives were Oton Župančič and Ivan Cankar, the second of whom is regarded as Slovenia's finest ever prose writer – a prolific and highly politicized essayist, novelist and polemicist, Cankar was also one of the first to champion a southern Slav union.

The coexistent movements of expressionism and social realism that had dominated both the artistic and literary landscape prior to, and just after, World War II, eventually gave way to western literary trends, notably **symbolism and existentialism**. Foremost amongst these writers was the dissident politician and ex-Partisan Edvard Kocbek, whose opposition to communist ideology and socialist repression manifested itself in a short story collection, *Strah in pogum* (*Fear and Courage*), and the diaries *Tovarišija* (*Comrades*) and *Listina* (*The Document*) – it also landed him a spell in prison. Similar critiques of the resistance movement were the preserve of other commentators at that time, too, including Dane Zajc and Tomaž Šalamun, the doyens of Slovene postwar poets.

Prominent amongst the **new generation** of writers are essayist and poet Aleš Debeljak – *The City and the Child* is one of his best volumes of poetry; post-modern fiction writer Andrej Blatnik, whose collection of short stories, *Skinswaps*, is a good introduction to his work; and poet and gay rights activist Brane Mozetič. Given that there's only a limited amount of Slovenian **literature in translation**, you're best off starting with one of the several excellent anthologies available: *A Bilingual Anthology of Slovene Literature* includes poems and prose by a panoply of Slovenia's literary greats, from Trubar and Prešeren, to Kocbek and Šalamun, while *The Imagination of Terra Incognita; Slovenian Writing 1945–1995* is the best available anthology of essays, poems and fiction by authors from the second half of the last century. A useful reference book is *Key: Slovenia: Contemporary Slovenian Literature in Translation*.

Film

Cinematography in Slovenia made its mark as early as 1905, with the short documentaries *The Fair at Ljutomer* and *People Leaving the Church*, shot by the pioneer of Slovene film, Karol Grossman. The development of the industry continued apace after World War II, a golden period for Slovene film thanks to the state-financed Triglav Film house, which produced several classics, such as *Kekec*, Jože Gale's enduringly popular 1952 film about a clever shepherd boy, and France Stiglič's 1956 film, *Dolina Miru* (*Valley of Peace*). Despite the fact that on average around just five films a year are made in Slovenia – one of the lowest outputs amongst central-eastern European countries – a fine crop of movies have been released in recent years, though, predictably, few of these ever make it beyond their own country or the occasional art film festival in western Europe. By far the most successful and celebrated of these – it was actually a joint Belgian-French-Italian-Slovenian project, and shot in the village of Bač near Postojna – was the Oscar-winning (Best Foreign Film 2001) *Nikogaršnje ozemlje* (*No Man's Land*) by Bosnian director Danis Tanovič. Featuring a Bosnian and a Serb as the two protagonists trapped together in a trench somewhere between enemy lines, it's an acute, compassionate, and darkly comic, dissection of a pitiless conflict, and without doubt one of the most affecting movies ever made about the Yugoslav wars. Another recent landmark Slovenian film, and winner of the prestigious Golden Lion award at the 2001 Venice Film festival, *Kruh in Mleko* (*Bread and Milk*) is the outstanding debut film by young director Jan Cvetkovič, a brooding social commentary on the effects of alcoholism and alienation in small-town Slovenia. Other films to look out for include Damjan Kožole's *Rezervni deli* (*Spare Parts*), a gritty drama about human trafficking across Slovenia, and *Zvenenje v glavi* (*Headnoise*), an unusual action flick centred around a prison uprising during a basketball match between Yugoslavia and the United States in 1970.

Slovenia stages a couple of excellent **film festivals** each year: the Festival of Slovenian Film in Celje during September, and the Ljubljana International Film Festival (LIFFe), which takes place in the capital in November (see p.84).

Music

As in other spheres of the arts and culture, Slovenia's musical heritage is surprisingly strong, and is manifest in ancient **folk** traditions and a **punk/rock** scene, which, during the 1980s, spawned some of the most exciting and controversial music in the former Yugoslavia. Whilst Slovenia has few **jazz** artists of its own, the genre has a small, yet devout following, as testified by the increasing number of bars with live music and a world-class summer jazz festival in Ljubljana. There's no shortage of other music events either, chief amongst which are the **world music** festival, Druga Godba, and Rock Otočec, which invariably attracts a strong international line-up; moreover, there are countless folk gatherings and **classical** music concerts staged around the country each summer.

Folk music

Whilst **Slovenian folk music** (Ljudska Glasba) generally belongs to the alpine, Austro-Bavarian cultural sphere, the best and most authentic song and dance emanates from the rural towns and villages of Bela Krajina and Prekmurje. The most traditional forms of Slovenian folk music are based on age-old folk literature and poems; this music would usually be performed for both ritual and entertainment functions (weddings, family holidays and religious ceremonies), and utilizes instruments such as the *okarina* (clay flute), *trstenka* (panpipe), *drumlja* (Jew's Harp) and the *gudalo*, a small clay pot over the top of which a pig's bladder is stretched – the bass sound emitted is made by rubbing the straw rod which extends up through the membrane. Although their role in everyday life has largely diminished you are likely to come across traditional music during local festivals.

Some of the best Slovene folk music in recent years has come out of the small village of Beltinci in Prekmurje, and in particular the remarkable **Beltinška Banda Kociper**, a kind of Mitteleuropean Buena Vista Social Club, whose members, who play the fiddle (a stock Prekmurje instrument), violin, clarinet, cimbalom, double bass and accordion, have been delighting audiences for more than half a century. The baton has now been passed down to a new generation of musicians from the same village, namely the four-strong **Marko Banda**, and the ten-strong, teenage **Mlada Beltinska Banda**. Other folk musicians to listen out for include the stunning all-female vocal group **Katice**, who specialize in interpreting classic harmonies from the Rezija mountain valley region on the Italian side of the Julian Alps; **La Zonta**, who perform traditional Istrian dances using bagpipes, fiddle and accordion; and the soloist, **Tomaž Podobnikar**, whose repertoire extends to playing the dulcimer and the amazing singing saw.

No self-respecting gathering is complete without some form of **dancing**, which, like songs, varies greatly from region to region. The oldest types of dances developed in Bela Krajina during the sixteenth century, and were heavily influenced by the Uskoks, bands of renegades from Serbia and Croatia who fled the Turks and settled in the region: the most popular of these is the *kolo*, an energetic, circular group dance performed to both musical and vocal accompaniment. The dances of Prekmurje are less exuberant affairs – typical is the *tkalecka* (weaver's dance), a kind of skipping dance whereby handkerchiefs are waved under the knees (reminiscent of an English Morris dance) – whilst those of Primorska are of an altogether more refined bent, having been established in bourgeois circles.

Although not strictly folk, Slovenia's best-known band, at least outside their own country, are **Terra Folk**, a group of four academically and classically trained musicians, whose free-ranging repertoire of Balkan, Gypsy, Folk, Klezmer, Irish and classical pretty much defies any standard form of categorization. Featuring an eclectic set of clarinet, bodhran (a kind of Celtic Drum played with a double ended stick), violin, flute, guitar, and occasionally double bass, Terra Folk's reputation has largely been built upon their entertaining live shows which combine ebullient musicianship with a roguish sense of humour. Their biggest accolade to date came at the 2003 World Music Awards in London, when they scooped the Audience Award, while that same year they also delighted audiences at the Edinburgh Fringe Festival. The group tour incessantly, and devote much of their schedule to playing in the UK as well as their homeland, so there's a good chance of catching them live somewhere. Terra Folk's clarinet player, Boštjan Gombač, also stars in the six-piece ensemble **Katalena**, another slightly unorthodox outfit who marry traditional folk forms with souped-up jazz and blues to beautiful effect.

Rock and pop

Although a number of creative bands emerged throughout Yugoslavia in the 1970s, Ljubljana was the first of all the Yugoslav cities to develop an authentic, home-grown musical scene of its own. In particular, it was the emergence of a local punk subculture in the late 1970s, alongside other so-called new social movements, that set the tone for the next few years. The most prominent of the first generation of punk bands were **Pankrti** (The Bastards), although they, like the majority of punk groups and their followers at that time were deemed a threat to civil society by the authorities, who attempted to associate the movement with Nazism; concerts were prohibited, persecution by the police was commonplace, and spurious accusations against punks abounded in the media. Decimated by the state in the early 1980s, the punk scene was eventually supplanted by other social movements, most notably an avant-garde collective called **Neue Slowenische Kunst** (New Slovene Art, or NSK), whose core members were the visual artists Irwin, the theatrical group Sestre Scipion Nasice, and the rock group Laibach.

Conceived in the industrial mining town of Trbovlje in 1980, shortly after Tito's death, **Laibach** produced some of the most uncompromising music and art ever to come out of the former Yugoslavia. Following an interview on national television in June 1983 – six months after the band's original singer and spokesman, Tomaž Hostnik, committed suicide – Laibach were summarily banned from appearing in public, the authorities reasoning that the band's use of the German language (Laibach is the German name for Ljubljana, and was used during both Habsburg rule and the Nazi occupation) and their apparent appropriation of Nazi images was just a cover for the resurgence of fascism. Laibach, meanwhile, maintained that, rather than espousing totalitarianism, they were in fact exposing its ugliest facets. Ostracized, the group embarked on the "Occupied Europe Tour" later that year, a tour that took them to countries on both sides of the Iron Curtain and exposed them for the first time to audiences outside their own country. Laibach marked the lifting of the ban in 1987 with a series of homecoming gigs (the "Bloody Ground-Fertile Soil" tour) in several Yugoslav cities, including Zagreb and Belgrade.

Returning to Belgrade two years later, the group delivered a typically incendiary speech, warning against the inflammatory rhetoric of Slobodan Miloševič, alongside a screening of a 1941 German propaganda film on the bombing of the Serbian capital.

Since their eponymously titled debut in 1985, Laibach have released more than a dozen albums. Their earlier recordings were wilfully experimental, avant-garde exercises, which drew heavily upon the electronic minimalism of Kraftwerk and DAF – as a result they do not make for easy listening. Towards the end of the 1980s the group moved towards a more overt and accessible rock sound (though still remaining faithful to their trademark militant Wagnerian soundscape), thanks in part to their predilection for doing cover albums, namely the Beatles' *Let it Be*, and the Stones' *Sympathy for the Devil*, neither of which will sound quite the same again once you've heard Laibach's version. The group returned to familiar ground with the 1994 release, *NATO*, which pointedly anticipated the expansion of western influence in the region, and included covers of Status Quo's *You're in the Army Now* and Pink Floyd's *Dogs of War*, while 1996's metal-driven *Jesus Christ Superstars* marked another shift in musical direction. After a seven-year hiatus, Laibach returned in 2003 with *WAT* (We Are Time), as direct and aggressive a record as any previously released and one that marked a return to the heavy techno/industrial rhythms of earlier albums.

Although few bands of note have emerged since Laibach's heyday, **popular music** has undergone something of a revival in recent years. Spearheading the charge is the youthful, six-piece band, **Siddharta**, whose melodic brand of stadium rock has made them the most successful and popular home-grown outfit since Laibach – interestingly, *B-Mashina*, a track from the band's second album, *Nord*, was covered (in English) by Laibach for their last album, *WAT* (see above). Other current popular acts range from mainstream pop groups (**The Elevators** and **Big Foot Mama**), to dance and techno-inspired performers like the multi-rooted **DJ Umek**, a regular on the European tour circuit. Two stalwarts of the Slovenian music scene are the singer-songwriter **Vlado Kreslin**, who has kept legions of fans in thrall for nearly two decades with his folksy brand of guitar-based rock, and the perennially popular poet and songwriter, **Zoran Predin**, who first came to prominence some twenty years ago as the founder of the rock group Lačni Franz (Hungry Franz). In addition to writing film and theatre scores, Predin now spends most of his time collaborating with other artists, such as **Šukar**, Slovenia's outstanding Romany group, with whom he has recorded an album of gypsy music. One of the most memorable events in recent years concerned a drag trio from Ljubljana called **Sestre** ("Sisters"), who caused a storm of controversy in Slovenia when they were selected – in somewhat dubious circumstances – to represent the country at the 2002 Eurovision Song Contest (dressed as air-stewardesses). Whilst the group is unlikely to go down in the annals of Slovenian popular music, this fractious affair did at least reignite the debate over gay rights in Slovenia.

Discography

The following list is merely a pointer to some of the recordings available, a few, but not many of them, internationally; rooting around stores and record shops in Slovenia will yield the many more CDs that don't have international distribution.

Folk music

Katalena *(Z)godbe* (RTV Slovenija). Luscious sounding album of traditional songs from Slovenia's multifarious folk regions – Prekmurje, Istria and Bela Krajina, as well as the Rezija Valley in Italy.

Mlada Beltinska Banda *Prekmurje Musical Heritage* (KUD Beltinci). Traditional folk music from the Prekmurje region, as performed by the young Beltinci Band.

Modern Folk Music in Slovenia Volumes I & II (Folk Slovenia Cultural Society). This enjoyable two-disc set is the best introduction to Slovenia's contemporary folk artists, including the female vocal group Katice, Styrian folk trio Kurja Koža, and the Marko Banda from Prekmurje.

Slovenian Folk Songs (RTV Slovenija). Four-disc set of narrative folk music recorded on-site by the Institute of Ethnomusicology in Ljubljana. Drawing upon themes of heroes, legends and love, this voluminous collection brings together poems, songs and instruments from the country's multifarious regions. The excellent sleeve notes help make some sense of it all.

Terra Folk *StereoFolk Live* and *Jumper of Love* (Music Net). The band's two releases to date are both live outings, recorded in clubs across Slovenia. Both are packed with their trademark effervescent tunes, though the second album, *Jumper of Love*, is a touch more diverse. A studio album is in the pipeline.

Rock/popular music

Laibach The band's earliest works are cassette-only affairs, and very difficult to get hold of. Otherwise, selected albums available on CD include: *Laibach* (Ropot, 1985); the double box-set *Rekapitulacija 1980–1984* (this is a re-mastered, redesigned edition of the 1985 original released on the Hamburg independent label, Walter Ulbricht; Mute, 2002); *Nova Akropola* (Cherry Red, 1987); *Opus Dei* (Mute, 1987); *Krst Pod Triglavom* (the soundtrack to NSK's theatre performance that same year; Sub Rosa, 1987); *Let it Be* (Mute, 1988); *Sympathy for the Devil* (Mute, 1990); *Nato* (Mute, 1994); *Jesus Christ Superstars* (Mute, 1996); *The John Peel Sessions* (recordings from two sessions, in 1986 and 1987, with the legendary British DJ; Strange Fruit, 2002); and *WAT* (Mute, 2003).

Siddharta *ID*, *Nord* and *Rh-* (Menart). Released between 1999 and 2003, these are the bands' three albums to date. A limited edition English version of the third, and best, album, *Rh-*, is also available.

Romany

Šukar *Prvo Ti* (*First Snow*; Nika) and *En Concert 1990-2002* (Etno Karavana). Whilst the best Romany music from the former Yugoslav republics is largely the preserve of musicians from Serbia and Macedonia, these two offerings (the second a live album) by Slovenia's standout Romany group – a young, five-piece tamburica ensemble from Ljubljana – feature sumptuous reworkings of traditional gypsy dance songs and ballads. *Mentol Bombon* is an album of songs recorded with singer songwriter, Zoran Predin.

Language

Language

Language

Although the earliest written records in Slovene date from around 1000 AD, it has existed as a literary language since the middle of the sixteenth century, when the first printed books – including a translation of the Bible – came into being. Today it's spoken by nearly two million people within Slovenia, and around half a million more outside its borders. Slovenian is a Slavic language, a branch of the Indo-European linguistic family, and is most closely related to Croatian and Serbian, with which it shares quite a few identical words and phrases.

Whilst attempting to speak the odd word or phrase of **Slovenian** will be appreciated, and can be a fun experience in itself, generally speaking there will be little call for it, as the standard of **English** amongst Slovenes – especially the young – is exceptionally high. Many older generation Slovenes speak **Serbo-Croatian** (as it was formerly called), whilst **Italian** is widely spoken in the Primorska region, and **Hungarian** in Prekmurje. Regional variations of Slovene abound, and the language is characterised by nearly fifty dialects and subdialects.

Basic grammar

Slovenian is grammatically complex with **six cases** for nouns, adjectives and pronouns, three genders (masculine, feminine and neuter) and **four verb tenses** (although only three are used in everyday language). Besides the singular and plural in the Slovene grammar, the **dual number** is also used (for two persons or objects): for example, not only *gora* (mountain) and *gore* (mountains), but also *dve gori* (two mountains). The matters become very complex when one considers special endings for gender, numbers and different cases. In Slovenian the **prepositions** are important because the forms or the following noun, pronoun and adjectives are dependent on them. Slovenian has no articles (such as "a" or "the") and the gender of the word is defined by its ending. The script is Roman and there are 25 letters, the specialty being s, c, z with a caron (a small "v" or hook) on top of each, which indicates sh, ch and zh sounds.

Pronunciation

Slovenian has free stress – it may fall on any syllable of a word. Like English, there are different values for vowels; vowels can be stressed or unstressed, long or short, open or closed, with further subtle variations in the pronunciation. The Slovene consonants are mostly pronounced as they are spelt. Letters not included below are pronounced as in English. There are no explosive or aspirated consonants.

A short **a** as in cat, long **a** as in father

C ts as in bats

Č ch as in church

D d as in dog (dan), **t** as in sit (grad)

E short **e** as in met (več), **ea** as in pear (mleko)

I short **i** as in hit (ris), long **ee** as in been (sin)

J y as in yet

L l as in leap

O short **o** as in hot (voda), long **o** as in short (sok)

R r pronounced with the tip of the tongue like a Scottish "r"

Š sh as in shop

U oo as in foot (kruh)

V v as in vat (voda), **w** as in word (avto)

Ž zh as in measure

Words and phrases

Slovenian distinguishes between formal and informal means of address. The formal (polite) way is very often used. The informal way is used among friends and people you know well. In the phrases below the polite form of address has been used.

Basics

Yes	Ja
No	Ne
I am from	Sem iz
...Britain/Ireland/ America/Canada/ Australia/ New Zealand	... Velike Britanije /Irske/Amerike/ Kanade/Avstralije/ Nove Zelandije
Slovenian	Slovensko
Slovenian person	Slovenec (male) /Slovenka (female)
Slovenian language	Slovenščina
Do you speak	Govorite...?
English	Angleško
German	Nemško
French	Francosko
What's your name?	Kako ti je ime?
My name is	Ime mi je
I (don't) understand	(Ne) Razumem
Please	Prosim
Excuse me	Oprostite
Two beers, please	Dve pivi, prosim
Thank you (very much)	Hvala (lepa)
You're welcome	Prosim / ni za kaj
Hello (informal)	Živijo
Goodbye	Nasvidenje
See you later (informal)	Adijo
Good morning	Dobro jutro
Good day	Dober dan
Good evening	Dober večer

Good night	Lahko noč
How are you?	Kako ste?
Could you speak more slowly?	Lahko govorite počasneje?
What do you call...?	Kako se reče...?
Please write it down	Lahko prosim napišete?
Hurry up!	Pohitite!
Entrance	Vhod
Exit	Izhod
Arrival	Prihod
Departure	Odhod
Open	Odprto
Closed	Zaprto
Free admission	Prost vstop
Toilet	Stranišče / WC (women's – ženske, men's – moški)
Shop	Trgovina
Market	Trg
Hospital	Bolnica/bolnišnica
Pharmacy	Lekarna
Police	Policija
Caution/beware	Previdno/pozor
Help!	Na pomoč!
I'm ill	Bolan (bolna) sem
No smoking	Kajenje prepovedano

No bathing	Kopanje prepovedano
Where is/are?	Kje je/so?
What?	Kaj?
Why?	Zakaj?
When?	Kdaj?
Who?	Kdo?

Accommodation

I'd like/we'd like	Rad(a)**/radi bi
when speaker is male	**rad
when speaker is female	**rada
How much is it?	Koliko stane?
Per night	Na noč
Per week	Na teden
Single room	Enoposteljna soba
Double room	Dvoposteljna soba
Rooms for rent	Sobe/oddaja sob
Hot (cold) water	Topla (mrzla) voda
Shower	Tuš
It's very expensive	Zelo drago je
Do you have anything cheaper?	Ali imate kaj cenejšega?
Do you have a student discount?	Ali imate študentski popust?
Is everything included?	Je vse vključeno v ceno?
Is breakfast included?	Ali je zajtrk vključen v ceno?
Full Board	Polni penzion
Half Board	Pol penzion
Can we camp here?	Ali lahko tukaj kampiramo?
Can I see the room?	Ali lahko vidim sobo?
I have a reservation	Imam rezervacijo
The bill please	Račun prosim
We're paying separately	Plačamo posebej

Getting around

Where's the...?	Kje je...?
Campsite	Kamp
Hotel	Hotel
Railway station	Železniška postaja
Bus station	Avtobusna postaja
Bus stop	Avtobusno postajališče
Inland	Notranji promet
International	Mednarodni promet
Is it near (far)?	Ali je blizu (dalečč)?
Which bus goes to...?	Kateri avtobus pelje v...?
A one-way ticket to... please	Enosmerno vozovnico za... prosim
A return ticket to...	Povratno vozovnico za...
Can I reserve a seat?	Ali lahko rezerviram sedež?
What time does the train/bus leave...?	Kdaj odpelje vlak/avtobus...?
When does the next train/bus leave for...?	Kdaj odpelje naslednji vlak/avtobus v...?
Do I have to change trains?	Ali moram prestopiti?
Towards	Proti
On the right (left)	Na desni (levi)
Straight ahead	Naravnost
(Over) There/here	Tam/tukaj
Where are you going?	Kam greste?
Is that on the way to...?	Ali je to na poti v...?
I want to get out at...	Rad(a) bi izstopil(a) v...
Please stop here	Prosim ustavite tukaj
I'm lost	Izgubil(a) sem se
Arrivals	Prihodi
Departures	Odhodi
To/from	V/iz
Change	Prestop

Numbers

1	Ena	30	Trideset
2	Dva	40	Štirideset
3	Tri	50	Petdeset
4	Štiri	60	Šestdeset
5	Pet	70	Sedemdeset
6	Šest	80	semdeset
7	Sedem	90	Devetdeset
8	Osem	100	Sto
9	Devet	101	Stoena
10	Deset	150	Stopetdeset
11	Enajst	200	Dvesto
12	Dvanajst	300	Tristo
13	Trinajst	400	Štiristo
14	Štirinajst	500	Petsto
15	Petnajst	600	Šesto
16	Šestnajst	700	Sedemsto
17	Sedemnajst	800	Osemsto
18	Osemnajst	900	Devetsto
19	Devetnajst	1000	Tisoč
20	Dvajset	**Half**	Pol
21	Enaindvajset	**Quarter**	Četrt

Time, days and dates

Either the 24 or 12-hour clock is used. When the 12-hour clock is used, "in the morning" (*dopoldan*), or "in the afternoon" (*popoldan*), is usually added. Halves and quarters are used: 4.30 is either *štiri trideset* or *pol petih* (half five), the latter being more common; 4.15 is either *štiri petnajst* or *četrt čez štiri* (quarter past four). Duration is expressed by the prepositions *od* (from) and *do* (to). To ask the time, say: *Koliko je ura?*

Day	Dan	**In the evening**	Zvečer
Week	Teden	**At midnight**	Ob polnoči
Month	Mesec	**At night**	Ponoči
Year	Leto		
Today	Danes	**Sunday**	Nedelja
Tomorrow	Jutri	**Monday**	Ponedeljek
The day after tomorrow	Pojutrišnjem	**Tuesday**	orek
		Wednesday	Sreda
Yesterday	Včeraj	**Thursday**	Četrtek
The day before yesterday	Predvčerajšnjim	**Friday**	Petek
		Saturday	Sobota
In the morning	Zjutraj		
Before noon	Dopoldan	**January**	Januar
Noon	Opoldan	**February**	Februar
Afternoon	Popoldan	**March**	Marec

April	April
May	Maj
June	Junij
July	Julij
August	Avgust
September	September
October	Oktober
November	November
December	December

Spring	Pomlad
Summer	Poletje
Autumn	Jesen
Winter	Zima

Food and drink

Basics

Bedro	Leg
Dober tek!	Bon appetite!
Dunajsko	Vienna style (deep fried in breadcrumbs)
Dušeno	Steamed
Gorčica/senf	Mustard
Kis	Vinegar
Kisla smetana	Sour cream
Kruh	Bread
Kuhano	Boiled
Malo krvavo	Underdone/rare
Maslo	Butter
Med	Honey
Na žaru	Grilled
Na zdravje!	Cheers!
Ocvrto	Fried
Pariško	a la Parisienne (deep fried without breadcrumbs)
Pečeno	Baked
Poper	Pepper
Praženo	Roasted
Prsi	Breast
Sladkor	Sugar
Smetana	Cream
Sol	Salt
Z*emlja / štrucka	Bread roll
Zapečeno	Well done (fried)

Soups (*juhe*) and stews (*enolončnice*)

Fižolova juha	Bean soup
Gobova juha	Mushroom soup
Goveja juha	Beef broth
Jota	Sauerkraut soup
Kisla Juha	Sour soup
Krompirjeva juha	Potato soup
Mineštra	Minestrone (mixed vegetable stew)
Paradižnikova juha	Tomato soup
Prežganka	Soup made by browning flour on lard and adding water
Ribji brodet	Istrian fish soup
Ričet	Barley and pork broth
Telečja obara	Veal stew
Zelenjavna juha	Vegetable soup

Appetizers – cold or hot (*predjedi – hladne ali tople*)

Jetrca	Liver
Narezek	Slices of cold meats
Olive	Olives
Pašteta (jetrna, račja, ribja)	Pates (liver, duck, fish)
Pršut	Dry-cured Italian ham / smoked ham
Rižota	Risotto
Sir (kozji, kravji, ovčji)	Cheese (goat, cow, sheep)
Šunka	Ham
Tatarski biftek	Raw mince with spices spread on toast
Testenine	Pasta

Salads (*solate*)

Salads are usually served with vinegar and oil (vegetable, olive or pumpkin). Other dressings often include yogurt. Many restaurants have salad bars.

Fižolova solata	Bean salad
Hobotnica v solati	Octopus salad
Krompirjeva solata	Potato salad
Kumarična solata	Cucumber salad
Mešana solata	Mixed salad
Motovilec	Lamb's lettuce
Paradižnikova solata	Tomato salad
Radič	Radicchio
Rdeča pesa	Beetroot
Regrad	Dandelion
Sezonska solata	Fresh salad or whatever is in season
Zelena solata	Lettuce
Zeljnata solata	Cabbage salad
Šopska solata	Mixed tomatoes, cucumbers, red / green peppers and cheese

Fish dishes (*ribje jedi*) & seafood (*morski sadeži*)

Brancin	Seabass
Lignji	Squid
Losos	Salmon
Morski list	Sole
Ocvrta riba	Fried fish
Orada	Dorada
Oslič	Variety of cod
Postrvi	Trout
Rakci	Prawns
Sardele	Anchovies
Skuša	Mackerel
Škampi	Shrimps
Školjke	Mussels
Tuna	Tuna

Meat dishes (*mesne jedi*)

Čevapčiči	Minced meat, grilled in rolled pieces
Divjačina	Venison
Dunajski zrezek	Wiener schnitzel
Golaž	Goulash
Gos	Goose
Govedina	Beef
Goveji zrezek	Rumpsteak
Jagnjetina	Lamb
Kranjska klobasa s kislim zeljem	Sauerkraut with sausage
Mesne kroglice	Meatballs
Meso na žaru	Assorted grilled meat
Ovčetina	Mutton
Perutnina	Poultry
Piščanec	Chicken
Polnjene paprike	Peppers stuffed with meat and rice
Puran	Turkey
Raca	Duck
Sarma	Cabbage stuffed with meat and rice
Svinjina	Pork
Svinjski kotlet	Pork chop
Telečja (svinjska) krača	Veal (pork) shank
Telečja (svinjska) pečenka	Roast veal (pork)
Telečji zrezek	Roast cutlet
Teletina	Veal
Vampi	Tripe
Zajec	Rabbit
Žrebickov zrezek	Horse steak

Sauces (*omake*)

Gobova omaka	Mushroom sauce
Paradižnikova omaka	Tomato sauce
Sirova omaka	Cheese sauce
Smetanova omaka	Cream sauce
Tatarska omaka	Sauce made of mayonnaise, mustard, garlic and parsley
Vinska omaka	Wine sauce

Accompaniments (*priloge*)

Ajdovi ganci	Buckwheat porridge
Krompir	Potatoes
Kuhan	Boiled
Pečen	Roasted
Pire	Mashed

Pommes frittes (pomfri)	French fries
Krompirjevi cmoki	Potato dumplings
Kruhovi cmoki	Bread dumplings
Riž	Rice
Testenine	Pasta
Kuhana zelenjava	Boiled vegetables
Žlinkofi	Slovene type of ravioli

Vegetables (*zelenjava*)

Artičoka	Artichoke
Beluši/šparglji	Asparagus
Brstični ohrovt	Brussels sprouts
Bučke	Courgette
Čebula	Onions
Česen	Garlic
Cvetača	Cauliflower
Fižol	Beans
Gobe	Mushrooms
Grah	Peas
Hren	Horse radish
Jajčevec/melancana	Aubergine/eggplant
Korenje	Carrots
Koruza	Sweetcorn
Krompir	Potatoes
Kumara	Cucumber
Paprika	Red/green peppers
Paradižnik	Tomato
Peteršilj	Parsley
Por	Leek
Rdeča pesa	Beetroot
Redkev	Radish
Repa	Turnip
Špinača	Spinach
Zelena	Celery
Zelje	Cabbage

Fruit (*sadje*) and nuts

Ananas	Pineapple
Breskev	Peach
Češnja	Cherry
Ribez	Currant
Grozdje	Grapes
Hruška	Pear
Jabolko	Apple
Jagoda	Strawberry
Lešnik	Hazelnut
Limona	Lemon
Lubenica	Watermelon
Malina	Raspberry
Mandelj	Almond
Marelica	Apricot
Melona	Melon
Oreh	Walnut
Pomaranča	Orange
Sliva	Plum
Figa/smokva	Fig

Desserts (*sladice*)

Gibanica	Pastry filled with apples, cheese and poppy seeds baked in cream
Palačinke z orehi, čokolado ali marmelado	Pancakes with walnuts, chocolate or jam
Potica (orehova ali pehtranova)	Cake (walnut or tarragon)
Štruklji (ajdovi, orehovi ali sirovi)	Rolls (buckwheat, walnut or cheese)
Zavitek (jabolčni ali sirov)	Strudel (apple or cheese)

Drink

Pivo	Beer
Sok	Juice
Vino (belo, rdeče)	Wine (white, red)
Voda	Water
Mineralna voda	Mineral water, usually with gas

Glossary of Slovenian words and terms

Avtobusna postaja	Bus station
Avtobusna postajališče	Bus stop
Avtocesta	Highway
Banka	Bank
Bolnica	Hospital
Center	Centre
Cerkev	Church
Cesta	Road
DDV	Goods tax, equivalent to VAT
Denar	Money
Dolina	Valley
Gostilna	Inn
Gora	Mountain
Gozd	Forest
Grad	Castle
Hiša	House
Hrib	Hill
Jama	Cave
Jezero	Lake
Kmečki turizem	Farm tourism
Letališče	Airport
Mestna hiša	Town hall
Mesto	Town, city
Morje	Sea
Most	Bridge
Nakupolvani center	Shopping centre
Otok	Island
Plaža	Beach
Ploščad	Platform (at the station)
Pokopališče	Cemetery
Polje	Field
Pošta	Post office
Pristanišče	Port
Reka	Piver
Restavracija	Restaurant
Samostan	Monastery
Sejem	Fair
Slap	Waterfall
Šola	School
Toplice	Mineral baths with therapeutic properties
Trajekt	Ferry
Trgovina	Shop
Trg	Square, market
Ulica	Street
Vas	Village
Vodnjak	Fountain
Vozni red	Timetable (bus and train)
Vrt	Garden
Železniška postaja	Railway station

Rough Guides

advertiser

...music & reference

frica & Middle East
ape Town
gypt
he Gambia
erusalem
ordan
enya
lorocco
outh Africa, Lesotho & Swaziland
yria
anzania
unisia
Vest Africa
anzibar
imbabwe

ravel Theme guides
irst-Time Around the World
irst-Time Asia
irst-Time Europe
irst-Time Latin America
ay & Lesbian Australia
kiing & Snowboarding in North America
ravel Online
ravel Health
Valks in London & SE England
Vomen Travel

estaurant guides
rench Hotels & Restaurants
ondon
ew York
an Francisco

laps
lgarve
msterdam
ndalucia & Costa del Sol
rgentina
thens
Australia
Baja California
Barcelona
Boston
Brittany
Brussels
Chicago
Crete
Croatia
Cuba
Cyprus
Czech Republic
Dominican Republic
Dublin
Egypt
Florence & Siena
Frankfurt
Greece
Guatemala & Belize
Iceland
Ireland
Lisbon
London
Los Angeles
Mexico
Miami & Key West
Morocco
New York City
New Zealand
Northern Spain
Paris
Portugal
Prague
Rome
San Francisco
Sicily
South Africa
Sri Lanka
Tenerife
Thailand
Toronto
Trinidad & Tobago
Tuscany
Venice
Washington DC
Yucatán Peninsula

Dictionary Phrasebooks
Czech
Dutch
Egyptian Arabic
European
French
German
Greek
Hindi & Urdu
Hungarian
Indonesian
Italian
Japanese
Mandarin Chinese
Mexican Spanish
Polish
Portuguese
Russian
Spanish
Swahili
Thai
Turkish
Vietnamese

Music Guides
The Beatles
Cult Pop
Classical Music
Country Music
Cuban Music
Drum'n'bass
Elvis
House
Irish Music
Jazz
Music USA
Opera
Reggae
Rock
Techno
World Music (2 vols)

100 Essential CDs series
Country
Latin
Opera
Rock
Soul
World Music

History Guides
China
Egypt
England
France
Greece
India
Ireland
Islam
Italy
Spain
USA

Reference Guides
Books for Teenagers
Children's Books, 0–5
Children's Books, 5–11
Cult Football
Cult Movies
Cult TV
Digital Stuff
Formula 1
The Internet
Internet Radio
James Bond
Lord of the Rings
Man Utd
Personal Computers
Pregnancy & Birth
Shopping Online
Travel Health
Travel Online
Unexplained Phenomena
The Universe
Videogaming
Weather
Website Directory

so! More than 120 Rough Guide music CDs are available from all good book and record stores. Listen in at www.worldmusic.net

STANFORDS
EXPLORE DISCOVER INSPIRE

THE ROUGH GUIDE TO THE MUSIC OF EGYPT
Egypt
MUSIC ROUGH GUIDE
Cairo to Nubia: the source of Arabic music
THE ROUGH GUIDE TO VENEZUELA
Venezuela
MUSIC ROUGH GUIDE
salsa, gaita, parranda: a kaleidoscope of sounds
THE ROUGH GUIDE TO BRAZILIAN ELECTRONICA
Brazilian Electronica
MUSIC ROUGH GUIDE
evolution & revolution: future sounds of Brazil
THE ROUGH GUIDE TO SALSA COLOMBIA
Salsa Colombia
MUSIC ROUGH GUIDE
THE ROUGH GUIDE TO BOLLYWOOD LEGENDS: ASHA BHOSLE
Asha Bhosle
MUSIC ROUGH GUIDE
ORIGINAL RECORDINGS
Bollywood diva: action, suspense & romance
THE ROUGH GUIDE TO CHICAGO BLUES
Chicago Blues
MUSIC ROUGH GUIDE
mojo working: electric blues in the city

small print

and

Index

A Rough Guide to Rough Guides

In the summer of 1981, Mark Ellingham, a recent graduate from Bristol University, was travelling round Greece and couldn't find a guidebook that really met his needs. On the one hand there were the student guides, insistent on saving every last cent, and on the other the heavyweight cultural tomes whose authors seemed to have spent more time in a research library than lounging away the afternoon at a taverna or on the beach.

In a bid to avoid getting a job, Mark and a small group of writers set about creating their own guidebook. It was a guide to Greece that aimed to combine a journalistic approach to description with a thoroughly practical approach to travellers' needs – a guide that would incorporate culture, history and contemporary insights with a critical edge, together with up-to-date, value-for-money listings. Back in London, Mark and the team finished their Rough Guide, as they called it, and talked Routledge into publishing the book.

That first *Rough Guide to Greece*, published in 1982, was a student scheme that became a publishing phenomenon. The immediate success of the book – with numerous reprints and a Thomas Cook prize shortlisting – spawned a series that rapidly covered dozens of destinations. Rough Guides had a ready market among low-budget backpackers, but soon also acquired a much broader and older readership that relished Rough Guides' wit and inquisitiveness as much as their enthusiastic, critical approach. Everyone wants value for money, but not at any price.

Rough Guides soon began supplementing the "rougher" information about hostels and low-budget listings with the kind of detail on restaurants and quality hotels that independent-minded visitors on any budget might expect, whether on business in New York or trekking in Thailand.

These days the guides – distributed worldwide by the Penguin group – offer recommendations from shoestring to luxury and cover more than 200 destinations around the globe, including almost every country in the Americas and Europe, more than half of Africa and most of Asia and Australasia. Our ever-growing team of authors and photographers is spread all over the world, particularly in Europe, the USA and Australia.

In 1994, we published the *Rough Guide to World Music* and *Rough Guide to Classical Music*; and a year later the *Rough Guide to the Internet*. All three books have become benchmark titles in their fields – which encouraged us to expand into other areas of publishing, mainly around popular culture. Rough Guides now publish:

- Travel guides to more than 200 worldwide destinations
- Dictionary phrasebooks to 22 major languages
- History guides ranging from Ireland to Islam
- Maps printed on rip-proof and waterproof Polyart™ paper
- Music guides running the gamut from Opera to Elvis
- Restaurant guides to London, New York and San Francisco
- Reference books on topics as diverse as the weather and Shakespeare
- Sports guides from Formula 1 to Man Utd
- Pop culture books from *Lord of the Rings* to Cult TV
- World Music CDs in association with World Music Network

Visit **www.roughguides.com** to see our latest publications.

Rough Guide Credits

Editor: Alison Murchie
Layout: Umesh and Jessica
Cartography: Katie Lloyd-Jones, Miles Irving and the Delhi Team
Picture research: Joe Mee
Proofreader: David Price
Editorial: London Martin Dunford, Kate Berens, Helena Smith, Claire Saunders, Geoff Howard, Ruth Blackmore, Gavin Thomas, Polly Thomas, Richard Lim, Lucy Ratcliffe, Clifton Wilkinson, Fran Sandham, Sally Schafer, Alexander Mark Rogers, Karoline Densley, Andy Turner, Ella O'Donnell, Keith Drew, Andrew Lockett, Joe Staines, Duncan Clark, Peter Buckley, Matthew Milton; **New York** Andrew Rosenberg, Richard Koss, Yuki Takagaki, Hunter Slaton, Chris Barsanti, Steven Horak
Design & Pictures: London Simon Bracken, Dan May, Diana Jarvis, Mark Thomas, Jj Luck, Harriet Mills; **Delhi** Madhulita Mohapatra, Umesh Aggarwal, Ajay Verma, Jessica Subramanian
Production: Julia Bovis, John McKay, Sophie Hewat
Cartography: **London** Maxine Repath, Ed Wright, Katie Lloyd-Jones, Miles Irving; **Delhi** Manish Chandra, Rajesh Chhibber, Jai Prakash Mishra, Ashutosh Bharti, Rajesh Mishra, Animesh Pathak, Jasbir Sandhu, Karobi Gogoi
Cover art direction: Louise Boulton
Online: **New York** Jennifer Gold, Cree Lawson, Suzanne Welles, Benjamin Ross; **Delhi** Manik Chauhan, Narender Kumar, Shekhar Jha, Rakesh Kumar
Marketing & Publicity: **London** Richard Trillo, Niki Hanmer, David Wearn, Chloë Roberts, Demelza Dallow, Kristina Pentland; **New York** Geoff Colquitt, Megan Kennedy
Finance: Gary Singh
Manager India: Punita Singh
Series editor: Mark Ellingham
PA to Managing Director: Julie Sanderson
Managing Director: Kevin Fitzgerald

Publishing Information

This first edition published July 2004 by
Rough Guides Ltd,
80 Strand, London WC2R 0RL.
345 Hudson St, 4th Floor,
New York, NY 10014, USA.
Distributed by the Penguin Group
Penguin Books Ltd,
80 Strand, London WC2R 0RL
Penguin Putnam, Inc.
375 Hudson Street, NY 10014, USA
Penguin Books Australia Ltd,
487 Maroondah Highway, PO Box 257,
Ringwood, Victoria 3134, Australia
Penguin Books Canada Ltd,
10 Alcorn Avenue, Toronto, Ontario,
Canada M4V 1E4
Penguin Books (NZ) Ltd,
182–190 Wairau Road, Auckland 10,
New Zealand
Typeset in Bembo and Helvetica to an original design by Henry Iles.

Printed in Italy by LegoPrint S.p.A

368pp includes index
A catalogue record for this book is available from the British Library

ISBN 1-84353-145-3

1 3 5 7 9 8 6 4 2

Help us update

We've gone to a lot of effort to ensure that the first edition of **The Rough Guide to Slovenia** is accurate and up-to-date. However, things change – places get "discovered", opening hours are notoriously fickle, restaurants and rooms raise prices or lower standards. If you feel we've got it wrong or left something out, we'd like to know, and if you can remember the address, the price, the time, the phone number, so much the better.

We'll credit all contributions, and send a copy of the next edition (or any other Rough Guide if you prefer) for the best letters. Everyone who writes to us and isn't already a subscriber will receive a copy of our full-colour thrice-yearly newsletter. Please mark letters: **"Rough Guide to Slovenia Update"** and send to: Rough Guides, 80 Strand, London WC2R 0RL, or Rough Guides, 4th Floor, 345 Hudson St, New York, NY 10014. Or send an email to **mail@roughguides.com**

Have your questions answered and tell others about your trip at **www.roughguides.atinfopop.com**

Acknowledgements

Thanks to Alison Murchie, my inordinately patient editor, Kate Berens and Geoff Howard for setting up and overseeing the project, Claire Saunders for finishing things off, and Katie Lloyd-Jones, Miles Irving, Manish Chandra and the team in Delhi for maps. Thanks also to David Price for proofreading and Umesh Aggarwal for typesetting.

Thanks to Jana Kovač and Špela Jurjak for the language section, and Tim Burford, for climbing, and then writing about how to climb, Triglav.

A very special thanks to Karin Tomažič, Nika Božič, Jana Kovač, Špela Jurjak and Irena Škulj for some fantastic help and evenings of fun in Ljubljana and elsewhere; Tatjana Radovič, Verica Leskovar and Petra Čuk at the Ljubljana Tourist Board; Majda Dolenc, Katja Počkaj, Mateja Kuhar and Anja Goršič at the Slovenian Tourist Board; Vesna Čuček at the Association of Tourist Farms; Jurij Šarman in Ptuj; Mitja and Matej Karun; Angela Rennie and the team at Slovenija Pursuits.

Thanks are also due to Tjaša Borstnik, Jo Chandler, Uroš Eržen, Janez Fajfar, Miro Gračanin, Lidija Ivanšek, Saša Jereb, Marko Koščak, Peter Krečič, Tanja and Vladimir Krmpot, Igor Lebar, Tomaž Lukančič, Gaby Lukič, Dejan Luzar, Barbara Majcar, Branka Marolt, Igor Misdaris, Miha Mlinar, Liljana Ošterbenk, Matjaž Pavlin, Suzana Plevel, Eva Štravs Podlogar, Milan Razdevšek, Robert Schilling, Tomaž Šegina, Mateja Škrlj, Lisa Spratling, Joško Štajer, Kristina Stanovič, Alojž Troha, Ana Tušar, Andrej Vršič, Roman Vucajnk, Sanja Žurga, the guys at humanfish.com, Rob, Dave and the rest of the crew at ISIS, and most of all, Biljana.

Photo Credits

Cover credits

Main front Julian Alps © fototeca

small front top picture Fountain Cathedral Ljubljana © Robert Harding

small front lower picture Cathedral Ljubljana © Robert Harding

Back top picture Piran © Robert Harding

Back lower picture Lake Bled © Robert Harding

Introduction

Winter on Snežnik mountain © Janez Skok, Corbis

Swans on Lake Bled © Tim Thompson, Corbis

Art Nouveau windows, Maribor © Robert Harding

Ljubljanica riverside, Ljubljana © Martin Barlow, Trip

Lipica stud farm © IPA Press/Panos

Haymaking, Stara Fužina © N & J Wiseman/Trip

Trenta Valley in the Julian Alps © Janez Skok, Corbis

Vineyards, Maribor region © Paul Almasy/Corbis

Rafting on the Soča © Robert Harding

Lake Cerknica © IPA Press/Panos

Proteus Anguinus aka Human Fish © IPA Press/Panos

Predjama castle © Otto Lang/Corbis

Piran harbour © Alamy

Things not to miss

01 Water spring in the Karst region © IPA Press/Panos

02 Logar Valley © Alamy

03 Gibanica © Ace

04 Wine cellar © Aldo Pavan/Photographers Direct

05 Ljubljana, Shoemakers' Bridge © Phil Robinson © Travel Ink

06 Franja Partisan Hospital © Martin Barlow/Trip

07 Pršut © Ace

08 View from Napoleon Bridge, Soča Valley © Alamy

09 Lake Bohinj © Martin Barlow/Trip

10 Boats on Lake Bled © Greg Balfour Evans

11 Hanke bridge, Škocjan Caves © IPA Press/Panos

12 Boy at Ptuj Kurent © Roy Clark/Photographers Direct

13 Lake near Jasna, Julian Alps © Janez Skok/Corbis

14 Skiing, Krn Mountain © Janez Skok/Corbis

15 Lent Festival, Maribor © Paul Almasy/Corbis

16 Piran, view from castle © David Forman, Travel Ink

17 Cycling in the Slovenian countryside © IPA Press/Panos

18 Ptuj at night © Alamy

19 Predjama castle © Sandro Vannini/Corbis

20 Planica ski-jumping © Murray Cohen/Photographers Direct

21 Whitewater rafting on the Soča © Brecelj Bojan/Corbis Sygma

Black and white photos

House front, Ljubljana © Bernard Martinee/Greg Evans (p.50)

Plečnik's Triple Bridge, Ljubljana © Phil Robinson/Travel Ink (p.65)

Vintgar Gorge © Alamy (p.88)

Signpost, Velika Planina © Robert Harding (p.95)

Seventeenth-century Karst house © Janez Skok/Corbis (p.150)

Otočec castle © IPA Press/Panos (p.210)

Kočevjski forest © IPA Press/Panos (p.257)

Wine press, Jeruzalem vineyards © Alamy (p.260)

Taking hay from a hayrack © Robert Harding (p.285)

Index

Map entries are in **colour**.

K

L

M

Map symbols

Maps are listed in the full index using coloured text.

Motorway
Road
Steps
Railway
Funicular railway
Footpath
Ferry route
Wall
Chapter division boundary
International boundary
Point of interest
Mountain peak
Ruins
Castle
Fortress
Monastery
Church (regional maps)
Synagogue
Monument
Mansion/stately home
Border crossing
Mountain refuge
Skiing

Lighthouse
Statue
Gate
Cave
Waterfall
Airport
Boat transfer
Bus stop
Gardens
Museum
Hotel
Campsite
Parking
Hospital
Tourist office
Post office
Building
Church
Park
Cemetery
Saltpan
Marshland
Beach